Calypso Magnolia

. . . .

· ·

New Directions in Southern Studies

This series is devoted to opening new lines of analysis of the American South and to becoming a site for redefining southern studies, encouraging new interpretations of the region's past and present. The series publishes works on the twentieth century that address the cultural dimensions of subjects such as literature, language, music, art, folklife, documentary studies, race relations, ethnicity, gender, social class, religion, and the environment.

Calypso Magnolia

The Crosscurrents of Caribbean and Southern Literature

JOHN WHARTON LOWE

The University of North Carolina Press   Chapel Hill

Cover illustration by Alyssa D'Avanzo

Library of Congress Cataloging-in-Publication Data
Lowe, John Wharton, author.
Calypso magnolia : the crosscurrents of Caribbean and Southern
literature / John Wharton Lowe.
pages cm — (New directions in southern studies)
Includes bibliographical references.
ISBN 978-1-4696-2888-2 (cloth : alk. paper)
ISBN 978-1-4696-2620-8 (pbk : alk. paper)
ISBN 978-1-4696-2621-5 (ebook)
1. American literature — Southern States — History and criticism.
2. Caribbean literature — History and criticism. 3. Caribbean Area —
In literature. I. Title. II. Series: New directions in southern studies.
PS261.L75 2016   810.9'975 — dc23
2015022647

This book was digitally printed.

To my mother,

    KATHERINE MORGAN LOWE,

and to the memory of my father,

    JOHN WHARTON LOWE JR.

Their love of the tropics led the way.

Contents

Preface

When I began thinking about the issues that became *Calypso Magnolia*, I was reminded of resources in my own history. I grew up in Atlanta but my mother was from Miami, and we went to Florida almost every summer, usually to Miami, but also to Daytona, Tampa, Clearwater, and Eau Gallie, where my Aunt Mary and Uncle Willie had a tropical nursery, hard on the banks of a black-water river that threaded through a lush jungle. Until Castro took over Cuba, my parents would deposit their children with my Aunt Nita in Hialeah while they flew the short hop over to Havana to party at the Tropicana and other night spots. I still have a banner from the club's restaurant. My Daddy spoke fluent Spanish and had many Cuban friends, who visited us in Atlanta, bringing painted Cuban ties and cigars. I used to go deep-sea fishing with Daddy, and he would point over the water to where Cuba was. After the revolution, my relatives in Hialeah became surrounded by Cuban neighbors, whose spicy food wafted enticing aromas across the hibiscus-festooned yards.

Living in Louisiana for many years placed the Caribbean squarely in front of me, as its great approach, the Mississippi River, abutted the campus I went to almost daily. New Orleans has long been said to be more Caribbean than Southern—although surely it is both—and its vibrant, diverse neighborhoods (and not just the ornate French Quarter) are right now being rebuilt and painted in bright, pastel colors that are also common to the Caribbean. The city's Haitian, Guadeloupean, Jamaican, Guatemalan, Honduran, and Puerto Rican citizens enliven the ethnic neighborhoods and markets. Much of the recovery work after Hurricane Katrina was done by Mexicans, who are an increasing presence in the Crescent City.

Louisiana's tropical flora, fauna, and climate are all replicated in the other areas of the Caribbean, and its swamps and jungles once resonated with the cries of Maroons, black runaways from plantations, who often forged alliances (including marriages) with Native Americans. Maroons played similar roles across the Caribbean, particularly during the Haitian Revolution.

The tropical flora and fauna of the circumCaribbean cross artificial boundaries too. In 1944, the naturalist Thomas Barbour wrote of the way hurricanes have of redistributing forms of plant and animal life. He remarks on the several varieties of snails that are common to both Florida and Cuba as a result of storms and adds that "a very large number of West Indian plants are found in South Florida. . . . Hurricanes have played a very great part in bringing them to Florida" (Barbour, 1944, 67–68). He also attributes the presence of species of birds in both areas to hurricane dispersal.

Foodways circulate around the basin as well. The unique cuisine of Louisiana has many affinities with those of the Caribbean, particularly of the French islands of Guadeloupe and Martinique, but Cajun cookery also resembles the spicy offerings of Jamaica. The state's waterways and bordering Gulf comprise, as Chef John Folse has stated, the greatest pantry God ever created. Louisiana's fishermen—now buoyed and energized by immigrant Vietnamese—suffered a grievous blow from Hurricanes Katrina and Rita but have mounted a strong comeback, aided by the increasing appetite of the nation for the state's seafood. Florida, too, like the rest of the circum-Caribbean, has historically played a key role in hemispheric fishing, and seafood occupies pride of place in circumCaribbean cuisine.

While I believe this book answers some pressing needs, and does so, I confess, by at times providing more questions than it does answers, it has grown organically out of the work I did in Louisiana for two decades. Until this new century, my own scholarly efforts had been concentrated on African American, Southern, and ethnic literatures of the United States, although my degree in comparative literature and my many years as director of the summer program in Italy of Louisiana State University (LSU) led me to courses in Italian literature and to teach Shakespeare's Italian plays in the cities that inspired them, which set my transnational registers quivering. However, my lifelong interest in opera has always made me aware of the uses Verdi, Mozart, Puccini, and other composers made of overseas cultures and ethnicities as they shaped Italian or Austrian music, even when the libretto was set in a foreign land, as in Verdi's *Aïda* (Egypt), Mozart's *Die Entführung aus dem Serail* (Turkey), or Puccini's *Turandot* (China), and I had always been aware of the extensive use of foreign settings in key works by American literary masters, such as Melville's *Typee*, Hawthorne's *The Marble Faun*, most of Henry James's and many of Wharton's works, Twain's *The Prince and the Pauper* and *Connecticut Yankee*, Baldwin's *Giovanni's Room*, and the African novels of Hemingway, Bellow, and Updike.

In 2000, many of us in Southern Studies, history, French, and Spanish at LSU began to talk with colleagues from music, geography, anthropology, and oceanography about setting up a program in Louisiana and Caribbean

Studies, which would honor the culture of our state while also attending to its myriad connections and the rest of the circumCaribbean. As we pondered a title for the program, several people insisted that we be precise—shouldn't we say it was really a Gulf and Caribbean program? Later, when many of us were engaged in planning a hire in Atlantic Studies, we once again faced the problem of defining a wide cultural region and came up with the term "circumCaribbean," which embraces the coastal Gulf and the Caribbean, as well as the islands that dot the seas and the western Atlantic.

At that time, many misconceptions about the Caribbean were beginning to be swept away by our former LSU colleague Édouard Glissant. As he notes in *Caribbean Discourse*, rather than the insularity the geographical reality would seem to indicate, "each island embodies openness. The dialectic between inside and outside is reflected in the relationship of land and sea. It is only those who are tied to the European continent who see insularity as confining. A Caribbean imagination liberates us from being smothered" (1989, 139). This study will proceed from this *aperçu*, in an attempt to achieve an openness that paradoxically can help us see ourselves anew, while understanding what has seemed foreign as related, necessary, and, indeed, local. Concurrently, Caribbean Studies can likewise profit from a move beyond the islands, which are centered in a vast region whose seas wash the shores of complementary, if sometimes radically different, cultures. As Glissant, Michel Foucault, Homi Bhabha, Paul Gilroy, and Brent Staples have asserted, culture is dynamic, nomadic, flowing. The myriad ships, boats, steamers, airplanes that have crisscrossed the circumCaribbean for centuries are now accompanied by instant electronic forms of communication and media, annulling distance and forming new micro-communities. It is time to unlock old geographical and cultural restrictions, as we reconfigure cultural formations and interactions that have always themselves overflowed artificial boundaries.[1]

I have researched and written this book in part as a "response" to James Clifford's "call": "It is more than ever crucial for different peoples to form complex concrete images of one another, as well as of the relationships of knowledge and power that connect them; but no sovereign scientific method or ethical stance can guarantee the truth of such images. They are constituted—the critique of colonial modes of representation has shown at least this much—in specific historical relations of dominance and dialogue" (1988, 23). I do so, however, knowing full well that there is resistance to this kind of effort. Sophia McClennan, who has worked for some time in inter-American and Latin American Studies, has accused North American scholars who are turning their gaze southward of representing "the latest variation on the Monroe Doctrine of patronizing Latin America. . . . Latin Americanists might see such a move as signaling a transition from covert to overt invasion of the rich Latin American canon." She has particularly objected to Jan Radway's endorsement of the "transatlantic turn" in American Studies, claiming, "What would an inter-American studies housed in English and History departments in the United States and taught by monolingual faculty be, if not an example of US intellectual expansionism?" (2005, 402). Of course she herself is an American scholar, as are many experts in the literature she wants to protect from "poachers," and many of these latter figures in fact do speak at least one of the basin's languages. Her position is somewhat understandable; however, let's turn that around. How many scholars of Latin American literature have also studied U.S. Southern literature in depth? In fact, there are at least four who have done so with notable and applauded effect. George Handley's *Postslavery Literature in the Americas* (2000) and Deborah Cohn's *History and Memory in the Two Souths* (1999) have shown how fruitful such studies can be, albeit from the other side. Elizabeth Russ has given us *The Plantation in the Postslavery Imagination* (2009), which pairs twentieth-century texts from the U.S. South with similar narratives from the Spanish Caribbean (for instance, Russ juxtaposes Teresa de la Parra's *Iphigenia* [1924] with Ellen Glasgow's *The Sheltered Life* [1932], focusing particularly on the role race plays in discrete regions). These three expansive works are complemented by José E. Limón's *American Encounters: Greater Mexico, The United States, and the Erotics of Culture* (2000), which often meditates on links between Mexican and U.S. Southern literature. His notion of a "greater Mexico" overlaps with my concept of the circumCaribbean.

This study concludes with a meditation on the dazzling writing that has been produced over the past three decades by Cuban American writers, much of it set in the fabled city of Miami. For me, Florida will always seem an integral part of the South I knew as a child. My grandfather migrated there from Georgia after World War I and set up the community's first salvage business. He came to a new city, which had only been established in 1896, and it was full of hustlers. At that time, Miami billed itself as both "Magic City" (proleptic of Disney's later "Magic Kingdom") and "Jewel of the South" (Shell-Weiss 2009, 76). My grandfather's quick profits, however, literally went up in smoke when his house burned, and another home was destroyed by the devastating hurricane of 1926, which killed over 400 people. Like my relatives, most of the older residents had migrated to South

Florida from other parts of the South, and the restaurants and cafés they frequented served not only seafood but also grits and biscuits. The mom-and-pop motels that proliferated outside of Miami Beach were owned by white Southerners but maintained by Southern African Americans, who lived in segregated neighborhoods. Even before the Cuban Revolution, there were many from that island in Florida, and in later years, my aunts and uncles in Hialeah had many Cuban friends. Later, of course, Hialeah would become almost totally Cuban.[2]

My grandfather, like other businessmen, employed black workers (some of them Bahamian), but blacks began to leave the city in the 1920s after the Ku Klux Klan staged huge rallies, and a series of violent racial incidents encouraged many local blacks to join their upper South relatives in the "Great Migration" to Northern cities.[3] Miami was at this time very much a Southern city, and this was true in terms of genteel Protestant surface morality, which increased after Prohibition became the law of the land. While the city's exponential growth during the first two decades of the new century set it off from other Southern cities, it was all too like them in terms of the violence that permeated its racial and labor conditions. These patterns (which led to increasing numbers of white Miamians) continued until the end of World War II. At that time, over 80 percent of the city's residents were born outside Florida, but of these, 80,000 (including my relatives) were from Georgia, followed by those from New York (26,000, many of them Jewish) and Ohio (12,000) (Shell-Weiss 2009, 96, 129).

Growing up in Atlanta but often visiting Miami, I entered into decades of comparison and contrast, especially after my cousins in Florida took to bragging about their "magic city." It has been exciting and informative to see Miami anew through the eyes and creativity of our Cuban American compatriots.

I summoned up some of these memories when my friend David McWhirter asked me to be one of four participants in a symposium on "Southern Literature/Southern Cultures: Historicizing Southern Literary Cultures," held at Texas A&M in 2002. The other speakers, Michael Kreyling, Trudier Harris, and Patricia Yaeger, were receptive to my paper—also called "Calypso Magnolia"—and offered helpful comments and suggestions. My excellent commentator, A&M's own Kimberly Brown, provided sharp and extremely useful suggestions for improvement, which were published as "Sniffing the Calypso Magnolia" when *South Central Review* brought out all the symposium papers.

A second signal event in the fall of 2002 started this project percolating—the pathbreaking conference held in Puerto Vallarta on "Postcolonial Theory, the U.S. South, and New World Studies." Sponsored by the Society for the Study of Southern Literature and the American Literature Association and masterminded by the energetic impresario Jon Smith, the conference brought together scholars of varying ages and rank from across the country, to rethink the U.S. South in a global context. While our glamorous setting on the Pacific was paradisiacal, it actually was quite a hike from the town itself, so people mostly stayed put. All the sessions were plenary; we therefore learned a great deal from each other because we heard *all* the presentations, and everyone participated in a stirring roundtable after the panels concluded. Most of the papers and the transcript of the roundtable were published in two special editions of *Mississippi Quarterly*, a feat also engineered by Jon Smith. Some of the people I am about to thank were at the conference, where I met many of them for the first time. Over the years, I have made a point to read the publications the group has produced, and I always attend panels that participants present at various conferences.

· · · · ·

This study would not have been possible without the assistance of three grants. A Freehling Fellowship at the Virginia Foundation for the Humanities for the spring term of 2007 gave me access to the University of Virginia's splendid collections, vital and informative fellowship with other fellows of the institute, including Chip Turner, Lawrie Balfour, Wayne Driscoll, and Bill Freehling, and advice and encouragement from the staff, especially Roberta Culbertson, Pablo Davis, Anne Spencer, and Rob Vaughn. My Charlottesville stay also included many good times and conversations with my dear friend Deborah McDowell, who gave me both encouragement and a careful reading of my Delany/Pickens chapter. Bob Jackson proffered advice in the breaks we took between our racquetball sets.

An ATLAS grant from the Louisiana Board of Regents enabled me to keep up the head of steam I had generated in Charlottesville after I returned to Baton Rouge. The staffs of Middleton and Hill Memorial libraries at LSU were ceaseless in their efforts to find and secure holdings that we did not have in our collections, and in some cases they alerted me to treasures that *were* there. A final year of writing and research was made possible by a Research Fellowship from the National Endowment for the Humanities. I am very grateful to the NEH for allowing me to postpone my fellowship year so that I could accept the ATLAS award from the Louisiana Board of Regents.

My research was augmented by my excellent research assistant, Erin Breaux, whose diligence, resourcefulness, and wicked wit sustained me through the early stages of this process. The first part of her appointment was sponsored by the Program in Comparative Literature at LSU, headed by Professor Greg Stone, who generously set up Erin's assistance. I also want to thank my splendid former chair, Professor Anna Nardo, who spared me department duties and made sure that I continued to get travel funds, which permitted me to share my work in progress with colleagues across the nation and in Europe. At the Rollins College archives, Wenxian Zhang and Gertrude Laframboise were expert guides to its valuable collections.

Parts of this manuscript were delivered as conference papers or keynote addresses at the University of Bucharest, the Center for the Study of the American South at the University of North Carolina at Chapel Hill, Emory University, Washington University at St. Louis, and Georgia State University. Audiences at these locales and elsewhere asked thoughtful questions and offered warm encouragement. I thank my hosts at these universities for their kind invitations to speak and their hospitality: Anca Peiu, Fred Hobson, Barbara Ladd, Rafia Zafar, and Gina Caison.

Writing a book is always difficult, but taking on this many writers and cultures all at once is a Herculean—and maybe foolhardy—task. I could not have completed this project without the strong support and advice of a host of friends, who have been willing to confer and contest with me on the phone, in emails, and over drinks and/or dinner at various conferences. Some of them—Debbie McDowell, Barbara Ladd, Susan Donaldson, Peter Schmidt, Bill Boelhower, Bill Demastes, Keith Cartwright, Ifeoma Nwankwo, Harry Stecopoulos, Kathleen Diffley, Jesse Alemán, Valérie Loichot—provided vital and helpful reading of individual chapters. My chief saint, however, in this connection, has been Veronica Makowsky, who carefully read and commented on the entire manuscript. Charles Reagan Wilson, my series editor, also provided an essential review.

In the final stages of preparation, I was blessed to have Linda Wagner Martin and Keith Cartwright as readers for the University of North Carolina Press. Their informed and rigorous reviews made every part of this work stronger. Mark Simpson-Vos, my editor at the press, could not have been more patient, encouraging, and insightful. His perusal of the final manuscript showed me how to slim down my chapters, straighten the seams, and highlight my insights.

In addition to advice, other friends graciously wrote letters of support for the grants. Many hosannas to Fred Hobson, Jerry Kennedy, Eric Sundquist, Bob Brinkmeyer, Suzanne Jones, Thadious Davis, and Werner Sollors.

Some of my best insights have come from conversations with my students, especially those who took my graduate seminars at LSU and the University of Georgia on the South and the Caribbean and on the Black Diaspora: *gracias* to Jordan Stone, Ilana Xinos, Richmond Eustis, Kirstin Squint, Craig Slavin, Cherry Levin, Matt Dischinger, Tomohiro Hori, Telba Espinosa, Benjamin Forkner, Gabrielle Fuentes, Jacquelyn Van De Velde, Sarah Harrell, Chris Bollini, Chris Shearhouse, Tamika Edwards, Sonia Sharmin, James Edge, Tareva Johnson, and Christen Hammock.

Let me also express gratitude to other friends and colleagues not listed above who have offered helpful suggestions and wonderful talk over the years: Ann and Dale Abadie, Eric Anderson, Juan Barrosa, Michael Bibler, James Borders, Keith Byerman, Doug Chambers, Deborah Cohn, Joe Comaty, Leigh Anne Duck, Femi Euba, Barbara Ewell, Genevieve and Michel Fabre, Cyle and Mary Ellen Ferguson, Christian Fernandez, Bill Ferris, Frances Smith Foster, Carl Freedman, Peggy Galis, Joanne Gabbin, Ernest and Dianne Gaines, Cristina García, Fred Gardaphe, Marcia Gaudet, Nancy Grayson, Trudier Harris, Taylor Hagood, Katie Henninger, Paul Hoffman, Tom Inge, Michael Kreyling, Joyce Marie Jackson, Suzanne Jones, Vera Kutzinski, Rebecca Mark, Jack May, Katie McKee, Brenda Marie Osbey, Berndt Ostendorf, Solimar Otero, Margaret Parker, John Pizer, Deborah Plant, Jim Payne, Noel Polk, Jo Ann Pope, Marco Portales, Peggy Prenshaw, Gary Richards, Riché Richardson, Malcolm Richardson, Adam Rothman, Adelaide Russo, Charles Rowell, Mona Lisa Saloy, David Shields, Joe Skerrett, Hongsheng Sui, Srinivas Thouta, Annette Trefzer, Natasha Trethewey, Les Wade, Carolyn Ware, Jay Watson, Dana Williams, Anthony Wilson, Charles Reagan Wilson, Mary Ann Wilson, and Reggie Young. Special thanks to Virgil Suarez; his counsel for the Cuban American chapter was invaluable.

Most of this was written during my years at LSU, but the final version was done at the University of Georgia, where I have taught for the past three years. I am blessed here with superb colleagues, a great library, and a very supportive administration. Special thanks to Nicholas Allen, Doug Anderson, Stephen Berry, Jim Cobb, Cody Marrs, Mike Moran, Hugh Ruppersberg, Jace Weaver, and most of all, Barbara McCaskill, for friendship, conversation, and encouragement. I also thank my colleagues at UGA's Latin American and Caribbean Studies Institute, especially our splendid director, Richard Gordon.

One of the best things about my move to Georgia has been closer proximity to my family, especially my wonderful brothers, Stephen and Jim, and our feisty, frisky, and brilliant mother, Bird (aka Katherine). Our joyous family gatherings have offered welcome respite from my scholarly duties. As always, my deepest debt is to my wife, June Conaway Lowe. Her love, wit, and wisdom illuminate every aspect of my life.

Calypso Magnolia

. . . .

Introduction

· ·

What the map cuts up, the narrative cuts across.

—Michel de Certeau

The past two turbulent decades have forced much rethinking about nation and national boundaries. The rise of multinational entities and the advent of transnational markets have sharpened our awareness that cultural configurations have always ignored real and imaginary sovereign borders. This premise has often been true for regions as well, particularly the most fabled part of the United States, the South, whose permeable borders hug the former states of the Confederacy—although Kentucky, Oklahoma, Maryland, and West Virginia sometimes get thrown in too. We now recognize, however, that the U.S. South—especially the coastal states of Texas, Louisiana, and Florida—is in many ways the northern rim of the Caribbean. In this study, I employ the inclusive concept of the circumCaribbean, which takes into account the basin's islands, the Gulf of Mexico, and the rims of these inland seas, namely the Southern coast of the United States, the eastern coast of Mexico, and the northern coast of South America. Immanuel Wallerstein calls this wider South the "extended Caribbean" and maps an area reaching from Brazil to Maryland, recognizing the transnational spread of the plantation economy that gripped the New World from its inception well into the twentieth century (2011, 166–67). While I accept his premise, I prefer the term "circumCaribbean."[1] Following this geographical conception into its transnational and transcultural manifestations, this book lays out the myriad ways the "South of the South" has affected the inhabitants of the U.S. South, particularly those dwelling in the tropical and subtropical zones of the region. I will also provide illustrations of the U.S. South's effect on its southern neighbors.

The Shifting Tectonics of Culture

The age of contact, exploration, and conquest had no strict sense of boundaries; early maps were constantly morphing into new formulations. Pre-

1

contact southern America had broad bands of differing cultures. Powerful Native American nations in the circumCaribbean, such as the Natchez, the Choctaws, the Creeks, and, in the wider Caribbean, the Mayans, Aztecs, Arawaks, and Caribs, were drawn into complex relations and often war, first with each other, and then with European explorers and colonizers, including the French, the Spanish, the English, and the Dutch. As conquest proceeded, New World Creoles were constantly shifting identities; they often intermarried or cohabited with Native Americans, African Americans, other Caribbeans, and, later, Asian immigrants. There were, of course, ties among the subjects of the various Western colonial powers. The United States had affinities with English-speaking Jamaica and Barbados; French Louisiana had ties with Haiti, Martinique, and Guadeloupe. We now remember that before the Louisiana Purchase, whose bicentennial we marked in 2003, New Orleans was the crown jewel of a Franco-Caribbean empire that spread French culture up the Mississippi River and across the Gulf of Mexico. Spanish Florida (and then Spanish Louisiana) was administered by governors in Havana and had links with the many other Hispanic colonies of the New World. The Spanish legacy, however, was also manifest in other Southern states, especially Texas. St. Augustine is the oldest continuously inhabited town in the United States, and its vibrant city to the south, Miami, now resonates as a kind of Latino capital, where business and culture often as not are negotiated in Spanish.

The congealing of regional identities in the United States during the nineteenth century increasingly led to the identification of the South as the opposite or "other" of the North. The idea of Southerners as opposed to the shaping emphases of the Founding Fathers (even though many of those men were Southerners) had emerged earlier, shortly after the American Revolution, and accelerated in the buildup to the Civil War. Part of the process consisted of linking the South negatively with the Caribbean, which also featured a slave economy, a debilitating climate, tropical diseases and epidemics, hostile jungles, and a feudal agricultural and social system that enriched a relatively idle upper class at the expense not only of the slaves, but of the common white folk of the region as well.

Conversely, the U.S. South saw its similarities with the Caribbean in a positive light. After all, many Southerners had properties in both the coastal South and the Caribbean. The plantations of the circumCaribbean generated great wealth and, to the minds of the property owners, enabled the creation of a refined, cultured ruling class, which made New Orleans, Charleston, Natchez, St. Pierre, Cap François, Havana, and Vera Cruz sophisticated and beautiful cities. The South was not immune to the nation's appetite for new lands, and antebellum Southerners looked to Cuba as a possible new state, whose annexation would provide senators and congressmen who would support slavery. Filibusters based in the South attempted to conquer not only Cuba but other Latin American countries too, and one of these men, William Walker, became president of Nicaragua for a time. Southerners felt ideally suited for such missions. They often had more in common with the "South of the South" than with the U.S. North, especially in terms of the transnational operations of slave economies. As explorers, travelers, and soldiers penetrated the circumCaribbean, they saw their own cultures in new ways as they contrasted them to those they were experiencing for the first time; concurrently, inhabitants of the islands and the more southern shores of the wider Caribbean began to have new ideas about *their* cultures, as contact with their northern neighbors proceeded, a process that would expand exponentially as the web of relationships grew and strengthened.

Often these encounters were martial. U.S. invasions of circumCaribbean nations, beginning with Mexico, resulted in the introduction of U.S. goods, customs, and culture, influences that grew rapidly as capitalist- and U.S.-dominated political and economic nets spread across the region. These events and their cross-cultural results helped form the idea of the circum-Caribbean, a concept certainly based on geographical realities, but also on increasingly complicated overlays of agriculture, trade (including the sale of human beings), religion, and traditions.

The rise of sugar production in the lower South after the expulsion of French planters from independent Haiti made for extensive links with Cuba, another new site for cane production. Engineers and merchants from the South and the Caribbean had myriad and beneficial influences on each other as circumCaribbean industry developed, particularly after the advent of labor-saving machinery. Similarly, cotton was always seen as a bridge between the peoples of the Americas, and the need for enslaved labor in both sugar and cotton production made the slave trade a demonic hemispheric priority.

In the decades before the Civil War, however, a real difference emerged between concepts of the South and of the Caribbean. After the forging of a common purpose in the debate over slavery and the subsequent Civil War, the South firmly believed in its own distinct history and identity, unlike the Caribbean, where centuries of imposed colonial rule made Spain, England, or France the "mother country" and the source of national myths. The longing many Southerners had for annexing the realms South of the South clearly had much to do, first, with U.S. and Southern perceptions of "blank" territory, which supposedly lacked history and development. Such tropical topicalities were thus ripe for reinterpretation and/or appropriation, be it imaginative or literal, as areas to be read through the spectrum of Southern culture, aspirations, and projections. Southerners also perceived the many geopolitical similarities between the two realms, which for centuries were in fact contiguous, sans national boundaries, and, in the case of Spanish, French, and British imperial networks, part of the same juridical and cultural control—likewise the similarities (in spite of the myth of a bichromatic U.S. South) in hybrid populations.

The defeat of the South in 1865 put an end to Confederate dreams of an empire, but many ex-Confederates immigrated to Mexico, Brazil, and other points south, thereby creating a new network of relationships, one that would intensify as Northern capital began to force mono-crop agricultural colonization in the Caribbean, a practice that often involved Southern engineers and workmen and the utilization of important Southern ports. Emancipation did not end the need for cheap labor but rather ushered in new forms of labor exploitation, such as sharecropping, and also far more extensive circumCaribbean trade networks. As Natalie J. Ring reminds us, the 1895 Cotton States and International Exposition in Atlanta was chiefly intended to foster stronger trade relations between the South and partners throughout Mexico, Central America, and South America: as Ring writes, the exposition was a "global celebration of the South" highlighting extensive relations in the wider circumCaribbean region (2012, 101).

Postbellum U.S. military incursions into the Caribbean began with the Spanish American War, which brought Puerto Rico and Cuba into the nation's orbit of power. Later, armed invasions of several Latin American countries (including a fifteen-year occupation of Haiti) brought many Southern soldiers and sailors to the South of the South.

Boxing In the Region: The Rise of Southern Studies

As we shall see, all of these events and influences had an effect on circum-Caribbean literature. The U.S. academy, fixated on a strictly defined literary canon of white, native-born, male writers, for the most part ignored circum-Caribbean texts, even in the U.S. South itself. Paradoxically, the scholarly subfield of Southern Studies, which began as an effort to counter negative images of the South, in many ways mimicked patterns in American literary studies and the quickly following new field of American Studies. Both of these latter disciplines eschewed comparative study in favor of scholarship that focused on American exceptionalism and strident nationalism. Presenting an equally "exceptional" view of the U.S. South and similarly concentrating on the achievements of white men, Southern Studies took hold in Southern colleges and universities in the early twentieth century and accelerated with the advent of the Fugitives/Agrarians at Vanderbilt and the social theorists at the University of North Carolina. There were significant differences in the stances of these two groups, but all these scholars and artists were operating to counter negative concepts of the region held by dominant Northern academics, journalists, politicians, and businessmen. Nevertheless, both the Nashville and the Chapel Hill theorists proceeded to develop similarly monolithic profiles, closely adhering to white, masculine, Protestant cultures, with scant attention paid to transnational connections, influences, or histories. (There were exceptions to this, as in Andrew Lytle's historical novel concerning the Spanish in Florida, or the popular novels of the African American writer Frank Yerby, who often traced connections between the South and the Caribbean.) The emergence of William Faulkner as the centerpiece of narrowly focused notions of Southern identity seemed to crystallize the inward-looking aspect of the discipline, even though there were always transnational aspects in Faulkner's work and, for that matter, in the fiction of many of his Southern contemporaries, such as Katherine Anne Porter, Thomas Wolfe, Evelyn Scott, Richard Wright, and Zora Neale Hurston.

The Local, the Global, and New Concepts of Region

In moving beyond these narrow conceptions, I draw on theorists such as Homi Bhabha, who has stated that "counter-narratives of the nation that continually evoke and erase its totalizing boundaries—both actual and conceptual—disturb those ideological maneuvers through which 'imagined communities' are given essentialist identities" (1990, 300). Likewise, as Benedict Anderson has demonstrated, national boundaries are really nothing more than veritable dotted lines around imagined communities (1983, passim). Constituting the Caribbean world to include its center and rim(s) as a new kind of imagined community is in fact a counter-narrative that questions and critiques both the totalizing concept of nation, which blinds its people to the multiple connections with those outside its borders, and the subset enclosure of region, which has been employed as a stereotypical and negative rendition of what the encircling "nation" is not. Very often national powers have a vested interest in preventing these new kinds of recognitions and extensions of cultural and topographical zones, for they may lead to efforts at secession and attempts to form new nations. In the more mundane world of "Southern-Lit-Nation," there may well be resistance to the kind of argument I am making here, as it can be read as a threat to the hegemony of the platitudes that have reigned in Southern Studies for decades. However, as I hope to suggest, we can better understand the local through the lens of the transnational and the global, and Southern literature and culture have always transcended the physical boundaries of a geographical South. While I have included references to, and readings of, many of the authors I have mentioned already, this work will provide extended readings of the following writers from the nineteenth century: Victor Séjour, William Clark Falkner, Raphael Semmes, Arthur Manigault, Martin Delany, Lucy Holcombe Pickens, Constance Fenimore Woolson, Lafcadio Hearn, and George Washington Cable; and from the twentieth century: Claude McKay, Zora Neale Hurston, James Weldon Johnson, William Faulkner, Arna Bontemps, Richard Wright, George Lamming, Édouard Glissant, Madison Smartt Bell, Virgil Suarez, Roberto Fernández, Gustavo Pérez Firmat, Ana Menéndez, and Cristina García. Why have many of these writers been ignored in Southern literary scholarship? Too often, narrow definitions of region have become blinders. Over the many decades of South watching, our notions of the South's history and culture have been circumscribed by what people have wanted and expected to see. Stereotypes have eclipsed reality, and transnational, shared cultural traditions have been ignored. As Salman Rushdie wickedly notes in *The Satanic Verses*, the trouble with the English is that so much of their history happened overseas, so they don't know what it means (1989, 264). Surely the same has been true for Southerners.

The New Southern Studies has rightly been criticized for focusing too much interest on the work of William Faulkner. While I will briefly consider his circumCaribbean aspects here (particularly in *Absalom, Absalom!*), I will not elaborate, partly because he has been closely examined from this perspective already, but also because other U.S. Southern writers have more to tell us about the circumCaribbean, and some of them have rarely been associated with Southern literature, let alone the narratives of the transnational South. While I will treat the entire basin, I will be especially interested in the history and literature(s) of Mexico, Cuba, Haiti, Jamaica, Barbados, Louisiana, and Florida.

Further, simply in terms of U.S. Southern literature, it is high time to quit worrying about where writers were born, how long they lived in the South, or if there is a static "Southernness" that needs attention. Culture is always fluid and dynamic, and it pays no attention to constructed borders. I want to pursue narrative as it cuts across maps that create artificial lines around peoples and cultures. There will be no focus here on the Civil War or Reconstruction except as those events influenced the writers I present who were configuring a transnational South during and after those events. I will, however, examine the Mexican American War, which involved massive numbers of combatants from the U.S. South (many of them in command positions), but I will do so with an eye to the impressions these men received of the circumCaribbean, rather than attending to military and political history, although both these topics will be considered.

I am attempting a new direction here, but it needs to be stated that leading scholars of the U.S. South urged the methodology I now practice some time ago. In 1986, C. Vann Woodward called on scholars to break out of the deadening dichotomy of North/South studies: "Comparison . . . offers [the] possibility of redefining traditional problems, revealing what needs explanation, shaping fresh periodization, discovering unsuspected relationships, proving what seemed ordinary to be rare or unique and what was assumed to be exceptional to be common" (1986, 123). What happens if we conjoin this insight to the adjacent circumCaribbean? According to Glissant, this area

> may be held up as one of the places in the world where Relation
> presents itself most visibly. . . . This has always been a place of en-
> counter and connivance and, at the same time, a passageway toward
> the American continent. Compared to the Mediterranean, which is an
> inner sea surrounded by lands, a sea that concentrates . . . the Carib-
> bean is, in contrast, a sea that explodes the scattered lands into an
> arc. . . . What took place in the Caribbean, which could be summed up
> in the word *creolization,* approximates the idea of Relation. . . . But the
> explosion of cultures does not mean they are scattered or mutually
> diluted. It is the violent sign of their consensual, not imposed, sharing.
> (*Poetics,* 33–34)

Understanding the CircumCaribbean

As we do this work, we must also be mindful of the complex history that has shaped and reshaped the circumCaribbean and how the invention of national units has obscured a conception of a cultural and geographical region. As Barbara Ladd asserts, "The South's places have never been simply geographical—especially where literature and literary criticism are concerned. . . . We might . . . reconceptualize place as a site of cultural dynamism. . . . It enables us to shift our focus from moments or sites of narrative (or historiographical) stability to moments/sites of narrative and historiographical process" (2002, 48–49). Ladd, after addressing the plantation system as circumCaribbean rather than merely Southern, suggests reading plantation narratives from across this transnational region side by side: thus far, however, she notes, "novels like Mitchell's [*Gone with the Wind*] and like Stark Young's *So Red the Rose* have not been read with novels of the Caribbean like Claude McKay's *Banana Bottom*" (2002, 49). While I don't make this comparison, I do read McKay's unjustly neglected novel side by side with Zora Neale Hurston's *Their Eyes Were Watching God*, with an eye toward the common heritage of postslavery people of the black diaspora.

Throughout this book, I will be concerned with this African diaspora, as all the islands, states, and nations I consider were part of both the tragic history of slavery and subsequent forms of racial oppression, some of which continue to this day. On the other hand, to use Thadious Davis's helpful terminology, these locales became "black spaces" that generated startlingly creative, and occasionally joyous, New World cultures (1986, 3). As Paul Gilroy suggests in his paradigmatic *The Black Atlantic* (1993) (a term I will also employ here), the African diaspora took different forms, not only in differing states of the U.S. South and North, but also in the circumCaribbean, where the history of colonialism and imperialism—mainly executed by Spain, France, England, Holland, and then the United States—shaped the lives of African-descended people rather differently.

The circumCaribbean contains elements of other diasporas as well. The "coolies" that were brought to the area from India form part of South Asia's continuing diaspora and played an essential role in the Caribbean. James Clifford notes that diasporic discourse has proliferated because of 1) decolonization; 2) increased immigration; 3) global communications; and 4) transport (1997, 249), factors that were present in earlier ages as well. Certainly one of the most significant effects of diasporic movements on the U.S. South has been the continuing migration to the region from both Cuba and Mexico.

Again and again, we will encounter writers, often on ships, contemplating the Caribbean through the lens of their Southern background and/or experiences. In terms of the two cultures and the ways in which their confluence and overlay(s) can shape identity, T. Minh-ha has claimed that identity "lies at the intersection of dwelling and traveling and is a claim of continuity within discontinuity (and vice-versa)" (1994, 14). According to Minh-ha, these vectors lead to a third space, one that proceeds from hybrid constructions, and this space can generate new forms of expression that differ from those of the first two spaces of *home* and *abroad*. While these concerns will surface throughout this study, they have special relevance to my consideration of the travel writers of the late nineteenth century, who capitalized on the new fascination with tropic climes.

Accordingly, I will consider some of the writers and many of the characters I have assembled here as "tropicopolitans," a term Srinivas Aravamudan employs bivalently, to refer, first, to writers who address the tropics, and second, to those who seek to create tropological change. Not surprisingly, texts that seek to explore new territories in a new way operate in both registers. Some of the writers I examine early on, for instance, employ tropological denigration of Africans and African Americans, while others attempt to change the basic trope of *blackness* as *unchangeable uselessness* (as Aravamudan explains its usage during the eighteenth century). Further, he proposes the term "tropicopolitan as a name for the colonized subject who exists both as fictive construct of colonial tropology *and* actual resident of tropic space, object of presentation *and* agent of resistance. In many historical instances, tropicopolitans—the residents of the tropics, the bearers of its marks, and the shadow images of the more visible metropolitans—challenge the developing privilege of Enlightenment cosmopolitans" (1999, 4).

You will find that many of my chapters pair texts by two different writers. In creating these couplings, I bear in mind George Handley's sense of the circumCaribbean's common roots, and his notion that "what is . . . indicative of cultural identity in the hemisphere are moments when texts resonate synchronically with one another and thereby provide telling evidence of divergent authorial and discursive agency within common sets of representational choices" (2000, 30).

While some of the texts I treat are centered in one discrete culture of the circumCaribbean, all of them, like clumps of grass, are connected to the others through a rhizome-like cultural grid that underlies the entire circum-Caribbean. Glissant, expanding on the original literary use of this concept by Gilles Deleuze and Felix Guattari, explains: "The root is unique; it is a stock that takes all upon itself and kills everything around. . . . The rhizome . . . is a multiple root, stretched out in nets in the earth or in the air. The notion of the rhizome maintains the fact of rooting but challenges the idea of a totalitarian root. The epistemology of the rhizome is at the heart of what I call a cross-cultural poetics, according to which each identity extends out in contact with the other" (1997, 23).

As the ensuing chapters demonstrate, one of the most extensive rhizomic structures developed among African American writers who visited and/or wrote about the Caribbean, especially after they came into contact with migrants from the basin who came to the United States, either in person or in print. Eventually, James Weldon Johnson, Zora Neale Hurston, Langston Hughes, Richard Wright, and other black Southerners would venture into the Caribbean themselves, doing research, writing, or fulfilling diplomatic functions, like Frederick Douglass before them. There were, of course, many others comparing and contrasting areas of the circumCaribbean, including anthropologists, sociologists, engineers, diplomats, missionaries, fruit company employees, and mercenaries. Until recently, however, the most penetrating work of remapping this part of the Americas has come from heirs of the black diaspora, many of them natives of the Caribbean islands. One of them, the distinguished writer and scholar Wilson Harris, has characterized his own work in terms that I find most persuasive, instructive, and inspiring: "To convert rooted deprivations into complex parables of freedom and truth is a formidable but not hopeless task. The basis of our inquiry lies in the conception that one may address oneself to diverse fictions and poetries as if they are the art of a universal genius hidden everywhere in dual rather than monolithic presence, in the mystery of innovative imagination that transforms concepts of mutuality and unity, and which needs to appear in ceaseless dialogue between cultures if it is to turn away from a world habituated to the pre-emptive strike of conquistadorial ego" (1983, 137). Harris's reference to "rooted deprivations" offers a variant on Glissant's notion of underground rhizomes, and his subsequent remarks add urgency to the search for a circumCaribbean dialogue between cultures, which can provide a key antidote to totalizing systems of oppression, be they aesthetic or political.

Rhizomes and roots can reach under and beyond any walls erected to contain them. The boundaries of the region's interests and connections have been charted only as far as traditional geographic limits. It is time for us to understand the South, its people, and, above all, the idea of the South as seen and expressed by its writers, as connected to the world in myriad ways, but in particular to that part of the world that is contiguous—the Caribbean. We can make a start by uncovering and reading the many texts in canonical and noncanonical Southern literature that link the two heretofore separate entities and peoples. The South has long since ceased to be merely a New World garden, and in any case, as Fernand Braudel declared, "history can do more than study walled gardens" (1972, 1:22).

Beyond the Racial Binary:
Reconfiguring Region as Heteroglossia

The circumCaribbean, like the Mediterranean, has been a cradle of culture and has always been multiethnic and multiracial. John Kennedy Toole's hilarious posthumous novel, *A Confederacy of Dunces* (1980), presents a tropical New Orleans that similarly connects with myriad cultures through its Creole history and its Caribbean character. The inscription to the novel, from A. J. Liebling, claims that New Orleans *is* Mediterranean, with allusions to the Greeks, the Italians, the Lebanese, and the Egyptians, a comparison that takes in three continents and the Afro-Asiatic roots of Western culture. Tellingly, Liebling goes on to subtly parallel the rim of the Old World's lake of commerce with the New World's, the Caribbean: "Like Havana and Port-au-Prince, New Orleans is within the orbit of a Hellenistic world that never touched the North Atlantic. The Mediterranean, Caribbean and Gulf of Mexico form a homogenous, though interrupted, sea" (1980, n.p.). This inscription suggests much, especially when we consider the way it annuls boundaries and ethnicity, like the humor that is the central driving force of the narrative. However, we need to ponder the more serious aspects of Liebling's claim, as in effect he insists on a criollo cultural model of coastal rims, ideally thought of as a cradle of myth and legend. Certainly Derek Walcott's *Omeros* (1990), a Caribbean refiguring of Homer's *Odyssey*, takes a similar tack. The linkage of the Greek epic to the Caribbean is hardly surprising when one considers the military and trade histories of the two seas, so often coupled with the national mythologies of the surrounding cultures. Then, too, we recall some of Homer's opening lines, describing his hero Odysseus: "Many pains he suffered, heartsick on the open sea," lines redolent of the traffic in the Caribbean in human bodies and the Middle Passage. The poet calls for the Muse to "start from where you will—sing for our time too," speaking of the continuing need for myth, one centered on "one man alone . . . his heart set on his wife and his return—Calypso, the bewitching nymph, the lustrous goddess, held him back, deep in her arching caverns, craving him for a husband" (1996, 77–78). The Caribbean has always been seen singing a siren song, and it has been sung in myriad registers. Today it seeks to lure tourists, but in earlier centuries the islands beckoned to Southerners as places where great fortunes could be made. Certainly William Faulkner's Thomas Sutpen, to name just one fictional hero, heard this call.

As we reconfigure the South and the Caribbean, we must be conscious of the fact that too many of us are unable to do work in French or Spanish, or both. Mexico's tangled history of colonization, revolution, and natural catastrophes, all of it preceded by centuries of magnificent preconquest cultures, remains a mystery to too many. Central American countries are often merely names, whose realities are difficult to place on a mental map. And yet all the shores of the Caribbean have had an impact on Southern literature, history, and culture, and vice versa.[2]

The tangled utterances of the circumCaribbean offer a superb example of Mikhail Bakhtin's celebrated notion of heteroglossia: "At any given moment of its evolution, language is stratified not only into linguistic dialects . . . but also . . . into languages that are socio-ideological: languages of social groups, 'professional' and 'generic' languages, languages of generations, and so on . . . literary language itself is only one of these heteroglot languages — and in its turn is also stratified into languages . . . stratification and heteroglossia widen and deepen as long as language is alive and developing" (1981, 272). Attending to these myriad voices requires supporting, encouraging, reading, and appreciating comparative studies and ceasing to consider that discipline marginal.[3] We need similar work that brings in the islands and the northern coast of South America as well; we need the kind of concept for the Caribbean that Braudel created for the Mediterranean. For the Caribbean, too, as he said of his sea, "speaks with many voices; it [too] is a sum of individual histories" (1972, 1:13).

Glissant often made the point that Guadeloupe and Martinique in scholarship have all too often been sequestered from their fellow islands because they are considered a part of France, and thus "other." This case becomes relevant in a more contemporary way when we look at the exclusion of Cuban, Dominican, Mexican, Vietnamese, and Haitian Southerners from the current biracial concept of the Southern canon. Glissant's most trenchant discussion of these issues emerges in his essay "The Quarrel with History." He acutely notes the cost of the "French" identity of Martinique and Guadeloupe: "The French Caribbean people did not relate even a mythical chronology of this land to their knowledge of this country, and so nature and culture have not formed a dialectical whole that informs a people's consciousness." Considered dispassionately, this statement assigns at least partial blame for disjuncture to the folk themselves, in terms of allegiances that are counterproductive, which could in fact be true for some erstwhile Southerners such as the Cubans in Miami. But the overriding scholarly issue remains the lack of recognition among the larger community of new subsets. The ultimate effect, as Glissant notes, is unfortunate, because "the creative link between nature and culture is vital to the formation of a community"

(1989, 63). Glissant and Antonio Benítez-Rojo find a solution to the isolation of discrete islands through the element that unites them—that is, the sea. This monumental fact of nature creates similarities for cultures, both shaping and (like Glissant's aforementioned rhizomes) connecting them, particularly in terms of folklore and myth.[4]

Grappling with the Caribbean Imaginary

Before employing any of these theories of place, region, and nation, however, we must come to terms with what I will call the "Caribbean Imaginary." The presence of two Western mythologies—Calypso and Prospero/Ariel/Caliban—weave in and out of island histories, whatever the language or background. These sorcerers/spirits are powerfully evocative of the symbolic and often erotic reveries the Caribbean has conjured up in explorers, tourists, and sometimes natives of the region.[5] The various "spells" cast by the island are obviously part and parcel of the most important religious overlay, the African-inspired religions that are variously known as hoodoo, voodoo/vodoun, Candomble, and Santería. The tropical allure of the circumCaribbean has been a kind of magical imaginary for readers and romantics north of both the South and the Caribbean. In addition to the magic of spells, critic Michèle Praeger argues, the "imaginary" aspect of the Caribbean has many facets; two of the most important are those that suggest the fictional, since "imaginary" can also be defined as "conjectural, dreamlike, ethereal, fabled, fabulous, fanciful, fantastic, fictional, hypothetical, illusory, immaterial, incorporeal, insubstantial, invented, make-believe, metaphysical, mythical, non-existent, romantic, speculative, supposed, theoretical, and unreal" (2003, 1). On the other hand, Praeger writes, the term refers to the fact that "[Caribbeans] have everything to invent, as they cannot return to a particular culture or tradition. Some Caribbean writers and thinkers, Aimé Césaire in particular, have in the past been tempted by the idea of a return to Africa, but this ideology seems obsolete in the contemporary Caribbean as Caribbean writers know that their origins, like the origins of language, are irretrievable. Yet they do not see, or do not want to see, their foreclosed past disappearing irretrievably" (2003, 2).

J. Michael Dash usefully historicizes this "Caribbean imaginary" by noting that the archipelago, "conceived as an absolute 'elsewhere,' as irreducibly different, was from its very inception invented as a blank slate onto which an entire exoticist project could be inscribed," a project generated by the industrialization of Europe, which created "the need to see in the Tropics [and here, the implications of Dash's argument would extend to Africa, Asia, and the Pacific as well] an antidote to Europe's sense of loss," and thus serve as a kind of "romantic otherness, a fetishistic opacity" (1998, 17).

Recently, people with African ancestry have discovered a common North American/Caribbean heritage, as they have come together in the great Northern cities of the United States and Canada, but also, increasingly, in those of the American South. Folklore, in particular, has been a source of connection and community, and this phenomenon demonstrates Glissant's sound observation that folklore, rather than myth, enables people to repossess historical space and to create a worldview that is both fortifying and useful for social change (1989, 83–85). Further, Benítez-Rojo has helpfully situated the concept of performative style as a distinction of Caribbean culture and has asserted that much of the power of Atlanta's Martin Luther King Jr. came from his understanding and practice of a performing art much like that of the Caribbean (1992, 24). Rogelio Martínez Furé has argued that there is definitely a "Caribbean civilization," one that includes the cultures of the islands but also the coastal rims and their cities, such as New Orleans, noting in particular that Cuba's *caringa* dance tradition, of Congo origin, has a counterpart in the *calinda,* which was performed in the Crescent City's Congo Square. Finding these links, he states, will strengthen others, "of both culture and revolutionary struggle, which unite us and make us an integral part of *Our America*" (1993, 115–16).[6]

Since Zora Neale Hurston's germinal *Tell My Horse* appeared in 1934, millions of Caribbeans—including the children of the Haitians, Jamaicans, and Bahamians Hurston studied—have immigrated to the United States. They and their progeny have written many books set in the Caribbean, or in both places. These writers include, most notably, Brooklynite, born of Barbadian parents, Paule Marshall; Haitian writer Edwidge Danticat; Antigua's Jamaica Kincaid; Dominicans Julia Alvarez and Junot Díaz; Puerto Rican Judith Ortiz Cofer; and a host of Cuban authors. Marshall, who has set many of her narratives in her father's Caribbean, lived for years in Richmond and has been influenced in important ways by Southern African American history, literature, and culture. Many of her powerful novels have Caribbean settings but constantly interbraid diasporic concerns that prominently include the American South. Edwidge Danticat has recently moved to Miami and has begun setting her narratives there. As my concluding chapter indicates, Florida in particular has become the home and/or subject for an increasing number of talented circumCaribbean writers. Inevitably, there will be more Southern/circumCaribbean writers in our future, and they must be linked with the patterns of colonization, immigration, and settlement that preceded them in connection with the history, literature, and culture of the South.

We have already begun to accept broad cultural patterns as more important than actual residence in a place as a foundation for culture-based fiction. For example, Jewel Parker Rhodes has written powerfully about Louisiana's Marie Laveau in *Voodoo Dreams* (1993), even though Rhodes grew up in Pittsburgh. The story developed, however, out of her cultural roots, specifically her grandmother's experience with conjure. As Rhodes cogently puts it, "The portrait of my grandmother redrawn in *Voodoo Dreams* speaks to my immediate community and, I think, by extension, to the larger, global village of ancestors and our intergenerational heritage and attachment," a statement that connects the South, the Caribbean, and the African diaspora.[7]

The "Inaudible Voice of It All" and the Tropical Sublime

Virtually all of the writers considered here devote much attention to limning tropical landscapes and the effect these settings have on their characters, some of whom have been shaped by these surroundings since birth, while others, thrust into these exotic realms by chance, are irrevocably changed. As I will demonstrate throughout this study, subjects such as these are quite difficult to write about, as they involve what Zora Neale Hurston called "the inaudible voice of it all," things that lie beyond language. This problem, however, has never stopped writers from attempting to wrest at least a suggestion of the unsayable from language, and one of the tools they have employed in Southern realms is the language of what I am calling the "tropical sublime," an extension of the usually Eurocentric concept of the sublime that began to be conceptualized in the classical era by Longinus, who was primarily concerned with elevated forms of rhetoric, which attempt to address the sublime. I will employ my concept of the "tropical sublime" extensively in the chapters that follow.

Despite the many works that reflect this interest, the South's concept of the sublime has been little studied. Although Rob Wilson's *American Sublime: The Genealogy of a Poetic Genre* (1991) claims a national scope, the only Southern writer who receives extended attention is Edgar Allan Poe. At least one of the reasons for this neglect has been the tendency to associate the sublime with Northern landscapes and, in particular, mountains, rather than with the tropical. Yet another might be the focus on fiction and poetry that critics have favored, to the neglect of travel writing, a popular genre in both the North and the South in the nineteenth century. Such pieces were a big part of popular magazines such as *Harper's*, in which many of the articles focused on the topography of the U.S. South, increasingly depicted as contiguous to, and comparable to the circumCaribbean.

Warfare, Filibusters, and Insurrection

Mexico, a nation colonized by the Spanish, the French, and then the Americans, provides the setting for Chapter 1, which examines the literary legacy of the Mexican American War, using the narratives of William C. Falkner, Arthur Manigault, and Raphael Semmes.

Two states and two islands loom large in this tropicopolitan panoply: Louisiana, Florida, Haiti, and Cuba. As colonial possessions of France and Spain (at different times, Louisiana was owned by both), these entities, which form part of the circumCaribbean rim, have generated some of the most important transnational literature of the West. New Orleans often served as a launching point for filibusters, the U.S. military, and writers embarking for the South of the South. Cuba became the richest pearl of the Caribbean, taking over revolutionary Haiti's role as major sugarcane producer. Always a coveted prize for various U.S. political leaders and businessmen, Cuba also functioned as a kind of mirror image of the United States, particularly in terms of its struggles for independence, its reliance on slavery, its multiracial population, its dynamic folk cultures, and, more recently, its mythic stature as a lost homeland for the Cuban diaspora. The island appears first here in a study of Martin Delany's *Blake* and its relation to filibuster narratives of the time, which I represent with Lucy Holcombe Pickens's fictionalized account of the Narciso Lopez filibuster missions in Chapter 2.

Haiti before its bloody revolution was the richest colonial possession in the world, but at a terrible cost: thousands of enslaved Africans were literally worked to death in the production of addictive sugar. Amazingly, the uneducated but religiously inspired Africans, under the leadership of, first, Toussaint-Louverture and then Jean-Jacque Dessalines and Henri Christophe, defeated the forces of the French, Spanish, and English, achieving independence in 1804 after a brutal thirteen-year war. This revolution, the subject of one of my chapters, was inspiring and/or terrifying to millions and has been written about by an impressive array of U.S. Southern and Caribbean writers. I examine the ways in which the Haitian Revolution, always a taboo subject in Southern letters, nevertheless exerted a powerful influence between the lines of many narratives and took on central importance in the imagination of African American writers. After a survey of early Southern literary reflections of that event, I relate those views to those of the Caribbean writers who limned the conflict in its various stages; I also consider the effect Haiti had on African American writers in the twentieth century, especially Harlem Renaissance celebrities James Weldon Johnson and Zora Neale Hurston, both Floridians who saw this new landscape through the lens of the tropical state that produced them and much of their writing. Hurston's little-studied *Tell My Horse: Voodoo and Life in Haiti and Jamaica* (1938), a nonfictional account of her anthropological trips to the Caribbean, offers one of the most arresting examples in all of Southern literature of the dramatic influence of the "indigo sea" on a Southern writer—in this case, a woman of color. Based on research Hurston did in the islands in 1936 and 1937, the book is inextricably bound up with *Their Eyes Were Watching God* (1937), which was written in Haiti, and *Moses, Man of the Mountain* (1939), wherein that patriarch is presented as the greatest hoodoo conjurer in history. Another writer in this school, Louisiana-born Arna Bontemps, wrote a historical novel about the revolt, *Drums at Dusk* (1939).

The Haitian Revolution would find impassioned chroniclers in the Caribbean too, including Victor Séjour, C. L. R. James, Alejo Carpentier, Derek Walcott, Aimé Césaire, Édouard Glissant, and many others, and their works will form an important component in this chapter.

This survey of texts that treat the history and culture of Haiti culminates in a reading of *All Souls Rising* (1994), the first volume of the Tennessee writer Madison Smartt Bell's trilogy on the insurrection; his work was strongly influenced by his Caribbean predecessors, but also by his lifelong involvement with U.S. Southern letters.

CircumCaribbean Travelers: The Roots and Routes of Narrative

The aftermath of war inevitably produces exile and diaspora; it generates retrospection and also an urge to recover equilibrium through escapist literature. Citizens in both the North and the South found relief from the pressures and problems of Reconstruction through travel writing, which enjoyed a new vogue following the exciting narratives coming out of Africa during the age of that continent's colonization and exploration. Exotic areas of the United States, it was discovered, could produce similarly compelling narratives of penetration and revelation. Chapter 4 focuses on the travel writing and fiction of Constance Fenimore Woolson and Lafcadio Hearn, ponders the implications and achievements of this genre and its influence on fiction, and demonstrates the myriad ways in which travel accounts limned a new sense of the circumCaribbean. This discussion will be complemented by consideration of key theorists of the circumCaribbean who have preceded me in thinking about new configurations of either Southern Studies or Caribbean Studies, or of both.

Chapter 5 turns to two other noted travelers, the Jamaican Claude McKay and the Floridian Zora Neale Hurston. As noted, I consider Hurston in my Haitian chapter, but I bring her back for an encore here, especially in terms of the research she did in Jamaica, which I believe included a reading of McKay's *Banana Bottom* (1933). This work has long been considered a masterwork of Caribbean literature, but in the United States it has been eclipsed by his key contribution to the Harlem Renaissance, *Home to Harlem* (1928), and more recently by *Banjo* (1929), which now constitutes a key text in the canon of the Black Atlantic. Here, I suggest that Hurston's work in Jamaica prior to writing *Their Eyes Were Watching God* included a careful and influential reading of *Banana Bottom*.

A writer contemporary with Hurston who shared her Southern background and scientific training was her sometime nemesis, Richard Wright. In the 1950s, Wright published a fascinating study, *Pagan Spain* (1957), which claimed that the Iberians, ostensibly devout Catholics, were really still pagan. Hurston makes precisely the same claim for Haitians, who are nominally Catholic but in reality "deeply pagan" (1938, 91). Wright never set a novel in the Caribbean, but he lived in Argentina for almost a year and visited Trinidad and Haiti. Later, he would write an introduction for George Lamming's moving 1954 autobiographical novel *In the Castle of My Skin*, which depicts a Barbados undergoing transformation from rural to industrial society. The effect on Lamming's protagonist is much like Wright's own life story in *Black Boy*. Chapter 6 thus explores Wright's experiences in the Caribbean and South America and demonstrate the strong relation between these two foundational texts—texts that have strongly registered with subsequent writers of the African diaspora, who have admired Wright and Lamming's delineations of the parallels among diasporic peoples.

Chapter 7 turns to a group of writers I see as part of U.S. Southern literature, the Cuban American writers of Miami and South Florida. The routes and roots of the Cuban diaspora involve contrasting attitudes toward Castro's revolution and the island homeland, and this has generated a fascinating set of texts that have many unexamined connections with U.S. Southern literature and culture. Virgil Suarez, Roberto Fernández, Gustavo

Pérez Firmat, Ana Menéndez, and Cristina García are dazzling talents who have added a striking new component to Southern letters, as we shall see.

Methodology in comparative studies demands practices that are not usual in narrowly defined canonical approaches. Because I deal with writers and texts in this study who are not widely known (Faulkner, Hurston, and Wright are three notable exceptions), I have provided more plot summary than I would for, say, a study of Faulkner or Eudora Welty. Many scholars of Southern literature are unfamiliar with even major figures of Caribbean literary traditions, and conversely, until lately, scholars in Caribbean studies have rightly been concerned with their own fields of interest (frequently dictated by the language group in question) or, at most, the other traditions of the Caribbean islands. I hope that this book speaks to scholars and also to students and general readers. The issues I consider here all find expression in this eclectic but dialogic grouping of texts; and to create maximum understanding of my points, an awareness of plot's intersection with issues seems crucial. For readers who do know many of these texts, I ask patience on this issue and also understanding. Plot details are essential for close readings; we should remember that our understanding of canonical texts in every case rests on the foundation of precise readings by early scholars—like Cleanth Brooks's magisterial interpretations of Faulkner. Most of the writers I am considering, with few exceptions, have not been given this kind of scrutiny. Gustavo Pérez Firmat has issued a challenge on this point: "It is time we brought close reading out of the closet. There is no reason to avoid it, to apologize for it, or to dress it up as something other than what it is. Close reading remains the fundamental form of engagement with works of literature" (2008, 70).

By looking to the dynamic history of a circumCaribbean that is partly constituted by the Deep South, we can break through to a new and more expansive understanding of both the U.S. South and the wider Caribbean. In this respect, we are following the lead of Fernand Braudel's magnificent two-volume study, *The Mediterranean and the Mediterranean World in the Age of Philip II* (1949). Braudel, building on the sweeping changes in historiography by his great predecessors, Marc Bloch, Lucien Febvre, and the Annales school, ignored sovereign boundaries to map a history of region and culture that was based on the lives of ordinary and extraordinary individuals, public and ecclesiastical documents, trade patterns, and census reports, and tied it all together across and upon the currents of the great sea he loved. However, in his extensive revision of the first edition in preparation for the work's translation into English, he attempted to address the Ottoman Empire, which at its height controlled more than half of the shores washed by the Mediterranean; he admitted, however, that he was unable to do justice to this task, for much of the information needed was in inaccessible archives in Istanbul—documents, he neglects to say, which were written in non-Western languages.

The shores of Mexico, Central America, and northern South America are our versions of Braudel's Ottoman coast, and we stand poised to explore it. The ever-accelerating pace of travel, migration, and forced exile has shattered barriers of all kinds, including those in the academy. Many of us have begun to explore adjacent areas—disciplines, languages, cultures, texts—because all of them have made appearances in our subject realms and, often, in our neighborhoods. Operating from a dual perspective is nothing new; since shortly after the American Revolution, Southerners have functioned as both part of the nation and its stepchild, particularly after secession and the Civil War. As such, its people have had to straddle two identities. Similarly, circumCaribbeans, who have had to deal with colonial and postcolonial doubled identities, have faced this situation as well. Indeed, migrants to the South, such as the Cubans I consider in my last chapter, have had to juggle a triple identity in this respect. As Salman Rushdie, speaking in particular about exiles from India, but in reality, about immigrants in general, remarked, "Sometimes we feel that we straddle two cultures; at other times, that we fall between two stools. But however ambiguous and shifting this ground may be, it is not an infertile territory for a writer to occupy. If literature is in part the business of finding new angles at which to enter reality, then once again our distance, our long geographical perspective, may provide us with such angles" (1991, 15). It is my hope that this book provides exactly this kind of solid geometry.

Many of the writers here challenge themselves and their readers by boldly examining what at first sight seems strange, exotic, or even terrifying. All of them—and many other figures considered in this book—would understand Toni Morrison's declaration that "the ability of writers to imagine what is not the self, to familiarize the strange and mystify the familiar, is the test of their power" (1992, 15). As we shall see, the writers of the circumCaribbean have met this challenge triumphantly.

1 Crossing the Caribbean

Southerners Write the Mexican American War

. . . .

As was originally the case with the U.S. colonial coastal states, tropical realms "South of the South" were often described as a new paradise by writers and visitors from northern climes during the nineteenth century. Very often, the appeal of such locales came to be expressed in terms of desire and/or matrimony, with the island or country feminized in order to be "taken" by her northern lover, the United States. Cuba, for instance, often lauded as the "Queen of the Antilles," was eroticized: she was said to admire "Uncle Sam, and he loves her. Who shall forbid the bans? Matches are made in heaven, and why not this? . . . She sits, like Cleopatra's burning throne, upon the silver waves, breathing her spicy, tropic breath, and pouting her rosy, sugared lips? Who can object? None. She is of age—take her, Uncle Sam!" (cited in May 1989, 7). Mexico, too, was seen as an appropriate "bride" for the United States, as was Nicaragua.[1]

Nowhere is this more noticeable than in the writing that developed before, during, and after the Mexican American War. The following discussion will situate that conflict as a watershed event in the relation of the U.S. South and the circumCaribbean. I will argue that when two cultures collide—especially when they are congruent—their confluence and overlay(s) can shape identity. While I will consider quite a number of commentators on the war here, I will concentrate on military/travel memoirs by Maryland's Raphael Semmes and South Carolina's Arthur Manigault and a sensationalist novel by Mississippi's William Clark Falkner (the Nobel Prize winner's great-grandfather). All three men were combatants in the war, and they clearly had read widely, including histories of Mexico and the various novels that were written about the conflict in the United States. As thousands of Mexicans, U.S. citizens, and foreign conscripts collided, the operations of the war were facilitated by repeated crisscrossing of the circumCaribbean and involved much interchange among the crucial ports of New Orleans, Vera Cruz, and Havana. We find registers of the hybrid constructions created by these seismic events in the prose and fiction that was generated during and after the conflict, sometimes by the combatants, but more often by writers who never set foot in Mexico.[2] General Scott's war arena was not just Mexico but encompassed the circumCaribbean, and Semmes and Falkner emerged from the conflict with sharp memories of the climate, the terrain, the culture, and the people.

The overarching pattern of this book is the movement of Southerners, both physically and imaginatively, out of the constructed boundaries of the Southern United States into the wider world of the circumCaribbean, a process that unsettled notions of exceptionalism and nationalism alike, while simultaneously, and paradoxically, creating a vision of a new Southern empire, which would conjoin slave-owning states with the plantations and territories of the Caribbean, Central America, and beyond. The path from New Orleans to Vera Cruz was the first important and large-scale trail, trace, or mapping of the circumCaribbean that is the subject of this study.[3]

As I will demonstrate, the Mexican War had much to do with the emergence in the 1850s of the idea of the South more as a nation than merely a region, one that could attempt to redeem the original revolutionary concepts of the Founding Fathers while simultaneously becoming a hemispheric power. Subsequently, it could spread its doctrines into the benighted countries to the south through adjustments of the existing plantation economy and slavery, moves that would graft more efficient and productive Southern versions of this agricultural machine onto the existing hacienda/habitation/peonage models. The coherence of these concepts during the Mexican American War led first to the many filibuster scenarios, which I discuss in the next chapter, and then to the basic conceptual building blocks of the Confederacy.[4] It is worth noting that the presumed authoritative history of Mexico in this era had been written by a near-blind scholar who had never set foot there. William H. Prescott's monumental 1843 *History of the Conquest of Mexico* revealed the country's ancient Aztec and Mayan cultures and the chronicle of their tragic encounter, led by their Emperor Montezuma, with the Spanish conquistadores, under the leadership of Cortés. Mindful of this history, many U.S. officers and enlisted men sought out and climbed the pyramids, and the phrase "in the Halls of Montezuma" found its way into popular culture. Informed by Prescott's romantic views of landscape, which were yoked to his graphic views of warfare, combatants found an ideal template for their present. As Prescott had told them, employing the language of the tropical sublime: "The features of the landscape become grand, and even terrible. His road sweeps along the base of mighty mountains, once gleaming with volcanic fires, and still resplendent in their mantels of snow. . . . All around he beholds traces of their ancient combustion . . . vast tracts of lava, bristling in the innumerable fantastic forms. . . . Perhaps, at the same moment, as he casts his eye down some steep slope, or almost unfathomable ravine . . . he sees their depths glowing with the rich blooms and enameled vegetation of the tropics" (1843, 1:5).[5]

Invading U.S. soldiers could also justify their mission by the fact that Prescott repeatedly situated current-day Mexicans as a "degenerate people," fallen away from the lofty standards of their ancient Aztec forebears. In this regard, he draws a parallel between the ancient Egyptians and Greeks and their current avatars, who have been so debased by centuries of conquest that they lack the ability to appreciate the sublime constructions and achievements of their classic ancestors (1843, 1:51). U.S. armies can thus function as "redeemers" of a great heritage and restore the country to its former greatness via democratic reforms and Yankee ingenuity.[6]

Prescott's focus on the "South of the South" had been preceded by other writers, including naturalists, diplomats, and explorers, most notably the German Alexander von Humboldt, who had published accounts of the land, its flora and fauna, and its people. His works fed into the tremendous vogue in the United States for travel writing. Inevitably, this led to the introduction of Caribbean and Latin American subjects and motifs in American painting, but also in writing of all types.[7] Prescott's history thus was used as a guide for "seeing" tropical nature and people, in the same manner that Humboldt was a guide for Darwin, who stated that when he made his first trip into a tropical forest, he was seeing things through Humboldt's eyes, after reading the latter's texts of exploration.

All this is relevant, too, to ways of "framing" Manifest Destiny, which required Americans to read foreign landscapes as potentially part of an expanded nation. So how to begin this process? It requires sorting out a doubled image of landscape, people, and culture. As we shall see, a bifurcated myth of Mexico—on the one hand, a land once ruled by a martial, creative, yet barbaric people who practiced blood rites and human sacrifice, and on the other, a blushing virgin in need of protection and productive fertilization—is reflective of the deeply contradictory nature of the U.S. doctrine of Manifest Destiny itself, which employed similar iconography as the nation pushed west and south, simultaneously embracing the language of a crusade against barbarism, and that of chivalry, rescuing the "virgin land" from primitive inhabitants who had no notion of how to make "her" "bloom."[8]

To Prescott's dismay, the expeditionary forces saw themselves re-creating the march of the original Spanish invaders, using *The Conquest* as a kind of military Baedeker.[9]

The war was preceded and caused by Anglo settlement in the Mexican territory of Texas, where the new immigrants were assured by the Mexican Cortes (the national legislature) in 1824 that eventually the area would be organized as a sovereign state. However, in the following decade, the tyrant Bustamente, acting as president, forbade further immigration and instituted martial law. After Santa Ana succeeded Bustamente, he invaded Texas and was defeated in 1836 in the battle of San Jacinto, resulting in the creation of the Texas republic. Mexico reacted furiously in 1845 when Texas applied for admission to the United States, leading President Polk, a Southerner from Tennessee, to send troops as a precautionary measure, which in turn precipitated an attack by Mexico.[10]

One of the most interesting tales that emerged from the conflict was William Clark Falkner's novel *The Spanish Heroine* (1851). After his dramatic military career in Mexico, Falkner served in the Confederate military, rising to the rank of colonel, thus earning his family sobriquet, "the Old Colonel." Although his Mexican tale often lapses into tired clichés and unbelievable plot contortions, it offers myriad insights into the culture and politics of the circumCaribbean of the time, which ultimately came to influence his great-grandson William's literary production. It also displays a fascination with both the tropical sublime and the native female body, which interestingly is paired with the paragon of male beauty, the American man, whose white, Celtic masculinity comes to stand for a kind of racial sublimity.[11] Falkner's novel, however, also needs to be understood through the actual history of the conflict, which was copiously documented by a variety of figures, including many military officers who participated in both the conflict and the ensuing occupation. Accordingly, I will discuss the Mexican War narratives of Raphael Semmes and Arthur Manigault as a way of foregrounding a reading of Colonel Falkner's novel.

These three Southern writers are part of a much larger group of participants in the conflict who recorded their experiences in Mexico during and after the war, in both fiction and nonfiction. Then there were other writers who never set foot in Mexico but who wrote detailed novels set there during the conflict. Finally, as Jaime Javier Rodríguez has recently demonstrated, many Mexican writers of that time and later wrote quite different accounts of the war, often excoriating the imperialist designs and actions of the United States.

To provide a context for the readings that follow, we need to get a sense of the broader picture that has been provided by the myriad letters, journals, and newspaper accounts that were generated by the conflict. The stirring accounts of international love that appeared in sensationalist fiction treating the war stemmed from the fact that many soldiers and sailors, like Colonel Falkner, had romances with Mexican women, learning some Spanish but also local customs as they proceeded. Town dances (*fandangos*) drew local women, whose American partners whirled them around to the music of Mexican tunes played on violins, guitars, and mandolins. While many women were attended by duennas—chaperones—others were not, and there was, in fact, a high degree of sexual disease among the troops. One surgeon confided to his diary, "Venereal disease [is] prevalent to an extent that could not be imagined in our land of steady habits where this gross licentiousness is restrained by a wholesome condition of public opinion" (McCaffrey 1992, 104).

The feared "mongrelization" of the Caribbean that would presumably follow from such dangerous liaisons found an analogous form in the motley populations of the conquered cities, such as Matamoros, which quickly developed into a hellhole with the arrival of U.S. troops. As an American officer observed, "About the principle corners loiter groups of men of all colours and countries are collected cursing, swearing, fighting, gambling and presenting a most barbarous sight. . . . Murder, rapine and vice of all manner of form prevails. . . . It is . . . the receptacle of all the dregs of the United States . . . a disgrace to our country; for our own citizens are much worse than the Mexicans who are mixed up with them. Oh vice! How hideous are thy features!" (Foos 2002, 99).

While diaries, journals, and letters home often waxed eloquent over the sublime tropical scenery—particularly the native plants and flowers and the majestic, snow-topped mountains—there were even more complaints about the reptiles, thorns, and insects, especially mosquitoes and ants, and the fleas and lice that infected bedclothes.

The racially various inhabitants of Mexico were also strange to many U.S. soldiers. An 1842 census listed the population at just over 7 million, consisting of 4 million Indians, 2 million mixed bloods, 1 million whites, and 6,000 blacks (Winders 1997, 174). The appalling poverty and illiteracy of the general population in the countryside was noticed by many U.S. combatants and was seen as a strong contrast to the more refined citizenry of the capital. The categories of Creoles and mestizos were familiar to Louisianans, but not to other soldiers.

Religious sensibilities came in for a shock as well. There was much anti-Catholic sentiment among the mostly Protestant U.S. Army, and many were offended by the bullfights, cockfights, gambling, and drinking that went on Sundays (Winders 1997, 182). Catholic soldiers from the coastal U.S. South, however, were not so shocked, as their home states were in many ways quite similar to the tropical lands further south. As William Freehling has noted, in New Orleans at this time, one could, on Sunday, see Edwin Booth perform Shakespeare, hear a piano concert or a Jenny Lind recital, take dancing lessons, watch horse races or cockfights, or attend the circus. "What city," he asks, offered more ways to violate the Sabbath?" (2007, 150). Well, Mexico City, for one. Even though many Americans were taken aback by the lack of pews in churches and what they felt was overly ornate decoration (especially statues of the Virgin and the saints), quite a few attended services and were thus introduced to the Catholicism that would soon feature in many Eastern and Southern port cities, because the flood tide of immigration caused by European political unrest began just as the Mexican War was concluding (McCaffrey 1992, 72). Some soldiers had had similar experiences in the churches of New Orleans while waiting on transport to Mexico, so yet another line of connection was being understood between the coastal South and Latin America.[12] Indeed, the Caribbean aspect of the war may be seen in part through the centrality of the ports of New Orleans, Havana, and Vera Cruz. One of the salient aspects of the narratives examined here is that they underline the importance of these three harbors and the triangular trade between them, which was considerable.[13]

Colonel Falkner's presentation of creolized cities of the Americas confirms Édouard Glissant's claim that nineteenth-century Creole cities such as Havana, New Orleans, Port-au-Prince, Kingston, Manaus, and Belém resembled each other; they favored the baroque, loved carnival, and were towns noted for every sort of hedonistic pursuit. He adds that "throngs of condemned slaves and free persons of color [practiced] every possible occupation . . . a mixture of almost every race of the world. . . . In these cities, the friendliest openness coexisted with the cruelest prejudices. . . . These cities were extensions of the Plantation system and could not be imagined without them" (1999, 246).

In terms of the linkages between New Orleans and Vera Cruz, legal and extralegal profiteers and soldiers of fortune had been preying on Mexico out of the Crescent City for decades, and much of the U.S. military might unleashed on Mexico embarked on ships from Louisiana. Many of them were glad to leave New Orleans, which had been devastated by the yellow fever epidemic of 1847. The city's population at this time was swollen with adventurers, who saw the Mexican expedition as an opportunity for looting; others enlisted because they thought newly conquered Mexican lands would be deeded to them on the spot (Foos 2002, 54). Nor were the lower classes alone in their enthusiasm. New Orleans merchants had grown wealthy trading with their neighbors to the south, but they also profited from the outfitting of Manifest Destiny groups bound for Texas, and the war promised further profits. The major American expeditionary force, embarking from New Orleans, landed in Vera Cruz in 1847, completing a pincer-like operation that began with the seizure of upper California, New Mexico, and portions of northern Mexico.

Paradoxically, it was in New Orleans that Latinos mounted one of the most vigorous campaigns against the war. *La Patria* (originally known as *El Hablitor*) was the most important Spanish-language newspaper in the United States during this period. Edited by Victoriano Alemán and Eusebio Juan Gómez since 1845, the paper was distributed to Spanish speakers throughout the nation. The editors expressed suspicion of U.S. motives: noting what had happened in Texas already, they pointed out that the invasion of Mexico went against supposedly essential American values, labeling it unjust and "dangerous to the North American Union" (Gruesz 2002, 116). This, however, would prove to be a minority view, especially after gifted writers created both memoirs and fiction about their reputedly necessary and redemptive mission into the South of their South.

The Mexican Stylistics of Semmes and Manigault

One of the more prolix observers of the Mexican American War was Maryland-bred Raphael Semmes, whose treatment of the conflict, *Service Afloat and Ashore during the Mexican War* (1851), runs to 480 pages. A U.S. naval lieutenant who served both at sea and on land, he begins his narrative by claiming that during his six months in Mexico, he "mixed freely with the inhabitants, and made himself familiar with their history, manners, customs, etc.," which made him realize "the grandeur of the scenery" of this *"terra incognita"* and the "great disparity between the two people" (v–vi). Semmes clearly wrote his account with volumes on Mexican history, maps, travel accounts, and other documents before him, as he provides a mini-history of Mexico interlarded with his own experiences. He explains, for instance, his reference to a *terra incognita*, by noting that Spain kept Mexico hermetically sealed against trade with other countries, permitting commerce through only one port, Vera Cruz.[14] His compassionate portrait of the unlanded and uneducated four-fifths of the population, coupled with his indictment of the wealthy class and the church, gives this text an almost proto-Marxist tinge, although that is often offset by his jingoistic sense of American exceptionalism and by his theory that the downtrodden majority is doomed because of its "mongrel" mixture of Indian and African blood. Eventually, Semmes declares that the slaves in the United States are superior in intellect and situation, owing to the natural "kindly feeling" masters have for their dependents there and the slave's perception that he is part of "his master's family" (17). Ultimately, this argument, which was shared by many filibusters and their supporters, used the "global" perspective to support the status quo of the "local," that is U.S., slavery.

At the time he was writing, however, Semmes and many other commentators on the war were at pains to emphasize both difference and affinity between the bordering countries. The similarities are dwelt on to disarm those who drew back—as many did upon the occasion of the Louisiana Purchase in 1803—from the possible infusion of polluting alien bodies and culture into the national imaginary. As these writers knew, the United States was about to incorporate, at one gulp, nearly half of a foreign, Catholic, mostly Indian, and "dark skinned" country.[15] Sometimes Semmes added substantially to racist fears with lurid descriptions of the *Leperos,* a dissolute species of "roving vagabonds," whose women are "without chastity" while the men are "petty rogues and thieves." He estimated there were at least 10,000 *Leperos* in Mexico City alone. Yet such "differences" had to be stressed in order to justify the invasion and need for a colonizing "improvement" of a mismanaged geography, one that could be "redeemed" by the transformations and translations of Manifest Destiny. Echoing Prescott's lamentations about a "fallen" people, Semmes goes into exhaustive detail about the deficiencies of the Mexican economy, particularly in terms of landownership, labor, onerous taxes, corruption of officials and the military, lack of transportation systems for commerce, and foreign ownership of the mines. Presumably, Yankee ingenuity and institutions could provide antidotes.[16]

There were other aspects to Semmes's work, however, that made for a somewhat sympathetic view of Mexico. He came from a six-generation Catholic family in Maryland, was thus much more interested than his colleagues were in the church's history and operation in Mexico, and was especially attentive to the beauties of the churches and cathedrals. His extensive reading in the history of the era of contact and discovery gave him an invaluable background for interpreting Mexican and Caribbean cultures. In the 1840s, when not on active duty, he was mainly occupied with mapping and surveying on the Caribbean/Gulf rim, which made him in demand when the U.S. Navy entered the Mexican War but also meant that he was much more aware than others would be of topography, climate, and cultural monuments. His service took him all over the Caribbean and to South America and eventually to the Mediterranean. After attending the Navy School at Norfolk, he had served in the Seminole wars, navigating small boats up the Withlacoochee River. This experience in the Indian country of the tropical South made him unusually attentive to native cultures of Mexico later. We will see this pattern repeatedly in this study, as initial observation of exotic tropical topology and cultures in the coastal United States dictates modes of perception as the viewer/writer/soldier/ethnographer ventures into the South of the South. This has obvious parallels to the syndrome we examined earlier, where Humboldt and Lyell influenced Darwin, and Prescott shaped views of Mexico by the invading U.S. officers.

We also note that Semmes always sees Mexico as part of the circum-Caribbean, partly because of his naval peregrinations. In 1845, shortly before his involvement in Mexico, Semmes's vessel was sent to Santo Domingo City to obtain information about the new nation by that name that had just declared its independence from Haiti. Semmes also visited Havana during this voyage and took copious notes. He was inspired by Columbus, whom he knew through Washington Irving's popular biography, and he visited the explorer's tomb in the Havana cathedral and the cell in which he was incarcerated in Santo Domingo. Havana harbor also drew Semmes's interest, as he contemplated how U.S. annexation of Cuba would secure a magnificent port that could be used to "harass the enemy's commerce and pick up his single ships" (Spencer 1997, 17). Clearly, he saw a constellation of related points in the circumCaribbean operating in tandem in a projected expansion of the imperial United States.

Semmes provides a "prequel" to his account of the Mexican War by sketching in the movement of Stephen F. Austin and a band of settlers to Mexican Texas and their subsequent prosecution by Mexicans, who resented the political involvement of what Semmes calls "a superior race." Astonishingly, while providing a rather conventional, racially charged linear history of the events that led to Anglo Texan revolution, he suggests that if things had followed a more tranquil path in Texas, "in a generation or two, the radical differences of the two races would entirely have disappeared—the flaxen hair and the blue eyes of the Anglo-Saxon taking a darker shade, and more brilliant light, from the Hispano-Mexican. We should have thus conquered

Texas—and ultimately all Mexico—as Greece conquered Rome, by civilization and the arts, instead of the sword" (1851, 43). This argument by amalgamation seems rather incredible, coming as it does from a Southerner whose native region had an elaborate bulwark between the races, although one that was undermined and overtopped every night, when white men appropriated the bodies of black women. There is no hint, however, in this "vision" that Semmes has of racial mixing, that there will be a "one drop" rule governing racial definitions. His theory here ultimately involves just another form of colonization, for presumably the "whitening" of "Hispano-Mexicans" would require a vast influx of "Anglo-Saxon" immigrants.[17] His attitude, however, was certainly not shared by all Southerners. In 1847, John C. Calhoun warned that "more than half of the Mexicans are Indians, and the other is composed chiefly of mixed tribes. I protest against such a union as that! Ours, sir, is the Government of a white race" (Robert E. May 2002, 15). Other Southerners were against annexing Mexico too, since that nation had abolished slavery in 1829 and because the climate and topography were viewed by many as not favorable to slave economies—and therefore would dilute the power of slave-owning states.

Interestingly, Semmes asserts that the navy assembled by the Republic of Texas really won the war—for Mexico, in order to successfully invade its former province, would have had to proceed in boats from the Gulf, because the long stretches between Mexico's interior and Texas were barren wastes, devoid of water. While it is a commonplace today to attribute the rise of Houston to its enormous port, opening onto the trade routes of the Atlantic, we have perhaps forgotten how important sea routes were at this time for intra-national travel, in all parts of the world. Control of Galveston and the surrounding waters was a vital requirement for U.S. mastery of Vera Cruz, and for the subsequent invasion of Mexico. Moreover, as Elizabeth DeLoughrey has rightly observed, the global South needs to be understood as a space "constituted by far more water than land and thus an apt place to consider the ways in which maritime histories and the transoceanic imaginary have been constituted in relation to landfall and settlement" (2007, xi).[18]

Semmes concludes his wrap up of the prelude to war by declaring, "The passage of our race into Texas, New Mexico, and California, was but the first step in that great movement southward, which forms a part of our destiny. An all-wise Providence has placed us in juxtaposition with an inferior people, in order, without doubt, that we may sweep over them, and remove them (as a people) and their worn-out institutions from the face of the earth.

We are the northern hordes of the Alani, spreading ourselves over fairer and sunnier fields, and carrying along with us, beside the newness of life, and the energy and courage of our prototypes, letters, arts, and civilization" (1851, 67). This imperial bombast situates the United States, as many did in this era, as the new Rome, destined to spread liberty and prosperity to the benighted South of the South. Similarly, after describing the fall of Vera Cruz, Semmes details the many improvements made by Americans: "Signs of the energy of our race began to appear, in the improvements. . . . The apathy and indifference to improvement, amounting almost to contempt, of the Hispano-Mexican, had given place to the go-ahead-a-tiveness—new phases of society must have new words—of Brother Jonathan" (145–50), an insertion of U.S. mythology into Caribbean linguistics that parallels Roman chronicles of conquered Gaul and provides yet another example of the constant parallels that have been drawn between the Mediterranean and the Caribbean.

In his account of the complicated naval battles and blockades off the Mexican coast, Semmes provides the reader with a good sense of the strategic aspect of the connecting sea, the topography of the coast, and of the centrality of Vera Cruz. This imposing citadel and city was the only major port open to large vessels, yet it was strongly defended against any hostile incursion by its fort and cannons. The other major ports in Yucatan—especially Laguna del Carmen—were also contested, and Semmes shows us the relation of these harbors to the dynamics of sea battle. Yucatan at this time was in rebellion against Mexico and was a key supply source for fresh food and water for U.S. vessels, which were repeatedly tracing a web of connection between the U.S. South and the western rim of the Caribbean.

Details like these stud other sections of the manuscript as well, providing context and historical background for the events described. The narrative, however, always circles back to the military conflict, and there can be few better accounts of nineteenth-century U.S. naval combat in the annals of maritime history. Yet Semmes also gives detailed descriptions of the sublime views offered of the coast and its towering mountains, the vicissitudes of the Gulf weather, and the myriad ways the seasonal *vomito* (yellow fever) plays havoc with Mexican industry and trade because of the frequent closures it causes of the port of Vera Cruz, through which three-fourths of Mexico's foreign commerce was negotiated. Astutely, Semmes employs a circumCaribbean geometry, as he observes that the "*vomito* of Vera Cruz resembles, in all its essential features, that of Havana and New Orleans" (1851, 115). The relation of Havana receives further detail when Semmes reveals that Santa Ana has been in exile there, amusing himself with fighting cocks and *monte* games, activities that still occur across the Caribbean basin, including Louisiana, where cockfighting remained legal into the twenty-first century.

As we have seen, most combatants in the war left the United States through New Orleans, and many of them entered Mexico through Vera Cruz. All these troops—including Semmes—were struck by the many similarities between the two ports, whose rich histories as generators of trade, mobility, and military operations gave them a centrality, in terms of the Atlantic World, that they would eventually come to lack, as national centers eclipsed ports, making them peripheral rather than commanding.

We see this division between the port and the interior when Semmes is dispatched to inland locations. His journeys allow him to provide accounts of Santa Anna's country estate, the tropical flora and fauna, and the dwellings and fields of the Indians, so different from the lordly *haciendas*. Semmes, perhaps thinking of the appeal of popular tourist guides of his time, refers to the vistas he sees as "singularly romantic; hills, now and then welling into mountain-peaks of the most fantastic and rugged outlines. . . . The view would open upon the country below, and the eye would wander over many leagues of a wild and barren waste, until it rested, in fatigue on the distant horizon" (219). This passage rehearses the language of Sir Walter Scott and the Romantic poets but also mimics the concept of "eye" employed by the great nineteenth-century American landscape artists and their concepts of the romantic sublime.[19] These supposedly "empty" landscapes play into the iconography of imperialist narrative, creating divine "voids" that cry out for "fulfillment." Semmes seems to understand that his readers want to read natural landscapes through the conjoined lens of memory, desires, and history.[20]

The operations of the "eye" have yet another register. As Mary Louise Pratt has noted, "advance scouts" for capitalism (and despite his ambivalent feelings about Mexico, Semmes surely can be counted among this company) usually "encode" terrains they survey as "*disponsible*, available for improvement. . . . The improving eye produces subsistence habitats as 'empty landscapes' meaningful only in terms of a capitalist future and of their potential for producing a marketable surplus" (Pratt 1992, 61).

Another aspect of Romantic iconography, the ruin, plays an even more important role in this narrative, for in addition to creating a meditative and picturesque *memento mori*, the ruin signifies the moral and political decay of Mexico, which the invasion, if taken to its most extreme potential (annexation of the entire country), could reverse through a program of imperial restoration and Americanization. Semmes in this sense (and many others) is following the lead of Prescott, whose meditations on the great Aztec ruins, which he saw as equivalent to those of Egypt and India, denote both a grand past that can be recaptured and a sign of the moral decay of the monument builders' descendants. These awe-inspiring ruins are matched by the vistas of the Mexican landscape, which Prescott describes as "grand, and even terrible," consisting as it often does of "mighty mountains," "volcanic fires," "unfathomable ravines," and the "enameled vegetation of the tropics" (1843, 1:5). In passages such as these, sublime mystery is rendered in a tropical key, but it is also employed to imagine an imperialist and racist future, one cloaked under the guise of progress and (white) liberation.

These terms are taken from classic concepts of the natural sublime but rendered through a tropic lens. Prescott and Semmes were by no means unique in employing such imagery and language. "The tropical sublime" offers a way of seeing, notating, and meditating, as the multiple writers I consider struggle to put the inexpressible into words. Accordingly, I shall be concerned with the ways in which the sense of the sublime has been conjoined and/or expressed through the tropical, another large term that has taken on many meanings. Well before William Bartram's botanical travels in the tropical United States in the eighteenth century, the strange new panoramas of *La Florida* and its surrounding islands and coasts caused Ponce de León, De Soto, and other early explorers to marvel, as they experienced something beyond the ordinary range of their experience. Cortés and his conquistadores had the same experience in tropical Mexico. Throughout Southern and circumCaribbean history, writers have sought words to express what is apparently inexpressible, for, as Philip Shaw states, "sublimity . . . refers to the moment when the ability to apprehend, to know, and to express a thought or sensation is defeated" (2006, 3). Words, in this case, are a good example of what Faulkner's Addie Bundren calls a "shape to fill a lack," or what Zora Neale Hurston termed "the inaudible voice of it all." Words often fail spectators who view things for the first time, and this is characteristic of many of the writers in this study, who are often experiencing new subjects and landscapes of the circumCaribbean tropical zone and groping for a new language in which to express it.

Since the classical age, the sublime has been associated with the vastness of natural spaces and objects, which emerged in unexpected new forms during the age of discovery and began to accelerate in the sixteenth century. Historians, military men such as Semmes, Manigualt, and Falkner, and travel writers, awed by tropical landscapes that defied standard modes of depiction, sought a new language to capture the sublime nature they were experiencing—a new descriptive vocabulary, one that could do justice to aspects of nature and sometimes material culture that were too immense or complex to contain in language. They had a ready resource in the preceding century's extensive literature on the concept of the sublime, which delineated the difference between knowing and feeling. The sublime is never far from violence. The tropical swamp and jungle—especially if the latter includes volcanic mountains—offer compelling visions of pleasure and danger. The monumental and awe-inspiring Aztec ruins (which when climbed, offered sublime vistas for contemplation) were doubly thrilling when spectators came to them aware, through Prescott's history, of the human sacrifices enacted there eons ago.[21]

In the case of the U.S. invasion of Mexico, the aesthetic appreciation of these "new" lands had to be balanced against the political and moral imperatives of the colonizing army and navy. Immanuel Kant felt that one could only encounter the sublime as an interior moral law or through the majesty of nature, and the invasion interbraided these two factors. He also proclaimed that "natural beauty carries with it a purposiveness in its form, by which the object seems as it were predetermined for our power of judgment, so that this beauty constitutes in itself an object of our liking. On the other hand, if something arouses in us, merely in apprehension and without any reasoning on our part, a feeling of the sublime, then it may indeed appear, in its form, contra purposive for our power of judgment, incommensurate with our power of exhibition, and as it were violent to our imagination, and yet we judge it all the more sublime for that" (1790, 245).[22]

These kinds of reactions were common to the writers we consider here, as they balanced romantic conceptions of the sublime with more practical, utilitarian observations based on concepts of commodity and productivity. We see this in Semmes's detailed and appreciative description of the relatively wealthy city of Puebla and the once-prosperous town of Tepeahualco (today spelled Tepeyahualco). The former, Mexico's second-largest municipality, whose magnificent churches are still today full of Indian-mined gold and silver, is eyed as having "every facility for becoming the great workshop of Mexico"—producing paper, porcelains, leather goods, jewelry, and soap, but especially textiles, which could use the South's cotton. Semmes notes that the painstaking hand manufacture of leather goods by the Indians could easily be speeded up by the use of Yankee machinery.

Taking another tack—bemoaning "ruins" as symptomatic of decay but also as sites of possible renewal through colonization—Semmes considers Tepeyahualco's church. It had once been "an elegant, building; but was now, like almost every noble relic of the past one meets with in Mexico, in a state of decay, fast verging toward dilapidation." The surrounding area was so poor that Indians actually lived in caves, "real troglodytes . . . like so many rabbits. . . . Every hut and cavern was filled with naked children" (1851, 228). Semmes understands very clearly that what prosperity Mexico has came from the victimization of the Indians, who had miserable lives in the 1840s. The town of Napolucan, for instance, Semmes shows us, owes its present economic health to the virtual slavery of the Indians of the area, whose poverty and nakedness led Semmes to "exclaim, with Madame Roland, 'Oh! liberty, what crimes are committed in thy name!'" (233).[23] As Madame Roland was a revolutionary whose failure to go along with Robespierre's excesses led to her execution (and her quote here was made in front of the statue of the Goddess of Liberty as she was carted to the guillotine), Semmes's blindness to the discrepancy between his passionate outburst and his slave owning is rather striking—however, the concept of "freeing" Indian slaves was grist for the mill of conquest. Semmes also seems to be reading these Indians through the lens of the history he has mastered before writing his narrative, for he often talks of the magnificent cities Cortés encountered during the conquest, especially Tlascala and Cholula, which were the fabled predecessors of the current city of Puebla. Again ironically, Semmes's method seems to be to suggest how the Spanish invasion ruined early cultures, but with the ultimate inference that the Spanish bungled what the Americans can now not only rectify, but do right—a *benign* form of colonization, in short. Semmes's source here had to be Prescott, whose history of Mexico devotes chapters 2 through 7 to the Tlascalan/Chololan cultures. Semmes also frequently refers to the "master race" observations of Cortes and Diaz, who are cited in Prescott.

Like other Americans who had described Mexican topography, Prescott employs a romantic and classically minded gaze. The resulting argument from the sublime, which proceeds from the ubiquitous raptures over Mexican landscape, links Mexico to North American concepts that are manifest in the conventional tropes of nineteenth-century landscape writing and painting. These concepts had been memorably expressed in Thomas Cole's allegorical paintings, *The Course of Empire*, which were exhibited to great acclaim in New York in the 1830s. Cole was vehemently opposed to the expansionist agenda of presidents from Andrew Jackson to James K. Polk and hated the prospect of the Mexican war. His allegorical cycle, in fact, included Caribbean/Latin American images of the dangers of revolution, such as exploding volcanoes, menacing foliage, and swarming, chaotic populations. His early scenes depicting the republic, however, are classically serene and Arcadian in a northern sense, more like the Hudson River Valley that was being limned by the luminist school.[24] In the same era, however, other American painters such as Albert Bierstadt and Frederic Church (who actually traveled in the tropics) were linking the continents with sublime, often imaginary, but definitely tropical landscapes of Mexico and Central and South America. These expanses had much in common with those being painted in the coastal South by figures such as Audubon, Marie Adrien Persac, and others. Church's painting *Cayambe* (1858) of Ecuador's snow-peaked mountain, offers a sublime view of a tropical landscape leading up to the peak itself, which emerges majestically from the clouds. Church's South American landscapes, so similar to those being done of the American West but with tropical touches, added to the Edenic image of the Southern Hemisphere, including the concept of land to be conquered, since virtually all of his vast expanses contain few signs of habitation. Bierstadt is famous for his Western landscapes, yet he also did tropical scenes, particularly those set in Nassau, and one of his more striking historical vignettes, *The Landing of Columbus*, provides a Caribbean panorama that features some very Western-looking natives.

While most of these painters of Latin landscapes were Northerners, their work provided images that linked the tropical zones of the two continents and the islands, helping to blur the lines of national boundaries through a hemispheric imaginary. Again, Semmes, who was conversant with these artistic and literary traditions, uses these conventions to advantage in making Mexico a prize worth winning and a landscape worth inhabiting and improving. Either "empty" but grand, or populated by degraded people yearning to be free, amid ruins in need of restoration, the landscape translates into a rationale for recolonization.

Semmes's embrace of narrative language to present the same vistas speaks to the unity of approach of Americans as they aestheticized the impulses of Manifest Destiny. As Rob Wilson explains, the notion of the American sublime was a way of sacralizing force, as the genre fostered a consolidation of American identity that was based on notions of landscape, immensity, and wildness—the latter read as power (1991, 7).[25]

Eventually, Semmes turns his eye to the fertile lands surrounding Puebla and decries the primitive methods of farming that could so easily benefit from American plows and scientific approaches to husbandry, whose effectiveness he had seen on the plantations of the coastal states of the United States. Significantly, he winds up his peroration with an endorsement of Southern workers—slaves—as he bemoans the virtual slavery of the Mexican Indians under the *mozo* system: "This is the boasted freedom of the Mexican soil, about which there has been so much senseless declamation in our congress. . . . The well-fed and well-cared-for dependent of a southern estate, with us, is infinitely superior, in point both of physical and moral condition, to the *mozo* of the Mexican hacienda. The 'hewers of wood and drawers of water' are slaves everywhere, as I have found; and whether the slave is so, *lege scripta*, or *lege necessitatis*, is, as the lawyers say, a distinction without a difference" (1851, 250).

This rationale carefully inserts, without saying so, the inference that colonization of this territory would benefit from American slavery, which would replace the *mozo* system. We note, too, that while the Indians in Mexico are deemed slaves, Semmes does not use that word in describing the "*dependent of a southern estate*" (my emphasis), a practice he and his ancestors had used for generations as slave owners.[26]

The racial stock of Mexico—even the "white" variety—is always seen as lacking, and, indeed, the Mexican women seem to feel this is so, for Semmes asserts that they pine for the "comely and manly forms of our younger officers, whom they could not but contrast, favorably, with their more puny husbands and *beaux*" (267). Later, he claims that Mexican women who have married Americans become totally converted to the standard of Anglo-Saxon male superiority. He cites one such lady who thinks "one good specimen of a northern man equal to at least a dozen *floxos Mexicanos*—weakly Mexicans!" (268).[27] Clearly, for Semmes (and, as we shall see, Colonel Falkner), amalgamation—impossible with black people—is a good thing when the race to be lifted is only mildly "colored" and the refining element is the blood of a stalwart white man. We should note too, that amalgamation has to be between a white man from the United States and a Mexican woman, never between a white U.S. woman and a Mexican man. The preoccupation of both Semmes and Colonel Falkner with the Adonis-like beauty of the prototypical U.S. male verges on the homoerotic but seems to be employed for ideological purposes of Manifest Destiny. This line of persuasion, however, goes well beyond male physical beauty. Aspersions cast on Mexican men in general are given more focus as Semmes critiques the Mexican generals, who are portrayed as constantly fighting among themselves, particularly

Santa Anna, the top commander, and his second, Valencia, who disgraced himself by fleeing the battle of Contreras, a fact also mentioned in Colonel Falkner's novel. The presentation of such scenarios makes a case for the fraternal bonds between U.S. men as yet another point for colonization, as male unity seemingly fosters industrialization and progress.

Semmes's 1851 memoir is one of the most detailed accounts of the war and its wider cultural aspect, and it is fascinating for a number of reasons. First, it offers an explanation for what must be seen as a kind of cultural shorthand in Colonel Falkner's text, and second, it displays little of the anti-Northern animus of accounts of the Mexican War that were created after the Civil War, when a retrospective memory seems to have operated on the part of bitter Confederate veterans such as Arthur Manigault. Third, Semmes's 480-page account was very influential, for it became a best seller, primarily because it was highly critical of General Winfield Scott (a subject I am unable to address here) and thus became campaign propaganda against the general when he ran for president in 1852. It was especially credible because Semmes was a valiant and involved leader at key battles, including the siege of Vera Cruz, the storming of Chapultepec, and the crucial battle of Churubusco, which receives a thrilling presentation here, perhaps because it leads to Semmes's devastating criticism of Scott for ordering this arduous, but ultimately unnecessary, siege in the first place, rather than pressing on to Mexico City. Finally, Semmes was an exceptionally well-educated man, who understood basic principles of art, philosophy, literary theory, rhetoric, and the history of military tactics, among other things. His narrative profits from extensive if judicious cribbing from prior historians and travelers and has the benefit of following a military campaign that echoed an earlier one, namely Cortés's path of conquest against the Aztecs, which gets extensive rehearsal here as Semmes educates his reader about history both contemporary and ancient. Above all, however, Semmes constantly compares Mexican landscapes and people with those of his native coastal United States, which will apparently constitute a model and paradigm for the redemption of Mexico.

But make no mistake—despite Semmes's regional set of comparisons, the narrative relentlessly proclaims the *national* right of Americans to invade and conquer Mexico, to spread slavery, and to congratulate themselves on the conduct of the war. As he asserts,

> To disgrace ourselves by sack and rape, no one thought of such things. . . . Indeed, in whatever light we regard this campaign, it is

one of the most wonderful on record. It is not wonderful that we triumphed over Mexico. This was to have been expected from her physical, and still more from her moral weakness. But like the knights of old [perhaps a reference to Scott's *Ivanhoe*, immensely popular in the antebellum South], we seemed to have scorned to avail ourselves of the weakness of our enemy. . . . With a mean force of ten thousand men, we landed in the season of tempests, on a coast where pestilence annually sweeps off its thousands, and marched through a nation of eight million. (1851, 467–68)

In his summary, Semmes employs the grandest phrases of Manifest Destiny: "The salvation of our institutions depends, in a great degree, upon a reasonable extension of our limits. This is the only thing which will rob faction of its bitterness. . . . As our territorial limits increase, the individual states will become less and less important." He also predicts the total assimilation of Mexico into the United States: "It is impossible to place two people, of such widely differing constitution and temperaments, in juxtaposition with each other, without one of them being absorbed by the other—But this absorption need not be violent . . . if she profit by the lessons of the war. . . . While the Sibyl is spinning the web of her fate, she should civilize and educate herself, to render herself the more worthy of the embrace of the young bridegroom to whom she is affianced" (476). Yet he also states that "our turbulent and proud sister has been taught to respect us" (479), so this looming marriage seems to be incestuous. Continuing his matrimonial metaphor, Semmes goes on to argue for total amalgamation of the mistreated Indians into the general population, for "I regard the Indian, in most parts of Mexico, as physically, the superior of the compound of the Celt and the Moor, which is there denominated the white man" (477), and in the very last sentence, he cries, "The next generation of Mexicans may have cause to look back with satisfaction upon the struggle of their country with the United States, as the starting point whence a new impetus was given her, in that great race of civilization, which is to fit her for her ultimate incorporation in the Anglo-American family" (479).

Semmes's remarks reveal a bifurcated stance toward the native strain in Mexican culture. While he professes admiration for the "physically superior" Indian, he nevertheless predicts an eventual benefit for Indian Mexicans in future racial amalgamation with the "Anglo-American family." As we shall see, Colonel Falkner consistently portrays his Mexican heroine Ellen as "Spanish" rather than Mexican (and therefore part Indian). This is characteristic of most of the romances of the period that involve unions between Mexican women and U.S. men. As Octavio Paz has explained, Mexico is the most Indian country in Latin America, whereas in the United States, Indians were either exterminated or confined to reservations. "This . . . is the major difference between our two countries. . . . The United States was founded on a land without a past. The historical memory of Americans is European, not American. . . . The opposite is true of Mexico. Mexico City was built on the ruins of Tenochtitlán, the Aztec city that was built in the likeness of Tula, the Toltec city that was built in the likeness of Teotihuacán, the first great city on the American continent. Every Mexican bears within him this continuity" (1985, 362–63). The war received a far less romantic reading by others. South Carolina's Arthur Middleton Manigault, who later became a brigadier general in the Confederate army, wrote a Mexican War narrative that detailed his service with the Palmetto Regiment. According to him, most deaths during the war were due to diseases "common to the climate of Mexico" (1983, 299).

In fact, the Mexican War was the deadliest in American history; 110 out of every thousand troops lost their lives to combat, accidents, or, most often, disease. The association of the tropics with new forms of disease cast a pall over more Edenic aspects of the country. Even the Civil War was less lethal, during which 65 out of every thousand died (Winders 1997, 139).[28]

The war was virtually over after the fall of Mexico City, and Manigault returned home to Charleston via Vera Cruz and Mobile after nearly two years of military service. Despite the graphic portrayal of war's miseries in his account, he concludes, "In spite of the privations fatigue and dangers to which I was at times exposed they were perhaps the happiest & most romantic period of my life" (1983, 320), a claim that is supported by an ensuing, rapturous account of the beauties of Mexico City. While there, Manigault attends plays, ballets, and opera and enjoys dinners at the lavish "fondas," or restaurants. He observes the extensive casinos but does not admit to gaming himself. He finds the climate "perfection."[29]

The ugly American statement, "Paris would be perfect if it weren't for the French," finds a hemispheric equivalent here: after praising the perfection of the Valley of Mexico, Manigault states, "Were it not for the inhabitants & the miserable government with which this country is cursed I would if it were possible, of all other places in the world which it has been my fortune to see, select this valley in which to pass my life" (322). The locale clearly seemed familiar to Manigault in another way as well. He remarks on the fertile haciendas, which he correctly interprets as "plantations or farms" (323). "The owners of these are as a general rule the true Aristocracy . . . men of great wealth," a fact that he approvingly finds consonant with the culture back home in South Carolina.

One of the most disturbing elements in the narrative comes at the very end, in a passage that perhaps accounts for Manigault's earlier assertion that the war, despite its privations, constituted the most "romantic" adventure of his life. "The Mexican women are not handsome but are well made with good figures, small feet & an exceedingly graceful carriage, coquettish & ready always for a flirtation. Their costume is exceedingly pretty & becoming and altho coming into their country with an invading army, yet many of our officers found but little difficulty in mingling freely with them" (324). Manigault, who had avoided sexual references earlier, seems to be unable to resist this final addition to his text—its repression earlier perhaps suggests that any invasion, conquest, or transformation of a tropical Caribbean country, of necessity involves "free intercourse" with native women, whose bodies are inevitably associated with the landscape itself. Manigault's stance here would be echoed by Julius Garesche, who wrote home that he was "reconciled to their dark complexions" but found it "impossible to entertain any respect for their morality" (cited in Foos 2002, 129).

Naturally, the racial sublime usually registered most powerfully in narratives of uplift through amalgamation (although mergers with African peoples remained taboo). The configuration of an imperial imaginary found its most popular form in the novel, where the exotic appeal of Southern climes was figured through the body of a native woman. Melville had done this in his first novel, *Typee* (1846), a tale of the Pacific islands, with the fetching native figure of Fayaway, the hero's beloved. Similarly, following the imperialist notion of Mexico as an appropriate "bride," after the war with Mexico, U.S. novels began to appear that involved the union of an American man— often a military figure—and a dark-skinned senorita.

As David Spurr has stated, in classic colonial discourse, "the body of the primitive becomes as much the object of examination, commentary, and valorization as the landscape of the primitive" (1993, 22), and this is certainly the case in U.S. accounts of the Mexican War, in both nonfiction and fiction. The primitive/colonized body has been described by Spurr as the final object of penetration for the Western gaze. "The body, rather than speech, law, or history, is the essential defining characteristic of primitive peoples" (22). A seeming corollary to this in the works of the military figures we are addressing in this chapter is the seemingly irresistible attraction native women have for their comely male conquerors, whose bodies are routinely valorized above those of native men.

Colonel Falkner's Fandango with History

Now that we have seen firsthand military accounts of the conflict, we may turn to a fictional treatment, Colonel William Falkner's circumCaribbean novel *The Spanish Heroine* (1851). As noted earlier, the conflict with Mexico was the first foreign war for the United States, and as such, it introduced thousands of soldiers—many of them from the U.S. South, like William Falkner—to the Caribbean. The great enthusiasm for the conflict, stoked originally by overwhelming support for the independence movement of U.S. settlers in Mexican Texas, was massively covered in the U.S. press, drew unprecedented numbers of volunteers, and occasioned the construction and movement across great distance of the greatest military apparatus in U.S. history up to that time. New Orleans, as the most important English-speaking circumCaribbean city, with its nine newspapers, became the mouthpiece for war reportage for the nation, giving reports a strongly Southern perspective. As Robert W. Johannsen has noted, this was the first U.S. war to be covered by correspondents, and foremost among them were stringers from New Orleans (1985, 17). The many stories in the press led to dime novels and later still, hard-bound novels, plays, paintings, and military histories. Interestingly, a number of the earliest fictions based on the war featured women soldiers who disguised themselves as men, as in Harry Halyard's *The Heroine of Tampico* (1847) and *The Warrior Queen; or, The Buccaneer of the Brazos* (1848). Works like these, which enjoyed wide popularity as late as 1860, relied on melodramatic thrills and rarely attempted any kind of social uplift. The motif of a woman cross-dressing in order to fight for her country (often alongside her man) provided an easy way to sexualize military narratives. William Falkner may have read one or many of these myriad tales of the war in American popular culture, or when in Cincinnati he may have seen a play based on the conflict. The most likely candidate for a model, however, if there is one, is Ned Buntline's (Edward Zane Carroll Judson) 1847 epic, *The Volunteer; or, The Maid of Monterey*, which like Falkner's tale, featured the Mexican battle site and a female warrior. Further, she falls in love with a Kentucky soldier, just as Falkner's Mexican Ellen adores her Appalachian lover Henry.[30] Even earlier, however, Robert Montgomery Bird's first novel, *Calavar; or, The Knight of the Conquest* (1834), a tale ennobling the fallen Aztecs while condemning the Spanish conquistadores, featured a cross-dressing Moorish woman who has migrated to Mexico after the fall of Islamic Granada in 1492. In a bizarre intervention into history, Bird has Leila and her father instruct the Aztecs in modes of Western warfare, finding revenge against their enemy by helping another invaded people in the New World. They declare this to be a war of "tyranny against freedom" (2:169). This thematic was used by all the American commentators on the war, who felt they were carrying the ark of liberty into a benighted country.[31]

As many critics have noted, William Cuthbert Faulkner, who found few reasons to admire his own father, found a male role model in this heroic great-grandfather, William Clark Falkner. A figure of the Mississippi frontier who combined a ruthless desire for success with reckless courage, Falkner established a considerable legend in Southern history through his military exploits in two wars, his pioneering development of the state's railroads, and his extensive literary career, which was often based on his travels, occasioned by both war and leisure.[32]

Falkner, like all U.S. combatants, configured the new culture he was exploring with his own "place of dwelling," in his case, northern Mississippi, but he had also lived on the frontiers of Tennessee and Missouri before that. Vexed issues of gender, race, class, trade, and agriculture were features of all those locales, and he remarked on Caribbean and Mexican manifestations of these and other aspects of his home domain as he toured the Southern climes. The processes of travel, spectatorship, participation in a new culture, and creative construction of a new hybrid narrative inevitably shaped the way that Falkner wrote ever afterward. But what, exactly, did he see and do in the circumCaribbean? According to his only biographer, Donald Duclos, William Falkner left Mississippi with volunteers of the Second Mississippi troops, sailing from Vicksburg for New Orleans in January 1847. They left that port on January 28 and proceeded to Matamoras, Mexico, arriving in early March. They had no military action until April. Military records reveal that Falkner was shot by Mexican guerrillas and sent home to Ripley, Mississippi, to recover. He returned to Mexico but was soon mustered out, on October 31, 1847, after doctors determined he was unable to resume full duty (he had been wounded in the foot and also lost three fingers of his left hand). Falkner received a pension and public land, prompting his enemy, Thomas C. Hindman, to challenge the award. His son, Robert Holt Hindman, had served with Falkner in Mexico; Falkner subsequently killed him in a duel in Ripley. The elder Hindman claimed that his son had told him that Falkner had been illegally away from camp, had indecently propositioned a Mexican woman, and had been shot by her kinsmen, thus spinning out a romantic Mexican tale of his own that would snare Falkner.

Spinning gold out of his troubled Mexican experiences, Colonel Falkner constructed a long narrative poem, *The Siege of Monterey* (1851), and *The Spanish Heroine* (1851), a short novel. Despite his focus on the conflict in Monterey, that battle had occurred well before he enlisted, so his account had to be based on those of others.[33] Colonel Falkner's poem and novel were published at his expense in Cincinnati in 1851. Duclos quickly passes over the novel in favor of the poem, which concerns the love of two Mexicans, Bibo and Isabel, but also has much about the Colonel's own life after the war, which attracted Duclos. The poem is modeled after Byron's *Don Juan* and consists of eight cantos. As in *The Spanish Heroine*, the heroine, Isabel, disguises herself as a man and fights in the war. While various real Americans appear in the poem as heroes, most of it concerns the incredibly melodramatic separations, reunions, and eventual bliss of the central couple (although there is an almost pornographic description of a striptease dancer early on).[34] *The Spanish Heroine* proves far more interesting than *The Siege* and should be seen as an early example of a hemispheric and transnational novel. Full of maritime journeys, shipwrecks, captivities, drownings, and storms at sea, the narrative crisscrosses the Caribbean and the Atlantic as it progresses, and several scenes are laid in Cuba. Falkner displays intimate knowledge of Mexico City and Vera Cruz; these metropolises were closely linked at the time, since seagoing visitors to the interior of Mexico usually disembarked from vessels onto the wharves of Vera Cruz and then went inland on horseback or in coaches. The novel is situated in one of the most important decades in American literary history, which saw the advent of Nathaniel Hawthorne's *The Scarlet Letter*, Herman Melville's *Moby-Dick* and *Benito Cereno*, Harriet Beecher Stowe's *Uncle Tom's Cabin*, Walt Whitman's *Leaves of Grass*, Frederick Douglass's *My Bondage and My Freedom*, and John Rollin Ridge's (Yellow Bird) *The Life and Adventures of Joaquin Murieta: The Celebrated California Bandit*. In terms of American works dealing with the Caribbean, Falkner's novel predates Martin Delany's *Blake; or, The Huts of America* by eight years and precedes Lucy Holcombe Pickens's *The Free Flag of Cuba* by three years. Falkner's story makes many connections to the U.S. South, as it creates a circumCaribbean imaginary. Because this Mexican tale inspired great-grandson William Faulkner's setting of Civil War cross-dressing in *The Unvanquished* (1938), it is also fascinating to compare it with the recently rediscovered Civil War narrative of Loreta Janeta Velasquez, *The Woman in Battle* (1876), which also features a Latina female soldier.[35]

Still, Colonel Falkner's novel is hardly a record of the war, as will shortly become clear when we compare it to the military accounts of the conflict we have examined. It was, however, very much working in the service of U.S. imperialism, even though it was calculated to attract members of the general reading public, especially those addicted to dime novels such as those of Ned Buntline. While setting their sights on a popular audience that doted on flamboyant melodrama and swashbuckling adventure, Buntline and Falkner, by creating transnational romances (usually between a U.S. man and a Mexican woman), helped set the stage for imperial dreams, and even though they represented the U.S. North and the U.S. South, respectively, both endorsed slavery, hierarchical racial codes, and the glorification of U.S. military might.

This by no means indicates that Falkner was merely copying prior writers such as Buntline. Unlike his literary competitors, Colonel Falkner had experienced the war personally. However, as a sophisticated and literate man of his time, who subscribed to many periodicals and owned a large library, Falkner no doubt had read many sensationalist texts, including those that treated the Mexican War he had witnessed. Apart from his own experience, he was aware that the Siege of Monterey had a particularly convenient mythical aura, for, according to Ulysses S. Grant, the American forces under General Zachary Taylor (like President Polk, a Southerner) were outnumbered by General Ampudia's Mexican unit roughly 10,000 to 6,500 (1990, 75). Further, as his use of Byron's *Don Juan* as a model for *The Siege of Monterey* suggests, Colonel Falkner was writing a fanciful romantic fantasy about his own amorous adventures with "Spaniard" women South of the South. As Prescott had stated, Spaniards were the "true representatives" of the romance, and of course *Don Quixote* began the tradition of the romantic novel. Byron's *Don Juan* took this attitude as well. Both of these classic texts make close links between the romantic and the chivalric, which is exactly what Colonel Falkner does in this novel. We see yet another European influence in the romances of Scott, whose *Rob Roy* in particular appealed to the Scotch-Irish Falkner, who was steeped in the Scott-inspired chivalric traditions of the nineteenth-century U.S. South.[36]

Colonel Falkner's novel begins in 1840, when the poor white Henry leaves his Kentucky mountain home to seek his fortune, something the Old Colonel had done himself, walking from Missouri to northern Mississippi, after attacking his elder brother with a hoe. Henry, sixteen, and of "a voluptuous beauty" (U.S. male pulchritude, which we noted as a thematic in both Semmes and Manigault, is a constant topic here), seems to leave home because of problems with his stepfather. On the Ohio riverboat *John H. Nichol-son*, he draws the attention of the "dark eyes" of fourteen-year-old Ellen Aakenza, who is returning to Mexico City with her father and brother after being educated in Philadelphia. Ellen spies him leaning against a column (emphasizing his phallic potential) and is fascinated by his "fair features" (8). This metaphor of "dark," "Spanish," or "native" eyes gazing with desire on a U.S. youth would be repeated in colonizing narratives for decades, as it reifies the concept of tropical nations, always feminized, in need of "matrimony" with an invigorating and strongly masculine Northern neighbor. All these narratives, once again, repeat axioms set forth by Prescott, who proclaimed that the modern Mexican man, the Aztecs' descendant, has been broken by the Spanish: "They no longer tread their mountain plains with the conscious independence of their ancestors. In their faltering step and meek and melancholy aspect we read the sad characters of the conquered race. . . . The moral characteristics of the nation, all that constituted its individuality as a race, are effaced forever" (1843, 1:52). Colonel Falkner varies this a bit, however. The "Spanish"/white Ellen has been engaged by her father to the evil Mexican Galvez, and part of Henry's mission is to save her from this figure, who represents the "fallen" state of native masculinity.[37] Tellingly, Ellen's brother Alveza immediately recognizes the strength and potency of Henry but interprets these aspects negatively; when Ellen begs her brother to employ the poor Henry in the family's Mexican store, Alveza declares, "We have no right to care for an American boy, who would murder us in a minute if he had the chance" (10), a proleptic remark, since Henry does indeed kill Alveza. This initial triangle of a brother and sister, plus an ethnic "Other" beloved by the sister, prefigures Henry, Judith, and Charles Bon in *Absalom, Absalom!* and the fact that Henry and Ellen are two prominent names in that text suggests that Faulkner was thinking about this prior triangle when he structured his own, as does the saga of a poor Appalachian being scorned by wealthy aristocrats from Southern climes (read: Thomas Sutpen). But the more salient reversal here lies in the fact that the two Mexican/Caribbean figures are portrayed—at least in Alveza's mind— as ethnically superior to the American.

Melodramatic cross-racial and transnational plots like this were very prominent in Europe and the United States during the nineteenth century, especially in gothic thrillers such as Matthew Gregory Lewis's *The Monk* (1796) and Mrs. Radcliffe's *The Mysteries of Udolpho* (1794). As in these popular and sensational novels, Falkner's story is highly sexual. The physical beauty of virtually all the characters, male and female, is dwelt on at length, with particular care taken with "bosoms" and "breasts." Ellen's is said to be "as white as driven snow," perhaps an effort to differentiate her from the Indian-descended Mexicans who appear later in the narrative, but we still have a bifurcated presentation of her in terms of her "dark eyes" and "white skin." Ellen fixates on Henry's "manly form" and murmurs his name in her sleep, causing her brother to cry, "I must part them forever. . . . I would much rather follow her to her grave than she should ever love the name of an American" (12), again reversing the racial formula while duplicating Henry Sutpen's physical reply to the unstated question, "Would you want your sister to marry one?" As such, we may locate the romance of ethnicity as a kind of screen story, which has the frisson of the sexual transgressions of slavery under its surface. Here the highly polished and cultivated Alveza contrasts strongly with the handsome but crude Henry, who in this sense closely resembles Henry Sutpen, whose "hobble-de-hoy" (*Absalom*, 74) bumpkin status similarly contrasts so strongly with the cosmopolitan sophistication of Charles Bon. In both texts, the cosmopolitan is murdered by the "bumpkin."

We note here that the initial unfolding of the book takes place on the bosom of the Mississippi River, North America's great estuary, which is also the major gateway to the Caribbean. Colonel Falkner's hero, from the Appalachian frontier, meets his destiny here; two differing cultures fuse as his eyes meet Ellen's, and they proceed, born on the turbulent waters of emotion, history, and myth, into the circumCaribbean.[38]

The highly romantic imagery of the book is balanced by a corresponding naturalism. When the riverboat burns, Falkner describes the "shrieks of the parents whose children were burning in the flames . . . heartrending beyond anything ever witnessed by mortal man" (12), a method he employs throughout the narrative. Henry saves Ellen but appears dead himself on the shore, till revived as his "fair young face" is nestled "on her heaving bosom. . . . Modesty would have forbidden it, but did she not owe her life to him?" (14). Falkner reminds us of Henry's original goals, however, while extending the narrative out to the wider circumCaribbean world of buccaneering: "Henry has found a gem far more valuable than all the shining mettle of California, of the diamonds of Golconda" (15), a translation of conventional tropes of conquest into a sexual language that nevertheless is based in "mining resources"—albeit of a human kind—in a tropical and clearly inviting realm. We remember here Thomas Sutpen's motivation to make his fortune in the Caribbean: "I learned of the West Indies," he tells General Compson, where "poor men went in ships and became rich" (*Absalom*, 242).

The ethnic diversity of New Orleans finds expression in dialect-speaking, stereotyped "Africans" and "Frenchmen." Henry's escape on a schooner is correctly described, as boats then were towed to the mouth of the Mississippi, as here. Henry sets out for Galveston and then Santa Fe on a trading expedition, again signaling the expanding tentacles of American adventurism. On his return, he is forced into a duel with Alveza; mortally wounded by Henry, Alveza forgives him and tells him to marry Ellen. Alveza is buried in the waters of the mediating Gulf, always a dramatic backdrop for the story and a symbol of the divide between the two lovers.

As noted, most of the regiments from the Ohio and Mississippi valleys embarked for Mexico from New Orleans, the fourth-largest metropolis in the United States and a strange and amazing city to most recruits, many of whom spent extended time there waiting for transport. The strongly Caribbean aspect of the metropolis, with its many brothels, bars, and strange foreign languages and dialects spoken by a transnational population of sailors and the city's complicated world of color, was not lost on the soldiers, and this became their introduction to the circumCaribbean world they would explore by boat and on foot in the months to come. It would be inevitable that they would compare and contrast these two tropical and exotic realms and see many connections between them, in terms of architecture, tropical foliage and climate, proximity to the sea, the dominance of the Catholic Church, the Spanish heritage, and the many affinities between the two great harbors. Both Vera Cruz and New Orleans are portrayed by Falkner as international ports, largely populated by Englishmen and Spaniards, whose adventures in these cities reveal the corruption and excitement of dynamic but dangerous crossroads of exchange. As Gruesz has noted, Vera Cruz, like New Orleans, was the major Mexican city for carnival, and it long played "the representational role of Mexico's appealing and dangerous periphery, where hybridized Afro-Indo-Caribbean forms like the *danzón* and the *son jarocho* reflect its history as New Spain's premier slave market" (2006, 479), a description that also applied to New Orleans.

One of the more curious aspects of the Colonel's novel lies in the introduction of Pedro, Ellen's fifteen-year-old servant, who is always at her side. Indeed, he sleeps in her room as her guardian. The reader at first thinks he is a black slave, especially when Ellen's father and the suitor he favors, Gabbez, decide he should be sold to the former's brother in Cuba. Pedro laments to his mistress, "To a foreign shore I must go, and be compelled to toil under the lash from early dawn till the close of day" (78), a rather surprising passage in a novel by a slave owner in Mississippi in the 1850s.

It turns out, however, that Pedro, originally a foundling, is actually Spanish, and a Count too, despite his dark skin.[39] Ellen has him buy boy's cloths for her disguise, prompting some homoerotics on Pedro's part: "She loves him [Henry] dearly, and I don't blame her for loving such a noble young man. I love him myself, and I don't know what I should do if I was her, but I think I should love him as well as she does" (47), a reverie that reminds us of Henry Sutpen's love for Charles Bon and of the homosocial exchange the latter's marriage to Henry's sister Judith would facilitate. Here the Old Colonel magnifies the traditional yearning after handsome U.S. youths by native women by extending it to native men as well, further justifying colonial appropriation.

More homoerotics arise. As in Shakespeare's tales of gender disguise—perhaps another source of Falkner's portrayal of Ellen's cross-dressing—sailors find this "boy" among them appealing: "His beautiful dark eye. . . . Look at his tender little white hand and wrist. . . . His countenance is sufficient to set the heart of any maid on fire. Look what a set of limbs he has got; I have never seen such a neat little foot and ankle . . . the most perfect figure I have ever seen." They marvel further at the profound grief this "boy" evinces on hearing (falsely) of Henry's death.

As part of Ellen's disguise, she paints her face "the color of the darkest Mexican," yet another differentiation between "Spanish" and "Mexican" figures, even though both groups presumably reside in Mexico.[40] Clearly, this raises the issue of the predominance of Indian heritage in the general Mexican population, a fact that continues to this day. U.S. soldiers were not favorably disposed toward Mexico's predominantly Indian population; after all, many of the Native Americans of the U.S. South and West had just been killed in "Indian Wars" or forced to relocate on Western reservations. U.S. soldiers had only recently been engaged in a series of wars against the Seminoles in Florida, a conflict accompanied by similar racial propaganda. The fact that most U.S. soldiers viewed almost everyone in Mexico as "colored"—especially the Indians—made such assertions more common than not. The same argument used against U.S. Indians—that they were unworthy of the custodianship of such a potentially fertile and productive land—was made against the Mexicans.

Falkner employs many of these sentiments in his narrative as well. Back in Vera Cruz, we see tropical luxury but colonial depravity too. Falkner presents Vera Cruz in particular and Mexico in general as spaces for shape changing and experimentation. Even further removed than New Orleans from rigid categories of identity practiced in the noncoastal South, the circumCaribbean offers a liberating arena of personal freedom. Falkner suggests this through his plot but also through imperial, often sublime, scene painting: "A silver mass of curling smoke hangs over the golden city. . . . The proud eagle looks down . . . the beautiful jackdaw sat perched among the orange trees. . . . The blood-stained banner was streaming from the tall dome of the mighty castle of San Juan, while the solemn strains of martial music, as it called the war worn soldier to take his stand . . . could be heard" (55). More scene painting of the type rendered by Semmes develops when Ellen travels home to her mother. We view the "tall peaks of the snow-capped mountains," the "boundless plains, the "thousands of cattle, sheep, and goats grazed on the verdant plain" (58). This sublime image of the Caribbean world as Eden is enhanced further: "The road-side was lined with an endless variety of luscious fruit—pine apples, bananas, oranges, figs, lemons, pomegranates. . . . All the fruits of the tropics are to be found in abundance between the cities of Vera Cruz and Jalappa" (60). Nor does Falkner ignore the inhabitants: "Each side of the road was lined with young Indian girls, dressed in loose gowns, with baskets on their arms, going to market" (58). Ellen, however, is never associated with these "Indian" maidens, or even Mexican ones; she is always described as "Spanish," which places her among what Ulysses S. Grant called "the better class."

Numerous examples of this "type" of Mexican are found in Falkner's most detailed urban landscape, Mexico City, on whose lake "floated a thousand little Gondoliers, filled with young *Simareters* from the city . . . engaged in bathing . . . in fishing . . . others in sporting with the young Umbras. . . . Several hundred bells might be heard ringing at the same time." The grand *alameda*, a park used by the upper crust of the metropolis as a pleasure ground, abuts Aakaiza's dwelling, which is surrounded by fruit trees and flowers, a veritable bower of bliss. This provides the setting for Ellen's sentimental reunion with her mother. Thus the novel takes us from the corrupt, turbulent, peripheral city of Vera Cruz, into a penetration of the heartland, culminating in the interior Eden of the capital, which is the epitome of the urban tropical sublime. From there, the novel's pattern unfolds in a series of trips, voyages, shipwrecks, escapes, and reunions. Many of the scenes occur on water, be it rivers, lakes, or oceans. In this sense, it is truly a Caribbean narrative, and the lines of travel bring together the various rims of the great waters. Édouard Glissant has asserted that the Caribbean is "not an American lake. It is the estuary of the Americas . . . [where] the dialectic between inside and outside is reflected in the relationship between land and sea. . . . A Caribbean imagination keeps us from being smothered" (1989, 139). Thus, in this fluid realm, Ellen and Henry can imagine a "space between" cultures for their love. Ellen dreams of Henry mounted on a "noble white war-house, with a star of honor shining on his manly breast; two golden epaulets rest on his shoulders; a golden plume streams from his military hat, and a golden sword swings by his side. . . . [He] leads on his regiment to the charge amidst shouts of victory. . . . The blood stained banner floats majestically. . . . She sees a ball pierce his noble breast" (62–63). This dream comes true; the lovers meet again during the siege, which is partly described in poetry, "whilst swift the Anglo-Saxons march along the field" (96), as Henry rides forward with General Quitman, a real commander, against the city. Realistic prose describes the carnage: "The polished walls were smeared with brains and blood" (97). A Spanish officer (Ellen, in male garb), on a jet black horse, is killing Americans right and left, leading the Mexicans toward victory. When Henry, who in parallel fashion has been mowing down Mexicans, is unhorsed, a soldier prepares to kill him; suddenly, however, the Mexican commander cuts this soldier's arm off and bears Henry into a house.[41] The fact that Ellen immediately ceases her deadly attacks upon finding her beloved sacrifices sensationalist gore, horror, and, yes, patriotism, to sentimental formula, but also sets the stage for her energies to be rechanneled into the processes of Americanization.

Appropriately, here Falkner yokes romantic and naturalistic tropes: "Darkness now spread her sable mantle . . . whilst the hungry wolf strode proudly across the bloody plain, lacerating the gallant bodies of those who had died in freedom's cause, and glutting his maw with gallant gore—the hungry dogs likewise claimed a share of the luscious feast" (99). The claim that this invasion is "freedom's cause" has an eerily familiar ring for today's readers. Further, the ugly reality of the conflict was that camp followers immediately stripped the bodies of both clothing and valuables, which may be the literal reference for the "wolves" and "dogs."[42]

The battle ended, the lovers reveal their identities and fill each other—and us—in on what happened during the past few years. Like Delany's *Blake*, which we will consider in the next chapter, the novel concludes with multiple weddings that create a circumCaribbean web of affiliation, although the central characters wind up living in Kentucky. One might suppose that the liberating aspect of the "feminine" Caribbean finds final expression here, as the domestic and maternal emerge triumphant, with a newly grafted Latin strain strengthening America's hardy stock. Kazanjian, commenting on the prevalence of these multiple marriages at the conclusion of many of the potboiler novelettes of the war, claims that they reverse the frantic cross-national, cross-racial, and sexual instability of the body of the text, substituting a ritual of foreclosure that tames, thereby allegorizing "the transformation of white settler colonialism and manifest destiny into neocolonial white civility" through ritual enactments of heteronormative white culture (2003, 196). Amy Kaplan has argued that the discourse of domesticity was used to "negotiate the borders of an expanding empire and divided nation" (1998, 28). This was necessary because it was feared that annexation would endanger national purity, and thereby the domestic space (28). Colonel Falkner symbolically solves this problem by, first, demonstrating the possibility of marrying only Mexican women of "pure Castilian blood" (that is, white, non-Indian) and, second, bringing the bride (along with her equally symbolic dowry) back into the safe confines of U.S.-centered domesticity. Presumably, the rich family estates in Mexico will be administered by functionaries under the direction of Henry. In a passage frankly metaphoric of the U.S. theft of half of Mexico, Colonel Falkner intones that Henry is stealing that "which he values higher than all the gold of Sacramento [another city taken by the United States]. . . . She will prove to be a treasure far above all wealth or fame . . . she is worth stealing" (34).

The subtitle of *The Spanish Heroine*—"A Tale of War and Love"—would seem to suggest that these seemingly opposite concepts are equally dislocating, disruptive, and violent. Both the martial and the romantic plots include racial and ethnic problems, engagement with the natural world, and gender confusion, especially through female cross-dressing. The hierarchies of color and the ways in which racial and ethnic roles get performed, dissolved, and refashioned in the more fluid realm of circumCaribbean narrative make the novel quite instructive in terms of understanding the basic aspects of the Old Colonel's legacy for his great-grandson.

Ellen's male garb, particularly as a fighting officer, clearly laid out a pattern for Faulkner to use in his characterization of the cross-dressing Confederate Drusilla Hawk in *The Unvanquished*. There, however, we are more concerned with the aftermath of the war than with the actual fighting, as Drusilla must face a new front of combatants, the ladies of Yoknapatawpha County, who are scandalized by her life in the camps alongside John Sartoris. The upshot of the episode is the refeminizing of Drusilla as the hoopskirt-clad new bride of her former commander.

Ellen, like her "descendant" Drusilla, is not only a wealthy woman; she is also an aggressive and sometimes quite violent woman warrior. While William Faulkner likely based his portrait of Drusilla partly on our Spanish Heroine, it seems possible that he was also aware of the central role women played in the more recent Mexican Revolution of 1910. The Zapatistas numbered many *soldaderas* among their ranks; indeed, Elena Poniatowska has recently claimed that "without the soldaderas, there is no Mexican revolution" (16). In a cruel conflict that involved massive rape of Mexican women, wearing men's garb and fighting as a man offered one form of protection against bodily violation. Famous Zapatistas such as Rosa Bobadilla and Maria Esperanza Chavira dressed as men and led troops in battle. Another woman, Petra "Pedro" Herrera, blew up bridges and rescued other women from rape. She raised a company of 1,000 women while acquiring a mythic identity in Mexican memory. All these women were in the tradition of ancient Indian figures such as Toci, the Earth Mother who carried a shield, and Xochitl, a Toltec queen who led a battalion of women (2006, 20–27). The Mexican Revolution of 1910–20, which the young William Faulkner avidly followed in local newspapers, was the first successful revolution of the twentieth century and would be paralleled by wars of liberation in Russia, Iran, and China. Severe economic imbalance caused by foreign domination and the excesses of the long-running Diaz government had led to the control of 90 percent of Mexico's industry by foreigners in 1900 (Hart 2000, 436).[43]

William Clark Falkner would go on to write several other book-length works, including novels and travel narratives covering his extended stays in Europe, where he arranged for stonecutters to create a life-size statue of him for his grave. His early attempts to present an exotic Caribbean world paid dividends later, when he mounted much more expansive and complicated readings of different cultures. Like Constance Fenimore Woolson, a writer we will consider later who wrote contemporaneously with him, reading both the South and the tropics later provided lens for the bewildering city-states and multicultures of Europe. His travelogue, *Rapid Ramblings in Europe* (1882), employs exuberant writing and an abundant sense of humor and testifies to the sophistication of the Old Colonel, whose great-grandson William would similarly enjoy his own "rapid ramblings in Europe" as a young man.[44]

The Mexican War was repeatedly put forward in the United States as the logical way to sustain and extend white Anglo-Saxon dominance in the Western Hemisphere. Obviously, this is a kind of mythic racialist stance, one deeply embroiled in the prevailing romanticism of the late eighteenth and early nineteenth centuries. As Paul Foos has demonstrated, extant diaries and letters of U.S. combatants are "steeped in romantic, heroic rhetoric" (2002, 4), so it was to be expected that fiction based on the conflict would be even more flamboyant, as is the case with Colonel Falkner's novel and

Manigault's memoir. As noted above, we see here the strong imprint of Sir Walter Scott on the Southern *and* circumCaribbean imaginary. As Georg Lukács has demonstrated, Scott's novels, like Falkner's (and many of his great-grandson's) dramatize history through the conflict of classes, as in works such as *Rob Roy* and *Ivanhoe*, where battle temporarily suspends economic and social barriers. Racial ideology certainly played a large role in this meld.

The trajectory of these narratives I have discussed depicts the war in stages, beginning with the voyage from New Orleans across the tropical waters, sometimes involving a stop in Havana, and arrival in Vera Cruz. Scenes of battle then alternate with descriptive, spectacular, and often sublime scene painting of the paradise that Mexico in some ways is, but, more often, *could be*, with the proper discipline and leadership, which U.S. soldiers, citizens, and, ultimately, colonists could provide. The final stage involves the U.S. occupation, which leads to all kinds of cultural, social, and racial exchange, often depicted as a mutually beneficial and certainly pleasurable, at least for the U.S. military, time of "amalgamation" following the cessation of hostilities. As many accounts indicate, the U.S. military enjoyed, in virtually every way, a ten-month occupation. Dance halls, coffee shops, bars, and restaurants opened their doors, and soldiers began employing their rudimentary Spanish as they wandered Mexico's towns and cities. Their spending, in fact, helped the Mexican economy to recover (Vasquez 2000, 367).

For the United States, however, uncertainties about the newly annexed territories and its people and the possibility of swallowing the rest of Mexico evoked a deeply ambivalent racial posture, in that most felt development of Mexico's mines and haciendas would necessarily involve slavery. At the same time, despite the valorization of the "pure Castilian/Spanish blood" of elites, U.S. writers displayed equally deep ambivalence at the prospect of diluting the predominantly "white" U.S. citizenry through possibly inevitable amalgamation with Mexicans, who so often have Indian and/or African roots.[45]

As these accounts indicate, the circumCaribbean war and its aftermath provided a true cultural education for U.S. troops, many of whom were from the South. The resultant knowledge of the circumCaribbean gave rise to new perspectives on their homeland but also on previously unknown and, to some extent, feared populations south of the border and in the inland sea, thereby helping to generate schemes for expanding Southern slavery into Mexico, Cuba, Puerto Rico, and elsewhere.[46] Indeed, the war with Mexico, which raised the issue of annexation even more powerfully than the incorporation of Texas into the union, had much to do with the ensuing debate over the expansion of slavery that led to the Civil War. In following decades, Mexico would remain entangled with the United States, in several ways. The rebel politician Benito Juarez was exiled in New Orleans before returning to Mexico just before America's Civil War to become president and wage a civil war on a rival president, General Félix Zuloaga, after establishing a base in Vera Cruz. Although an Indian himself, Juarez had fought the Mayan uprising in coastal Yucatan and had later become president of Mexico's Supreme Court. He sided with the faction that confiscated church properties and drew ecclesiastical enmity. Juarez was installed as president in June 1861, just two months after the firing on Fort Sumter. His ascension, however, led him to milk as much customs duty as possible from the Caribbean cash port of Vera Cruz. The ensuing opportunistic French invasion, a protracted and bloody struggle that produced the coronation of Maximilian as a French emperor in 1864, outraged many in the United States; seemingly it was all right for *them* to seize almost one-half of Mexico, but the Europeans had no business in what had become "an American lake." Subsequently, the increasingly effective guerrilla warfare of Juarez and his allies, coupled with the unpopularity of the French regime, led French emperor Napoleon III to order a phased pullout of French troops, a situation very akin to the later disasters suffered by both the French and then the United States in Vietnam. In 1867, the troops of Porfirio Diaz captured much of the country, and Maximilian and his generals were caught and executed on June 16, 1867, after President Juarez refused clemency.

What does all this have to do with the U.S. South and the Caribbean? Mexico's extensive reforms after Maximilian's fall were designed to lead to the modernization of a rural land. Under the rule of Juarez, a full-blooded Indian (who is often referred to as the "father" of modern Mexico), mestizos were brought into the government. But when Juarez died of a heart attack in 1872, the period of true reform was over. His successor, Porfirio Diaz, though endorsing modernization, was soon taking the country back to its old ways. This historical pattern runs quite parallel to that of the South, where the temporary advancements of Reconstruction were also cut short — first, as in Mexico (although some years later), by the death of a president, and then by the failure of the liberal party to carry through its reforms. The ascent of indigenous politicians was halted, and although Mexico prospered through Diaz's program of greatly increased exports of raw materials, only the upper classes benefited, a picture that unfortunately was mirrored in Henry Grady's "New South," where class inequities also had a racial aspect.

Both Mexico and the South continued to suffer from dependent capitalism, in both cases in relation to the industrial North of the United States. As we shall see, many other Latin American countries and the islands of the Caribbean were increasingly in this position, especially after the entrance of U.S. mining, sugar, and fruit interests into the region.

There is still another major aspect of the war, which I am unable to pursue here. Jose E. Limón has stated that one could say that "the American South served as midwife—and not a gentle one—at the birth of greater Mexico" in 1848; however, he notes that this "birth" really began in 1826 with immigration into Texas by Southerners, who came with their black slaves. Limón repeats and seconds Clement Eaton's earlier pronouncement that the "Mexican War was an adventure in imperialism of the South in partnership with the restless inhabitants of the West. It was provoked by a Southern president and fought largely by Southern generals and Southern volunteers" (Eaton 1949, 365). As we have seen, however, most of the dime novels that have served as the popular literary record of the war were composed by Northerners, most of whom had never been to Mexico. Reading the narratives I have considered here helps us to see these cross-cultural encounters in a different perspective, from the viewpoint of Southern combatants.

The Mexican American War generated the first massive exposure of U.S. citizens from the South to Caribbean culture, and it thus has much to tell us about the complicated relations between the South and the Caribbean and has rightly been seen as an important precursor to the Civil War. As U.S. Grant noted, "The southern rebellion was largely the outgrowth of the Mexican war. Nations, like individuals, are punished for their transgressions. We got our punishment in the most sanguinary and expensive war of modern times" (1990, 42). Grant's commander, Zachary Taylor, executed a martial North-South remapping, but Southern combatants—including Semmes and Falkner—were simultaneously forging a South-South chart, and we find an intersection, or crossroads of cultures, in the texts these Southerners left us. Although they wholeheartedly participated in what can only be understood as a war of imperial aggression, they also began a massive new intercultural dialectic, one that would only intensify in the years to come.

The Mexican War brought the nation together to face a new challenge and to spread both its domain and its political potency. At the same time, however, the war operated on two tracks, as the Southern states won their objective of slavery in a new state—Texas—while laying a foundation for further annexation that would benefit the South, particularly in the Caribbean, where Cuba was eyed as a new state or states that could, like Texas, add new congressional power supportive of the peculiar institution. As such, the Mexican War brought *Southerners* together more tightly as they braced themselves for the decade of the 1850s, when the issues that divided the North and the South would ignite and then burn out of control. Further, the South's major contribution, in terms of both soldiers and officers for the U.S. military effort in Mexico, suggested that any new nation created out of the Southern states would have the basic ingredients of a powerful military force.[47] Immediately after the Mexican conflict, however, the South was more interested in expanding the reach of slavery in the hemisphere than in separating from the North. Dreams of an expanded South soon found realization in the various filibuster movements that sought to colonize the South of the South. These efforts will be our focus in the next chapter.

2 Liberating Fictions

The Caribbean Imaginary in the Novels of
Lucy Holcombe Pickens and Martin Delany

. . . .

Cuba, for many years the richest of the Caribbean isles and the closest to the
United States in both distance and cultural connections, has always exerted
a magical spell for all the peoples of the Americas, be it one of attraction or
repulsion. The Founding Fathers cast a covetous eye on the island. Jefferson
wrote to James Monroe in 1823, "I candidly confess, that I have ever looked
on Cuba as the most interesting addition which could ever be made to our
system of states" (1905, 479). In our own time, Castro's regime has reversed
this formula for many.

Unlike today's era of legal restrictions and trade embargos, from the beginning of the contact era of colonial settlement there were almost no lines
of distinction between South Florida and Cuba, which were both colonized
by Spain. St. Augustine and Havana were sister cities, and the conquistadores roamed both places as part of a whole. Further, we should remember
that a third metropolis, New Orleans, was under Spanish control from 1763
to 1803, and during this time, those three ports formed a vital triangle of
the circumCaribbean, throbbing with the rhythm of commercial trade and
cultural exchange. By the age of the filibustering expeditions to Cuba and
Latin America in the nineteenth century—and many of these trips began
in and/or obtained important support from the city of New Orleans—the
United States had controlled Louisiana's great port for over forty years, yet
the city still had vital connections with the Spanish Caribbean. As we saw in
the preceding chapter, thousands of Southerners had experienced the Caribbean and its western shore through participation in the Mexican American
War, with boats running repeatedly between New Orleans, Havana, and
Vera Cruz.

As Thomas Sutpen's tale in Faulkner's *Absalom* suggests, the Caribbean
was perceived by nineteenth-century Southerners as an arena where one
could prove one's manhood while earning a fortune. Others felt manhood
would come through battles of liberation. Interestingly, this part of the

Southern narrative had two registers, one white, one black. In Lucy Holcombe Pickens's *The Free Flag of Cuba; or, The Martyrdom of Lopez: A Tale of the Liberating Expedition of 1851* (1854), white filibustering Southerners join forces with heroic Latinos to achieve the island's liberation from Spanish despots. Pickens (1832–99), who would later become the wife of the Civil War governor of South Carolina, earned the soubriquet of "the uncrowned Queen" of the Confederacy. Her lofty, regal sentiment in 1850 was that Cuba's destiny would best be served through union with an imperialist United States, and she assumed that the island's slave system, comfortingly similar to that of the South, would continue after annexation; further, Cuba would then furnish congressmen favorable to the "peculiar institution."

Pickens's novel had its counterpart in many articles published before the war that advocated a vast slave economy for the Americas, one controlled by the United States and centered on the profitable plantations of the South and the Caribbean. For others, however, the Creole Cubans' long struggle to throw off the Spanish yoke meant revolution. The great Cuban poet Plácido's heroic martyrdom in 1844 inspired other oppressed people of color throughout the hemisphere and so fascinated U.S. writer Martin Delany (1812–85) that he made him a central character in his 1859 serialized novel, *Blake; or, The Huts of America*, which was published in final book form in 1861, at the outbreak of the Civil War.[1] It has often been cited as one of the first African American novels, but it should also be recognized as an early version of the transnational novel in the Americas. This would be more apparent if the only version of the novel currently available used the original, and more revealing title, which was *Blake; or, The Huts of America: A Tale of the Mississippi Valley, the Southern United States, and Cuba* (noted in Levine 1997, 191). Delany is central to the overarching theme of my study since he was the first African American writer to closely link the American South and the Caribbean in a work of fiction. Later in his life, he would mount the first scientific expedition to Africa, significantly done in tandem with a Caribbean scientist, the Jamaican Robert Campbell, thereby creating an early strand across what we now term "the Black Atlantic."

Paul Gilroy, who coined that phrase in his eponymous study, has perceptively noted that *Blake* helps us move beyond a binary notion of the supposed opposition of national and diasporic perspectives. For him, Delany presents a "webbed" black network stretching across the Atlantic, thereby challenging empty nationalist perspectives, including those based on ethnicity (1993, 29). I would add, however, that *Blake* also points to the possibility of a Caribbean that can shift its shape in accordance with any given congruence of interests/vectors of neighboring or associated entities, be they nations or cultures, which is amply displayed by comparing the various ways in which this setting is employed in the works of Pickens and Delany.

Both writers saw the affinities of the coastal South with the Caribbean lands and had their characters crisscross Gulf waters—and in the case of Delany, the Atlantic as well—in an effort to expand the canvas for the issues that impassioned them. However, unlike the chroniclers of the Mexican War, they spend little time detailing the wonders of flora or fauna or, with a few exceptions, meditating on the lessons that a sublime nature can bring to bear on contemporary issues. This no doubt is due to the fact that neither author had ever visited Cuba.[2] However, there is another factor at play here. In the military narratives we have considered, the authors want to dramatize the battles but also need to appeal to other interests of their readers, who were used to travel writing, romantic readings of nature, and biased histories of Mexico. Pickens and Delany have more focused interests in that each is obsessed with the issue of slavery and colonization, but from radically different perspectives. Both pay lip service to the conventions of the sentimental domestic novel, whether following the model of Harriet Beecher Stowe (often the case with Delany) or forging the conventionally romantic path that would shortly be followed by Augusta Jane Evans (Pickens), but the real interest lies in the political and ideological. Pickens preceded Delany on the international stage, and it may well be that Delany intended to signify on her work. Even earlier, however, there were more than a few resemblances between Delany's various plans to colonize Central America (and, later, West Africa) and the machinations and maneuvers of the white/Latino filibusters, who sought to conquer and/or annex Caribbean or Latin American countries for themselves or the United States. Filibusters were usually American adventurers who recruited soldiers of fortune to join them in attempts to invade and, ideally, conquer foreign countries, even if there was no quarrel between the target nation and the United States. After all, as Edward Said puts it, "at some very basic level, imperialism means thinking about, settling on, controlling land that you do not possess, that is distant, that is lived on and owned by others" (1993, 7). We need to keep this in mind as we ponder the filibusters, their champion Pickens, and the fiery black revolutionary and advocate for black emigration, Delany. We should also remember that even Frederick Douglass could be guilty of a colonizing gaze. After serving on a government commission on Santo Domingo, he went on record as favoring annexation. In an 1873 speech, he declared that the citizens there desired it: "They want Saxon and Protestant civilization. . . . Let us lift them up to our high standard of nationality" (cited in Levine 1997, 228). Further, Douglass and Delany alike were impatient with the restrictions of an artificial geographical border. As Douglass proclaimed, and as Delany would illustrate in his fiction, "In some sense we [now] realize the sublime declaration of the Prophet of Patmos, 'And there shall be no more sea.' The oceans that divided us, have become bridges to connect us" (1848, cited in Foner and Taylor 1999, 105).

At the same time, many exiled Cubans in the United States were working with U.S. leaders, both black and white, and with their compatriots in the homeland to throw off the yoke of Spanish oppression, and although many in this contingent enthusiastically supported expeditions like that of Lopez, they did not always have a clear view of the self-serving motivations of such leaders, or of plans to sustain slavery.[3] As noted, neither Pickens nor Delany had been to Cuba, and there is no evidence that either spoke Spanish. Both of them, however, created novels that mix fictional and actual personages; that are set first in the American South and then in Cuba; and that concern transnational insurrection. We can therefore say that they each construct a "Cuban imaginary" in order to frame and animate their investigation/presentation of contemporary historical events and to push their own ideological/political projects. Both authors are fixated on race and myths of manhood and provide a spectrum of racial "types." Further, despite her gender, Pickens, like Delany, does not hesitate to create scenes of torture, murder, and death. Both demonize the Spanish and raise cries for liberation and justice. The ultimate ends they seek, however, could not be more different. Pickens wants to extend slavery, while Delany is determined to end it. Ultimately, he would take part in the Civil War and play a heroic part in Reconstruction in South Carolina, in effect helping to "dethrone" the state's first lady, Pickens. His concern for enslaved Cubans, however, went tragically unanswered during his lifetime, as slavery was not ended on the island until 1886, the year after his death.[4]

Both Pickens and Delany had histories, travelers' accounts, and newspaper and journal articles at their disposal as they mined Cuban culture for the cause of both liberation and publication. Both were obsessed with breaking through national boundaries to create new, hybrid fictions that could advance their respective causes. Both writers were, *au fond*, revolutionaries. Pickens envisioned a new Cuba, one freed of the Spanish yoke, which would facilitate a revamping of what she saw as a mismanaged slave system. Lopez, to her, was a Latin version of George Washington, whose heroic stature would draw thousands to his banner once the invasion was accomplished. The ultimate entry of Cuba into the Union as, possibly, several states would add to the South's congressional delegation while increasing the output and potential of the cotton empire the South already enjoyed. Presumably, this new state would involve amalgamation between the whites of Cuba and the South, but the merging of the two slave systems would necessarily lead to intermarriage between the many different diasporic peoples who populated the two slave cultures. Further, a linguistic and cultural accommodation would have to be reached, as these components were integral to the operation of a smoothly functioning economic system.

Delany, by contrast, while stating his preference for "pure African blood" throughout his fiction, accepts people of all types within the race and within the hemisphere. His presentation of the various tribal roots of enslaved Africans demonstrates his awareness that diasporic culture had benefited from the intertwining of distinct continental cultures. His plan for a new colony of emancipated people from its inception envisions incorporation of different ethnic heritages and languages, and the last chapter of the existing manuscript presents several mixed marriages that reflect the hybrid nature of the new country/culture he envisions.

Pickens and Delany were not unique in their creation of imaginary versions of real geographies and cultures. Anna Brickhouse has recently demonstrated how many U.S. novels written between 1826 and 1856 created a "transamerican literary imaginary." As she explains, this imaginary, full of contradictions, reflects a nation struggling with expanding borders and narrowing racial boundaries (2004, 6–7). What Brickhouse does not do, however, is provide a portrait of how Southern writing created variants on this larger pattern. In the cases of Pickens and Delany, we see contrasting racial visions of the Caribbean imaginary, as each writer interacts with other strands of circumCaribbean political and literary culture.

A Belligerent Belle(triste)

Lucy Holcombe Pickens would have been a remarkable figure in Southern and American history even if she had never written a single word. A famous beauty who married Francis Wilkinson Pickens, the Confederate governor of South Carolina, she was attracted to martial power and played a key role in Confederate politics and cultural life. She was prominent enough to draw the ire of the more celebrated chronicler of the times, her fellow South Carolinian Mary Chesnut. Pickens is remembered, however, primarily for her novel. The book's acceptance came more easily due to her use of a male pseudonym (H. M. Hardimann) and because she made it a "man's book" by avoiding most (but not all) of the woman-centered conventions of the sentimental-domestic novels that were popular in her time. Logically, her book was brought out by one of the leading publishers of filibuster texts, the New York firm of DeWitt and Davenport. Her real-life hero, Narciso Lopez, was truly a man of the Atlantic World. Born in Venezuela in 1797 on his father's plantation, he had held various official appointments in Spain and Cuba before his military campaigns. His position on the island was cemented by marriage into a leading family. He blamed the failure of his various enterprises on the Spanish colonial government and had to flee to the United States after a coup that he attempted failed in 1848. In 1849, he was about to lead an invasion of Cuba from Round Island, off Mississippi, but he and his men were blockaded by the anti-filibuster Taylor administration. In 1850, he and a band of supporters actually landed in Cuba and took possession of a town but were unable to go further. In 1851, he led a final expedition, but when locals failed to rally to his banner, he was captured and publically garroted by a black executioner.

Pickens seems to have been passionate about the Lopez affair because her first love, Colonel William L. Crittenden, was part of the 1851 invasion force, and she saw his ship off in New Orleans personally (Burton and Burton 2002, 17). She took great pride in Crittenden's supposed final words before Cuban authorities executed him, "An American kneels but to his God," and uses them in his fictional counterpart's execution scene. As such, she may have seen herself as "co-conspirator." We should remember, too, that Martin Delany was involved in conspiratorial gatherings with John Brown when he was writing *Blake* (Moses 1978, 151), so there was a kindred feeling between these two authors and their characters.

Pickens also shared Lopez's concern that Spain was about to allow the "Africanization" of Cuba by freeing the slaves. Such an example would set a dangerous precedent only a few miles across Gulf waters from Florida. There were two alternatives: creating a new Cuban republic after a liberatory invasion and revolution or annexing the island to the United States. Both of these options would have the same effect: the preservation of slavery. Always a part of slaveholding families, after she married the much older Pickens, she became the very engaged mistress of over 300 slaves. Throughout her life, she had a vested interest in protecting the prolonged value of such "property," which would fire her determination to both spread and stabilize slavery, be it through political maneuvers, covert military operations, outright revolution, or sensational fiction.

We need to remember, however, that Lopez was supported by non-Southerners too. He was a hero to the exile Cuban society in the Northeast-ern United States. Indeed, many politicians and citizens outside the South saw good reason to expel Spain from Cuba, in the name of Manifest Destiny. As Amy S. Greenberg notes, Lopez rallies in New York, Pittsburgh, Balti-more, and other Northern cities sometimes drew crowds numbering in the tens of thousands. She explains that the rallies appealed to men who saw Manifest Destiny as a way of asserting and performing their manhood. The invasion of Cuba was seen as revenge for Americans who had already lost their lives fighting for Cuban independence, but also as the first step toward what was then seen as the inevitable American domination of the entire hemisphere, including Canada. Further, annexing/freeing Cuba promised an opening for U.S. businesses, especially in terms of trade, port activities, and potential real estate dealings. It was said that New Orleans alone would realize increased trade of $25 million annually (Greenberg 2005, 191–92). Thus, although Lopez would be immortalized along Southern lines by Pick-ens, he was also valorized elsewhere in the nation for different reasons.

The overwhelming interest of many U.S. citizens in annexing or buying Cuba was signified by the notorious 1854 Ostend Manifesto, written in Bel-gium by the U.S. ambassadors to Spain (Pierre Soulé), Great Britain (James Buchanan), and France (John Mason) and then leaked to the press. Soulé had failed to persuade Spain to sell Cuba; there were plans to try that ploy again, but the three drew up a document that posited further action should the sale not go through. As they arrogantly decreed, "We shall be justified in wresting it from Spain if we possess the power; and this upon the very same principle that would justify an individual in tearing down the burning house of his neighbor, if there were no other means of preventing the flames from destroying his own home. . . . We should be recreant to our duty . . . should we permit Cuba to be Africanized and become a second St. Domingo, with all its attendant horrors to the white race, and suffer the flames to extend to our neighboring shores" (cited in Levine 1997, 202). Pierre Soulé offers an excellent example of a transatlantic "operator" of the period, and as a diplomatic parallel to the filibuster. Born in France, he was exiled for anti-Bourbon activity; pardoned in 1818, he became a lawyer in Paris but was once again arrested for revolutionary endeavors. He escaped, eventually going to Haiti, but soon took up the practice of law in French-speaking New Orleans, where he quickly rose in the Democratic Party, eventually serving as U.S. senator and, subsequently, minister to Spain. He was imprisoned by the Union after the Civil War and lived for a time in the Caribbean, first in the Bahamas and later in Havana, but died in New Orleans, where he is buried in the historic St. Louis Number Two cemetery (John Preston Moore 1955, passim). We see, through his myriad roles that led him to crisscross the Caribbean and Atlantic repeatedly, that there were public men whose pattern of activity and movement echoed those of the filibusters and the fictional creations of Pickens and Delany.

Pickens's novel, while ostensibly focused on Lopez, also sang an anthem to other filibusters such as William Walker, whose invasion of Nicaragua briefly made him president but ultimately led to his dethronement and execution. Figures like Walker and Lopez, in her mind, were needed in order to spread, solidify, and strengthen the slavocracy's power throughout the hemisphere. However, the real Lopez was viewed by some as little more than a piratical adventurer.[5] Clearly, Pickens fervently wanted everyone to see Lopez not only as normative but, ideally, as paradigmatic and necessary for the urgent work of Manifest Destiny—hence her investment of his story with stirring narrative. She was hardly alone in endorsing such projects. Only three years earlier, Melville's Ishmael had cried out: "Let America add Mexico to Texas and pile Cuba upon Canada; let the English over swarm all India, and hang out their blazing banner from the sun; for two thirds of this terraqueous globe are the Nantucketer's. For the sea is his; he owns it" (1851, 158). Of course the end of the *Pequod* and Lopez's mission are not dissimilar, making the narratives that these events constitute at least doubled in meaning.

Sharing a pattern used by many other writers of the period, Pickens links the two Caribbean cities of New Orleans and Havana. The actual facts that underlie her fiction kept her from using the more familiar setting of her native South Carolina's Charleston. Two of her aristocratic protagonists, Genevieve Clifton and Eugene de France (both Catholics), are from Louisiana, as is the enslaved African American figure Scipio. Of course, the expedition did in fact draw much of its support from New Orleans, but Pickens seems interested in making use of the complementary exoticisms of the two locales and of the opportunities such tropical realms offered for romance and intrigue. Her inscription for the first chapter reads, "The past but lives in words," while her prologue, decrying historical forgetfulness, declares that the writer has "dreamed of those scenes" and that she will endeavor "to share our dream," thereby generating a "rise from the ashes" of the expedition, "a bird which shall avenge them all" (Pickens 1854, 53–54). This image figures the legendary phoenix, which rose from its own ashes in rebirth. Significantly, it would become the central figure in the great seal of

Atlanta after its destruction by fire in the Civil War. The motif of revenge, however, raises the question of against whom it will be waged—does she have Cuban despots in mind, or the U.S. government, which failed to support the invasion?

The entire narrative is based on the belief that Lopez was fighting to extend freedom to Cuba, "that fatally loved isle" (55), despite the opposition from President Fillmore, who forbade filibustering in a presidential neutrality proclamation in 1851 (which Pickens roundly criticizes). But Pickens knows that the best way to argue the case for filibustering is to dramatize it. Genevieve Clifton begs her lover Ralph Dudley not to join Lopez, as the Cubans are not worthy of freedom. He demurs, claiming that the Cuban people "will gladly flock" to support the invasion. Arguing for a nineteenth-century version of "regime change," Dudley concludes, "We have but to land, and our numbers will be swelled to a formidable army. . . . A republican government will be established which looks to America as its model" (70). Ralph sees himself as both Genevieve's champion and Cuba's Lafayette, enforcing the mythical dimension of the novel as a reprise of both the American Revolution and chivalric days, à la Scott. Delany also figures his characters as contemporary versions of the Founding Fathers.

Like future Plantation School writers such as Thomas Nelson Page and Joel Chandler Harris, Pickens employs a cast of faithful black retainers. Indeed, old black Marmion, the butler, in effect raised Dudley after his parents died, and Scipio fought side by side with his master in the Mexican War. As was usual in Southern literature of the time, the blacks are naively comic but also strangely wise, and all of them are dedicated to their "white folks." Marmion scorns the freedom Dudley offers him, crying "Marse Ralph! Don't 'sult dis grey head in yo' own dead father's house!" (100). Genevieve, too, is surrounded by comic but seemingly all-knowing female servants, and all these black folk speak dialect, unlike the white figures, who speak standard, even elevated, English, as do the Spanish characters.

Like the Yankee visitors in early plantation fiction such as John Pendleton Kennedy's *Swallow Barn* (1832), Mabel, descended from New England Puritans, is a surrogate for the reader, as she learns the virtues inherent in Southern mores. But Pickens also makes her a feminine mouthpiece for Lopez, as she blasts the federal government's anti-filibustering policies. At dinner, she cries out, "Don't say filibusters! Call them by their proper name,—'Patriots!' 'Liberators!'" (108). Indeed, the title of the novel comes from Mabel's handiwork, for she has fashioned a tiny version of the "free flag of Cuba" for Eugene. Pickens's astute yoking of this sentimental domestic wing of the scheme to conquer Cuba was the Southern front of a national campaign that had a Northern component bent on colonization not of Latin America but of Africa. We remember that Harriet Beecher Stowe's *Uncle Tom's Cabin* (1852), one of the sources for Delany, advocates, through the figure of George Harris, African resettlement. Sarah Josepha Hale ceaselessly argued, through her editorship of *Godey's Lady's Book* and her novels *Northwood* (1827, 1852) and *Liberia* (1853), that the problem of slavery (she was not for abolition) could be solved by sending educated slaves to Africa to make it a Christian civilization, thereby preparing the way for resettlement there of all enslaved people of the United States. Like Pickens, who saw Cuba's "emancipation" as the opening wedge for a campaign of liberation in the hemisphere, Hale projected that "the whole continent of Africa will be regenerated. . . . The Republic of Liberia will be the great instrument in working out this regeneration" (Hale 1853, 303). As Amy Kaplan has observed, this foray of American domesticity into the international sphere was intended to extend the doctrines of Manifest Destiny but also to police the national domestic realm, purging blacks from the imaginary white national family. Delany makes a case like this, but for different reasons; blacks cannot succeed—in evangelizing or anything else—until they are free *within a predominantly colored nation*, because of the inherent racism of whites. Including Pickens among this group brings a new register to the concept of domestic Manifest Destiny, as she represents both the masked imperialism of her Northern sisters and a proslavery, filibustering viewpoint that seeks an expansion of the political, economic, and racial horizons of her native region.

Lopez's flag first flew on the masthead of one of his ships, the *Susan Loud*. It had been designed for the second of Lopez's expeditions in 1850 by Jose Teurbe Tolon, the editor of the New York newspaper for Cuban exiles, *La Verdad*, and a member of that city's Consejo Cubano organization. Its design—blue stripes and single star against a red backdrop—was based on the Texas Lone Star flag, which had similarly inaugurated the tradition of a "new" nation (Chaffin 1996, 119). The flag, like many others of the period, also echoed the colors and tradition of the French tricolor, always a symbol for glorious revolution by the people, and the Old Glory of the United States. We remember that the various flags of the Confederacy also kept these colors in play, in keeping with an appropriation of the revolutionary values of national independence established in the 1770s.[6]

Except for a brief appearance in the opening chapter, Lopez himself is kept offstage until well into the narrative. Pickens fully portrays him first at a reception held in New Orleans, where he has been living, appropriately, in the Lafayette quarter. The narrator rhapsodizes: "The beauty of the noble head was of the highest order. . . . The broad full-veined brow . . . seemed so fit a temple for the holy visions . . . the glorious falcon eyes . . . burning with all the fire of a southern sun. . . . He came to you in all the majesty of old romance—a Hero" (120). This florid description has much in common with the hymns to male beauty in Colonel Falkner's *The Spanish Heroine* and is misleading—the real Lopez was hardly prepossessing, and many accounts state that he was quite dark. As Amy Greenberg notes, he was repeatedly "whitened" in popular accounts, including illustrations that accompanied them in newspapers.[7] Although others stated he was a dissolute womanizer and gambler (Chaffin 1996, 218), Pickens portrays him as a paradigm of virtuous manhood in the Americas. Above all, she equates Lopez with the *beau ideal* of Southern masculinity, the Gentleman (who was also epitomized in the character representing Pickens's deceased fiancé). As we shall see, Martin Delany paints a similar portrait of Henry Blake, who ultimately is revealed as a Cuban grandee, a device that is also employed with other characters.

The scene introducing Lopez is the hinge of the book, as all that precedes it takes place in the United States and the following chapters are set in Cuba. Once she takes readers to the island, Pickens creates melodrama by bringing the Spanish commander Concha on stage as a tyrannical villain and certainly no gentleman. He, "of gory fame," paces restlessly, like a wild animal, with "glittering . . . cold eyes" that echo "the assassin's steel. It was a coward's face. . . . No mercy had ever softened the relentless heart of Cuba's dark oppressor" (125), a description that is the pendant and exact opposite of the description just rendered of Lopez, and one in keeping with "the dark legend" of Spanish colonial oppression. Concha is aware of the expedition and in fact has sent false letters to Lopez that promise he will be met by a popular uprising.

Pickens intrudes on the narrative to give a mythic history of Cuba, that "island queen" whose "wondrous beauty" is of an "ocean-born goddess." The Spanish, she tells us, "with false promises on their lips . . . encircled in their dark, treacherous arms the fairest child of the southern waters. Once possessed, the deadly grasp of avarice and oppression crushed and marred her glorious loveliness, sending from her torn bosom a piteous and continued cry for mercy and relief" (130). This description clearly figures a white Cuba, raped and abused by a black Spain, thereby conjuring racial specters already present in the white South in abundance after the Haitian Revolution and internal slave revolts. Moreover, Cuba here is a child, making Spain a predator, providing a Freudian variant of the famous "Black Legend" of Spanish colonialism.[8]

The actual invasion is thwarted because Concha has cleverly evacuated towns that might rally to Lopez's flag. Crittenden and his men are captured and executed in a scene that rouses the imagination and indignation of the author, who compares them to Crusaders meeting their deaths at the hands of the "infidels," thereby linking the Spaniards to the medieval Moslems (as Muslims were termed at the time), despite the fact that both Lopez and his enemies are presumably all Catholic. Expanding her inappropriate metaphor, Pickens exclaims, "Love of their holy religion took the Saxons from their homes, sending them across the blue waters of the Mediterranean. Is not the principle of liberty in reality the religion of our people?" (141). Here, as we shall see, her artistic contortions prefigure Delany's, as his heroes Blake and Plácido attempt to build a new secular religion of liberation on the framework of traditional Christianity. We are also struck by yet another linkage of the Caribbean to the Mediterranean, whose myths and legends, from Troy to Caliban, find constant reanimation in the Americas. Finally, the use of religious rhetoric for political ends registers powerfully here as well, in terms of both Southern and national imperatives, not identical but rather fraternal twins of Manifest Destiny. The fact that Pickens had not given up the dream of conquering Cuba when she wrote the book is again implicit in her defiant cry, "The eagle of Columbia shrieks hoarsely for vengeance over her slaughtered sons, *and she shall not shriek in vain*" (143).

In one of Lopez's most revealing utterances, he asserts that Spain, rather than lose Cuba, will free the slaves: "The Spaniard would cast upon her the undying stain of African equality. He would bid the Cuban grasp his slave as a brother, and together kneel before a crown whose pollution, fiends might blush to wear" (173). This speech, which comes rather late in the novel, aligns Lopez tightly, and on strictly racial terms, with Pickens and her fellow Southerners and introduces the motifs of infection and social anarchy that miscegenation suggested in the South.

Dudley and the enslaved Scipio take Lopez's body back for ceremonial burial in New Orleans, where portraits of Lafayette and Washington are draped in black. The flags of the United States and Cuba are interbraided above his coffin. Once again, rituals of death entwine nations, historical eras, and the races. Similarly, the novel concludes three years later, when Dudley, newly flush from California ventures, at last marries Genevieve, in a double ceremony with Mabel and her new beau Stuart Raymond. This tableau provides a life-generating coda to the earlier ritual of death.

While Pickens does not choose to detail Dudley's enterprises in the Golden State, she would have been keenly aware that California had been taken from Mexico—deemed an inappropriate and wasteful custodian of rich lands—and from a largely Spanish culture that lacked "Saxon" industry and know-how. Dudley's success there could be seen as offering the message that he would have "improved" Cuba too if the invasion had been successful, and that it was not too late "to seek a better world" there.[9]

In the concluding chapter, Pickens allows herself a speech. Depicting Cuba as a chained figure rising from the waves—thereby combining the mythical Venus with Hiram Powers's famous statue, the enchained "Greek Slave"—she calls for "young America, the nation-knight," to release her from her bonds. Decrying the failure of the nation to come to Cuba's aid, she calls on citizens of the United States to honor the cause of freedom—for now, in addition to the affinities Americans should feel for a people who crave liberty, "there is a link of *blood* which holds her to every American heart." Cuba has been newly consecrated, "deluged with the blood of our kindred and countrymen" (212). We note that the blood she refers to on both sides of the waters is purely that of whites. Significantly, the wedding banquet that precedes this rhetorical flight concludes with a comic toast offered by "Scipio Africanus" (the first time his name has been listed as such), but it is really serious, despite being rendered in dialect. He addresses the wedding party but also alludes to the filibusters John Quitman and Lopez, and to Jefferson Davis, "an' all de solgers we took to Mexico an' Cuby; in fac', sir, I drink to all our boys, dead an' 'live" (209).

Letting Scipio have the last word keeps the spirit of the occasion light because of the humor involved, but it also unifies all the characters, white and black, in the cause of Manifest Destiny, while simultaneously papering over the glaring irony of the filibusters—fighting for freedom, but not freedom for all. This use of racial ventriloquism pushes readers to reflect: if an enslaved black endorses limited freedom, what's the problem? Scipio also pulls together the expansionist aspect of the Mexican American War with the Cuban expeditions and proleptically looks forward, with the reference to Jefferson Davis, to a Confederacy that Pickens could only dream about at this point in her career. Finally, Scipio's privileged position in this scene supports the old shibboleth about the biracial plantation family as well as the notion that while blacks could not be kin by blood (even though, of course, many white families in the South had black kin through interracial rape), they could, by "consent" rather than "descent," function as important and supportive elements in Southern dreams of expansionism.[10]

Delany and the Dream of Hemispheric Revolt

Only five years after *The Free Flag* appeared, Martin Delany's *Blake; or, The Huts of America* (1859) would make very different use of a Cuban setting. As the novel abundantly demonstrates, the most shameful connection between the South and the Caribbean island was the slave trade. The importation of slaves to Louisiana began in 1719 with shipment of 500 captured Guineans, but soon enslaved Africans were imported from the Caribbean as well, particularly from Saint Domingue. But after that island's slave revolt began in 1791, it was felt that the introduction of workers from there would foment revolution, and the Spanish governor Hector banned slave imports from the West Indies. Nevertheless, covert trade continued, and thousands of enslaved Africans were brought to Louisiana alone after Haitian planters and their retainers were ejected from Cuba in the early 1800s. There were always numerous planters who had plantations and slaves to work them in both the coastal South and Cuba, a fact that Delany employs tellingly in his novel.

Martin Delany was born free in Virginia but came to maturity in Pittsburgh. He studied medicine at Harvard but had to leave when white students objected to his presence. He moved to Canada in 1856, where he wrote part of *Blake*. Delany opposed the emigration of blacks to Liberia and instead advocated for Central America as a site for black colonization. After traveling widely in Africa in 1859–60, however, he favored Niger Valley resettlement projects. Ever protean in his outlook, after serving as a major in the Union army, he came to think of the United States itself as promising for blacks, and he worked to fulfill this possibility in various occupations in South Carolina for many years, at first with the Freedmen's Bureau. He lived in the South until shortly before his death in 1885 and wrote about it extensively even before moving there, so it is certainly time to acknowledge him as a Southern writer. Further, as I hope this chapter will demonstrate, there is much to be gained by considering Delany against the backdrop of the South and his depiction of it in *Blake*. First, the ways that he imagines Cuba have everything to do with his conception of the South, which he accurately saw as linked to Cuba in myriad ways through the hemispheric plantation industry. He was keenly aware of the literary campaign Southerners like Pickens were waging, in terms of bolstering slavery and of extending it through colonization of the Caribbean. Recentering diasporic culture in the circumCaribbean rather than in merely the U.S. South was clearly a central objective for him—hence the importance of *Blake* for my project, which has, in this respect, the same aim.

Blake would seem by its very title to be evidence of the Southern/Caribbean heritage, as the full subtitle *The Huts of America: A Tale of the Mississippi Valley, the Southern United States, and Cuba* refers to the hemispheric system of slavery. Free himself, Henry discovers that his enslaved wife has been sold into slavery in Cuba. Posing as a slave, he enters the island, obtains his wife's freedom, and works with the mulatto society there to foment revolution. Eventually, he sails to Africa, describes the slave trade in gruesome detail, and demonstrates the sordid ties that bind the Black Atlantic together. Blake's travels through the Southern states offer a landscape of Hell, à la Dante, and the subsequent portrait of slavery in Cuba provides a grim pendant. He also celebrates pockets of resistance, like the Maroon society in Virginia. The stance of these groups becomes his inspiration as he foments revolution across the South and the Caribbean.

Blake ostensibly differs dramatically from Pickens's narrative, in that Delany would have characters like her Scipio engage in covert activities to free themselves, rather than helping the cause of liberation for white Cubans. However, Delany, like Pickens, is ultimately interested in what we could call another brand of filibustering, in that he was obsessed for many years with black colonization plans, which would have involved the appropriation of territory owned by natives. In a revealing essay, Timothy Powell has identified what he calls the "self-cloaking" aspect of American colonization, wherein the arguments made by figures such as Lopez, Walker, and Pickens's fictional Dudley are "self-cloaking" stratagems for imperialism and colonialism. Obviously, the fiction that "we paid"—the sums involved were minuscule—for vast appropriations of land such as those seized from Mexico—fits in here too. Powell also uses postcolonial theory to demonstrate how Delany's Henry and enslaved Africans and African Americans are being forced into "external colonization" (that is, the establishment of free colonies outside the United States) as opposed to the creation of internal outlaw colonies such as those of the Maroons. In this reading, "Blake completely dismantles this self-cloaking mechanism of American colonist discourse by reconfiguring the colonizer/colonized binary such that Creoles and blacks are clearly seen to be the colonized while Americans and Spaniards are grouped together as colonizers" (2000, 360–61). Powell does not consider the fact that Delany's efforts to affect black colonization in both Latin America and Africa also constitute colonization in Edward Said's sense—that is, settlement of land already belonging to other people—or that there may be "self-cloaking" aspects of Delany's rhetoric that are uncomfortably close to those of the filibusters.

Like Pickens, Delany uses dialect for slaves while his educated heroes speak elevated standard English, and he too relies on a conventional romantic ending, with multiple marriages. Still, in most of the narrative, he strives to eliminate romantic clichés, an effort helped by his background as a newspaper editor, which included two years co-editing the *North Star* with Frederick Douglass. The transnational aspect of *Blake*, however, came from his equally trailblazing work of 1852, *The Condition, Elevation, Emigration, and Destiny of the Colored People of the United States, Politically Considered*. His advocacy of a new state for persons of African descent was based on his opposition to the Liberian settlement movement.[11]

Henry's preference for extreme measures—a violent revolution on the order of Haiti's—clearly stemmed from Delany's deep pessimism about racial prospects in the United States. In an 1853 letter to Frederick Douglass, he predicted that in order to save the Union, the North would eventually reinstall slavery (Levine 2003, 225). Moreover, he believed that men of color could never succeed except in societies in which they were the majority, which explains his choice of Latin America and, later, West Africa. It should be remembered that virtually all African American leaders at this time despaired about racial progress, as the triple catastrophe of the Missouri Compromise, the Fugitive Slave Act, and the *Dred Scott* decision created powerful props for the slavocracy and for its plans to expand slavery beyond the nation's borders.

In this connection, we note a principal thematic in an ostensibly jointly authored document, "Political Destiny of the Colored Race on the American Continent," which is signed by twelve black men, but with the name of Martin Delany at the top of the list. The essay argues that blacks can never achieve justice in the United States, as they will never be a majority. Therefore, as Delany did repeatedly elsewhere, the argument is made for a majority-black colony noting that great civilizations of Egypt, Greece, and Rome had fallen because they had lost a pure original identity, while Great Britain, Russia, Turkey, and France of his day had ostensibly retained it. One wonders what Delany would think about the current multicultural composition of not only the United States, but, increasingly, of the other countries he lists.

Delany supposes that emigration to a country where racial characteristics are shared would create the kind of group identity necessary for nationhood. Later, however, when he went to Africa to explore the Niger River area as a site for immigration, he saw clearly that there would have to be tremendous American-style changes in Africa in order for African Americans to set up a ruling junta. Why would Delany—who decried colonization by "Saxons"—decide to attempt it himself? In his speech "Political Destiny of the Colored Race on the American Continent" (1854), he lists all the countries of the world that had been colonized in the preceding decades, so much so that two-thirds of the world's people—all colored—are now ruled by one-third (the whites). Delany declares: "Shall we stand still and continue inactive—the passive observers of the great events of the times. . . . Shall the last vestige of an opportunity, outside of the continent of Africa, for the national development of our race, be permitted, in consequence of our slothfulness, to elude our grasp, and fall into the position of the whites? . . . Black men [should] . . . take advantage of the opportunity, by grasping hold of those places where chance is in their favor, and establishing the rights and power of the colored race. . . . The West Indies, Central and South America, are the countries of our choice" (2003, 253–54).

Likely because of Spain's iron-fisted control of Cuba, Delany never seems to have seen that island as a prospective site for his black colony. Still, like virtually everyone of that time, he understood that the central location, large size, and natural resources of Cuba made it a controlling force in the future of the Caribbean, and, indeed, of the hemisphere. The liberation of enslaved Afro-Cubans would be a vital step toward his dream, in that such a nation—rather than a new slave-owning Southern state of Cuba—could be a buffer zone and possible ally for a black colony on some southern shore of the inland sea. Cuba could, in this respect, echo the revolutionary achievement of Haiti, while avoiding that island's ultimate isolation and impoverishment. Further, Delany was well aware that, despite laws forbidding the transatlantic slave trade, ships regularly embarked from New Orleans and other Southern ports to take on cargoes of slaves in Havana, human commodities that were then dispersed throughout the cotton states via the Crescent City. As Delany declared, "Cuba is the great western slave mart of the world, containing the barracoons or refining shops to the slave factories of . . . pirates on the western coast of Africa. It is the great channel through which slaves are imported annually into the United States, contrary to the law of the land" (Levine 2003, 161). The liberation of Cuba's slaves would cut off an illegal but continuing supply of enslaved peoples for the U.S. South.

Delany explained his preference for Central and South America and the West Indies as potential destinations for African American emigrants in some detail in his 1852 volume, *The Condition, Elevation, Emigration, and Destiny of the Colored People of the United States*. He claims there that the varieties of climate in Central and South America echo those of the U.S. South, as does the productivity of the soil. Mineral resources, waterways, shipping ports—all these are viewed favorably as well. Above all, however, Delany declares, there are no racial inequities, and people of color—"our brethren"—vastly outnumber whites. Again, like Lopez and the other filibusters, he asserts that "the people stand with open arms ready to receive us. . . . Go we must, and go we will, as there is no alternative. To remain here in North America, and be crushed to the earth in vassalage and degradation, we never will" (1852, 207).

Like *The Free Flag of Cuba*, *Blake* is neatly divided into two parts, with the second part set in Cuba and Africa. Populated by diasporic characters from all over the globe, the novel steadfastly refuses to privilege African Americans. As such, Delany's magnum opus constitutes an important forerunner of the kind of Pan-Africanism espoused by W. E. B. Du Bois and others later in the century. Yet it has uncomfortable affinities with the filibustering narratives we have examined. Still, the inscription to *Blake*, from Harriet Beecher Stowe, which Pickens would no doubt agree would apply to Cuba too—at least in spirit, for she would of course have no use for the author— has truer meaning here: "I have sworn to right the wrong, / I have pledged my word unbroken, / For the weak against the strong."

As the reference to Stowe suggests, Delany was much indebted to *Uncle Tom's Cabin*. The opening gambit of the plot is to show that the favored slave of the mistress, Maggie, is in danger of being sold.[12] This echoes the first scene of Stowe's novel on the Shelby plantation, where the master's gambling debts dictate the sale of not just any slaves, but the *best* slaves like Uncle Tom and Eliza. Just like her predecessor Eliza in Stowe's epic, Maggie has a child, Little Joe, who is also in danger, despite the fondness their mistress, Mrs. Franks, has for them. A Northern visitor, Arabella Ballard, Franks's kinswoman, bridles at the kindnesses showered on Maggie, and when possible, mistreats her, even slapping her—but worse, she plots to buy Maggie from the Franks. This seemingly domestic struggle between Franks and Ballard has large implications for the narrative, as the latter and her husband have a country home near Havana, where she means to take Maggie. The Ballards' ownership of estates in both the South and the Caribbean shows that plantation economics spread their tentacles across national boundaries, a fact made plain by the designation of slave bodies as portable capital/commodities, and by the parallels—particularly between Louisiana and Cuba—in crop husbandry, particularly sugarcane. Cuba had taken on much greater importance in the Western Hemisphere after the conclusion of the Haitian Revolution, which led to drastically decreased sugar production in that country, formerly the leader in the world market. Cuba quickly took Haiti's place in that role, which then led Spain to exact crushing new taxes from its newly rich colony, thereby causing internal foment and the threat of revolution but also increased temptation on the part of the United States—particularly the South—to annex the island. In his powerful 1849 essay, "Annexation of Cuba," Delany sounds the alarm on this subject, calling the plan for annexation a "perfidious wicked design" (2003, 161). His arguments note, as well, the long-standing (and illegal) practice of traders from the coastal states going to Cuba, "the great western slave mart of the world," to transport black bodies to New Orleans for resale throughout the South. In a ringing conclusion, which suggests much about the subsequent setting of half of *Blake* in Cuba, Delany declares that "at the instant of the annexation of Cuba to these United States, it should be the signal for simultaneous rebellion of all the slaves [of] the Southern States, and throughout that island" (165). In a subsequent essay that same year, "The Redemption of Cuba," he encouraged enslaved black Cubans to look to the example of Haiti, and to the martyrdom of Cuba's own Plácido (2003).

Sowing the Seeds of Southern Revolt

Delany was aware that these prose declarations of principle lacked the magnetic power of fiction. Accordingly, *Blake* presents a Cuban imaginary replete with sexual horrors that are consonant with those enacted in the United States. Colonel Franks—whose sins span the coastal South and the Caribbean, along with his holdings—agrees to sell Maggie to her husband, Blake, for as we learn, she has spurned his sexual overtures. Still later in the novel, this offense becomes monstrous, when we learn that Maggie is his natural daughter. William Faulkner would use this horrific motif in his novel *Go Down, Moses* (1942), in which the antebellum patriarch Carothers McCaslin impregnates his daughter, causing her slave mother to drown herself.[13] Throughout the novel, Delany has slaves reveal that black women are constantly raped by white men. Still, Delany always has white characters abort conversations about interracial sexuality before they become too detailed, presumably because he knows his refined readers might throw down the book if sexual propriety is violated in print, even though the crimes involved cry out to heaven. Frederick Douglass suffered under similar constraints, as did all slave narrators.

Like George Harris, Eliza's husband in *Uncle Tom's Cabin*, Henry scorns stoic acceptance of Maggie's sale and trust in "de Lawd." Also like George, Henry, unlike the other slaves, speaks in standard English rather than in dialect, as in this stirring denunciation of his kinfolk's biblically inspired obedience: "Don't tell me about religion! . . . My wife is sold away from me by a man who is one of the leading members of the very church to which both she and I belong! Put my trust in the Lord! I have done so all my life nearly, and of what use is it to me? . . . I'm tired looking the other side; I want a hope this side of the vale of tears. . . . I and my wife have been both robbed of our liberty, and you want me to be satisfied with a hope of heaven" (16). This is in sharp contrast to the slaves in Pickens's narrative, who reject freedom and, in one case, actually suggest that their destitute master sell them to raise money.

Unlike Stowe's mulatto intellectuals, Henry is "black—a pure Negro— handsome, manly . . . of good literary attainments . . . educated in the West Indies, and decoyed away when young" (16–17). Here Delany forges yet another line of connection between the South and the Caribbean, suggesting better possibilities for people of color in the islands, where there were indeed many more free blacks. Further, the fact that Henry, originally free, was captured into slavery, creates an affinity with Solomon Northop, a free man of New York who was kidnapped and enslaved in Louisiana. His narrative, *Twelve Years a Slave* (now an acclaimed movie), which was published in 1853, was surely an influence on *Blake*. Finally, the generic location, "West Indies," is purposely vague, for it keeps Henry's exact origins mysterious, thereby providing punch for the surprise revelations that change everything midway through the novel.[14]

Franks promises to sell Henry to Van Winter, who will take him with her to Cuba, and thus to Maggie. But Franks learns of this and sells him to an unscrupulous trader for more money, causing Henry to run away, taking his son Joe with him, for "I'd bury him in the bottom of the river" rather than leave him in slavery.[15] Henry has $2,000 for his escape, stolen over the years from his master. This use of a providential "stash" has its mirror in Pickens's novel, but there the slave Scipio sacrifices his savings to secure his master's well-being, rather than to buy his own freedom. Importantly, Delany has Henry's flight prefaced by a meeting with three male slaves from other plantations, Sam, Charles, and Andy. "Clasping each other by the hand, standing in a band together, as a plight of their union and fidelity to each other, Henry said, 'I now impart to you the secret, it is this: I have laid a scheme, and matured a plan for a general insurrection of the slaves in every state, and the successful overthrow of slavery!'" (39). Thus Delany creates a communal dimension *in ovo*, so to speak, which will radiate out as Henry travels onward and meets with other enslaved communities.[16]

Henry also challenges the meaning of the line "standing still to see the salvation" from the Bible, which has already been used by Mammy Judy in an effort to constrain Henry. Instead of reading it as advocating passivity, he uses it repeatedly as a call for revolution. As he declares, "We must now begin to understand the Bible so as to make it of interest to us" (41), a strong endorsement of using the tools of the master against him. Henry gives his friends an example of how to do this immediately, as he urges them to steal from their masters to enable freedom: "God told the Egyptian slaves to 'borrow from their neighbors'—meaning their oppressors—'all their jewels'; meaning to take their money and wealth wherever they could lay hands upon it, and depart from Egypt" (43). Throughout African American history, the two most important books of the Bible have been Exodus and Revelation, which concern, respectively, liberation from bondage and return to the promised land and the dream of Apocalypse and the defeat of evil. *Blake*, in its complicated plot, envisions all of these possibilities, projecting a scheme that encompasses the South, the Caribbean, and Africa, the triangle of the Black Atlantic. Indeed, the anthem Henry raises here conjoins geography: "My watchword 'Freedom or the grave!' / Until from Rappahannock's stream, / To where the Cuato waters lave [a stream in Cuba] / One simultaneous war cry" (44), as Virginia and Cuba become a common ground of struggle.

The Cuba connection is strengthened when Delany introduces Major Armsted, Franks's business associate and, like Ballard, a landowner in Cuba. The conversations between the two offer Delany a mode of presenting varieties of white (and hemispheric) master-class ideology. Ballard, a Northerner, like his wife, endorses slavery. "My large interest . . . in the slave-labor products of Cuba, should be, I think, sufficient evidence of my fidelity to Southern principles" (60), prima facie evidence of the North's collusion in both imperialism and slave labor.

Judge Ballard applauds the recent *Dred Scott* decision (although it is never named) and inveighs against blacks' privileges in Cuba. "I consider that colony . . . a moral pestilence, a blighting curse. . . . Cuba must cease to be a Spanish colony, and become American territory. Those mongrel Creoles are incapable of self-government, and should be compelled to submit to the United States" (62). This utterance represents a classic imperialistic pose, one in keeping with parallel arguments that had been made in the preceding decade to justify the seizure of almost half of Mexico. Further, the fact that he himself has been a judge reveals the corruption of the U.S. judicial system, even in the North.

The rhetoric of contagion employed by Ballard is also revealing and contrasts to the use of that term by Blake. As Edward Said has demonstrated, the "incapability" of natives to govern themselves is always used as justification for conquest, and the "infection" argument—that the "pestilence," or "blight," of racial and geographical mismanagement can spread and thus must be contained—is another familiar theme in both filibuster texts and arguments for Manifest Destiny. Race, of course, trumps everything. Here it seems that Ballard, unlike many white New Orleanians of the time, views "Creole" as inevitably including the African, which accounts for the equation Creole-equals-mongrel.[17]

This scene also raises the old adage—common among Southern blacks as well—that in the North, they don't mind giving you rights as long as you don't get too close, while in the South you can get close but can't get rights.[18] Major Armsted twits Ballard by telling him that the cigar he is smoking was not only made by slaves, but that they often draw cigars through their lips during the manufacturing process to make them cohere. But all the food the whites eat is prepared by black hands too.

The ties between Louisiana and the Caribbean are underlined when we learn that Maggie was sold to Peter Labonier, a Louisiana planter now living in Cuba, after Ballard found her to be difficult. Ballard, Franks, and Armsted ride out to Grason's plantation to see an eleven-year-old boy, Reuben, perform Jim Crow capers under the application of a whip. Franks laughs, but Ballard stops the show, leading Franks to say, "Not quite a southerner yet Judge, if you can't stand that!" (67). Delany tells us that Reuben dies that night from loss of blood. This "raree" show has been imported from the United States to Cuba, an "infection" of cruelty that proves epidemic. Delany makes it clear that violence in the pursuit of freedom is permissible, for Henry kills a white overseer during his flight.[19] Pausing at the Red River to pray, he thinks of Moses and intones, "Could I but climb where Moses stood, / And view the landscape o'er; / Not Jordan's streams, nor death's cold flood, / Could drive me from the shore!" (69). Clearly, Delany figures the Red River as the Red Sea, with Henry becoming a modern-day Moses. Subsequently, Henry learns that a black overseer, Jesse, beats slaves unmercifully. The next day, Jesse is missing, presumably murdered by Henry. We remember that Moses killed an Egyptian overseer for similar reasons, so this is an extension of the basic comparison on Delany's part. Underlining this is the recruitment on this plantation of old Moses, who is said to have taken the life of a white overseer in Virginia, replicating Henry's crime.[20] Delany sums up a string of adventures: "From plantation to plantation did he go, sowing the seeds of future devastation and ruin to the master and redemption to the slave, an antecedent more terrible in its anticipation than the warning voice of the destroying Angel in commanding the slaughter of the firstborn of Egypt" (83). Here the topic of "pestilence" and "plague" that the white men speak of in the Caribbean becomes real for the South, through Henry's "infection" of the local black populace.[21]

And there is more. A positive variant of infection, "sowing . . . seeds," here appropriates one of the chief symbolic modes of colonization. As Jill H. Casid has demonstrated, botanical references pepper all discourses of imperialism, through a "founding paternal gesture of possession. . . . With the materializing metaphor of planting scattered seed, that is, the practices of agriculture and landscaping as (hetero)sexual reproduction, to plant was both to produce colonies and to generate imperial subjects to sustain them" (2005, xiv). Delany thus shrewdly employs both contagion—the "infection" of liberty—and the master's discourse of "sowing"—and thus "improving" and propagating the New World garden, an activity ironically enhanced through the "sowing" of the master's seeds in the bodies of enslaved women, whose children would do the very real sowing and reaping of capitalist production.

Delany's tropical swamps and jungles support Maroon alliances and cultures, as in the West Indies. While slaves did escape to such settings, the most famous Maroon community in the United States was created by Seminole Indians, whose communities in the Everglades after Andrew Jackson's effort to exterminate or relocate them ensured them a permanent place in Florida, both physical and mythical. In his use of these historical enclaves and communities, Delany shows us that stories of such societies and social alliances circulate beyond the Caribbean rim far into the interior and, as such, function as the kind of "infection" that Henry seeks to inculcate through his plot.

In North Carolina, Henry meets Maroons in the Dismal Swamp, allowing Delany to rehearse the great history of runaway communities in that setting and other wetlands, a syndrome familiar to readers of that time through Stowe's *Dred: A Tale of the Dismal Swamp* (1856). Henry's meeting with confederates of the sainted Nat Turner offers yet another mode of "remembering," a term that should be read in two ways, in terms of memory but also as growing new "limbs" for the struggle to come. One of these veterans is Gamby Gholar, Turner's conjurer, who claims that he had prophesied Henry's coming. After combing through his gourd of mystic elements, he presents Henry with a sacred bird breastbone as a charm. The tales of his glorious predecessors seem to revitalize Henry, who is anointed as a priest of the order of High Conjurors in a cave guarded by a huge serpent, no doubt a sign for the African god Damballah. This passage never signifies belief on Henry's part in conjure, but effectively counters the devout if militant Christianity espoused by other rebels earlier in the text while linking the South with the voodoo practitioners of the islands, who form another section of the black diaspora. As these Conjurors endorse Henry's uprising, we understand that their normal proselytizing for new disciples will now have a double purpose, giving a dual aspect to the "infection" thematic, which is now strongly Caribbean too. Significantly, old Maudy Chamus brags that he and "Gennel Gabel fit in de Malution wah"—or as Henry translates for us, "the Revolutionary War for American independence, father" (113). Here, Henry's appellation of "father" creates filiation for liberation and also links up with the concept of national "Founding Fathers," claiming a space in that company for black men. Honoring Maudy Chamus also mitigates the disdain readers might have for him because of his dialect, which here rightly becomes the folk-drenched vehicle for communal wisdom. Further, this declension from the Revolution to the current impulse for armed insurrection (a device, as we have seen, employed by Pickens as well) makes the actions of Henry and his partisans throughout the book profoundly American rather than terrorist, as whites of the time would charge.

Father Maudy's use of the "mad dog" image for the slave insurrectionist Gabriel Prosser returns us to the concept of freedom as an "infection," a usage employed by both blacks and whites in the novel, although the slave owners see this infection as a "plague" and a menace, one equivalent to terrorism rather than a desire for freedom. As Eric Sundquist has noted, Prosser's conspiracy was thwarted, yet it "achieved in the arena of terror and propaganda many of the effects of successful revolts" (1993, 43). Nevertheless, as Don De Lillo has stated, "people who are powerless make an open theater of violence. True terror is a language and a vision. There is a deep narrative structure to terrorist acts, and they infiltrate and alter consciousness in ways that writers used to aspire to" (DePietro 2005, 84). Declaring that Henry and his co-conspirators seek freedom does not change the fact that they seek to spread terror among the whites, just as was done in Prosser's Richmond and, much more pervasively, in Haiti. The logic of such plans and deliberations does indeed lead to a "deep narrative structure" that informs the novel from beginning to end. The spread of terror as a cleansing fire appropriates and reverses the common trope of Haiti-equals-contagion/ infection. These scenes set among the Maroons inevitably bring to mind Haiti's original rebels in the mountains. As Vera Kutzinski has remarked, "Haiti, unable to be contained geographically and temporally, becomes an archetype grafted onto those other spaces where it leaves traces of Jacobean rebellion and spreads cultural Africanisms of various kinds that, surreptitiously but persistently, call into doubt paradigms that encode and disseminate beliefs in racial purity" (2001, 66).

Maroon culture was yet another way in which the South and the Caribbean had affinities. As Richard Price and contributors to his collection *Maroon Societies* have shown, there were numerous communities of runaway slaves in virtually all Southern and Caribbean locales, especially in swamps, but also in mountain recesses and forests. Herbert Aptheker posits fifty such communities from 1672 to 1864, with the largest and most famous situated in the Virginia/North Carolina Great Dismal Swamp, the locus of Stowe's novel *Dred* and a site of interest in Delany's narrative, as we have seen. Over 2,000 runaways living there illegally traded with people on the borders of the swamp (1996, 155–56).[22]

Creating a Cuban Imaginary

At almost the exact midpoint of the novel, Henry engages himself as a valet on a ship bound for Cuba, and we begin the Caribbean part of the novel. The ties between Louisiana and the Caribbean are signaled yet again when we meet Captain Garcia and his Louisiana bride.

It seems she has brought the bad habits of the South with her, for, like Stowe's Mrs. St. Claire, she has her slaves beaten regularly. Mr. Garcia is a slave trader, and later Henry sails with him to Africa for human cargo. We learn for the first time that Henry speaks perfect Castilian (so the earlier information that he is from the West Indies would now seem to narrow to the Spanish isles), and the Garcias naturally assume he is from Cuba. Searching for Maggie, he visits a plantation owned by a Louisianan and takes shelter with the Grandes, who seem to represent the hemispheric scope of slavery and, indeed, the entire black diaspora. They are "native African, having learned English on the coast, French Creole at New Orleans, and Spanish at Cuba; but ten years having elapsed since they were kidnaped, the whole family by chance getting together. Their African name was Oba, the Cuban, Grande" (172). Their background and their linguistic abilities pull the various heritages and histories of the circumCaribbean into a narrative nexus, adding a familial diasporic thematic that complements more familiar stories of enslaved individuals whose lives involve migration across national borders, as is the case in the slave narratives of Olaudah Equiano and Mary Prince. Further, the impressive multilingual ability of the family speaks to a similar facility found in thousands of the enslaved, a factor seldom noted in most historical and fictional accounts of the period or in examinations of diasporic cultures.

After Henry is reunited with his broken-down and abused wife, Maggie, he resolves to buy her, and Cuban law permits such a transaction. At this point, readers are amazed to find that Henry is really Carolus Henrico Blacus, a Cuban of good family who went to sea at age seventeen, only to find he was on a slave ship. After returning to the Americas with human cargo, the slave trader sold Henry along with the others, and that is how he wound up on the Franks plantation. He tells all this to his cousin Plácido, who was a very real and famous mulatto poet. Henry reveals that his program for revolution was inspired by reading his cousin's verses in a Spanish journal in New Orleans, thereby emphasizing again the Caribbean aspect of that city as well as the transnational struggle for emancipation and the role of literacy in that effort. Plácido reads a recent poem that has a poignant line in it all too apropos of Henry's current situation: "One look upon my tortured wife, / Shrieking beneath the driver's blows, / Would nerve me on to desp'rate strife, / Nor would I spare her dastard foes!" (196).

Why did Delany decide to insert this real figure into the narrative? Ifeoma Nwankwo has given us a careful and helpful reading of the historical Plácido, whose role in Cuban history was quite different from the one presented in Delany's fiction (2005). The poet's early biographers tell us he was abandoned as a newborn in 1809 on the steps of a Havana orphanage by his mother, Concepción Vázquez, a white dancer, and her hairdresser at the theater, a quadroon named Diego Ferrer Matoso. The child was named Diego Gabriel de la Conceptión (Stimson 1964, 45). Eventually his father reclaimed him, and he grew up spending time with both parents. Obviously, this equates with Blake's kidnapping and separation from *his* parents, and, indeed, the narrative gives us no reason to believe that he reveals himself to them as their son during the course of the novel, thereby eliminating the kind of melodramatic reunion of lost children and parents that we saw in *The Spanish Heroine* (in which Pedro's sudden elevation from servant to wealthy nobleman offers a similar shock).

Plácido's poems drew the Spanish government's ire, and he was imprisoned for six months after being falsely accused of plotting a Negro insurrection. He was subsequently executed in 1844 for the "high treason" of playing a role in the Escalera insurrection of 1843 in Matanzas, when thousands of slaves were imprisoned, not just from Matanzas, but from all over Cuba. Many were tortured on ladders (*escaleras*).[23] The charges specified that he had visited many spots on the island, organized cells of conspiracy, and urged extermination of all whites. Finally, and most interesting for our connection with Pickens, it was said that his belongings included the flag of the filibuster Lopez, that is, the "free flag of Cuba," the flag Pickens uses so extensively in her novel (Stimson 1964, 80).

There are no credible biographies, however, that definitively credit Plácido with plots to exterminate whites, and there is no historical proof that he ever killed anyone. Nevertheless, the Spanish authorities asserted that they had testimony from thirty-two co-conspirators that implicated Plácido as the key figure in the plot. On the other hand, they also charged that he and the other rebels were following orders of the white British consul, David Turnbull. Mulling over the various accounts of the Escalera episode, Nwankwo has demonstrated how Plácido and the issue of his identity became a "crucial battleground," as he was turned into a symbol by radically different constituencies—white and black abolitionists, Cuban *pardos* and *morenos*, and the agents of the Spanish colonial government (2005, 34–44).

The fact that Delany did not read Spanish makes it likely that his best ideas about Plácido were taken from William Henry Hurlbert's (1827–95) biographical sketch, published in the *North American Review* in 1849. A central tenet of this portrayal of the poet came not from Hurlbert himself but from one of his footnotes, where a "lady from Massachusetts" is quoted from Boston's *The Harbinger* of 1847: "His [Plácido's] deep-laid and almost barbarous schemes of revenge upon the oppressors of his race . . . have not destroyed the sympathy of the best hearts in his country and our own, for the victim of institutions which *breed* revenge" (quoted in Stimson 1964, 94). This portrait is much more congruent with Blake's own stance than that found in any other of the various biographies of Plácido.

It is revealing that Delany substitutes poems written by others (notably James M. Whitfield and perhaps some written by himself) that in fact fit his purposes better than Plácido's actual poems would have. Nwankwo has profitably read Plácido's poems and makes a persuasive case for their revolutionary fervor.[24] However, living as he did under a very repressive regime, the criticisms of slavery that he makes in his poems (as Nwankwo admits) are coded in many cases, and are nowhere as militant as Whitfield's ode to Cinque, the leader of the *Amistad* revolt.

After leaving Maggie with his parents, Henry signs on as mate of the *Vulture*, a slaving vessel, and sails for Africa. This ship is the very one we saw at the beginning of the novel, when it was called the *Merchantman*. Now illegally refitted to accept the packed bodies of enslaved Africans, it is indeed a vessel that feeds on death, and it thus closely resembles, in its symbolism, the monstrous *San Dominick* in Melville's *Benito Cereno* (1855), whose prow, stripped of its original figurehead, sports the skeleton of the captain's best friend, Aranda, with the penciled motto "follow your leader" under it, indicating that Americans are in the thrall of a deadly enterprise that will eventually consume them as well—thereby making Melville, as many have noted, proleptic, in prophesying (along with many other writers of the period) the Civil War.

Delany's ability to shift tone and technique is signaled by the introduction of the comic character of Gascar: "Irony and satire abounded in almost everything he said, so that he became the attraction of all on board." Gascar, presumably a Cuban, nevertheless sings a song in dialect that a footnote tells us was taken from a little black boy Delany encountered in the American South: "I'm a goin' to Afraka, / where de white man dare not stay; / I ketch 'im by de collar, / Den de white man holler; / I hit 'im on de pate, / Den I make 'im blate! / I seize 'im by de throat— / Laud!—he beller like a goat!" (210). This passage, because of its origin and context, again unites the South and the Caribbean and shows Delany's willingness to mix sources and folk wisdom from both areas at will. The comic song, however, also shakes out the irony of a black figure singing of future freedom in Africa while sailing on a ship that will enslave natives. And there is more. The song apparently rejoices in the fact that while slaves are drawn from Africa, the white man has yet to conquer the continent itself, which is still under the rule of the kings of Dahomey and Ashanti (who are mentioned prominently in the text).[25]

The international scope of slavery becomes apparent when the character of Ludo Draco, the Portuguese factor and a friend of Geza, king of Dahomey, is introduced, a reminder of the key role the Portuguese played in introducing slavery into the Americas. This portion of the book brings the diaspora into full perspective as Draco and the white slavers discuss the market and the best place to hawk their full cargo of 2,000 souls. Cuba and the United States are said to be optimum and quite similar in their approach to slavery, which is being condemned in Brazil. Delany sets up a rather sentimental mechanism for his presentation of the African end of the slave trade by creating an African, educated, and Christian wife for Draco, Zorina, whose life is a misery because of the shame caused by her husband's trade. The stand-in for the reader is her daughter Angelina, who has been away for years studying in a convent in Lisbon. She asks Zorina about the details of the barracoons (slave pens) and the ships, employing an innocence quite reminiscent of that of Little Eva in Stowe's *Uncle Tom's Cabin*. When Zorina explains the burning and whipping that prepares the slaves for "packing" in the bottom of the ship, Angelina vows never to accept support from her father again. Later she faints when she witnesses the branding of the slaves and seems to be dying. Stricken, Draco vows to renounce his trade, thereby causing the miraculous recovery of Angelina, his "good angel."

Delany begins the voyage back to the Americas by describing the white sails, the fine weather, and the fair wind, but this is a contrasting prelude to our Dantesque descent below deck into the stalls, with the stench of "the half-suffocated beings closely packed in narrow stalls like brutes wallowing in revolting mire" (223). After forcing us to look at the bodies of asphyxiated children and the brutal hosing of the "cargo," the narrator aptly states, "The 'Vulture' like a monster was gliding and mounting the then increasing swells of the sea" (224).

In one of the most shocking scenes in American literature, the heartless Portuguese and American leaders of the ship, pursued by a British ship, tellingly run up the American Stars and Stripes before dead and dying enslaved Africans are thrown into the sea by the black sailors in order to lighten the ship and increase its speed: "Men, women, and children raging with thirst, famished, nauseated with sea sickness, stifled for want of pure air, defiled and covered with loathsomeness, one by one were brought out, till the number of six hundred were thrown into the mighty deep, and sunk to rise no more till summoned by the trumps of Heaven in the morning of the General Resurrection of all the dead, to appear before the Eternal Throne of God" (229).[26] The remaining slaves, however, are saved, as Blake, upon landing in Matanzas, contacts Plácido, and they spread the word that the slaves had been rebellious during the voyage, thus driving down their price and enabling emancipators posing as agents to purchase the entire cargo. Free, the Africans melt away into the populace, presumably as agents of the insurrection, perhaps the chief aim Blake had for making the voyage in the first place.

Auspiciously, all this is accomplished just before the gala day of the nativity of the Infanta Isabella. Delany uses the festival as an occasion for the assembly of all the prominent blacks in Havana at a grand reception. Two key moments in the convocation come when the hostess, Madame Cordora, asks a series of questions. First, she challenges Delany's assertion that pure blacks (with no admixture of white blood) are the equal to "pure" whites, which causes her to think he is devaluing racially mixed people of color — like her. His explanation that only when black and white are equal can "mixtures" also be seen as equal sets the ground for the necessary multi-hued composition of any revolution from below, which Delany knew had to follow the pattern set in Haiti, where all the many differently catego-rized people of color came together to foment rebellion. As Nwankwo has demonstrated, this point was made by Spanish authorities in the *Sentencia*, the official document that condemned Plácido and the other Escalera con-spirators (2005, 35). Thus, one of Plácido's chief offenses in the eyes of the Spanish authorities — and one parallel to Blake's — is the creation of a black community that in its unity possesses power, in effect echoing the motto of the United States, *e pluribus unum.*

Madame Cordora further inquires how the insurrection can be squared with the Catholic faith. Blake replies that almost all of them in the con-spiracy belong to numerous other denominations, but in any case, "we have agreed to know no sects, no denominations, and but one religion for the sake of our redemption from bondage and degradation, a faith in a common Savior as an intercessor for our sins. . . . No religion but that which brings us liberty will we know. . . . The whites accept of nothing but that which promotes their interests and happiness. . . . They would discard a religion, tear down a church, overthrow a government, or desert a country, which did not enhance their freedom. In god's great and righteous name, are we not willing to do the same?" (258). Like Frederick Douglass, Richard Wright, Malcolm X, and Martin Luther King Jr., Blake/Delany seems to know that it would be a mistake to not build the foundation for revolution on the strongly religious nature of African-derived cultures, and that a reconceptualized form of the Christianity that has been grafted onto this base offers a very useful unifying device for people from different lands and backgrounds. However, "our ceremonies . . . are borrowed from no denomination, creed, nor church . . . but originated by ourselves, adopted to our own condition . . . founded upon the eternal word of God" (258). This takes the narrative back to the beginning, when Blake insisted on using the Bible for his people's own ends rather than those of the master.

This scene offers ample justification for the anachronistic inclusion of

Plácido, for he complements Blake's ministerial and military stances by offering a reflective, creative, and philosophical perspective that echoes the academy, which he in many ways represents. In a great ode to Africa, he declares to the company, "Let us prove, not only that the African race is now the principal producer of the greater part of the luxuries of enlightened countries, as various fruits, rice, sugar, coffee, chocolate, cocoa, spices, and tobacco; but that in Africa their native land, they are among the most industrious people in the world . . . supplying . . . rice, coffee, sugar, and especially cotton, from their own native shores . . . and that race and country will at once rise to the first magnitude of importance in the estimation of the greatest nations on earth" (261–62). Plácido here, in an early form of Pan-Africanism, counters many of the ostensibly "economic" justifications for both slavery and colonization made earlier in the novel by members of the slavocracy, but unlike them he argues from both history and contemporary "enlightenment" logic. By making Plácido a man of ideas and Blake a man of actions, Delany knits together the twin impulses needed for racial unity and armed insurrection, but he also sets in motion a standard kind of literary device that animates many novels.

We saw how Pickens interbraided her tale of adventure and conquest with a rather conventional set of love narratives, culminating in a double wedding. Delany, while giving scant attention to such matters, also provides a concluding double wedding in Havana, when the chief caterer of the white Count Alcora, Gofer Gondolier, marries the Abyssinian Christian Aybssa, who was transported in the cargo on the *Vulture*. General Juan Montego marries the revolutionary and wealthy mulatta Madame Cordora. As Delany suggests, the double wedding signifies the coming together of Africa and the Americas, but also of the upper and lower classes, and the union of disparate complexions. Unity is key to the success of the insurrection.

These unions should also be seen in conjunction with the restoration of the union of Blake with his Maggie. Delany himself was married for many years and fathered nine children, whose names echoed his diasporic dreams: Toussaint-Louverture, Alexandre Dumas, Fastin Soluque, Rameses Plácido, Charles Lenox Redmond, Saint Cyprian, and Ethiopia Halle (Marsh-Lockett 1986, 75). Thus, in the domestic sphere of the family he created—symbolically and physically—he saw an expression of the black hemispheric empire that would unite all people of African descent. While the novel focuses on revolution, it is framed by the domestic, echoing Stowe but also reflecting Delany's basically conservative values and his alignment—despite his very masculine and radical orientation—with basic tenets held by later black women writers such as Pauline Hopkins, Anna Julia Cooper, and Frances Ellen Harper, all of whom highlight the black family and domestic enterprise as keystones for racial advancement.[27] Delany's colonization efforts are always conceptualized as the movement of families rather than of individuals, to the colonies in, first, Latin America, and then the Niger Valley. But it also aligns him with Sarah Josepha Hale, whose plan to colonize Africa we examined earlier.

At the wedding reception at his father's house, Blake again uses the Bible to predict success for the insurrection: "Ethiopia shall yet stretch forth her hands unto God; Princes shall come out of Egypt" (285).[28] This passage may relate to the significance of Abyssa to the narrative. Although she is originally from "Soudan," her name embodies Abyssinia (Ethiopia), as does her Christian faith, and she periodically cries out to Blake, "Arm of the Lord, awake!" (224, 260). This becomes a mantra for others too.

Delany, three times in this narrative, employs carnival settings, first at Mardi Gras in New Orleans, then at the festival of Infanta Isabella, and then at El Día de los Reyes, "Kings' Day" (January 6; Delany spells it King's Day, however). This festival, he tells us, parallels the "Congo Dance" performed in Congo Square in New Orleans (299). Conjoining the Havana and New Orleans carnivals links the South and the Caribbean, "blackens" both cities in a festive but also religious sense, and braids together Christian and African religious ritual. Delany, however, retreats, letting an unknown expert tell us about the day, an expert who is obviously white: "This is the only day the black can call his own. . . . No master has the right to refuse his slave permission to go out for the whole day. . . . They generally assemble according to their tribes. The Gazas, the Lucumis, the Congoes, and Mandingos. . . . As it is the sights, the sounds, the savage shrieks, the uncouth yells suggest very uncomfortable thoughts of Negro insurrection. One cannot help thinking of the menace of the Spanish Government that Cuba shall be either Spanish or African. . . . It would be easy on King's Day for the Negroes to free themselves, or at least to make the streets of Havana run with blood" (299–301). Thus carnival days provide a mask for revolutionary activity, because permitted, if temporary, rupture of the rules inevitably reveals their injustice.[29]

Daniel E. Walker has provided a detailed history and comparison of the Kings' Day rituals and those conducted in Congo Square in New Orleans. As he notes, the festivals combined the sacred and the secular, African and Catholic religious traditions, and both reflected a resistance ethos for the enslaved in both cities. Each metropolis had accommodated large numbers of Haitians of all racial categories after the revolution on that island. As the majority of enslaved Haitians had been born in Africa, both cities were "re-Africanized." The processions, drumming, dancing, and African dress one experienced at Congo Square events and in Havana were syncretic, blending many separate secular/religious traditions of the peoples of West Africa, who had been influenced by each other's cultures in the crucible of enslavement (2004, 45).

Blake seems to be building to a climax when Henry and his army prepare to mount the insurrection on this carnival day of permitted excess. As Bakhtin has noted, carnival is a time when life is turned inside out, "the reverse side of the world." Further, "The laws, prohibitions, and restrictions that determine the structure and order of ordinary, that is noncarnival, life are suspended during carnival: what is suspended first of all is hierarchical structure and all the forms of terror, reverence, piety, and etiquette connected with it . . . everything resulting from socio-hierarchical inequality. . . . Carnival is the place for working out . . . a *new mode of interrelationship between individuals*" (1984, 122–23).

This reversal of custom had counterparts on other Caribbean islands. Sean Goudie has noted that West Indian slave rebellions were often planned to coincide with the Jonkunno (John Canoe) festivals, when slaves were permitted to mock their masters and exhibit otherwise proscribed behavior (2006, 164). Indeed, J. Michael Dash has claimed that "Carnival is a tempting trope for Caribbean writers because it so obviously facilitates an exploration of a free flow of time and space as well as the permutations, randomness, and eclecticism that are essential to the cultural diversity of the Caribbean" (1998, 128).

Delany seizes the paranoia of white Havana as a pretext for linking that city to other slave-owning capitals: "Few people in the world lead such a life as the white inhabitants of Cuba, and those of the South now comprising the 'Southern Confederacy of America.' A dreamy existence of the most fearful apprehensions, of dread, horror and dismay; suspicion and distrust, jealousy and envy continually pervade the community; and Havana, New Orleans, Charleston or Richmond may be thrown into consternation by an idle expression of the most trifling or ordinary ignorant black" (305). Such is the life of circumCaribbean whites, who have, as Jefferson expressed it, "the wolf by the ears" (1891, 481).

The narrative ends abruptly, after Plácido and Ambrosina Cordora, in two separate incidents, are physically and verbally abused in public. Fears of the rumored insurrection have caused heightened animosity toward Cubans of color. Scholars have been divided over whether Delany intended for the narrative to break off here, as a kind of "call" for an actual revolutionary response, or whether there are indeed lost chapters that tell of the beginning of an armed hemispheric racial revolt.

While the defeat of filibusters such as Lopez, Walker, and others was completely justified, some others saw it as an extension of a pattern of failure to "liberate"—however that term was defined—Latin America and the Caribbean. Although Delany's novel ends inconclusively, there was never, in fact, a successful Central American colony of former U.S. slaves. We would do well, however, to remember that the long and often oppressive history of Spanish colonization of the circumCaribbean, which was mimicked by the subsequent (and competing) operations of France, England, the Netherlands, and Portugal in terms of the introduction of slavery into the hemisphere, intersected again and again with the citizens and culture of the U.S. South, as this chapter has revealed. Ironically, the same "free flag" that Pickens celebrates became a rallying cry in the twentieth century for Castro's revolution, and that flag flies today over a defiant Havana.

Coda

The disasters of Lopez's expeditions led to despair among the Cuban exiles in the United States, epitomized by "To Cuba" of 1852, written by the aforementioned Tolon, which was published in New York's *La Verdad* newspaper:

Oh Cuba! Sweet Cuba! My fatherland
Home to my parents, nest to my love—
You hold that which I cherish
And all, so sad, that I had. . . .
Eden so blessed by the Inca's God
Will it be that I have lost you forever. . . .
But no, the Gothic power will soon
Fall in defeat, the yoke of tyranny cracked
Cubans will have fatherland, home, and liberty.
    (Cited in Lazo 2002, 6–7)

As this chapter has demonstrated, the sentiments of this poem would have been championed by Pickens, Lopez, and Delany, but for different reasons. Here, once again, we have references to the tropical sublime, but also to riches. The "Gothic" reference relates the Spanish to oppressive invaders of the past, but also to romantic concepts of European decay and decadence. Yet Tolon also links the island to the wider New World, through his reference to the Indian culture of South America, specifically the once-magnificent Inca people, implying an extension of the long hemispheric struggle to escape the Spanish yoke (Peru had been liberated by Bolivar in 1824). By including all Cubans—not just those actually enslaved—as victims of the "yoke of tyranny," Tolon's "Cuban imaginary" maximizes the possibilities of partisan efforts to free the island. But, as people of color across the hemisphere knew all too well, the promise of "fatherland, home, and liberty" would ring hollow without emancipation.

Walter Mignolo has usefully suggested that capitalism's early origins led to a bifurcated imaginary, the "formalization of 'purity of blood' and the 'rights of the people,'" which are contradictory to their aims. "The first was repressive, the second was expansive," but the tandem "connected the Mediterranean with the Atlantic," where a new imaginary was emerging for a modern/colonial world system (2000, 38). Pickens's ostensibly liberatory but actually oppressive campaign operated from a belief in the "purity of blood," while Delany's secular gospel offered liberation for both whites and blacks, ironically through projected (but never realized) colonization, thereby effecting an expansive notion of human identity and possibility, one that would take more than a century to bring about in the United States, when the civil rights movement and resultant juridical changes demolished the racial citadel of the U.S. South.

3 Unleashing the Loas

The Literary Legacy of the Haitian Revolution in the U.S. South and the Caribbean

. . . .

The Haitian Revolution was a volcanic eruption that shattered the Americas and Europe and gave hope to enslaved peoples across the world. For whites, it was an omen and warning and was even seen as a sign of a coming apocalypse. In both the South and the Caribbean, it had an effect on literature, but much more so, until recently, in the tropical zone. In this chapter, I will consider many instances of Haiti's presence in Southern literature, but I want to also note its centrality in the Caribbean imagination, for writers of many other islands and shores have written about this event as if it were their own. The Trinidadian historian C. L. R. James's passionate chronicle, *The Black Jacobins: Toussaint L'Ouverture and the San Domingo Revolution* (1938), reads like a novel and has had a literary legacy, certainly in the classic *The Kingdom of This World* (1949) by Cuban novelist Alejo Carpentier. It is no wonder that James's history has a dramatic pulse, for he had already written a play, *Toussaint L'Ouverture* (1936), which was produced in London starring Paul Robeson. Some of the other principal texts depicting the revolt have also been plays, including Martinican Aimé Césaire's *The Tragedy of King Christophe* (1970); St. Lucian Derek Walcott's Haitian trilogy, *Henri Christophe* (1948), *Drums and Colours* (1958), and *The Haitian Earth* (1984); and, most memorably, Martinican Édouard Glissant's masterful *Monsieur Toussaint* (1961).

Accordingly, this chapter will trace a trajectory between works dealing with Haiti, and especially the Haitian Revolution, by Caribbean and U.S. Southern writers, concluding with a reading of the first volume of Madison Smartt Bell's monumental trilogy of novels based on the Haitian Revolution, *All Souls Rising* (1995), *Master of the Crossroads* (2000), and *The Stone That the Builder Refused* (2004). As Bell discovered, outrages were committed on all sides, and African-descended writers of the Caribbean have said so in their works. In one of the Walcott plays, a key character condemns the colonial powers for their roles in the island nation's tragic trajectory but also

93

assigns blame to the dictator kings, Dessalines and Christophe. Employing a grand, lofty tone that owes much to Walcott's attentive reading of Shakespeare, his three Haitian plays alternate between poetic profundity, irreverent puncturing of historical pieties, and frequent embrace of folk culture. Rhonda Cobham (1979, 18) has hailed the London production of the first play in Walcott's trilogy, *Henri Christophe*, in 1950, as a milestone in the Caribbean nationalist period (1948–58). Walcott has stated that, during this time, "full of precocious rage, I was drawn, like child's mind to fire, to the Manichean conflicts of Haiti's history. The parallels were there in my own island, but not the heroes: a black French island somnolent in its Catholicism and black magic. . . . The fire's shadows, magnified into myth, were those of the black Jacobins of Haiti . . . Dessalines and Christophe, men who had structured their own despair" (1970, 11).

The powerful relevance of the insurrection for black Caribbean writers was inevitable. But why does a meditation on the treatment of Haiti in Southern and Caribbean literature seem so timely today? As Eric Sundquist has noted, the discourse over slavery in the nineteenth century ultimately led to a "return to the fraternally divisive energies of the revolutionary generation." Further, he states, "when the major issues are reoriented only this slightly, not New England and New York but rather the South and the Caribbean become the significant geography, the social and political soil on which a cultural renaissance could occur" (1993, 30). Saint Domingue, the richest colony in the world, occasioned envy and desire on the part of mainland Southerners, but also dread and dismay, particularly in terms of the supposedly barbaric slaves, many of whom were African rather than Creole and thus closer to the continental "heart of darkness."

In 1803, the French community of New Orleans was by no means happy that the old colonial regime was ending; many, in fact, felt their world was crashing around them. They could take comfort, however, that the Louisiana Purchase was a relatively peaceful transformation, unlike the Haitian Revolution, whose bicentennial commemorated Dessalines's 1804 proclamation of the final independence of the former Saint Domingue, an event that concluded almost fourteen years of bloody conflict involving rebellious slaves, Creoles, mulattoes, and the military forces of several European nations.

The Haitian Revolution paved the way for the Louisiana Purchase. Napoleon had intended to regain Louisiana, which could then provide food for a recolonized Saint Domingue once General Charles Leclerc's troops took back the island and reinstituted slavery. The collapse of that effort led to abandonment of plans for a continental empire. Eventually, too, slavery expanded in the United States, as sugar operations were transferred to Cuba and Louisiana and as cotton increasingly became the cash crop. The specter of Haitian-style revolt provided slave owners ammunition for their campaigns to more strictly control slaves. The incredible victory of the islands' combatants against the great European powers sparked revolt after revolt and inspired writers such as Frederick Douglass, Martin Delany, and a host of others to dream of organized black resistance to, first, slavery and, after the Civil War, Jim Crow de jure segregation.

The great theorist of the tradition of circumCaribbean connections has been Édouard Glissant, who endorses Edward Kamau Brathwaite's dictum that the peoples of the Caribbean are linked by a transversal, submarine unity. The sea, Glissant asserts, evokes "all those Africans weighed down with ball and chain and thrown overboard whenever a slave ship was pursued by enemy vessels and felt too weak to put up a fight. *They sowed in the depths the seeds of an invisible presence*" (1989, 66–67), an utterance that logically extends to the thousands of blacks killed in the liberation of Haiti.

Clearly, the embrace of the Haitian narrative by circumCaribbean writers not from the island indicates their eagerness to adopt the Haitian Revolution as a unifying and inspiring saga for the archipelago, which has been fragmented for centuries by the legacy of multinational colonialism, a process that actively pitted natives of one island or group of islands against others.[1] As what follows demonstrates, the Haitian Revolution shocked the Western world, even though it had been preceded by, and in fact inspired by, the American and then the French revolutions. The revolt of thousands of uneducated, mostly African slaves against European armies was, as Laurent Dubois has stated, "unthinkable," yet it happened, although it took thirteen years and thousands of deaths to accomplish. Today we are beginning to honor that revolution and its meaning for circumCaribbean and world cultures, but historians, in both the United States and Europe, suppressed its full dimensions for decades.[2]

"Forgetting" History

Michel de Certeau has remarked that Western history is always arranged in sections set off from each other by ruptures or "breakage," which is based on a distinction between what "can be *understood* and what must be *forgotten* in order to obtain the representation of a present intelligibility." Yet he cautions that these discarded "shards" always come back, constituting a return of the repressed (1988, 4). In what follows, we will see that courageous writers have fought to reassemble these shards of memory, honoring a revolution that brought forth the first black nation of the Western Hemisphere.

The suppression of narrative also has a medical analogue, the effort to stamp out pollution. Throughout this study, we have repeatedly noticed the thematic of blackness as "infection." No event in Western history promulgated this obsession more than the revolution "from below" in Saint Domingue. "Forgetting" is thus inextricably linked with "disinfecting"—stamping out memories of black agency and revolution. We find a comic inversion of this morbid fear in Ishmael Reed's 1972 experimental novel, *Mumbo Jumbo*. There he relates what he calls "neo-hoodoo" to the spread of an epidemic in America called "jes grew," a parody of the Africanization of American culture, particularly through music and dance. The prologue to the novel takes place in New Orleans, which is where the epidemic began. In yet another novel, *Flight to Canada* (1976), a parody of the slave narrative, Reed states that Guede, one of the chief loas in vodoun, is in New Orleans, and that "Guede got people to write" (9). Reed in these comic riffs underlines the Haitian heritage of the coastal South while simultaneously seizing on the old shibboleth of blackness as infection, then transforming it into a liberating, expansive trope, one that celebrates a dynamic and creative culture. Notice that he associates it, too, with writing, that is, narrative. Reed, of course, is repeating, perhaps unconsciously, the metaphor Delany chooses for Blake's plan for insurrection, a gradual spread of revolutionary cells, a "smallpox" of emancipating contagion. As Glissant's remark above suggests, black rebellion has an intimate counterpart in the equally dreaded concept of "miscegenation," which was indeed seen as a stain, a threat, and a menace. Miscegenation laws that made mixed marriages illegal were in effect in the U.S. South well into the twentieth century, and the rhetoric justifying them employed the same concept of pollution, one based on the idea that once encouraged, it could spread, like a contagion. Reed turned all this on its head by emphasizing the liberating aspects of Africanization—that is, cultural "amalgamation." As he shows throughout his work, the liberating nature of African American culture grew out of centuries of oppression, its converse. While this impulse took many cultural forms, the narratives it generated constitute a genre, which Patrick Taylor, following Erich Auerbach (1957, 18), has defined as "liberating narrative," which "grounds itself in the story of lived freedom, the story of individuals and groups pushing up from below to reveal the ambiguity and multilayeredness of reality" (1989, 3). Such writing, however, when it aspires to the universal, refuses to provide mythical closure and circles constantly around the question of freedom for all peoples.

History, as we have seen, has provided the framework for liberating narrative, especially in the slave narrative tradition. Many of those authors were thrilled and given hope by the example of the Haitian Revolution (1791–1804), the only successful African slave revolt in world history, as the mostly African blacks of the island rose up to defeat the armies and navies of France, England, and Spain. Conversely, however, the Haitian Revolution terrorized hemispheric whites, especially those who owned slaves. The revolt was spoken of in hushed tones throughout the U.S. South after the insurrection erupted in 1791. The volcanic force of the uprising, and its strong association with narratives and myths of revenge, validated the slavocracy's worst fears—namely, that where blacks had critical mass, they could emulate the horrors already inflicted on them, by raping, torturing, and killing their hated masters and destroying the imprisoning and brutalizing plantations and farms. "Jes' grew," indeed; the fear of infection from Haiti found confirmation in the numerous slave rebellions that punctuated Southern history from 1791 to the outbreak of the Civil War. It was feared that black revenge would be exacted *after* that war as well, which had much to do with the swift creation of the Ku Klux Klan, new restrictions on black liberty, and the neo-slavery of sharecropping.

Forgotten Caribbean Connections

After the Haitian Revolution, thousands of Haitians, white and black, migrated to Louisiana, and for good reason. Before the Louisiana Purchase, whose bicentennial we marked in 2003, and prior to the Spanish reign in Louisiana that began in 1762, New Orleans was one of three crown jewels of a Franco-Caribbean empire that spread French culture up the Mississippi and across the Gulf of Mexico. The other gems were the most profitable colony of New France, Saint Domingue, whose sugar cultivation would spread to the coastal United States, and the sophisticated capital of Martinique, St. Pierre. Like Louisiana, the island of Hispaniola had originally been inhabited by Native Americans. But well before the time of the insurrection, their enslavement and decimation by Western diseases had wiped them out. Native slavery had been tried and abandoned on the continent too; subsequently, across the circumCaribbean, the importation of slaves from Africa became the chief labor supply for the plantation factories.

Louisiana, partly because of its own multiple similarities with Haiti, including Native American history, French colonization, flora, fauna, climate, and agriculture, especially sugar production, and above all, its reliance on African slavery, was horrified and transfixed by the Saint Domingue insurrection that began in 1791, a rupture that broke almost a century of sustained contact, trade, and cultural commerce between the two circumCaribbean societies. Despite the fact that there were many echoes of both the American and the French revolutions in the revolt, most whites saw only the specter of racial massacre. Prior to the uprising, the French colony had 655 sugar plantations, 1,962 coffee plantations, and 398 cotton and indigo plantations (Ott 1973, 6, 9). Half a million slaves labored in these fields, and their high death rates were paralleled by the high profit margins of the plantations, where unspeakable cruelties were practiced by plantation owners and overseers. There were only 40,000 whites and 28,000 free blacks (including often prosperous mulattoes) on the island, but the *grand blancs* commanded the military and the arsenals and kept strict vigilance over their human "property" (Hunt 1988, 9).

African Religions, Rituals, and Creolized Identities

Despite their efforts to dehumanize such "chattel," slave owners were well aware that they had been unable to erase deeply instilled cultural practices from their workers. As virtually all African-derived writers of the hemisphere have described in their works about Haiti, enslaved Africans were fortified by the African-inspired religion of vodoun, which was largely based on Rada and Petra gods, figures they combined with Catholic saints so as to escape the censure of their masters. The loas, African deities, were primarily drawn from the adjoining African territories of Dahomey and what is now Yoruban Nigeria. The Rada gods are generally seen as positive and come from Dahomey; they include Damballah (the serpent god of the sky, rivers, thunder, wind, lightning), Agwe Arroyo (the sea), Erzulie Freida (love, femininity, fertility), and the trickster god of the crossroads, Legba. The Petro gods, many of them of New World origin, include Legba-Petro, Baron Samedi (cemeteries, death), Marinette/Erzulie Mapionne, the raging variant of Erzulie Freda, and Damballah ge-rouge. Rada rites also involve the Nago loa Ogoun/Chango (fire, iron, and power, especially political). Maya Deren attributes the rise of the sterner, often violent Petro gods to the anger of enslaved Africans, whose trance/possessions at the time of the revolt were instigated by the Petra loas, who invade and "ride" their human "horses."

The revolution supposedly began, in fact, at a secret vodoun ceremony presided over by the *hûngan* (vodoun priest) Boukman. An old black woman, possessed, sacrificed a black pig, whose blood was consumed by the Petro celebrants as a sign of their enlistment in the original insurrection (1953, 62–85).[3] Many other variations exist. However, in practice, the principal gods overall are Ogoun, as the god of power and war; Ghede, god of the dead; and Erzulie, goddess of love. An intermediary figure, who in some cases takes on an even greater importance because of his position between man and the gods, is Legba, also known as Esu-Elegba or Esu-Elegua. His position as ruler of the crossroads makes him a central figure in all complex transactions of life.

The overwhelming numbers of Africans on the island and the fact of absentee landowners meant that these African deities had far more influence than in the continental United States, because far less control of the enslaved was possible after work hours than on U.S. plantations. The continual influx of the newly enslaved meant that African retentions in general were far more extensive and ritualized. In August 1791, after an infamous vodoun gathering in the forest, 2,000 slaves, acting on the guidance of loas and priestly networks, invaded white plantation households, raping, burning, murdering, and pillaging. As the preeminent historian of the revolt, C. L. R. James (1989), noted, they destroyed ceaselessly. "Like the peasants in the Jacquerie or the Luddite wreckers, they were seeking their salvation in the most obvious way, the destruction of what they knew was the cause of their sufferings; and if they destroyed much it was because they had suffered much. . . . From their masters they had known rape, torture, degradation, and, at the slightest provocation, death. They returned in kind. . . . Vengeance was their war-cry, and one of them carried a white child on a pike as a standard."[4] As James points out, however, the uncontrolled violence receded under the leadership of the black general, Toussaint-Louverture, but after his incarceration and death in a French prison, Dessalines, his successor, first promised amnesty to the whites but then executed most of those who were left. The conflict, which eventually led to takeover efforts by the British, the Spanish, and, finally, the French under Napoleon, went on for over thirteen years. It was on January 4, 1804, that Dessalines proclaimed the former colony as Haiti, adapting the name the now-vanished natives of the island had used for their island.

Reverberations of the Revolution in Black and White

The example of Haiti was cited often and repeatedly in the writings of escaped and freed slaves. One of these writers, Frederick Douglass, would become minister to Haiti in 1889. William Wells Brown, once a Southern slave, published *St. Domingo: Its Revolutions and Its Patriots* in 1855. "Let the slave-holders in our Southern States tremble when they shall call to mind these events," he wrote. "The day is not distant when the revolution of St. Domingo will be reenacted in South Carolina and Louisiana" (32).

Haiti's horrors were sensationally publicized in Philadelphia in 1808 through Leonora Sansay's *Secret History; or, The Horrors of St. Domingo*, an epistolary narrative that is more interested in domestic and romantic tales than in the revolt. Nevertheless, it offers glimpses of the horrors that were perpetrated; a young white woman refuses black sexual embraces and as a result is hung by a "monster" on an iron hook in the marketplace, where "the lovely, innocent, unfortunate victim slowly expired."[5] But with few exceptions, most white Southern writers, including those in New Orleans, kept monumental silence on the subject, both before and after the Civil War.[6] This is most surprising in the case of the Crescent City writers, as thousands of refugees from Haiti poured into the city after the revolt began in 1791, and more followed in 1809 when refugees who had first fled to Cuba were expelled from that island. But merely telling the story could give it circulation and possibly encourage mainland slaves to revolt. Indeed, many Southerners were certain that news via the "slave grapevine" of the events in Haiti spawned many of the subsequent insurrections in the states, particularly in Louisiana, South Carolina, and Virginia.

As Sybille Fischer has reminded us, the silencing of the Haitian Revolution was observed in other slave cultures of the Caribbean as well. From 1791 to 1805, the leading Havana newspaper of the time, *Papel Periódico*, made no mention of 1) the revolt; 2) the abolition of slavery; 3) the defeat of Napoleon's troops; or, 4) the establishment of the independent nation in 1804 (2004, 3). Napoleon's defeat at the hands of black slaves was a disaster for slave owners everywhere. The "infection" of the hemisphere's first black republic had to be contained, and it was.

Haiti was shunned by other nations for decades, in a manner similar to the attempted "containment" of Castro-style communism on the part of the United States after the fall of Batista in the mid-twentieth century. Trade dwindled to a trickle as the collapse of the plantation system destroyed sugar and coffee production, which moved to other locales in Louisiana, Brazil, and Cuba. It is no accident that U.S. and, later, Confederate interest in colonizing Cuba increased dramatically around this time.

On the eve of the revolution, in 1791, there were 39,000 whites in the colony, 27,000 mixed bloods, and 452,000 slaves, two-thirds of them born in Africa (Bell 1995, xii). The high percentage of Africans resulted from the fact that slaves were literally worked to death through a system of agriculture set up mostly by absentee plantation owners. Fear of insurrection led to brutal punishment of any disobedience, including death, necessitating the importation of more Africans.

Enslaved Africans in Saint Domingue seized the opportunity provided by the rupture of the French Revolution to mount their island insurrection. Abolitionists in the United States linked the struggle to the American Revolution as well. But the rebels' brutal massacres of whites and the ensuing chaos in the new nation provided slave owners of the circumCaribbean ammunition in their argument against emancipation. Haiti took on a menacing new aspect after Gabriel Prosser's slave conspiracy of 1800, Denmark Vesey's in 1822, and, most significant, Nat Turner's Virginia slave rebellion, which terrorized the white South in 1831. Charleston editor Edwin C. Holland thundered that "our Negroes are truely the *jacobins* of the country . . . *anarchists* and the *domestic enemy* . . . who would, if they could, become the destroyers *of our race*" (cited in Sundquist 1993, 33).

Southerners were well aware of the parallels between these insurrections, which stemmed from a shameful history they had created. The most damning connection between the South and the Caribbean was the slave trade. The importation of slaves to Louisiana began in 1719 with shipment of 500 slaves from Guinea (which was usually referred to as Guinée during this period). But soon slaves were imported from the Caribbean as well, particularly from Saint Domingue. The French governor of Louisiana, Jean-Baptiste Le Moyne de Bienville, proposed exchanges of his colony's enslaved Indians for enslaved Africans from Saint Domingue. But after the island's insurrection began in 1791, it was felt that the introduction of Saint Domingue blacks would foment revolution, and the Spanish governor, Francisco Luis Hector de Carondelet, banned slave imports from the West Indies (Hanger 1996, 4).

Once the revolution broke out, Gallic Louisiana, where French was the common language, clearly offered the best U.S. refuge for exiles. In 1791, New Orleans had 4,446 inhabitants. By 1797, the population had doubled, largely from absorbing exiles from Saint Domingue. By 1809, after refugees were expelled from Cuba, 1,887 whites, 2,060 free Negroes, and 2,113 slaves had migrated to New Orleans. Creoles soon were publishing newspapers, devoting much space to the events in Haiti. Gradually, they began to espouse the survival of Francophone culture (they founded the fabled French Opera House in the city), and in cultural terms Creoles ruled Louisiana long after the Louisiana Purchase.

The transfer of thousands of black Haitians—both slaves and affranchis (the mulatto class)—to New Orleans, meant that the already existing African-inspired religions, particularly hoodoo, became transfused with a more directly African form, Haiti's vodoun (the word was Dahomean for deity or spirit). This religion, which was practiced by many of the leaders of the Haitian Revolution, had a definite political and empowering element at the time of its admixture with New Orleans hoodoo. The hoodoo spirits took on more profoundly African aspects, because existing modes of ritual and cultural performance were directly influenced and directed by the Haitian traditions.

Details of what had actually happened on the island were best known in the Crescent City, which drew more exiles from Saint Domingue than any other American port, earning it the name of "Creole Capital of North America." The connections between Saint Domingue and the South were by no means limited to New Orleans, however, and preceded the Haitian Revolution. Mulatto soldiers from the island had fought in the American Revolutionary War, most notably in the siege of Savannah, which involved André Rigaud, a future Haitian military hero, and, some have said, Henri Christophe, who would eventually become the black republic's king.[7]

Although Francophone New Orleanians welcomed white Creoles, they had grave misgivings about the accompanying slaves and free people of color. Louisianans were certain that the largest slave rebellion ever mounted in the United States, which was led by the slave Charles Deslondes in Pointe Coupee parish in 1811, was an infection spread from the island nation.[8] The most notorious example of the influence of the Haitian rebellion in the United States was the 1822 slave revolt in Charleston led by Denmark Vesey, who had come to South Carolina from Haiti. Other insurrections following the Haitian model, in addition to the ones listed above, also occurred in Venezuela and Barbados. The most important insurrection outside Haiti, however, was the 1812 rebellion in Cuba, led by the Haitian José Antonio Aponte, who employed images of Toussaint, Dessalines, and Christophe, the recently designated king of Haiti (Geggus 2001, xiii).

Haiti became a watchword as the United States inched closer to the Civil War. Abolitionists and slave owners alike used it as a warning—abolitionists of the consequences of avoiding emancipation and slave owners of the reverse. The Haitian Revolution particularly terrorized slave owners in states such as Louisiana, Mississippi, and South Carolina, where sections or the entire state were predominantly black. Jefferson had warned that Americans had "the wolf by the ears" in slavery, and Haiti brought that lesson home. Indeed, even before the revolution broke out in Haiti, Jefferson had mused that "deep rooted prejudices entertained by the whites; ten thousand recollections by the blacks, of the injuries they have sustained; new provocations; the real distinctions which nature has made . . . will produce convulsions which will probably never end but in the extermination of one or the other race." After the revolt broke out, he predicted that all whites would eventually be driven from the Caribbean islands (Scherr 2011, 21).

Jefferson was more prescient than he knew. As Frantz Fanon has stated, decolonization "is quite simply the replacing of a certain 'species' of men by another." And further, "The violence which has ruled over the ordering of the colonial world, which has ceaselessly drummed the rhythm for the destruction of native social forms . . . that same violence will be claimed and taken over by the native at the moment when, deciding to embody history in his own person, he surges into the forbidden quarters. To wreck the colonial world is henceforward a mental picture of action. . . . The destruction of the colonial world is no more and no less than the abolition of one zone, its burial in the depths of the earth or its expulsion from the country" (1963, 40–41). This is precisely what happened in Haiti.

Historians have suggested that the events in Saint Domingue hardened the South's resistance to emancipation while simultaneously leading to far harsher treatment of rebellious slaves. The very word "Haiti" was sufficient to silence conversation. African American writers, however, venerated the Haitian rebels and used them as a watchword in their own literary works. The island had figured prominently, however, in the North American consciousness well before the Haitian Revolution, and the conflict began to register in some detail with the publication of Baron Vastey's 1816 biography of Toussaint-Louverture, which detailed the author's service under the general. Eugene Genovese has demonstrated the extensive impact the revolt had on both the enslaved in the United States and black abolitionists and intellectuals in the North, who were forging ties with liberation movements across the hemisphere.[9]

That influence ultimately led to powerful fiction from the region's diverse writers. We will begin our survey of the influence of Haiti on the writers of the U.S. South in New Orleans with the work of Victor Séjour (1817–74). Born to free parents of color, one from Saint Domingue and the other from Louisiana, Séjour received a fine education before being sent to Paris for further study. Meeting Dumas *pere*, the abolitionist Cyrille Bisette, and others, he began to write journalism and plays after the publication in the Paris-based *Revue des Colonies* of his remarkable short story "The Mulatto" ("Le Mulâtre") in 1837, which became the first published African American short story. As Anna Brickhouse has noted, the journal in which Séjour chose to publish his piece was in many ways a mouthpiece for many displaced Caribbean writers, whose work, like Séjour's, could never have been published in the repressive societies of the New World, many of which still practiced slavery. Even Haiti, ostensibly a black republic, suffered under the repressive censorship of the Jean-Pierre Boyer administration (1818–43). Haitian writers in exile therefore used the *Revue* to correct the many misconceptions about their island nation and to publicize the continuing horrors of enforced slavery. Indeed, as Brickhouse notes, the *Revue* was a major factor in France's decision to end slavery in its colonies in 1848, while simultaneously demonstrating, in its wide spectrum of genres written by a full range of New World writers, the possibilities of a transnational literary realm, or what Brickhouse suggests we would today call a "comparative American literature" (2004, 88).

Séjour's story is rendered initially by an unnamed narrator, a traveler in Saint Domingue before the Haitian Revolution, but he soon hands the reins over to an old black man, Antoine, who relates a tale of a beautiful African girl, Laïssa, who is sold to a young planter, Alfred. After Alfred rapes her, she gives birth to a son, Georges, but the father tires of them and sends them to live in destitution on the outskirts of his vast properties. Laïssa dies after Georges promises not to look at the portrait of his father she leaves in a bag until his twenty-fifth birthday.

Laïssa's funeral rites are clearly African and no doubt derive from Séjour's knowledge of such practices brought to New Orleans by Haitian slaves after the revolution. Georges, grown, and a father himself, saves Alfred's life, but soon afterward Alfred tries to rape Georges's wife, Zelia, who defends herself and is thereby sentenced to be hung. Georges, unable to persuade Alfred to save her, takes his son and joins the Maroon colony in the forest. Years later, Alfred, now married, has fathered another son. Georges poisons the wife and kills Alfred, but the latter's dying words reveal he is his murderer's father, causing Georges to commit suicide.

Séjour no doubt was attracted to the Haitian scene because he knew it would resonate with his new audience in France, but also because he had knowledge of the island and its revolution from his parents and from the Haitian refugees in New Orleans communities of color. The story, however, also echoed many tales of interracial rape, mixed parentage, and revenge that were common in Southern literary narratives, particularly among African Americans, who would begin to write about such situations in increasing numbers after emancipation. There were Maroon enclaves all over the South, including several in the swamps surrounding New Orleans. The themes of incest and the planter's passionate desire for a white son, while rejecting his black progeny, look forward to Faulkner's Thomas Sutpen and his Haitian son, Charles Bon.

In 1893, Delany's onetime colleague, fellow editor, and friend, Frederick Douglass, a recent consul to Haiti, gave an address to dedicate the Haitian pavilion at the Chicago World's Fair. He proclaimed that black liberty as it existed in 1893 would have been impossible without the example of Haiti. Repeating the phrase, "Until she spoke," he noted that no nation before 1791 had abolished slavery, and that the Christian churches of the world sanctioned it. Douglass got to the heart of the scorn in the United States for the island nation: "Haiti is black, and we have not yet forgiven Haiti for being black or forgiven the Almighty for making her black" (Jackson and Bacon 2010, 202). Yet, as David Brion Davis notes, Douglass had notably left Haiti out of his addresses before 1863, knowing that the mere mention of the country reinforced the claim that emancipation could lead to racial genocide and rape and the destruction of plantations dependent on slave labor (2001, 4).

The absence of Haiti, however, in white Southern letters after the Civil War was, with few exceptions, total. The general index to the seventeen-volume *Library of Southern Literature* (1907) has no entry for Haiti or Saint Domingue, and certainly not for Delany. Perhaps the editors, Joel Chandler Harris, Edwin Anderson Alderman, and Charles William Kent, were just working with what they had, for Haiti is notably absent in the literature of the South before the twentieth century. To speak of Saint Domingue was to summon the specter of bloody black revolt against whites; the risk of "infection" bred a monumental silence.

The index does list, however, voodoo, and the very first volume concludes with an eerie tale by Mississippi-born Sherwood Bonner (1849–83), "The Hoodoo Dance" (originally published in *Harper's* in 1881). While the story is not set specifically in Louisiana, it has a strongly Haitian cast to it. The white young "missy" Dina goes in protective disguise with her Maum Dulcie to observe a nighttime hoodoo rite. The details of the story make it clear that the participants are being "mounted" by loas, that they are hoodoo "horses." When Dulce is accused of two-faced behavior, stripped, and thrown into a pit with a straw effigy, her white mistress reveals herself and demands Dulce's release. The hoodoo priest menaces Dina, but she is saved by the sudden appearance of a white gallant with a pistol, pointedly named Marion West, who cries out, "You hounds . . . fall back!" (461). This association of hoodoo with black rebellion is quite consistent with the Haitian legacy that proved pervasive in New Orleans and also in surrounding states. Bonner, an independent woman who left her child and husband in the South to pursue a journalistic career in Boston, perhaps felt less of the constraints her Southern peers had about Haiti, but her interest in African American culture, reflected in her "Grandmammy" sketches, made her a sympathetic observer of the folklore of the African diaspora.

Another entry in the collection, written by the New Orleanian Charles Gayarré (1805–95), "At the Old College of Orleans," concerns an old man, Jules Davezac, who has immigrated to Louisiana from "St. Domingo." The narrator, Fernando de Lemos, informs us that "many of the French, when driven from that island by the negroes, had fled to the neighboring one of Cuba, from which they had again been expelled when Napoleon invaded Spain. About four hundred of that unfortunate population had at last taken refuge in New Orleans, where they met with much sympathy and the most liberal support." Indeed, Lemos suggests that Saint Domingue exiles soon were a majority on the College Board of Regents, for they had "affiliated with the natives" quickly and had acquired "marked influence." Despite the fact that many key figures in this narrative came to New Orleans from Saint Domingue, the narrator never details any of their prior suffering, which of course would involve the unspeakable "horrors." Gayarré, author of *Romance of the History of Louisiana* (1848), would quarrel with his fellow Louisianan writer George Washington Cable about the latter's supposedly negative presentation of Creole culture (which to Gayarré was white, not mixed race). Nevertheless, Cable credited the older man's call for a Louisianan Walter Scott who could make history understandable for a general audience.[10]

Grace King's (1852–1932) little-known but extensive history, *New Orleans: The Place and the People* (1895), is in fact dedicated to Gayarré and contains detailed description of the exiles from Saint Domingue. However, the horrors of the Haitian Revolution never emerge fully; instead King concentrates on the cultivation of the luxury-loving exiles. As she states, "As a biographer of the times explains, thankful for the escapes they had had from unmentionable horrors, all were contented, satisfied, happy, and more charming men and women than ever (1915, 171)." The closest she comes to the bloodshed is, "What tales of their escapes the St. Domingo ladies had to tell . . . the alarm, the flight, the cries of the blood-infuriated blacks in pursuit, the deathly still hiding-place in the jungle; and always, in every tale, the white sails of an English vessel out in the Gulf, watching for signals for rescue . . . a grandmother spattering with her brains the child in her arms, — or a child shot away from a mother's breast, or a faithful slave expiring with her arms clasped about her mistress's knees, or — every combination of heart-breaking horrors. There were always in each family, God be thanked, faithful slaves (172–74)."[11] This mythic chord would be sounded again by Margaret Mitchell, when her Scarlett is saved from attack by her former slave. It is telling that the rupture of the white families in Saint Domingue is not accompanied by a consideration of how black families were regularly separated by slavers and slave owners, including those depicted in this affecting scene.[12]

The great novel dealing with the immediate effect of the Louisiana Purchase is by King's hated nemesis, George Washington Cable (1844–1925), who would come to be recognized (at least in the North) as the greatest New Orleans writer. Although a native of the city, his German background and Protestantism kept him out of the Creole elite that fascinated him, as did his growing outrage over slavery and the injustices of the Jim Crow South. His novel *The Grandissimes* (1880), which King detested, opens in New Orleans in 1803, the year of the Louisiana Purchase and just a year before Haiti's establishment as the only black independent nation in the hemisphere. The book was first published serially in *Scribner's* in 1879. Depicting the clash of the Creoles and the invading Americans, the novel also closely examines both communities' relationship to slaves and free people of color. The Grandissime family is divided into white and colored branches, each featuring an Honore Grandissime. The great inset story of the novel, however, concerns an African prince who has recently been bought by the Grandissimes, a muscular giant they call Bras Coupe. He and other Africans in the novel are depicted in a detailed, virtually anthropological way by

Cable, whose chief source on African cultures and religions was M. L. E. Moreau de Saint-Méry's *Description topographique, physique, civile, politique, et historique de la partie française de l'ille Saint-Domingue*. This monumental work was especially valuable in its description of the Jaloff people, who had been brought to both Saint Domingue and Louisiana. In the course of the story, Bras Coupe becomes enamored of his mistress's slave Palmyre, who dreams of her champion instigating a slave revolt. Bras Coupe eventually escapes to the swamps, successfully practices vodoun on his white enslavers, is captured and tortured, has his ears cut off, and is hamstrung. The story rehearses, without mentioning it specifically, the island insurrection. The similarity of Louisiana's harsh Code Noir with that of white-controlled Saint Domingue, the parallel Maroon communities, and the Western African origins of vodoun, which was practiced in both locales—all these factors are suggested by the text. Above all, however, the tale illustrates the potency of the combination of African mysteries with the justified rage of a suppressed people. On the other hand, the power of vodoun registers when, early in the novel, Cable acquaints us with the fact that "many of our best [that is, white] people consult the voudou horses" (55). The most prominent of these "horses" (she is really a *hûngan*, or priestess) is Palmyre Philosophe, the onetime slave of Aurore Nancanou. Now, as a free woman of color, she has an extensive clientele. Palmyre, an admixture of Creole and African Jaloff ancestry, presents a combination that was quite common in Haiti. Moreover, she and she alone inspires fear in the Creole patriarch Agricole Fusilier, a token of the "infection" of the black arts, which have a Haitian background (significantly, Palmyre refers to the heroism of Toussaint).

Aurora, a devout white Catholic, nonetheless follows vodoun practices in her daily life, carrying a mirror, a coin, and a broom into her new house to protect it from spirits. She knows what to do when she pricks her finger sewing and how to follow African formulas for avoiding misfortune in almost every aspect of daily life. She consults Palmyre for rituals that will help her pay the rent. Agoussou, the demon of love, and Assonquer, the "imp of good fortune" (74), are featured here.

Cable's silence on the subject of Haiti is far more remarkable in his nonfiction work of 1885, *The Creoles of Louisiana*, a popular history. He barely mentions the revolt when he gets to the 1790s, and it only receives lengthier treatment when he comes to the second migration of Saint Domingue refugees of 1809, when thousands who had originally fled to Cuba were ejected from that island as Spain and France went to war. Cable states that over thirty-four boats arrived, bearing whites, free mulattoes, and slaves in about equal numbers. Others soon came from other Caribbean isles, swelling the refugee population to over 10,000, almost doubling the city's existing population of 14,000. The new American quarter objected strenuously, but the local Creoles welcomed their West Indian brethren, as they substantially strengthened their communal and Francophone power. Cable is notably silent, however, about the revolution itself, or about the wide fear all New Orleanians had that "San Domingo" fever would spread to the local slave population.[13] He was more willing, however, to discuss contemporary racial injustices; his "The Freedman's Case in Equity" (1885), a fiery indictment of Southern racial policy, fed the anger against him that eventually led to his exile in the Northeast.[14]

In the twentieth century, sensationalist accounts of the Haitian Revolution began to appear in the United States, as the nation began hungering for a Pan-Caribbean empire. White-written accounts of Haiti, like Frederick Ober's, made incredible claims. Ober insisted that Haitians practiced cannibalism (*In the Wake of Columbus*, 1893). Books written in the wake of the U.S. occupation of Haiti from 1915 to 1934 took similar tacks. John Houston Craige's *Black Baghdad* (1933) and *Cannibal Cousins* (1934) depicted a primitive, brutal nation obsessed with voodoo. Edna Taft's *A Puritan in Voodoo-Land* (1938) features a trembling white woman listening to the drums, fearful of the jungle, and thanking God for the American occupation. Such books had prompted W. E. B. Du Bois in *The Crisis* to note in 1935: "There seems to be a rule that requires travelers to Haiti to offer for the palate of sedentary readers as gruesome and weird a picture as possible of voodoo practices and beliefs. . . . There has been far too much play upon the barbaric and the weird in dealing with things Haitian. A common sense attitude with a sound scientific approach is a crying need" (cited in Dash 1984, 47).

The Haitian-inspired Southern novel that engendered the most interest until recently is William Faulkner's *Absalom, Absalom!* (1936). The story was likely inspired by Faulkner's absorbed reading of his great-grandfather's transnational/circumCaribbean novel, *The Spanish Heroine*. Thomas Sutpen, like the hero of Colonel Falkner's novel, is a poor immigrant from Appalachia who seeks his fortune in the circumCaribbean. In Haiti, he marries a wealthy planter's daughter and fathers a son. "I learned of the West Indies," he tells General Compson, where "poor men went in ships and became rich" (242). Compson himself describes Haiti as "a spot of earth which might have been created and set aside by Heaven itself as a theater for violence and injustice and bloodshed and all the satanic lusts of human greed and cruelty . . . a little island set in a smiling and fury-lurked and incredible indigo sea, which was the halfway point between what we call the jungle and what we call civilization, halfway between the dark inscrutable continent from which the black blood . . . was ravished." The incredible abundance of the sugarcane is seen as "recompense for the torn limbs." The irony, of course, is that this description could also be of Mississippi. Faulkner knows enough of voodoo to describe the tokens the French planter finds ominously laid on his pillow. But there is little in the narrative to suggest any deep involvement on Faulkner's part with the American occupation of Haiti in the twentieth century, as some have claimed. For that matter, as Richard Godden has shown, Sutpen could hardly have returned from Haiti with slaves after an insurrection, as the Haitian Revolution had preceded his stay there by some years and the French had abolished slavery in 1793 (1997, 57). More recently, however, John T. Matthews has demonstrated that Faulkner more likely intended to show that Sutpen, ever an "innocent" of sorts, thought he was working for whites who were really "affranchis," the mulatto class of the island (2004, passim). Dessalines had killed or exiled virtually all whites in the early 1800s.

In any case, Faulkner clearly found the concept of Haiti compelling as something radically different, alien, and at the same time terrifyingly familiar. Faulkner's lifelong love of the French and the French language must have made this setting appealing as well. It is interesting to note that in the story that inspired and preceded *Absalom*, "Evangeline," Bon is never pictured as West Indian. Still, Barbara Ladd is correct to observe that both Haiti and the South are "tropic sites" within the narratives of nationalism and amalgamation (1996, 155). The novel eventually suggests that Sutpen set his Haitian family aside when he discovered its African ancestry; he then began his struggle to found an estate and patrimony in northern Mississippi, where most of the events of the novel transpire. Sutpen certainly must speak Creole French and would presumably have acquired many social characteristics of the Franco-colonial society into which he married. However, the novel is notably lacking in these particulars. It is rather Charles Bon, Sutpen's son, who has acquired the polish and politesse—some might add guile—that distinguished this group.

However, Sutpen would also have become familiar with the complicated mestizo world of the Caribbean, with the various classes based on color. Sutpen retreats to Mississippi and thereby rejects Haiti's alternate view of race that permits high-class distinction for people of color.

It should be noted here that Mr. Compson's characterization of Haiti, cited earlier, is notably condescending and clearly linked above all to race. The slaves Sutpen brings back are described to us too by Mr. Compson as virtual animals, and it is true that white Southerners were always fearful of slaves imported from Haiti, as the history of insurrection there was well known. Just as important, however, was the fact that many if not most of the plantations in the islands had absentee landowners who left their plantations in the hands of overseers. Consequently, slave culture in the islands allowed for far more African retentions and led to less interracial sexuality. When it did occur, however, the children were often accepted and educated.

The appearance in Oxford and then on Sutpen's plantation near Jefferson of Charles Bon, the Haitian son, brings a Caribbean flavor to the book, especially when his activities in New Orleans (which include his octoroon mistress and their son) become known. Barbara Ladd (1996, 142 ff.) points to the ways in which *Absalom* reflects how U.S. nationalism drifted into imperialism. She sees a connection between the racial fears and desires for new territories common to slaveholders and those of late nineteenth-/early twentieth-century national imperialism. There is no question, however, that whatever he knew about Haiti or the Caribbean, Faulkner made indelible use of the replication and interbraiding of the racial complexities and resultant tragic histories of the islands and his own Mississippi. Glissant has commented that "everyone who has spoken of his work has been touched by Faulkner's stunning prophetic finesse, particularly in his return to the primal issues in which everything is given (yet hidden)" (1996, 113). Faulkner's decision to situate the "revolt" in the Sutpen family in the person of an African-descended Haitian surely stems from his understanding of the myriad ways in which all hemispheric whites saw the "primal event" of the uprising in Saint Domingue as whites reaping the whirlwind they instigated through the sin of slavery. Freud would call this the "return of the repressed," and it is to Faulkner's credit that he enfolds this psychological dimension into his story as well, which symbolizes the much larger repression of Haiti in general in the white Western imagination.

Ramon Saldivar profitably dissects this aspect of the novel; the latter views the book as Faulkner's "most enthralling encounter with the colonial and emerging postcolonial subject" (1995, 97).[15] But he usefully reminds us that Faulkner had considered the plight of the ethnically divided subject before in *Light in August* (1932). Ah yes, you are saying, Joe Christmas, whose father was either black or a Mexican—but Joanna Burden's father's first wife, Juana, was Mexican, and Joanna has her name. Thus the issues of color and ethnicity are intermingled, employing the colonized Mexicans—who also share the Caribbean circumference—as other and creating split personalities in each of the doomed lovers, whose tortured and shifting sense of self leads to mutual annihilation. Faulkner saw the links between the plantations of Mississippi and the Caribbean and the multiple ways in which they served as interchangeable parts of a lucrative hemispheric system of labor and production. As he understood, the South and the Caribbean were united by their production of raw commodities for distant factories.[16] We see Sutpen's activities in Haiti, however, only through Mr. Compson's bemused second-hand account. Faulkner himself never visited Haiti. His incorporation of the Caribbean into a notion of an expanded South must be considered a pathbreaking gesture, especially in terms of the twentieth-century writers treated here, who went much further in this direction.

Filtering the Caribbean through a Southern Lens

A Southern writer who certainly knew both New Orleans and Haiti and writing at the same time as Faulkner was penning *Absalom* was Zora Neale Hurston (1891–1960). Her little-studied *Tell My Horse: Voodoo and Life in Haiti and Jamaica* (1938), a nonfictional account of her anthropological trips to the Caribbean, offers one of the most arresting examples in all of Southern literature of the dramatic influence of the "indigo sea" on a Southern writer. Based on research Hurston did in the islands in 1936 and 1937, it is inextricably bound up with her two greatest novels, *Their Eyes Were Watching God* (1937), which was actually written in Haiti, and *Moses, Man of the Mountain* (1939), wherein the biblical prophet is presented as the greatest hoodoo conjurer in history. While it does not directly address the Haitian Revolution, her work in Haiti and the writings it inspired offer an indelible example of the effect the Caribbean had on a figure we now see as one of the most important Southern writers, who also, I argue, increasingly saw her work as circumCaribbean.

Hurston would have heard about the Caribbean long before her visits to the islands. An interest in the Caribbean was natural for African American writers, as they always understood it as part of the African diaspora. As James Clifford states, although diasporas usually "presuppose longer distances and a separation more like exile[,] a constitutive taboo on return, or its postponement to a remote future," they also "connect multiple communities of a dispersed population" (1997, 246). Hurston's native Florida was drawing more and more circumCaribbean immigrants, whose stories, legends, and jokes were contributing in an important way to that state's folklore. We remember as well that the fabled Harlem Renaissance (1919–40) attracted black writers from diverse hemispheric cultures. U.S. writers in this group were often not eager to admit such immigrants to their circles; Caribbean characters derogatorily called "monkey chasers" appeared in many stories, plays, and novels. Conversely, more positive images of such figures appeared when the writer himself or herself was from the Caribbean, as were Claude McKay and Eric Walrond. The islands made their first appearance, however, in Eugene O'Neill's electrifying *The Emperor Jones* (1920), his Freudian primitivist play about a Southern "darkie" who rises to bombastic Emperorhood on an unnamed and exotically limned West Indian island that often seems much more like Africa than the Caribbean. Jones's superstitious and growing fear of the beating tom-toms and the menacing world of the jungle echo the stereotypes associated with Southern blacks in Plantation School writing.[17]

Hurston arrived in New York in 1925 and was soon the toast of Harlem and the recipient of several literary prizes. She was mainly occupied, however, in the pursuit of a graduate degree in anthropology at Columbia, where several of her teachers were vitally interested in the cultures of the Caribbean. The connection between Hurston's anthropological work and her novels is quite logical too, since, as many scholars have reminded us, writing in anthropology has much in common with the writing of fiction, and particularly historically based fiction. Indeed, Hurston wrote a successful Guggenheim Fellowship application in 1935 to "make an exhaustive study of Obeah (magic) practices" and "to search for the Moses legends among Negroes," which she would then use to write a novel about Moses. In the same application, she noted that she wanted to do her work in the Caribbean because "the lore [there] stands between that of America and Africa." Further, she stated that her "ultimate goal" was "to collect for scientific scrutiny all phases of Negro folk-life and to personally produce or create fiction out of this life that shall give a true picture of Negro life at the same time that it entertains." Hurston began her grant by living for over six months with a Maroon community in Jamaica. She then continued on to Haiti, where she wrote *Their Eyes Were Watching God*, in seven weeks, while continuing to do field work. Similarly, *Horse*, based on her Caribbean work, appeared in 1938, quickly followed by *Moses, Man of the Mountain*, her third novel, in 1939. So the interplay among her research, academic writing, and fictional narration continued apace—indeed, at a rather frantic pace. Hurston's relative failure in both academic and novel-reading circles in these years perhaps stemmed from her overriding interest in sketching cultures in toto, rather than in a starkly scientific listing of facts or, in fiction, in a narrative centered on the career and/or loves of one compelling figure.[18] Her work gathering folklore in Florida initially led to a scholarly essay, "Hoodoo in America," which took up an entire issue of the prestigious *Journal of American Folklore* in 1930. Because of her work with Melville Herskovits in New York, she was keenly aware of both the similarities and the differences between hoodoo and Haitian vodoun. Still, part of Hurston's subsequent interest in the Caribbean stemmed from her firm belief that her native Florida, which she had researched extensively for the Federal Writers' Project in the 1930s, was the heir of the African diaspora via the Caribbean: "The drums throb. Africa by way of Cuba; Africa by way of the British West Indies; Africa by way of Haiti and Martinique; Africa by way of Central and South America . . . Florida, the inner melting pot of the great melting pot America" (Bordelon 1999, 67). She claimed that Tampa's air was flavored with "Cuban songs, dances, and folk ways," and that Miami was "a polyglot of Caribbean and South American cultures," with "more than 30,000 Bahamians with their songs, dances, and stories, and instrumentation . . . Haitian songs, dances, instrumentation, and celebrations," while the area from Key West to Palm Beach had "Bahamian and Cuban elements in abundance" (Bordelon 1999, 66). Hurston, we remember, did not think the "primitive" was to be despised, so when she says that Bahamian folk culture is "more savage," she sees it as more authentic. According to her, "The Bahamian and the West Indian Negro generally, has had much less contact with the white man than the American Negro. As a result, speech, music, dancing, and other modes of expression are infinitely nearer the African. Thus the seeker finds valuable elements long lost to the American Negro." She goes on to say that American Negroes were not allowed to stay in tribal groupings, whereas that was not the case in the West Indies, where owners were often absent. She claims one can easily identity the tribal origins of many Bahamian tunes. And this has had an enriching effect in the American South: "Nightly in Palm Beach, Fort Pierce, Miami, Key West, and other cities of the Florida east coast the hot drumheads throb and the African-Bahamian folk arts seep into the soil of America" (Bordelon 1999, 91). These remarks provide ample proof that Hurston was thinking of the Black Atlantic long before Paul Gilroy came on the scene.

There is no question that Hurston's biblically inspired novel, *Moses, Man of the Mountain*, was equally influenced by her time in Haiti, where she experienced a culture steeped in the traditions of African conjuration. In writing of Moses, Hurston was tapping into the long tradition in African American culture of looking at the whole syndrome of transatlantic diaspora, although this is not the term she used.[19] Hurston would have been schooled in the concept of diaspora by her mentor, Franz Boas, who as early as 1909 complained that knowledge of the black race was hampered by a reliance on inadequate research solely on Southern blacks. "Nothing that may be observed in our own country can show what the capacities of the race may be in other surroundings; a broader treatment of the question will require a consideration of the achievements of the negro under other conditions" (cited in Herskovits 1953, 114–15).

Probably because of her previous painstaking research on the hoodoo of U.S. black cultures, the most striking thing about *Tell My Horse*, her 1939 anthropological study of the folklore and history of the Caribbean, is its respectful exploration and delineation of voodoo, or vodoun. Hurston, an initiated hoodoo priestess but also an anthropologist, was the ideal investigator of this neo-African religion. As she describes the main loas (gods), the rituals that attend them, and, above all, the way these gods inhabit people—the way they "ride their horses," to use the vernacular—makes for a fascinating and illuminating study.

Hurston's research in Haiti stretched from September 1936 to September 1937, a period that followed the American occupation of 1915–34.[20] In chapter 6, "Rebirth of a Nation," Hurston offers a thumbnail sketch of Haiti that begins with a markedly biblical tone—"A prophet could have foretold [peace] was to come to them from another land . . . when these symbols shall appear . . . a voice in the night. A new and bloody river shall pour from a man-made rock . . . a black plume [in the sky]." Her shorthand is explained as standing for the 1915 revolution against the tyrant Guillaume Sam by General Bobo and the army. Hurston dramatizes the events of the U.S. takeover of the island that year by supposedly quoting the inhabitants: a black peasant woman falls upon her knees with her arms outstretched like a crucifix and cries, "They say that the white man is coming to rule Haiti again. The black man is so cruel to his own, *let the white man come*" (71). Hurston employs a kind of Grand Guignol in these passages, graphically reporting the mob's dismemberment of the dictator Guillaume Sam's body, which permits the United States to come in under a plume of black smoke, bringing peace, with an echo of Moses's fire and cloud. Now that the nineteen-year American occupation has ended, Hurston ponders the future. Here she very much resembles Richard Wright's deliberations on the newly freed African state of Ghana. Both Americans adopt what can only be seen as a colonizing gaze.[21] As Annette Trefzer has pointed out, however, Hurston's simultaneous presentation of voodoo rituals as strategies of resistance to colonialism makes the text maddeningly ambiguous in a political sense (2000, 299).

Hurston's satiric survey of Haitian history acknowledges the heroism of the black revolutionaries of 1791 but rues the fact that "Haiti's curse has been her politicians" (74). Lest this seem overly harsh or patronizing, let me point out that Hurston is just as hard on American racial leaders in this pointed comparison: "These talking patriots [men who 'rattle' the bones of Toussaint-Louverture and Dessalines for the peasants' benefit] . . . are blood brothers to the empty wind bags who have done so much to nullify opportunity among the American Negroes. The Negroes of the United States have passed through a tongue-and-lung era that is three generations long. These 'Race Men's' claim to greatness being the ability to mount any platform at short notice and rattle the bones of Crispus Attucks . . . and *never* fail to quote, 'We have made the greatest progress in sixty years of any people on the face of the globe. . . . It made us feel so good that the office seeker did not need to give out any jobs'" (76–77).

The heart of the book is Hurston's presentation of voodoo, which she describes as "the worship of the sun, the water and other natural forces." Moreover, although many claim that voodoo practitioners worship Catholic saints, Hurston claims that these images are merely approximations of loas, or African deities. These are either the "good" Rada gods, originally from Dahomey, or the evil Petro gods from the Congo. Damballah and Baron Samedi are the chief gods of the respective groups. Hurston identifies Damballah (who is often represented by Saint Patrick, as both are symbolized by snakes) as Moses, whose symbol is also the snake. Here, at last, Hurston, who would go on to write a novel based on Moses the next year, links Haitian practices to the United States:[22] "All over the Southern United States, the British West Indies and Haiti there are reverent tales of Moses and his Magic" (116). She provides graphic accounts of the sexual aspects of the worship ceremonies and seems to delight in the account of the cult of Erzulie Freida, the "Venus" of voodoo, who takes human husbands in exotic rituals.

Hurston's attendance along with the mambo/priestess at the compounds of Archahaie—a remarkably African settlement presided over by the patriarch Dieu Donnez—teaches her the intricate rites of the island. Supposedly, Hurston witnesses a dead houngan (Hurston's spelling—elsewhere we find it as *hûngan*) rising up and splitting from his loa (spirit). The authenticity of this section is heightened by the photographs Hurston took of activities and also of key figures in the clan, such as Mambo Etienne. Hurston also photographed what she claimed was a zombie, a dead woman recalled to life by a Bocor (an evil type of houngan/voodoo priest) for manual labor. Hurston's insistence that we accept this supernatural event will find an echo decades later in Madison Smartt Bell's novels of the Haitian Revolution, where the reader is once again asked to accept a zombie as real. These scenes link Haiti to the hoodoo scenes Hurston includes in her earlier book of African American folklore, *Mules and Men* (1934), and posit a continuum of African-inspired religion across the circumCaribbean, a fact that has expanded exponentially lately as Haitians, Cubans, and Jamaicans have brought fresh infusions of vodoun, Santería, and Obeah to new ethnic communities across the U.S. South.

Although Hurston does not provide detailed consideration of the Haitian Revolution, her reading of Haitian culture had a great deal of influence on subsequent Southern writers who set the conflict in fiction. Madison Smartt Bell has told me that Hurston's book was an important influence on his trilogy. Bell's intricate presentation of Haitian vodoun, and of the daily lives of enslaved Africans and Maroon communities in Haiti, has many correspondences with passages in *Tell My Horse*, particularly in the ways in which he portrays the mounting of a practitioner (a "horse") by a loa, or spirit. Bell's exhaustive glossaries display an impressive knowledge of the terms of the religion, some of which he may well have received from Hurston, among others.

Another great African American who took an interest in Haiti was Hurston's fellow Floridian James Weldon Johnson (1871–1938), one of her most valued friends. An elder statesman of the Harlem Renaissance, songwriter, novelist, poet, and diplomat, he was appointed U.S. consul in Venezuela in 1906, and he later served in this role in Nicaragua. In 1916, he became field secretary for the NAACP, a position he held for fourteen years. Significantly, Johnson begins his little-read but absorbing autobiography, *Along This Way* (1937), by revealing that his great-grandmother Hester Argo, who had three children with a French army officer in Haiti, left that island in 1802. One of her children, Stephen Dillet, became a leading political figure in the Bahamas and then postmaster. His daughter, who migrated to the United States, was Johnson's mother. Haiti, therefore, loomed large in Johnson's imagination, and he brought this heritage with him to the island in 1920, when he gathered materials to support the effort to end U.S. occupation, which began in 1915. Cushy jobs had been set up for democratic party office seekers, and protesters in Haiti were deemed "bandits." Meeting with leading Haitian intellectuals, he learns that a sophisticated culture has been sustained over the years and that Port-au-Prince is a vibrant city. Johnson clearly delineates the differences between the Haitian Revolution and the aftermath of the U.S. Civil War in the South: "Our Civil War freed the slaves in name only. It left them illiterate, penniless, and homeless, and at the economic mercy of their former masters. . . . In Haiti, the large plantations were cut up into small parcels . . . [which] the former slaves cultivated . . . as independent farmers. . . . There was no such thing . . . as a peon class" (346). After his trip, Johnson met with Warren Harding, who used the irregularities of the occupation as a campaign issue, although, once elected president, he reversed course and let a whitewash proceed. Johnson's several articles on Haiti in the *Nation* and *Crisis* (1920), however, had a salutary effect on efforts to liberate Haiti, which was accomplished in 1934. Like Hurston, Johnson had originally favored the occupation, but he came to see its oppressive aspects through an NAACP investigation he led in 1920. He exposed the U.S. abrogation of national rights; the imposition of a new constitution that reversed the nation's rule against foreign ownership of land; the abolishment of any meaningful form of Haitian representation in a government after the imposition of U.S. martial law; and the absolute control of Haitian finances by the National City Bank of New York. Most important, however, he charged the United States with the murder of over 3,000 Haitians.

Johnson obviously felt freer to make serious charges in the pages of the black-owned *Crisis*, where he made a direct link between the oppression of Haitians and the American South: "Americans have carried American prejudice to Haiti . . . because the Administration has seen fit to send southern white men to Haiti. . . . What the Washington Administration should have known was that in order to do anything worthwhile for Haiti, it was necessary to send men there who were able and willing to treat Negroes as men, and not because of their ability to speak poor French, or their knowledge of 'handling niggers'" (1920, 219).

The revolution's legacy for Johnson was powerful, and he found a visual expression of it when he made the long climb up the mountain to view the ruins of Henri Christophe's gigantic fortress, La Ferriere, the largest defense edifice erected in the Americas, which was built as a last stronghold against the possibility of the French trying to retake the country and reinstall slavery. As such, the building had great symbolic power, not just for Johnson, but for all people of color in the circumCaribbean. Today it has been restored, and it constitutes Haiti's most important national site, featured on stamps and national documents. Built to quarter 30,000 soldiers with the enforced labor of 20,000, Johnson proclaims it as the most wonderful ruin in the Western Hemisphere. He photographed it and lectured on its importance upon his return to the United States, and he suggests that two important books about Haiti, William B. Seabrook's *The Magic Island* (1929) and John W. Vandercook's *Black Majesty* (a 1928 study of Christophe), were partly inspired by his efforts. Johnson's awed account offers a superb example of how a manmade edifice, set prominently in nature, can evoke the tropical sublime.

Johnson by no means, however, felt that Haiti could not profit from various examples set by the United States. In his meetings with prominent Haitians, he insisted they should adopt a program like the one he and his colleagues had formulated at the NAACP to foster literacy. In particular, he urged the institution of Creole, rather than French, as the national language, but he made little headway with the elite, who prided themselves on their proper French and looked down on the black masses.

Traveling home on a rough steamer, Johnson hears drunk whites call out, "Never let a nigger pick up a tool." Although he does not make the connection, the long isolation of Haiti, coupled with the refusal of the educated, mostly mulatto elite to concern themselves with the people, makes this racial slogan applicable to the world's reaction to the Haitian Revolution itself, which has continued to this day. When we think of the thousands of Haitians who board leaky, overcrowded boats in a desperate effort to get to the United States, we might consider Johnson's summation, that "no condition under which he struggles oppresses the Negro more than the refusal of a fair and even chance to earn a living" (1933, 355). Clearly, Johnson viewed the situations he found in the Caribbean through the lens of his own experience as a black man who grew up in the U.S. South. His anger at the behavior of U.S. Marines during the long occupation was exacerbated by the fact that many of them were Southerners who brought their prejudices and cruelties with them across the waters.[23]

Johnson's friend and fellow Harlem Renaissance figure, Louisiana-born Arna Bontemps (1902–73), was also drawn to the Haitian Revolution, partly because his ancestors had migrated to the United States after the conflict began on the island. His novel *Drums at Dusk* (1939) has always existed in the shadow of his much stronger novel *Black Thunder* (1936), which portrayed Gabriel Prosser's 1800 slave rebellion in Virginia. Still, *Drums at Dusk* has reminded readers of the importance of the ignored "third" revolution of the Atlantic World. In addition to his Haitian ancestry, Bontemps was born not far from Pointe Coupee parish, the site of a large slave rebellion that was inspired by the revolt in Haiti. *Drums at Dusk*, however, is far more restrained in its presentation than one might expect. Perhaps aiming for large sales, Bontemps deals mainly with the white colonials who ruled Haiti and only treats the opening years of the revolution. The French protagonist, Diron Desaultels, belongs to the revolutionary group in France that helped foment the Haitian Revolution, Les Amis des Noirs. He has links with the Maroon communities of runaway slaves that are hotbeds of revolutionary activities and vodoun rites. As in Bell's novels, Toussaint is a character, but he is pictured in a much less vigorous manner and does not come to central stage until relatively late in the novel, when the rebel leader Georges Biassou leads an attack on Toussaint's plantation of Breda.[24] The emphasis then shifts to Toussaint, who is given more prominence than he in fact had, ignoring other leaders and the fate of the country after Toussaint was taken prisoner and removed to France. In this way, it echoes the problematic mode of the award-winning movie *Gandhi*, which suggests India's independence owes everything to the title figure, rather than to the range of historical figures who were active in the struggle.

Drums at Dusk has been criticized recently by Mark Christian Thompson for fostering a kind of "voodoo fascism," one that ultimately led to the horrors of the two Duvalier regimes in the twentieth century. As Thompson points out, vodoun itself is kept offstage, along with any real glimpse of the Maroons, and, although a few brutal scenes unfold, the extremes of the slaves' long oppression and the resulting horrors of the initial revolt are not dramatized. For all its faults, however, Bontemps's novel offered a necessary intervention after sensational works such as John W. Vandercook's *Black Majesty* (1928) and Orson Welles's *Voodoo Macbeth* (1931) had kept outsiders fixated on stereotypes of Haitians as voodoo-dominated near savages, an image that had helped sustain the long American occupation of the island (1915–34).[25]

As we have seen, most of the writers of the U.S. South who saw the events in Haiti as hopeful and liberating rather than terrifying and to be kept out of mind were black. Paul Gilroy has amply demonstrated the benefits of refiguring the history of the Atlantic through a postnational lens, but also through the perspective of people of color, whose diaspora in multiple ways became the *real* underlying history of the hemisphere, one that is still characterized today by racial struggle and conflict. The history of colonialism in the New World was for centuries also the history of slavery — at first Native American bondage, but increasingly, and then overwhelmingly, African slavery. Consequently, many of the hemispheric writers who have sought to create an alternate history to the ones written by white academicians during the nineteenth and early decades of the twentieth century were men and women of color, who as historians — actual or literary — were following the example of W. E. B. Du Bois. His monumental *Black Reconstruction* (1934) provided a paradigm for overturning false histories. Just four years later, the Trinidadian historian C. L. R. James's passionate chronicle, *The Black Jacobins: Toussaint L'Ouverture and the San Domingo Revolution* (1938), took up Du Bois's challenge to reread the Haitian Revolution.[26] James understood that this seismic event encapsulated the hemispheric struggle for black liberation and, in broader terms, the struggle for all New World peoples, regardless of color, to break free of colonial chains. His chronicle reads like a novel and has had a literary legacy, certainly in the classic *The Kingdom of This World* (1949), by Cuban novelist Alejo Carpentier, and also in many other key texts of the circumCaribbean.

Many Southern writers who did not know Caribbean literature have nonetheless been compelled to rupture the artificial boundaries of region and nation to reach out to the inland sea. We find compelling evidence of this in the work of Faulkner. The continuing study of his works appears to be inexhaustible, perhaps because, whatever one thinks of his views on any given subject, he seems to have engaged most of the difficult issues that continue to dominate modern life. Race, class, and gender in his work have long been fermenting in critical discussions, and now we realize he had thoughts on colonialism and postcolonialism as well, many of them engendered by his state's and his region's long connection with, and indeed immersion in, the Caribbean, which laps the shores of Biloxi and the aptly named Gulfport, new meccas for trans-Caribbean gamblers.

From C. L. R. James onward, writers have also recognized that the complicated hierarchies of race and color in Haiti also mirrored similar conventions and conflicts (many within the race itself) in other colonies and nations of the New World. Some of the principal historical narratives that have followed in this tradition have been plays, including Aimé Césaire's *The Tragedy of King Christophe* (1970); Derek Walcott's Haitian trilogy, *Henri Christophe* (1948), *Drums and Colours* (1958), and *The Haitian Earth* (1984); and, most memorably, Édouard Glissant's masterful *Monsieur Toussaint* (1961). While I cannot address many of these narratives here, I would like to briefly consider the great Martinican statesman, essayist, poet, and dramatist Aimé Césaire, who spent seven months in Haiti in 1944. He had already prominently featured Toussaint in his 1939 epic poem *Notebook of a Return to the Native Land*, and in 1960 he would also publish a biography of the general. His most striking Haitian subject, however, was one of Toussaint's successors, Henri Christophe, a freeborn Grenadian cook turned revolutionary soldier, who eventually became king of Haiti, ruling from 1811 to 1820. His reign, described in *The Tragedy of King Christophe*, was devoted to grand public works and an equally grand European-style court. The drama begins with a cockfight between "Petion" and "Christophe," named for the antagonists who became rulers of the south and the north of Haiti, respectively. We learn that many scorn the pretension of Christophe's grand palace and court, but Baron Vastey shrewdly notes that civilization is all form, and that Haiti must have France's respect if the European powers are to be prevented from reinstalling slavery. Throughout the play, a tension exists between the parody of Christophe's grand erections—his palace of Sans Souci and the great fortress of Ferriere—and his ironclad dedication to the freedom of his people. He orates powerfully on the "ship" he will build to secure this, which turns out to actually be the imposing La Ferriere, which will be built high on an interior mountain. It is referred to as a ship, as it will cancel forever the specter of the slave ships that brought two-thirds of living Haitians to the island by providing true security against foreign occupation.

Christophe's tragedy is partly that in order to prevent the reinstallation of slavery, he has to utilize a form of it himself, as 20,000 enforced laborers are necessary to build the gigantic fortress. Part of the play shows Christophe laboring with these workers and standing undismayed when lightning strikes his arsenal. In a powerful scene, the feast of the Assumption is celebrated, employing both Catholic and vodoun rituals, featuring the king's hand-chosen five African youths, his "bonbons." Christophe falls, paralyzed, after seeing the ghost of the bishop he had killed, crying out to St. Toussaint and St. Dessalines. When his men desert him and enemies approach, Christophe kills himself, offstage, and is buried in a vat of still-wet mortar at the fortress, where we learn he has been taken by the loa Shango, in keeping with his appeals to the African spirits in the latter part of the play. Critics were quick to note the parallels between Christophe's growing corruption, his use of vodoun, and his brutal retinue and that of Haiti's dictator of the 1960s, Duvalier, whose Tonton Macoutes had turned the land into a police state.

In a 1967 interview, Césaire repeated his earlier claim that it was Haiti that gave him his celebrated sense of *Negritude*, essentially an embrace of his culture's African heritage that was designed to combat the alienation caused by colonization. "I love Martinique, but it is an alienated land, while Haiti represented for me the heroic Antilles, the African Antilles . . . a country with a marvelous history, the first Negro epic of the New World was written by Haitians, people like Toussaint Louverture, Henri Christophe, Jean-Jacques Dessalines. . . . Haiti is the country where Negro people stood up for the first time, affirming their determination to shape a new world, a free world" ([1955], 2000, 90). Implicit in these comments we find an indictment of France, which first colonized Martinique and Guadeloupe and then made them departments of France; both actions erased local history and replaced it with that of the French nation.[27] Further, Haiti, while a poor and troubled country, is presented here as having a glorious history, one that inspired heirs of the black diaspora across the circumCaribbean. Césaire's insistence on the history of Haiti as an epic helps explain its attraction for writers, particularly as it constitutes the greatest epic narrative, that of a people seeking freedom.[28]

Madison Smartt Bell's Haitian Epic

In one of the ironies of history, the most complete and graphic account of the Haitian revolt has come in a trilogy of historical novels—a dramatic fictional epic—by a white Southern writer from Nashville, Madison Smartt Bell.[30] The concluding volume was published in 2004, the year of the Haitian Revolution's bicentennial. *All Soul's Rising* (1995), *Master of the Crossroads* (2000), and *The Stone That the Builder Refused* (2004) are magnificent achievements that raise the standard of historical fiction. Although they are based in Haiti, they relate in myriad ways to Bell's native South. I have argued that, despite the literary and intellectual embargo the U.S. South's writers, politicians, and social leaders maintained over the centuries, the Haitian Revolution was a foundational event for the circumCaribbean, including the states of the Old Confederacy. Yet, as we have seen, only African American writers of the U.S. South proclaimed the importance of this traumatic and highly symbolic insurrection.

Bell, recognizing the myriad intersections between the Haitian revolt and his native South, also saw crisscrossing lines of influence and mythology radiating back and forth from *all* segments of the circumCaribbean, particularly after he absorbed the many plays, novels, essays, and stories that have been based on the event by writers from many circumCaribbean nations. Accordingly, his trilogy knits together past narratives, in the nature of epic, for all great epics contain elements of those that have preceded it. While all three novels deserve extended commentary, I will mainly address *All Soul's Rising* here. The book demonstrates, at least to anyone who knows something about Haitian history or Afro-diasporic cultures (the two, alas, are not always as connected as they should be), that its author did dedicated, detailed research into not just history, but racial history; not just philosophy but also religion; and not just Haitian Catholicism but also, and more important, vodoun and the various avatars of religious systems of Africa as practiced in the New World. The trilogy is the product of Bell's sustained research into Haitian history, religion, and culture and profits from his expertise in French, Haitian Creole, and African-derived rituals of possession.

Since Bell was not known for writing about these subjects before, it is helpful that in interviews he reminds us that he has always been concerned with matters of the spirit. A self-confessed disciple of the Catholic-convert novelist Walker Percy and an adherent, if not to their racial biases, then to their ecological stances, of the Nashville Agrarians, Bell has dedicated the trilogy to "les Morts et les Mysteres, and for all souls bound in living bodies, I have burned this offering." This tribute, like much of the book, is double-sided. On the one hand it conveys the deep respect evident everywhere in the book that Bell has for African-derived New World religions. On the other hand, the concept of souls bound in living bodies follows the Christian idea of the superiority of the soul to the body, but simultaneously seems to refer to the most fabled aspect of Haitian culture, the cult of the zombie. And, in effect, the relentless dissection of the horrors of both slavery and the bloody revolution it took to end it in Saint Domingue suggests that all peoples — black, white, mulattoes — suffer terribly from the practice and then from the bloody abolition of the institution, and thereby are indeed locked within a prison of flesh. The powerlessness implied here leads to the figure of the zombie, which is delineated here as real, as is true with the zombie figure Hurston photographed for *Tell My Horse*.

On the other hand, Bell's tribute relates eloquently to Ishmael Reed's comments on his aforementioned concept of "jes grew," the joyous, life-affirming infection of African American culture: "The ultimate purpose of

Jes-Grew is to manifest processes that we as mortals cannot perceive and these processes are used for the purposes of art. . . . If we want to go to Haiti and Africa, Legba is a catalyst[,] and even in Christianity [there is] the Christ figure, who reveals the world invisibles to the world visibles, to the real world" (Gaga 1995, 55). As Bell's title for the second volume of the trilogy, *Master of the Crossroads*, indicates, he sees Toussaint as a crucial Esu-Elegba figure, the catalyst and shaper of the revolution, whose relentless crisscrossing of the island and many switches of allegiances in his relentless campaign for freedom did indeed make him, for a time, master of the crossroads, and in his mystical connection to his troops and his people (which is most prominently manifest in the ruminations of Riau), a champion of the "world invisibles."

Bell has stated that Toussaint-Louverture "could, when he chose to, take possession of a wholly European mode of perception and response, and at other times inhabit a mind almost purely African. Indeed, he claimed a freedom of passage between many very different worlds" (Carnes 2001, 205).

The divided emphases of the narrative—particularly through the triangular foci of Hebert, Toussaint, and Riau—create a dynamic energy. On the one hand, we have realistic, naturalistic, often horrific images and scenes, all of which require an almost detached, even clinical method. On the other hand, Bell's decision to honor the spiritual, the unexplained, the "mysteres," coupled with the inclusion of many poignant depictions of the varieties of human love and sacrifice, offers a counterbalance, and therefore a tension, which animates the multiple narratives.

Bell's novel is indebted to several narratives of the revolution that preceded his. The structure he employs, which alternates between scenes of Toussaint's imprisonment in France and the events of the revolution from 1791 up to the 1800s, clearly was inspired by Glissant's play, *Monsieur Toussaint* (1961), which takes place in the general's cell in France as he reminisces about his past life. In the introduction to the published version of the play, Glissant admits his own debts to Aimé Césaire's *Toussaint Louverture*, C. L. R. James's *The Black Jacobins*, and Victor Schoelcher's stirring biography. Yet Glissant declares that his drama is "*a prophetic vision of the past*. . . . To renew acquaintance with one's history, obscured but obliterated by others, is to relish fully the present, for the experience of the present, stripped of its roots in time, yields only hollow delights. This is a poetic endeavor" (2005, 15–16).

Bell's decision to follow his great Caribbean predecessors in writing about these events (we should note that none of the writers I have cited were from Haiti either) seems to have included a principled determination to do justice, in a way never before achieved in fiction, to both the tragic experience of enslaved Africans and their heroic revolt against it, but in a way that would reflect the terrible realities of that struggle. Treated barbarically themselves, their revolt was barbaric in turn, and Bell does not flinch from depicting atrocities. But in keeping with his idea, which he shares with Douglass, Du Bois, and other great black intellectuals, that slavery was damning to all who encountered it, all the groups he depicts—the *grand blanc* slave owners, the *petit blancs* poor whites, the mulattoes, and the slaves themselves—commit horrible deeds. The slaves' determination to exact revenge on their masters was seen by white racists as a manifestation of African people's tendency to depravity, yet the whites, who initially are in control in the narrative, are brutal without this justification. Their earlier violations of the enslaved wind up scripting their own. Bell tempers his portrayal of torture, rape, and murder by providing fully rounded portraits of numerous people of color in the story, including, of course, the actual figure of Toussaint. Perhaps the most poignant and arresting figure, however, after the general, is his soldier Riau, who, like two-thirds of the Haitian slaves, was born in Africa. His portion of the narrative has a freshness and an immediacy; spoken in first person, it is accented with Creole and is richly figured with allusions to the African religious pantheon that he and many other black characters in the novel follow. As Riau tells us, referring to the whites, "Their story is not the same as ours. This is a story told by god, but a different god chose me" (27). Riau's personal narration of the rebellion, his life among the Maroons, and his role in a sexual triangle with Merbillay and her other lover, Achille, a *hûngan*, provides symmetry to the other main sexual triangle formed when Dr. Hebert forms a liaison with the mulatto courtesan Nanon, who was previously linked with both the wealthy, embittered, and cruel mulatto Choufleur and his white father, Sieur Maltrot.

In terms of his adaptation of "blackness," Dr. Hebert has a counterpart in the character of Claudine Arnaud, whose drunken brutalities toward her servants at the start of the novel initiate the reader into the horrific world of slavery. In the first of many unbearable episodes that demonstrate the demonic possibilities inherent in owning human beings, an inebriated Claudine beats, slits open, and thus murders the black maid her husband has impregnated, after realizing that the girl was sold in Africa in a manner not so different from her own parents' betrothing her to Arnaud in Nantes. As Bell reveals, "All over the island masters and slaves were expressing their relation in similar ways, and it was nothing to lop an ear or gouge an eye, even to cut off a hand, thrust a burning stake up a rectum, roast a slave in an oven alive, or roll one down a hill in a barrel studded with nails. All these were as sacraments, body and blood" (89). Viewed as contrast, the vodoun rituals come off as therapeutic and life affirming, despite the fact that they ultimately contribute to the torture, rape, and death of the white population.

One-third of the way into the novel, the insurrection ruptures a peaceful scene of country dancing at the Lambert habitation, where Dr. Hebert has stopped and encountered Claudine. In the lurid glare of the burning cane fields, Claudine sees "a larger host of devils than any hallucination had figured forth for her till now" (158). The men are brutally murdered, and all the women except Claudine and Marguerite, who huddle in a ditch with Hebert, are raped. The survivors are saved from a band of marauders by Claudine, who madly cuts off her finger when a crazily dressed rebel demands her ring, astonishing the attackers, who let them pass. This scene seems taken from Toni Morrison's *Sula* (1973), where the title character behaves similarly. Bell strikes sparks anew when he once again presents the scene of Claudine amputating her finger, but here seen through Riau's eyes, who was apparently present: "When she spoke it sounded like the voice of a *loa*" (175). Eventually, in fact, Claudine, ridden by guilt over her crime (she has visions of Mouche as a zombie), does indeed become an initiate of vodoun, and she ministers to the young and the sick, thereby conjoining her with Dr. Hebert, both in perception of African-derived wisdom and custom and in therapeutic cross-racial ministration.

In seeking a poetic prose for these and myriad other events, characters, and histories, one that can simultaneously evoke horror, sensuality, and profound meditation, Bell is following the Caribbean writers I have named as his predecessors artistically, yet he seems to feel that this history is also his—and why not? C. L. R. James from Trinidad, Carpentier from Cuba, Glissant and Césaire from Martinique, Walcott from St. Lucia—all have felt that this is true for them.[31] As Bell has stated, "I've always felt that the Haitian slave revolution is a microcosm of American racial history, and I saw it as very relevant to the plight of the United States today" (Hogan 1997, 1).

Riau is the most salient example of Bell's determination to tell the story of the insurrection from "below," that is from the burning volcano of the enslaved, and their desire for liberation. His mastery of vodoun, its loas and mysteries, brings the narrative into a virtual other/parallel plane and demands that the reader accept what in other discourses has been called the "marvelously real," as when we must believe that a zombie has actually died and been reborn into a second slavery.

Riau's role in the novel persuades me that Bell has been profoundly influenced by arguably the most important history of Haiti after C. L. R. James's, that of Carolyn Fick, who in *The Making of Haiti: The Saint Domingue Revolution from Below* (1990), as her title suggests, steers readers away from loading the whole history of the revolution onto the shoulders of the hero Toussaint. Instead, she makes a case for the black and mulatto masses, whose African backgrounds, relation to the land, and cultural arrangements on the island gave them a peculiar vision of history.[32] Bell, following Fick's lead here, is more attentive than perhaps any of the other chroniclers to the outrage of the free persons of color, who prior to the installation of the *code noir* by the French in 1685 had not been subject to any deliberately discriminatory laws, although they were not entitled to full French citizenship (Fick 1997, 55). The burning intensity of the privileged mulatto Choufleur is meant to represent that of an entire class, whose animosity toward the whites above them and the blacks below them had much to do with the shifting alliances formed before, during, and after the initial revolt.

In a sense, one could locate the struggle "within the race" in the novel as one between the motivations and aims of Toussaint and of Choufleur. The actual historical figure Toussaint—a Creole, not an African—created a hybrid identity for himself from his African heritage—particularly his role as "root doctor" and healer—and his literate, intellectual side that has resulted from his social mimicry of his masters, which has had to suffice in light of his slave status. Choufleur, by contrast, has been afforded luxuries and a European education. His dissolute lifestyle has been fully supported by his indulgent white father, who nevertheless has no intention of acknowledging Choufleur as his son and successor. Choufleur has inherited all the base qualities of his father. Both abuse their common mistress, Nanon, and, ultimately, Choufleur's lack of concern for anyone and his tendency to excess and cruelty align him, despite his education, with the most brutal insurgents, whose mad torture, rape, and pillage are going nowhere until the energies of the revolt are harnessed and channeled by Toussaint.

Tellingly, Toussaint attempts for years to work within the French governing system for citizenship for the emancipated slaves, only to see that emancipation revoked. Further, in his personal life, Toussaint saves his former master and his family and envisions a future wherein the former planters can continue to work with the freed slaves in a new plantation economy.

Choufleur, however, gets caught up in the madness of revenge and, in the most chilling scene in the book, binds his white father and systematically flays him alive, taking out and handling his organs, and stuffing the old man's penis into a snuff box as an ironic and chilling gift for Nanon.

By yoking actual and fictional stories in this way, Bell forces a reconsideration of the implications of the revolution, in all its many aspects. Layering—and often alternating—accounts of telling events of the time, Bell decenters existing historical doctrines, by assembling a dialogue of voices, representing the conflicting desires and struggles of all the various groups, be they the *petit blancs,* the *grand blancs*, the citizens of color, black enslaved Africans, soldiers, plantation owners, servants, field hands, courtesans, sailors, nursemaids, officers, priests, *hûngans*, or mambos.

The trilogy has received an interesting (if somewhat superficial) reading lately from the eminent South watcher Michael Kreyling, whose several reservations about the trilogy I cannot treat here. However, I do note that Kreyling charges Bell (and, by implication, scholars of the wider region, including me) with "annexation." As he states, "I am interested in the risks mainland southern writers (and the critics who strive to interpret them) assume when, as in Faulkner's case, they attempt to 'remember' a place they have never visited, or, as in Bell's case, a place to which they are not native" (2010, 121). Not surprising, this leads him to suggest that Bell resembles William Styron, who famously "appropriated" the narrative, first of Nat Turner (1967), and then of concentration camp victims in *Sophie's Choice* (1979). This position ignores the myriad achievements of historians and writers of the past, who similarly were not "of the culture" themselves, but who nevertheless created detailed, well-researched histories and fictions. This notably includes the many non-Haitian Caribbean writers who have written narratives based on the revolution. The argument should not be, as William Faulkner's Quentin Compson claimed, "You would have to be born there," but rather, "You didn't do your homework." However, as Kreyling himself notes, the distinguished Haitian historian Michel-Rolph Trouillot has had extensive discussions with Bell, beginning in the period when Bell was completing *All Souls Rising*, and by Bell's own account, Trouillot's counsel and, of course, his written work have been major influences, particularly on the second and third volumes of the trilogy. What Kreyling does not consider is that Trouillot, J. Michael Dash, and several other key Haitian scholars and intellectuals have been virtually unanimous in praise of the trilogy, as the best account yet written of the meaning of Haiti's great struggle and triumph.[33] Finally, although Bell *did* go to Haiti before writing the second and third volumes of the trilogy, the entire work deals with the Haiti of two hundred years ago, which topographically, culturally, and economically varies dramatically from the Haiti of today.

A key achievement of Bell's work is his determination to present the usually ignored thoughts and feelings of the enslaved, rather than just concentrate on the brutalized whites or the major figures of the revolt, such as Toussaint and Dessalines. For this reason, among others, we need to attend more closely to Riau, who gives us access to the immediate antecedents of the armed revolt, when Boukman and other leaders visit Maroon communities and plot death for the whites, thereby following in the tradition of the Macandal poisonings that terrified white Haiti in 1757.[34] During the sacred rites, the African loas "ride" humans, who in effect become the gods. Achille is ridden by Ghede, the greatest vodoun deity, while Merbillay becomes Erzulie, chief female deity, and Riau is ridden by Ogun Feraille, the god of war and iron. As Erzulie is often pictured on the arms of two concurrent lovers (Jahn 1958, 45), Bell's plot is apt, and we can extend this aspect of Merbillay to her female counterparts, the mulatta Nanon and the white women Elise and Isabelle. These scenes involving African religions are totally convincing and demonstrate Bell's mastery of the works of Hurston, Janheinz Jahn, and, above all, Alfred Métraux. We come to understand characters' *ti-bon-ange* (the little good angel that is their unique identity) and their *gros-bon-ange* (their life force that maintains life and returns to the gods once death occurs). We trace the *veve*, or sacred designs of the loas, and sing their songs along with the characters, learning some Creole along the way.[35]

The rituals, the songs, the descent of the loas, create an alternate site, one that is impregnable by the slave owners. As Michel de Certeau explains, such imagined spaces are "utopias," which coexist with "that of an experience deprived of illusions." The oppressed peoples thereby "subvert the fatality of the established order," creating a "song of resistance" (1984, 17). It is worth noting that early in the book, when Claudine has had her husband's black concubine Mouche strung up in the barn, she is infuriated when she hears her singing an African chant, understanding that even her brutalities have not penetrated into the inner being of the slave, who is, indeed, singing a "song of resistance." Tragically, this provides the spark to Claudine's madness and leads to Mouche's evisceration and death.

Riau introduces us to Toussaint, the coachman of a kind master, Bayon de Libertat, as the two visit the Heberts when the Maroons are poaching the edges of the property. The old lecher Sieur Maltrot, fresh from Paris, brings news of the French Revolution there and the celebration of the executed mulatto rebel Oge, who had attempted an uprising in 1790, resulting in his death by torture in Le Cap, then the principal Haitian city. Bell provides the back story of the revolution several times, but in pieces, always through recounting narratives; importantly, however, he makes sure we see past and present events through multiple perspectives, especially black and white.

The main cast of characters is completed when Dr. Hebert lodges in town and meets his childhood friend Captain Maillart, accompanies him to the theater, and spies the courtesan Nanon in a box. Later he pays a call on Isabelle Cigny, his sister Elise's friend, a bored wife whose multiple affairs lend piquancy and complications to the novel, particularly when she crosses the color line, as do many of the other characters. When we first meet her, she gossips about a Polish woman who gave birth to a black child, ascribing it to being startled by a black coachman when she was pregnant. "That explanation wouldn't wear well here. . . . It would become rather *too* universal, do you not agree? And *all* our children would be black" (99). Toward the end of the trilogy, she herself has a black child. The child is adopted by Dr. Hebert, who has wed Nanon. Nanon gives birth to his mulatto son about the same time, and the boys are raised as brothers. Ultimately, Haiti declared all citizens in its borders at the time to be "black," while denying any future rights to whites, so Madame Cigny's fanciful speculations indeed come true and lead, at the trilogy's end, to the survival of some of the white characters, although the narrative proper concludes before Dessalines's ascendancy and the final extermination, under his orders, of the remaining whites (an afterword to the trilogy, however, by an aged Riau, delineates the fate of most of the white characters).

Riau's accounts of black history and legend, especially in the second and third volumes of the trilogy, echo many sections of Carpentier's *The Kingdom of this World* and demonstrate Riau's affinities with the Cuban writer's fictional narrator, Ti-Noel, a peasant who lives through decades of revolution, rather like the centenarian Miss Jane Pittman, Ernest Gaines's fictional narrator, who is born a slave and lives to see the civil rights movement. In both cases, the author finds a fictional way to do what Carolyn Fick does as a historian, that is, to tell the story "from below." In this sense, Ti-Noel, Riau, and Miss Jane not only provide alternate histories; they "right"/write history.

The story of how Macandal, forced into service as a shepherd after his accident, learns the properties of plants, aligns him with both Toussaint and Dr. Hebert, who have a similar ability. Indeed, Dr. Hebert learns to supplement his medical knowledge with local plant lore and eventually uses this knowledge as the attending physician for Toussaint's army. The opposite of therapy, however, is death; Macandal distributes poisons to slaves, who kill thousands of whites and farm animals before he is captured and burned alive. Here we might consider that the German word *Gift* actually means poison, and thus is definitely *not* a cognate. For the enslaved Africans, however, Macandal's poisons *are* a gift and inaugurate the thematic of contamination/infection that laces through histories, fictions, and myths of the Haitian Revolution.

Riau provides the history of this first revolt in African terms and does the same with the story of Boukman and the oath of insurrection he has slaves swear at a ritual dominated by Damballah in the Bois Cayman. This legendary, possibly apocryphal, event comes alive through Riau's very African interpretation; the union of Rada and Petra drums brings together the two strands of vodoun, as mulattoes and blacks join in the ritual. Legba is invoked, and he rides a horse, as Riau muses: "There were so many to be drawn up from the Island Below Sea [Guinée]. I knew that our living people outnumbered the white men ten to one. The whitemen knew it too and were afraid—this was the fear that drove the whip. But what the white men never knew was that every one they killed was with us still" (118). In a powerful scene, Toussaint and Riau watch the ritual oath and see Damballah; a huge mosquito feeds on Toussaint, who does not kill it but brushes it off. Riau suggests it is Macandal, who was said to have transformed himself when being burned at the stake into a mosquito and flown away. This fictional transference from the long-dead mystic to the living coachman pulls together the various histories of the book and lays a foundation for all that follows.

Riau, in the role of griot, provides us with an oral history of the string of rebellious acts that began with Macandal's scheme to poison Haiti's whites in 1757. Transmitted to him orally, such narratives offer an alternative history "from below" for readers, but in Riau's Haiti, these shared narratives, family history, and heroic memories constitute basic components of community consolidation. His addition of the Boukman ceremonies to this string of events creates a clear sense of decades-long struggle and a sense of more to come, with pulsing, if hidden, communal memory as combustible transmitted psychic fuel.

The tangled relations within the book all involve hybridity, and vodoun is traditionally presented as a fusion of various African religions with Catholicism. Bell, however, provides a variant of this in his novel by having a Catholic priest, Père Bonne-Chance, exhibit transgressive qualities, including an unsanctioned union with a mulatto woman with whom he has several children. He is a remnant of the Jesuit order, which has been expelled from the country, and a drunkard. Eventually, in a tragic turn of events, Bonne-Chance (whose name is deeply ironic) is confused with a rogue priest who has played panderer to black chieftains, and with his wife watching, he is "broken on the wheel" (a cruel form of execution where the condemned, bound spread-eagled on a wheel, has his bones broken by an executioner with a hammer). More of a Christ figure than almost any other character, his lusty life and saintly end recalls the doomed heroes of Graham Greene's more spiritual novels, while underlining the Catholic dimension of the cultures at whose crossroads he literally lives.

Always alternating viewpoints, Bell forces us to see the initial attacks on the whites through Riau's eyes, who, during the initial stage of the revolt, eagerly joins raids on the plain's plantations with other Maroons. Here he refers to himself as Riau, indicating that he has been mounted by Ogun. He murders and rapes, without comment on either action, as pandemonium and horror reign. Later in the novel, after Revolutionary France has betrayed the black rebels in favor of the mulattoes, Toussaint unleashes Riau and men like him to kill again, but in a more circumspect way, teaching them to follow the Western mode of combat arms, replete with drill and weapons maintenance, both necessary skills for the looming combat with French battalions now en route to the island.[36] At the same time, Toussaint adapted European methods to fit his tropical setting. The Maroon fighters so numerous in his cadres knew the secret passages over the mountains and were used to waging guerrilla attacks; it was Toussaint's ability to create a new hybrid form of warfare that led to his ultimate success. As Srinivas Aravamudan puts it, the insurrection "opportunistically tropicalized the French Revolution into a Haitian Revolution." He also cites the popular legend that Toussaint had read Abbé Raynal's 1780 edition of *Histoire des deux Indes*, where, after noting the "two colonies of black fugitives" already active in Saint Domingue, he states, "These streaks of lightning announce the oncoming thunderbolts, and the blacks only need a leader courageous enough to lead them towards vengeance and carnage" (cited in Aravamudan 1999, 301).

American blacks appreciated Toussaint's role in taming the energies of the African-born troops through discipline. James Holly's 1850s studies of the Haitian Revolution commented on this "judicious self-control" that first Toussaint and then Dessalines instilled in their troops, which, Holly asserted, led to Haiti's eventual ability to conduct national affairs and a "thrifty commercial trade" conducted by a population "equal to the demands of the nineteenth century" (1850, 365), words black nationalist writers of the time such as Martin Delany relished.

When Maillart rejoins Toussaint, now a general, he is impressed by the martial bearing of the soldiers, former slaves and mostly born in Africa: "Congos, Mandingoes, Ibos and Senegalese . . . a year or five years since they would all have been fighting each other with bows and lances and clubs. Now, but for the masks of tribal scarification, the filed teeth, dyed locks and feathers braided in the hair, there was not so much in their bearing to distinguish them from the Creole blacks and the scattering of colored men" (467), a vision that Bell does not have to overtly compare with those describing the unruly mobs of the early narrative. But they still bear scars from slavery on their backs.

Riau assists Biassou in creating a *coup poudré* made from ground toad, puff adder, skulls, and graveyard dirt, a mix that will destroy the hated Chacha, who stumbles over the *veve* that they have traced on the ground outside his hut; that night he dies. But three days later, he is raised by Biassou as a zombie, and there is no question that we must accept him as such. This magic causes Riau to shed his uniform and to run away to the Maroon community and his wife and child. "I was Riau again, only Riau, and I was glad to be running away to Bahoruco" (476).

Riau's inconstancy seems to punctuate the book, but it is to be understood as an ultimate loyalty to the ancient loas and to the black family and community found in the Maroon enclave, which for Riau represents not only his own freedom, but his historic identity, an extension of Guinée into the misty mountains of Haiti.

Gruesome scenes of torture, murder, and rape are repeated again and again, and it would be pointless to focus on more details. Suffice it to say that Bell refuses to spare us, anymore than the slaves were spared their agonies before the revolt. Kafka said that the role of the artist is to break through the frozen heart of the reader, and here Bell's theater of cruelty matches the irruptive shock of his predecessors, such as Jerzy Kosinski, the creator of the Grand Guignol of *The Painted Bird*. But we find scenes like these in Faulkner, Wright, Ellison, and other U.S. Southern writers as well, when racial conflict is being portrayed.[37]

This form of carnival obeys the rules of the genre—as Mikhail Bakhtin states, the more usual joyous carnival permits the latent sides of human nature to emerge into expression; all combinations are possible, and all orders can be inverted (1984, 123). Bakhtin does not take this where I am going, into demonic carnivalization, which is another expression for insurrection of the most extreme kind, as was practiced in Haiti. Nowhere is this seen more powerfully than in the scenes where several muscular black men, after raping and murdering, don white women's dresses and wigs. Riding frantically through the burning plain, their growing drunkenness leads the marauders to injure themselves. Riau reflects, "This was the hell where Jesus sends people who serve him poorly, and I saw that he had made it here for the whites as they deserved but that somehow we must be in it with them too" (175), an insight that can be applied to the system of slavery now being dismantled too. Frantz Fanon, we remember, declared that decolonization is a world of "complete disorder": "You do not turn any society, however primitive it may be, upside down . . . if you have not decided from the very beginning . . . to overcome all the obstacles that you will come across . . . to [be] ready for violence at all times"; yet "this violence . . . invests their characters with positive and creative qualities" (1963, 37, 93). Thus demonic carnivalization unleashes not only terrible violence, but also creative energies for reimagining a world.

Employing one of the most notorious images recorded from the massacres, Riau reports Jeannot as brandishing a white baby stuck onto a spear, still moving its limbs, echoing an earlier scene when a white man for no reason spears a toad. But Bell has Riau add, as early white reporters of the outrage did not, "I knew this was a thing the white men had done before. They carried colored children on spears" (176). As this passage suggests, horror breeds horror. In Le Cap, the *petit blancs,* thinking the mulattoes have led the revolt, begin massacring and raping them and looting their opulent homes, which have drawn their jealousy. One should also read the slaves' demonic carnivalization as a form of mimicry, as they replicate the horrors inflicted on them before the revolt, which Bell illustrates, as we have seen, at the beginning of the narrative.

Dr. Hebert at one point, wounded, scales a palm tree and is tormented by rebels with pikes, but he is saved by Toussaint, who mocks him as an ape, but then asks, "Why don't you come down here and be a man with me?" (225), a key moment in the narrative, because for most of the rest of the novel Hebert will cast his lot with this rebel leader, becoming a field doctor and, eventually, more or less "black." Toussaint's question is also meant for us as readers. Bell asks us to read history quite differently, and to cast our lot with Toussaint. Indeed, Bell has stated, "In writing the book I came to realize that the real subject of the argument was who counted as being human and who didn't. Those who got categorized as less than human could be butchered" (Jack Stephens 2000, 4). This is in keeping with his observation that, of the American, French, and Haitian revolutions, only the latter "extended . . . ideas of natural human rights to all people, not just white people—and was thus more complete, more radical and more successful, though from our point of view more obscure" (2). Further, by characterizing the central white character as "an ape" who is asked to "become a man" like Toussaint, Bell reverses the dogma of social Darwinists, suggesting that white Europeans have a long way to go toward true "civilization," and that they can be assisted by presumed inferiors, who are, in fact, more aware of the true meaning of humanity and justice.

Warfare requires doctors. This issue of therapy—which contrasts with the alternate thematic of infection—perhaps explains the invention of Dr. Hebert, who starts out as an observer but becomes a participant, and whose attentive eye to nature reveals its medicinal qualities, yes, but also its tropical beauty. In a limpid and tranquil scene, which limns the tropical sublime, Dr. Hebert bathes off the coast, mingling with pink octopi, sea urchins, and minnows in "translucent turquoise" waters. His rapture, however, is balanced scientifically: his wound is "healing nicely with no more treatment than the ocean soaks and the herb poultices he'd learned while prisoners of the blacks" (328). Throughout the novel, we see the breathtaking beauty of eighteenth-century Haitian mountains, jungles, fields, and seas through his eyes, and yet his perceptions are made more fleeting and poignant because of the underlying terror of the war-torn country, providing a keen sense of the tropical sublime while simultaneously reminding us of the tragic ecological disaster that is today's Haiti.

Similarly, after the initial horrors, the long combat of forces begins, and Bell signals the break by having us explore the mountains and rain forest alongside Toussaint and Hebert, taking packed, ancient trails made by the now-extinct Carib Indians, trails that later facilitate Toussaint's army's miraculous transits from battle to battle. In terms of Bell's impressive re-creation of the lush plantations and the densely verdant mountains and rain forests that surround them, we find one of the most powerful examples of the tropical sublime in our survey of circumCaribbean texts, a portrait that is more impressive knowing that Haiti's forests have literally gone up in smoke, for firewood, denuding the country almost completely. Bell's lyrical portrayal of this now-vanished topography extends backward in many ways to Longinus, Burke, and Kant, and yet also forward to Lyotard and Žižek, as we consider the sublime aspects of terror that unfold against this magical backdrop. An ambush can erupt from the gorgeous foliage at any moment, and more than once it does.

Further, the narrative explores the various aspects of the racial sublime, as the multiple registers of color in enslaved culture, free mulatto culture, and white culture of the island are plumbed. All of this becomes even more impressive when we remember that this finely nuanced fiction is firmly based in a minutely observed and balanced historical framework, one that constantly seeks to resurrect and honor the history of the islands' enslaved combatants and victims, particularly by voicing that history through both fictional black characters and actual personages of the island's history.[38]

In these scenes, Bell reminds us of the verdant paradise that today's treeless, parched Haiti once represented, when it was indeed the "pearl of the Antilles." Toussaint informs the doctor that the Caribs are all dead because "they would not be slaves" (253), a stance that now of course has been transferred to the Africans. In the mystical green light of the mountain, under a purple sky, the doctor "understood he was in the presence of God" (253), and it is here, at last, that he meets Riau and that the diverse strands of the novel meet. Appropriately, the narration shifts to Riau; he has returned to the Maroons and Merbillay and their new baby, Pierre Toussaint, after seeing the rebels acting all too much like their former masters in Jeannot's camp. In a brilliant passage, his disgust at Jeannot's brutality is rendered from an African perspective: "Jeannot had made himself like a little king of Guinée. . . . A mean spirit ruled him. Erzulie-gé-rouge was his *maît'tête*, all spite. . . . Each morning . . . he drank a mixture of blood and tafia from the round top part of a whiteman's skull . . . on each fifth post a whiteman head was stuck. . . . He would try to think of new ways to kill them slowly" (255). Eventually we learn that Jeannot learned many of his ingenious forms of torture from his old master, Bullet.[39]

But for a time Riau deserts the army, and when he returns, Toussaint, at first enraged, seems ready to kill him, but he softens and reads a passage to him from a book that had inspired him years ago by Abbé Raynale: "*Already there are . . . two colonies of fugitive negroes. . . . A courageous chief only is wanted. Where is he, that great man whom Nature owes to her vexed, oppressed and tormented children? . . . He will appear, doubt it not: he will come forth and raise the sacred standard of liberty*" (420). Toussaint then declares that Riau's son, Little Toussaint, was born free, and to remember it. But, Riau thinks, "it was Toussaint who forgot that Riau was born free in Guinée, while only he, Toussaint, was born to slavery" (421).[40] Similarly, in one of the book's most powerful utterances, Riau wonders why white men think only Christ could come back from the dead, for the men from Guinée like him survived the "death" of the Middle Passage. Now he and Maillart are fellow captains, who must learn from each other—Riau, the arts of Western war, Maillart, the culture and courage of Riau's fellow Africans. Their earlier roles as twin amanuenses of Toussaint now expand into military arms.[41] We note as well that Riau's griot orality has now merged with the West's tradition of creating history through documents, since Toussaint's missives are destined to shape formal accounts of the time.

In these passages, Bell reminds the reader that two-thirds of the slaves were, like Riau, born free in Africa, and although this novel portrays Toussaint as the hero he was, it also refuses to valorize him above those who brought the revolution "from below" with the aid of their loas. Moreover, there are few occasions when vodoun is fused with Catholicism, which was often the case on other islands and in New Orleans, as Bell constantly impresses on us that most of the rebels were in fact born in Africa, so their Petra and Rada loas tend to be unadulterated.

In a brilliant stroke, Bell has Toussaint take up Riau because he knows how to write, and he needs someone other than the doctor to record his messages. Both men take dictation at once, signifying the divided stream of the novel itself, which is intent on telling the story of the revolution from both a European and an African perspective, which in fact fuse in the mysterious figure of Toussaint. "You must teach him," Toussaint calls to the doctor, "the way I taught you herbs" (274). Writing and herbs thus both represent good health, wisdom, and futurity.

Bell's narrative echoes that of Séjour's in that Choufleur's obsession with Nanon largely stems, it seems, from the fact that she was his white father's mistress. In what is perhaps the most charged scene in the novel, once the insurrection has broken out, this bitter mulatto Choufleur has his white patron, Maltrot, tied to a tree, as the older man protests that he has been kind to him, educated him in France, and given him money and slaves. Ultimately he admits that he is his father too, to which Choufleur replies, "You gave me a nigger to be my mother" (235), before he systematically flays him alive. Once again, Bell doubles our agonized gaze, as Dr. Hebert appears and reports the scene, giving it added dimension and demonic horror, as Choufleur slits his father open and handles his organs. Simone Vauthier notes that scenes such as this, where social redress and parricide mingle, are not unusual in mythic literature, because they are "imbued with an abundance of psychoanalytic significance and revolutionary relevance" (1980, 90–91). Because Choufleur's venom is partly caused by his father's appropriation of his childhood sweetheart, Nanon, his story echoes Séjour's *Le Mulâtre* so closely that the tale may be a direct influence. The episode has a chilling aftermath beyond that of Séjour's, however, for, as noted earlier, Choufleur, enraged at Nanon's liaison with Dr. Hebert, presents her with his father's snuff box; inside is his parent's severed and shriveled member. As in Séjour's tale, the Oedipal configuration of the Haitian Revolution here becomes underlined, as Choufleur (the murderous son, who has appropriated the body of his father's mate) becomes a demonic personification of the new nation. Ironically, although he is the child of a colonizer himself, he is part of the revolutionary generation that eventually will kill or exile all white people — thus the point of the severed member of the father/France, and the end of the imposed history of the father country. Michel de Certeau has observed that there is no law that is not inscribed on bodies. The marks on Choufleur's face are thus not accidental, but rather a reminder of the ways in which the law has marked and circumscribed him. As Certeau states, "A body is itself defined, delimited, and articulated by what writes it" (1984, 139). Thus the "writing" Choufleur does with his knife/pen creates a new "law" and exacts punishment on the body that ironically doomed his own.

Bell's monumental trilogy builds on scholarship that has been done on Caribbean and Southern history, studies of African religions (particularly vodoun), and other novels, plays, and anthropological texts that deal with slavery and/or Haiti. But his works also extend and amplify the anxieties and influences Haiti generated and bestowed on the American South. The first novel concludes with a very helpful and quite accurate "Chronology of Historical Events," extending from 1757 to 1805, when Dessalines began the extermination of all whites remaining in Haiti. The inclusion of this timetable offers evidence of Bell's determination to create historical fiction that is, in fact, largely true to actual events. However, his multilayered narrative, which takes care to provide insights from the slaves, mulattoes, and *petit* and *grand blancs*, as well as the various European groups represented on the islands, generously embroiders on these facts, offering a dramatization of history through individual and compelling stories, thereby following the method Tolstoy employed in *War and Peace,* according to which actual historical figures such as General Kutuzov interact with fictional families. While Toussaint and many other real personages of the conflict come alive again in Bell's prose, Tolstoy's fictional Prince Andrew, Pierre, Natasha, and Helene, and their families find equivalents in Doctor Hebert, Ninon, Choufleur, and, most important, Riau. Bell also provides a preface, which summarizes and brings to life what the chronology lays out in cold facts later.

The novel concerns itself with every aspect of life and death, including birth. In an extended scene, late in the novel, Nanon gives birth to her first child with Dr. Hebert, who watches somewhat helplessly as huge, black Maman-Maig' works a black midwife's mojo. Hebert sees that the boy resembles his grandfather—but then he realizes that his son is "not himself, not Nanon, but a mingling—something new. This, the doctor realized, was what all the trouble was about" (345), the intercourse—of all sorts—between the races. This final scene, of escape, refuge, and reunion, offers up many strands of the novel's great subject, hybridity and its role in survival. As Bell comprehends, these issues did not find closure with the establishment of the Haitian nation. More broadly, he, like the other circumCaribbean writers whose treatments of the Haitian Revolution he mined, understands the Haitian chronicle as a metaphor for what W. E. B. Du Bois correctly predicted would be the dominant issue of the twentieth century—the conflict around the color line. The great epic struggle of the past century in the U.S. South was the civil rights movement, a crucible that shaped Bell himself and his entire generation. His published interviews indicate a hope on his part that a return to the Haitian story might give us new modes of perception as we begin to search for answers to enduring racial and social problems across the artificial lines of geographic/national demarcation. Haitians may be struggling today to remove the rubble and heal the wounds of their latest catastrophe for years to come, but they will be inspired in this work and in the building of a better future by their great national story of emancipation.

· · · · ·

Like his Caribbean peers named above, Bell has constructed a mythic counter-history, one that takes very seriously the side of the island's insurrectionists. As David Cook and Michael Okenimkpe have stated, "Selected images, events, speeches and individuals embody certain needs of a people. Myths draw upon history. But writers who develop national myths are using history as part of a continuing process which can help determine and shape the future by encouraging certain possibilities in society and perhaps discouraging others. To such writers history is not static, but is material out of which social and economic realities have created the present, providing various openings for the future" (1983, 161).

Bell's recognition of the penetration of African elements into the creolized cultures of the lower U.S. South and the South of the South led him to see, along with James, Glissant, Walcott, Césaire, Carpentier, and the many other circumCaribbean writers not from Haiti, the centrality of that island nation's revolutionary achievement and how elements common to its history and theirs, such as a concentration of African people, Maroon cultures and histories, and the power of the African religion of vodoun, helped create a spirit of resistance and creativity. This spirit has, over the centuries, not died with the specific failures within Haiti, but to the contrary, has, as in Reed's novel, "jes grew" into a standard of struggle and achievement for people everywhere.

Throughout the trilogy, Bell relentlessly portrays new combinations of people, events, catastrophes, and more mundane things, such as novel combinations in herbal medicine, adaptations of Carib Indian ways, and legacies from mixed ancestries, that profitably commingle in various ways. The story is profoundly Caribbean but has many affinities to the literature of the U.S. South that gave Bell his first introduction to fiction when he was growing up in Nashville. Space prevents exploration of these thematics and patterns in the final two parts of Bell's trilogy, but I would like to close with a consideration of how these novels fit into a larger framework of circumCaribbean writing and into our new conception of a transnational South. Bell's reminder of Haiti's contribution to the hemisphere's continuing search for liberation, social justice, and transnational community and prosperity could not come at a better time. The concept of Haiti's revolutionary triumph as an infection to be feared—an eruption of blackness and barbarity into the sacrosanct "white" societies of the Western world—has found modern forms in the last decades. The eruption of the HIV virus, supposedly brought to the United States from Haiti by a promiscuous flight attendant, has transformed what started as a political infection into one of blood. However, part of the Haitian specter was biological from the outset, in terms of the fear of racial amalgamation, either through rape or through the syndrome of "passing," which presumably would have been easy for Creoles of color, like Faulkner's Charles Bon. The recent Haitian earthquake has flushed out, yet again, the concept of contagion and impurity, most notably through white evangelist Pat Robertson's declaration that God brought down the earthquake as retribution for Haitians selling their soul to the Devil as the price for their 1804 liberation. Barbara Browning has delineated the myriad forms metaphors of infection have taken over the decades, not just in connection with Haiti, but with all manifestations of the spread of African culture in the Western world (1998, passim). Bell reminds us that the negative mythologies surrounding Haitians and their history have found all-too-similar reflections in the U.S. South, where people of color—most recently Mexican immigrants—have been stereotyped, scapegoated, and used as a psychic dumping ground—the "not us" that therefore supposedly defines "us."

The preceding chapters of this study form a foundation for my reading of Bell's masterly historical narratives, which resulted from his ceaseless and meditative braiding together of histories and fictions of the U.S. South and the Caribbean. The fact that his work has been widely admired by Caribbean writers—including very prominent Haitian figures—offers confirmation of his achievement and of the challenge it presents us as we rethink nation, region, the transnational, and the diasporic. Bell's trilogy, a virtual palimpsest of reaccentuations of prior texts, reinterprets the myriad preceding narratives in an epic form, as all epics do.

Bell's role might be to claim not just Toussaint but all the heroic figures of the Haitian Revolution for a newly configured circumCaribbean history that includes the U.S. South, for the "submarine" connections of the diaspora extend powerfully into the full gamut of Southern literature and culture. While Bell is white, the overall thrust of his project—like that of African American writers, particularly those in the South—is not different from what J. Michael Dash has described as the point of departure of Caribbean literature, namely "the effort to write the subject into existence" by tracing efforts to find individual and communal identity. "The heroic prodigal, the solemn demiurge, the vengeful enfant terrible, outspoken Caliban—these are some of the pervasive images of the transcendental subject in Caribbean literature" (1989, xiii).

All of these aspects find powerful representations in Bell's trilogy, in both character and actions. As Bell demonstrates repeatedly, the Haitian Revolution, as upheaval, reconstituted the world. Classes, colors, cultures, all were caught up in the vortex of change, and new combinations inevitably resulted, a kind of "cosmic" hybridity whose sign, to the *ancien regime*, would indeed be the feared "miscegenation." Glissant has stated that "Haiti, the Caribbean, the elsewhere . . . is a place where, one suspects, the stain of miscegenation marks every corner of the plantation. There, mixture is a threat and a menace" (1999, 87).

The "pollution" of "color" also stands, for those invested in "whiteness," for the "infectious rhythm" that Barbara Browning has identified as metaphors for the "contagion" and "spread" of African culture. Bell, like many of his colleagues across the color line, regularly inverts this scheme to show how *Western* influence is a pathogen. Like Reed in his masterful and wickedly funny *Mumbo Jumbo*, Bell, in a much more serious vein, shows again and again how African cultures of the New World—especially those in Haiti—yes, *are* contagious, but they lead to invigoration, creativity, and life-sustaining intercourse of all kinds between peoples and cultures. The real tragedy of the Haitian Revolution—the snuffing out of many of its hopeful possibilities through sustained and purposeful isolation and punishment of the new nation by Western powers over centuries—has to be inferred by the reader—a reader who concludes the trilogy with a new awareness of her or his preconceived ideas about blackness, hemispheric history, and cultural value and integrity. As Bell is well aware, these issues, methods, and subjects have been inherent in most black and some white U.S. Southern literature for centuries. The parallels between the northern rim and island center of the basin become obvious as the trilogy progresses.

The heretofore "hidden history" of the Haitian Revolution and its role in shaping both social and literary developments in the U.S. South emerges forcefully in the trilogy, which illustrates many of the points made—or purposely obscured—by Bell's predecessors in Southern/circumCaribbean letters. The narratives we have considered in this chapter offer an ideal example of the kinds of voices Stuart Hall has identified as crucial in Caribbean narrative (which I have extended to circumCaribbean discourse): Présence Africaine, Présence Européene, and Présence Américaine. For Hall, the first of these is the "site of the repressed"; the second is the "colonialist, hegemonic construction of knowledges"; and the third is a New World site of "cultural confrontation, possibility for creolization and points of new becoming" (2003, 233). Bell's brilliant interrogation of a history we thought we knew forcefully participates in Caribbean *creolité*, a process that unites the oral and the written, the dead and the living, the seen and the unseen, the act and the spirit that lies behind it. The elements he assembles form a whole, but each remains distinct, a powerful antidote to the deadening dualistic molds of Western history. By pointing to the violence of history, the novels reveal a parallel Caribbean story that complements the tragic racial history of the U.S. South and the nation. More generally, these narratives force the complacent reader to confront history with less detachment and with more awareness of the lives that have been lost in the quest for full humanity and freedom.

Constance Fenimore Woolson and Lafcadio Hearn

Extending the Boundaries of the Transnational South

· ·

Every story is a travel story—a spatial practice.

—Michel de Certeau

After the U.S. Civil War, the pace of the industrial revolution quickened in the North, and although most of the money generated went into the pockets of monopolists and oligarchs, a rising middle class soon found itself with leisure time, disposable income, and a newly developed yen for travel, either through the pages of popular periodicals, which fathers would read to assembled families around the parlor lamp, or through actual visits to exotic/ quaint/picturesque sites. These visits might be extended stays in Europe, which would soon become the scene of Henry James's "international" novels, but they could also be to places relatively nearby—as Sarah Orne Jewett's short stories demonstrated, the islands off the coast of Maine could be as "foreign" and intriguing to even Boston residents as an African savannah.

Ambitious writers soon realized that travel writing had a lucrative counterpart in local color fiction, especially when it was set in the most exotic region of the nation, the tropical South. Constance Fenimore Woolson (1840–94), the grandniece of James Fenimore Cooper, was unusual for this era in making a living entirely from her writing. Early in her career, she alternated between travel pieces and short stories about the Midwest, where she was reared. Later, however, her invalid mother required a warmer clime, and they wintered in St. Augustine, Florida. The state's circumCaribbean history and its magnificent but dangerous swamps, waterways, and jungles offered myriad possibilities for her pen, while the region's painful adjustment to the devastations of the Civil War and the ordeal of Reconstruction created an interface with both Northern and Southern readers. Woolson's travel pieces, like "The Oklawaha," made ample use of the tropical sublime and were often published by *Harper's*, one of the nation's most popular magazines.

Concurrently, *Harper's* was publishing pieces by the New Orleans journalist Lafcadio Hearn (1850–1904), whose many "local color" articles drew on the sharp journalist's eye he had developed as a roving reporter, first in Cincinnati and then in New Orleans. In this chapter, I will draw a contrast between these two writers. Their personalities and styles were quite divergent, but the overall patterns of their lives, their interest in the tropical and the sensuous, and their penetrating sense of the effect of landscape and climate on people and events make them fascinating figures of comparison. My purpose in placing them together, however, has not been to trace a set of ideas specific to these writers but instead to show that their work was part of a new approach to the circumCaribbean, one that proceeded from an understanding that the coastal U.S. South was inextricably linked with the wider basin, its islands, and its southern rims.

The nineteenth century was an age of discovery. Charles Gordon's exploits on the Nile and David Livingstone's journeys into Africa (and Stanley's in search of him) were only two of the more sensational kinds of travel writing. People were eager to learn about other lands, yes, but also about strange, unthought-of realms within the nation itself. Well into the twentieth century, especially in the pages of the *National Geographic*, readers relished accounts of expeditions to the Amazon, the polar icecaps, or the exotic islands and nations of the Pacific and Asia, but they were also fascinated by backwoods Georgia, Louisiana, Florida, and the Appalachians.

Within the United States, the American South had always had a siren's call for many Northern residents, as Walt Whitman memorably indicated in his poem, "O Magnet-South!" Much was known about Charleston, New Orleans, and Savannah, particularly after the Civil War brought Northern soldiers to those cities. The little-visited tropical South fascinated most of all, especially Louisiana and Florida. Writers who concentrated on these coasts were naturally drawn to outlying U.S. islands, but also to the further islands of the Caribbean, the shores of the circumCaribbean, and the connecting maritime traffic, which had long ago brought both the colonial powers and African slaves into the region. The criollo cultures of the coastal South in this sense were immediate links with the transnational history of the great basin. Inevitably, writers used their knowledge of the U.S. South as a lens for reading the new "South of the South," an exploration that was expanding exponentially with the rise of "armchair tourism" that mass print culture had invented, but also with the birth of actual hemispheric tourism, which took on new urgency after the Civil War.

Two momentous publishing events generated interest in accounts of the tropical South: the first was the appearance of one of the nation's first best sellers, the two-volume edition of *Picturesque America* (1872–74).[1] Published by the aggressive and ambitious D. Appleton and Company, it began as a series of travel sketches of exotic and/or remote areas of the expanding nation. Significantly, the very first sketch in the collection featured tropical Florida: "A Journey up the St. John's and Ocklawaha Rivers" had text by Old Southwest humorist Thomas Bangs Thorpe (1815–78) and illustrations by the series' most accomplished artist, Harry Finn. Rather than picturing the landscape as pestilential and dreary, Thorpe employed picturesque language, limning the swamp's wild beauties and the endless variety of scenes as the boat navigated the twists of the channel. The views took on especially exotic aspects at night, when black crews kept torches burning on the roof. Thorpe suggested that the tree trunks, meeting overhead, were like the pillars of Gothic cathedrals, while the hanging moss comprised "tattered but gigantic banners, worm-eaten and moldy, sad evidences of the hopes and passions of the distant past" (582).

The second important publishing event also came in 1872, when Josiah Gilbert Holland, attempting to capitalize on the fevered interest in Henry Morton Stanley's account of searching for David Livingstone in central Africa, employed Edward King to create a series of articles on the Reconstruction South. The 1875 compilation, *The Great South*, made extravagant claims as to the novelty of its "discoveries," which were achieved through "penetration" and "investigation." As Jennifer Greeson has demonstrated, both Holland and King sought to situate the South as a kind of "domestic Africa," which was indeed not too different from racist Northern impressions of the region. Greeson asserts that the representation of the Reconstruction South as a colony of the North — one paralleling European global holdings — made the United States equal to the European powers. This "global reframing," she feels, was a major achievement of *The Great South* (2010, 244).

Louisiana occupies a prominent position in King's book, partly because of its exotic tropical topography but also because of its colonization by France and Spain, which had created many ties to the circumCaribbean. Formerly Spanish Florida acquired a similar aura, and, as Greeson observes, the imperialist interests of the nation explain why these two states, which train the eye southward, became the most popular settings for travel writers, displacing an earlier fascination with the states of the upper South like Kentucky and Virginia (Greeson 2010, 507). Other writers preceded Woolson and Hearn on this path. In the same year of *The Great South*'s book publication, one of the Confederacy's most celebrated writers, Sidney Lanier (1842–81), a poet, novelist, and talented musician, sought to capitalize on the craze for travel writing. *Florida: Its Scenery, Climate, and History, with an Account of*

Charleston, Savannah, Augusta, and Aiken, and a Chapter for Consumptives; Being a Complete Hand-Book and Guide opens by declaring that the state "by its very peninsular curve whimsically terminates the United States in an interrogation-point" (1875, 9), which leads to his assertion of the many questions Florida raises with its bewildering diversity and, sometimes, its inaccessibility. Lanier was capitalizing on the public's hunger for "penetration" into unknown realms; accordingly, he depicts "another world," albeit one with a fabled history. The tropical nature of the landscape is abundantly portrayed in the book's many illustrations. Lanier is better known for his lyrical poetry, much of it focused on the rivers and marshes of his native Georgia. His travel volume, however, deserves consideration as an early example of a popular genre, which increasingly took the Sunshine State as its subject.

Woolson followed Lanier's example and published her own version, "The Oklawaha," in the January 1876 volume of *Harper's*.[2] She quotes the early naturalist William Bartram and, like him, employs the language of the tropical sublime, rather than the gothic, to limn the enchanting beauty of the swamp. To factor in the frisson of the sublime, she shrewdly adds the swamp's dangers—like the huge alligators and serpents. The terror and awe of the sublime are thrilling because of the protected perspective of the comfortable boat and its capable crew. Since antiquity, the sublime has been associated with the vastness of natural spaces and objects, which emerged in unexpected new forms during the age of discovery that began to accelerate in the sixteenth century. Writers seeking to capitalize on these developments strove to develop a new descriptive vocabulary, one that could do justice to aspects of nature (and sometimes material culture) that were too vast or complex to easily express in words.

The sublime exposes the difference between knowing and feeling and is never far from violence. The tropical swamp and jungle—the latter including volcanic mountains—offer a compelling vision of pleasure and danger. Further, in Woolson and Hearn, these locales represent the tangle of emotions felt by both the passengers and, to a certain extent, the authors. Woolson seems to envision the sublime in the manner of Kant, who felt that one could only encounter sublimity through an interior moral law, a principle presented through the conversations of the passengers.

In New Orleans, meanwhile, Hearn published "Saint Malo," which involves a trip to a little village inhabited by Filipino fishermen and alligator hunters in the wetlands south of New Orleans. The tale describes a tropical liminal place, between the sky and sea, the United States and the Caribbean, and underlines the multiethnic nature of the wide basin. Subsequently, in 1887, just after Woolson published her compelling Florida novel, *East Angels*, Hearn took a steamer to the West Indies, a trip he used as material for a series of published sketches. He fell in love with Martinique and returned there after a brief sojourn in New York; he lived and wrote in the capital, Saint Pierre, for two years. There was, in a sense, a feeling of "return" on Hearn's part, as he had been born on the Greek island of Levkas (his first name came from the ancient term for the island) and was raised in the British Isles. He always felt somewhat of an isolato, too, and his peregrinations across the globe created a sense of island realms as appropriate for the isolated artiste. Hearn had explored and vacationed in the islands just off Louisiana's coast; the multicultural, free-wheeling inhabitants, many of them fishermen, smugglers, or fugitives, captured his imagination. His first novel, *Chita: A Memory of Last Island*, was set on L'Isle Derniere, which had been devastated by a legendary hurricane, the subject of the narrative, and his first step toward the islands that lay beyond.

It is remarkable to note that Hearn's Caribbean writings were created at precisely the same time that Woolson was recognizing Florida as a Caribbean culture. Her Southern stories, first published as a collection under the title *Rodman the Keeper* in 1880, had appeared earlier in magazines, starting in 1875. Hearn's New Orleans pieces began to appear only two years later. He too had visited Florida and contemplated writing about it, noting there was a ready market for the subject, perhaps thinking of Woolson and Lanier in that regard. (Indeed, the frontispiece to his *Collected Works* is a picture of the Oklawaha, which he also visited and wrote about.) Woolson's six winters in Florida and other Southern locations were succeeded by years in Italy, primarily Venice, another realm of islands, and Hearn found such a setting when he migrated to the island nation of Japan after his Caribbean years. Like Hearn, Woolson became entranced by her new culture and would write admiringly of Italian peasants and their rural surroundings. Ultimately, however, Hearn married a Japanese woman and became a father and an admired figure in the country, while Woolson became increasingly isolated—particularly after her rupture with her close friend Henry James—and she eventually jumped to her death from the window of her Venetian palazzo. Woolson and Hearn died early, both at the age of fifty-four.

Woolson and Hearn, who never met, were aware that the wild landscapes that had enthralled them were paradoxically diminishing with the advent of the same commercial tourism they were advancing. In Hearn's first novel,

Chita, he laments, "The cane-fields have degenerated into sandy plains, over which tramways wind to the smooth beach;—the plantation-residences have been converted into rustic hotels, and the negro-quarters remodeled into villages of cozy cottages for the reception of guests" (7–8).

Neither of these figures have been previously described as either Southern or circumCaribbean writers, partly because neither was from the region, and both eventually left it. The writing they later did in Europe and Japan, respectively, and the close friendship Woolson developed with Henry James have tended to overshadow their circumCaribbean writing. Their tropical narratives, however, have much to teach us about the ways in which nineteenth-century writers were ignoring artificial national boundaries to consider broader cultural zones, which were united by topography, climate, folkways, and slavery's legacy.

To accomplish these readings, I will employ a variety of tools, including postcolonial theory, which most people rightly associate with the literatures produced by formerly subject people in Asia, Africa, and the Caribbean. The de facto recolonization of the South after the Civil War was pointed out early on by C. Vann Woodward in *The Rise of the New South*, and his point has been echoed more recently by critics such as Greeson and Walter Benn Michaels. Michaels has reread Plantation School narratives through the lens of postcolonial theory. Southerners did indeed see their region as a victim of Northern invasion and colonization from 1865 to around 1917, and many Confederates migrated to Mexico and Brazil.[3] Postcolonial literatures—particularly those that rehearse wars of oppression, exile, and genocide—often build narrative on a foundation of mourning and memorial. As Tzvetan Todorov has noted, "Commemoration is always the adaptation of memory to the needs of today" (cited in Lowe 2005, 221).

Southern Reconstruction can easily be read through the lens of displacement, disruption, exile, loss, and commemoration; in fact, that is exactly the way it *was* read by Reconstruction Southern novelists such as Thomas Dixon, Thomas Nelson Page, and Harry Stillwell Edwards. Their fictions, however, were counterposed by strong writing by African Americans such as Anna Julia Cooper, Charles Chesnutt, and, later, W. E. B. Du Bois (especially in *Black Reconstruction*). This group of writers, in fact, has virtually eclipsed their white counterparts at this date in literary history. However, I argue that we cannot hope to see the power of African American writing about Reconstruction, the Nadir—the terrible decades of lynching before and after the turn of the century—and the early twentieth century without concurrent study of the literature that so many African Americans read, disliked, and then sought to subvert and displace.

Woolson's fiction in this sense could be said to occupy a mediating position between these schools of writers. Capitalizing on the North's colonizing maneuvers in the ruined South, the fictional fruit of Woolson's Florida sojourns were her superb short story collection *Rodman the Keeper* (1880) and three novels: *East Angels* (1886), *Jupiter Lights* (1889), and *Horace Chase* (1894). Many of the characters in Woolson's Southern narratives are in mourning for the "lost homeland," even if they are still living on it. The decaying mansions, the tattered rags of former finery, the barren fields, the empty quarters—all of these are decried by Woolson's blacks, whites, Minorcans, and others. Many figures leave, in a Southern diaspora that extends into the American West, Europe, and, very often, the tropics South of the South. According to Plantation School narrative, ex-Confederates retain a powerful memory of an exalted, pastoral past, which evolves into myth, and they yearn for a restoration. This is to be accomplished through new modes of controlling the emancipated African Americans and through education of Yankee oppressors—which is often engineered through the stratagem of intermarriage, usually between a Yankee officer and a Southern belle, but also through the romantic attentions of a cavalier Southern gentleman to a young Yankee maiden. As James Clifford explains, "Maintaining connections with homelands, with kinship networks, and with religious and cultural traditions may renew patriarchal structures" (1997, 259), and ultimately, this is exactly what happened in the South.

Several of the stories in *Rodman* concern the devastated landscape, the poverty of all classes, black and white, and the vacuum caused by the death of a generation of young men. Woolson, however, never indulges in a romantic portrait of life before the war or in notions that slavery had its merits. Still, one can read her implied indictment of the North's failure to honor the aims of Reconstruction as a critique of what was rapidly becoming an imperialist enterprise.[4]

The Caribbean had always produced anti-imperialist writing, because of the region's colonial history, which in the nineteenth century was still very much in place. As we look for links between Woolson's and Hearn's "Southern" narratives and the circumCaribbean elements of subsequent writing, we might ponder the ways in which theorists have tackled the issue of how to talk about the Caribbean as an entity, a particular problem because of the very different forms the area's colonialism took under the regimes of the French, the Spanish, the British, and the Dutch, all supplemented by enforced slavery, first of Native Americans, then of Africans, and later of indentured South Asians.

CircumCaribbean/Transatlantic Linkages

Woolson's Florida characters are surrounded by water—swamps, rivers, lakes, sounds, oceans—and they travel on steamers, yachts, trawlers, fishing vessels, and canoes. These bodies of water are described idyllically or realistically, as scenes of the sublime or as turbulent, dangerous cauldrons. They are links to the outside world, to avenues into the primeval, to sources of life through the harvest of the sea, and to death.

In her Southern tales, Woolson continually refers to Africa, a presence suggested by the Africans and African Americans that surround her in Florida, but also in the circumCaribbean. The connectedness of the waterways of the Americas she references suggests Glissant's observation of the subterranean convergence of Caribbean history, whose unity is "submarine" (1989, 67), particularly in terms of the thousands of black bodies thrown overboard by slave vessels. As Woolson suggests, more than just African Americans are linked through these submarine histories. The Southern communities that Woolson depicts are all far from urban centers, and, in fact, most of them are "islands," either in reality or in function. As such, they bear comparison to what Benítez-Rojo has termed the "repeating island" aspect of Caribbean culture. He refers to the ways in which cultures have been ignored and marginalized and identifies several contributing factors, including fragmentation, instability, reciprocal isolation, uprootedness, cultural heterogeneity, lack of historiography and historical continuity, contingency, and impermanence (1992, 1). All of these conditions applied to the postbellum South in Woolson's fiction. She plays a doubled role as author in these works, namely, to make aesthetic capital out of these conditions, but also to displace or reform them. Certainly, her histories of Florida highlight the long trajectory of events that began in the contact era and encompass the centuries of Native American and then Spanish dominance. At the same time, she embraces cultural heterogeneity and attempts to take readers beyond the usual racial binary of Reconstruction fiction and mythology. She has a different sense of history and the future to come than the Lost Cause group of writers.

Earlier, I referred to Braudel's history of the Mediterranean (1972) and his acknowledgment that his book was a partial statement, in that he was unequipped to discuss the great sea's Ottoman coast, which represented unknown territory for European scholars. In Woolson's time, the Florida coast (with the exception of St. Augustine) and most of the Caribbean were "unknown territory" for most readers. As Hearn stated, there was a ready market for books on "Gulf-coasts and shifting dunes, sands, winds, and tides, storms and valiant saving of life" (Bisland 1906, 1:381).

Antonio Benítez-Rojo has attempted to analyze aspects of Caribbean culture in an effort "not to find results, but processes, dynamics, and rhythms that show themselves within the marginal, the regional, the incoherent, the heterogeneous, or if you like, the unpredictable that coexists with us in our everyday world" (1992, 3). This was Woolson's project as well. As both these figures recognized, the great engine that developed both the South and the Caribbean was the plantation. Woolson is often vaguely considered as operating in the Plantation School tradition in her Southern narratives, and many have thought this meant she was influenced by Thomas Nelson Page or Thomas Dixon. These writers, however, published after Woolson, and she must therefore be considered as a major progenitor of Southern local color fiction and of transatlantic fiction of the circumCaribbean. When she chose to set her stories in her own time rather than in the antebellum period, she inevitably was going to write about the temporary destruction of the "plantation-machine." The great sugar mills, the cotton farms, the orange groves—all these are in decline in the Florida she paints. But by choosing this moment of stasis and despair, she sets in motion the thematics she most cared for, namely those of dignified poverty, renunciation, and constant struggle, including the fight for social progress, both personal and communal, which ultimately can lead to redemption and renewal. Her delineation of the coastal South comes from her own close inspections rather than from other literary influences. Indeed, there were few fictional accounts of this terrain before her.

I now turn to illustrations of some of these issues in Woolson's Southern texts—principally the collection *Rodman the Keeper* and her best novel, *East Angels* (both 1886).[5] The story "Rodman the Keeper" begins this way: "In the little town . . . everything was monotonous, and the only spirit that rose above the waste was a bitterness for the gained and sorrow for the lost cause. The keeper [Rodman, the "keeper"/caretaker of the cemetery, which is based on the actual federal burial ground in Andersonville, Georgia] was the only man whose presence personated the former in their sight, and upon him therefore, as representative, the bitterness fell . . . so Rodman withdrew himself, and came and went among them no more" (11–12). This opening tableau emphasizes "silences," a dominant motif in Woolson, for she constantly maintains that the people of the South—be they British, Spanish, cracker, African, or Native American—have been "silenced" by defeat and colonization. Henry James recognized this aspect of her work, speaking of her Southern tales' high value, "especially when regarded in the light of the *voicelessness* of the conquered and reconstructed South" (1930, 4). This thematic was possibly related to Woolson's own growing deafness, which became a great source of depression for her in the years preceding her suicide.

The silence of colonized/conquered people is a note often sounded in postcolonial theory and discourse; their chronic economic dependency has often led to situations such as the one in Martinique, where Aimé Césaire remarked on a people "so strangely garrulous yet silent" (cited in Dash 1989, xxii). Woolson, although from New England and the Midwest, seeks to provide a voice for these conquered people. She renders region through a multitude of voices, and many of them are redolent of both the wider South below Florida and the myriad connections of the Atlantic World, including the Black Atlantic. Her intermittent financial struggles made her sympathetic with the impoverished citizens of the South, particularly the war widows and newly enfranchised but often underemployed African Americans.

Then, too, Woolson of course knew that a grieving North might lend a more sympathetic ear to Southern chronicles if approached through mourning and commemoration. The mood of death and ruin that dominates the beginning of "Rodman the Keeper" has a sequel later when the Union veteran Rodman relates his personal history, one that involves the deaths of both of his parents and his two brothers, the loss of the family home, his fortune, and his health, and the admission that he sought the keeper's job because the Southern clime would aid his recovery. Miss Bettina, similarly grieving over her dead kin, except for her parallel and obstinate loyalty to the Lost Cause, now seems a possible mate for Rodman, especially after she comes secretly to the Union cemetery to honor the dead, despite her pride.

Woolson atones for her "darky" imagery in parts of the story by featuring a moving procession of the town's black folk that appears on the national memorial day to honor the fallen Yankees who helped set them free. They ask Rodman to "head . . . de processio" [sic] as they scatter flowers on the graves. Woolson tells us that "it was a pathetic sight to see some of the old men and women, ignorant field-hands, bent, dull-eyes, and past the possibility of education even in its simplest forms, carefully placing their poor flowers to the best advantage. . . . They knew dimly that the men who lay beneath those mounds had done something wonderful for them and for their children; and so they came bringing their blossoms, and with little intelligence but with much love" (33). While we reject the paternalistic, even dismissive depiction of the "dim" recognitions of the black tribute bearers, this story offers a sense of the ways in which Woolson differs from the Southern writers who celebrated the Lost Cause. While she strongly sympathizes with the suffering of both blacks and whites during Reconstruction and seems to recognize both the beauty and the graciousness of Southern culture, she has no identification at all with claims for "states rights," ladies' memorial societies, or the insidious forms racism took after emancipation. This story, more than anything else she wrote, speaks to her profound admiration for the achievement and sacrifices of the Union army.

Despite a common sense of loss, Bettina's and Rodman's rituals of mourning take on very different meanings, and they ultimately part. Rodman kisses her hand just before she leaves for a lonely teaching job in Tennessee. The reader has had every reason to suspect that these two will become lovers, yet Woolson disappoints that expectation, although one can think that Miss Bettina will return one day. This hope is engendered by Rodman going to the new owner of her old family home, a Yankee, and requesting cuttings of the tropical vines she planted there. The concepts of "grafting" and memory speak to the ways in which Woolson sees the nation coming together again in an overlapping set of mourning rituals. Additionally, this story creates the thematic that opposites attract, which is extended with circumCaribbean aspects in ensuing tales.

Accordingly, the second story in the collection, "Sister St. Luke," has a fascinating introduction, as we confront three pairs of "Spanish eyes"—the "swarthy Pedro," a "figure in black," and a nun (the title character) on an island near Pelican Reef in the former Spanish territory of Florida. The Minorcan Pedro's role as keeper of the old lighthouse, which was built by the Spanish, remodeled by the British, and then redone by the United States, echoes the "keeper" role of Rodman. Here, as there, what is "kept," the lighthouse, like the Union cemetery, is a marker of history and a symbol of warning against the reefs of the world and of warfare. As readers, we identify with Carrington and Keith, two vacationing Northerners staying at the lighthouse; they are the real focus of the narrator as the story begins, rather than the title's nun. Her vocation is at odds with Pedro's wife, Melvyna, who is not Spanish but rather a fierce Protestant from Vermont who unaccountably accepted Pedro's offer of marriage, since she hates the "lazy tropical island" and the Catholic Church in equal measure.

Woolson signals the link to the Caribbean by referring to the ships that sweep by on their way to the "Queen of the Antilles"—presumably Cuba—

and to the "far Windward and Leeward Islands" (44). Later, a sea-bean is imagined by Keith as adrift from "one of the West Indian islands . . . let us say Miraprovos—a palmy tropical name, bringing up visions of a volcanic mountain, vast cliffs, a tangled gorgeous forest, and the soft lapping wash of tropical seas" (62). This vision is in keeping with Keith's romantic view of nature. Earlier, upon finding Pedro's lost boat in the marsh, he rhapsodizes that "a salt marsh is not complete without . . . an abandoned craft, aged and deserted, aground down the marsh with only its mast rising above the waste," a figure that rehearses the basic elements of the Romantic era's notion of a ruin as a metaphor of the relation between man and nature. However, the mast rising above the waste also mirrors the situation of the virtually abandoned lighthouse. Woolson rehearses early history, stating that the early Spanish "keepers" kept a sharp eye out for "damnable Huguenot" sails, which find their current referent in Pedro's New England Puritan wife. Nor does Woolson forget the rest of the Atlantic, for the waves surge from "the distant African coast." Enslaved Africans, she need not say, occasioned the great war that had devastated the United States.

A sick Sister St. Luke was taken in by Melvyna after the death of the latter's infant, which had elicited sympathy from the nun. Keith and Carrington take the nun on fortifying walks: "They treated her," Woolson tells us, "partly as a child, partly as a gentle being of an inferior race" (49), and they "instruct this unformed, timid mind, to open the blinded eyes . . . to listen to the melodies of nature" (49). Sister Luke stands in for the reader as Carrington and Keith inform her about the strange natural world around her.

Woolson provides a detailed description of the twenty-mile-long island, noting exotic plants, the salt marsh, crabs, jellyfish, gulls, pelicans, hawks and eagles, and varieties of seaweed. The rather sugary narration is ruptured when a tornado hits the island while the men are out at sea. Sister Luke climbs up into the lighthouse's lantern room to look for them—ominously, it is full of dead birds and shattered glass. Seeing her friends clinging to what is left of the reef, their boat destroyed, she fearlessly sets out in the other vessel that the men taught her to sail, to save them. In her notebooks, Woolson made a note of a good plot structure: "To imagine a girl (or woman) doing some extraordinarily brave and heroic action, and then immediately afterward being afraid of a mouse" (Benedict 1930, 126). This story follows this pattern, yet we note the heroism of an "ethnic and religious Other," rather than that of a Southern belle. On the other hand, Sister St. Luke could be read as the "colonized," who has been taught by the "colonizers"—Keith and Carrington—so that the colonizer can profit, which they do, as we shall see.

Part of the story's method is to strip away the habit of the nun. Melvyna removes the wimple, leaving only a veil, and during the jaunt to the ridge and marsh, Keith sweeps that off too. This effort on the part of the men to remake and educate her is quite opposite to the other strand of the story, the uncovering of Spanish history, which is made evident when the Anglos discover the wreck of a Spanish galleon, which has emerged from the eroding sands where Keith sunbathes: "I never imagined I was lying on the bones of this old Spaniard" (63). The story suggests history as palimpsest, for Sister St. Luke in effect is a descendant of the old Spanish sailor, and the Minorcans like Pedro have helped create the paradise that the Anglos gratefully inhabit while their Northern climes are shrouded in snow and ice.[6] The male protagonists' lack of respect for Sister St. Luke's Spanish-inflected English and her Catholicism is part and parcel of the ways in which their "innocent" tourism is an extension of the imperialism the nation was practicing during this same period, which included the posting of Protestant missionaries in Catholic countries in the Caribbean and Latin/South America.

The story in this sense has much in common, in many ways, with Henry James's transnational novel *The American* (1877), in which Claire de Cintré winds up in a Carmelite convent, much to the dismay of the title figure, the Californian Christopher Newman, who has lost her. Claire tells Newman that he does not understand—she will have peace and refuge from her corrupt family. Woolson, similarly, paints a portrait of Sister St. Luke's convent life that is serene and, indeed, beguiling, replete with doves, a charming courtyard, orange trees, and soft music. Sister St. Luke's love for her single life, in fact, is quite reminiscent of Mary Wilkins Freeman's famous story, "A New England Nun" (1891), which similarly embraces the notion that a woman can live quite happily without a man. The convent, here, however, is in the United States, not France, and Woolson makes us accept it as part of the fabric of Florida and part of its complex history. We do indeed see it through "Spanish eyes." But the story also reads Florida through Northern eyes, as Keith and Carrington's "teaching" of Sister St. Luke proceeds from "lessons" they have learned themselves. The actual marriage of Pedro and Melvyna and the impossible one Woolson nevertheless makes us imagine between Keith and Sister St. Luke cross cultural and religious lines and point to the hybrid nature of American history and society.

Today, the South has been transformed yet again by thousands of Mexi-

cans who have come in search of work and, in many cases, a new homeland. They have transformed large areas of Atlanta, Nashville, and Charlotte. Miami's revitalization as a scintillating crossroads of the Caribbean
and, indeed, the hemisphere accelerated with the influx of refugees from
Castro's Cuba and then from other Latin American countries. Latinos/as
have created a dazzling new brand of salsa-seasoned Southern culture. The
Spanish heritage of Florida has had to be rethought yet again, and Woolson's
ruminations help us to see connecting histories rather than rupture. "Sister
St. Luke" concentrates on the Florida coast, but Woolson also finds rich fictional terrain in the interior. The swamp has always been a vital component
of Southern literary expression and also a locus for refuge and freedom in
African American literature. Because the swamp plays a key role in Woolson's novel *East Angels*, her short story "The South Devil" deserves close inspection. It opens at the edge of a burned plantation home, as robust orange
grower Mark Deal and his consumptive stepbrother Carl enjoy the warm December weather.[7] Buildings on their property were burned by Indians, and
the narrator reminds us of the Spanish past, when plantations flourished, yet
"the belief is imbedded in all our Northern hearts that, because the narrow,
sun-bathed State is far away and wild and empty, it is also new and virgin,
like the lands of the West; whereas it is old—the only gray-haired corner
our country holds" (142). Woolson excels in her sublime description of the
cypress-shadowed realm of the surrounding swamp, detailing its myriad
plants and animals but simultaneously creating an atmosphere of menace.
Carl sees beauty in the watery jungle, where Mark sees danger. Both, in
fact, are present, and both represent the sense of beauty and terror that
we locate in the tropical sublime. Mark shoots a moccasin that is about to
strike, but Carl, oblivious, has climbed the swamp canopy because "above[,]
the long moss hangs in fine, silvery lines like spray . . . mixed with . . . air-
plants, sheafs, and bells of scarlet and cream-colored blossoms." Dreaming
or dozing, he falls.[8] Mark, by contrast, necessarily sees nature as his enemy,
as he has to hack his living out of it. Woolson's detailed description of the
moccasins that Mark has to kill repeatedly reveals her revulsion but also her
fascination with snakes. Carl's desire to make music on his violin from the
sounds of the swamp recalls the method of the modern composer Olivier
Messiaen (1908–92), whose *Oiseaux Exotiques* does exactly what Carl wants
to do, but for an orchestra.

The crisis comes when the con-man Schwartz gets Carl drunk, cheats him
at cards, and demands Mark's hidden money. Schwartz then books passage
for Key West, "bound South," where there is "smuggling and illegal trading,

with which the waters of the West Indies are infested. . . . All the harbors, inlets, and lagoons of the West Indies were open. . . . Pursuit would be worse than hopeless" (163). Here, South Florida, and the islands beyond that echo it, extend the negative reading of the swamp as a figuration of the lawlessness of the American tropics in general, but the serpents are men. The reference to the South Atlantic as an outlaw terrain ties it to mythologies of the frontier and has much to do with the tangled webs of imperialistic conquest and piracy—which were quite similar—in the centuries preceding Woolson's tales.

The thin but effective plot of "The South Devil" functions as overlay to Woolson's constant examination of the different terrains of Florida, from the swamps to the palm region, from the shore to the scrub. After Carl dies from consumption, Mark takes his body in a canoe through the swamp. Woolson provides a lush, lyrical description of the flowers, the alligators, the myriad birds, and asks us, "Did Deal appreciate this beauty?" The answer is no, as his New England perspective and the constant memory of his scornful beloved up north keep him from any kind of sympathy.[9] Arthur Hobson Quinn early on noted Woolson's achievement in this tale: "The way [she] establishes the mystical relation between the great swamp and Carl, the young musician who hears the harmonies the swamp sings only to him, and who cannot keep away from it though it may mean death to him, reveals her great power of understanding the relations of place and human character" (1936, 334). There is a third, largely unexamined way of comprehending and reading the swamp. The old huntsman who supplied Mark with game is said to have "rather mixed descent, having probably Spanish, African and Seminole blood in his veins" (165). Later, Woolson refers to him as the "mongrel old hunter" (168). This primordial man represents the transnational South but has no voice, like many other subaltern figures of the culture. His entire life has been an education in reading the lessons of the tropics, but the central characters seemingly ignore his wisdom.[10]

Once again, as in "Sister St. Luke," we have two Northern transplants who react to the swamp in radically different ways; both, however, read it as sublime, in that its power and danger awe and repel Mark, while Carl hears its mysterious music as enchanting and a call to reverie. Further, the sublime refers to "a moment when the ability to apprehend, to know, and to express a thought or an emotion is defeated. Yet through this very defeat, the mind gets a feeling for that which lies beyond thought and language" (Shaw 2006, 3). Carl cries, "The wish that haunts me—drives me—is to write out the beautiful music of the South Devil . . . the song of a Southern swamp" (154). While Carl fails to achieve this goal, the story itself achieves it triumphantly.

The Latina title character of the story "Felipa" is racially marked as "dark-skinned, yellow-eyed," a fisher girl dressed in men's clothing who has seen only three women before in her life. Vacationers Catherine and Christine (yet another pair of Northern tourists) are already enchanted by the paradise they find in Florida, and Felipa seems almost part of the landscape. Indeed, she is compared to the little brown deer. Felipa plays a racial card when she exclaims she likes the silver skin of her new friends better than the brown ones of the Indian and Spanish women she knows. As is usual with Woolson, Felipa's Minorcan relatives are disparaged as "slow-witted . . . part pagan, part Catholic, and wholly ignorant; their minds rarely rose above the level of their orange-trees and their fish-nets" (199). Christine confides to Catherine, "Teach a child like that, and you . . . ruin her happiness" (200), an "ignorance is bliss" argument repeated for centuries in colonial cultures, a convenient twisting of Rousseau's theory of the noble savage.

When Catherine paints Felipa and her dog Drollo, Christine sees an image of "an ugly little girl," although Catherine means it to embody "latent beauty, courage, and a possible great gulf of love" (203). Once again, as in "The South Devil," friends view the same thing very differently, a point Woolson makes over and over; fictions often circle around an object or idea from every possible angle in an effort to make the reader see things in their multiple aspects. Henry James, a strong influence on Woolson, excelled in this method.

In a telling scene, Felipa dresses in borrowed female finery and causes the narrator, Catherine, to laugh. Felipa drags her to the mirror and cries, "You are not pretty either. . . . Look at yourself!" Here the colonizing gaze is reversed, and our perspective as readers shifts as well. This would seem to describe Woolson's method in much of her fiction—to reverse perspectives and to reveal truths, which sometimes are not so pleasant, about dominant culture and perhaps about the reader too. Further, although the other stories often portray men as colonizers of women, here Catherine and Christine fill that role, reversing the pattern. These two women even use language imperiously. The story, though narrated in English, is multilingual, in that the Anglo characters all speak Spanish with Felipa, but when she appears to be learning the English they use to shut her out, they resort to French. These are the imperially imposed languages of the Caribbean.[11]

Ultimately, Felipa, who has adored both Christine and her lover, Edward, turns on the latter when Christine finally gives in to his suit, thereby shutting Felipa out of what she had seen up until then as a trio. In this sense, she strongly resembles young Frankie in Carson McCullers's 1946 Southern drama, *The Member of the Wedding*. However, Filipa, after eating paints and letting a snake bite her, stabs Edward in the arm, then asks to die at Christine's feet, with "her white robe over me" (220). She recovers, however, and the Anglos leave, but not before the old Minorcan grandfather sums things up: "It was two loves, and the stronger thrust the knife" (220). The shock of the ending is that the reader, too, has seen Felipa's love for Edward and Christine as dog-like devotion. It is worth pondering that the great slave revolts of the South and the Caribbean put an end to the myths of the blind devotion of black servants to their white masters.

What are some conclusions we might glean from these Southern stories? First, Woolson, as has often been noted, obviously drew from the Plantation tradition, but with a difference, as she approached it with Northern eyes, and often through those of Northern characters. Second, she was keenly conscious that Florida was a different part of the South, and her constant concern for the Spanish and Indian past, even if she sometimes tended to portray both heritages along with African American culture as racially inferior, speaks to her interest in transnational issues that would result in her move to Italy. Third, her fascination with tropical flora and fauna dictates that we consider her, as no one yet has, as part of the group of Caribbean writers who have made capital out of the basin's ecology. Fourth, these stories depict Northern tourists as colonizers who are often blind to cultural nuance, history, and the profound lessons to be learned from tropical nature. Fifth, the gendered depictions of colonization indict men far more often than women. Sixth, we see in every tale her interest in multiple perspectives and polyphonic dialogics, and often this causes her to point to the interchanges of the Caribbean languages of English, French, and Spanish.

Writing *Rodman the Keeper* was a great rehearsal for Woolson's finest novel. Henry James reserved his highest praise for *East Angels*: "She has expended on her subject stores of just observation and an infinite deal of the true historical spirit" (1930, 10). The novel opens with a meditation on the difference between the tropic, blue skies of Florida and the icy, snow-covered North. A New England visitor, who has the historic Puritan name of Evert Winthrop, basks in the sun, while Edgarda ("Garda") Thorne, one of his hostesses in the South, yearns to experience winter, perhaps because her mother, née Melissa Whiting in New England, has told her about the colder climes. Winthrop has come to Florida after hard work has made him a multimillionaire; hating the cold climes that produced him, he seeks tropical warmth and perhaps a wife. Winthrop was raised alongside his cousin Lanse Harold by his Aunt Katrina Rutherford; eventually Lanse married the handsome, wealthy, but retiring Margaret, but soon tired of her and left for years in Europe. When Mrs. Rutherford and her entourage come for a stay in Gracias-a-Dios, she brings Margaret, who has become her companion, with her. Soon, a vexed relationship between Winthrop and Margaret is resumed (he feels she must have been to blame for the failure of her marriage with his cousin).

The exotic, Spanish aspect of the Thornes' home, East Angels, is signaled by the name of the hamlet, Gracias-a-Dios, and Woolson embroiders on the transatlantic, Caribbean influences on this place throughout the narrative. For example, despite her displacement in Florida, Mrs. Thorne was a staunch Confederate and applauds the British for their sympathy for the Lost Cause: "They were with us—all their best people—as to our patriarchal system for our servants." To her, the Civil War was "the late unhappy contest" (6). The Thornes themselves, however, have been in Florida for generations, originally during the British occupation, and then afterward under the Spanish, when a Thorne married a Duero. Their son also married a Spaniard, which accounts for Garda's doubled ancestry. As Mrs. Thorne puts it, "Edgarda is the portrait of her Spanish grandmother painted in English colors" (7), a clever construction that has embedded within it an assertion of racial purity. The exotic nature of Garda—which is quite removed from the usual type of the belle in Plantation School literature—is reinforced when Winthrop associates her "naturalness" with Native American maidens he encountered out west—whom he did not care for.[12] But Garda, somehow, is different, indicating a shifting racial line running through his categories of exotica. Ruined by the war, the Thornes remain proud. Despite their poverty, they have a "jet-black" retainer, Raquel, a fourth-generation servant who is loyal to the family. Significantly, she and her husband, the gardener, Pablo, both have Spanish names.

Winthrop's tour of East Angels allows Woolson to display her expertise with flora and fauna, as the avenue of live oaks, the cultivated magnolias, the Cherokee roses, the towering palms, the orange arcade, and the lively pet crane, Carlos, all get considered. The house, though decayed, has specifically tropical magnificence, with a pomegranate wainscot and shell masonry construction; it forms a parallelogram around a Spanish courtyard, replete with a balcony with green blinds. Winthrop's introduction is also ours: he discovers "traditions and legend . . . which had nothing to do with Miles Standish . . . [, having] more richness and color and a deeper perspective than that possessed by any of the rather blank . . . American history farther North. . . . Like most New Englanders, he had unconsciously cherished the belief that all there was of historical importance . . . was associated with the Puritans. Thinking of Europe, he muses, 'When Raphael was putting into the background of his pictures those prim, slenderly foliaged trees which he had seen from Perugino's windows in his youth, the Spaniards were exploring this very Florida shore'" (16).

This reference to the Italian Renaissance brings a forceful congruity to privileged art and New World conquest and draws the parameters of the Americas into a different configuration. Further, Winthrop's formulation reflects Woolson's own transatlantic perspective, leaving out only the Midwest of her upbringing. Winthrop sums up: Before the Puritans sailed for New England, "on this Southern shore had been towns and people, governors, soldiers, persecutions, priests" (16). Indeed, as Winthrop learns more about Florida, he declares, "I am ashamed of myself for staring about and applying adjectives in this way to the people and scenery here, as though it were a foreign country; it ought to be as much a part of me, and I of it, as though it were Massachusetts Bay" (83), a sentiment Woolson wants her readers to share.

The dark Adolfo Torres disturbs Mrs. Thorne when he asks to "address" Garda—she tells Winthrop she prefers someone more "Saxon" (144)—like him, of course. The issue of Spanish racial identity seems vexed in the novel. Garda, after all, is half Spanish, and her dark good looks relate her to both her local Latino suitors, Manuel Ruiz, of Patricio Plantation, and Torres, of Giron Plantation. When Garda names these men as leading figures in Gracias, Winthrop exclaims, "A tropical list," to which Garda replies, "I'm tropical myself" (18). Under the surface of this exchange is racial coding, and it is worth remembering that although Garda briefly marries the blond, carefree Anglo-Saxon Lucian Spenser, she ultimately winds up with Torres.

Although the novel eventually focuses in on the frustrated lovers Winthrop and Margaret, Garda in many ways is the fulcrum of the book, and of its transnational thematics. Her grandmother taught her Spanish, and a friend taught her French. Thus Garda has at her command the three languages of the Caribbean and can converse with Torres, born in Cuba but educated in Spain—he speaks only Spanish. Perhaps to reflect the suspected African heritage of Cubans, Woolson describes him as a "dark-skinned youth, with dull black eyes . . . ungainly" (38–39). He is strongly contrasted to the Spanish American Manuel Ruiz, a "remarkably handsome young man" from the neighboring estate; fluent in English, he is compared to a romantic

Italian tenor. The contrasting silence of Torres through most of the novel is compensated for occasionally when Woolson enters into his consciousness or "translates" his conversations with Ruiz, Ruiz's uncle, or Garda. Rather than condemn Woolson for the more usual silence of her Latino characters, we might see this as an example of what Glissant calls "opacity," a mode of representation that represents "a positive value to be opposed to any pseudo-humanist attempt to reduce us to the scale of some universal model" (1989, 162).

The name "Garda" relates to the Spanish verb "guardar": to keep, to put away; to look after; to guard; to observe; and, with the reflexive "se," to be careful not to. Garda, more than any of the other characters, truly "sees" nature and guards against yielding to conventional strictures of her culture(s). As a child of a New Englander, she naturally inherits Emersonian traits of self-reliance and independence, which some readers have translated as egoism and selfishness. But Woolson clearly wants us to see both her and Torres as criollos of the Americas, and it is really not surprising that they wind up with each other at the end, except for the fact that Woolson is an Anglo author who might be expected to constantly "improve" her characters by, as Mrs. Thorne might say, further "Saxonizing" them.[13] Ivanhoe, after all, is attracted to the dark and Jewish Rebecca but marries the fair Saxon Rowena.

Woolson's attempt to instill a new awareness of American identity and hemispheric and Atlantic connectedness is revealed in her arresting metaphor for the shape of Florida: "Stretching like a finger pointing southward from the continent's broad palm into the tropic sea" (26). The most obvious import of this is the link with Cuba and the Antilles, but this finger also points us to a creolized culture, where the polyglot peoples of the Caribbean jostle, interact, and create new hybrid forms of expression and material culture. Her confident approach to this creolized world is quite different from Sidney Lanier's, who asserted that Florida, "by its very peninsular curve whimsically terminates the United States in an interrogation-point" (9), thereby pondering the state's identity—is it Southern, Caribbean, or both? (This is a question still being asked today, as we shall see in the final chapter on Cuban American writers and Miami.) Woolson, however, confidently links the creolized state with the Caribbean.

Edward Kamau Brathwaite defines creolization as "a cultural action— material, psychological, and spiritual—based upon the stimulus/response of individuals within the society of their environment and—as white/black, culturally discrete groups—to each other" (1971, 296). The mixed community of Gracias certainly fits this description. The two churches, Anglican and Catholic, sit side by side, as do their parishioners. Although a perceived ethnic and racial hierarchy prevails, the public occasions of the town involve everyone, as Woolson demonstrates throughout the narrative, liming cultural interdependency, hybridity, and often harmony.

Woolson, as narrator, discourses on the history of Gracias-a-Dios, which was named by grateful Spanish sailors fleeing a storm. She idealizes the original British and the later immigrants from Georgia and the Carolinas, thus elevating the Thornes. But there are more recent newcomers, predators who want to open health resorts, land speculators, builders of canals, and drainers of swamps, who want to rape the landscape and ignore its history, who pronounce "gracias" as "grashus." This line of complaint against "invaders" has frequently been voiced by natives of the Caribbean, and tourists and entrepreneurs had invasive counterparts earlier, in the form of pirates, wreckers, and smugglers who holed up in the Florida Keys.

"Invaders" can be comic. Woolson creates humor out of the contrast of Mrs. Rutherford's Yankee maid and the black servants of the nearby Seminole Inn, who have never seen a white retainer before. Here Woolson inserts more Caribbean color, for Telano, thinking Minerva a witch, shakes a voodoo fetish at her and practices conjure in his room, what Woolson terms "pagan rites." Minerva, by contrast, loves Telano's songs and hums "these bones," thinking the words refer to rheumatism. A fervent Protestant, she is appalled that they are living over an old Franciscan monastery. It is significant that Woolson's ethnic/cross-cultural humor often comes at the expense of the ostensibly "white" figures.

The complications surrounding Garda increase when Lucian Spenser, a sometime engineer and dilettante painter, joins the circle and incites jealously, particularly Manuel's, since he is deemed to be just as handsome, and he is an Anglo—indeed, descended from Virginia's Byrd family. Once again the racial line of distinction emerges, although it is complicated by the fact that Spenser speaks Spanish and takes an interest in Torres. Spenser's blonde good looks and noble ancestry should make him the ideal of the "Saxon" Mrs. Thorne has wished for to supplant Manuel Ruiz. Yet he disquiets her and many others in their set. We mainly see these reservations through the eyes of Winthrop. He seems to know this "type" of dilettante wastrel, who can charm any woman and who is seen by many as a fortune hunter. It also seems likely that Woolson is critiquing the loss of ambition and focus in even the best Southern families after the war. Winthrop and Margaret, usually at odds, share concerns about Lucian's attentions to Garda and agree the locals do not see a threat because it is "an idyllic society" (183). Margaret then reveals she is thinking of taking Garda north for lessons—"as you say, irresponsible people have made their way in here. . . . We shall not be able to keep the place, and Garda, idyllic simply to please ourselves" (184), a colonizing statement condemning the wrong sort of invader.

When Winthrop buys East Angels from Mrs. Thorne (partly as a way to provide income for the impoverished family), Woolson has a tailor-made opportunity to once again provide Spanish-era history, as the deeds are examined. The original grant to Admiral Juan de Duero in 1585 was directly from the Spanish crown and was regranted later by the British sovereign, and on and on, including three raids by buccaneers and several by Indians. And Indians have survived; we learn at one point that Margaret has made a shirt for the Sioux chieftain Spotted Tail, a fact that prompts Winthrop's declaration, "They don't want shirts, they want their land. . . . We should have made them take care of themselves long ago, but we shouldn't have stolen their land" (207), yet we have just learned that Winthrop has not paid much for East Angels.[14] The colonization of Indian lands thus seems a parallel to the Northern colonization of Florida.

We wonder, when the Northern-born Mrs. Thorne lies dying, whether her confession to her fellow Yankee Margaret is partly Woolson's:

"Oh! I so hate and loathe it all—the idle, unrealizing, contented life of this tiresome, idle coast. They amounted to something once, perhaps; but their day is over. . . . Every idea they have is directly contrary to all the principles of the government under which they exist. . . . They think themselves superior. . . . I have stood up for them. . . . The first Spaniards were blue-blooded knights and gentlemen, of course; *they* never worked with their hands. But the Puritans were blacksmiths and ploughmen and wood-choppers . . . but *gentlemen* they were not. . . . [But] in my heart I have always . . . ranked the lowest Puritan far, far above the very finest Spaniard they could muster. . . . They caught the poor Indians and made them work for them; because they imported Human Flesh, they dealt in negro slaves! . . . Their country here will be opened up, improved; but not by them. . . . They will dwindle in numbers, but they will not change. . . . *Could* I leave Garda to that . . . knowing that she would live over there . . . on that forlorn Ruiz plantation, or down the river in that tumble-down house of the Girons—that Manuel with his insufferable airs, or that wooden Torres with his ridiculous pride, would be all she should ever know of life and happiness—my beautiful, beautiful child?" (220–21)

Reading between these lines, however, we see that Mrs. Thorne is guilty of Saxon pride; she provides a moving and extensive list of all the labors and thrifts she has had to endure to make ends meet over the years; however, she does it with the idea that her sacrifices have been exceptional. She never considers that her neighbors—especially the emancipated workers—must have been going through similar trials. She confesses that in her determination to make herself over as a Thorne, "I even swallowed slavery—I, a New England girl . . . abolitionist to the core! . . . I covered every inch of myself with a southern skin. But if any one thinks that it was easy or pleasant, let him try" (224). We note, too, how skillfully Woolson lards this address with a mini-history of Florida and the circumCaribbean.

Poor whites of the current day get their due as well. In Woolson's long, lyrical description of the pine barrens Winthrop favors for his canters, she inserts a "cracker" for the first time, "astride his sorry pony. . . . Packed into the two-wheeled cart behind him, all his family, with their strange clay-colored complexions and sunburnt light hair, would stare. . . . They were a gentle, mummy-like people, too indolent even to wonder why a stranger should wish to know [directions]" (274). At least this reader wonders at the way Woolson constantly applies the word "indolent" to most of the residents of Florida, including Latinos, blacks, whites, and Indians, when her wealthy Northern main characters, who might expend a tourist's energy on walks and canters, are hardly fountains of industry. She was far from alone in employing this kind of depiction, however. Edward King's *Great South* not only exclaimed over the failure of the local whites to exploit the vast mineral and agricultural potential of the region, but also included many engravings of slack-jawed, simianized "crackers" alongside similarly caricatured African Americans (Greeson 2006, 503–4).[15] We noticed the same attitude on the part of U.S. military officers surveying a conquered Mexico, whose people similarly have supposedly been poor husbandrymen of a potentially prosperous land, and similar descriptions of natives of the Caribbean have been employed for centuries. Why? As Mary Louise Pratt has demonstrated, a desire for, and implementation of, the systemization of nature was a core component of Western colonization of the New World (1992, 36), and the advance of Northern capital and investment in the Reconstruction South operated similarly.[16] This convenient classification of natives as indolent and ignorant has an ancient pedigree in hemispheric history, particularly in regard to the appropriation of Native American lands.

Woolson creates yet another shock when Lanse Harold, Margaret's estranged husband, finally appears, after adulterous years in Rome. Winthrop, in love with Margaret, meets her husband in the little post office on the pier at St. John's River. Lanse is sitting in the "United States" chair. This location suggests the transatlantic correspondence and travel that dominates the novel and creates the suggestion of a crossroads, one that was surely there for centuries, for the Indians, the Spanish, the frontiersmen, and now for the modern folk who are changing the face of the state and the South after the war. Winthrop's arrival on the *Hernando* (named after de Soto) and the coonskin-wearing postmaster suggest this rich past, but the latter's archaic dress also contrasts sharply with the present. Amazingly, rather than present Lanse as a European American, Woolson has him take Winthrop out in a birchbark canoe into an inlet, where old Joe, born in Africa, shows them a huge rattlesnake and alligator he has killed. Moored among the reptiles, Lanse tells the story of his rupture with Margaret years before, revealing his adulterous, base conduct and Margaret's saintly silence. We understand why Woolson chose this strange place for the confession, for a young black boy comes by with the young white girl he is babysitting. When a moccasin falls into their boat, Lanse saves them but is bitten and paralyzed as a result, necessitating reunion with Margaret. His heroism partly redeems Lanse's sins but also results in his deserved retribution.

When Margaret and Winthrop must brave a storm to canoe into the swamp to find the missing Lanse, old Rose, terrified, cries out: "Please missy, *no*. Not inter de Munloons in der *night, no! Ghosessess dar!*" (464). She and Dinah sing a spiritual as Winthrop and Margaret push off: "Didn't my Lord delibber Dan-yel, Dan-yel?" These pronouncements create a gothic frisson but at the same time Africanize the swamp/jungle, as was the case in descriptions of voyages up the Oklawaha. This desperate and dangerous canoe trip into the heart of the swamp brings out the full arsenal of Woolson's tropical colors, as she sketches a scene not really Southern but more Caribbean, in its tangled vegetation, strange beauties, and deadly reptilian dangers.

The tropical sublime, with its serpentine shapes, dark and twisting waterways, tangled vegetation, and superabundant, wildly variegated foliage (often heavily scented), is the product of vegetable and animal sexuality and exudes powerful metaphors of human desire. Freud argued for the centrality of the repressed in human consciousness, and the swamp has always functioned as a psychological symbol of this in fiction. It has also, however, simultaneously been seen as a refuge and a site for freedom, as in the Maroon communities of escaped slaves, a motif that registers powerfully in Harriet Beecher Stowe's *Uncle Tom's Cabin* and *Dred: A Tale of the Dismal Swamp*, but also in many slave narratives and in fiction spun out of the Haitian Revolution.[17] Margaret and Evert are looking for a "clear path" through the swamp, but also for a moral one. This is nothing new; in addition to functioning as a site for reverie and meditation, the swamp has always been the locale for numerous love stories, where the struggle against an extravagant, beautiful, dangerous, and seductive environment offers a metaphor for the emotions within them. It is no accident that the search for Margaret's husband in the nocturnal world of the tropical swamp waters engenders the most intimate scenes between her and Winthrop.[18] Henry James commented on Woolson's "remarkably fine" interlude: "The picture of their paddling the boat by torchlight into the reaches of the river, more or less smothered in the pestilential jungle, with the personal drama, in the unnatural place, reaching an acute stage between them—this whole episode is in a high degree vivid, strange, and powerful" (1920, 14), understanding, of course, that the tortured and gigantic outgrowths of the terrain were an expression of the powerful emotions that the two characters must, and do, contain.

The scene in the swamp brings to a climax the repressed love that Margaret has had for Evert for years, which he secretly reciprocates. The journey also brings them into cooperation for once; he paddles, she navigates, as she knows the terrain from her earlier visits with Lanse.[19] But their close confinement in the boat, she moistening his head with a bit of her lace, is mimicked as they enter a luxuriantly flowered and overpoweringly fragrant narrow channel, so intoxicating that Margaret faints: "The atmosphere became so heavy that they could taste the perfume in their mouths" (472). Ultimately, however, this heated scene must yield to renunciation. Later, Lanse partially recovers from his accident and returns to his mistress in Italy. Eventually his infirmity returns, paralyzing him from the waist down. This leads him to return, and he demands that Margaret nurse him, which she dutifully does. The lack of a sexual relation between the couple ironically underlines the repression of what Margaret yearns for, sexual union with Evert. Her ultimate situation, then, does indeed accord with a nun-like existence; also recall that we have exactly that life portrayed in "Sister St. Luke" but with a much different perspective.

In her fiction, Woolson's refusal to situate a bounded identity for the South—in terms either of its citizens or its topography—brings her in congruence with our age of postnational studies of the Americas. As Glissant has stated, "The struggle against a single History for the cross-fertilization of histories means repossessing both a true sense of one's time and identity: proposing in an unprecedented way a revaluation of power" (1989, 93). While it would be an overstatement to say that Woolson shared this agenda, in her own way she let her strong feeling for Florida, the Caribbean, and their shared landscapes, seascapes, folkways, climate, and history guide her to a surprisingly broad vision of a transnational realm, indeed validating her conception of Florida as a finger pointing southward, a proleptic gesture fraught with the possibilities and problems of our complicated present.

Lafcadio Hearn's Caribbean Idyll

When Hearn moved to St. Pierre in 1887, the city seemed familiar to him, and no wonder—Hearn had always associated New Orleans with the Caribbean. During his early years in the Crescent City, he wrote a study of the similarities and differences between Louisiana dialect and Martinique Creole (McWilliams 1946, 100). His 1877 essay "At the Gate of the Tropics" situated New Orleans as portal to all that was South of the South. But he also saw the Crescent City as linked to many of the world's other great ports as he surveyed the ships in the harbor: "Steamers, with East Indian names, that have been to Calcutta and Bombay; strong-bodied vessels from Norway . . . tight looking packets from English ports; traders under German, Dutch, Italian, French and Spanish flags . . . shapely craft from West Indian harbors" (*Inventing*, 2001, 7). Hearn had friends in New Orleans who had migrated from the Caribbean, including the bookseller Julien, whose Creole parents fled the Saint Domingue revolution, and Hearn sat for hours, entranced by Julien's tales of the islands (Tinker 1925, 108). He also became fascinated by the Creole or "gombo" language of black New Orleanians and began to study it with his intellectual friends Dr. William Henry, Dr. Alfred Mercier, Louis Claudel, and Professor Charles Gayrarré, leading to his book of Creole proverbs, *Gombo Zhèbes* (1885).[20] Because many of these expressions were also common in the Antilles, they proved invaluable to Hearn during his time there.[21]

The proud white Creole families Hearn met would have been scandalized at his account of their mixing with other people. He wrote to his Cincinnati friend, the music critic Henry Edward Krehbiel, in 1878 of these "white" families: "Blending with Creole immigrants from the Canaries, Martinique, and San Domingo . . . their characteristics offer an interesting topic, and the bastard offspring of the miscegenated French and African, or Spanish and African, dialects called Creole offer pretty peculiarities. . . . Creole music is mostly negro music. . . . There could neither have been Creole patois nor Creole melodies but for the French and Spanish blooded slaves of Louisiana and the Antilles" (Bisland 1906, 1:188–89).

Hearn's interest in Creole culture, and particularly in the African components of its music, was vastly increased through his growing friendship with the celebrated writer George Washington Cable (1844–1925), who at the time of their meeting, had yet to publish his collection of New Orleans stories, *Old Creole Days* (1879). These two men, both of short stature, made frequent collecting excursions to various communities, particularly those of Creoles of color. Cable would write down the music, Hearn the words. Cable showed Hearn the romance of the gorgeous city. Another friend, the writer/priest Adrien Rouquette, who had lived in France but also among Louisiana's Native Americans, acquainted Hearn with the area's lush forests and swamps and regaled him with native tales. Rouquette, whose fanciful poems (especially *La Nouvelle Atala*) were inspired by Chateaubriand (particularly *Atala*), was, like Hearn, an aficionado of French literature, which operated as a kind of filter for his views of Louisiana.

These two writers thus became guides for Hearn to the city and the country and to myriad forms of folk cultures. But the musical elements of the region most excited him, and he knew his friend Krehbiel would be vitally interested in the Creole tunes he and Cable were uncovering. He had become close to Krehbiel when both of them wrote for Cincinnati papers, and he shared with him his interest in Creole cultures (especially music) and folklore of all types, including African American. Krehbiel respected Hearn's intellect and took his advice to leave the Midwest to try his fortunes in the East, eventually becoming music critic and reporter for the *New York Tribune,* and Hearn always tried to see him when he was in New York City.[22] Hearn wrote more letters to Krehbiel than to anyone else, and his increasingly combative tone stemmed from underlying moral differences between the two men. Krehbiel, a Protestant minister's son, was appalled by Hearn's morbidity and eroticism, while Hearn deplored his friend's "gothic" prudery, which seemed to detest beauty. This impasse proved useful, however, as Hearn went to great lengths to try to make Krehbiel "see" and also *feel* things the way he did, which helped Hearn to develop his language of the tropical sublime.

Hearn's interest in Creole music naturally included the work of the composer Louis Moreau Gottschalk (1829–69), who had traveled widely in the Caribbean and used its musical traditions in his compositions. Hearn wrote several articles on Gottschalk and appreciated his efforts at hemispheric musical creation. He was aware that the composer, like him, had noted similarities between the Afro cultures of the coastal South and the Caribbean. He told Krehbiel that Gottschalk "found the theme for his Bamboula in Louisiana—*Quand patate est chinte,* etc.—and made a miracle out of it" (Bisland 1906, 1:337).[23]

In 1877, Hearn had written a piece on "Los Criollos" that shows us his growing knowledge of the Antilles he would soon inhabit:

> The Creoles of the Antilles seem to have felt more pride in the lin-
> guistic curiosities of their native isles than the Creoles of Louisiana
> have. . . . In Trinidad fine collections of Creole legends and proverbs
> have been made, and an excellent grammar of the dialect published;
> in Martinique, hymn books, *paroissiens,* and other works are printed in
> Creole; the fables of La Fontaine and many popular French fairy tales
> have found Creole translators in the West Indies, while several remark-
> able pamphlets upon the history and construction of the West-Indian
> dialects are cited in Parisian catalogues of linguistic publications. But
> it was not until the French publishers of *Mélusine* showed themselves
> anxious to cull the flora of Louisiana Creole that the Creole themselves
> made any attempt to collect them. Happily the romantic interest
> excited throughout the country by George Cable's works stimulated
> research. (*Inventing,* 2001, 38)

Hearn's consciousness of this literary "vogue" no doubt assured him that there would be material of this nature worth mining in Martinique.

Hearn was also aware of the many connections between New Orleans and Cuba. His account of the famous fencing master Pepe Llula (who had served on slave ships from Africa to the Caribbean as a youth) mentions the lat-ter's employment in the trade between the Crescent City and Havana, and, more important, Llula's service to the Spanish ambassador, whose life was endangered by the passion excited in the city by the Narciso Lopez expedi-tions of the 1850s that we examined in an earlier chapter. Hearn situates New Orleans as the long-existing center of filibustering. Siding with Spain, Llula defied the Cuban insurgents of the 1860s, through posters, challenges, and successful duels, making him a great hero in Havana and Madrid. Cuban ladies wove a portrait of Llula for him with their own hair (*Inventing,* 2001, 56–57).[24]

Hearn viewed the Creole cultures of New Orleans and the Caribbean as profoundly "Latin." Writing to Krehbiel in 1880, he declared that "now I am with the Latin; I live in a Latin city;—I seldom hear the English tongue ex-cept when I enter the office. . . . I see beauty here all around me,—a strange, tropical, intoxicating beauty. . . . Were I to tell you all that I have seen and heard in these years in this enchanted City of Dreams you would verily deem me mad rather than morbid" (Bisland 1906, 1:217–18).

Yet Hearn also practiced literary realism in his work. Many times, in his reportage and fiction alike, he would describe, in gruesome detail, the effects of fever on ravaged bodies, the stench of sewers, the decay of ruins and dead bodies. Allied with these perceptions was Hearn's recurring desire to escape imprisoning cities, even New Orleans. Writing Joseph Tunison in 1889 while unhappily visiting New York, Hearn confided: "I want to get back among the monkeys and the parrots, under a violet sky among green peaks and an eternally lilac and lukewarm sea, —where clothing is superfluous. . . . Civilization is a hideous thing. Blessed is savagery! Surely a palm 200 feet high is a finer thing in the natural order than seventy times seven New Yorks" (Bisland 1906, 1:444).

Yet nature, too, he knew, was full of grim realities as well, despite its beauties, which often concealed underlying violence. It was the sea, above all, that offered a fundamental sign of nature's twinned sublime beauty and brutality. He wrote to his friend Matas from Grand Isle: "I wait for the poet's Pentecost—the inspiration of nature, the descent of the tongues of fire . . . when the wild skies brighten, and the sun of the Mexican gulf reappears . . . with hymns of wind and sea, and the prayers of birds" (Nishizaki 1956, 87). On another occasion, sounding like the Melville of *Moby-Dick* and "The Encantadas," he spoke of schools of fish being devoured by porpoises and sharks, and above them, in the "murderous bands of air—squadrons of shrieking gulls, and wheeling eagles, and fish-hawks. . . . The birds feed upon the eyes only . . . enormous slaughter! —appalling cruelty! destruction symbolizing grimly the great contests of human life in which the fiercest and strongest and swiftest survive to exemplify Nature's mystic and merciless law" (*An American Miscellany*, 1925, 56–57), a thrilling but also appalling example of the tropical sublime's fascination with nature's raw feeding frenzies and the terror it inspires. Like European theorists of the sublime, Hearn also found it in the ocean's opposite, mountains, which evoke the melancholia lurking in the sublime perspective: "The blue multitude of the peaks, the perpetual telling of Nature's eternal youth . . . something like the fullness of a great grief begins to weigh at the heart. . . . For all this astonishment, of beauty, all this majesty of light and form and color, will surely endure" (227).[25]

Hearn's gaze on sublime scenes, however, was peculiar; a childhood accident cost him the sight of his left eye, which became disfigured. His "good" eye required spectacles, and he never had good vision (Cott 1990, 28, 29). Because of his partial blindness, Hearn was keenly aware of the visual, in every dimension. His first job at the *New Orleans Item* led him to illustrate his pieces with graphic and compelling woodcuts of street vendors, laundresses, exotic plants, and tombstones, sometimes drawing faces right from Honoré Daumier. He gained this visual and descriptive ability from the "exposé" pieces he wrote for newspapers in Cincinnati, and his nocturnal wanderings with questionable companions testify to his taste for the morbid, bizarre, and grotesque, which are the flip side of his desire for strange beauty, the exotic, and the sensual. Hearn called these pieces "fantastics," describing them to Krehbiel as his "impressions of the strange life of New Orleans" (Bisland 1906, 1:221). His taste for such things found satisfaction for a time in the Crescent City, but he yearned for more intensity, which he felt he would find "South of the South" in the Caribbean, whose maritime colors and scenes he had tasted in Louisiana's outlying isles and whose splendors were less adulterated by the detritus of modern urban life.

After the success of his first novel, *Chita*, gave Hearn a momentary prosperity, he set out for the Antilles, hoping to sell resultant travel articles to his new friend Henry Alden, the editor of *Harper's*, who had accepted *Chita*. An excited Hearn wrote to a friend, "In Trinidad I can see South American flora in all their splendor. . . . I can get good chances to study those Creole types which are so closely allied to our own" (cited in Elizabeth Stevenson 1961, 154). Hearn was particularly eager to visit Martinique, as he had spent long hours hearing about the island from his friend Leona Queyrouze's Martinican maid, Marie (Elizabeth Stevenson 1961, 155). Once in St. Pierre, he knew he had found what he was looking for. Writing to Krehbiel, he enthused: "For romantic material the West Indies offer an unparalleled field of research. . . . The ground is absolutely untilled, and it is not in the least likely that anybody in the shape of a Creole is ever going to till it" (Bisland 1906, 1:410).[26]

Two Years in the French West Indies

Hearn begins *Two Years in the French West Indies* (1890), by indicating that he himself is the object of scrutiny. On the boat bound for Martinique, he feels the gaze of "a pair of peculiarly luminous black eyes—creole eyes. Evidently a West Indian" (1). And, indeed, by living under the gaze of the West Indians, Hearn comes to see himself anew, as he gradually acquires a new vision of the tropics, one he had originally encountered through the screen of various stereotypes, like those "creole eyes." As his boat nears the Virgin

Islands in October 1887, he keeps ruminating on the various colors of blue, matching them against what he has heard about the fabled hue of the waters. On the fourth day he awakens "unspeakably lazy;—this must be the West Indian languor" (2). His fellow passengers indulge in similarly conventional daydreams of what lies before them: "pleasant tempting things,—tropical fruits, tropical beverages, tropical mountain breezes, tropical women. . . . It is a time for dreams" (3).[27]

The enchantment of the tropics was always, for Hearn, partly caused by what he called "Azure Psychology." In an essay by that title that he wrote in Japan, he looked back on his first voyage to the Caribbean and the astonishment he felt at the blue of the Gulf Stream and the overarching sky. The color was "a magical splendor that made me doubt my senses—a flaming azure. . . . A million summer skies had been condensed into pure fluid color" (1923). For Hearn, blue is the breath of the planet, suggesting altitude, vastness, profundity; it is, in short, the color of the sublime (a word he does not use). But it also suggests space in time, for it is the color of "distance and vagueness" (*Exotics*, 1905, 232). As Yi-Fu Tuan observes, such "landscape pictures" permit us to "organize visual elements into a dramatic spatio-temporal structure" (1997, 123), as Hearn does here.

Hearn was a notorious womanizer who delighted in women of color. In Cincinnati, he had been briefly married to a beautiful ex-slave, Alethea "Mattie" Foley, and he indulged his carnal appetite freely during his years in New Orleans, making frequent nighttime visits to brothels and opium dens with his landlady's ne'er-do well nephew, a hulking Irishman, Denny Corcoran, a 300-pound "bodyguard" to the diminutive Hearn. Corcoran, fleeing the law, had taken refuge in the West Indies, and he intrigued Hearn with tales of the dusky beauties of the island women (Tinker 1925, 212–13).[28]

The sublime allure of the tropics, in Florida and in the Caribbean, always floats on hidden dangers. Approaching land, Hearn's ship attracts naked black boys, who swim from shore to dive for tossed coins, despite the danger of sharks under the waves. There is also, Hearn tells us, the menace of sunken reefs. Landside, the charming Spanish ruins seen from the boat (which recalls the ruins explored in *East Angels*) were, Hearn tells us, the site of a slave revolt in 1878. Later, he muses dreamily on the fantastic variety and alluring mystery of the tropical tangle of the island's forest but soon punctures the mood by warning: "To enter these green abysses without a guide were folly. . . . Nature is dangerous here. . . . There are trees distilling venom, there are plants that have fangs; there are perfumes that affect the brain, there are cold green creepers whose touch blisters flesh like fire; while in all the recesses and the shadows is a swarm of unfamiliar life, beautiful or hideous, —insect, reptile, bird, —interwarring, devouring, preying" (34), especially the deadly fer-de-lance, which seems to be everywhere in the jungle. This advice echoes the lesson of the swamp journey in *East Angels*, which would have indeed been folly if Margaret had not been able to function as a guide. Here Hearn leaves romanticism behind in favor of graphic gothic description of both the snake and the results of its venom.

This fear of serpents heightens Hearn's dread of the seemingly impenetrable jungle; he finds a way to examine its flora safely, however, in the secure realm of the neglected but still lovely Jardin des Plantes, which had parallels in European cities. Created during the French revolutionary period, the garden's statue of Martinique's native daughter, Napoleon's Empress Josephine, inspires Hearn's romantic reveries on her transatlantic history, but the surrounding ordered beds prompt respect for the regimenting concepts of the French botanists. Musing under the cathedral-like canopy of huge trees, Hearn marvels at the singular impression of awe tropical nature projects, an example of his sense of the tropical sublime; he also notes the omnipresent odor of decay, musing that "where Nature is most puissant to charm, there also is she mightiest to destroy" (39), a belief that keeps him from penetrating the actual jungle, with its fer-de-lance.[29]

We note here, as well, the juncture of fascination and dread that seems emblematic of the Western gaze on the tropical landscape. In 1887, Hearn wrote that myopia like his can heighten artistic sensibility: moreover, his damaged sight gave him a peculiarly individual notion of the sublime. In "Artistic Value of Myopia," he declared that good eyesight may be a hindrance to those feelings of sublimity that exalt the poetic imagination:

The more visible the details of a large object—a mountain, a tower, a forest-wall—the less grand and impressive that object. The more apparently uniform the mass, the larger it seems to loom; the vaguer a shadow space, the deeper it appears. An impression of weirdness—such as that obtainable in a Louisiana or Florida swamp-forest, or, much more, in those primeval and impenetrable forests-deeps described so powerfully by Humboldt—is stronger in proportion to the spectator's indifference to lesser detail. . . . There is no possibility of mysterious attraction in wooded deeps or mountain recesses for the eye that, like the eye of the hawk, pierces shadows and can note the separate quiver of each leaf. (*Editorials*, 1926, 344–45)

He quotes a poem by Andrew Lang to make his point: "'Try spectacles,' one's friends intone; / 'You'll see the world correctly through them.' / But I have visions of my own /And not for worlds would I undo them!" And once again, he cites Baudelaire approvingly, who, in his "Curiosités Esthétiques," had claimed that the greatest schools of painting "were evolved among hazy surroundings—Dutch fogs, Venetian mists, and the vapors of Italian marsh lands" (*Editorials,* 347).[30] History can be presented. Nature and humanity, however, prove illusive and must often only be suggested. Musing on these subjects, Srinivas Aravamudan steers us to Jean-François Lyotard's notion of the "unpresentable in presentation itself," which he associates with Edmund Burke's concept of the sublime, a conjoining of fear and obscurity that was based in concepts of dread, monstrosity, and coercion. Aravamudan builds on Michel Foucault's assertion that the two great mythological experiences for eighteenth-century philosophers were travelers seeing new sights in strange lands and fables of blind men being made to see (1999, 191). The two strands are powerfully interconnected by the sight-impaired Hearn, an indefatigable traveler who delighted in the strange, the exotic, the gigantic, the terrifying.[31] Hearn's insistence on these "visions of his own" evinces a preference for the fantastic, which is another way of saying the obscure, and all this presupposes a predilection for the sublime vision.[32]

Most of the first part of *Two Years in the West Indies* consists of Hearn's leisurely exploration of other islands of the Lesser Antilles. Again and again, he compares and contrasts varying tropical locales and muses on their interconnections. Port of Spain, Trinidad, is "somewhat Spanish looking—a little like St. Pierre, a little like New Orleans" ([1890] 2001, 59). In Georgetown, Demerara, he marvels at the ventilated rooms, the latticed windows, the shaded porches and balconies, which, he theorizes, may well have been designed by British colonizers who had first spent time in India. Trinidad's "coolies" (immigrant workers from India) fascinate and appall Hearn. Although he admires the women's sensuality, he declares that "under the dark fixed frown [of Indians] the eye glitters like a serpent" (54). His racial biases emerge forcefully as he views the seemingly threatening throngs of Trinidad: "As you pass through the black crowd upon the wharf [one sees] a population as nearly African as that of Barbadoes. . . . When a white face does appear . . . under . . . an Indian helmet . . . the physiognomy of one used to command . . . this bearded English visage takes something of heroic relief;—one feels, in a totally novel way, the dignity of a white skin" (60). This kind of racial panic does not emerge in Hearn in Martinique, where the many gradations of color keep him from feeling submerged in pure blackness. Homi Bhabha has observed that "the object of colonial discourse is to construe the colonized as a population of degenerate types on the basis of racial origin, in order to justify conquest and to establish systems of administration and instruction" (1994, 70), and we see elements of this in Hearn's colonizing gaze.

Concluding his initial circuit of the Lesser Antilles, Hearn sailed to New York, where he was overjoyed by the sale of his travel accounts to *Harper's* for $700. Splurging on a camera that cost $106, he bought a one-way ticket back to St. Pierre, revitalized by the realization that his love for the tropics could possibly lead to financial security through further reportage, which became *Two Years in the French West Indies*. In that account, bound back to Martinique, Hearn deplores the increasing loss of whites in the islands, which depletes the Caucasian army needed for "ethnic struggle" (72). Emancipation, he makes plain, has ruined local agriculture (particularly sugar production), and new battles loom between black islanders and mixed races, "beautiful fruit-colored populations." The mutual hatreds between these groups, coupled with the black citizens' superior ability to thrive in the oppressive climate, prompts Hearn to predict a future of "universal blackness . . . perhaps universal savagery" (73–74).

At other points, Hearn shifts from racial panic to bemoan the lost economic potential of the islands; in Martinique, for instance, some beaches have sands composed 90 percent of steel ore, yet Western industries have been frightened away, Hearn claims, by universal suffrage and the high cost of marine transport (99). Similarly, the rough seas around Grand Anse preclude profitable shipping, and planters on that coast are often ruined by an inability to get crops to the safe harbor of St. Pierre, since no one has taken the initiative to build a railroad across the island. Further, the decline of agriculture in general has caused the islands to become dependent on imported food: "The island does not feed itself: cattle, salt, meats, hams, lard, flour, cheese, dried fish all come from abroad, — particularly from America" (229). The natives associate the sound of a tin can opening—"bom"—with the United States, and call the U.S. vessels "bom-ships."

Hearn uses these vessels as a departure point for an inset story of two black boys, Stéphane and Maximilien, who join their peers in the sea to dive for gold coins thrown out by wealthy passengers. The boys' craft is made from a U.S. lard-box, and a strong current takes them far out to sea, where they are marooned for days. Eventually, they pass out. Maximilien is revived on the deck of the *Rio de Janeiro* with the dead Stéphane beside him, while white voices murmur "poor little devils" (241). The tale is quite drawn out and contains much Creole, which Hearn unobtrusively translates for the reader. In its naturalism and situation, the tale recalls Stephen Crane's masterful "The Open Boat" (1897), especially when Maximilien thinks about a cricket he once saw on a bark chip, drifting out with the tide. "Then he understood that he himself was the cricket,—still alive. But some boy had found him and pulled off his legs" (his own are seemingly immobile at this point) (240). Hearn perhaps inserts this fable of the quest for imperial gold, mounted in a boat that represents the detritus of colonial oppression, as a tragic indictment of capitalist corruption of native youths.

These opening sketches, which were originally separate from the longer study of Martinique, were intended by Hearn to be "Impressionist work,—always keeping to my dream of *poetical prose*." He expected to concentrate on tropical foliage in Trinidad, then to focus on "Creole types . . . which are so closely allied to our own" (Bisland 1906, 1:382–83). Readers who know the history of the island must feel a sense of poignancy as Hearn describes his impressions of the power and majesty of Mt. Pelée and the town it overshadows, the charming St. Pierre, "the quaintest, queerest, and the prettiest . . . among West Indian cities." In 1902, the volcano erupted with terrific force, instantly destroying the town and 30,000 inhabitants.[33] In a particularly ironic passage, Hearn remarks on the azure light that tints everything, comparing it to the pale colors Coomans used in his Pompeiian studies (28). Even more piercing is Hearn's musing on the St. Pierre cemetery: "Some day there may be a great change in the little city of St. Pierre—there may be less money and less zeal and less remembrance of the lost. . . . The green host [the jungle vegetation] will move down unopposed" (29). Indeed, chapter 7 of the book is entirely devoted to La Pelée, and to an overt question: "Is the great volcano dead? . . . Nobody knows. . . . For the moment[,] it appears to sleep" (202).[34] In the shadow of the volcano cliffs originally formed by eruptions, "the Confederate cruiser *Alabama* once hid herself, as a fish hides in the shadow of a rock, and escaped from her pursuer the *Iroquois*," a link between the islands and the U.S. South, where legends like that of the devious *Alabama*, a famous Confederate gunboat, offered solace for the overall defeat.

Hearn marvels at the many religious statues but also claims that the black bell ringers of the churches create an African feeling, and everywhere in the ensuing narrative we find evidence of both African retentions and the synthesis of diasporic culture with European heritage, particularly in religion. Hearn had seen exactly such hybridity in New Orleans, which had been "re-Africanized" by the many black Haitians who migrated there after the revolution; the bell ringers at St. Louis Cathedral had also been black.[35]

Not surprisingly, Hearn "reads" St. Pierre from a Louisianan perspective: "The architecture is quite old; it is seventeenth century, probably; and it reminds one a great deal of that characterizing the antiquated French Quarter of New Orleans." On the other hand, although he had initially loved the Crescent City—largely because of its "tropical" color, people, foliage and weather—he had eventually come to hate it as it had become increasingly urban, more and more like Hearn's least favorite city, New York. St. Pierre took him back to his early days in New Orleans, to a feeling of "primitive" simplicity and freshness. As he stated, the climate was "heaven on earth, no thieves, no roughs, no snobs; everything primitive and morally pure" (cited in Kinnard 1912, 152).[36]

In keeping with his interbraiding of the primitive and the exotic, Hearn constantly "orientalizes" the islands, as in, "A population fantastic, astonishing—a population of the Arabian Nights. It is many-colored; but the general dominant tint, is yellow, like that of the town itself—yellow in the interblending of all the hues characterizing *mulâtresse, capresse, griffe, quarteronne, métisse, chabine*. . . . You are among a people of half breeds,—the finest mixed race of the West Indies . . . fine warm tints of this tropical flesh . . . those rich costumes Nature gives to her nearest of kin and her dearest,—her honey-lovers" (20–24).[37] Intoxicated by the rush of colors he sees in the people, the flowers, and especially the dress and jewelry of the women, he declares that they "suggest the Orient," while the "full-dress coiffure . . . is so strikingly Eastern that one might be tempted to believe it was first introduced into the colony by some Mohammedan slave" (20). So struck was Hearn by this apparition, that he used a portrait of a *métisse* wearing this elaborate headdress for his frontispiece.[38]

Speaking directly on the concept of tropical beauty in an 1888 letter to George M. Gould written in St. Pierre, Hearn remarked: "When you think of tropical Nature as cruel and splendid, like a leopard, I fancy the Orient, which is tropical largely, dominates the idea. Humanity has a great beauty in these tropics, a great charm,—that of childishness, and the goodness of childishness. As for the mysterious Nature . . . it was understood by the ancient Mexicans, whose goddess of flowers, Coatlicue, was robed in a robe of serpents interwoven. She is rich in death as in life, this Nature, and lavish of both. I would love her; but I fear she is an enemy of the mind,—a hater of mental effort" (Bisland 1906, 1:436).[39]

On other occasions, Hearn would speak more directly on the mixture of the races, which characterized both Creole New Orleans and Martinique. In 1890, the same year that *Two Years* appeared, he published an essay in *Cosmopolitan*, "A Study of the Half-Breed Races in the West Indies," wherein he claims that the mixed races of the islands had been locked in a struggle "to become white," and that the mulattoes born of slavery had become an "all-powerful element of discord, and finally appeared in the rôle of an enemy of whites and blacks alike—forcing the parent races apart forever. By its superior intelligence and cunning, it was able to illuminate the simple minds of the blacks as to the injustice of their situation, and separate them morally from their owners by destroying the credulous idea of duty and that artificial sentiment of filial affection which the old patriarchal system had cultivated." And yet he does see that the hatred of the mulattoes stemmed from the horrors of slavery: "Its aggressive vice represented only the consequence of crime avenging the crime in Nature's way." Moreover, as always in the Caribbean, these racial conundrums find reference to Haiti: "Long before the great insurrection of Santo Domingo, far-seeing writers had predicted the ruin of the colony by the vengeance of its half-breeds. Old West Indian histories and narratives of travel teem with prophecies against them, and warnings of their future advent to power as a calamity" ("Study," 1925, 221–22).[40] But he reports that after the revolution, blacks in Haiti "exterminated" mulattoes, knowing that a two-caste system would otherwise evolve; he refuses to indict the massacres ordered by Dessalines, as blacks had no reason to love civilization and only wanted to restore an "African mode of life." According to Hearn, Martinique was spared Haiti's fate only by the takeover of the island by the British in 1794. Although they restored slavery, they maintained order and kept the Haitian Revolution from infecting the island. After the French return to Martinique, slavery is abolished and the mulattoes take control and rule over blacks while keeping whites out of positions of power.

Glissant has remarked that written elitist narratives of the Antilles—originally that of the colonists and plantation owners but then of the travelers to the islands (like Hearn)—sought to fantasize legitimacy: "One condition of the process was that the conventional landscape be pushed to extremes—the gentleness and beauty of it. . . . There is something of an involuntary Parnassus in the novels and pamphlets written by colonists of Santo Domingo and Martinique; the same propensity to blot out the shudders of life, that is the turbulent realities of the Plantation, beneath the conventional splendor of scenery" (1990, 70). Hearn's years in Martinique were in this sense doubled; much of the "turbulent" colonial plantation life was indeed ignored in his work. However, he himself *lived* in and for the "shudders" of life, and they eventually find their way into his work, although perhaps not in terms of economic oppression. "Shudders" were also located by Hearn in the African religions of New Orleans and Martinique.[41]

Two Years reminds one constantly of prior accounts of life in the tropics, such as Melville's *Typee*, in which the author delights in providing ornate inventories of fruits, flora, sunsets, and stately palms.[42] Like Melville's Tommo, Hearn as narrator initially insists on reading the scene before him Edenically, thereby fitting into his preconceived stereotypes of tropical life. The people, he claims, are all perfectly healthy, with fine, rounded limbs. He attributes this partly to good diet but also to "race-crossing, climate, perpetual exercise, healthy labor—many conditions must have combined to cause it" (27). The many rapturous passages that describe the sunsets, the purple mountains, the flaming and fragrant flowers—all these had direct antecedents in his earlier reports to friends north about New Orleans. Here is an example from that time: "Life here is so lazy,—nights are so liquid with tropic moonlight . . . summer is so languid with perfume and warmth,— that I hardly know whether I am dreaming or awake" (McWilliams 1946, 111). We know, however, that an important literary source for such raptures was the work of Pierre Loti (Louis Marie Julien Viaud, 1850–1923), whose novels were full of exotic settings and liaisons of white men with native women.[43] Hearn and Loti were the same age, and the latter's career as a French naval officer afforded him the opportunity Hearn yearned for—to see the world. Loti's travels to Turkey, Japan, Tahiti, and elsewhere led to exotic fictions, which inevitably involved East/West romances that echoed Loti's real life affairs, with both men and women (although his homosexual adventures were not part of his published works). Also a talented travel writer, Loti delighted in "going native," wearing the costume of the country and mingling with the common people, as did Hearn. Above all, however, Loti's feverish, gorgeously painterly prose was employed to render nature's more flamboyant modes, particularly sunsets, the sea, and tropical foliage.[44] There were, to be sure, other extravagant writers who influenced Hearn, such as Théophile Gautier, whose steamy stories lacked tropical settings but offered plenty of sex.[45] Like Loti, Hearn's focus naturally gravitated to the native women, and in particular to "Les Porteuses," the subject of his first Martinique chapter, women who carry goods in loads of a hundred pounds long distances across the island in baskets on their heads. Their fortitude and stern beauty, Hearn states, make them like Greek caryatides, thus linking them—through a Caribbean/Mediterranean comparison—to his own native culture. In the twenty-five pages he devotes to *les porteuses*, Hearn uses what they see on their cross-island transports to introduce readers to the sublime landscapes. Here—especially in the comparison to the caryatides—Hearn concentrates on the crossroads between the tropical sublime and what Chris Bongie has termed "exoticism," which he defines as a "discursive practice intent on recovering 'elsewhere' values 'lost' with the modernization of European society" (1991, 5).

One of the reasons Hearn looms so important at the juncture of the U.S. South and the Caribbean stems from his bilingualism. His fluent French enabled him to converse with the inhabitants of the island. Still, as we just saw, he sometimes rejected their accounts. He accepts the white version (rather than the black one) of the myth of Father Jean-Baptiste Labat (1663–1738), who blacks claim introduced slavery into the island. Hearn pored over the six volumes of island history Father Labat contributed, and they provided Hearn with a blueprint for his own study. Combining Labat's writings with the complementary biography of Labat written by Dr. Etienne Rufz, Hearn portrays the Dominican from Paris, who volunteered to serve in the West Indies, as a true Renaissance man of many talents. During his twelve years on the island, Labat took a bankrupt plantation, improved it scientifically, and made it the richest one. He built fortifications, did the same in Guadeloupe, and participated in battles against the predatory English, alongside allied buccaneers and filibusters. He traveled the West Indies, gathering materials for travel accounts, which filled six volumes, built convents and churches, and governed his order, before being sent on a permanent mission to Rome. Supposedly he was not permitted to return to the island because he spoke too freely about the "family origin and personal failings of various colonists considered high personages" (126). Hearn describes Labat's volumes as "full of quaint drawings, plans, and odd attempts at topographical maps. . . . What particularly impresses the reader. . . is not so much the recital of singular incidents and facts as the revelation of the author's personality. . . just by nature, yet capable of merciless severity" (126). He also admires Labat's sly sense of humor and his fondness for gourmet treats, such as roasted parrots.

However, it seems that Labat saw nothing wrong with slavery, employed it on the church lands, and "regarded the negro as a natural child of the devil,—a born sorcerer—an evil being wielding occult power" (128), perhaps because he recorded many instances of African-derived sorcery, particularly rainmaking. He once had a black wizard lashed 300 times, followed by an application of fiery peppers, for prophesying a sick slave's death, which did indeed follow. As a result of such terrors, the local population has understandably forgotten Labat's positive contributions and use him as a ghostly specter to scare children into obedience (Temple 1974, 95–96).[46] Blacks rightly indict Labat as an evil colonizer, yet Hearn, despite his love of the Caribbean people, dismisses their account of the island's history and bemoans the fact that "all the wonderful work the Dominican accomplished has been forgotten by the people" (132). Hearn concludes his musings on Labat and the Catholic Church by noting the decline in influence that came with universal suffrage: "All local positions are filled by blacks or men of color; no white creole can obtain a public office or take part in legislation; and the whole power of the black vote is used against the interests of the class[;] thus politically disinherited The Church suffers in consequence."[47] This passage no doubt created horror among his white readers, who had feared just such an outcome from Reconstruction in the United States.

Increasingly, Hearn transcends his racial biases by showing us that African elements lie behind virtually every aspect of island life. For instance, he indicates that the omnipresence of Catholic statues and icons is misleading, for the blacks on the island have always conflated their African gods with Catholic images. "The old enemy of Pére Labat, the wizard (the *quimboiseur*) already wields more authority than the priest, exercises more terror than the magistrate, commands more confidence than the physician" (138).

Certainly one aspect of African tradition in the island that is guaranteed to intrigue white readers is the figure of the zombie, which we encountered in *All Souls' Rising*. A native woman tells Hearn that "it is something that makes disorder at night . . . the zombis go everywhere; the dead folk remain in the graveyard" (144). A zombie can be a gigantic dog more than five feet high; a three-legged horse; or the maker of magical fires that lure travelers forward into pits. Hearn eagerly absorbed many zombie tales from his housekeeper/mistress Cyrillia, the middle-aged *capresse* (a mixed-race woman with reddish skin) who managed his tropical household.[48]

The supernatural could have a comic side as well. Like Hurston, Hearn provides a wealth of Caribbean legends and folktales, such as the story of Yé and the Devil, an interchange involving a *bitaco*, a much-maligned "lazy" negro from the mountains. Although the comic tales confirm Yé's shiftless ways, they also detail his great suffering; clearly, the Devil is a stand-in for cruel masters during slavery. As Hearn concludes this section, he sympathizes: "Poor Yé!—you still live for me. . . . I have seen you cutting cane. . . . I have seen you climbing from plantation to plantation with your cutlass in your hand, watching for snakes . . . to look for work, when starvation forces you to obey a master . . . always hungry,—and always shiftless!"

(320). Hearn does not read the Devil in the tales as a double of the master, but rather as a symbol of demon rum, "tafia," which has destroyed so many Yés. Indeed, in a repetition of the sentiments of post–Civil War whites in the United States, Hearn declares, "There is no Bon-Dié to help you. . . . The only Bon-Dié you ever really had, your old Creole master, cannot care for you anymore, and you cannot care for yourself; [his masters kept Yé] innocent as a child of the struggle for life. . . . But you feel that law now! You are a citizen of the Republic! you are free to vote, and free to work, and starve if you prefer it, and free to do evil and to suffer for it;—and this new knowledge stupefies you so that you have almost forgotten how to laugh!" (320).

The biracial family of the U.S. South finds its counterpart in the Caribbean, where white planters often sire black and white families. Hearn dramatizes this with two small girls, both named Mimi, both ostensibly white. The well-dressed one who wears shoes, however, gets in trouble for playing with her shoeless counterpart. Hearn reports that they had fallen in love with each other at first sight, a sentiment in keeping with the conceit of instinctual attraction toward one's biological kin, even when true identity is unknown.[49] Hearn rightly locates this kind of situation in biblical myth: "Human nature has little changed since the day that Hagar knew the hate of Sarah" (158). The "black" Mimi, her two sisters, and their mother become part of Hearn's extended portrayal of the plagues that strike the island during carnival celebrations, whose witches and devils seem to embody the evils nature is causing through smallpox and typhoid. Eventually, the three little girls are left orphans. The two Mimis have differing economic situations because, although their white father made provision for them both before he died, his white heirs undid his legal arrangements.

As a former citizen of New Orleans, Hearn was fascinated by Antilles carnival, and some of the participants, in fact, directly echo the blackface minstrelsy of the Crescent City's Krewe of Zulu: "The 'Molasses Negro' wears nothing but a cloth around his loins;—his whole body and face being smeared with an atrocious mixture of soot and molasses. He is supposed to represent the original African ancestor" (163). Several maskers are costumed as the devil woman who lures men from the cane fields, never to return. She is called *la guiablesse*, and although Hearn indicates this is a singular legend of the island, Hurston reports a similar manifestation in her study of Haiti.

As he did with *les porteuses*, Hearn lavishes many pages on the fabled *blanchisseuses*, or washerwomen, whose work in the island's rushing streams— punctuated by their dreamy tragic narrative songs—receives romantic treatment. Hearn's peculiar focus on the *blanchisseuses*, like his earlier portrait of *les porteuses,* offers yet another example of his fixation on the bodies of native women, this time as they carry out *plein air* work. As David Spurr has noted, "The material value of the body as labor supply, its aesthetic value as object of artistic representation, its ethical value as a mark of innocence or degradation, its scientific value as evidence of racial difference or inferiority, its humanitarian value as the sign of suffering, its erotic value as the object of desire" (1993, 22) are all valorizations of colonial narrative, and we find all of this in *Two Years in the French West Indies.*

Elsewhere, Hearn bemoans the fact that his delighted observation of cane workers bundling sheaves in the warm sunlight is not often possible, for "the introduction of the piece-work system has destroyed the picturesqueness of plantation labor throughout the island" (213). Painting here and elsewhere rural work with words, in the way Jean-François Millet and Camille Corot did on sentimental canvases in France, Hearn compromises his credentials with the reader as a dispassionate observer of island life, although his accompanying complaint about the mechanization of agriculture certainly places him in good company with the early modernists who hated the advent of "the machine in the garden." On the other hand, he deplores the rampant destruction of local trees of every variety for use as charcoal, a practice taken to an extreme in nearby Haiti, which today has been stripped of its formerly lush rain forests.

Repeatedly, and more frequently than Woolson does in her fiction (not surprising, in light of the dominance of African ancestry in the Caribbean as opposed to Woolson's St. Augustine), Hearn posits the relationship of the island to Africa: "Directly east is Senegambia: we are well south of Timbuktoo and the Sahara . . . [and] the vegetation is African. The best alimentary plants, the best forage, the flowers of the garden, are of Guinea;—the graceful date-palms are from the Atlas region: those from Senegal. Only in the touch of the air, the vapory colors of distance, the shapes of the hills, there is something not of Africa; that strange fascination which has given to the island its poetic creole name,—*Le Pays des Revenants*" (226).[50] Hearn saw the African element of New Orleans as well, and in both Louisiana and Martinique he was quick to read whatever he saw through an intoxicated filter of nineteenth-century racial romanticism, a product of his absorbed reading of French writing of the time.

As Hearn keeps circling back to the women of the island, he considers them as custodians of a dynamic folk culture (particularly in terms of dress) and as figures in a ladder of color, the result of a complicated system of black female/white male relations that ultimately led to the various color "types."

Chapter 9, "La Fille du Couleur," replete with seven elaborate engravings of various types of women, entertains notions of sexual/racial mixing that today we find problematic.[51] Hearn seems to agree with "experts" who state that the original women from Africa were "hideous," but over the years, he claims, racial admixture has led to charming varieties of color and facial types. "It was not uncommon for a rich man to have many 'natural' families," he reports, and indeed, only one in twenty-five was listed as legitimate (254). Hearn's adoration of the *fille du couleur* is based on her childishness, her ready submission to her white lover, her refusal to demand legitimation for their children, and her resigned acceptance of his eventual marriage to a white woman. Still, he maintains that such women retain something "savage" and are increasingly—as white islanders immigrate elsewhere—likely to cohabit with a mulatto *homme du couleur*. This group of men, Hearn tells us, might be handsome and industrious but are said to be debauched and fickle and are hated by whites because of their social aspirations and by blacks because of their superior airs. In almost all these respects, Hearn rehearses—but without any reference to—the system of *plaçage* as it was practiced in New Orleans.

Hearn's own sexual life finds covert presentation. In a late chapter of the volume, "Ma Bonne," Hearn describes his housekeeper/cook, the middle-aged woman of color, Cyrillia. Hearn does not state that she was also his lover, but a perceptive reader soon figures this out. Hearn yields to her ministrations, avidly soaks up her stories, and clearly associates these with his appetite, since most of the chapter is about island fruits, vegetables, and culinary concoctions. He admits, late in this section, that he is "a little bit overfed . . . the stranger in the tropics can not eat like a native" (285).[52]

Satiety apparently accompanied other problems. In the penultimate chapters, Hearn, who has largely painted an image of Martinique as an earthly paradise,[53] describes in detail the debilitating effects of the tropical climate on an immigrant from the North. Growing lassitude, fevers, decreased appetite, can eventually lead to madness and/or death. The lack of books and high culture make for monotony, as does the interdiction against nocturnal movement caused by serpents. He wants us to understand "why the tropics settled by European races produce no sciences, arts, or literature,—why the habits and thoughts of other centuries still prevail where Time itself moves slowly as if enfeebled by the heat" (307).[54] Hearn was hardly unique in this view. Two decades later, Ellsworth Huntington's *Civilization and Climate* (1915) would indict the ways in which the tropical climate precluded the development of advanced "civilization," and how white folk who chose to reside there would, like Hearn, fall victim to "tropical inertia."[55] Woolson's characters, like Hearn and several of his acquaintances in New Orleans and St. Pierre, often fall victim to fever; Margaret Harold, the heroine of *East Angels*, almost dies of it at one point. The leitmotif of disease, which runs through that novel, necessitates the important participation of Dr. Kirby, the community's physician.

This litany of conditions closely echoes Hearn's earlier take on the cultural scene of New Orleans: "I do not wonder the South has produced nothing of literary art. Its beautiful realities fill the imagination to repletion. It is regret and desire and the spirit of Unrest that provoketh poetry and romance. . . . The North . . . is the land of imagination and poetry" (McWilliams 1946, 111). In several ways, all these sentiments echo the early twentieth-century charges of H. L. Mencken in his indictment of U.S. Southern culture, "The Sahara of the Bozart." The sage of Baltimore, however, is not as cognizant as Hearn clearly is of the killing effects of tropical climate. It is interesting here that Hearn does not make overt linkage to the equally oppressive weather of the New Orleans he had just left, which in terrain, flora, annual rainfall (including hurricanes), and temperature was so similar to Martinique, a resemblance that obviously made Hearn more aware of the conditions he found on the island.

And yet Hearn *did* prove productive during torrid times in both Louisiana and Martinique. He became, like his subsequent narrative transformations, "tropicalized." As Aravamudan has reminded us, while tropicalization has been used to describe "the acclimation of flora, fauna, and even machinery to warmer habitats . . . the same could be said for ideas, habits, and attitudes," and as such, is similar to Mary Louise Pratt's notion of "transculturation," which in the more vulgar terminology of the past represented "going native" (Aravamudan 1999, 6). Woolson, too, despite the heat, tropical diseases, and frequent enervation, was unusually productive in Florida.

Two Years ends melodramatically, as Hearn, who has spent the last several chapters revealing the horrors of tropical life, now waxes nostalgic as he prepares to leave. At the center of his version of the trip north is the tale of a little governess leaving her native island to work in New York. As they enter the great Northern harbor, Hearn depicts "Lys" shrinking back with white lips, as he blesses her in Creole. The interchange between the opening and closing of the book—with a naive Hearn at the beginning and a virginal female traveler going in the opposite direction at the end—pulls the book into transnational configuration. However, it also, without saying so, suggests a median in the tropical South—particularly New Orleans—that Hearn also knew and recognized as part of a circumCaribbean quite apart from the frozen North overcast with the "gray sky of Odin." This final reference to the "bitter" and "spectral" element that is so opposed to the "eternal summer's green" forces a reconsideration of the reservations Hearn had in the penultimate chapters and, further, creates a clearer understanding of his realization that the South of the South was part of a cultural and climatic orbit quite alien to that of the triumphant military and industrial juggernaut of the postbellum North.[56]

Hearn always associated the tropics with what we would now call "primitivism." His ideas about native culture were not so different from those of Paul Gauguin, whose Tahitian idyll led to paintings that used Pacific images and people to refigure biblical mythology. Hearn, however, went back further in his references, as a letter to his eye doctor, George Gould, indicates: "Grace is savage, or must be savage in order to be perfect; that man was never made to wear shoes; that in order to comprehend antiquity, the secret of Greek art, one must know the tropics a little . . . and that the question of more or less liberty in the sex relation is like the tariff question—one of localities and conditions, scarcely to be brought under a general rule" (Bisland 1906, 1:438).

This crucial assertion has much to do with many of the writers in this study. The tropics—and especially the tropical sublime—could be a lens for reading not only ancient cultures, but also adjacent ones, such as that of the U.S. South. If Hearn, Raphael Semmes, William Clark Falkner, and many of the other writers we have considered here tended to read the tropics through the lens of their Southern experiences, the reverse was true as they engaged in "questions of travel." In 1889, in the North, Hearn wrote that "the tropical Circe bewitches me again—I must go back to her" (Bisland 1906, 1:469). Circe, like Calypso, was both an enchantress and a teacher.

Chita

We find a complement to Hearn's memoirs and travel writings in the two circumCaribbean novels he composed, *Chita* and *Youma*. His knowledge of the islands off Louisiana's coast expanded in 1884 when he vacationed in Grande Isle with his friend Marion Baker. They found a hybrid creolized population, including combinations of French, Italian, Spanish, Andalusian, Portuguese, Malay, and Chinese ancestry (McWilliams 1946, 167).[57] He must have seen similarities between this culture and that of Atlantic Florida, where he traveled the next year; he was fascinated by the Spanish history of that state (particularly Ponce de León's expedition, memorialized in Silver Springs). Unfortunately, his immersion in the icy-cold "fountain of youth" spring caused him to suffer from fever once back in New Orleans.[58] Hearn's intense interest in Native American and Spanish influence in Florida stemmed naturally from his research into these two groups' influence on the similarly criollo culture of Louisiana and aligns him closely with Woolson's presentation of *La Florida*.

Hearn followed this Florida sojourn with a second jaunt to Grand Isle, which caused him to circle back to his earlier meditations on the 1856 catastrophe of the L'Ile Dernière hurricane. These visits led to the publication of two short sketches, "Torn Letters" and "The Post Office" (both 1884), which formed the kernel of *Chita*. Hearn's Spanish friend and a doctor, Rudolph Matas, helped him with the Spanish dialogue in the novel. The two friends enjoyed playing Spanish, Mexican, and Cuban music, trying to ascertain their differences, an exercise in circumCaribbean/Hispanic diasporic culture (McWilliams 1946, 186).[59]

Chita begins geographically: "Traveling South from New Orleans to the Islands, you pass through a strange land into a strange sea, by various winding waterways" (3). This watery mixture of land and sea is also a dream image of scrambled geography, as we first encounter a series of thatched houses on stilts erected by Malay fishermen in the style of their home wetlands and then a Chinese settlement. Ultimately, however, we arrive at L'Ile Dernière, clearly a part of the Caribbean, albeit also part of the United States. Along the way, Hearn enumerates and names other islands of Louisiana's coastal archipelago, many of which have now vanished or been decimated by hurricanes—most recently Katrina. His words from the nineteenth century have an ironically doubled tragic heft today: "Many and many a mile of ground has yielded to the tireless charging of Ocean's cavalry. . . . The porpoises . . . play where of old the sugar-cane shook out its million bannerets; and shark-fins now seam deep water above a site where pigeons used to coo" (9). The narrator, after limning the luminous tints of the majestic waters and the skies above and listing the ranks of creatures that inhabit both realms, takes us back thirty years prior to the day of August 10, 1856, as this world trembles before the first ominous winds of the great hurricane that will destroy the island and almost all upon it.

The 400 carefree dancers in the great hall of the island's hotel seem modeled on the gay party in Poe's "The Masque of the Red Death" and in the embedded poem "The Haunted Palace" in that author's "The Fall of the House of Usher."[60] We remember that Hearn greatly admired Poe and called himself "the Raven." And yet Hearn wants to make this a specifically "Southern" idyll too, so he includes the following: "Slave-servants circled through the aristocratic press, bearing dainties and wines, praying permission to pass in terms at once humble and officious—always in the excellent French well-trained house servants were taught to use on such occasions" (26).

We might suspect, as well, that Hearn was thinking of his friend George Washington Cable's magnificent short story, "Belles Demoiselles Plantation" (1874). At the conclusion of that fanciful but tragic tale, a plantation home on the banks of the Mississippi falls into the flooded river with the seven beautiful daughters of the house, who are sponsoring a festive dance: "Belles Demoiselles, the realm of maiden beauty, the home of merriment, the house of dancing, all in the tremor and glow of pleasure, suddenly sunk, with one short, wide wail of terror—sunk, sunk, down, down, down, into the merciless, unfathomable flood of the Mississippi" (142).[61] Both Cable's story and *Chita* depend on this sense of impending doom, but the thematic of the dance of death is figured through myth, dancing, and youth, a combination that found repeated power in the plantation tradition, culminating in the ball scenes of *Gone with the Wind*. Here, however, the French/circum-Caribbean setting of an actual hurricane makes the story resonant of turbulent climactic history. A horrified sea captain, struggling to keep his boat afloat, exclaims, "Waltzing! . . . God help them! . . . *The Wind waltzes to-night with the Sea for his partner!*" (27).

Hearn ruptures the tragic romance, however, as plunderers appear after the storm. They represent the "motley crew" of the circumCaribbean, an international, scurvy set so like the gulls and hawks that accompany them: "Sicilian and Corsican outlaws, Manila-men from the marshes, deserters from many navies, Lascars, marooners, refugees of a hundred nationalities" (31), a tip of the hat to the smuggling/piratical legends of the greater Caribbean, but also a chillingly realistic portrayal of unscrupulous harvesters of disaster. Dead fingers are snapped to get at rings. Cold beauties are denuded of their still valuable finery. Earrings are torn out.

A childless Spanish fisherman, Feliu Viosca, and his wife, Carmen, find a living baby and decide to raise it. The little girl takes the place of their daughter, Conchita, who died in Barcelona before they immigrated to Cuba and then to this archipelago. This child, Lili, speaks French; she knows her parents were named Julien and Adéle, and her referents to their home indicate they were well-off, but no further information is forthcoming.

Readers learn, however, that Julien La Brierre survived, unlike his wife, and that he presumes that daughter Lili is dead too. He is stunned when he finds a tombstone relatives have erected with his name on it in New Orleans. Standing before his wife's tomb, he notices the grave of a Cuban-born friend who blew his brains out after losing his wife in the storm: *"Ramirez . . . Nació en Cienfuegos, isla de Cuba"* (65). Here, and everywhere in the story, Hearn delights in larding the texts with other languages—French, Spanish, and Creole too. The ensuing flashback to Julien's wild youth reveals that he fought a duel with the same Laroussel who was present when Lili/Chita was found, but he did not recognize her. Hearn thus laces up pieces of the plot for a tighter, and more ironic, unity, but he also underlines the interplay within Latin cultures between desire and violence.

As Chita develops, she receives little formal education, but Hearn wants us to know that she nevertheless is absorbing ancient Nature's wisdom, a tenet of his "paganism" that he took with him around the world. "Unknowingly she came to know the immemorial sympathy of the mind with the Soul of the World . . . days of windy joy, hours of transfigured light" (82), but all of this was tempered by her profound fear and respect for the terrible sea. Her foster father, aware of this, teaches her to swim and thus to draw strength from the ocean she has now mastered. Nevertheless, the child seems to have vestigial racial codes, which is signaled when she shocks her adoptive mother by scorning the *nègues marrons* and by demanding a white virgin to pray to rather than Carmen's "negra" Virgin of Guadalupe. Hearn thus underlines the more relaxed racial codes of the islands, so different from those of New Orleans in the decade before the Civil War.

Ultimately, the narrative skips forward sixteen years to a plague-ravaged New Orleans, where Julien, a doctor, ministers to the ill. He leaves, however, to attend to a call from Viosca's Point, where his father's old friend lies close to death. Readers of course think Julien will recognize Chita as his lost child. After the Italian boatmen Sparicio and Carmelo ferry him to the island (permitting Hearn to demonstrate his mastery of Italian), Julien learns the old man has already died, thus clearing the way for a seemingly inevitable encounter with Chita. Julien does indeed become riveted by her resemblance to his dead wife, but before he can question Carmen, he falls ill and dies, despite Carmen's ministrations.

Chita, composed before Hearn sailed to the Caribbean, offers a kind of literary bridge between New Orleans and Martinique. The Louisiana islands were and are a kind of "in-between" zone, a wetland that at that time was a mélange of foreign and U.S. cultures and a magical landscape for Hearn's yearning and flamboyant imagination. It was also a further development of his sense of a wider-ranging tropical "South," an idea that brought him closer to the feverish imagination of his idol, Pierre Loti. Further, Julien's miraculous "resurrection" finds an echo in his near-recognition of his daughter; she has been nourished and sustained by the culture of the islands, which could possibly have made Julien whole again as well. Hearn may have intended Chita to represent a hybrid multicultural future, but one with little knowledge of the past.

Youma

Hearn wrote *Youma*, his Martinique novel, in 1888, when he was staying home to avoid a yellow fever epidemic that was sweeping the island. *Youma* opens by explaining the meaning of the Creole word *da*—which referred, in the era of colonial Martinique slavery, to a "Creole negress,—more often, at all events, of the darker than of the lighter hue,—more commonly a *capresse* than *mestive*" (1). The *da* was a Caribbean variant of the South's "mammy," functioning as a second mother of white Creole children. The *da* showed her charges the wonders of the tropical world, told them slave tales, and catered to their every wish. This meant, Hearn intones, that the *da* was more loved than the white mother—at least during childhood. He also points out that a *da* might serve more than one generation of a white family (which we remember was the case with Faulkner's "Mammie Callie"). Further, she usually "ended her days with her masters; although she was legally property, it would have been deemed almost an infamy to sell her. When freed by gratitude . . . she did not care to make a home of her own; freedom had small value for her except in the event of her outliving those to whom she was attached. . . . She represented the highest development of natural goodness possible in a race mentally undeveloped, kept half savage by subservience, but physically refined in a remarkable manner by climate, environment, and all those mysterious influences which form the characteristics of Creole peoples" (4–5).[62]

Unlike the freed mammies of the U.S. South, however, the *da* of Martinique quickly disappeared, Hearn states, after the black majority supposedly took control over the whites through universal suffrage: "The races drew forever apart when they needed each other most. Yet there are a few das left, still with their white families, still practicing the ancient verities."[63] Youma is introduced only after this first chapter on the *da* figure. She is said to be a pretty *capresse,* the "pet slave" of her godmother Madame Léonie Peyronnette and constant companion to madame's daughter Aimée. When the latter marries M. Louis Desrivières, Youma accompanies them to their new home. Thirteen months later, Youma becomes *da* to Aimeé's daughter, Mayotte, a duty that becomes more serious when Aimeé unexpectedly dies.

Throughout the text, Hearn describes local, quotidian customs, such as the inspection of the feet of the children for parasites, the transport of goods to anchored merchant ships by *gommiers*, the huge canoes rowed to the beat of *tam-bou-belai* drums. He does not neglect religion, dramatizing the local priest's instruction of the catechism to slave children in a mixture of French and Creole. The most dramatic moments come, however, when Youma tells Mayotte *contes Creoles* that involve talking serpents, crabs, magical woods, and wicked witches. One night, a real serpent invades Mayotte's bedroom, and Youma courageously stamps on it while calling for the men to come help her. Gabriel, a very dark man who kills the snake, becomes Youma's admirer, and asks her master for her hand. Physically imposing, a hard worker, he is nevertheless deemed inferior because of Youma's pampered upbringing as a house servant. As Desrivières correctly predicts, "No; Madame Peyronnette would never hear of such a union; the mere idea of it would revolt her like a brutality!" (78). Indeed, the lady thinks that Youma's fascination is "purely physical, or, as she termed it, animal. Madame had purposely declined the fervent entreaties of her daughter Aimée to free Youma, as she intends that Youma will one day marry 'a thrifty and industrious freedman . . . able to make a good home for her. . . . In such an event she was to have her liberty . . . perhaps a small dowry'" (20).

This story is remarkably like one by Kate Chopin, "La Belle Zoraïde" (1894) and may well have inspired Chopin's tale. However, the thematic is quite common in African American literature. Madame Peyronnette's theory that "a girl innocent enough to become enamoured of the first common negro who made love to her, needed looking after" (83) is the same sentiment that Nanny in *Their Eyes Were Watching God* (1937) has when the young Janie becomes infatuated with the worthless Johnny Taylor. As we shall see, many view the educated Bita Plant's preference for her father's "blue black" workman Jubban (in Claude McKay's *Banana Bottom*) similarly, just as the people of Eatonville feel about the older Janie's selection of the much darker day laborer Tea Cake. In all of these cases, the authors seem to be indicting such "color-struck" and class-defined attitudes as racial philistinism.

Unlike Chopin or Hurston, however, Hearn interprets his black heroine's love for her supposed social inferior differently. As he puts it, Youma's anger at her separation from Gabriel causes a revolt: "Something long held in subjection within her,—something like a darker passionate second soul, full of strange impulses and mysterious emotions,—had risen to meet him, bursting its bonds, and winning mastery at last; the nature of the savage race whose blood dominated in her veins" (84–85). This revolt, however, had been brewing for some time. Confined to refined child rearing in the big house, "she sometimes found herself envying the lot of others who would have gladly changed places with her; the girls who traveled singing over the sunny mountain roads [*les porteuses*], the negresses working in the fields, chanting *belai* to the tapping of the *ka*" (87). A change of setting in the narrative contributes to the expansive yearning of Youma's character as well. When Aimée dies, Youma and Mayotte are sent to the child's father's plantation in rural Anse Marine, on the other side of Martinique. Hearn delights in limning this location as a veritable paradise, painting its tropical foliage, abundant fruits, pastel sunsets, and praising the abundant Africanisms, especially as found in dialect-driven folktales straight out of Africa. He relishes re-creating the privileged days of slave dancing that featured *bamboulas* and *caleindas*.[64] Despite the realistic folkloric details, however, Hearn sugarcoats the life of the slaves in these passages just as fulsomely as the apologists for slavery did in books like Mary Henderson Eastman's *Aunt Phillis's Cabin* (1852), written as antidotes to Stowe's *Uncle Tom's Cabin* (1851).

As is often the case in circumCaribbean literature of the African diaspora, the text suggests that the further "outback" a slave community is, the more African the Creole culture. The *contes créoles* told by old African women to the enslaved children are variously "purely African invention" or "African adaptation of old-world folk-lore and fable," but Hearn considers them "a reflection of colonial thought and life as no translation can preserve" (39). Ultimately, Hearn's story is quite different from the "mammy" narratives of the nineteenth-century U.S. South, and from Faulkner's relationship with his elderly black nurse too, in that Youma is a young, beautiful woman who obviously is an object of desire. Until Gabriel appears, however, Youma is indifferent to the gazes she attracts. Besides, "there were few young whites . . . who would have presumed to tell their admiration to Youma: there was something in the eyes and the serious manner of the young slave that protected her quite as much as the moral power of the family in which she had been brought up" (15).

Hearn's explosion of stereotype is provocative. In the Old South formula, the mammy is an old, very black woman, often of ample size, her head bound in a kerchief. The "mammy" stereotype developed as a Southern response to the revelations of abolitionists before the war, who decried the rampant sexual appropriation of the bodies of enslaved black females by their masters, overseers, and other white rapists. By suggesting that the usual relation between white men and black women was maternal, slavery's apologists created a screen for sexual and racial transgression.[65] By contrast, Youma, young and beautiful, is unusually taciturn and rarely displays emotion, and the text tells us her face suggests that "indefinable" visage of the Sphinx (14). William Faulkner uses the identical trope for *Absalom*'s enslaved mulatto Clytie, who is similarly taciturn and mysterious. Hearn, however, allows Youma's innate passion to erupt before the end of the story, setting up a tension that sets the stage for her ultimate sacrifice. Her mistress's refusal to sanction the marriage with Gabriel causes Youma to realize for the first time that she really is enslaved, "helpless to resist the will that struck her" (84). Hearn tells us that her "darker passionate second soul" had risen to meet Gabriel's, expressing "the nature of the savage race whose blood dominated in her veins" (85). Moreover, Gabriel's vehement indictment of slavery, replete with telling details, offers evidence of the horrors of the institution that Hearn knew existed, even though he usually chose to keep them in the background of his romantic stories.[66] This fictional crisis has a historical context. Emancipation appeared as a possibility with the proclamation of the French Republic. Hearn sets the scene by acquainting us with a racial census. There are 12,000 whites on the island and 150,000 black and "half-breeds" (as he calls them), and all of them are aware of the precedent of the bloody Haitian Revolution of 1791–1804: "Masters and slaves alike were haunted by a dream of blood and ire, — the memory of Hayti" (154). As Hearn reveals here, in both the U.S. South and in the Caribbean the image of the faithful slave provided an antidote to the residual fears of black rebellion. Other islands had experienced slave revolts after Haiti's, and thus the stage is set for the novel's final act—racial revolution in St. Pierre that leads to the torching of the mansion that houses Youma and her ward, Mayotte. To underline Youma's eventual sacrifice, Hearn has her white master offer her the chance to flee to colored neighbors before the mob attacks. First, however, old Monsieur Kersaint appeals to the mob: "What do you want, my sons?" generating the mocking response, "Are you our father? . . . There are no more 'my sons'—there are only citizens" (165). This is an ironic reminder to the reader of both racial hybridity and the old plantation myths of the biracial family that were used so successfully to control enslaved people— people like Youma. Hearn concludes the onslaught with a grimly realistic account of the deaths of the white aristocrats, the trashing of the mansion, and its destruction by fire. Youma, sequestered in the locked upstairs apartments with the terrified white survivors, damns the mob from a window, reminding them of advantages the masters gave them and condemning their cowardice in burning women and children. Gabriel is unable to persuade Youma to leave, and she is last seen at the window, the blond child in her arms, in a tableau recalling the Blessed Virgin, "Notre Dame du Bon Port." Hearn says her stance reminds one of the night she stepped upon the serpent, and many renditions of the Virgin depict her as standing on a serpent that represents Satan. The novel ends ironically: "And the same hour, from the other side of the world,—a ship was running before the sun, bearing the Republican gift of liberty and promise of universal suffrage to the slaves of Martinique" (193).

Hearn has been praised for choosing black Creoles as his doomed lovers here, and it is true that he has Gabriel indict slavery and ultimately transforms him into a racial revolutionary.[67] Still, the two figures in many ways replicate stereotypical characters used by Harriet Beecher Stowe, and indeed, white Southern writers, as Youma's final allegiance is to her white owners, who in her mind, have given her so much that she is willing to repay them with her life. Ultimately, then, this Caribbean *da* is identical to many "mammies," from Scarlett O'Hara's to Caddie Compson's. This examination of Hearn's circumCaribbean texts reveals that he came to his presentation of the Antilles through the lens of his New Orleans experiences, and that he saw the two realms as closely related, primarily because of the enveloping heritage of the black diaspora and the inevitable effects of the tropical environments both realms shared. Glissant groups Hearn among the many creators of "erotic literature" who came to the islands from the seventeenth century to the end of the nineteenth century. They were not, Glissant admits, without charm, but essentially they crafted a literature of illusion. "The supposedly receptive lasciviousness of the slaves, mulatto women and men who were of mixed blood, and the animal savagery with which the Africans were credited, produced an abundant supply" of material (1997, 70). Hearn, trained as an international reporter but also steeped in romantic travel and adventure writing like that of Pierre Loti, gave his readers an engrossing, sometimes realistic, but more often fantastically embellished, account, conjuring a world that he thought he saw but that ultimately was only imagined. Inevitably, New Orleans, the Gulf islands, and finally the Antilles became mirror images of his innermost desires, demons, and fears; everything beautiful had a dark, dangerous underside, as in the work of his adored Edgar Allan Poe, who declared that all true beauty possessed an element of "strangeness."

5 A Proper Order of Attention

McKay and Hurston Honor the Hardy Peasant

· ·

In the 1930s, Aimé Césaire and Leopold Senghor codified a new black aesthetic in response to colonial oppression, which we now call "negritude." Their valorization of "peasant" culture, after centuries of its scornful dismissal, became the basis of decolonization and took many differing forms across the black diaspora. These two writers were inspired, in part, by one of the greatest examples of their principles, the existing work of the Jamaican Claude McKay (1890–1948). After limning his native Jamaica's pastoral beauty in some juvenile poems, his subsequent wanderings took him to colleges in Alabama and Kansas, to the artistic and sexual ferment of the Harlem Renaissance, and then to Europe, where he was swept up by both the avant-garde and the communists, eventually traveling to Russia and enjoying the largesse of various white patrons as he variously drank and wrote his way around the Old World. Eventually, however, he would settle in Morocco, whose tropical setting brought back memories—and new perceptions—of his native island.

In the United States, while McKay was touring and working in Europe, Zora Neale Hurston was enjoying herself as a literary and social doyenne of the Harlem Renaissance, while pursuing a graduate degree in anthropology at Columbia University. Like McKay in his later life, her experiences away from her native Florida and her new understanding of social constructions made her reflect on the culture that produced her and on the rich repositories of folklore that were its crowning glory. This chapter demonstrates how these two superb writers each recast their perceptions of the "hardy peasant" culture that produced them, resulting in two masterworks that reflect Afro-Caribbean culture, *Banana Bottom* (1933) and *Their Eyes Were Watching God* (1937). Finally, I suggest that Hurston's reading of McKay's novel inspired and influenced the writing of *Their Eyes*, as she began to better understand the profoundly Caribbean aspects of her Florida and its people.

Claude McKay was a very serious artist who immediately saw dramatic possibilities in the new mixed worlds of color he was experiencing, first in

New York, and then in Paris, Marseilles, and Tangier, where many Africans and people of African descent had started immigrating from the French colonies around the world. His enduring classics, *Home to Harlem* (1926) and *Banjo* (1929), throb with the energies of new black communities in Manhattan and Marseilles, respectively. The latter book, however, is far more political and introduces colonial issues into the racial conversation McKay had started in New York about color biases, within the race and without as well. These works were strengthened by McKay's parallel nonfiction writing and his poetic endeavors, as well as his extensive relationships with modernist writers of all races and backgrounds. Both of his first two novels, however, are highly picaresque and therefore very masculine in point of view and in terms of action. Moreover, neither Harlem nor black Marseilles had the kind of rootedness and history necessary for an in-depth study of communal tradition and culture—which is not to say that these novels do not contain a multitude of rich scenes, complex ideas, and brilliant use of an innovative black modernism. In his final novel, *Banana Bottom* (1933), set in Jamaica, McKay was imagining, after his cosmopolitan experiences in newly created black metropolitan clusters, the "warm . . . fraternity of olden days." McKay was also aware, at this point, of the work of his Harlem colleagues, such as Zora Neale Hurston, Eric Walrond, Langston Hughes, and Sterling Brown, who had made magnificent poems, plays, and fictions from the materials of black peasant cultures of the U.S. South and the Caribbean.

Accordingly, toward the end of his life, McKay, disabused of the false promises of Western political parties and movements and living a pastoral, even agricultural, life in Morocco, cast his thoughts back to his native Jamaica and the rural folk whose values he had never really forgotten.[1] Like Hurston, whom he resembled in a surprising number of ways, he now was equipped with new lens of perception that made him see his origins in a more penetrating and poetic way. Just before writing his Jamaican novel, he had written and published *Gingertown* (1932), which featured several charming short stories set in Jamaica, including "The Agriculture Show," a richly detailed tale about a local festival, a visit from the governor, and the complications of color hierarchies, most of it told from the perspective of a young boy. Busha Glengly and his family play key roles, and this patriarch and his son appear in *Banana Bottom* as well. The story "Crazy Mary" details how a schoolmaster is accused of raping his young student Freshy, while another tale, "The Strange Burial of Sue," contains forbidden affairs, communal gossip, and religious thematics. Writing these Jamaican short stories planted the seeds for the novel in McKay's mind.

Generally ignored by U.S. and European critics, *Banana Bottom* has from its inception been seen as a classic of Caribbean literature. But I will argue here that it almost certainly inspired other "peasant" novels by U.S. Southern writers, and it has other strong parallels in the works of subsequent circumCaribbean writers as well, including Hurston, DuBose Heyward, and Jacques Roumain.[2] *Their Eyes Were Watching God* has many parallels with McKay's last novel, and it is entirely possible, indeed likely, that Hurston had read this work as part of her preparation for her research in Jamaica. I will be more interested, however, in demonstrating how her experiences in the Caribbean led her to see connections between her own culture in Florida and that of the islands, particularly in terms of the African heritage common to both and the interplay of multiethnic peoples in both realms. My analysis will cover white and black religious traditions of the two areas, gender conceptions, economic models, the legacy of slavery, agricultural practices, and the methodology McKay and Hurston develop to present what they both call "peasant" life. Further: as *Banana Bottom* was written after McKay's extensive interactions with U.S., French, Russian, Moroccan, and African diasporic cultures (particularly in Marseilles), it inevitably involves a much more searching and comparative method of analysis than any he might have employed had he never left Jamaica. His political activity gave him a new appreciation of his islanders, as both "proletariat figures" and heroic creators of a dazzling culture. His time in the U.S. South and his agricultural studies also gave him a new sense of the plantation history and new agricultural potential of the South of the South. Similarly, *Their Eyes* was written not only through the lens of Hurston's Caribbean experiences (which included extended stays in New Orleans, Jamaica, the Bahamas, and Haiti), but also through what she called the "spy-glass" of anthropology, following her graduate work at Columbia, her field research under the direction of Franz Boas, and her extensive intellectual encounters with writers, professors, musicians, and immigrants in Washington, Baltimore, New York, coastal South Carolina, and her native Florida. Her new understanding of the myriad aspects of her own peasant culture influenced and deepened her appreciation of the Caribbean world that was both similar to and different from Florida.

Another critic who has examined these novels in tandem (if briefly) is Hazel Carby, whose influential reading of *Their Eyes Were Watching God* has inspired a number of like-minded critics to severely chastise Hurston for sins of omission, rather than of commission. Carby, a Marxist critic who favors ideologically driven, urban-centered texts that aim for social change, accuses both McKay and Hurston of "romanticizing" the folk by creating "utopian" peasant communities.[3] In fact, neither McKay nor Hurston are depicting "utopias" in their fiction. While they appreciate the beauty of the natural environment, the expressive richness of black folk culture, and the productive husbandry of the land, they do not hesitate to reveal the envious backbiting, anti-intellectualism, religious bias, color prejudice, and vicious gossiping of the "peasants," or the amorous betrayals, neglect of progeny, and acts of violence and bestiality. Further, the people are devastated by unwise mono-crop husbandry, hurricanes, droughts, and floods, and although McKay does not include an earthquake, Kingston was almost totally destroyed in 1907 by a forceful set of tremors. Carby raises, however, some crucial points about the depiction of folk culture, and we will return to her observations in what follows.

Hurston had done extensive field work in Jamaica and wrote *Their Eyes* in Haiti when she was recovering from an intense but doomed love affair with a very dark man much like both Jubban and Tea Cake. Her surroundings at the time surely led her to emphasize the tropical nature of her novel's Florida setting and to valorize more than ever the common folk of the town, whom she now understood as masters of deeply meaningful folk culture that had extensive links to the Caribbean. Both she and McKay made a conscious effort to pay homage to the achievement of black folk speech, employing a form of dialect that was pungent and expressive but never demeaning. Further, they demonstrate how powerfully this kind of language is based in the natural, tropical world the characters inhabit, thereby illustrating many of the principles of language Emerson laid down in his seminal essay "Nature."

Hurston's background as the daughter of John Hurston, a popular Eatonville minister who also served for a time as mayor of the all-black town, is well known. Living in an eight-room house with seven siblings, Hurston was encouraged by her mother to read and dream, and when she later studied in famous Eastern schools, she never tried to "get above her raisings." On the contrary, most of her fiction brought her hometown and its surroundings to joyous life, as she paid homage to the rich folk culture of central Florida and to its African heritage. In her autobiography, Hurston provides a portrait of Eatonville's early origins, which are remarkably Caribbean: "This had been dark and bloody country since the mid-1700's. . . . Spanish, French, English, Indian, and American blood had been bountifully shed." And she describes the Maroon communities the Seminoles and Negroes created in the swamps, so like those of the Caribbean (*Dust Tracks*, 1942, 12).

McKay also grew up in virtually all-black surroundings, in a remote village in the central hills of Jamaica. He was born in 1890, just one year before Hurston. His father bragged about descent from the Ashantis in Africa and told Anancy tales to his children. Like Hurston's father, he was quite religious and served as an elder in the church but refused to participate in Obeah rituals (Ramesh and Rani 2006, 14–15).

The plot of *Banana Bottom* was inspired by McKay family history. Claude received a solid education, one modeled on British culture. His brother Uriah was a schoolteacher with access to a good library, and he encouraged his brother to steep himself in the British classics and to write mimetic verse, such as his early and stilted poem "Old England." Young Claude took pride in speaking correct English and became the protégé of an expatriated Englishman, Walter Jekyll, an unusual man who deeply admired Jamaican folk culture, which he collected and published. He encouraged McKay, particularly in the writing of dialect poetry, and this led to the publication of young Claude's two collections, *Songs of Jamaica* and *Constab Ballads* (both 1912). The latter collection drew on his angry memories of serving as a colonial policeman in Kingston and Spanish Town. Jekyll became the model for Squire Gensir in *Banana Bottom*.

Hurston read McKay's Harlem Renaissance work, and her comments on his nonfiction indicate she felt a sense of kinship with him. Reviewing his *Harlem: Negro Metropolis* (1940), she said that McKay "knows what is really happening among the folks. . . . He fixes a well-traveled eye on the situation and thus achieves proportion. . . . He has spoken out about those things Negroes utter only when they are breast to breast, but by tradition are forbidden to break a breath about when white ears are present. The book is as frank and open as twelve o'clock noon. For that reason it will not find favor among the large class of Negroes who plump for window-dressing for whites. Yet it is valuable to both races" ("Review," 1941, 95–96). McKay consistently refers to his people as "peasants." His patron Walter Jekyll wrote in his preface to McKay's *Songs of Jamaica* that the poet is a "Jamaican peasant of pure black blood" (1912, 9). One of McKay's first published dialect poems, "Peasants' Way o' Thinkin" (published in *Daily Gleaner* in January 1912), uses a folk persona to argue not only for help for the poor, but respect for their ideas (Wayne Cooper 1987, 50). In his posthumously published memoir, *My Green Hills of Jamaica* (1979), he notes, "My youth in Jamaica was not unhappy. In our village we were poor enough but very proud peasants. We had plenty to eat. We had enough to wear, a roof against the rain, and beautiful spreading trees to shade us. . . . Alligator pears and mangoes grew stoutly on the brink of the banks. . . . They fell on the road and anybody could pick them up" (3–4).[4] His sense of peasant culture had been strongly reinforced through his trip to Russia and his absorbed reading of Russian writers, particularly Tolstoy and the "peasant" poet Sergei Yesinin (*Long Way*, 1937, 88–97). In *Banjo*, the Haitian intellectual Ray (in many ways a fictional avatar of McKay) declares, "You're a lost crowd, you educated Negroes and you will only find yourself in the roots of your own people. . . . Turn your back on all these tiresome clever European novels and read about Russian peasants, the story and struggle of their lowly, patient, hard-driven life. . . . Be interested in native African dialects and though you don't understand, be humble before their simple beauty instead of despising them" (201). George Lamming claimed that the Caribbean novel is usually concerned with the poor "and has served as a way of restoring these lives—this world of men and women from down below—to a proper order of attention; to make their reality the supreme concern of the total society" (*Castle*, 1953, xxxvii). Many classic texts of the literature of the U.S. South and the Caribbean have shared this impulse, especially during the Depression, with books like Erskine Caldwell's *Tobacco Road* (1932), Henry Roth's *Call It Sleep* (1934), Horace McCoy's *They Shoot Horses, Don't They* (1935), John Steinbeck's *The Grapes of Wrath* (1939), and Richard Wright's *Uncle Tom's Children* (1938). These classics of 1930s literature galvanized a nation around the struggles of the suddenly representative peasant cultures of both rural hovels and urban slums. Depression-era writers sought to foreground the dignity and strength of the poor. Hurston and McKay, while endorsing these aims, also wanted to highlight the creativity and exuberance of peasants, especially as they shape their mother wit into subversive weapons against oppression.

In her paradigmatic study, *Southscapes* (2011), Thadious Davis lays out a new definition of what has until now been seen as a forcibly segregated, and therefore carceral, black community, the one that preceded the Civil Rights Acts of the 1960s. Her study points out the myriad ways in which African Americans created a vital communal, social, economic, and creative culture in "black space," despite the strictures of Jim Crow (Davis, 79).

Robert Stepto, in laying out the principle of his study of cultural ascent and immersion narratives in African American culture (1979), ties ascent to literacy, which in the slave narrative is linked to the seminal journey north. McKay and Hurston certainly attained literacy in their own "peasant" communities, but they achieved a higher education after leaving Jamaica and Florida, respectively, in "journeys north," through institutions of higher learning, life experiences, and contacts with scholars, intellectuals, and artists (particularly in New York, and later for McKay, Paris and Marseilles). Both, however, knew they had learned much from peasant culture before their departures. Each had a deep dedication to what Hurston called "the Negro furthest down" and strove to meet and understand common people within the race wherever they were, be it in Port-au-Prince or Marseilles. Most important, they yoked the two concepts of ascent and immersion in their principal characters, Bita and Janie, suggesting that a fully integrated person must be anchored in the "soil" of folk culture, so that the "flower" of full expression—and of course this includes the Western-influenced aesthetic production of the individual authors as well—could emerge as a hybrid, complete, manifestation of healthy, conjoined, racial culture.

Stepto bases his theory in part on Victor Turner's famous formulation of *communitas*, which Turner uses to describe relations between people jointly undergoing ritual transition. Yet, as Turner also pointed out, "*communitas* does not merge identities; it liberates them from conformity to general norms" (cited in Stepto 1979, 69). Stepto's theory also involves the concept of *genius loci*, employing Geoffrey Hartman's sense of how "local integrities" or "imagery of the tribe are given bounding outlines" through special spaces, "even though as expressions of spirit of place they depict place (ritual grounds), and as expression of 'race-spirit' or 'race-message' (W. E. B. Du Bois's terms) they provide the currency of exchange, as it were within the realm of *communitas*" (Stepto 1979, 70).

Thus Eatonville, the "Muck," and Banana Bottom emerge in these two texts as symbolic geography, marked by the agricultural life of the inhabitants, their "peasant" culture, and their interaction with the flora and fauna, the weather, and the changing seasons. Above all, however, Hurston's evocation of Florida makes it akin to the Caribbean; in both spaces, people of African descent are in the majority and African-derived culture predominates in the popular imagination. Still, both McKay and Hurston dramatize key moments of conflict with dominant white cultures, particularly in terms of Jamaica's colonial structures of oppression and the rigged social and juridical systems of the U.S. South.

Woolson's description of the Florida peninsula as a finger pointing south connects Hurston's *genius loci* with McKay's, and the marked Caribbean quality of Hurston's novel underlines that connection. Further, both novels point to the strong influence of the local climate and its growing seasons and the close connection between the people and the land the climate controls. Finally, both narratives conclude with a devastating hurricane, one that changes the parameters of both the main characters and the communities they inhabit, while laying bare racial inequality and capitalist manipulation. As such, catastrophe "clears the ground" for new, sustaining rituals, which begin in death but lead to rebirth. This motif fits with Kenneth Ramchand's accurate appraisal of the novel and its central action: "[Bita] gradually strips away what is irrelevant in her English upbringing. . . . [She] is the first achieved West Indian heroine and *Banana Bottom* is the first classic of West Indian prose" (1983, 259). As we shall see, Tea Cake's death and the erasure of the community on the muck lead to Janie's reintegration—in new terms—with her home *genius loci* of Eatonville, through the interweaving of her story with the imaginations of her neighbors. Tea Cake's bundled seeds, which Janie brings with her, are signifiers of the fertilizing effect of his and Janie's story. McKay uses the hurricane and its aftermath to similar affect. It brings about the death of Jordan Plant and Mr. and Mrs. Craig and the need for new plantings in the community, which is symbolized by the grafting of the "flower" of Bita onto the "root" of the black peasant, Jubban, leading to the rebirth of her father in the naming of their son after him.

Robert Stepto importantly notes that Hurston's novel is "quite likely the only truly coherent narrative of both ascent and immersion, primarily because her effort to create a particular kind of questing *heroine* liberates her from the task (the compulsion, perhaps) of revoicing many of the traditional tropes of ascent and immersion" (1979, 164). Of course many of these (although Stepto does not say this) involve issues of masculine identity, as predicated by the slave narrative. I will claim here that *Banana Bottom* (which has always been—perhaps rightly so—categorized as a Caribbean novel) also functions as both ascent and immersion narrative, in quite similar ways.

McKay, Hurston, and Tropical Founts of Identity

Claude McKay has been best known recently for his angry, stirring poetry and his seminal novel, *Home to Harlem* (1926), which offers a vibrant sense of the multiple layers of the cultural matrix of the New Negro's beehive in New York. More recently, Paul Gilroy, Jeff Karem, and others have directed our gaze across the Atlantic to Marseilles, the setting of McKay's very different narrative of the black diaspora, *Banjo*. McKay's third novel, *Banana Bottom* completes the triangle of the Black Atlantic with the story of Jamaica's Bita Plant, a transnational heroine who comes home to her island roots after seven years of education in Britain.[5] The novel has been neglected in favor of McKay's other works, but the issues I have raised thus far should amply indicate why I believe this text deserves a place in any discussion of the affinities between Southern African American and Afro-Caribbean writing.

McKay's novel begins in the small town of Jubilee, pictured throughout the novel as a refuge from the incursions of the colonial world of the bigger cities such as Kingston. Bita Plant, seated at the piano, has brought culture—literacy and Western musical training—to Jubilee back from her education in England. She returns to a communal "lovefeast" that resembles gatherings in Hurston's Eatonville, accompanying—and thus participating in—the performance of the "Coloured Choristers." Bita has always had music in her life, for her father, Jordan, was a renowned fiddler in his youth, and McKay takes pains to show us how music, both European and Afro-Caribbean, permeates every aspect of Jamaican social and religious culture.

Because Bita has spent those seven years (the traditional stint of bondage in the Bible) in England, without any contact with her native culture, the reader perhaps expects someone who will put on airs. But despite the fact that she wears a "princess" gown—aligning her with British royalty—she knows she is at last among "her own folk." At first, this would seem to include the white Reverend Malcolm and Priscilla Craig, who "had taken Bita like a child of their own" when she was "a hoyden," "improved" her, and then sent her to England.[6] There are signs of resistance to the colonizing program of the Craigs from the start, however, even among this refined group. The Coloured Choristers, led by the appropriately named soprano Belle Black, are "in no way intimidated by Bita's years of higher and foreign culture. Indeed they were united in testing it" (2), but Bita can keep up with the frantic tempo that Belle sets. "Bita had passed *their* test," an "exam" that asks whether Bita's fancy education has made her unable to "play" (in every sense) with them, and at their pace. This idea of testing dominates the novel, as Bita, and also the other key characters, are "tested" by a variety of differing measures.

Bakhtin has identified "testing" of this sort as one of the most fundamental organizing concepts in the novel, which radically distinguishes it from the epic, where any concept of doubt regarding the hero is "unthinkable." He uses the German term *Prüfungsroman* to signify this testing aspect. Usually the heroism or fidelity of the central character goes under trial (*Dialogics*, 1981, 388). In the above scene, we have a relatively benign example of this syndrome, but there are many other such "testings" in the novel, of Bita, of the Craigs, and of Jubban. But, significantly, in this first example, it is the *assembled folk* who test and then approve.

McKay brings a shocking and sexual revelation into this polite gathering, for while Bita is kissing and being kissed, he informs the reader that she is "a girl with a past. . . . She had been raped by Crazy Bow Adair" (2). We remember here that in *Their Eyes*, Janie's mother, Leafy, and Janie herself are products of rape. McKay's description of the rape of Bita, rendered in a short flashback, is quite ambiguous, in that she teases and embraces Crazy Bow passionately as they romp in the wood: "She clambered upon him again and began kissing his face. Crazy Bow tried to push her off. But Bita hugged and clung to him passionately. Crazy Bow was blinded by temptation and lost control of himself and the deed was done" (10). McKay uses this flashback—and others related to it—to point to the ways in which peasant culture can be negative. Jordan Plant, Bita's father, would have liked to have hushed up her rape, probably because he knows the details and because he cares about her reputation, but gossiping women spread the story far and wide and Crazy Bow must go to the asylum. Later, jealous peasant women look back at Bita's rape as a kind of fortunate fall, and McKay even has some of them wish that they had been raped in her place, for it led to her being "lifted up" by the Craigs through her privileged English education and her later "adoption" by the couple as part of the work of their mission.

Just after the rape, the villagers compose a cruel but creative ditty (one of many communal creations in the book), which they sing as "a toothsome tale," for they are jealous of Jordan's success:

You may wrap her up in silk,
You may trim her up with gold,
And the prince may come after
To ask for your daughter,
But Crazy Bow was first. (14)

The association of "silk" and "gold" here refers to Jordan's prosperity and to the foolishness of trying to shield juicy truth from the folk, what Hurston, in a sense of both admiration and approbation, called "mouth-almighty." There are many other incidents in the novel of the envious, "basket-of-crabs" syndrome among the Antilleans, which is identical to that in the U.S. South: if one crab tries to escape from the fisherman's basket, the others, jealous, reach up and pull it back. Hurston's envious villagers of Eatonville welcome Janie's apparent "fall" as she returns to the hamlet alone, in mud-stained overalls. In *Banana Bottom*, the "toothsome" tale of Bita's fall spreads through the vicious gossip of Sister Phibby, who habitually "stirs the pot" of local mischief by spreading tales of "ruint" women and scandalized men.

This part of Bita's history affords McKay an opportunity to offer an alternative to the white "adoption" of the Craigs, for Crazy Bow is a third-generation descendant of a Scotsman who married a "Negress" (McKay does not give her a name) and then launched a program of providing land for black Jamaicans, and not just for his own huge flock of descendants. McKay comments: "The Highlander's blood has flowed down into a dark-brown stream deep sunk into the soil. His children's children are hardy peasants. Some are reliable artisans" (3).

Here McKay sets up a model of another kind of "adoption," namely that of blood. This Scotsman felt no abhorrence of blackness, unlike the British, who rarely intermarried with subject peoples in any Anglo colony, although, as McKay will demonstrate, they did have black mistresses and sired many of the mulattoes who came to dominate Jamaican second-tier culture. Indeed, the Scotsman's wife was "one of the blackest of them" (2). Jordan and his neighbors live on the high ground of Banana Bottom, which in many ways resembles Hurston's hometown of Eatonville. It was established by old Adair but became a virtually all-black, peasant enclave, just as Eatonville did in Florida. Banana Bottom, McKay tells us, is "among the first of independent expatriate—Negro villages" (9), and Eatonville was the first all-black incorporated town in Florida.

Jordan's family stands in contrast to the white missionaries, the Craigs, but they become linked to the black community through their apparently autistic and mute only child, Patou (the patois word for screech-owl).[7] Patou's presence in the novel operates on several levels; first, the Craigs, for all their refinement, have produced a child whose perceived animal-like nature places him on the lowest rung of island life, despite his whiteness; further, Mrs. Craig chooses Bita over Herald Day as a candidate for "adoption," for she cannot bear the idea of supplanting her own son with another, a visible sign of rejection. Finally, when a dazed and confused Mrs. Craig, viewing a local exhibit of African art, has a delirious vision of being surrounded by whirling black masks (199, 202), Patou's face becomes one of them, before she, too, lapsing into mobile fantasy, joins in frantic dancing. The dream would seem to indicate that Mrs. Craig understands, through the agency of the child she has produced, that the "primitive" is in her too, and that the chaos it symbolizes—the whirling, mad dancing—has been in her body, which may be proven by the gestural but incoherent physicality of her natural/unnatural son. And indeed, earlier, quite consciously viewing the real masks in the missionary hall, she had been troubled by the thought that "they seemed to take on a forbidden actuality and potency, as if they were immortal. . . . She discerned something of their spirit in the decadent practices of the Obi-worshipers. . . . Those objects were unholy. . . . There was much more behind their exhibition than they thought. The objects were so positively real. Surely they possessed some elemental force. . . . She was troubled to think that they might have their origin in some genuine belief . . . that the night-wrapped creatures of Africa might also have had there in the dim jungles their own vision of life" (198). The dream itself offers a fine example of what Suzanne Césaire claimed about Surrealism, that it was "a state of mind . . . the domain of the strange, the marvelous and the fantastic . . . the metamorphoses and the inversion of the world under the sign of hallucination and madness," which she prophesied would "supply the rising people with a punch from its very depths" (cited in Kelley, 2000, 16).

The Craigs are skewered, however, from the beginning by the acid-tongued narrator, who describes Bita as "the transplanted African peasant girl that they had transformed from a brown wildling into a decorous cultivated young lady." This description maintains the "plant" imagery and constitutes the Europeans as the "husbandrymen" of the colonial "garden," as Bita is "one precious flowering of a great work" (11). The Craigs are aware of their link to the generations of white missionaries who had come to the islands to preach to "the Quasheees. To bring to the jungle creatures Light" (12).

This ecological imagery is also seen in the name "Plant." The name strongly roots both Bita and Jordan in the native flora and fauna, which play an important role in the development of the novel. The "dark-brown stream" of Jamaican culture was the original nourishment for Bita, and she has been hungry for its sustaining energies, we find, the whole time she was in England. A sensitivity to actual plants and flowers operates symbolically in the novel, for Jubban, while hunting, spies a rare and lovely flower growing in the armpit of a tree. He does not remove it, as he knows that the botanically inclined Englishman, Squire Gensir, Bita's intellectual white patron, will be interested in it, and that the latter likes to collect specimens himself, as "the villagers were careless doing it" (171). The local population sees nothing special in a lovely plant, or for that matter, in Bita Plant. Both Jubban and the Squire *do* appreciate the marvelous and rare. However, Jubban's deferral to the Squire's usual wish that others not pick the flower results in it not being collected, as the Squire is unable to locate it. This small episode has much to do with the overarching symbolism of the novel and with the colonial impulse. As we have seen, the Craigs think of Bita as the "precious flowering" of *their* great work, which stands for the overall project of British colonialism. Squire Gensir, while ostensibly far superior to the Craigs, also emerges from this episode and elsewhere as the face of colonialism, for his appreciation of the merits of the island and its people's culture is based on superiority; *they*, the peasants, are too ignorant to appreciate it. But Jubban saw and correctly identified the flower. There is no question about the identity of the source for Squire Gensir (whose name must be a satiric shorthand for a triple redundancy, Squire Gentleman Sir). He is based on Walter Jekyll (1849–1929), a well-off Englishman who had come to Jamaica to escape the rapid industrialization of England and Europe. Like Gensir, he relished black Jamaican culture and language and urged McKay—who spoke perfect English—to write poems in dialect. McKay wrote eloquently of the effect Jekyll had on him in his autobiography.[8] It is worth noting here that Squire Gensir and Bita (and for that matter, their models, Jekyll and McKay himself), are in effect mirror images, in that each of them represent what J. Michael Dash has termed "hybrid personalities . . . whose legitimacy is equal to that of the native inhabitant" (1998, 101).

The Craigs and their brethren fit into what McKay calls a "species of white humanity" (4). This group recoils in horror from the racial mixing that the island's emancipation supposedly produced, and yet they favor light-skinned blacks such as Crazy Bow (before his incarceration), whose wunderkind musical abilities, on the piano, the fiddle, the banjo, and the guitar, link him to Bita. But, despite these musical abilities, his light skin would seem to dictate a bureaucratic post, "one of the little polite places that were always the plums of the lighter-skinned coloured people" (4), and he is sent to a private school. Learning the piano and the fiddle, however, like the artist in Plato's theories, carries him into madness, as he seemingly communes with the gods of music, leading him to Dionysian bouts of playing and drinking orange wine at the rambunctious "tea meetings" that dominate the social life of poorer and darker blacks on the island, and which provide a constant setting for the novel, a realm of "testing" where we and the white characters strain to see how well Bita meets the temptations of sensuous peasant culture.

The locals have very different standards, however, because of their colonization and their "backwoods" mentality. When whites feel moved to label Crazy Bow's talents according to Western ideas, they call him a "coloured Paganini," but "the peasants laughed at the idea of greatness in him. Greatness could not exist in the backwoods. . . . To them and to all the islanders greatness was a foreign thing" (8). They are much more accepting of Bita's elevation, as she has indeed become a "foreign thing."

Repeatedly, in the first section of the novel, McKay refers to the "peasants" and makes us care for their feelings and opinions far more than those of the Craigs, who are missionaries but also colonists, as they seek to change the people into model Brits. Further, the use of the term "backwoods" perhaps reflects McKay's time in America, when he would have seen the sharp distinction between not just urban and rural blacks, but also between small-city citizens and folk who live in agricultural communities, in the "backwoods." Certainly, in Hurston's novels and stories, even the citizens of tiny Eatonville feel themselves superior to the "country" folk who live in Polk County, working in the "backwoods" sawmill and turpentine camps. This thematic of "backwoods" figures largely in other writers of the South and the Caribbean, such as Mark Twain, Marjorie Kinnan Rawlings, Zora Neale Hurston, William Faulkner, Edward Kamau Brathwaite, Erna Brodber, and Derek Walcott.

McKay, like Hearn, carefully provides the math of color caste on the island, since it will be a repeated refrain throughout the narrative. Three-fourths are descendants of slaves and are dark; one-fifth is light brown, because of white blood. The rest are white, East Indian, or Chinese—yet admixtures are common. Later, he discusses the ways in which all these communities are drained by immigration outward. Jordan Plant had four brothers, but three left to work on the Panama Canal and the fourth joined the army. Only Jordan, "rooted in the soil," does well.

The Panama Canal was a jealously fought-over project, in terms both of its location (Panama, Nicaragua, or Mexico) and its control (the Vanderbilts, filibusters, or the United States). It was yet another locus for drawing together the various peoples of the Caribbean. As Bita proudly points out to the Craigs, who bitterly resent the drain of outstanding peasants, "they make more money there . . . eight times more gain. . . . They say the construction is a mighty work and the black labour the best down there, especially the Jamaicans and Haitians" (35), an early indication of her respect for black industry and black men.[9]

McKay's use of the term "hardy peasants," his indication of their vital contribution to the building of the Panama Canal, and the myriad other passages that show what he means by that term could well be a tip of his hat, not only to Tolstoy, but also to Thomas Hardy (1840–1928), whose sympathetic and compelling portraits of British peasants in works such as *Tess of the D'Urbervilles* (1891) suggested the potential of contrast between peasants and upper-class British. Like Hardy, who lovingly depicts mundane activities such as the shearing of the sheep in *Far from the Madding Crowd* (1874), McKay provides a similar tableau when Bita takes part in the harvesting of the pimento crop, a scene that comes alive through radiant natural description.

The minor characters provide much of the color and "peasant" wisdom of the book. Another of Bita's suitors, Hopping Dick, dancer and dandy, is the son of the wily horse trader Amos Delgado. His girlfriend, Belle Black, may sing in the choir, but she is looked down on, as her father, Nias, won't marry her mother or become a church member, nor will she. Significantly, Nias is an expert drummer, aligning him with African heritage, and both he and his daughter frequent the "ungodly" tea meetings. Hopping Dick is roundly disliked by the Craigs' servant Rosyanna, who considers him "a grogshop customer, a horse-gambler and a notorious feminine heart-breaker" (43). But she also is offended when he tells Bita not to carry heavy loads herself, like "big-foot country gals," as she (Rosyanna) is both big and barefooted. Here McKay offers two excellent examples of both resistance to and acceptance of colonizing standards. Rosyanna objects to Hopping Dick's attention to Bita because he is "low-down," not up to white standards of quality, unlike the prissy Herald Day. Yet her country identity objects to his put down of her from the viewpoint of precisely the same set of authorities—white standards of propriety. Local color is also rendered through food and the peasant market where exotic fare is sold. But the market is also the community's crossroads where all come together in convivial discourse while simultaneously engaging in commerce. Both the crossroads and the market are favored sites for the African orisha Esu-Eleggua, whose propitiation is a sine qua non for any ritual—in this case Bita's drawn-out "immersion/baptism" in folk culture.[10] The market draws out the poet in McKay:

> Broad warm faces of all colours between brown and black, sweating comfortably, freely in gay calico clothes, the full hum of their broad broken speech mounting and falling in strong waves under the sheer outdoor sun. Bita mingled in the crowd, responsive to the feeling, the colour, the smell, the swell and press of it. It gave her the sensation of a reservoir of familiar kindred humanity into which she had descended for baptism. She had never had that big moving feeling as a girl when she visited the native market. And she thought that if she had never gone abroad for a period so long, from which she had become accustomed to viewing her native life in perspective, she might never had had that experience. (40)

The trope of "baptism" annuls the "false birth" that is the fantasy of the Craigs, who think they have "baptized" Bita into the white world as their adopted child, and shows that Bita has in fact been only prepared for the *real* baptism here, which so closely echoes the theory of immersion and ascent put forward by Stepto in his seminal study, *Behind the Veil*. These perceptions of Bita in the market also closely parallel Hurston's remarks after returning to Eatonville from her years in the North to gather folklore for her Ph.D. degree in anthropology at Columbia. She had always known the traditions of her native South, but her training at Barnard and Columbia had given her both distance from her culture, and therefore perspective, and new lens through which to see it. As she put it, it had previously been too close to her, which had earlier fit her "like a tight chemise. I couldn't see it for wearing it" (*Mules*, 1935, 3).

The scene at the market identifies island produce with the natives, and this finds extension in Bita's first meal back home, which firmly indicates the Afro-Caribbean nature of this "backwoods" culture: "Thick Congo-pea soup, seasoned with salted beef and scallion . . . stewed goat meat, the sauce high-coloured with annatoo, and . . . an assortment of native vegetables, the yellow and flowery afou yam, bourbon-pink cocoes and fine mashed choo-chos. It was pure native cooking" (53). The emphasis on "purity" rather aligns McKay (at least in this novel) with Delany, who similarly validated "pure" African blood and traditions in *Blake*.

Banana Bottom, a kind of saving remnant of "pure" peasant culture, replicates an irony in Toni Morrison's *Sula*, where the black neighborhood of "The Bottom" is actually high up over the white town. We "ascend" with Bita when she is called home to care for her Aunt Nommy, who is ill. Jordan Plant's substantial six-room home is situated in a flower garden "full of heavy-scented hot-country flowers growing untidily thick together, bell-flowers and bluebells, the night jasmine and the creeping jasmine . . . the running bramble, crotons of many colours, the climbing sweet-william trailing its tiny but strong vermilion bloom along the veranda, and the exquisitely speckled tania flowers and the delicate variegated painted-ladies" (50–51). This passage, one of many we could point out in the novel as replicating Walt Whitman's addiction to providing lists of plants, animals, and people, makes Banana Bottom a kind of Eden, and indeed Bita has crossed over to Jordan, her father, while *ascending*, to use the word so key to Stepto's formula, and also *immersing* herself in folk culture.

These inventories can also, as with Janie's pear tree in *Their Eyes*, take on a highly sexual aspect: "The bellflowers were lovely cream-white and the coffee roses had spread all over the place. In the breadkind garden there was the old akee tree . . . full of fruit, the vermilion husks opening to view the deep-cream lobes and shiny black seeds" (58), a description that summons up images of Georgia O'Keefe's highly suggestive paintings of flowers and shells. Compare Hurston's famous portrait of sexual awakening in *Their Eyes*: "She was stretched on her back beneath the pear tree soaking in the alto chant of the visiting bees, the gold of the sun and the panting breath of the breeze when the inaudible voice of it all came to her. She saw a dust-bearing bee sink into the sanctum of a bloom; the thousand sister-calyxes arch to meet the love embrace and the ecstatic shiver of the tree from root to tiniest branch creaming in every blossom and frothing with delight. So this was a marriage! She had been summoned to behold a revelation. Then Janie felt a pain remorseless sweet that left her limp and languid" (24). The ability of peasant folk like Jubban and Janie to read sublime aspects of nature underscores their unsuspected sensibilities, suggesting the sustaining power of a proper relation to nature.

Man, of course, is part of nature as well, and both McKay and Hurston configure the human body with fruits of nature. In a magnificent scene, Bita undresses at home and looks at her body in the mirror: "She caressed her breasts like maturing pomegranates, her skin firm and smooth like the sheath of a blossoming banana, her luxuriant hair, close-curling like thick fibrous roots, gazed at her own warm-brown eyes. . . . 'Only a nigger gal!' Ah, but she was proud of being a Negro girl. And no sneer, no sarcasm, no banal ridicule of a ridiculous world could destroy her confidence and pride in herself and make her feel ashamed of that fine body that was the temple of her high spirit. For she knew that she was a worthy human being. She knew that she was beautiful" (266). This scene echoes the sentiment, if not the details, of the scene in *Their Eyes* when Tea Cake has Janie look in the mirror to admire her beauty. He too, like Jubban, is a man of the people and is black. Even earlier, however, when Jody dies, Janie remembers: "Years ago, she had told her girl self to wait for her in the looking glass. It had been a long time since she had remembered. Perhaps she'd better look. She went over to the dresser and looked hard at her skin and features. The young girl was gone, but a handsome woman had taken her place. She tore off the kerchief from her head and let down her plentiful hair. The weight, the length, the glory was there" (135). The use of strongly local natural imagery to describe Bita's beauty is a tactic Hurston also uses in describing Janie's body as she comes back to Eatonville after Tea Cake's death: "The men noticed her firm buttocks like she had grape fruits in her hip pockets; the great rope of black hair swinging to her waist and unraveling in the wind like a plume; then her pugnacious breasts trying to bore holes in her shirt" (11).[11]

McKay, however, takes the relationship between man and surrounding nature and extends it to the entire community. The congregation of the rural church, acting out what Hurston called the "Negro will to adorn," brings nature's bounty inside; the church sports "arches of plaited palm fronds, roses and hibiscus, marigolds and buttonflowers, long bamboo branches . . . banana suckers . . . ropes of running ferns," appropriate decorations for a Caribbean ceremony that includes a recitation:

Sow the seeds of children's love
So that they may grow
Flowering plants that God above
Blesseth here below
Scatter flowers for children's day,
Flowers so pure and bright
That along life's pathway they
E'er may be our light. (61)

This is countered, however, when we learn that the prize books given to these same children are all European in origin, be it the Grimm brothers, Hans Christian Anderson, or Bible tales. "Tales of all children, except Negro children, for little black and brown readers" (61), hardly the right kind of literary "flowers" to guide them. Similarly, during the Harvest Festival post office ritual, little notes are passed; however, the tradition seems British, since the color references are to "blue eyes," an "ivory hand," and "golden hair." As McKay mockingly states, "Miss Chocolate Lips shrilled with unfeigned delight over "I adore your cherry lips." Such moments remind us that even in upland black pockets of the island, colonial-imposed mimicry prevails. A more positive example of this is found in the big Independence Day picnic, which is significantly held on Tabletop, the plateau at the top of the mountain, where African drumming is conducted as celebrants march up to the cricket field, a fusion of the colonized and the colonizer, but also a distillation of productive and proud peasant hybridity. Again, the location and the occasion illustrate perfectly Bita's continuing experience of ascent and immersion.

Tack Tally, recently returned from Panama in flamboyant garb and loaded with jewelry, is deemed a "hurry-come-up," "a have-nothing who had risen to be a have-something, but also one of bad reputation," a male-negative to Bita's female-positive. Significantly, when Tack, ruing the fact that he cannot approach Bita, rehearses the Crazy Bow story, Jubban, Jordan's driver, a strapping, velvety black man, defends her, beating him, later stating—and again significantly, in dialect, "Teach him to keep am mongoose mout' offen folkses bettarn him" (70). As this is the man who will eventually marry Bita, it is important that he is closely aligned with her father, defends feminine virtue, and speaks the pithy dialect of the people Bita so loves. Further, his massive strength and dark good looks identify him, as we eventually realize, as a strong counterpart to his chief rival, the stiff, smarmy, and very British Herald Newton Day.

Near the end of the novel, it is Jubban who takes Bita home after her "vision" and fall at a revival, which causes her to see him as "a responsible person in the family" (252). The fact that his gentle ways with animals have led to a medal from the Society for the Prevention of Cruelty to Animals underlines his keen understanding of a farmer's necessary respect for animals, but it also suggests the tenderness Bita is looking for in a partner, as a balance for masculine strength. Finally, this seemingly small detail is a telling contrast to Herald Day's bestiality (he falls from grace after having intercourse with a goat).

McKay rather insists on Jubban's color and its beauty. Years before the scene above, when Bita first moves to Banana Bottom to care for ailing Aunt Nommy, she becomes "conscious of the existence of her father's drayman for the first time, remarked his frank, broad, blue-black and solid jaws, and thought that it was all right for her father to have confidence in him" (115). It is significant that this is just after we have been informed of her sexual interest in Hopping Dick, a ne'er-do-well, and her physical repugnance for her fiancé, Herald. This embrace of a "blue-black" man on Bita and McKay's part challenges the color prejudice within the race that Frantz Fanon noted. Indeed, he declared, "The number of sayings, proverbs, petty rules of conduct that govern the choice of a lover in the Antilles is astounding. It is always essential to avoid falling back into the pit of niggerhood, and every woman in the Antilles, whether in a casual flirtation or in a serious affair, is determined to select the least black of the men" (Fanon 1967, 47). Reversing this, McKay and Bita valorize and aestheticize Jubban's color, especially in the scene late in the novel at a tea meeting, when he wins the right to kiss the queen, Bita, who thinks: "His skin possessed a velvety indigo-black tone like an eggplant [another natural description of beauty] and that among all the men gathered there at that tea-meeting he was the most appealing" (279).

This issue of color at first threatens to send Bita into Herald's arms. After she agrees to marry him, she thinks, "What could a cultivated Negro girl from the country hope for better than a parson. . . . If she had happened to be born a light-brown or yellow girl, she might, with her training, easily get away with a man of a similar complexion—a local functionary. . . . But she was in the black and dark-brown group and there were no prospects of her breaking into the intimate social circles of the smart light-brown and yellow groups" (101), a bitter commentary stemming from McKay's own ostracism because of color in Jamaica, sentiments similar to those examined in Wallace Thurman's acidic novel centering on a dark oppressed heroine, *The Blacker the Berry* (1929). It is to McKay's credit that he shows Bita looking at all sides of the question of color, especially in terms of her own place and chances of positioning within its hierarchies. Yet, when challenged by Herald, she exclaims: "Let me tell you right now that a white person is just like any other human being to me. I thank God that although I was brought up and educated among white people, I have never wanted to be anything but myself. I take pride in being coloured and different, just as an intelligent white person does in being white. I can't imagine anything more tragic than people torturing themselves to be different from their natural unchangeable selves" (169). This aligns Bita with Hurston, who once proclaimed, "I am not tragically colored. . . . I do not belong to the sobbing school of Negrohood who hold that nature somehow has given them a lowdown dirty deal. . . . No, I do not weep at the world—I am too busy sharpening my oyster knife" ("How it Feels," 1979, 153).

Color, however, is only one aspect of race. It is at a tea meeting that the thematic of dance is introduced, a key concept of both the Harlem Renaissance and the gestural language of Southern African American and Caribbean literature. Bita, who had learned Western dance forms in London, now significantly joins a "grand altogether breakdown": she "danced as she had never danced since she was a girl . . . wiggling and swaying and sliding along, the memories of her tomboyish girlhood rushing sparkling over her like water cascading over one bathing upon a hot summer's day . . . forgetting herself . . . dancing down the barrier between high breeding and common pleasures under her light stamping feet until she was one with the crowd" (84). This passage is the heart of the novel, and it employs the abundant water imagery McKay favors. Here the "baptism" becomes the more natural island phenomenon of standing under a waterfall, with the refreshment of reviving memory. Further, McKay tells us, "the crowd rejoiced to see her dance," indicating reciprocal union.

In another scene involving water and memory, evoking Melville's assertion that meditation and water are wedded forever, Bita, after seeing nude pubescent boys swimming and discussing their pubic hair, takes a dip herself in a sequestered pool. "She turned on her back to enjoy the water cooling on her breasts. . . . How delicious was the feeling of floating! To feel that one can suspend oneself upon a yawning depth and drift, drifting in perfect confidence without the slightest intruding thought of danger" (117). While this scene leads to other consequences, it also centrally figures the "immersion" thematic of the narrative. Just before she slips into the water, Bita muses on her village: "All of her body was tingling sweet with affectionate feeling for the place." Once in the water, she idly sorts through European memories, including one of a white boy she had liked. But her assurance of "confidence" is misplaced, for the rogue Tack Tally has watched her, just as she watched the boys, and has stolen her clothes. Wrapping herself in ferns, she pursues him, a Caribbean Eve, calling him an "ugly monkey! I'll have you arrested" (118). Here, as elsewhere in the novel, McKay sets up the possibility of another rape, or at least of Bita's seduction, but it never happens. Instead, he plays the scene as a comic signification on Eden, and has Bita, who is very black herself, use a racial epithet that was heard often in Harlem, where Caribbean immigrants like McKay and Eric Walrond were called "monkey chasers."

Significantly, echoing the multivalent implications of the novel, the Plant family is multihued itself, like the culture it expresses. Jordan and Bita are black, his wife, Aunt Nommy, is "cocoa-plant" brown, while her son from her first marriage, Barnaby (Bab), is "banana"-colored. Consistently, McKay delights in using positive natural referents when describing the colors of his characters, a pattern he had used earlier in the worlds of color he limned in his Harlem and Marseilles novels, and he embraces the full spectrum without qualification.

Any consideration of McKay and Hurston must take into account their associations with the concept of "primitivism," which meant something quite different during the Harlem Renaissance—particularly among black artists—than it does today. A pairing of these two novels offers an opportunity to consider black/white divides on the issue, for both McKay and Hurston were supported by white patrons who were keenly interested in the "cult of the primitive." McKay himself saw nothing wrong with the term, nor did Hurston. Speaking of the mistaken idea that his character Jake in *Home to Harlem* was an alter ego, McKay lamented, "I couldn't indulge in such self-flattery as to claim Jake . . . as a portrait of myself. My damned white education has robbed me of much of the primitive vitality, the pure stamina, the simple un-swaggering strength of the Jakes of the Negro race" (*Long Way*, 1937, 229).

We should remember that Jake, who reappears in *Banjo*, hails from the Southern United States, and McKay's portrait of him utilizes everything he had learned about black Southerners from his time in Alabama, but also, and primarily, from the black Southern immigrants to Harlem, who added so much folklore, dialect, and down-home humor to the discourse of the Age of the New Negro. Two of McKay's constant companions in his New York base during this period (1917–19), "Mr. Morris" and Manda, taught him much about the black South, as did the people he met in the cabarets and clubs: "It was not until I was forced down among the rough body of the great serving class of Negroes that I got to know my Aframerica." McKay, however, found a contrast between the "spontaneous . . . loose freedom" of these new friends and "the definite peasant patterns by which I had been raised" (cited in Wayne Cooper 1987, 87), which accounts for his admiration of the "purity" and "vitality" of figures like Jake. McKay's 1940 *Harlem: Negro Metropolis* draws several lines of connection between Southern and West Indian blacks but also notes differences. Cults and mystic chapels were run by both Southern conjurors and West Indian Obeah practitioners, and they had much in common. Immigrants from the South routinely played the numbers game, which was controlled for a time by a Cuban black named Messolino. However, McKay notes that West Indians were frequently resented for their overly serious demeanor, their boasting about (largely fictional) better conditions in the island, and their (to McKay) rather absurd loyalty to the mother country that was oppressing them. The great coming together of the two groups, however, was in Garveyism. Marcus Garvey (1887–1940) was from Jamaica, and his elaborate back-to-Africa plans (replete with a steamship line, a new black religion, and a hierarchy of nobility) united Southern and Caribbean blacks (*Harlem*, 75, 108, 132–34, 150ff.).[12] Garvey was a part of the cult of the primitive in Harlem, and his romantic presentation of Africa to the masses had correspondences in the poetry of McKay, Countee Cullen, Langston Hughes, and many other writers of the Harlem Renaissance.[13]

The primitive was also, in some ways, a label for the ordinary folk of Florida and Jamaica, whose lives McKay and Hurston reverently recorded through a presentation of the quotidian aspects of African American and Afro-Caribbean life. McKay, responding to criticisms of *Home to Harlem*, complained about "not a line of critical encouragement for the exploitation of the homely things—of Maudy's wash tub, Aunt Jemima's white folks, Miss Ann's old clothes for work and wages, George's Yessah-boss, dining care and Pullman services, barber and shoe shine shops, chittling and corn-pone joints—all the lowly things that go into the formation of the Aframerican soil into the formation of the Aframerican society, still has its roots" (Wayne Cooper 1973, 133). In *Banana Bottom*, however, he would vastly expand the inventory of items such as this, with greater effect, as he knew that culture far better than that of the rural South, which he alludes to in the passage quoted. Hurston, of course, knew *both* that world and the Caribbean.

McKay's early role in the Harlem Renaissance and his friendships with black and white modernists would have made him conversant with the various interpretations of the "primitive" and of the fear such concepts could evoke in whites, in terms both of its manifestations in blacks and the suspicion that such dangerous concepts could be contagious; even worse, could contact with the "primitive" bring out hidden elements of it in one's own atavistic past?

In *Banana Bottom*, Squire Gensir comes across as a positive influence on Bita and as someone who believes in a rather pure definition of "primitivism." Bita herself criticizes his severely simple two-room "hut": "it's so primitive," to which he replies that "primitive living was more complex than his visitor imagined. That it was the art of knowing how to eliminate the non-essentials that militate against plastic living and preventing accumulations, valuable or worthless" (120). Significantly, this is not an utterance by Squire Gensir but a summary of what he said to Bita by the author, and it clearly proceeds more from a reaction to Eurocentric excess than to African-inspired aesthetics. Editing, which is the real thrust here, is quite opposed, in fact, to what Hurston has called the African impulse toward "adornment," as even a cursory glance at African court aesthetics would reveal. Gensir's perspective, in fact, has more to do with European interpretations of African art—such as that of the sculptor Brancusi—than with anything specifically African. His appreciation of Caribbean music, however, is more to the point, as is his feeling that "some of our famous European fables have their origin in Africa. Even the mumbo-jumbo of the Obeahmen fascinates me. . . . Obeah is only a form of primitive superstition. As Christianity is a form of civilized superstition" (124). This declaration fits Franz Boas's concept of cultural relativism and is a good example of how the term "primitive" did not necessarily mean something negative to McKay and Hurston, who were in basic agreement with the forward-thinking sociologists and anthropologists of the time.

It should also be noted, however, that Squire Gensir's conversations with Bita reveal quite a few points of difference between them, and that, although they both learn from and enjoy each other's company, Bita's final choices in the novel are hers. Gensir may act as a catalyst, but he is hardly the controlling puppet master some suggest. The key statement he makes might be: "Obeah is part of your folklore, like your Anancy tales and your digging jammas. And your folklore is the spiritual link between you and your ancestral origin. . . . My mind is richer because I know your folklore. I am sure you believe the fables of la Fontaine and of Aesop fine and literary and the Anancy stories common and vulgar. Yet many of the Anancy stories are superior" (125). Elsewhere, he notes a close resemblance between a Jamaican folk song and a piece by Mozart.[14]

Both Gensir and McKay seem to share, as Hurston certainly did, Franz Boas's refutation of the common assumption that primitive peoples lacked complexity. In his authoritative study *The Mind of Primitive Man* (1916), which Hurston, and perhaps McKay too, had read, Boas showed conclusively that "primitive cultures" were and are, in fact, often more complex than contemporary Western societies in some ways, particularly in regard to music, religion, and regulated social custom. As noted, the Squire delights in the Anancy tales, which like the comic and satirical ditties the folk in this novel create, use humor to deal with complicated situations, but also to bring the distant object close, in order to examine and "test" it. Through these devices, which initially seem cruel, the community eventually embraces Bita.

In connection with Gensir's remarks about religion and superstition, we remember that Delany's Blake has a very similar reaction to conjure, an American counterpart to Obeah. While he respects the sustaining elements of it, he ultimately feels it is superstition. The difference, however, lies in the fact that despite his criticism of Protestant Christianity as whites practiced it, Delany *did* believe in that faith, unlike Gensir and, until his late life conversion to Catholicism, McKay. This becomes manifest in Ma Legge and Yoni's visit to the cave of the Obeahman Wumbe. His rituals and trappings are described respectfully, but his advice about a rival—which implicates Bita—reveals the falsity of his authority, as does his exorbitant fee of two pounds, which is Yoni's salary for two months.

Perhaps one of the reasons that McKay withholds any satirical treatment here is that this scene prepares us for a tragedy that follows, although it is set in motion comically. The gossip Sister Phibby spies Tack being admitted by Yoni to the church annex where she works. "'Ah ketcham!' she ejaculated to herself. 'So dat's what. Jes' a twat like any udder in de fox grass wid all har preening and primping an' fanning har 'long de road like a high lady. Widouten shame fer de mission and de school!'" (143). Her exposure of Yoni brings down the wrath of Pa Legge upon Tack, who responds to the old man's rage by choking him.[15] Although Pa dies of a heart attack, Tack thinks he has killed him and flees, and all assume he has gone back to Panama. Wumbe, on his way to his cave, sees a white vulture, a sure sign of disaster; he then finds Tack's body swinging from a tree in front of the cave, a suicide's rebuke to the conjuror whose Obeah seemingly failed him.

This seemingly tangential story has many uses, for Yoni's path could have been Bita's, who is similarly "tested" many times, and once by Tack, whose sexual allure does not escape her, despite her overall contempt for him. And her stronger appreciation of the other dandy, Hopping Dick, offers another dangerous parallel. Moreover, Tack, like Bita, has gone away from Jamaica, earning an "education," although that of a sporting man in Panama. Yet temptations, superstitions, and false forms of masculine codes doom him.

Tack's irreverence and disruptive nature—acquired in foreign parts—relate him to his name, for the 1760 slave revolt known as Tacky's Rebellion was one of the legendary events in Jamaican history. Tacky was one of the warlike Coromantee people of West Africa and became an overseer after being enslaved in Jamaica. Working with Obeahmen, he and his followers united many slaves and instigated a revolt on Easter Sunday. The Obeahmen prophesied that the powder they dispensed would protect the combatants. The revolt was crushed, but over 400 blacks and 60 whites were killed. To refute the Obeah prophecy, whites hung an Obeahman, with his ornaments of teeth, bones, and feathers. Edward Long reported that Tacky was supposed to be able to catch all the bullets fired at him in his hand, and that he would then fling them back at the whites (1774, 451–52). Yet Tacky was shot, and his head was severed and placed on display. His surviving men committed suicide in a cave near what is now known as Tacky's Falls.[16] It is easy to see many of these details in the scenes involving the Obeahman and Tack, especially when the latter finds Tack hanging outside his cave. The text reads, "Convinced that he had murdered Pap Legge, Tack remembered that he had recently paid Wumbe well to protect him from Evil," perhaps a conscious parallel to the false promises of the Obeahmen during Tacky's Rebellion. The local minister preaches a great sermon against Obeah after Tack's body is found at the cave, claiming, "The continent we came from is cursed and abandoned of God because of magic. We brought along the curse with us from over there. It is sapping our strength [and making] for disunity," but we quickly see his real motive: "The Obeah is robbing the churches. . . . The preachers can hardly make a living. . . . Throw the jungle out of your hearts and forget Africa" (153–55). This echoes the shrewd observations of Squire Gensir, in that one "superstition" seeks to weed out another, but more from a sense of self-interest than from faith.

The "test" of Tack takes a new form later when Bita begins to be interested in the book's other dandy, Hopping Dick. Mrs. Craig's refusal to let Bita join him at a party initiates the clear realization in her that she has always been Mrs. Craig's "pet experiment," and that she now has a "natural opposition" to her white mother. The word "natural" is not used lightly; in a rush of perception, she and we see that "the profession of religion left her indifferent . . . this religion that had been imposed upon and planted in her young mind. She became contemptuous of everything—the plan of her education, and the way of existence at the mission, and her eye wandering to the photograph of her English college over her bed, she suddenly took and ripped it from its frame, tore the thing up and trampled the pieces under her feet" (212). This scene needs to be read with some care. It initially suggests that Bita rejects her entire experience in England. Yet we know she has come to appreciate literature, music, and any number of other subjects she studied there. These interests continue after she marries Jubban and settles down amid "peasant" culture. This scene reflects her suddenly full perception of the colonizing educational project, and the costs of such a program, in terms of her personal identity and her relation to her original culture.

Bita's recognition here constitutes a preamble to the rather comic and final break with Mrs. Craig. Told by the latter she is to have no more contact with Hopping Dick, Bita finds a dance tune in her head: "Just going to do the thing I want / No Matter who don't like it." This leads her to impishly remark to Mrs. Craig, "I like Mr. Delgado. Like him much more than I ever did Herald Day. After all he is a biped and not a quadruped" (219). This overt reference to Herald's bestiality—and thus a naked reference to perverted sexuality—proves to be the final straw for the repressed Mrs. Craig, and Bita goes back to Banana Bottom for good.

Their Eyes Were Watching God builds to a climax with the onset of a terrible hurricane. McKay, however, who eventually employs this catastrophe, precedes it with a three-year drought, reversing the watery image. Earlier, telling of a Scotsman who sired a large multiracial family, McKay describes the enriching union of blood through water imagery—a stream. Here, the terrible drought provides an obverse portrait of this generative act. This catastrophe creates havoc for farmers because they have been led by colonizing U.S. fruit companies to place their confidence entirely in bananas, while wiser figures such as Bita's "peasant" father, Jordan, have maintained a better balance of crops, which sustains them during the drought.[17] This section of the novel, like many others, is strongly reliant on biblical mythology, suggesting the wisdom of Joseph in Egypt. And, indeed, the rule of the British is put forward here as a kind of captivity. In this respect, we would do well to reconsider the popular "pastoral" notion of the novel, in several ways. As Edward Said has remarked, imperialism, an act of geographical violence, creates a loss of locality for the native, who must then somehow restore it, if only through the imagination (1993, 78). Predatory, colonial patterns of agriculture have indeed annulled the character of Jamaica. Jordan and Jubban have an antidote to this, partly through their protected and relatively isolated acres, but also in their adherence to their shrewd "peasant" knowledge of the land and its uses.

Upland Banana Bottom is less affected by the drought than other areas, but everyone seems to see the aridity as punishment for sin. A great revival takes place, led by a small white man who has previously failed in business enterprises. In describing these failures, McKay issues a critique of American trade patterns; local attempts to set up businesses have failed because American firms underprice them, selling goods in the islands for less than in the United States. Things are going badly in other ways too. Bita's cousin Bab, who had studied to be a civil servant, is undone by a switch from test results to selections made by sitting officials. Although some of them are black, they have light wives and children and refuse to hire dark Jamaicans, despite high scores. Worse is the hypocritical reason one gives: the dark peasants were "clever enough to pass the examination. Civil Service candidates . . . should come from respectable and refined homes" (235), an utterance at odds with the speaker's own origins in dire poverty.[18] A related economic issue is the importation of workers from India, "coolies," who take work away from blacks through cheaper wages, leading to more emigration of the island's young. Similarly, Chinese shopkeepers are said to offer shoddy goods in order to undercut local rivals. Here, and in many other moments in the narrative, McKay reveals a serious interest in the rupturing modernist economics that is transforming the island, belying Carby's claim that this is a romantic, utopian fable.[19] The thematic of tests and testing continues on multiple levels. Jubban comes to Bita's rescue when Tack Tally is tormenting her, and then again when she falls down helpless during a revival. His third and final test (the number echoes that of the traditional trials of the hero) comes when Arthur, the bastard mulatto son of a rich white planter, assaults and insults her: "You ought to feel proud a gen'man like me want fer kiss you when youse only a black girl" (262). Bita's dislike had already been evident before the attack, as she mused on his voice and dialect, "so different from the peasants' way of speech; their brief concise phrases, words dark and yielding as the soil and green as the grass wet with dew, pliant as supple-jacks and juicy as mangoes, sifted and moulded to give expression to simple Negro tongue" (262), sentiments that McKay originally received from Walter Jekyll, but then made his own, in glowing, poetic passages such as this. Though he is never mentioned in this reverie, Jubban, who is, we find, nearby, speaks this very tongue, and he uses it—not in poetry, but in an indictment—as he protects Bita. Rejecting Arthur's labeling of him as a "jigger-foot drayman," he declares, "Mi feets em cleaner than you' mouth. . . . You t'ink ah 'fraid a you 'causen youse a son of a bacra? Ise a drayman but a man all de same an' it wi' tek a bigger one than you to lick mi black bottom wid a supple-jack," and knocks off the planter's white helmet. McKay, perhaps overstressing the point, tells us that "the white helmet . . . rested upon the head of busha and planter like a halo of protection. Under it slave-owners and slave-drivers had goaded the black herds to toil. . . . In spite of changing times they still remained the lords of the tropics" (264). Saved by a blue-black man she is growing to love, Bita tells Jubban, "I loathed his touching me, the slimy white hog" (265).

Before Bita chooses Jubban, however, McKay creates a powerfully moving scene. Bita's rapist, the crazy and now aging Crazy Bow, joins her, with her consent, in concert practice, first brilliantly playing Handel's *Judas Maccabaeus*, and then several spirituals. "He made the people weep, recreating again the spirit of the ancient martyrdom that still haunted the crumbled stones and rusted iron of many a West Indian plantation." Soon afterward, however, the Craigs' disabled child, Patou, irritates him, and he tries to strangle him, which leads to his reincarceration and death in a straitjacket (258). Crazy Bow represents a Jamaican variant of the myth of Philoctetes, whose magic bow is his only if he endures his painful wound. McKay interbraids this with Plato's concept of the artist, who becomes mad by soaring up in creative frenzy into the firmament, mingling with the gods. He must be banned from the Republic, and so it is with Crazy Bow. Yet his place in the book is to demonstrate an affinity between the two cultures, for his mastery of both Western and Afro-Caribbean musical forms—and the tangled nature they play in his madness—offers a kind of commentary on yet another possible route that Bita has not taken, and perhaps a commentary too, on McKay's tortured identity, which by this point in his life had taken many twists and turns.[20] In a deadly hurricane, Jordan Plant dies in the arms of

Malcolm Craig as they are trapped in a flooded river. Devastated, Mrs. Craig succumbs to a stroke only days later.[21]

But the storm has also cleared the ground for new crops and broken the drought, while watering seedlings. Similarly, the death of the patriarch sets the stage for Jubban replacing Jordan. Bita remembers her father's many kindnesses to his beloved child, especially after she was raped: "How strange and terrible her father's face had been, yet he had been so kind and more fatherly than ever to her. A fine father. And she had loved him deeply with a love rooted in respect. All the men that she really respected had something of his character: Malcolm Craig, Squire Gensir, Jubban" (288). In a strange but fitting denouement to the deaths, Bita and Jubban make love in the wagon that bears her dead father's body home: "Her conscience fortified her with a conviction of the approval of his spirit" (289).

· · · · ·

Just as Jubban has profited by Jordan's "rooting" and "planting" of Bita, he now helps sell the varied produce to hungry people, crops that Jordan raised instead of bananas. Jordan and Jubban offer a restoration of native agricultural patterns, which help reclaim the local. Aimé Césaire wrote of how colonial masters' focus on cotton, coca, or mostly banana cultivation, or of foreign grapevines or olive groves, came at the expense of "natural *economies* that have been disrupted—harmonious and viable *economies* adapted to the indigenous population—about food crops destroyed, malnutrition permanently introduced, agricultural development oriented solely toward the benefit of the metropolitan counties; about the looting of products, the looting of raw materials" (43). This outrage is seen as partially corrected through the marriage of Bita with Jubban, whose expanded lands and wise husbandry may help restore these viable *economies*.

As in *The Free Flag of Cuba* and *Blake*, the novel concludes with a double wedding, as Yoni and Hopping Dick also unite. The effect of this resembles instances in Shakespeare's comedies where a "noble" and a "peasant" couple wed. As is often the case, the "peasant" groom is a comic figure; Hopping Dick cracks jokes repeatedly.[22] The feasting concludes with the grooms spirited away to be made drunk. Hopping Dick obliges, but Jubban comes home early. Later that night, he and Bita are awakened by a serenade from the people: "That was Teacher Fearon's gift, Bita thought. How beautiful it was, that low singing below her window just before dawn! Oh, it made her happy. Those singing voices were the most beautiful gift of all" (306).

This could have been the end of the novel, and a fine one. But McKay has more in mind. Squire Gensir returns to England to tend to his sister, but dies there himself. We learn he has left his house, piano, and 500 pounds to Bita. Seated at the piano, she cannot play, but she can reflect:

> This man was the first to enter into the simple life of the island Negroes and proclaim significance and beauty in their transplanted African folk tales and in the words and music of their native dialect songs. . . . He had found artistry where others saw nothing, because he believed that wherever the imprints of nature and humanity were found, there also were the seeds of creative life, and that above the dreary levels of existence everywhere there were always the radiant, the mysterious, the wonderful, the strange great moments whose magic may be caught by any clairvoyant mind and turned into magical form for the joy of man. (310)

The final scenes take place years later, when Jubban and Bita have settled down to steady life with their son, Jordan. "They had adjusted themselves well to each other. The testing-time was over"—the final example of the testing theme that has dominated the book. "Her music, her reading, her thinking were the flowers of her intelligence and he the root in the earth upon which she was grafted, both nourished by the same soil" (313). Bita understands that Jubban accepts and is proud of her education, and that it is equivalent, in many ways, to the "natural" wisdom he has acquired as a farmer. Indeed, K. Chellappan has suggested that this union emblemizes the real "dualism" in the novel, which is that of man and nature, rather than the one identified by many critics as British/native (1992, 37). However, nature wears many faces in this novel, as in *Their Eyes*—characters die through floods in both novels, and hurricane winds destroy crops and homes. Sexual urges often seem merely bestial—literally so with Herald Day—and sometimes lead to tragedy. Just as in farming, proper checks and balances—weeding, if you will—are necessary in a moral cultivation of one's "garden." Bita is several times endangered by sexual temptation, and in a scene at her nuptials where she has to control a runaway horse, we see an apt metaphor for the duality of control/liberty.

In a seemingly minor but significant part of *Their Eyes*, the front porch wags Sam Watson and Lige Mosely debate what keeps people from touching a hot stove—"caution" or "nature." Lige declares, "Caution is de greatest thing in de world. If it wasn't for caution—." But Sam interrupts him, claiming, "Show me somethin' dat caution ever made! Look whut nature took and done. Nature got so high in uh black hen she got tuh lay uh white egg. Now you tell me, how come, whut got intuh man dat he got to tuh have hair round his mouth? Nature!" (103).

Bita and Janie both employ "caution" but ultimately trust "nature." Pheoby warns Janie against marrying Tea Cake: "You'se takin' uh awful chance," to which Janie replies, "Dis ain't no business proposition, and no race after property and titles. Dis is uh love game" (171), a remark that builds on her earlier pronouncement, "Ah always did want tuh git round uh whole heap, but Jody wouldn't 'low me tuh. . . . Ah'd sit dere wid de walls creepin' up on me and squeezin' all de life outa me. Pheoby, dese educated women got uh heap of things to sit down and consider. Somebody done tole 'em what to set down for. Nobody ain't told poor me, so sittin' still worries me. Ah wants tuh utilize mahself all over" (169). These pronouncements fit Bita and her eventual choice of Jubban precisely, *except* that McKay rewards her choice with economic prosperity too, as Jubban's wise husbandry, coupled with the inheritance Bita receives from her black and white patriarchs (surely symbolic of both her spiritual and her cultural inheritance from Jordan and Gensir) leads to not only her family's prosperity, but to that of the community as well, through their example.

All these scenes demonstrate that employing a simple "Western/native" dichotomy plays havoc with the subtle nuances of the two novels' concerns. As J. Michael Dash has suggested, resistance of Caribbean writers to Western imperialism—particularly that of the United States in the early twentieth century—led to foundationalist narratives that presented cultural authenticity "as identical with physical terrain," one "outside of global modernity." Thus we had a renewed interest in "hinterlands . . . peasantry . . . and indigenous values as a means of healing the national psyche and fostering a renewed sense of place. The 'peasant novel' thus became the vehicle for rethinking the national 'terroir' in the face of the centralizing, alienating thrust of the occupation" (2008, 33).[23]

Kotti Sree Ramesh and Kandula Nrupa Rani have observed that the usual practice of viewing the conflict between Bita and the Craigs as a black/white binary discounts the former's Caribbean identity, which is hybrid, even before her "adoption" and British education. The body of the book, which presents many examples of the highly polyglot nature of both the islander's ethnic identities and the overall, multilayered culture, should mitigate against such a reductive conception of the novel's organization and purposes. As Ramesh and Rani argue, by reading the novel against the backdrop of Jamaican colonization, we can better conceptualize the dynamic, fluid, and hybrid aspect of both Bita and the culture(s) she epitomizes. As Bita moves through various avatars of the factors that have shaped and continue to shape her, she constantly performs "translations" of cultures, thereby creating a kind of "third space" of perception and being (2006, 158–68).[24]

I have elsewhere written in some detail about the comic aspects of *Their Eyes* (Lowe 1994), and the same approach could be employed here with *Banana Bottom*, which in many ways is also comedic and ends with a marriage, the traditional ending of comedies. I have been more concerned, however, with tracing out the confluences—but also the differences—between Southern and Caribbean cultures and, particularly in this pairing of texts, between two varieties of the black diaspora. Still, the vexed issue of Bita's only marriage and Janie's last marriage deserves consideration. As noted earlier in this discussion, several critics have severely criticized Bita's marriage to Jubban. One wonders exactly what Bita should or could have done instead. The role of women in Britain in 1933—white women—was hardly expansive, and Bita has no desire to settle there in any case. What, precisely, would these critics have her do? She could presumably teach, as McKay's brother did, but women were never afforded higher positions at this time in Jamaica educational circles, and positions were often dependent on color— and Bita is dark. Because she inherits land and property from both her father and Squire Gensir, her "dowry" enables Jubban, the chosen heir of her father, to replicate his mentor's achievements and expand them, by utilizing time-proven methods of agriculture, rather than the mistaken ideas taken from outside "experts" that have ruined the other peasants. As in *Their Eyes*, his "seeds," like Tea Cake's, are meant to nourish and inspire the people to resist colonial patterns of dependency.

Florida at this time was experiencing its own modernization, which Hurston would document in much greater detail in her last novel, *Seraph on the Suwanee* (1948). Orange orchards, expanding and modernizing fishing fleets, the real estate boom, sawmill and turpentine camps, and the advent of immigrants from Cuba, the Azores, the Bahamas, the Caribbean, and elsewhere made for a hybrid population similar to the polyglot composition of the Northern cities, whose poverty and troubled racial relations, Carby seems to think, should have been Hurston's focus. As Konzett asserts, "In the end, *Their Eyes* emphasizes the cross-cultural and transnational characteristics of Florida, demonstrating that modern social, demographic, and cultural changes occur differently in various regions across the United States" (2002, 89).

A better way to approach this pairing of McKay's and Hurston's novels might be to accept them on their own terms. The fact that *Banana Bottom* focuses on emotion, folk culture, and interpersonal relationships of all kinds hardly categorizes it as "romantic." Yet many of the critics who have condemned the book use this term very loosely to damn a text that concerns the folk—a focus that is presumably unacceptable, unless the folk are in overt rebellion, thus becoming a "proletariat." Frantz Fanon, however, was concerned not just with revolution, but with the day-to-day operations of racism and color prejudice within the race, and with methods of conquering the self-hatred that the whites had instilled in Antilleans. Repeatedly, he turns to Césaire, who in his poetry and theory embraced the common man: "Do you understand? Césaire has *come down* [a form of Stepto's *immersion*]. He is ready to see what is happening at the very depths, and how he can go up [*ascent* in Stepto's terms]. He is ripe for the dawn. But he does not leave the black man down there. He lifts him to his own shoulders and raises him to the clouds" (1967, 197).

Yet we are concerned here, mainly, with a black woman, one who chooses marriage and motherhood over a career in a white-dominated colonial society. Many critics have read this as Bita's "fall," and not in the positive sense of "immersion." Michael North, in a cursory reading of *Banana Bottom* (which is a prelude to his more intense interest in McKay's early poetry), has claimed that the novel reflects McKay's final tribute to Walter Jekyll, in that the latter's fictional counterpart Gensir guides Bita as she seemingly chooses between "dialect, tea meetings, obeah, and sex, on the one hand, and standard English, hymn singing, Scotch Presbyterianism, and loveless marriage on the other." North goes on to assert that both these poles, however, are defined by the British, and that McKay did not see that it was a trap, "a false dichotomy between rigid, life-denying Scotch Presbyterianism and free-life-affirming Jamaican paganism. . . . Both sides were actually defined by the English, and it was false because it posed England as culture against Jamaica as nature" (1994, 102). This wrong-headed reading denies agency to both McKay and Bita and assumes there can be no middle ground, no hybrid identity, which the details of the novel contradict. There is no indication at the end of the novel that Bita is rejecting her education and the insights it has afforded her, or that she is lost in a "primitive" world through her marriage to Jubban. Indeed, it seems evident that, like Hurston, her exposure to Eurocentric culture has helped her to fully appreciate her own. North's reading actually endorses a European myth—namely that Bita turns out to be a Pygmalion-type construct after all—the only difference being that her shaper has been Gensir rather than the Craigs. Similarly, Belinda Edmondson insists that Bita lacks agency at the end of the novel, for she has simply followed a path dictated by Squire Gensir (1999, 73). Rhonda Cobham, by contrast, sees Bita as erased by the combined actions of the Squire and Jubban (1979, 71, 75). Reading the facts of the novel through a circumCaribbean lens, as we have seen, indicates otherwise; the key role Jubban and Bita play in the community at the conclusion of the novel should guide us toward insights not dissimilar from those of Trinh T. Minh-ha, as she considers the role of women in agricultural Africa, which McKay clearly sees as similar to that of women in rural black Jamaica: "The notion of *woman* not as sexed individual but as *home*, of *etiquette* as *communal survival*, the idea of attributing woman's oppression to the advent of a monetary economy . . . a gendered life-style[,] implies that non-interchangeable men and women work together for the survival of their community. The contrary may be said of life under the regime of industrial economics" (1989, 108).

McKay, in his sketch "Boyhood in Jamaica," asserted, "The people of Jamaica were like an exotic garden planted by God. And today I see them as something more. I see them as a rising people, and sometimes I think that the negroes amongst them will give leadership to the negroes of the world in the great struggle that lies ahead" (145). As one example of McKay's assertion, we might ponder the ways in which the concluding focus on agricultural production goes to the heart of the contemporary colonialism McKay was critiquing. The imposition of mono-crop farming by foreign corporations like the United Fruit Company intersected with the cultivation of small individual plots by local farmers. As Erna Brodber has stated, the administration of the island "still lay in the hands of the larger plantation interests. . . . The plot's expansion to include a new generation depended on the willingness of the large landowners to sell. How to engineer this increased space was a constant question for young blacks, who saw making a living from own account farming as the way to independence from the plantations" (1887, 147). Jordan Plant, and Jubban and Bita after him, seem to be models for precisely the kind of leadership McKay called for in the "great struggle" that lay ahead.

The Caribbean Connections of *Their Eyes Were Watching God*

There are multiple ways in which *Banana Bottom* and *Their Eyes Were Watching God* reflect each other, and while it is likely that Hurston knew *Banana Bottom*, which appeared four years before *Their Eyes*, the similarities would seem to come out of the common cultural configurations of the communities involved, which have both been fashioned away from, but in response to, colonial governments in tropical surroundings. A key distinction here is the parallel infection in both cultures of what Wilson Harris calls "philistinism." Indeed, he asserts that Caribbean literature exists "against a background of a philistine middle-class establishment. Philistinism is a much more complex state of mind than one first thinks and possesses unique elements in the Caribbean. It is also the natural *persona* humanity wears in a dangerous world, it is a way of playing safe, it is a way of taking no risks. Philistinism appears in unlikely guises, in sophisticated lies, sophisticated laughter and debunkings of mental image or creativity. The denial of profound exile, the refusal to perceive its own dismembered psychical world, is basic to Caribbean philistinism. It has led to a body of education which describes, feasts upon, rather than participates in, the activity of knowledge" (1983, 122). This issue lies at the heart of both *Banana Bottom* and *Their Eyes Were Watching God* and is presented as a mainstay of racial stereotyping in the U.S. South (in both black and white communities) and as a prop of colonial domination in Jamaica. Philistinism rears its head with the Craigs, Herald Newton Day, Phibby, and many other characters in McKay's narrative. Many members of the Eatonville community, such as those who want Janie to marry the undertaker from Winter Park after Jody dies, display these values as well, but the key exponents of philistinism are surely Jody himself, his minion Hezekiah, and the pompous and color-struck Mrs. Turner, who urges Janie to leave Tea Cake for her more proper and lighter-skinned brother. Both McKay and Hurston situate peasant culture as the antidote for vulgar middle-class aspirations, which they indicate is part of social mimicry of white society in each case.

Hurston wrote *Their Eyes* after her years of research in the Caribbean, which resulted in two books of anthropology/folklore: *Mules and Men* (1934), which considers the black folk culture of the U.S. South, and *Tell My Horse: Voodoo and Life in Haiti and Jamaica* (1938). As Hurston discovered, Jamaicans, colonized by the English, naturally read texts from the United States, including books of folklore such as Joel Chandler Harris's *Nights with Uncle Remus*, which had much in common with Jamaican Anancy tales. McKay's mentor, Walter Jekyll, had collected and published these tales. In *Tell My Horse*, Hurston replicated the method of folklore collection she had employed when writing *Mules and Men*, focusing once again on dialect, African religious influences, and African-inspired tales, legends, dances, jokes, and mythic historical memories. Through a nonfictional account of Hurston's several anthropological trips to the Caribbean, *Tell My Horse* constitutes one of the most arresting examples in all of Southern literature of the dramatic influence of the "indigo sea" on a Southern writer, who in this case was also a woman of color. Based on research Hurston did in the islands in 1936 and 1937, the book is inextricably bound up with her two greatest novels, *Their Eyes Were Watching God* (1937), which was actually written in Haiti, and *Moses, Man of the Mountain* (1939), wherein the biblical prophet is presented as the greatest hoodoo conjurer in history.[25]

Hurston claimed that Miami was "a polyglot of Caribbean and South American culture. . . with more than 30,000 Bahamians with their songs, dances, and stories, and instrumentation . . . Haitian songs, dances, instrumentation, and celebrations," while the area from Key West to Palm Beach had "Bahamian and Cuban elements in abundance" (1999, 66). Hurston, we remember, did not think the "primitive" was to be despised; so when she says that Bahamian folk culture is "more savage," she sees it as more authentic. According to her, "The Bahamian and the West Indian Negro generally, has had much less contact with the white man than the American Negro. As a result, speech, music, dancing, and other modes of expression are infinitely nearer the African. Thus the seeker finds valuable elements long lost to the American Negro." She goes on to say that American Negroes were not allowed to stay in tribal groupings, whereas that was not the case in the West Indies, where owners were often absent. She claims one can easily identify the tribal origins of many Bahamian tunes. And this has had an enriching effect in the American South: "Nightly in Palm Beach, Fort Pierce, Miami, Key West, and other cities of the Florida east coast the hot drumheads throb and the African-Bahamian folk arts seep into the soil of America" (1938, 91).[26]

The most striking thing about *Tell My Horse* is its respectful exploration and delineation of voodoo, or vodoun. Hurston, an initiated hoodoo priestess but also a Columbia-trained anthropologist, was the ideal investigator of this neo-African religion. Clearly, she saw many links between the hoodoo of the American South and vodoun. Her description of the main loas (gods), the rituals that attend them, and, above all, the way these gods inhabit people—the way they "ride their horses," to use the vernacular—makes for a fascinating and illuminating study.

Hurston's observations in Jamaica also center on race. The system there privileges mulattoes, and all of them seem to want to be British. "There is a frantic stampede white-ward to escape from Jamaica's black mass. . . . One must remember that Jamaica has slavery in her past and it takes many generations for the slave derivatives to get over their awe for the master-kind. Then there is the colonial attitude. Add to that the Negro's natural aptitude for imitation and you have Jamaica" (6). She is amused by the generations of illegitimate black children who pride themselves on their illustrious white ancestors and considers it all from a Southern perspective: "It is as if one stepped back to the days of slavery or the generation immediately after surrender when Negroes had little else to boast of except a left-hand kinship with the master, and the privileges that usually went with it of being house servants instead of field hands." However, the idea of emulating whites has a fatal flaw—black folk keep having children! "This is the weak place in the scheme. The blacks keep on being black and reminding folk where mulattoes come from, thus conjuring up tragic-comic dramas that bedevil security of the Jamaican mixed bloods" (7). Hurston elaborates on this by reporting on a banquet given in Jamaica to honor the president of Atlanta University, John Hope, who was, she states, "quite white in appearance." "All went well until John Hope was called upon to respond to a toast. He began his reply with, 'We negroes—.' Several people [mulattoes] all but collapsed. . . . If a man as white as that called himself a negro, what about them" (8).

This entire first chapter of *Tell My Horse*, in fact, is called the "Rooster's Egg," because of Hurston's amusement over the celebration of white fathers and the banishment of black mothers. "You hear about 'My father this and my father that . . . my father who was English, you know.' . . . You get the impression that these virile Englishmen do not require women to reproduce. They just come out to Jamaica, scratch out a nest and lay eggs that hatch into 'pink' Jamaicans" (8–9). The critique in many Southern African American texts of those within the community who are "color-struck" makes this Jamaican syndrome familiar. Clearly, scenes such as these suggested diasporic points of convergence for Hurston, who had dealt with this issue herself in many texts based on Southern culture, including a play entitled *Color Struck* (1926) and in the famous Mrs. Turner episode in *Their Eyes Were Watching God* (1937).

As these remarks suggest, in *Tell My Horse*, Hurston once again uses humor to drive her narrative along. However, her comic pronouncements often foreground serious, even reverent subjects. Her trip to the Maroon settlement at Accompong is accomplished on a pop-eyed mule, whose duel with Hurston occasions much mirth. But once at Accompong she intones: "I could feel the dead generations crowding me. Here was the oldest settlement of freedmen in the Western world . . . men who had thrown off the hands of slavery by their own courage and ingenuity. . . . I could not help remembering that a whole civilization and the mightiest nation on earth had grown up on the mainland since the first runaway slave had taken refuge in these mountains. They were here before the Pilgrims landed" (22), a wry displacement of the myth of the Puritan origins of the American self, but also an attempt to rupture the artificial chronological and geographical boundaries of the Americas. Even more than McKay, Hurston seemed to comprehend what Jacque Stephen Alexis has called "zonal cultures," which spill over artificial boundaries: "One must wonder in the face of this confluence of national cultures in zones, if we are not witnessing in today's world the beginning of the creation of zonal cultures which, at a higher level, would dominate national cultures" (translated and cited in Dash, 1998, 95).

Throughout her visits, Hurston draws parallels between cultural phenomena. "First we talked about things that are generally talked about in Jamaica. Brother Anansi, the Spider, that great cultural hero of West Africa who is personated in Haiti by Ti Malice and in the United States by Brer Rabbit" (25).[27] Hurston points out the folk one would not find in the South too, such as the "Hindoos," who prepare the curried goat she eats at a feast and the ethnic Chinese who are invited guests. In perhaps the most intriguing and titillating passages, Hurston investigates the old women who instruct young brides and mistresses-to-be in the art of love, including proper positions, muscular control, and the like. The "balm bath" is given to "remove everything mental, spiritual and physical that might work against a happy mating" (19). It is fascinating to note that the African American writer Frank Yerby includes a bath and a massage just like this in his celebrated Louisiana novel, *The Foxes of Harrow* (1946), where Odalie, the previously frigid Creole wife of Stephen Harrow, seeks instruction from hoodoo women in order to win her husband back from his quadroon mistress, and just such a bath rouses her desire and enables her to triumph. The old woman Caleen thinks, as she massages Odalie, "So we give bride in marriage in the dark hills of San Domingo. And she go to her man no green girl. . . . Never from her own mind, could maitresse change. But I change her, me, by Dambala, by the Virgin, by all the saints!" (224). By reading Hurston and Yerby together, we see the boundary-crossing "zonal culture" of African folklore, a process especially evident in Louisiana, which acquired many slaves from the more Afrocentric Caribbean.

Everywhere Hurston goes, it seems, she finds the world invested with spirits. There are taboos against all sorts of actions, rules for most activities, all based on the rule of the duppies, or spirits. The affinity of Afro-Caribbeans with black Southerners is signaled in many places, but strikingly here, as the details of a Jamaican funeral—which seemingly is designed mainly to ward off duppies (ghosts)—echoes in complexity the details of both Lucy Pearson's and Lucy Hurston's death rituals in, respectively, the novel based on her parents' marriage, *Jonah's Gourd Vine*, and *Dust Tracks on a Road*, her autobiography. As Hurston had already written *Jonah* (1934) but would compose *Dust Tracks* (1942) after her Caribbean experiences, she may have thought about these similarities as she wrote her autobiography.

Hurston carefully explains that the duppy/ghost in Jamaica is more feared than ghosts in Florida; more often, however, as in her other collections of folklore, she steps aside to let folk who get together around her communally tell often comic and sometimes terrifying tales of duppies they have known. As she listens, she does so as part of a diasporic community, but also as an alien from the mainland who represents the reader. When the tellers employ Jamaican terms, Hurston simply translates them with parentheses: "We talked . . . of dumb cane and of bissy (Kola nut) as an antidote" (30). Thus she is both inside and outside, a participant in the exchange and yet also a novice, but presumably, after her research concludes, a translator and a guide. Here her text implicitly argues the case for greater expertise in hemispheric languages and for texts that present differing languages — even if only word by word — side by side.

In yet another overlap of folklore, Hurston reports that Jamaicans believe that some early Africans brought to the island flew back to Africa — any African then could fly if they had never eaten salt. The myth of slaves flying back to Africa was told in the American South too, and Toni Morrison makes central use of it in *Song of Solomon* (1977). Mention should be made here of another link between the two women writers. Hurston makes fun of herself as she submits to the rigors of a five-day wild boar hunt with the Maroons. This part of the book delineates the culture of one of the most important prerevolutionary groups that continued to exist up to Hurston's time — the bands of runaways who mounted armed resistance to the slave owners from jungle/swamp hideaways, figures we initially saw in this book in Delany's *Blake*, and much more extensively in *All Souls' Rising*. The Maroons have always functioned as mythic sources of narrative, and Morrison employs them as such in her Caribbean novel, *Tar Baby* (1981). Hurston heard about the Caribbean long before her visits to the islands. Her native Florida was drawing more and more immigrants, whose stories, legends, and jokes were contributing in important ways to that state's folklore. Further, during her time in New York City, thousands of immigrants from the Caribbean worked and partied side by side with recent arrivals from the U.S. South. Accordingly, characters called "monkey chasers" appeared in Harlem Renaissance novels and stories, particularly when the writer himself or herself was from the Caribbean, as were Claude McKay and Eric Walrond. As noted earlier, the islands made their first appearance in Eugene O'Neill's *The Emperor Jones* (1920). This primitivist play's West Indian island often resembles Africa more than the Caribbean. Jones's superstitious fear of the beating tom-toms and the jungle echo the stereotypes associated with Southern blacks in Plantation School writing.[28] McKay and Walrond, however, created more authentic characters for their Harlem tales and helped to spread awareness of the dramatic potential for Caribbean material among Southern writers such as Hurston, Benjamin Brawley, and James Weldon Johnson. The latter, from Jacksonville, had already written eloquently about the Cuban community in his hometown and was proud of his Haitian and Bahamian forebears.

Hurston's Caribbean-inspired *Their Eyes Were Watching God* opens precisely as *Banana Bottom* does, with a heroine returning to her former community, changed by her education in another culture. The novels are quite different, however, in the nature of these "other" worlds. Bita's education has been formal, Western, and British and has not involved a man, while Janie's has come "down on the muck" with migrant workers, Indians, and the "Negro furthest down," all supervised by her Orpheus-like younger and darker husband, Virgible "Tea Cake" Woods. At the same time, however, I would not want to conflate the people on Hurston's "muck" and those in Banana Bottom. J. Michael Dash has pointed out how negritude in its political applications in the 1950s tended to argue a kind of black universalism that transcended national and geographical boundaries, annulling distinctions that are in fact vital to mining local resources and traditions (1978, 77). The same kind of caution is in order here. Further, as we have seen, at one point Bita rejects the falsity of her time in England (but not the education she received).[29] While Hurston does not choose to give Janie an equivalent formal education, the many years of her marriage to the pompous philistine Jody Starks offers something of an equivalent; her return to the folk with Tea Cake is similar to Bita's return to Banana Bottom and, ultimately, her marriage to Jubban. Glissant has warned of the ways in which Western "education" can lead to the "disequilibrium" of the elite, and then to the subjugated overall community's passive surrender of its "potential development, its real culture. . . . A close scrutiny of this dispossession is one way of fighting against collective self-destruction" (1989, 11–12). Both *Banana Bottom* and *Their Eyes* offer a telling example of this kind of necessary "close scrutiny." *Their Eyes* differs in important ways from *Banana Bottom*, too, in that the latter has no "close scrutiny" of painful memories of slavery. Nanny tells her granddaughter Janie the story of her own rape by her master and of her mistress's brutal slapping of her after Nanny gives birth to a gray-eyed blond baby. Her flight to the swamp echoes that of the Maroons who were in the South and also the Caribbean.[30] "Ah knowed de place was full uh moccasins and other bitin' snakes, but Ah was more skeered uh whut was behind me" (35), but soon Sherman's army comes with news of her liberation. Significantly, Nanny lived near Savannah, so she was close to the sea and the great port that trafficked with the Caribbean. Her relocation to west Florida is not specified as to location but could be near or in another coastal city like Pensacola. Nanny's "Maroon" history may indicate a link with the Caribbean, for Nanny was a famous militant Jamaica Maroon and Obeah woman (McCarthy 2007, 76).[31]

When Janie cannot love Logan Killicks, the husband Nanny selected for her, Nanny accuses her granddaughter of wanting "some dressed up dude dat got to look at de sole of his shoe everytime he cross de street tuh see whether he got enough leather dere tuh mak it across. You can buy and sell such as dem wid what you got" (42), a description that could easily apply to either Tack Tally or Hopping Dick in *Banana Bottom*. What differentiates Janie from Logan is a lack of wonder on his part, a missing appreciation of the natural: "Janie waited a bloom time, and a green time and an orange time. . . . She knew things that nobody had ever told her. For instance, the words of the trees and the wind. She often spoke to falling seeds and said, 'Ah hope you fall on soft ground.'. . . She knew the world was a stallion rolling in the blue pasture of ether," all of this a language unknown to Logan. Bita Plant similarly reads nature this way, and so does Jubban, which in many ways accounts for their mutual attraction, and later in *Their Eyes*, Tea Cake will show he "knows things" like this too, as his name, "Virgible Woods," signifies.

Jody Starks buys 200 acres of land from the white folks to sell to other blacks who move to Eatonville, the all-black town that echoes the composition of Banana Bottom. The original settlement, however, was donated by the white Captain Eaton, just as Banana Bottom had been founded by the "Crazy" Scotsman Adair in the eighteenth century, whose many mulatto children settled next to other blacks who were attracted by the small plots Adair sold.[32]

Gossip and envy play a large part in the communities of both books. As Pheoby says of the "mouth almighty" neighbors' condemnation of Janie, "An envious heart makes a treacherous ear. They done 'heard' 'bout you just what they hope done happened" (16), and we remember that the old gossip Sister Phibby thinks Bita's rape by Crazy Bow was "a good thing, done early" (15), as Bita had been pampered by her relatively wealthy father and thus could be accused of acting "womanish." As Pheoby says of Eatonville's gossips, "So long as they get a name to gnaw on they don't care whose it is, and what about, 'specially if they can make it sound like evil" (17). And as Coker of Eatonville states, "Us colored folks is too envious of one 'nother. Dat's how come us don't git no further than us do. Us talks about de white man keepin' us down! Shucks! He don't have tuh. Us keeps our own selves down" (63), a sentiment obviously shared on occasion by McKay. As noted earlier, in both the South and the Caribbean, this syndrome is explained by the "basket of crabs" reference. Any crab that tries to climb out is pulled in by its fellows.

We noted the economic aspects of McKay's text, where white and black approaches to appropriate agricultural and business practices receive much attention. We should remember that Jody is an entrepreneur and politician par excellence, making a bundle right away on real estate and then prospering as store owner and mayor. Part of his success comes from image, in that he tells Janie to "dress up and stand in the store. . . . She must look on herself as the bell-cow, the other women were the gang" (66). On this occasion Jody provides treats for the crowd and is subsequently elected mayor. Like most successful politicians and salesmen, Jody is a "man of words," a concept also valued in the African Caribbean. By contrast, the bumpkin Tony Taylor's speech honoring Janie and Jody's arrival in the community is mocked because his tribute lacks eloquence. Jody also understands promotion and spectacle and arranges a festival to celebrate his erection of a streetlight, replete with a three-pig barbecue and a weeklong ritual display of the light before its erection. Brazenly, he appropriates biblical references to sanction his symbolic blasphemy—for he is "God" proclaiming "let there be light." But he actually says, "Dis evenin' we'se all assembled heah tuh light uh lamp. Dis occasion is something for us all tuh remember tuh our dyin' day. De first street lamp in uh colored town . . . let it shine, let it shine, let it shine [an obvious echo of the spiritual, "This Little Light of Mine," which Jody has similarly transformed from communal inspiration to a selfishly individual assertion of power]." "Brother Davis, lead us in a word uh prayer" (73). In Freudian terms, the erection of the lamp on the "straightest" cypress pole from the swamp signifies his own rampant, phallic power, but he cleverly makes the people feel it as a communal achievement, one sanctioned by God himself. Further, the cooption of the holy man to his charade demonstrates how the "peasants" can be dominated through religious methods, just as the Craigs do in Jubilee.

Small details relate how the town echoes the Caribbean. Jody drives

Henry Pitts out of town after Henry pilfers a load of cane from his employer Jody's field, causing a debate among the men. Sim Jones, after checking to make sure Jody can't hear him, complains, "Colored folks oughtn't tuh be so hard on one 'nother," offering a communal argument, to which Sam Watson, the sage of Jody's store porch and Pheoby's husband replies, "Let colored folks learn to work for what dey git lak everybody else" (77–78). But it seems the real complaint is about Jody's manner: "All he do is big-belly round and tell other folks what tuh do. He loves obedience out of everybody under de sound of his voice," and Oscar Scott complains, "You feel a switch in his hand when he's talkin' to yuh. . . . Dat chastising' feelin' he totes sorter gives yuh de protolapsis uh de curinary linin'." The discussion escalates into metaphor, as Jeff Bruce chimes in, "He's uh whirlwind among breezes," to which Sam responds, "Speakin' of winds, he's de wind and we'se de grass. We bend which ever way he blows . . . but a dat us needs him. De town wouldn't be nothin' if it wasn't for him. He can't help bein' sorta bossy. Some folks needs thrones, and ruling-chairs and crowns tuh make they influence felt. He don't. He's got uh throne in de seat of his pants" (78).

This sequence deserves scrutiny on several levels. As a study of folk linguistics, it reveals the riches of the local vernacular and the way in which common discussion can escalate into a kind of creative verbal dueling (hence the introduction of metaphor). Further, the largely comic exchange masks a quite serious discussion of racial and communal leadership and the problems it inevitably raises, particularly when the leader in question seems to be mimicking white values, or "showin' off his learnin'," as Hicks terms it, something the character Herald Day does repeatedly in McKay's text.

Eatonville's envy of Starks here echoes Banana Bottom's envy of Jordan Plant, but the grudging acknowledgment of the Florida town's need for Joe—and of his learning—also parallels the love/hate relationship Banana Bottom seems to have for Bita. It also seems time for us to examine Joe Starks more closely. Early treatments of the novel have rightly concentrated on Janie and her attempts to establish agency and voice. An unfortunate aspect of this kind of reading, however, has been to increasingly demonize Janie's three husbands, especially Jody. While I am among the majority that found much to dislike about the recent movie that was made of *Their Eyes*, I did think that it offered a more balanced portrait of Jody, who does, in fact, make a positive difference in many ways in the life of Eatonville, and for that matter, in the life of Janie, although ultimately, as many have noted, he becomes a patriarchal tyrant. A useful new treatment of all three husbands comes from Trudier Harris, who sees many of the positive aspects I have been mentioning here (2011, passim).

A link with *Banana Bottom* appears in the episodes dealing with Matt Bonner's mule. The men use the raw-boned animal as the butt of jokes, many of them implicating his hapless owner, but eventually they turn to physically tormenting the old animal, which moves Janie: "A little war of defense for helpless things was going on inside her. People ought to have some regard for helpless things. She wanted to fight about it" (90), and she is pleased when Jody buys the mule and sets him to graze and fatten in front of the store, as a sign of his largesse. She tells him, in front of the other men, that the deed "makes u mighty big man outa you. Somethin like George Washington and Lincoln. Abraham Lincoln, he had de whole United States tuh rule so he freed de Negroes. You got uh town so you freed uh mule. You have tuh have power tuh free things and dat makes you lak uh king uh something" (92). This constitutes her "maiden speech" on the porch, which causes Hambo to marvel, "Yo' wife is uh born orator, Starks. Us never knowed dat befo'. She put jus' de right words tuh our thoughts." Significantly, Jody does not object, as he has before, to Janie's speech, as it praises *him*. However, the irony lies in the fact that while he will free the mule, he won't free Janie, who labors in the store under his stern directives.

The link with Bita's story is through Jubban, whose tenderness is signaled to Bita by his loving care of his animals, which eventually earns him a citation from the Society for the Prevention of Cruelty to Animals. And, indeed, we initially see his kindness in a scene in which Jubban is grooming mules, "vigorously and yet so lovingly that the brutes were as gentle and docile as sheep under his hand. . . . Only Jubban could pick the ticks from under Mayfly's tail and groom her there. Any other person who wanted to do that had to rope up Mayfly's hind legs. . . . [He] had a way of coaxing and taming mules and horses and making them work willingly. . . . A colt broken in by him would turn out a better worker" (252).[33]

Jody forbids Janie to attend the mule's funeral, where he preaches a mock elegy over the dead animal that adds to his reputation among the villagers. This is consistent with his treatment of Janie over their decades-long union. She is to be the "bell cow," and is too good, as "Mrs. Mayor," to be associated with folk culture of any type. Even her hair must be hidden from view, and she is virtually silenced in the store, even as she has sales contact with everyone in town. Her stance here, a kind of black "trophy wife," has much in common with Bita Plant in terms of her relation with the Craigs. As their educated, properly dressed (as we have seen, in drab colors), agent at the mission, she is a sign of their good works, a useful commodity for religious—and thus social—domination. They forbid her to go to tea meetings or any other kind of peasant entertainment, even though she was taught to dance in England.

We noted McKay's mixed attitude toward Obeah. The conjurer Wumbe is mocked as an imposter, yet Squire Gensir says the ancestral/African religion should be respected. Hurston, we remember, was an initiated hoodoo priestess, wrote respectfully about vodoun in *Tell My Horse*, and proclaimed that the Western world had "a nerve" to speak disdainfully of African-derived religions as mere superstition. Still, when Jody gets sick—likely of cancer—and refuses to eat Janie's cooking, we learn that he and others in the town think that Janie has hired the local conjure man to "fix" him. Joe himself, in fact, has consulted this "faker," whom Janie calls a "trashy nigger dat calls hisself uh two-headed doctor" and "a multiplied cock-roach" (127–28), a description that could easily apply to Wumbe.

A number of critics[34] have noticed strong connections between the characters of *Their Eyes* and the West African loas. Maria Smith, in particular, has made a strong case that Hurston relies on vodoun mythic models for the novel. Employing postcolonial, anthropological, theological, and literary theory and convincing analyses of transatlantic forms of ritual and vernacular culture, she suggests that Janie's pear tree (following Maya Deren's reading of the Haitian loas) is a form of the *loa racine*, "roots without end," a preferred avenue of divine approach. In light of Bita Plant's name and the symbolism of leaves and grafting associated with her "rootedness" in Jubban, this suggestion becomes doubly intriguing. Janie is related to Erzulie, the goddess of love, but also, because of her ability to "split" herself into inside and outside, to Esu-Elegba, the trickster. Tea Cake, after his death, rises to the stature of ancestor, while the trajectory of the narrative is equated to a vodoun initiatory rite (Smith 2007, 19–55).

My own work suggests that Hurston's religious sensibility was syncretic rather than focused in vodoun, and that her overarching interest is in the retention of African traditions in general, including religious forms such as vodoun and Santería. Her circumCaribbean recastings of black Southern life can also take on a satiric edge, which often happens in African religions as well. The comic mule's funeral has a human parallel with the magnificent funerals Janie provides for both Jody and Tea Cake. The former's rites are "the finest thing Orange County had ever seen with Negro eyes." The fancy cars, "the gold and red and purple, the gloat and glamor of the secret orders . . . the Elks band . . . with a dominant drum rhythm. . . . The Little Emperor of the cross-roads was leaving Orange County as he had come—with the out-stretched hand of power" (136). The "Emperor" tag both mocks and praises Jody and suggests both Emperor Jones and Emperor Garvey (as do the references to the lodges). But above all, "emperor of the cross-roads" conjures up Esu-Elegba, the trickster, whose guile and cunning was always apparent in Jody, who undeniably used it to further himself, yes, but also the community. Finally, the "out-stretched hand" reference reminds us yet again of the biblical passage so central in Delany's *Blake*: "Princes shall come out of Egypt; Ethiopia shall soon stretch out her hands unto God" (Psalms 68:31). Tea Cake's funeral, however, is associated with Egypt, another mythical black culture, for he is consistently termed the "son of Evening Sun [Osiris]." Through Janie's expensive outlay for his funeral, he "rode like a Pharaoh to his tomb," accompanied by a band, as in circumCaribbean New Orleans funerals, which Hurston had studied.[35] These rites placate the community, which originally thought she had killed him so as to join Mrs. Turner's brother.

Jody's death causes Janie to reexamine the pattern of her life, and she finds she hates her grandmother for marrying her off to Logan Killicks: "Nanny had taken the biggest thing God ever made, the horizon . . . and pinched it in to such a little bit of a thing that she could tie it about her grand-daughter's neck tight enough to choke her. . . . She [Janie] had found a jewel down inside herself and she had wanted to walk where people could see her and gleam it around. But she had been set in the market-place to sell" (138). Similarly, Bita's proposed marriage to the priggish Herald Day (forestalled only by his perverted affair with a nanny goat) had been set up by Priscilla Craig, whose subsequent objections to Bita's keeping company with Hopping Dick underline the many ways in which she has restricted her over the years: "It would be impossible for her to stay when she felt not only resentment, but a *natural* opposition against Mrs. Craig. A latent hostility would make her always want to do anything of which Mrs. Craig disapproved. . . . . To Mrs. Craig, a woman whose attitude of life was alien to hers, and not to her parents, she owed the entire shaping of her career" (211, my emphasis). Of course the difference is that as Mrs. Craig's "pet experiment," Bita becomes the colonial subject par excellence; however, both Nanny and Mrs. Craig value "respectability" and social position over love and "natural" affinity.[36]

If Bita had married Herald Newton Day, they would have been false models for the community, in that they would be pillars of the colonial establishment—puppets for the administrative authority that demands allegiance to the cultural heritage of the "mother country" thousands of miles away. But Janie, married to Jody, propped up as a fancy-dressed icon on the porch of Jody's blindingly white "big house" store, occupies just that kind of false and, indeed, colonializing function, as her union with Jody mimics what he understands is the proper "white" presentation and operation of power and prestige. If she had married the proper undertaker from Sanford, as many wanted her to, her position as trophy wife would have been repeated.

The townspeople of Hurston's Eatonville, used to the role Jody assigned to Janie, take a dim view of her romance with Tea Cake: "Why she don't stay in her class?" (10). This is precisely what many in Banana Bottom eventually ask about Bita when she considers, first, Hopping Dick and then Jubban.[37] Hurston, herself, however, always felt an affinity for those that McKay called "hardy peasants." As she declared in her autobiography, "These poets of the swinging blade! The brief, but infinitely graceful, dance of body and axe-head as it lifts over the head in a fluid arc, dances in air, and rushes down to bite into the tree, all in beauty. . . . Sweating black bodies, muscled like Gods" (1942, 179).

Tea Cake, like Jubban, is presented as a very dark and handsome man. Janie, as narrator, comments on his "full, purple lips" the first time he enters the store, and later, as he teaches her to play checkers, she appreciatively notices "those full, lazy eyes with the lashes curling sharply away like drawn scimitars. The lean, over-padded shoulders and narrow waist. Even nice!" (146). These images expand, as do Bita's of Jubban's, until Janie admits to herself, "He looked like the love thoughts of women. He could be a bee to a blossom—a pear tree blossom in the spring. He seemed to be crushing scent out of the world with his footsteps. Crushing aromatic herbs with every step he took. Spices hung about him. He was a glance from God" (161).[38] Janie's Jody-wannabee storekeeper, the teenage Hezekiah, warns her against Tea Cake: "Ain't got doodly squat. He ain't got no business makin' hissef familiar wid nobody lak you" (156). Yet Tea Cake *does* have something—joy in life and many "natural" abilities. He is an expert fisherman and a fine blues pianist—presumably self-taught. An expert gambler, he makes Janie's $200 of honeymoon money turn a handsome profit in Jacksonville. As Sally Ann Ferguson has shown us, Tea Cake is a positive form of the "badman" figure in African American folk culture. He is also, as his skill with a piano, a guitar, and his voice demonstrate, a black Orpheus whose music, humor, and creative mischief makes him a favorite with everyone he meets. In this sense, he is quite different from Jubban, whose quiet demeanor is a good match for the untalkative Bita. Yet both men are heroic, in their strength, their dedicated love for their women, and their ability to fight—physically and morally—for their family and their people. Like Jubban, Tea Cake is "tested" several times, by Janie and by us as readers. His three disappearances, during courtship and honeymoon, prove nerve-racking, but the rewards each time—the car, the gambling money, the new guitar—offer the semiotics of our faith rewarded. He is also an expert hunter and teaches Janie to become a marksman, which of course sets up her tragic but necessary shooting of Tea Cake at novel's end.

As noted, both Jubban and Tea Cake are very dark. The near-white Mrs. Turner urges Janie to leave Tea Cake and "class up" with "light" people, like her and her available light-skinned brother. Her diatribe against "black" black folk is a litany of racist clichés: "Who want any lil ole black baby layin' up in de baby buggy lookin' lak uh fly in buttermilk? Who wants to be mixed up wid uh rusty black man, and uh black woman goin' down de street in all dem loud colors, and whoopin' and hollerin' and laughin' over nothin'?" (211). Mrs. Turner even hates Booker T. Washington (one of Hurston's personal heroes, and, at one point, before he read Du Bois, McKay's): "All he ever done was cut de monkey for white folks. So dey pomped him up. But you know whut de ole folks say 'de higher de monkey climbs de mo' he show his behind' so dat's de way it wuz. . . . He didn't do nothin' but hold us back—talkin' 'bout work when de race ain't never done nothin' else. He wuz uh enemy tuh us, dat's whut. He wuz uh white folks' nigger" (212). We find multiple ironies here: Mrs. Turner may be almost white, but her diatribe resonates with folk expressions turned inside out, and, clearly, if anyone is a "white folks' nigger," she's it. Also, Washington led in agricultural research, which he felt would facilitate black independence, a thematic, as we have seen, in the concluding chapters of *Banana Bottom*.

The two-room house the Woods happily inhabit on the Muck echoes the simple two rooms of Squire Gensir in *Banana Bottom*, and small as it is, their home becomes the center of the community, just as Jubban and Bita's does at the conclusion of McKay's novel. The muck, we learn, is a Caribbean world, with Bahamian drummers providing its rhythm and dances. Janie and Tea Cake become friends with the "Saws" and attend their fire dances. They also talk to the Indians, who are leaving the Muck after seeing signs a hurricane is coming. Soon the native animals—rabbits, possums, rattlesnakes—begin an exodus as well, and then deer, panthers, and buzzards. The buzzard is an important mythical bird in African culture, as the earlier surreal funeral of the mule indicated. Here, Janie/Hurston builds the exodus of animals to a climax that ends with them: "A thousand buzzards held a flying meet and then went above the clouds and stayed" (230). "Palm and banana trees began that long distance talk with rain" (230), lyrical language that emphasizes the circumCaribbean flora, fauna, and weather.

Many critics have commented on Tea Cake's failure to pay attention to the warning of the Indians and the animals, but the Bahamians have even more extensive experience with the storms; one of them, Lias, stops by to say he's leaving. He speaks a markedly different dialect and is more attune to the signs: "Man, muck is too low and dat big lake is liable tuh bust. . . . De Indians gahn east, man. It's dangerous. . . . If Ah never see you no mo' on earth, Ah'll meet you in Africa," a Caribbean-diasporic expression and warning. But not all the Bahamians leave. Motor Boat stays behind. His name reminds us of a lack, for there is no boat for an escape.

The parallels between the disasters in both these texts and the terrible recent reality of the destruction of New Orleans are chilling. In Hurston's account, just as in New Orleans in 2005, some people do not trust the warnings and stay behind: "The people felt uncomfortable but safe because there were the seawalls to chain the senseless monster [the Lake] in his bed" (234). Ignored warnings, an exploding lake, failed levees. Tea Cake, impressed to bury bodies in Palm Beach, becomes our guide to the destruction, describing bodies as "dead with fighting faces and eyes flung wide open in wonder. Death had found them watching, trying to see beyond seeing" (252), another echo of the title, which seems to question how God can do such things to man.

The hurricane clearly echoes the one in *Banana Bottom*, and, indeed, the fictional depictions were likely based on the same storm, the great Lake Okeechobee hurricane of September 6 to September 20, 1928, which caused over 2,500 deaths. It is still the second-deadliest natural disaster to hit the United States, after the Galveston hurricane of 1900, which killed at least 6,000. There were major hurricanes in 1933 as well, but McKay had already completed his novel at that point, as it appeared that year. Both Hurston and McKay, as circumCaribbean people, had been through many hurricanes before, including one Hurston experienced while in the Bahamas in 1929 and one in Haiti while writing *Their Eyes*.[39] As anyone who has experienced such a storm knows, it tests the abilities of everyone in its path. In both novels, the storms replicate the "testing" of the hero/heroine of the earlier narrative but also provide a challenge to the wider communities of which they are a part. Hurricanes are literally a "clearing of the ground," and although sublimely terrible and often deadly, they ironically create conditions for change, renewal, and resurrection. In both novels, deaths mark the end but also a beginning, especially in *Banana Bottom*, where Jubban and Bita make love for the first time in the wagon hauling her dead father's body. Janie, returning to Eatonville after burying Tea Cake, brings his symbolically regenerative seeds with her; the story she tells, which will enrich the community as Pheobe and her husband Sam retell it, is an equivalent. Janie leaves us as she ecstatically climbs the stairs, grateful for memories of her life with Tea Cake. He seems to be dancing in the air above her, summoning her to a new stage in her life.

In these two stunning novels, McKay and Hurston sought to preserve folk wisdom that had seemingly been lost in modern, technological cultures, a thematic that echoed throughout the Harlem Renaissance after perhaps the quintessential statement in Jean Toomer's *Cane* (1923), which both McKay and Hurston revered. Yet they reject the "swan song" intent of Toomer. They see their "hardy peasants" not only enduring, but prevailing, and marching on to new destinies. High literary culture of Western modernism had no use for the "peasant" novels I have highlighted and honored here, and therefore helped contribute to global imperialism. Colonial powers understand all too well that local narratives, if designed for liberation, are inimical to imperial objectives. For these reasons, in virtually every colonized area, local narratives have been either blocked or manipulated by the dominant power. Aiming for an authentic and empowering local narrative, McKay, Hurston, Roumain, Heyward, and many other writers of the circumCaribbean strove mightily to amplify the voices of the folk, whose counter-narratives made their transnational novels effective foils in a battle against cultural erasure.

6 Palette of Fire

The Aesthetics of Propaganda in *Black Boy* and *In the Castle of My Skin*

. . . .

Richard Wright, whose fiery *Native Son* exploded across the American literary firmament in 1940, has always been noted as a master of propaganda, and his lifelong commitment to writing as a force for social change has rightly been studied in depth. This critical approach, however, has often hampered a full appreciation of Wright's full arsenal of talents in all the techniques of rhetoric, poetry, and narrative. Nevertheless, from the beginning of his career, Wright has been ceaselessly pigeonholed by left-leaning critics, who prefer to ignore his aesthetic gifts in favor of his political realism, perhaps seen most in *Black Boy* (1945). This discussion will instead begin from the premise that Wright always saw his propaganda as art, and that he worked tirelessly throughout his career to incorporate both of these while simultaneously experimenting with new forms and techniques.

Viewing Wright this way can assist us as we reconfigure him in new hemispheric and transatlantic ways, for Wright always appealed to writers outside the United States through his propaganda and his art. Further, Wright had an especially strong influence on Caribbean writers, who were, in many cases, making an argument through their craft against European colonial oppression. I need not detail here how often a parallel has been made between the racial system of the pre–civil rights U.S. South and the colonial histories of the Caribbean, which were equally but differently structured around racial division. To demonstrate this influence, I will subsequently reveal a similar trajectory for the Barbadian novelist George Lamming, whose autobiographical novel *In the Castle of My Skin* seems a veritable homage to Wright, who indeed wrote the introduction for *Castle* when it appeared in 1953. Setting these two texts together reveals the many similarities between Southern and West Indian rural life, diasporic commonalities, and multiple instances of literary invention that stem from racial oppression.[1]

Further, Wright often spoke of the United States, the Caribbean, and Africa as a kind of triangular Black Atlantic. In an interview with George

Charbonnier in 1960, he claimed that "it is American Negroes, from the South of the United States and the Caribbean, who brought the idea of black nationalism to Africa. . . . We feel we are not really at home in our country. This is the origin, logically enough, of black nationalism. It begins with Marcus Garvey [a Jamaican] in the United States. After Garvey and W. E. B. Du Bois, George Padmore [from Trinidad] was at the root of this idea" (*Conversations*, 1933, 228). Thus the idea of black "homelessness" for Wright is a hemispheric, rather than a U.S., phenomenon, and Lamming would seem to him to be a fellow traveler in this respect. Both of these books were written by men who had fled into exile from their native homelands—Wright from Mississippi, Lamming from Barbados. Lamming's initial relocation to Trinidad was soon followed by permanent relocation to London. Wright, after years of political and literary work in Chicago and New York, finally went into exile in Paris, where he took on a new identity as a kind of elder statesman of the black literary diaspora. Exile was a stance, a topic, and a frame of mind for each man. Lamming, in his book-length *The Pleasures of Exile* (1960), declared, "The exile is a universal figure. . . . We are made to feel a sense of exile by our inadequacy and our irrelevance of function in a society whose past we can't alter, and whose future is always beyond us. . . . To be an exile is to be alive" (24). Edward Said has famously remarked, "Exile is strangely compelling to think about but terrible to experience. It is the unhealable rift forced between a human being and a native place, between the self and its true home: its essential sadness can never be surmounted." Said suggests that the only home available, after exile, is in writing (2000, 173–84).

Some years ago, Robert Stepto identified key strands of the slave narrative, which many find to be the fundamental structure for much of black literature of the diaspora. These elements are "the violence and gnawing hunger, the skeptical view of Christianity, the portrait of a black family valiantly attempting to maintain a degree of unity, the impregnable isolation, the longing and scheming to follow the North Star resolved by boarding the 'freedom train,'" and "the narrator's quest for literacy" (1977, 533). If we change the "North Star" and freedom train to Lamming's boat bound for London, we have a symmetry of effects in our two life stories that indeed bears resemblance to the classic slave narrative, which ends in flight—but to freedom, not to exile (although there were certainly elements of exile in the state of escaped slaves too). Lamming's equation of exile with life bears within it an implicit endorsement of writing as life. But as he usefully notes, the situation of an American black exile—and he uses Baldwin, not Wright, as an example—is different from a black West Indian in London, for the latter has to fight the imposition of the fiction that British culture is *his* culture, and that he will be judged by his mastery of it (he should know English literature, for instance, not Caribbean), and also that in Barbados there is no sense of being an oppressed minority, for blacks are the majority. While one may be condemned by blackness to poverty, one is not singled out for specific punishments for the fact of blackness, as in Wright's or Baldwin's United States (*Pleasures of Exile*, 1960, 33).

I believe George Lamming would approve of the aims and operations of *Calypso Magnolia*, and particularly of my linkage of *Black Boy* and *Castle*. In an interview, he professed to be disturbed and "astonished" at the exclusion of Afro-Caribbean literature from Black Studies courses in the United States: "It should be an immediate cultural concern for the United States, because the Caribbean is part of the Americas. . . . It would really be incomplete to think in terms of what has happened to the development of Black expression both politically and culturally without considering the role of the Caribbean, of the West Indian intelligentsia in exile in the United States, in that development. If you take a period like the Harlem Renaissance, you would not think of that without thinking of the importance of West Indian migration to Harlem, particularly the influence of Claude McKay and Marcus Garvey" (*Conversations*, 75).

When Lamming refers to "what has happened," he returns again to the concept of literature as an alternate history, and his emphasis on the links between the United States and the Caribbean bespeaks a need for consideration of the entire cultural region, but also its "fragmented" history, which is symbolically registered, as we shall see, in *Castle*, where the character of Pa rehearses the hemisphere-spanning Middle Passage. The migration of Caribbean people to Harlem also heightened cross-fertilization among them and transplanted black Southerners, who like Wright and Lamming after them, would find many points of convergence between the diasporic cultures.

A corollary to this approach will be the assumption that Wright and Lamming found their genius in their native settings, and that much of their greatest writing achieves its stature through shrewd, sometimes majestic employment of Southern and Caribbean culture, flora and fauna, folklife, weather, history, and language. Further, these testimonies came from memory, conjured up in exile, as Wright wrote after immigration to Northern cities and later to Paris. Lamming penned his works in London. Simon Gikandi has accurately observed that key Caribbean literary texts by Aimé Césaire, Frantz Fanon, C. L. R. James, V. S. Naipaul, and Lamming were produced in exile, which Gikandi defines as "a historical and existential condition" (1992, 33), and Wright belongs in this grouping as well. For both Wright and Lamming, grappling with memories in exile was always also a reconstruction of history and genealogy. Each writer proffers discrete Southern communities through the eyes of a black boy who claws his way into manhood. Rather than pondering whether these central figures are representative or not, we might consider how each of them functions as "eyes" for the reader. Both Wright and Lamming were aware that most whites had no notion of the worlds that were being presented in these texts. As such, the narratives are not only autobiographical—they are forms of "tours," armchair investigations of what many readers would consider fascinating but dangerous terrain. The word "eye" is used repeatedly in both texts, and, indeed, Wright once stated that "living in the South doomed me to look always through eyes which the South had given me, and bewilderment and fear made me mute and afraid. But after I had left the South, luck gave me other eyes, new eyes with which to look at the meaning of what I'd lived through" (*Conversations*, 81).

Through the Eyes of a Black Boy

In the 1920s, Boston's L.C. Page Company published a series of illustrated books in the Spell Series, which included a volume by Archie Bell, *The Spell of the Caribbean Islands*. In his detailed account of his visit to "Little England," Barbados, he warns the traveler to eschew British watering places on the island and to instead seek out "the life . . . that cannot be compared to any other in the West Indies; perhaps to none in the world," namely the black life of the island. "One does well, if he engages a boy" like the one he hired, one George. Like Wright's Richard, he yearns to leave his home and go north to the United States, but he cannot afford to pay both his passage and his mother's, and he won't go without her. "White folks has everything. . . . Us niggers don't seem to have much to do about running things." The narrator displays a good bit of racism throughout his tour. Still, he learns a great deal from George and ends his stay in Barbados by telling the reader that "one should not fail to be towed around by a Barbadian black boy . . . because to miss conversation with him is like going to Egypt and neglecting to visit the Sphinx . . . both are lovers of eternal sunshine, both are ever watchful, enigmatic, even mysterious—survivors from the bygone that is almost forgotten by the world" (348–49). Both *Black Boy* and *Castle* might be read from this popular vantage point, as a kind of magical mystery tour of a tabooed black world, where the Dante-like reader is led by the young black boys who function as Virgil did in the *Comedia*. As such, the reader sees things though the black "eye"/"I." Put another way, however, to fulfill the meaning of Lamming's title, the reader gets into the imprisoning "castle" of the narrator's *skin*. Lamming's title cleverly reverses its source, Derek Walcott's line, "You, in the castle of your skin, I the swineherd," relocating the center of interest from the white colonial master to the young black boy's fevered search for a transcendent identity.[2]

Black eyes, however, can lose what Du Bois called their "second sight." Wright was surprised by the black Francophone Africans and West Indians he encountered in Paris: "I found they were more French than black. . . . They had graduated to being French . . . [and] no longer identified with the lives of their people or with the brutal realities of colonial life" (*Conversations*, 120). Lamming certainly observed the same effect in London among many of his fellow black colonials. Clearly, Wright's and Lamming's narrators face this danger too, and both texts take great pains to dramatize the authenticity of their "tours" through dialect-driven vernacular, albeit as reported by a properly speaking—and imaginatively *seeing*—narrator.

Ample proof and examples for these assertions may first be found in one of Wright's greatest achievements, *Black Boy* (1945), the first part of the overall autobiography that concludes with *American Hunger* (1977). The narrative's intricate modes of narration, symbolism, sequence, image, and structure all contribute forcefully to the book's overall propaganda, but also to a powerfully moving and satisfying artistic product. My reading will take advantage of several recent studies of Wright and the aesthetics of propaganda, as well as new theories of the "local" as a component of the transnational and global. Finally, in light of Wright's increasing uneasiness in the United States, his already formidable record of international travel, and his eventual exile in Paris (which finds a parallel in Lamming's relocation to London), where he wrote three novels and several nonfiction books, *Black Boy* deserves to be read as a text that transcends its ostensible boundaries. For even though Wright situates it in the Mississippi that he knew all too well, its relentless exploration of the shaping of black identity in a Western society spoke and continues to speak to people of color throughout the black diaspora. One of those who heard this "call" was Lamming. Wright must have seen these lines of connection when he was asked to write an introduction for *Castle*, an exercise that summoned up his memories of, and meditations on, the "South of the South."

Wright never set a novel in the Caribbean, but his introduction recognizes that the account of Lamming's Barbados undergoing transformation from rural to industrial society — and its effect on the protagonist — was much like Wright's own life story in *Black Boy*. Wright declared: "I, too, have been long crying these stern tidings, and when I catch the echo of yet another voice declaiming in alien accents a description of this same reality, I react with pride and excitement, and I want to urge others to react to that voice. One feels not so alone, when, from a distant witness, supporting evidence comes to buttress one's own testimony" ("Introduction," 1953, ix). Wright's use of the terms "echo" and "pride" could be translated as a "response," indicating he saw *Castle* as answering the "call" of *Black Boy*.[3]

We might also note the temporal frames of the two texts. Wright's novel by no means concerns his entire life, but rather it concentrates on the years 1912 to 1927 (his first four years are understandably briefly summarized). Similarly, Lamming's novel, circling around the crucial year of 1937–38, concerns a similarly formative period in his youth, from about 1936 to 1946, encompassing his ninth birthday and his departure for Trinidad.

Wright seems to have always sensed a connection between black U.S. culture and the circumCaribbean. In a 1940 interview, he declared, "It is necessary that the black community of Latin America unite with that of North America. In this way, they will both come out ahead. . . . An association of American writers is needed. . . . The creative writers of the Latin American world should stand shoulder to shoulder with the creative writers of the English speaking peoples in the fight for Liberty and Justice" (*Conversations*, 33).

Wright expanded his physical knowledge of the hemisphere that same year, just as *Native Son* was astonishing and/or infuriating readers across the United States. He and his first wife, Dhimah, her two-year-old son from a previous marriage, and her mother, Eda, joined their friends Lawrence and Sylvia Martin in Cuernavaca, Mexico. The Martins found a rental property for the Wrights that cost only twenty-seven dollars a month. The trip south was accomplished by sea, on the SS *Monterey*, so Wright encountered the full majesty of the Caribbean physically, as a link between the South and Latin America, and he saw the similarities between the oppressive hacienda system and the plantation system back home. Wright found the weather and the foliage remarkably like that of Mississippi. As he wrote his boyhood friend Joe Brown, "Mexico reminds me a lot of the South. The climate is wonderful" (*Letters*, 1968, 9). Rejecting the house the Martins had located as too small, he installed his family in a villa with a swimming pool and started learning Spanish (Rowley, 2008, 195–96). Wright was no doubt impressed by the magnificent murals at the Palace of Cortés by his fellow modernist and socialist Diego Rivera, which depicted the Conquest of Mexico.

Wright eventually got beyond his palatial digs when he joined John Steinbeck and Herbert Kline on a scouting trip for locations. Steinbeck and Kline would film *Forgotten Village*, about Mexico's rural poor, which the three saw in abundance in the state of Michoacán. Race was not an issue in Mexico, where Wright lived in comparative freedom and luxury. When he left the country for good, he took a train to San Antonio. Once in the United States, he had to ride in the Jim Crow car and was baited by train personnel (Rowley, 2008, 208–9), a striking contrast that helped shape his concept of Latin culture as opposed to that of the South.

Wright's fascination with the South of the South would continue in the next decade. In 1950, he traveled to Curaçao, and then to Haiti. He met many prominent writers and started plans for a film on the island's liberator, Toussaint-Louverture, whose life had been immortalized in C. L. R. James's *The Black Jacobins* (1938). This program would have united Wright's growing interest in diasporic history and his desire to demonstrate the richness and variety of black cultures in his adopted homeland, France, which had a special interest in the Francophone Caribbean. His plan to play the leading role speaks of his identification with Toussaint. The project never developed, but Michel Fabre has shown that Wright took copious notes for it while in Haiti and intended to write about the history of the country, the causes of its poverty, and the despair of its young people (1998, 352).[4] We should remember that there was much interest in Haiti in the 1930s, for a variety of reasons. The occupation of the island by the United States from 1915 to 1934 led to a constant stream of newspaper and magazine articles, documentary films, and many books, both fiction and nonfiction. Orson Welles mounted a famous version of *Macbeth* set there, with the three witches transformed into voodoo priestesses. The production was a sensation, and Richard Wright made a special trip to New York to see it. His review in the *Daily Worker* noted that the play gave black actors work and that white audiences could hardly object to the subject matter, since it was the work of the Bard (Rowley, 2008, 553n7).

Wright's visceral experience with poverty made him align quite naturally with many writers in the Caribbean. As Lamming once stated, "The Novel has had a particular function in the Caribbean. The writer's preoccupation has been mainly with the poor; and fiction has served as a way of restoring these lives—this world of men and women from down below—to a proper order of attention. . . . There was also the writer's recognition [that] this world, in spite of its long history of deprivation, represented the womb from which he himself had sprung, and the richest collective reservoir of experience on which the creative imagination could draw" ("Introduction," 1953, xxxvii). Lamming had been inspired by Wright's impressive example of "restoration" in *Black Boy*. Other African American and Caribbean writers, however, had created similar texts. For Zora Neale Hurston, the truest repository of black culture lay in the "Negro farthest down," and she in her turn had been inspired by the earlier example of Claude McKay's fiction, as we have seen, which similarly insisted on a "proper order of attention" for impoverished workers of the black diaspora. But all these were peasant cultures that originated in slavery. As Lamming stated, "We inherited a region which was not designed for social living. It was intended exclusively for production . . . a source of fortune for hostile strangers" (*Conversations*, 78), a comment that is equally relevant to the rural South of Wright's childhood. We might think about the myriad ways in which this colonial practice has spread into many other cultures today, with disinvestment in social life and infrastructure. In this sense, Lamming and Wright functioned as canaries in the coal mine, warning us of social petrifaction.

Like many of his fellow African American writers, Wright was always alert in his travels over the globe to parallels that existed among diasporic peoples. More recently, many members of the black diaspora have discovered a common North American/Caribbean heritage, especially as they have come together in great cities of the hemispheric North, but also, increasingly, in those of the U.S. South. Folklore, in particular, has been a source of connection and community, and this phenomenon demonstrates the soundness of Édouard Glissant's observation that folklore, rather than myth, enables people to repossess historical space and create a worldview that is both fortifying and useful for social change (1989, 83–85). Further, Antonio Benítez-Rojo has helpfully situated the concept of performative style as a distinction of Caribbean culture and has asserted that much of the power of Atlanta's Martin Luther King Jr. came from his understanding and practice of a performing art much like that of the Caribbean (1992, 24). As Paul Gilroy has forcefully argued, Wright, increasingly aware of these kinds of connections, eventually came to see that colonial oppression—particularly of people of color—was inextricably intertwined with the patterns of Jim Crow America. Wright's embrace of global political efforts to root out imperialism and racism was not, however, an abandonment of his determination to delineate the struggles of U.S. blacks. Indeed, he interbraided these political strategies with his use of black vernacular (1993, 148).

This linkage became a political and aesthetic exercise. Writers in the Caribbean and in Latin America like Lamming admired Wright for his revolutionary fervor, but also for his mastery of his craft. Over the years, there has been general agreement that he fomented a fundamental redefinition of the role of black diasporic writing, forcing it into a highly confrontational form of racial propaganda and away from more "genteel" formulations, as he saw them. While there is much truth in this image, in the long run it has actually been a hindrance to Wright's overall reputation, because the flip side of such a view, although sometimes unstated, is that Wright—like Theodore Dreiser, say, or Harriette Arnow—was strong on power and short on aesthetics. It is my view that Wright's works also represent a high achievement in literary terms, but, further, that Wright was a protean artist who always experimented with forms and genres, *especially* when supposedly "aesthetic" manipulations could reinforce his didactic purposes.[5]

When critics approach *Black Boy*, they rarely mention the inscription, which is from Job: "They meet with darkness in the daytime / And they grope at noonday as in the night." Those who do consider the passage naturally link it with the didactic aspect of the book of Job. However, we might do well to reconsider these lines as profound, eloquent, and representative of Wright's intent to craft his story with equally powerful and aesthetic rhetoric. Although he had contempt for organized religion, he had been steeped in the Bible, and his constant use of biblical allusion throughout his career speaks to his reverence for the magnificent literary resource of scripture. Certainly the majestic and anguished complaint of Job before a seemingly indifferent (or even malevolent) God spoke to him in a powerfully personal way, especially in terms of his mother's intense suffering.

Black Boy makes it clear that Wright owed much of his biblical lore to his grandmother, a strict Seventh-Day Adventist. In an intriguing passage, Wright manages to render the majesty of the biblical imagery and rhetoric he absorbed, while simultaneously boasting about its failure to win his soul: "Her church expounded a gospel clogged with images of vast lakes of eternal fire, of seas vanishing, of valleys of dry bones . . . of God riding whirlwinds . . . a salvation that teemed with fantastic beasts." Yet at the end of this long, bravura passage, which in fact catalogs images and metaphors that Wright would repeatedly use in his own work, he asserts, "I was pulled toward emotional belief, but as soon as I went out of the church and saw the bright sunshine and felt the throbbing life of the people in the streets I knew that none of it was true and that nothing would happen" (89). Ah, but he came to see, however, that this apocalyptic language could indeed be harnessed to describe the many terrible events that *did* happen during his lifetime. And indeed, later in the narrative, he tells us he passed much time in his room poring over the Bible in an attempt to come up with some new verses for hymns, a process designed to win Granny's favor, but also one that trained him for typologically driven literary symbolism. This in fact leads him to write his first story, an incoherent tale about the suicide of a young Indian maiden. When his female neighbor fails to understand it, he is pleased, smiling the satisfied and superior smile of the artiste.

This prefigures Wright's later attempt at extended narrative, a florid tale entitled "The Voodoo of Hell's Half-Acre." The title alone signaled a use of alliteration and attention-getting pyrotechnics and an effort to mine African American exotica, which had a Caribbean ring to it in the Haitian term "voodoo." When it is published in the local black paper, his classmates, rather than congratulating him, find him strange; at home, Granny accuses him of creating lies. The lack of praise parallels his constant earlier motif of physical hunger—now he knows artistic hunger. But Wright summarizes his new desire to go north and become a writer in the language of the train sermons of the black church (which figure Christ, God, or sometimes, the Devil, as a rushing locomotive), but transposed into a negative, apocalyptic mode: "In the dead of the southern night my life had switched onto the wrong track and, without my knowing it, the locomotive of my heart was rushing down a dangerously steep slope, heading for a collision, heedless of the warning red lights that blinked all about me, the sirens and the bells and the screams that filled the air" (148). This magnificent passage exalts the fifteen-year-old Richard as never before—for he is now the rushing locomotive that often figures as Christ himself in the black pulpit.[6]

In order to understand this performative and symbolic stance, we might ponder Marian Wright Edelman's pronouncement about black identity in the United States, which also echoes the complaint of Job: "It is utterly exhausting being black in America. . . . There is no respite or escape from your badge of color. The daily stress of non-stop racial mindfulness . . . is wearing. The constant burden to 'prove' that you are as smart, as honest, as interesting, as wide-gauging and motivated as any other individual tires you out. . . . The bottom line, however, is to believe in yourself and not let anybody—of any color—limit or define you. . . . Race and gender are givens of God. . . . Being racist and sexist are a state of mind and a choice" (1992, 23). This statement finds powerful verification in Wright's works and, if we add an "s" to "America," in the work of South of the South writers such as Barbados's Lamming. Yet, as Wright himself acknowledged in 1945, books like his and Lamming's, which zero in on a somewhat narrow orbit of an individual life, albeit one situated amid a community, did not adequately fill a pressing need. As he put it, "There is a great novel yet to be written about the Negro in the South; just a simple, straight, easy, great novel, telling how they live and how they die, what they see and how they feel each day; what they do in the winter, spring, summer, and fall. Just a novel telling of the quiet ritual of their lives. Such a book is really needed" (*Letters*, 1968, 13). Implicit in this statement is his own sense of having failed to compose such a work, since his novels had been more focused on the terrible day-to-day ravages cited by Edelman. And yet we can find myriad passages in his writings that do indeed render a sense of black Southern life, a traditional mode of living in concert with the land and the seasons. This is not to say, however, that those passages are where we should look for evidence of Wright's artistry; he was equally adept at rendering apocalyptic scenes of racial conflagration. His creative ability, like that of the biblical sages, spanned the sublime and the horrific, and the coloration of these differing effects was drawn from the same artistic palette, which was inspired by the realities of his native region.

Richard Wright left the South for Chicago in December 1927. He was nineteen but already older than that in terms of the harsh lessons he had learned about his native culture. He talks of that course of instruction in the autobiographical sketch that opens his magnificent collection of short stories, *Uncle Tom's Children* (1938): "My first lesson in how to live as a Negro came when I was quite small. We were living in Arkansas" (3). The second sentence virtually explains the first; place is *all*. The conditions of domicile immediately stand for the larger social (and frequently physical) hunger felt by most Southern blacks. Their "skimpy yard" (an impoverished image of the American garden) is "paved with black cinders," an expression of black segregation and barren social privilege, but also of the wasteland motif of T. S. Eliot and of F. Scott Fitzgerald's valley of ashes. And, indeed, such is the vision of the world racism sets before young Richard, who languishes in a punishing world. The only "touch of green" the young Richard can see is "beyond the tracks" where the white folks live. But the young boy does not miss the green and in fact enjoys the cinders, for they prove to be fine weapons for firing at "woolly black heads" that "pop out from . . . another row of pillars" (3).

Again and again in his fiction, Wright focuses on the way black people attack each other. This scene finds profound extension in Wright's last published novel, *The Long Dream* (1958), when a teenage Fishbelly and his friends visit a touring carnival on "Colored Folks Day" and take turns firing baseballs at a black man, whose head protrudes from a hole in the canvas. Normally, this is a sport for white patrons. Some whites choose to attend the carnival on Colored Folks Day, too, and whites watch curiously as "real niggers" try to hit the "symbolic nigger." Fishbelly becomes embarrassed and "wanted to surrender his balls," but he and the other boys, inflamed by the shameful message sent out by the grinning circus employee, are intent on smashing the face that represents theirs, and they do. The lion tamer tells Tony, who bloodies the face, "As long as you can hit that nigger, I'll buy you all the balls you want, nigger" (45).

In "The Ethics of Living Jim Crow," the first section of *Uncle Tom's Children* (1938), young Richard is severely cut by a white boy's projectile and as a consequence is brutally beaten by his mother for not hiding (a passage Wright recycles for *Black Boy*). Our narrator shows us how the pastoral can become deformed into demonic signifiers: "The green trees, the trimmed hedges, the cropped lawns grew very meaningful, became a symbol . . . an overreaching symbol of fear" (5). Thus, in many ways, the pastoral, for Wright, becomes freighted with menace and pain. Further, ostensible folk games, like the one Wright would much later set at the carnival, are revealed as vicious racial shorthand. When the lion tamer promises "balls," he makes the price of "manhood" violence against one's fellow blacks, a form of racial masochism. This mode is foreshadowed in *Black Boy* when the narrator's friend Shorty allows white men to kick him in the rear in exchange for money. Throughout the narratives, one is said to be "lucky" if confrontations with whites do not lead to castration, death, or, in the case of women, rape by white men. The motif of "losing one's balls" emerges clearly in the passages cited above, and one of the key episodes in Wright's last published novel, *The Long Dream* (1958), involves the castration of Chris, a black bellboy, who has had sex with a willing prostitute.

As Wright sketches in aesthetic shorthand in *Uncle Tom's Cabin* the "lessons" he learns as a teen in Mississippi, he summarizes, "I learned to lie, to steal, to dissemble. I learned to play that dual role which every Negro must play if he wants to eat and live" (13). Throughout the sketch, Wright plays variations on the black man's predicament of always being caught between Scylla and Charybdis, a situation that presents the victim with the possibilities of both psychic and physical trauma. A white man accuses him, in front of another white, Mr. Pease, of referring to the latter merely as "Pease." The stratagem causes him to leave work, for to deny it would be calling the accuser a liar. This scene has many parallels in the piece and is solved only at the end, when, carrying an armload of packages, Richard is unable to remove his hat before white folks in an elevator. Rather than thank the white man who removes it for him, he pretends to almost drop his packages, "an acceptable course of action which fell safely between these two poles. . . . In spite of adverse circumstances [I] salvaged a slender shred of personal pride" (14–15).

These stratagems for preserving a shred of masculine dignity have a corollary with Richard's home, where he lives in severe poverty with disadvantaged women, without the steadying influence of a provider/father. Lamming's character G. has a similar experience but lives only with his single mother. In both books, the lack of a father stands for the lack of a strong identification with a homeland, for, in the U.S. South and Barbados, white culture, which defines all standards and, importantly, publically shared history, denies people of color a place in either the past or the present apart from servitude and submission. Although Lamming actually had a step-father, he subtracts him from G.'s story, perhaps in emulation of Wright, but also possibly because he wished to emphasize the quest for manhood by foreclosing the presence of an immediate source in the family.

Sound plays a dual role in Wright as well. Repeatedly, silence and uproar are contrasted as another example of polar opposites in black experience. In many confrontational situations, black characters are expected to respond only in silence before their white tormentors. Conversely, the mob violence that punctuates so many of the narratives constitutes a babel, an equally noncommunicative mode. The salience of this Southern polarity may be suggested by the ending of "The Ethics of Living Jim Crow": a black man comments, "Lawd, man! Ef it wuzn't fer them polices 'n' them ol' lynch-mobs, there wouldn't be nothin' but uproar down here!" At first glance, this utterance would seem to undercut the gist of the preceding material; but, in fact, this is prophecy and revelation, indicating that black silences mask communal, if internal, uproar—revolutionary rumblings that, if unleashed, would certainly drown out the roar of the lynch mob. Further, this dichotomy of the roar of the mob and the silence of the black community serves as a frame for the generation of voice, a salient feature of all these narratives and one at the heart of Wright's aesthetic. The bones of the victims, in fact, generate the voice of the poet. Finally, we note that the painful wisdom of this utterance is couched in an ironic vernacular, thereby giving it resonance and a sense of folk history. All of these inferences are repeated in Lamming's novel.

Yet another psychological component of Wright's harsh vision of life came from his strongly Freudian view of sexuality, which he came to see as a mixture of delight and dread.[7] In *Black Boy*, his first awakening of lust comes in the black church, where his adolescent fixation on the elder's wife seems later to him to have been stimulated by the "masochistic prayers" and the hymns that were so closely entwined with imagery from dreams. "If my desires had been converted into a concrete religious symbol, the symbol would have looked something like this: a black imp with two horns; a long, curving, forked tail; cloven hoofs, a scaly, naked body; wet, sticky fingers; moist, sensual lips; and lascivious eyes feasting upon the face of the elder's wife" (98). Such a symbol comes from the Boschean imagery of the Book of Revelation, which Wright's Granny has imposed on her grandson as a lesson and warning. His conscious identification with such a demonic image constitutes a rebellion but also a figuration of Freudian theory through African American religious iconography.

More often, however, realistic imagery predominates. As in most circum-Caribbean literature, nature plays a key role in all of Wright's early short fiction. In *Uncle Tom's Children*, an attentive eye plays over woods, pastures, cabins, vacant lots, and domestic interiors, registering both bleakness and beauty. Wright's subsequent nonfictional work, *Twelve Million Black Voices: A Folk History of the Negro in the United States* (1941), demonstrates conclusively how attentive this artist was to the relation between words and images, but his early work also has a highly tactile quality to it and in fact is much more visual than the didactic last part of *Native Son* and more philosophical works such as *The Outsider* (1953) and *The Long Dream*. As his interest in photography grew, however, Wright would reinstall highly visual, often poetic imagery in his prose, reinvigorating all his work from *Black Boy* onward, especially *Pagan Spain* (1957) and the original version of *Black Power* (1954), which initially was to include many of the hundreds of photographs Wright took in Ghana.

There was, however, a price to pay for the gift of vision. Wright shows us, in great detail, that his literacy and, even more important, his fervid artistic imagination make living the racist nightmare much worse for him than for others, who are blind (sometimes willfully so) to the wider spectrum of horrors he engages through his gaze and imagination. As he states, after learning of the lynching of a classmate's brother, "I was compelled to give my entire imagination over to it, an act which blocked the springs of thought and feeling in me, creating a sense of distance between me and the world in which I lived" (*Black Boy*, 151). We remember here that he wrote an unforgettable poem, entitled "Between the World and Me," which details finding the remains of a burned, lynched body, and we therefore can understand both passages better through this comment on the workings of the imagination.

Wright also includes a statement about the power of art (visuals and writing together) to do evil, even when—perhaps especially when—the art is crude and direct. This occurs when a kindly older man chides him for selling a newspaper that features racist cartoons and columns advocating lynchings. At least part of Wright's subsequent aesthetic lay in opposition to such "art," which constitutes a kind of soul-sullying racial pornography.

We also see that Wright's analysis of his childhood has been partly forged through the lens of his reading, which was certainly the case with Lamming too. Speaking of his grandfather's touching and futile attempt to get his Union army pension, Wright compares him to "K" of Kafka's *The Castle* (1926), and there are many other passages that relate to talismanic, symbolic, and surreal texts Wright has read. He admits that some of his early prose had been influenced by Horatio Alger stories, lurid magazine tales, and the like. However, we understand that from the very beginning his writing has, *au fond*, been his and his alone, however inflected by other reading. This is made unmistakably clear when the principal of his school attempts to write the valedictory address Wright was to make. Despite threats and the remonstrance of his uncle and others, he gives his address, in his own words. This, too, marks Wright's aesthetic independence from that moment forward.

Many of these points find illustration in the *Black Boy*'s opening account of how the four-year-old Richard, beset with boredom, accidentally sets the house on fire and then is beaten half to death by his mother. But this passage is followed by his pronouncement that henceforward he came to see that "each event spoke with a cryptic tongue. And the moments of living slowly revealed their coded meanings. There was the wonder I felt when I first saw a brace of mountainlike, spotted, black-and-white horses clopping down a dusty road through clouds of powdered clay. . . . There was the faint, cool kiss of sensuality when dew came on to my cheeks and shins as I ran down the wet green garden paths in the early morning" (7). These pastoral early passages encode a child's primitive philosophy, which will nevertheless grow into the man's creed: "There was the great joke that I felt God had played on cats and dogs by making them lap their milk and water with their tongues" (7), a prefiguration of Wright the writer's concept of God as cosmic joker.

These lyrical memories are coupled with graphic, more naturalistic ones: "There was the speechless astonishment of seeing a hog stabbed through the heart, dipped into boiling water, scraped, split open, gutted, and strung up gaping and bloody," lines akin to Walt Whitman's graphic description of the bloody suicide on the floor or the pimply neck of a prostitute in *Song of Myself*.[8]

Both of these modes, however, are essentially descriptive. For charged action scenes, Wright could summon an economical, clipped, highly verbal mode of presentation. Charged by his mother to go out again to brave the bullies who stole his grocery money, young Richard, desperate and caught between the twin furies of the street boys and his mother, becomes a fury himself: "I flayed with tears in my eyes, teeth clenched, stark fear making me throw every ounce of my strength behind each blow. I hit again and again. . . . The boys scattered, yelling, nursing their heads, staring at me in utter disbelief. . . . I stood panting, egging them on, taunting them to come and fight. . . . I ran after them and they tore out for their homes, scream-ing. The parents of the boys rushed into the streets and threatened me, and I shouted . . . telling them that I would give them the same. . . . That night I won the right to the streets of Memphis" (*Black Boy*,1945,16). Stripped of modifiers, streamlined into forceful strings of strong verbs, the passage mimics the hysteria of desperate self-assertion and survival through furious, instinctual actions of self-assertion and survival.[9]

Throughout *Black Boy*, Wright seeks to provide a truthful portrait of black rural life. In keeping with his documentarian impulses, and in synco-pation with the sociological photo-narrative volumes produced in the 1930s by teams of prominent writers and photographers, Wright sometimes inserts virtual "photographs," which are even more dramatic when they rupture the narrative proper. In one of the book's most famous scenes, speaking of the last time he saw his father as a boy, Wright interrupts his discourse to fast-forward twenty-five years to his ultimate reunion with his father in a Mississippi field. The son, now an educated and sophisticated Northerner, takes in the sight of his aged father standing alone on the red clay of a Mis-sissippi farm: "A sharecropper, clad in ragged overalls, holding a muddy hoe in his gnarled, veined hands. . . . I could see a shadow of my face in his face[;] though there was an echo of my voice in his voice, we were forever strangers. . . . He was standing against the sky, smiling toothlessly, his hair whitened, his body bent, his eyes glazed with dim recollection, his fearsome aspect of twenty-five years ago gone forever. How completely his soul was imprisoned by the slow flow of the seasons, by wind and rain and sun. . . . How chained were his actions and emotions to the direct, animalistic im-pulses of his withering body." And yet, "as a creature of the earth, he endured, hearty. . . . I forgave him and pitied him as my eyes looked past him to the unpainted wooden shack" (30–31). Abdul JanMohamed persuasively reads this scene as Wright's signal that he has triumphed over "social death," that is, he has managed, through hard work, education, and physical flight from the South, to avoid his father's fate. Further, he sees the scene as one of triumph (over the father who abandoned him) but also as an act "of deep mourning" (144).

I would add that the writing here itself offers a keen sense of differentiation, as Wright keeps his father mute, transforming him into a poetically rendered photograph, one not unlike the ones he had included of black peasants in *Twelve Million Black Voices*, where once again the people are mute, unlike the narrator. The eloquence of Wright's words here similarly ennobles the figure visualized but simultaneously erases him by denying him any kind of voice, which serves to further emphasize the stunning poetic pirouettes of the narrator's portrait. As we shall see, George Lamming uses this method to great effect as well.[10]

The negative readings of black folk that one might extract from this scene multiply in another passage, again in the voice-over of the mature narrator. Certainly one of the reasons many people give for not going forward to read other works by Richard Wright is their strongly negative reaction to one infamous section in *Black Boy*. It goes like this: "After I had outlived the shocks of childhood . . . I used to mull over the strange absence of real kindness in Negroes, how unstable was our tenderness, how lacking in genuine passion we were, how void of great hope, how timid our joy, how bare our traditions, how hollow our memories. . . . Negroes had never been allowed to catch the full spirit of Western civilization" (32). The passage, however, is situated in the past, and follows a description of his departure from the orphanage, when his mother is shocked by his indifference to the children he is leaving behind. But, as the narrator explains, "I kept my eyes averted, not wanting to look into faces that hurt me because they had become so thoroughly associated in my feelings with hunger and fear" (32). One should remember, too, that *Black Boy* is an aesthetically shaped product that draws much of its power from it creation of a proud, lonely hero, one much akin to those created by Wright's future Parisian colleagues, Jean-Paul Sartre and Albert Camus. Although it indeed tells the story of one Richard Wright, it is also a selective rendition of that person's life, and it is therefore artistic and perhaps in some cases actually fictional. We would also do well to remember that all these charges against the black community are contradicted at many other junctures in Wright's fiction and nonfiction, both before and after he wrote this text. It is a testimony to the power of his aesthetics that we take this passage so seriously, as it builds on a particular moment in the young boy's life to extend outward to poetic social commentary.[11] Moreover, this idea is contradicted time and again within this very book. When Richard's mother suffers a debilitating stroke, the neighbors nurse her, feed the children, and wash their clothes as they wait for family to arrive. And, indeed, seven of Ella's eight siblings rush to her bedside, from Detroit, Chicago, and various Southern cities, a powerful contradiction of the narrator's portrait of the lack of kindness in his race.

Despite such qualifications, because of the harshness of Richard's judgments of the black South, Wright was justified in being apprehensive about the reception *Black Boy* would get, for he knew many of the things he said like this would prove offensive to black readers. He was right—the book was judged more for his attitude than for how he said things. His old friend Ralph Ellison wrote a critical review and later told Constance Webb in a February 3, 1963 interview, "It was an attempt to get Dick to see certain things. . . . In *Black Boy* he cut his ties with Negroes" (Webb, n.d., n.p.). We should also recall Wright's comments about black stereotypes, which this book was designed to combat. As he charged, "There is something serious to be said about this legend that all Negroes are kind and love animals and children. . . . That legend serves to protect certain guilt feelings about the Negro. If you can feel that he is so different . . . naturally happy . . . and . . . smiles automatically you kind of exclude him . . . from the human race. . . . You don't have to feel bad about mistreating him" (*Conversations*, 65).

We might locate a rationale for this particular mode of presentation at this point in the book by looking at Wright's previously expressed theory of fiction, in his famous 1937 "Blueprint for Negro Writing," where he notes that merely holding a mirror up to a historical period is not always effective: "The relationship between reality and the artistic image is not always direct and simple. The imaginative conception of a historical period will not be a carbon copy of reality. Image and emotion possess a logic of their own" (48). This highly aesthetic posture says much about Wright's concept of propaganda that is also art.[12] Similarly, George Lamming feels that the political riots against colonial rule that erupted in 1937 in Barbados, Trinidad, and Jamaica fueled a Caribbean literary renaissance, "a creative literary explosion. . . . Its source may be found in the collective grievances that were beginning to bear fruit through political action" (*Conversations*, 117).[13]

Wright's notorious negativity in the cited passage *is* problematic, however, especially when—as is often the case—*Black Boy*, or perhaps *Black Boy* and *Native Son*, are the only Wright texts a reader knows. We can see immediately, however, that Wright had a more appreciative view of black culture in *Twelve Million Black Voices*. This collaboration with the celebrated photographer Edwin Rosskam followed in the wake of several seminal photonarrations concerning rural poverty, most famously Erskine Caldwell and Margaret Bourke-White's *You Have Seen Their Faces* (1937), Herman Clarence Nixon's *Forty Acres and Steel Mules* (1938), Dorothea Lange and Paul Schuster Taylor's *An American Exodus: A Record of Human Erosion* (1939), and in the same year, 1941, the publication of Walker Evans and James Agee's much more famous collaboration, *Let Us Now Praise Famous Men*. In a much-noted comparison of the Bourke-White and Evans photos, documentary scholar William Stott claims that the former represents sharecropper life as "an unrelieved abomination," while the latter presents it as an abomination but also reveals its beauty, "discounting neither," and always presenting the beauty as tragic, because "it can never be recognized or appreciated by those who create it" (1973, 271).

Although there has been little discussion of Wright and Rosskam's work, John Reilly has perceptively noted that the former created a new language for the book, one "akin to the style of the popular blues, spirituals, and sermons . . . a secularization of the sacred moral voice of the folk . . . rooted in localized tradition" (Reilly, 1982, 117). Or, as Henry Louis Gates might say, the book becomes a "speakerly text." This is in keeping with Wright's announced goal of seizing "upon that which is qualitative and abiding in Negro experience, to place within full and constant view the collective humanity whose triumphs and defeats are shared by the majority" (5–6). This is instantly clear in the pages of *Twelve Million Black Voices*. While the book ostensibly also takes in the world of Southern African American immigrants to the North, they are viewed throughout the work as Southerners. In this reading, the North's shabby tenements and oppressive working conditions are only an extension of "American Hunger," which was the original title of Wright's famous *Black Boy*.

William Stott has been highly critical of *Twelve Million Black Voices*, pointing out that some of the pictures have little relation to the text, and that, indeed, some are outright deceptive—one picture that means to illustrate the plight of black sharecroppers is actually of a poor white (1973, 232). Stott's ensuing discussion, however, demonstrates his own ignorance of African American history, for he claims Wright's description of the Middle Passage is overwrought, when if anything it is understated. He feels that Wright's depiction of African American life "as unmitigated hell" exaggerates and emotionalizes (234). Stott prefers Nixon's *Forty Acres and Steel Mules* to most of the photo-narration works of the time, for it supposedly treats the same matters "without emotionalism or oversimplification." One wonders how carefully Stott and other critics have studied *Twelve Million Black Voices*. Stott praises the academic background of Nixon, apparently unaware that Wright had acquired many principles of sociology and ethnology during his time with the academics of the University of Chicago.

Twelve Million Black Voices is the real "history written with lightning" that President Woodrow Wilson claimed for D. W. Griffith's *The Birth of a Nation*. Wright pressed his earlier drive to revise history through fiction into a new channel here, as he used photographs of actual people to illustrate his passionate commentary, and vice versa. At the same time, the pictures themselves struck a deeply poetic chord in Wright, one that in sounding seemed to awaken some kind of hope in this deeply existential writer. In viewing these faces, which seemed to "speak" to him of the resources of his people, which he had sometimes ignored in the past in favor of a presentation of victimization, he appears to have been revitalized, by both anger and the prospect of new communications and connections. It is important that this work, which connected the once-conjoined but now geographically and culturally separate black communities of the rural South and of Northern cities, prepared him for the circumCaribbean comparisons he would soon make, his transatlantic perspective of the Paris years, and, finally, his deep engagement with black globalism and international congresses of people of color. In terms of Lamming's presentation at the end of his autobiographical novel and in his subsequent works of the dislocation of thousands of people (especially *The Pleasures of Exile* [1960]), we see a further influence from Wright in the presentation of the history of black diasporas, both from Africa and then from the U.S. South and the Caribbean.

We have already seen a keen example of Wright's ability to frame a literary "photograph" in the scene with his aged father in the field. But he could create pendants for such scenes through psychological portraits as well. Certainly one of the strongest scenes in *Black Boy*, relating to the inscription from Job, comes when Richard's mother suffers her second stroke, which condemns her to the life of an invalid. Employing literary terms, Wright declares, "My mother's suffering grew into a symbol in my mind, gathering to itself all the poverty, the ignorance, the helplessness . . . the futile seeking, the uncertainty, the fear, the dread; the meaningless pain and the endless suffering. Her life set the emotional tone of my life. . . . A somberness of spirit that I was never to lose settled over me . . . that was to make me keep forever on the move, as though to escape a nameless fate seeking to overtake me" (87). This bravura passage operates on several levels. First, in terms of narrative, it sums up the preceding events, flashes forward to the future and, indeed, to the present moment of narration. It is simultaneously a reading of events and of the narrator's psyche. As such, this moment of fracture and trauma becomes a key to reading the rest of the book, and, indeed, the rest of Wright's works. Further, it forms a pendant to the virtual portrait of his aged father.[14]

Wright shows us that highly charged prose—accuracy be damned—was what he hungered for as a reader, even as a child, and there should be no surprise that he eventually wanted to create it too. A copy of *Bluebeard and His Seven Wives* creates a "thirst for violence . . . for intrigue, for plotting, for secrecy, for bloody murders. . . . [The] story of deception and murder had been the first experience in my life that had elicited from me a total emotional response. . . . I had tasted what to me was life" (*Black Boy*, 35), a passage that reveals much about the following trajectory of Wright's literary career, but also about the events he selected for aesthetic presentation in this, his life's story, which is shaped by hunger and trauma. Along these lines, one of the most moving portions of the book, too, comes late when on a white man's borrowed card, he checks out library editions of H. L. Mencken: "I was jarred and shocked by the style, the clear, clean, sweeping sentences. . . . I pictured the man as a raging demon, slashing with his pen, consumed with hate, denouncing everything American. . . . Yes, this man was fighting . . . using words as a weapon, using them as one would use a club" (218). These glimpses lead to other books, other styles; but the new knowledge awakens an awareness that he has "a new hunger," thereby extending the overarching theme of the book.

Wright, always conscious of his Southern heritage, makes the relocation of the family from a sterile Memphis to a verdant Arkansas bloom through short, impressionistic poetic descriptions of pastoral scenes and events in language strongly reminiscent of Walt Whitman's *Leaves of Grass*: "The days and hours began to speak now with a clearer tongue. Each experience had a sharp meaning of its own. . . . There was the feeling of impersonal plenty when I saw a boll of cotton whose cup had spilt over and straggled its white fleece toward the earth. . . . There was the excitement of fishing in muddy country creeks with my grandpa on cloudy days. . . . There was the dry hot summer morning when I scratched my bare arms on briers while picking blackberries and came home with my fingers and lips stained black with sweet berry juice" (*Black Boy*, 40–41). These charged one-sentence vignettes strongly presage Wright's later fascination with Japanese haiku and the splendid versions he created from his own experiences. Dan McCall has mocked these lines, calling them the kind of emotions one expects from a Miss Alabama (1969, 117). McCall, however, who was writing in the militant 1960s, displays that era's preference for the tough, the political and ideological, at the cost of the tender, the imaginative, the mystical—all once felt to be the province of the feminine, but which Wright always saw as a necessary component of his aesthetic palette, one that threw into sharp contrast his more militant prose. Wright tries on, as I have indicated, a variety of styles, and seems to relish all of them.

In another Whitmanesque passage in *Black Boy*, Wright belies his earlier statement about the poverty of African American culture by offering a list of nineteen sayings, such as "If I kissed my elbow, I would turn into a girl. If my right ear itched, then something good was being said about me" (63). The repetitions that are so characteristic of African American culture are part of what Wright describes as "magic possibilities," and the incantatory music of the lists mirrors the yearning in the narrator's boyish consciousness. Wright sums it up poetically: "Because I had no power to make things happen outside of me . . . I made things happen within. Because my environment was bare and bleak, I endowed it with unlimited potentialities, redeemed it for the sake of my own hungry and cloudy yearning" (64). Thus as Wright charts the growing power of fantasy to channel the young Richard's fears and hostilities, he projects a psychological development for us of a paranoid personality, but also of a fervid and vivid imagination, one that develops into a richly creative literary sensibility, which Lamming creates along similar lines for his G.

From all the styles, Wright extracts his own, achieving a new mastery of words as he makes final plans to head to Chicago with his family. He moves effortlessly from sweeping, detailed passages of introspection and self-analysis to hard, gem-like formulations: "This was the culture from which I sprang. This was the terror from which I fled" (225). This ceaseless, protean stylistic shape-shifting seems a by-product of Wright's attempt to master the art of saying the unsayable. Commenting on the brutal treatment he received from a variety of white workers at various jobs, he laments, "I knew what was wrong with me, but I could not correct it. The words and actions of white people were baffling signs to me. I was living in a culture and not a civilization and I could learn how that culture worked only by living with it. Misreading the reactions of whites around me made me say and do the wrong things. . . . I could not grin. In the past I had always said too much,

strongly presage Wright's later fascination with Japanese haiku and the splendid versions he created from his own experiences. Dan McCall has mocked these lines, calling them the kind of emotions one expects from a Miss Alabama (1969, 117). McCall, however, who was writing in the militant 1960s, displays that era's preference for the tough, the political and ideological, at the cost of the tender, the imaginative, the mystical—all once felt to be the province of the feminine, but which Wright always saw as a necessary component of his aesthetic palette, one that threw into sharp contrast his more militant prose. Wright tries on, as I have indicated, a variety of styles, and seems to relish all of them.

now I found that it was difficult to say anything at all. I could not react as the world in which I lived expected me to" (172). Fashioning a new aesthetic for autobiographical propaganda, Wright found a way to express what Zora Neale Hurston called "the inaudible voice of it all."

"A Charged and Poetic Prose"

In the Castle of My Skin (1953) famously splits the narration between first and third person, thereby blending the voices of the fictional persona and an autobiographical speaker. This fusion appropriately meets the challenge Lamming set himself of writing an autobiographical novel. I would argue that although Wright seemingly favors the latter voice, he in effect wrote an autobiographical novel himself in *Black Boy*, which is so consciously shaped and framed—editing out many aspects of Wright's actual life and reshaping others—that it needs to be considered a fiction, despite the fact that most of the major incidents actually occurred. Like Lamming, Wright intends his text to be representational; the title is not "Richard Wright" but *Black Boy*. Lamming, who was certainly influenced by Wright's text, similarly highlights race in his title, where the figured "skin" is definitely black.[15]

Black Boy, however, more clearly bifurcates/contrasts the living presence of "Richard," whose reactions to the events being described are both immediate and of that time, and the performed narration of the mature Richard Wright, who is selecting, shaping, and "performing" these events himself, quite apart from "Richard," in his more distanced commentary. James Olney has asserted that *Black Boy* would not really work if it did not employ its signal mix of "narration and commentary, past experience and present vision, and a fusion of the two in the double 'I' of the book"—both "Richard" and "Richard Wright"—the latter "a mature man, an urban intellectual, an accomplished writer brooding over his life and its meaning" (1990, 248). Lamming, also relying on the details of his own life, nevertheless casts his narrative as a novel, so the bifurcation in *Castle* is the more traditional kind between the central character and the omniscient narrator, even though he too is, like Richard/Wright, looking back on his youth. Further, the character Trumper provides numerous passages of folk philosophy that "trump" G., the central character, because he performs the commentary role that Wright himself takes on in *Black Boy*. Having been exiled for a time in the United States, Trumper has forged a new perspective on his native island, and he sees that, while class and social position have kept peasants in their place, so has race. It is this more than anything else that Lamming took away from Wright's presentations in *Black Boy*.

The biographical facts of the two lives have a remarkable symmetry. Lamming grew up in an oppressive colonial rural setting and "escaped" only through a hard-won education that enabled his immigration at the age of nineteen to Trinidad and a subsequent and permanent move to England four years later, in 1950. Wright left Jim Crow Mississippi in 1927 at the age of seventeen for Chicago. His later relocations to New York and, ultimately, to Paris, echo Lamming's moves to Trinidad and then London; ironically, in the last year of his life, Wright was trying to make a move to that city himself.

Lamming's strong sense of pride and individuality is signaled immediately in this title, since "castle," particularly in the British colonies, had a wide symbolic resonance, one that includes the sense of fortress, enclosure, royalty, warfare, strength, endurance, power, and bulwark. "Castle" has an exact referent in Lamming's novel in the landlord's imposing edifice, set on a hill. As such, the British family is protected from the devastating flood that marks the opening sections of the novel, when entire huts are swept away by the raging waters. A central symbol, the castle's wall, is surmounted by broken bottles. "It was a castle around which the land like a shabby back garden stretched" (29). In light of the title of the book, we are drawn to connect this "fortress" of value and power with the body of the protagonist, in his black skin. For it is the white colonizing power that assigns value to the terrain it surveys, and a black body ironically becomes an imprisoning mechanism for the human spirit as it is incarcerated by the colonizing gaze through "black" coding. Dungeons of the spirit can be paralyzing, while "castles" protect the empowered from "catastrophes." However, both Wright and Lamming point to the potential of social revolution, which could dislodge the "king" from his "castle." In fact, at the conclusion of Lamming's novel, the man-made rupture of the strikes causes the landlord to sell his holdings. Once again, however, the really poor people lose, as only the better-off blacks are able to purchase the properties. As in Wright, the complaint of Job applies to both natural and man-made disasters.

We might remember that Wright, in his powerful 1938 story "Down By the Riverside," and Zora Neale Hurston, in the preceding year's novel *Their Eyes Were Watching God*, had set actual historical floods—the great Mississippi River flood of 1927 and the Lake Okeechobee hurricane of 1928, respectively—and in each narrative, the consequences for poor blacks is much worse than for whites. *Black Boy* and *Castle* end in precisely the same way, with the protagonist preparing to leave his Southern home (Barbados/ Mississippi) for the North (Chicago/London), although in *Castle* the initial destination is the neighboring island of Trinidad. There is a key difference, however. Wright's narrator speaks to us out of isolation and alienation, totally alone. G., the narrator of *Castle*, ends his text in dialogue with old man Pa, who similarly is leaving on a journey, but one quite different, as he is heading to what he calls his "final resting place," the almshouse. After the old man bestows a paternal kiss on G.'s head and departs, the narrator tells us, "The earth where I walked was a marvel of blackness and I knew in a sense more deep than simple departure I had said farewell, farewell to the land" (303). Both narrators, however, would seem to agree with Wright about their own part of the larger "South": "The environment the South creates is too small to nourish human beings, especially Negro human beings" ("The Handiest Truth," 1945, 3). It should be mentioned, too, that Lamming (who is, as of 2015, still living) fared rather better in exile than did Wright. As he indicates in *The Pleasures of Exile* (1960), he developed a playful, creative style once in London. Despite the coldness he detected in the British toward colonials of color, he enjoyed many rich intellectual friendships and an appreciative literary audience, especially among the many West Indians who had migrated there. For the past decades he has held teaching posts in the United States and the Caribbean, where he spends much of his time in his native Barbados. Wright, by contrast, while the center of an expatriate black literary community in Paris and the confidant of French intellectuals such as Albert Camus, Jean-Paul Sartre, and Simone de Beauvoir, was still a solitary figure who constantly had to struggle to make a living for his family, and he never returned to Mississippi. Lamming always had, in both Barbados and London, a community that supported him, and that makes a difference in the worlds that they depict.

Still, at the conclusion of *Black Boy*, Wright declares: "I was not leaving the South to forget the South, but so that some day I might understand it, might come to know what it had done to me, to its children. . . . Deep down, I knew that I could never really leave the South, for my feelings had already been formed by the South, for there had been slowly instilled into my personality and consciousness, black though I was, the culture of the South. So in leaving, I was taking a part of the South to transplant in alien soil, to see if it could grow differently, if it could drink of new and cool rains . . . perhaps to bloom. . . . And if that miracle ever happened, then I would know that there was yet hope in that southern swamp of despair and violence" (228).

Remember, too, that this term "the South" could easily apply to the circumCaribbean world in general, a vast region drastically affected by the history and curse of slavery and plantation culture, a fact that Wright obviously understood. His effort to "escape" later came to encapsulate the restrictions of the Northern United States, but also the hemispheric culture of racism. His flight to Paris and, ultimately, his engagement with the struggles of people of color in both Europe and Asia exponentially expanded his sense that any fight for liberation would have to go beyond the bounds of the narrowly national concept of culture. Lamming, similarly, fled not only Barbados and then Trinidad, but also the Caribbean and the Western Hemisphere, all arenas of black diasporic oppression, whether at the hands of Jim Crow in the United States or under the ostensibly "civilizing" strictures of white British colonizers.

As Curdella Forbes (2005) and others have indicated, studies of Lamming—like those of Wright—for too long concentrated on his political role, particularly in terms of nascent Caribbean nationalism. This blinkered tradition has prevented a wider view of the global implications of his work. Forbes zeroes in on the great period of nationalism in the Caribbean—the 1950s through the 1970s—and demonstrates how one can, as she does in her own project, read Lamming in a transnational context through gender.[16] One can easily employ this same stance, with comparable results, with Wright, who similarly constructed an aesthetic framework built on metaphors of gender, particularly masculinity, as was the case with Lamming. It is worth noting, however, that Forbes's study concentrates on Lamming's later novels rather than on *Castle*, which she sees as overtly invested in masculine gender formation, whereas the later novels, beginning with the female protagonist of *Season of Adventure* (1960), interrogate the masculinist traditions of the West Indian novels that Lamming ironically had seemed to typify with 1953's *Castle*. Similarly, I argue, Wright, at the end of his life, was demanding that more attention be paid to the black woman's story; and his last published novel, *The Long Dream* (1958), and its unpublished sequel, *Island of Hallucinations*, provide strong female characters who speak with urgency and power about the plight and rights of women.[17]

In their metaphors of the "black earth" that has nourished them as children, both writers provide a foundation for this later concern with women, and for the strong role the central figures' mothers play in each text. We also notice that while both writers centrally employ a poetic sense of earth and its link to life, Lamming situates it as foundation, while Wright expands the metaphor, proleptically envisioning a "blossoming" from this black garden once a transplantation has taken place. Certainly, one way to read this passage is to see Wright figuring not just his own individual being, but the "blossoms" of his book-length works of fiction, which, I would argue, are always deeply rooted in his Southern past, especially *Uncle Tom's Children* (1938), *Eight Men* (1961), and *The Long Dream* (1958). The Chicago novels are also profoundly Southern, despite their setting, and the nonfiction Wright composed after exiling himself to Paris—especially *Pagan Spain*—are based on a Southerner's reaction to landscapes, cultures, and climates that he constantly compares to those of the South, and no wonder, as sensory and intellectual triggers bring forth powerful and inescapable memories, part of what Wright "was taking . . . to transplant" in the passage cited.

Both *Black Boy* and *In the Castle of My Skin* end with the hero's departure/ exile, but this thematic is introduced quite early in Lamming's text when he refers to the natives who have immigrated to Panama, where many Caribbean men traveled to find work. As we have seen, this is also a major motif in McKay's *Banana Bottom* (1933). Later in Lamming's story, we learn that the "everyman" figure of Pa was once wealthy with money he earned helping build the Panama Canal, a great works project that once offered hope for the impoverished people. As Ma plaintively notes, "'Tis a next Panama we need now for the young ones" (86), a line that looks forward to the ending of the text. This is also suggested when Pa predicts that the next Panama will be America, "Panama multipl[ied] seven times seven" (86), a biblical incantation and prophecy. Panama thus offers hope, just as immigration to Detroit or Chicago did for black Mississippians. But we should remember that in both situations movement away from the ancestral earth inevitably involves exile, loss, displacement, and a disconnect with individual, familial, and communal history.

It is worth noting, however, that, despite the nostalgia both writers occasionally evince for the folk/peasants of their Southern homes, each man takes pride in an ability to shake free of any tie to a particular locality. Wright, sounding much like his French existentialist friends, asserted in *Black Power*, "I like and even cherish the state of abandonment, of aloneness; it does not bother me; indeed, to me it seems the natural, inevitable condition of man, and I welcome it. I can make myself at home anywhere on this earth" (1954, xxix). Similarly, Lamming claimed, "This may be the dilemma of the West Indian writer abroad; that he hungers for nourishment from a soil which he (as an ordinary citizen) could not at present endure. The pleasure and paradox of my own exile is that I belong wherever I am" (*Pleasures of Exile*, 1960, 50). The two in this sense presage Homi Bhabha's more recent pronouncement of a "third space" between the colonizer and the colonized (1994, 36–39), which would seem to be available for flexible exiles. This also speaks, however, to Wright's strong existentialist streak, which is not as marked in the more communally minded Lamming.

Prosperity in Lamming's narrative is sought first, however, through the strike that the former schoolteacher Mr. Slime calls, which is reminiscent of the strike in Claude McKay's *Banana Bottom*—one that has such disastrous effects. There is really no equivalent to this in *Black Boy*, although we do find some in the powerful stories of black resistance in Wright's 1938 short story collection, *Uncle Tom's Children* (especially "Fire and Cloud" and "Bright and Morning Star"). Lamming's strike indeed leads to the redistribution of land with the landlord's defeat, but, sadly, it is sold to those with ready cash—the black bourgeoisie. The common peasants are displaced and presumably condemned to a life of urban day labor. In this sense, their movement "off the land" echoes the broader trajectory of the Great Migration in the United States of millions of blacks, including Wright and his family, which begins in the final pages of *Black Boy*.

The thematic of shame and public surveillance emerges powerfully early on in both texts. In Wright, the narrator is filled with horror and guilt when he accidentally sets his family's house afire and then, later, when he intentionally kills a kitten in a literal enactment of his father's offhand remark. Lamming, perhaps emulating these episodes in *Black Boy*, has his protagonist force-feed his pigeon castor oil, which kills it. "That night the pigeon died and I with a burning shame in my head buried my blessings in the pillow" (13), a shame multiplied exponentially when neighborhood boys and others gawk at his nude body as his mother washes him outdoors.

Buried in *his* pillow, Wright's protagonist famously dreams of enormous white udders dripping nauseating milk over his head: "Whenever I tried to sleep I would see huge wobbly white bags, like the full udders of cows, suspended from the ceiling above me. Later, as I grew worse, I could see the bags in the daytime with my eyes open and I was gripped by the fear that they were going to fall and drench me with some horrible liquid. . . . Each event spoke with a cryptic tongue" (6–7). Similarly, Lamming's protagonist sees "enormous phantoms with eyes of fire and crowned with bulls' horns stalking through the dark. . . . One came forward hovering over my head in a jeering silence" (13). Both images relate strongly to the apocalyptic symbology of the Book of Revelation, wherein shame, judgement, and terrible punishment are commingled with spectacle and surveillance. We note, however, Wright's seeming fear of the feminine and Lamming's contrasting dread of the masculine (the "horns"). Both passages evoke a psychological fear of castration.

Further, the bathing scene in Barbados introduces the thematic of the harsh, even cruel mother, who constantly "lashes" her son to make him do right, just as Richard's does in *Black Boy*, practicing a kind of "tough love" to season her son to face the oppressive white world. When Lamming's young hero fails to cover himself in the bathing scene, his mother hisses, "You little fool" (19), the identical words Richard's mother hurls at him after she discovers he has killed the kitten (11). In both texts, the "phallic mothers" demonstrate the truth of Wright's perception that words can often be powerful weapons, of both oppression and liberation.

Mothers, of course, employ such words as modes of correction. Neighboring women in Lamming's text cite the biblical passage of "Spare the rod and spoil the child" (21). It is G.'s friend Bob, however, who suffers most from a mother's beating. Lamming picks up Wright's suggestion that fierce black mothers, forced to operate as fathers would, ironically steal their son's manhood while seeking to foster it, which young Richard's dream indicates. At one point, the narrator's friend Gus employs Freudian terms to describe the effect of his mother's voice, so like the belt she inflicts on his body: "Her voice with the sharpness of a bullet castrated my glance" (114). Here and elsewhere, Lamming powerfully echoes Richard's rage against his mother, who beats him for fighting white boys and for challenging the racial order in general. As Jan Mohamed has argued, she in effect becomes an agent in such scenes for Jim Crow (2005, 152).

Certainly the absence of fathers in these two texts speaks eloquently of the "historyless" aspect of colonized cultures, whose economic deprivations often result in fathers abandoning their families. The rootlessness of Wright's matriarchal family throughout his early life finds complementary expression in Lamming's narrative, even though G. and his mother are comparatively stable. In neither case do these families own land. Instead, they are enmeshed in a community based on sharecropping, in a culture where white families hand down the large parcels of land from generation to generation, renting to peasants, who may stay, if permitted, or who may—especially in the U.S. South—move frequently from place to place. In Barbados, Lamming shows us, more extended residence is possible, but only at the pleasure of the landlord, who inhabits the "castle" that lords it over the peasants from the hill.

Communal habits and misconceptions are repeatedly cited by Lamming as a kind of Greek chorus of self-imposed oppression, one based in shame.

For peasants and the educated blacks alike, "the enemy was My People. My People are low-down nigger people. My people don't like to see their people get on. The language of the overseer . . . The myth had eaten through their consciousness like moths through the pages of ageing documents. Not taking chances with My People. They always let you down" (26–27).[18] One wonders if Wright, reading this passage, thought of his narrator Richard's statement in *Black Boy* that blacks lacked "real kindness." In any case, in his introduction to the first edition of Lamming's novel, he comments that the story was "a symbolic repetition of the story of millions of simple folk who, sprawled over half of the world's surface and involving more than half of the human race, are today being catapulted out of their peaceful, indigenously earthy lives and into the turbulence and anxiety of the twentieth century" ("Introduction," 1953, x). He approvingly noted that Lamming had appropriately employed "a charged and poetic prose" to tell this tale ("Introduction," 1953, ix), something he had done himself in *Black Boy*.

Unlike Wright's Richard, Lamming's narrator grew up in a predominantly black culture, albeit one, like Wright's, controlled by whites. We should be wary, however, of claims of "representation," or in Lamming's case, of his narrator operating as a representative of a "collective consciousness." In his famous 1983 introduction to *Castle*, which needs to be considered alongside Wright's earlier one, Lamming insisted that his *mode of narration* was chosen so as to present the "collective human substance of the village" rather than an individual consciousness (x). Simon Gikandi has forcefully argued that the community pictured in the novel, as in Wright's tale, is fractured in various ways, and that the narrator's self-portrait is designed, in fact, to show how difficult the struggle always is to differentiate the self from the master scripts of any traditional community, scripts that are inevitably mixed and in conflict (1992, 75). In Lamming's case, his culture was breaking down under the pressures of modernization, while Wright's world was disappearing because of the increased pressures of Jim Crow culture and the resulting Great Migration to the North, which the narrator joins at the end of the book. Gikandi's overall observation that "attempts to investigate family and communal history through narrative are bound to meet the issues of alienation, emigration, and exile" (77) have equal relevance to *Black Boy*—and for that matter, to Wright's last masterwork, *The Long Dream*, suggesting that conditions in both the South and the South of the South, based in the residual history of slave cultures, have much in common and produce similar social outcomes and destinies.

But there is a key difference between Southern black disdain and Carib-

bean black disdain for their fellow "folk." The standard employed in the Caribbean is not necessarily that of white neighbors, but of the British Empire.
The Barbadians who were trained in England return home "stamped like an
envelope with what they call the culture of the Mother Country" (*Castle*,
27). As this passage follows the scenes depicting cruel actual mothers, we
perhaps are meant to see a link between the colonizing mother culture and
the overly harsh actual mothering. Also, the class distinctions within the
black community in Barbados are different from the Southern situation,
where the divide is much more between blacks and poor whites; the latter
group's ferocious differentiation between itself and its black neighbors creates a false hierarchy that seems elevating.

Lamming creates a kind of folk philosopher in the figure of the shoemaker, who has learned from reading J. B. Priestly that colonial governors
can convince themselves that what is only a temporary privilege is actually
a permanent right. Through his reading of newspapers, he identifies with
riots taking place in Trinidad, a place he knows through cricket matches.
He understands that the contests between teams from various British-
dominated colonies instills in the subject people similar habits and customs
that are English, thus reinforcing their subject position through culture and
making the net of confinement more tangible by showing it extending over
the far-flung islands and territories of the British circumCaribbean. He tells
his friends that things have to change and that he is inspired by the example
of Marcus Garvey. Moving through a review of the world's great empires,
the shoemaker concludes that the British Empire too will fall. Mixing folk
idiom with shrewd historical analysis, he declares: "God don't like ugly, an'
whenever these big great empires start to get ugly with the thing they does
the Almighty puts His hands down once an' fo all" (103).[19]

In a telling discussion of why Garvey failed, the men agree that it was
because he summoned up a link with Africa, and, as the shoemaker remarks,
"If you tell half of them . . . they have something to do with Africa, they'd
piss straight in your face," to which one replies, "No man like to know he is
black" (104), which causes the shoemaker to look hard in the mirror, presumably not just at his own reflection, but at the group's. This Emersonian
moment seems to suggest "know thyself" in racial terms that are congruent
with Garvey's overarching message. The entire sequence, like many such
passages in Wright where black folk talk among themselves, has a gravity
tempered by ironic humor, because it is rendered in vernacular dialogue,
replete with folk idioms and bawdy humor. According to Hazel Rowley,
Wright could not endorse Garveyism, but he admired the racial pride of the

Jamaican's followers and their determination to find an alternative to their rejection in the United States (2008, 65).

Lamming's narrative differs significantly from Wright's in its use of humor and comic anecdote, particularly when it comes to courtship and marriage. In the middle of the book, the boys consider two instructive tales. One concerns Jon, who has children with Susie and then impregnates Jen, whose father demands he marry her. Marrying Susie will prevent that, but in his confusion Jon agrees to marry each of them in separate churches on the same day. Befuddled, he hides out in the churchyard between two graves, unable to choose—or perhaps unable to give up his freedom, which, as the symbolic graves suggest, has been doubly compromised, "buried."

This tale is interwoven with that of Bambi, whose two women, Bots and Bambina, live with him and their children. A German woman who takes notes (seemingly a caustic reference to trouble-making anthropologists) tells Bambi he should marry one of them; they cast lots and Bots wins. Strangely, Bambi begins to periodically get drunk and beat both of the women, in turn. Eventually, they blame each other for this, and they fight. Finally, Bambi dies of a heart attack, and the two women, with attendant undertakers, engage in a struggle over who will bury him, but it turns out neither has the money, and the state buries him in a pauper's grave.

Wright applauded the humor here but also saw it as doubled, "both ribald and pathetic," in the impact of Western concepts of marriage on "naive, paganlike minds" ("Introduction," 1953, xi).[20] The whole thing is told in dialect, and it seemingly has the moral of "never marry." But, as the bitterly wise Trumper concludes, "Those things never happen in histr'y, an' even if they did, histr'y ain't got eyes to see everything" (141). Still, as Trumper again tells us, such strange things do not usually happen, because people in the village "do so many things the same way. Everybody in the village sort of belong. Is like a tree. It can't kind of take up the roots by itself; we all live sort of together, except for those who don't really belong" (144). Both of the stories are told from a strongly masculine point of view and seemingly indict the controlling tendency of women (especially the German woman), which has already been shown in the behavior of the village's mothers. Jon's story is told first, mainly for laughs. Bambi's tale, however, offers a darker and more complicated treatment of issues raised in the first story and concludes with economic matters that underline communal poverty, even in death, where the dignity of a proper burial (a salient aspect of both black Mississippi and Barbados cultures of the time) is denied. Finally, the stories' telling, through the voices of the young boys, offers an alternate history that puts something before us that "hist'ry" (that is, "white history") would never even consider.[21] Bambi's story in this respect relates to various inset tales in *Black Boy*, such as the tragic story of Wright's Uncle Hoskins, another tale that "hist'ry" has ignored but that needs telling.[22]

Lamming, far more than Wright, invests his secondary peasant figures with hard-earned wisdom, be it the kind drawn from age and endurance, as in the character of Pa or the shoemaker, or through acquiring an inside view from the "outside," as with Trumper. It is significant that all these figures, who represent youth and age, speak in Barbadian Creole. Trumper informs us that "America make you feel . . . that where you been livin' before is a kind of cage." As a result, he urges the islanders to break out of theirs: "You think they dare move all these houses. . . . If every one o' you refuse to pay a cent on that land [the landlord's, which is eventually sold to middle-class blacks], and if all o' you decide to sleep in the street or let the Government find room for you in the prison house, you think they dare go through with this business o' selling the land?" (284–86). Wickedly playing on the Judas Mr. Slime's name, he says the latter's selling out is "the way of the world, and in a world o' Slimes there ain't no way out for those who don't know how to be slimy . . . a nasty crime" (286). This kind of dialect-driven folk discourse is in short supply in Wright, except in moments of levity. It is the dominant mode, however, of Zora Neale Hurston's "speakerly text," *Their Eyes Were Watching God*, which seeks to infuse folk expression into both dialogue and the omniscient narration.[23]

Trumper helps create a sense of reader/author irony, in that G. professes not to understand him, providing yet another example of what I have termed "bifurcated narrative." When the former proclaims, as Wright did in more formal language, that "this world is a world o' camps, an' you got to find out which camp you're in. And above everything else keep that camp clean," G. states, "This was all very cryptic" (288), but the reader understands Trumper very well, especially when he responds to G.'s question, "Who are your people," with "The Negro race . . . I didn't know it till I reached the States" (295).

The enabling power of literacy and education is signaled in each book, but in different ways. Lamming's narrator tells us that "language was a kind of passport. You could go where you liked if you had a clean record. You could say what you like if you know how to say it. It didn't matter whether you felt everything you said. You had language, good, big words to make up for what you didn't feel. And if you were really educated . . . if you could make the language do what you wanted it to do . . . you didn't have to feel at all. You could do away with feeling. That's why everybody wanted to be educated" (154).

In the years to come, this education is offered to the narrator, who does well on tests, but his cronies Boy Blue and Bob become drifters, Trumper migrates to America, and the narrator goes on to high school. The young boys in both books are dreamily wistful, wishing for a better future, and in each case, that means leaving home. In Lamming, they dream of going to America: "They say things good there" (168), just as their ancestors dreamed of Panama. As always, they quote Mr. Slime: "[He] call it the promise land an' some who been an' come back says 'tis the bread basket o' the world" (168). Lamming was familiar with this aspect of Wright's life too, for, miraculously, the young Richard also excels at school and in fact graduates first in his class.

Academic attributes, however, do not spare young black men from the stereotypes of being oversexed and obsessed with the bodies of white women. These myths, which had similar forms in both the U.S. South and the Caribbean, are used against the young narrator of *Castle* and his two friends when one night they sneak through the wall to the landlord's property and stumble upon his daughter being seduced by a sailor. They escape by joining a revivalist's outdoor ceremony and pretending to be "saved," but later they learn that the sailor spread the word that they had tried to attack the daughter, thereby reversing the actual facts and transforming them from boys into adult black rapists. This tale echoes the outset of Wright's powerful short story "Big Boy Leaves Home" (1938), in which innocent young black boys are seen bathing nude in a white-owned pond by a white woman, which initiates a deadly series of killings and, finally, a lynching, the latter partly instigated by the fiction that the boys attempted to rape the woman, when in fact they were the innocent figures in the original scenario. Both narratives employ the symbolism of forbidden fruit in the Garden of Eden.

The hysteria aroused by the false report of the boys' activities in *Castle* is strengthened considerably when Mrs. Foster's son Po King is shot dead from a tree and the strike raised by Mr. Slime leads to rioting and then looting by men from other locales. Twenty of them are prepared to kill the landlord, but Mr. Slime intervenes. Both Wright and Lamming show how supposed racial and sexual transgression can trigger an automatic script for mob violence.

Years pass, and the mythical Pa has a mystical, lyrical vision of Africa and the Middle Passage.[24] "Each sell his own. . . . The silver sail from hand to hand and the purchase was shipped like a box of good fruit. . . . We were for a price that had no value; we were a value beyond any price. . . . I make my peace with the Middle Passage. . . . If the islands be sick 'tis for no other reason than the ancient silver" (210), a chilling presentation of the continuing curse of slavery that goes on even after emancipation, and not just in Barbados: "I see the purchase of tribes on the silver sailing vessels, some to Jamaica, Antigua, Grenada, some to Barbados. . . . Families fall to pieces. . . . New combinations . . . make quite a different collection. Now if you hear some young fool fretting about back to Africa, keep far from the invalid and don't force a passage to where you won't yet belong. These words not for you but those that come after" (211). This mystical, memorializing section of the book bears a family resemblance to Beloved's famous re-creation of the Middle Passage in Morrison's great novel and may well have been an inspiration.[25] Pa also reminds us of the equally mystic and prophetic Father John in the concluding story/play of Jean Toomer's *Cane* (1923).

Wright, in his reflections on *Castle*, significantly undervalued Ma and Pa, perhaps because he tended to scorn "backward" looks, perhaps discounting the accumulated racial wisdom involved in such reflections, as he always favored struggles toward a better future. While he admired Ma and Pa as "superbly drawn character portraits" straight out of the Old Testament, he nevertheless classed them as "simple, peasant parents musing uncomprehendingly upon the social changes that disrupt their lives and threaten the destinies of their children" (xi), a kind of pat accompanied by a slap. This latter part of the description, in fact, is quite similar in sentiment to that in Wright's description of his reunion with his aged sharecropper father with his uncomprehending eyes.

As Lamming and Wright both see that the white man's history (which leaves blacks out completely) has led to a kind of social and national anomie for blacks, they also indicate that the white man's religion has been employed to keep blacks down. Wright most memorably shows this in the linked stories of *Uncle Tom's Children*, especially when Reverend Taylor of "Fire and Cloud" finally understands how his ministry has been used by white people as a method of control for black citizens. In Lamming's tale, the rebellious Trumper declares, in a dialect-driven outburst, "They turn us dotish with all these nancy stories 'bout born again, an' we never ever give ourself a chance to get up an' get. Nothin' ain't goin' change here till we sort o' stop payin' notice to that sort o' joke 'bout a old man goin' born again" (167). The term "nancy" suggests that white religion aims at a kind of symbolic castration, one that precludes the possibility of "chance." Ultimately, Trumper and the others yearn to leave the island for the "promised land" of

America, just as the narrator of *Black Boy* eventually flees his native Mississippi for Chicago, substituting a dreamed-of but very real alternative space for the imprisoning, colonized life of racially restrictive Mississippi and Barbados. Significantly, although he migrated there himself, Lamming's characters do not aspire to immigration to Britain, knowing that the racial codes that govern their island prevail on the larger, more northern one as well.

We now circle back to the fact that both of these texts were written in exile from the communities that inspired them. The escape—or banishment—from their native homes in each case permitted a former Caliban to become Prospero. These two Shakespearean figures long fascinated Lamming, whose island background drew him to the play. As he has stated, "There is no landscape more suitable for considering the Question of the sea, no geography more appropriate to the study of exile" (*Pleasures of Exile*, 1960, 96). Mastering Prospero's books can lead to sorcery, but it is compromised if it involves cutting off one's racial and cultural heritage. Perhaps for these reasons, Richard Wright came to feel ever more isolated in his adopted home of France, and at the end of his life he was considering relocating elsewhere. His vision of *The Long Dream*'s Fishbelly sinking into a life of squalor in France is appropriately entitled "Island of Hallucinations," and it is indeed a study of exile. Both Wright and Lamming, after they leave their native homes, found in exile an opportunity and a curse, and this situation inflected everything they wrote.[26]

The concept of the fragmented histories of people of African descent has been powerfully addressed by Édouard Glissant: "In the face of a now shattered notion of History, the whole of which no one can claim to master nor even conceive, it was normal that the Western mind should advance a diversified Literature, which is scattered in all directions but whose meaning no one could claim to have mastered. . . . Literature is not only fragmented, it is henceforth shared. In it lie histories and the voice of peoples. We must reflect on a new relationship between history and literature. We need to live it differently" (1989, 77). In the moving, disturbing life-narratives of Mississippi's Richard Wright and Barbados's George Lamming, we find a model for this reconnection of "fragments," and for living this *vitanuova*; their palettes of fire irradiate what begins as propaganda into pyrotechnic aesthetics of identity.

7 Southern *Ajiaco*

Miami and the Generation of Cuban American Writing

One of the least noted but largest lacuna in Southern literary studies has been the neglect of Latino/a writers of the region, whose literary legacy began with the establishment of Florida's St. Augustine in 1565. This omission originally stemmed from the fact that many key works in this tradition remained, until recently, only in Spanish. In our own time, however, this neglect proves even more puzzling, as over the past decades Latino/a writers living in and/or writing about the U.S. South have become increasingly productive and have been writing mostly in English.

Religious, cultural, and artificially constructed notions of both region and nation—which all played a role in the formation of a Southern literary canon—also stood in the way. As many critics have noted, the idea of the "American South" for many decades was concentrated on white, mostly Anglo-Saxon Southerners. Until the civil rights movement, African American writers were not deemed part of the canon or, indeed, of the culture itself, even though they had been crucial components of *actual* Southern society since Jamestown. A similar condition existed until recently for Native Americans writing in and/or about the U.S. South.

Yet another factor overlaps with these; many recent Latino/a writers were born in, migrated to, or have chosen to live in Florida. Significantly, Florida itself, although it has provided a rich literary harvest over the centuries, has often been ignored in Southern Studies. "South-watchers" have dismissively asserted that the state is really "New York South," basing their disdain on the large numbers of retirees from the North. But another reason might be that tropical Florida, which was still largely unexplored jungle in the late nineteenth century, has always been correctly seen as Caribbean, and therefore not only not Southern, but in many ways, not like the rest of the region or the nation. Today, this cultural shorthand has a ready metaphor in the polyglot but mostly Latino/a city of Miami.

Again, as with Florida, within the United States it is often said that Miami is not really a Southern city—yet it is located in one of the states of the

Old Confederacy, was originally settled by Southerners, and has become the most important major city in the southernmost extension of the United States. Miami in many ways has paralleled the past of its regional rival, Atlanta, which is also a center for communications, transportation, finance, and music. When three of the nation's largest airlines moved to Miami, it led to the opening of Miami International Airport in 1941, Atlanta's main aviation rival in the region to this day. Miami's major population group, however, unlike Atlanta's, is Latino/a; radio and TV stations, film facilities, and recording industries operate mostly in Spanish and for Spanish-speaking peoples of the Americas. Miami's airport functions as the chief international hub for the Americas, surpassing even Atlanta in hemispheric flights.

The location of all these cultural engines in Miami owes much to the legacy of the Cuban Revolution. Before the Castro-led insurrection triumphed in 1959, Havana housed leading hemispheric organizations, corporations, and communication centers, including magazine publishing. The U.S. embargo, coupled with the massive relocation of leading Cuban entertainers and entrepreneurs to the United States, shifted much financial and cultural capital to Florida. Certainly one of the key benefits of this shift has been the magnificent outpouring of Cuban American writing, which now has more than a half century of history.

In writing this book, I initially wanted to consider all the new ethnic writers of the U.S. South and the myriad ties many of them have to the wider circumCaribbean. That, however, would be a study unto itself, and a multivolume one at that. Accordingly, I decided to focus on arguably the richest vein in this mine, the literature Cuban Americans have produced in Florida, particularly in Miami. The writers I have chosen—Virgil Suarez, Roberto Fernández, Ana Menéndez, Gustavo Pérez Firmat, and Cristina García—offer a dazzling and representative sample of the variety and power of Cuban-Southern writing, as well as a microcosm of the impact new Latino/a immigrants are having on the rest of the region.

Earlier chapters of this study have traced the myriad effects Cuba has had on the U.S. South, particularly when the island was imagined as an additional slave-owning state, or states. Always, however, before the revolution, the numerous connections between the island and the lower South made it an integral aspect of transnational culture. After Castro's ascent, however, a kind of palm curtain was lowered after the U.S. embargo began in 1960. The mass immigration to Florida and elsewhere of thousands of Cubans—many of them from the educated and professional classes—ultimately resulted in a kind of simulacrum in Miami of Havana, which of course was called "Little

Havana." As Ana Menéndez notes, "They named even their stores after the ones they had lost; and the rabid radio stations carried the same names as the ones they had listened to in Cuba" (*Loving Che*, 2003, 2). Little Havana soon became a useful and colorful adjunct to the South Beach stereotype. Until Cubans became a "problem" population after the 1980 influx of the "undesirable" Mariel boatlift population, there was relatively little bias against Cubans, who were considered white, especially since most of them were well educated and often spoke some English before their exile. Wealthy Cubans had traveled to the United States and done business there. In Havana, they listened to American music, viewed American movies and TV, and read U.S. newspapers and journals. Just before and after Castro's revolution, Cubans who fled to Florida were welcomed, especially as many of them were educated, multilingual, and, in many cases, quite familiar with the existing culture of South Florida. As Gustavo Pérez Firmat tells us about his early years in Florida, "I cannot come up with one single example of feeling ostracized or discriminated against because I was Cuban" (*Next Year*, 1995, 70). Later, after "boat people" and then the Mariel boatlift brought poor and sometimes criminal Cubans to Florida, attitudes began to change, partly because many of the new immigrants were Afro-Cuban.

Throughout this chapter, the Cuban American writers I feature refer to Havana almost as a metaphor for the entire country, for many of the original Miami/Floridian exiles were from there. As Román de la Campa warns us, however, Havana before the revolution was far more Spanish and yet also more American than the rest of the country in its obsession with the creation of wealth and with its social hierarchies situating whites at the apex. By contrast, the rest of the country was more rural, much poorer, African in origin, and in many ways in opposition to Havana. De la Campa maintains, in fact, that the continuing deterioration of the capital has been the result of this long-held animus, which in some ways was concentrated in the far more Caribbean and African eastern city of Santiago (2000, 57–58).

Ricardo Ortiz is inclined to see what some might call "mimicry" of Havana in Little Havana as more substantial: "Miami Cubans can, in part quite legitimately, claim a closer connection to Cuba's traditions, hence to Cuba itself, less because of their geographic proximity to the island and more because of their success in having transplanted so much of the culture to their adopted extraterritorial home" (2007, 7). The stage set of Little Havana, however, provides a visual simulacrum, one that has been equated with those of Miami's South Beach, whose restoration of the Art Deco glories of once-dilapidated hotels and apartment buildings suggests to some that the city presents a gaudy, even vulgar, fake paradise, given to false facades, overblown ornamentation, and excessive display of wealth. Those who know history, however, are more inclined to recall the city's troubled racial past, its divided neighborhoods, and the poverty that lies just a few miles away from the glamour of Miami Beach.

One can, however, avert one's gaze from ugly realities. For those who do so, Miami has become not only a simulacrum of Havana; it has also become the eternal city of exiled Cuban dreams, just as Richmond and its Monument Avenue functioned for ex-Confederates. The new shrine commemorating the Elián González affair is an example. The concept of the simulacrum has been given special emphasis by Jean Baudrillard, whose theory of the image of the original (here, Miami as image of Havana) goes through four stages: "1. It is the reflection of a basic reality. 2. It masks and perverts a basic reality. 3. It masks the absence of a basic reality. 4. It bears no relation to any reality whatever; it is its own pure simulacrum" (1988, 173). Along these lines, we recall Pérez Firmat's observation that he finds

> this effort to recreate yesterday's Cuba in today's America both heroic and pathetic. Heroic because it tries to rise above history and geography. Pathetic because it is doomed to fail. No matter how intense and persistent, substitution cannot go on forever. At some point—after months or years or maybe decades—the immigrant begins to find it impossible to sustain, even precariously, the fiction of rootedness. Unsettling events reimpose a sense of reality. Someone dies and has to be buried outside the Cuban family lot; your children bring home friends (or worse: spouses!) who cannot trill their *r*s; the old radio stations switch to music that follows a different beat. The enclave is no longer *en clave*. (*Life on the Hyphen*, 1994, 8–9)

In the 1990s, the poet Carolina Hospital and the historian/journalist Jorge Cantera published *A Century of Cuban Writers in Florida*, which was intended to "take the younger writers and [put] them in the context of Florida history, all the way back to the 1700s." "I wanted to show," Hospital explains, "that *los altrevidos* . . . were part of a tradition, a connection that had been there between Florida and Cuba for two centuries" (Dick, 2003, 69–70). Hospital's preface to the volume rehearses what Pérez Firmat calls "yesterday's Cuba," (1994, 8), and the rich history of Cubans in Florida, where various revolutionaries, exiles, and indigent migrant workers found refuge for over a hundred years *before* Castro. As Hospital notes, the then small towns of Ybor City (Tampa) and Key West had Cuban mayors early in the twentieth century. During his fifteen years of exile in New York, the Cuban revolutionary, intellectual, and writer José Martí repeatedly visited Key West, Tampa, Jacksonville, Ocala, and St. Petersburg, sometimes giving speeches to crowds of thousands. Many of Cuba's greatest writers and thinkers spent time in Florida, wrote there, and contributed to Floridian journals and newspapers. Indeed, the nineteenth-century priest/philosopher and writer Félix Varela was born in St. Augustine and died there. Most writers and critics, however, have concentrated on Cuban American writing since the revolution (1996, xiv–xv).

Hospital and Cantera's survey leads us to fill in other gaps in popular memory. The ninety miles between Florida and Cuba has been crisscrossed repeatedly over more than four centuries, especially during the time that Florida was a Spanish possession, and thus had even more in common with Cuba, Puerto Rico, Louisiana, and the many other Spanish colonies in the New World. Cuba's history has unfortunately largely been collapsed into its fate since the Cuban Revolution. That cataclysm, however, must be seen as part of a much longer trajectory of events, which has always been intimately connected to Florida. Cultural exchanges began even before the contact era, when Cuba's Arawak Indians regularly traded with Florida's Tequesta people. In the sixteenth century, Hernando de Soto explored Florida with three Cuban Creoles. Still later, Cuban priests came to evangelize in frontier Florida, which was controlled by Cuban officials for almost 200 years. The mass exile of Cubans to Miami after Castro's ascension was dramatic, but it should properly be seen as a fairly recent wave in a centuries-long pattern of immigration and complex cultural exchange between the island and the U.S. South. The shift of sugar production to Cuba from Haiti after 1804 attracted planters from the United States, who set up Cuban plantations, later utilizing the modern machinery they had begun to employ in the United States—we saw an example of this in Martin Delany's novel *Blake*. Steamships began to link Cuba with the Southern ports of New Orleans, Mobile, and Key West as early as 1836. An underground cable was laid between Havana and Key West for telegraph service in 1867. All of these industrial developments were highly dependent on U.S. manufacturers for equipment, parts, and maintenance. After the Civil War, thousands of Confederates relocated to Cuba, including Generals John C. Breckenridge, Robert A. Toombs, Birkett Fry, John B. Magruder, and Jubal A. Early, and onetime Louisiana governor Thomas Overton Moore. Conversely, many Cuban firms did business in the United States, and Cubans were key factors in the establishment of cigar factories in cities across Florida. Increasingly, too, wealthy Cubans sent their children to the United States for a superior education. When they returned, they spoke English, had a passion for baseball (which quickly became a national pastime), and had *Yanqui* ideas of progress and liberty, which fed into the several armed insurrections against Spanish rule during the second part of the nineteenth century. This in turn led to thousands of *destierros*—exiles—migrating north. The Cuban patriot José Martí sought backers in Tampa and Key West and mounted one of his attempted invasions of his island from Jacksonville, shortly before the Spanish American War gave Cubans independence from Spain but placed the island under the control of the United States. Miami, founded in 1896, quickly supplanted Tampa and Key West as a place for Cuban relocation.[1]

Conversely, Miami's residents had a convenient recourse in their neighboring city of Havana. Cuba's popularity as a tourist site increased exponentially during the 1920s, as did the production of rum and other spirits. Casinos, racetracks, and boxing rings advertised openly, while brothels, drugs, and other illicit pleasures exercised their pull by word of mouth. Because of the proximity of Cuba to the U.S. South, many of the "northern" tourists were Southerners. Cuba's reputation as the "island of romance," endlessly trumpeted in popular sheet music and recordings of the time, fed into the Southern addiction to moonlight and magnolia motifs. American fascination with the rhumba and the mambo and virtually every form of Cuban music led to more cultural interchange; on the other hand, American films became an addiction for Cubans at every level of society during this period.[2]

Miami, like New Orleans before it, often functioned as a place of exile, where revolutionaries plotted invasions of the island. During the 1920s, over 1,000 Cuban radicals migrated to Miami to plot the 1933 overthrow of the dictator Gerardo Machado. Ironically, his supporters then selected Miami as an ideal spot for *their* exile (Gannon, 1996, 402). Similarly, Fulgencio Batista took refuge in Miami before his successful coup in 1952; subsequently, Fidel Castro raised money in Miami for *his* revolution against Batista.

On the cultural front, during the 1920s, American tourists began flocking to Havana for relief from the strictures of the prohibition era. Miami's architecture—particularly in the new development of lush Coral Gables—was consciously modeled on Spanish colonial lines by developers such as George Merrick and C. C. Lowe. Streets, subdivisions, and hotels were given Spanish names; nightclubs featured bands and singers imported from Havana; and day trips and longer cruises to Havana were organized by Florida tour lines. During the 1950s, Miami also increasingly became a banking center for Cubans nervous about Castro's increasingly powerful insurrection, and better selection and lower prices drew Cuban shoppers to Miami stores. Cubans reveled in the many similarities between Miami and Havana but also in the differences. Florida beaches were accessible, streets were clean, little corruption and chicanery was visible, and Spanish was spoken almost everywhere. The establishment of "Little Havana" after 1959 therefore was not as difficult as one might suspect.

The configuration of the two cities took on a racial aspect after the aforementioned Mariel boatlift of 1980 effected the removal from Cuba of 125,000 refugees, 26,000 of them with criminal records, to Florida, with Castro's consent and approval. It drastically changed the image of the Cuban American community and made non-Cuban whites associate the exile community with the drug- and crime-riddled black neighborhoods, such as Liberty City and Overtown.

Afro-Cubans newly located to the United States came from a troubled racial history on the island. After the United States inserted itself into the Cuban war for independence from Spain (1895–98), it took control of the island and all its institutions. The devastating war had left Cuba in ruins, and the newly minted citizens were suddenly ostensibly free. But in reality, they had been colonized anew by their neighbor to the north, which had tried at least seven times in the past to conquer and annex the island. Slavery had been ended legally in 1886, and the war for independence offered an opportunity for Afro-Cubans—50 percent of the rebels and 40 percent of the officer corps were of African descent. After the U.S. military withdrew in 1902, leaving puppet administrators behind, these black veterans began organizing to get their share of land and jobs, forming the Independent Party of Color. In 1910, this party was declared illegal, and a period of lynching, mass incarceration, and, in some areas, massacres began, especially in 1912, when blacks rose up en masse. This wave of oppression echoed what blacks in the United States call "the nadir" of racial relations in the United States, a period just preceding this one in Cuba.[3] While there were many negative effects from the dominance of U.S. culture in Cuba after liberation from Spain, one of the most serious was the way in which North American racial attitudes increasingly were adopted by Cubans, who had profited from their earlier tolerance of racial difference by the crucial involvement of people of color in the wars of liberation. The rise of large U.S.-owned sugar mills led to the demise of small black-owned farms; U.S. meddling with enfranchisement resulted in blacks losing the vote; and the white conservatives who came to dominate the government after the deaths of the more progressive patriots José Martí and Antonio Maceo saw to it that virtually no Afro-

Cubans were admitted into civil service jobs (Welch, 2001, 181–82). Black Cubans were quickly situated into a Cuban variant of U.S. sharecropping on the sugar plantations. This situation continued for decades. Arthur Schomburg, a prominent black U.S. intellectual, cherished his Puerto Rican heritage, which led to his championing of Afro-Caribbean rights, particularly in Cuba. In 1912 he brought this issue to the attention of readers of W. E. B. Du Bois's *Crisis*, declaring that "during the colonial days of Spain the Negroes were better treated, enjoyed a better measure of freedom and happiness than they do to-day. Many Cuban Negroes were welcomed . . . during the days of the revolution, but in the days of peace . . . they are deprived of positions, ostracized and made political outcasts" (1912, 144).

Years later, the hope for racial equality under Castro proved illusory as well, and the Mariel boatlift Afro-Cubans faced a new form of oppression in Florida. Racial riots had erupted in Miami in 1968 and again in 1980, when white police officers accused of beating a black motorcycle rider were acquitted. Another riot in Overtown in 1982 gave Miami the air of the last Southern redoubt of racial turmoil, summoning memories of eruptions in other cities during the 1960s and 1970s. As Joan Didion puts it, tensions were exacerbated by the influx of *Marielitos,* who often clashed with black Miamians, who, she claims, were more familiar with oppression from the "cracker South" (1987, 47). "Jobs and services [that blacks would ordinarily fill] . . . went to Cubans. . . . Havana bankers took jobs as inventory clerks at forty-five dollars a week" (48).[4]

Many of the texts treated here that recall the "golden days" of Little Havana ignore this history of Afro-Cubans entirely. But if Gustavo Pérez Firmat (2000) and George Yúdice (2003) are correct in asserting that Little Havana is only a shell of what it once was, most of the accounts I deal with in this chapter, recent though they may be, represent a bygone era. Indeed, some of the writers suggest this in their more recent publications, which note the movement of Cubans to the suburbs and the effect new immigration has had on the city's Latino/a population. As Rudy Pérez has stated, "Miami is no longer just Cuban or even Latin American. Now there are Italians, Russians, and other Europeans in addition to Brazilians, Columbians, Dominicans, Puerto Ricans, and Central Americans" (Pérez, cited in Yúdice 2003, 208).

Not everyone sees this as a bad thing. Cuban culture, much like that of the United States, has been concerned with fostering the idea of the integration of the various elements in Cuban society. As Antonio Benítez-Rojo states, even "popular cuisine . . . . expressed this same desire for integration. The oldest and most prestigious dish in Cuba, called *ajiaco,* is achieved by filling a thick, flavorful broth with native (maize, potato, *malanga*, boniato, chicken), and African (plantains and yams) ingredients" (1992, 53).[5]

Over the years, Cuba's *ajiaco* of cultures has more often than not been depicted on the streets of Havana. Miami as simulacrum of Havana is a product of, but different from, what I will call here the "Cuban imaginary" that has existed for centuries.[6] Like the island of Sicily, which is similarly located in the middle of a vast sea, Cuba has been fought over, colonized, and exploited by a host of pirates, filibusters, and national powers. As Alan West has aptly stated, Cuba has been variously figured as "Pearl of the Antilles, tropical paradise, whorehouse of the Caribbean . . . tourist haven/exotic folkloric locale (flesh depot, fun in the sun, shed your inhibitions), investment opportunity (source of cheap labor), or revolutionary menace/terrorist haven (as U.S. nightmare)" (1997, 2). But let me be clear: the "imaginary Caribbean" has more often than not been a fanciful fantasy. Delany and Pickens had never been to Cuba, yet they were able to construct convincing portraits of the island and its culture. A simulacrum, however, is based on very real knowledge of the original, and this has been the case with Cuban Miami as a re-created Havana. On the other hand, the younger generations—some of whom have never been to Cuba, let alone Havana—now operate more in terms of an "imaginary" than a simulacrum.

In a technological age, which has vastly expanded the meaning of what Walter Benjamin has termed the age of "mechanical reproduction," (1968, 214), advertising and many forms of capitalist endeavor have endlessly recycled shallow representations of reality, especially those with mythic cultural meanings, which are read with ever-appealing nostalgia. Baudrillard has shown us that this syndrome of simulation—which is perhaps most saliently presented in the Epcot world of Florida's Walt Disney World, or the Venice/Paris/Rome replicas of Las Vegas—is in fact evident at every level of postmodern life (1988, 170). For many Cuban exiles, it would be pointless to return to the actual Havana, because the simulated Havana they have created in Miami is truer than the one they left, which has been forever transformed by the Cuban Revolution.[7]

It should be noted that the U.S. South itself has been the subject of both positive and negative imaginaries. This inventory of Cuban-inspired fantasies has a remarkable parallel with the Southern imaginary as it has existed in the United States, and in many respects, with the South Florida imaginary. We are all familiar with the *Gone with the Wind* fantasies of the plantation and the "moonlight and magnolia" of popular fiction, film, and television scripts. Leigh Anne Duck is the most recent excavator of the more negative aspects of this cultural practice, which she has mapped as, first, a setting up of the South as what the nation was not and did not want to be, and then, after the Depression, of what the nation could become. Duck's point has been made more pithily by the satirical black Southern-born writer Percival Everett, who asserts, "The United States has used the South as a wonderful scapegoat. If you have a really awful member in your family, anytime you do something bad you can point to that member of the family and feel good about yourself—think you have done better. That's what the United States have used the South for. . . . The North and the large western urban areas have excused their behavior toward minorities, the American word for downtrodden and disenfranchised peoples, by blaming the South for all the evils in the land" (Julien and Tissut 2007, 231).

The group of Cuban American writers I will consider here range widely, and some of them pay little attention to Miami's identity as a Southern metropolis. The first group of literary exiles included Guillermo Carera Infante, Enrique Labrador Ruiz, Eugenio Florit, Severo Sarduy, Lino Novás Calvo, Lydia Cabrera, Marías Montes Huidobro, and Eduardo Manet. These figures came of age in Cuba and migrated to different locations. I will be more concerned with artists who may or may not have been born in Cuba and who have set their fictions in Florida. Many of those artists came to the United States as children—they belong to what Pérez Firmat calls the "one-and-a half" generation (*Next Year*, 1995, 5). Others were born in the United States to exiles. This younger generation understandably considers itself both Cuban and American. Each member of this generation has had a different relation to the issue of race within Cuba and Florida, and also to the African religious traditions of the island summarized under the rubric "Santería." Virgil Suarez talks in his memoir *Spared Angola* (1997 passim) about the everyday presence of this religion in his family. Cristina García, by contrast, has informed us that her family "provided no information on the santería. It was not something I grew up with. It was something the character Felicia [in her novel *Dreaming in Cuban*, 1992] led me to and then I had to scramble and research to keep up with the forays into santería" (Vorda 1993, 68).[8]

Román de la Campa's memoir, *Cuba on My Mind* (2000), comments on some early cultural miscues just after the revolution when he was attending the Florida Military Academy as one of the "Pedro Pan" children sent by their parents to the United States.[9] Relations between the dominant white Southerners and the growing numbers of Latin American students were sometimes troubled; Latinos/as were ridiculed for their looks and their English, but also for their clannishness. As de la Campa admits, this last criticism was perhaps just, for he now realizes that he and his peers, many from wealthy Cuban families, exhibited a sense of superiority and entitlement (35–36).

Joan Didion's now-dated 1987 approach to the city concludes with the assertion that the well-heeled Cuban community, then 56 percent of the population, was merely playing a waiting game for Castro's death and its return to island power, rather than thinking of acculturation as U.S. citizens. More demeaning, however, was her dismissal of the city at large as a vulgar, crime-ridden, cultural void. Didion's attitude has been echoed by a plethora of other meditations that have continued in a constant stream up until today. A few years ago, the *New York Times* devoted the front page of its prestigious *Book Review* to Steven Gaines's sensational exposé, *Fool's Paradise: Players, Poseurs, and the Culture of Excess in South Beach* (2009), which the reviewer Carl Hiaasen termed an "entertaining chronicle of sleaze and vapidity in the Florida tropics," adding, "Most people don't go there for intellectual enrichment; they go for the sex, dope and parties" (Hiaasen 2009, 1). In one of the ironies of history, before the revolution crowds of tourists went to Havana for "sex, dope and parties," and in the last decade, the Castro regime has looked away as a lucrative "sex industry" has developed as part of the expansion of tourism, particularly on Havana's beaches (as we will see, this has been dramatized in García's *The Agüero Sisters* [1997]).

More recently, as noted, the city has been the site of confrontations between Cubans and blacks—but the latter category now includes Haitian refugees, who have settled in the city in large numbers. As such, it presents a microcosm of ethnic politics in a postmodern world.[10]

"The South Shall Rise Again!" / "Next Year in Cuba!"

All of these thematics and issues emerge abundantly in the copious writing of one of the more important Cuban American writers, Gustavo Pérez Firmat, a novelist, poet, and essayist who has also carved out an impressive career as a professor of Spanish. While he currently teaches at Columbia, he states that he "lives" in North Carolina, where he for many years taught at Duke University. Two of Pérez Firmat's academic books are *Literature and Liminality* (1986) and *Life on the Hyphen* (1995). This latter text has been very influential, not only with Cuban American artists but with many other U.S. ethnic writers, as a kind of credo, one that turns an apparent negative into a positive frame of being and creating.

As his titles suggest, Pérez Firmat has throughout his career alternately cursed and relished his "in-between" state as a Cuban but also an American, as a man trying to straddle the divide between his very Cuban parents and his equally American second wife and children. The first part of his para-digmatic memoir, *Next Year in Cuba* (1995), concerns his family's affluent existence in pre-Castro Havana, which he tells us involved "big houses, big cars, a big yacht, big jewelry, big furs, big cigars." While most exiles faced much-reduced circumstances in Miami, the many rich Southerners around them sported all these things, adding to the eerie resemblances between the island and their new home. The stark contrast of blacks and other people of color living nearby in poverty was also familiar, especially since the Pérez Firmat household in Cuba was run by a black staff whose living standards were quite different.

To some extent, the main character in *Next Year* is Miami itself, especially what Pérez Firmat sees as its palpitating heart, Little Havana, the vibrant community clustered around Eighth Street, or as it is more familiarly known, Callé Ocho. As he notes, however, both Miami and Little Havana have under-gone tremendous change since he penned his memoir, as we shall see.[11]

The method of *Next Year* features a controlling narrator who oscillates between his present life as a professor of Spanish and critical theory at Duke University in North Carolina and his past life, first in Cuba, but then in Miami, particularly in Little Havana. The movement of the narrator in both time frames, from wherever he is—Ann Arbor, New York, or Chapel Hill—to and from Miami, creates a systolic synergy for the book, one that provides a dynamic metaphor for the metaphysical ambivalence of the author, whose doubled consciousness is various—a Cuban and an American; an academic and a Nuevo–Desi Arnaz; a macho lover and a cerebral writer; a sometimes distant father and son and a tribute-bearing family historian.[12]

Pérez Firmat calls these repeated visits to Florida "my pilgrimages to Miami" rather than visits to his family (although ostensibly, this is the main reason for the trips), and, indeed, the tropical palms and blue waters signify a Cuban Mecca, one invented and sustained not just for the narrator, but for thousands of his fellow exiles, for whom true repatriation to Havana and/or Cuba seemed impossible. Consequently, Miami—especially after a concentration of over a million Cubans came to populate the city—became a virtual second Havana, or as Pérez Firmat states, part of "greater Havana." In this sense, the city emerged as a preeminently liminal space, where the possibility of *communitas* somewhat assuages the originally overwhelming pain of exile.

This agony is shared by many diasporic cultures and people. Edward Said has declared that our age—"with its modern warfare, imperialism, and the quasi-technological ambition of totalitarian rulers—is indeed the age of the refugee, the displaced person, mass immigration" (2000, 174). And yet there are possibilities in this situation. There is no question that for the more conservative Cuban American writers such as Virgil Suarez and Pérez Firmat, hatred for Castro's regime and its legacy is paramount. But both of these writers go beyond the political to the social and cultural and see very clearly both the possibilities and the limitations that a Cuban-dominated Miami offers, creating what Lamming has termed "the pleasures of exile." As James Clifford has usefully explained, "Diasporic cultural forms can never, in practice, be exclusively nationalist. They are deployed in transnational networks built from multiple attachments, and they encode practices of accommodation with, as well as resistance to, host countries and their norms. . . . Diaspora . . . involves dwelling, maintaining communities, having collective homes away from home. . . . Diaspora discourse articulates, or bends together, both roots *and* routes to construct . . . alternate public spheres. . . . Diaspora cultures are not separatist" (1997, 251).

There is another side to Pérez Firmat's Southern identity, for his longtime residence in North Carolina clearly differed from his years in Florida. In an interview, he stated that as the father of two children "who were born not only in the States but in the South, I began to worry in a more deliberate way about issues of identity, culture, choice of languages" (Dick 2003, 144), a stance that suggests that not only "Yanqui" values can "infect." "Southernness" can apparently be contagious as well, although Pérez Firmat does not specify what these negative values are, and he often, in fact, valorizes Southern rituals and traditions.

These issues are common to diasporic cultures. We should return here to William Safran's characteristics of diasporas: "(1) [They are] dispersed from an original center to at least two 'peripheral' places; (2) they maintain a 'memory vision, or myth about their original homeland'; (3) they 'believe they are not—and perhaps cannot be—fully accepted by their host country'; (4) they 'see the ancestral home as a place of eventual return, when the time is right'; (5) they are committed to the maintenance or restoration of this homeland; and (6) their consciousness and solidarity as a group are 'importantly defined' by this continuing relationship with the homeland" (1991, 83–84). While other theorists have found Safran's categories useful, James Clifford (1997, 248–49) reminds us that for many in diasporic communities, the restoration of/return to a homeland is not a goal (many Jews—in the

United States and elsewhere—do not desire relocation to Israel, for instance, and as we have seen, large portions of the Cuban American community will not consider a return to Cuba).

Next Year in Cuba exhibits most of these characteristics. However, the narrator, while acknowledging the presence of many Cuban exile friends and relatives in other U.S. cities, particularly New York, always makes it clear that Little Havana is the nonpareil locus for the diasporic community. He and his parents' generation exhibit a strong "memory vision" of the old country, one that has been shared by virtually every writer who has emerged from the first generation and what is called the "one and a half" generation, which was brought to the United States as children. The author's parents and their generational friends and siblings seem to be more caught up in this "memory vision," perhaps largely because of their repeated hope that "Next Year in Cuba" there will be freedom and the possibility of return. As he ages, however, the narrator—like other members of his generation—realizes how unlikely this has become. Indeed, in the later part of the book, it seems the "time" will never be "right" for such a move, as it is really too late to go back to a purely Cuban identity, imbued as they are with the culture of the United States. And there is the tremendous change in Cuba itself.

The Cuban idea of "next year in Havana" has multiple parallels with not only "the South will rise again," but also with the sense of exile actual and fictional Southerners have when living elsewhere, manifest in works such as Willie Morris's *North toward Home* and Thomas Wolfe's several novels and in Quentin Compson's yearnings in Cambridge, Massachusetts, and James Wilcox's novels about homesick Louisianans living in New York.

Next Year in Cuba is studded with references to the South and its history, and the thematic of a "lost cause" reverberates everywhere. One of the most revealing aspects of the book is the way the concept of *regreso*, or return, changes for the narrator, his family, and his community over the decades. Just after arrival in Florida, his father sleeps with deeds to his Cuban property under his pillow. The Dade County auditorium becomes the venue for Cuban revues, with titles like "Havana Memories."

Pérez Firmat claims he has not been made into a good ole boy by the South but admits his fondness for Durham Bulls baseball games and skimpily clad Southern belles. "Sitting in . . . Bulls stadium, clad in Duckheads and sneakers and sipping warm beer, I feel like I've just stepped out of an Alabama CD. Surrounded by soft drawls and rebel yells, I forget that I haven't heard or uttered a word of Spanish" (*Next Year*, 7). He makes a strong distinction between North Carolina and Miami, but the same kinds of Southern experiences would be his in Florida if he ventured out of Little Havana, which he rarely does when there. As he tells us, Miami is really part of what he calls "Greater Havana," and indeed, Miami has more Cubans than any other city besides Havana.

The book begins with the story of the family's journey to the United States from Cuba, a tale that has been told many times, by many different writers who have had varying experiences. Pérez Firmat and his affluent family had no real difficulty in flying to Miami; later immigrants, however, often had to take their lives in their hands, boarding leaky boats in the dead of night, sometimes paying unscrupulous smugglers who might or might not follow through with their promises. Pérez Firmat's family were merchants in Cuba, and before the revolution they made yearly buying visits to Crowley, Louisiana, the center of the state's rice farms. And indeed, before the revolution, as we have seen, there was regular and extensive trade between Cuba and the South, particularly through the twin bustling ports of New Orleans and Havana. There was even a Bacardi Bowl in Havana, where American football teams such as Auburn fought for gridiron glory. The extensive networks of plantations that spanned Cuba must have seemed familiar to Southerners who traveled to the island for inexpensive tropical vacations.

Conversely, today only north and north central Florida maintain a strongly Southern flavor, but even Jacksonville, once called the biggest redneck city in the world, now has a vibrant international population. Tallahassee's Florida State University, set in the heart of the traditional coastal South, caters to a student body that is mostly Southern but also Latino/a and international in makeup. The English department offers creative writing classes with several leading Cuban American writers, most prominently Virgil Suarez and Roberto Fernández, but it also has non-Latino/a Southern writers and Southern literature scholars on the faculty.

Cuban American narratives like *Next Year in Cuba* therefore should resonate for white U.S. Southerners and their new Latino/a neighbors, and also for the broader U.S. citizenry, whose constant mobility often involves not just a sundering of ties with a natal place, but with many places in succession. This has been true for U.S. Southerners too, whose children often leave small towns for hubs such as Atlanta, Charlotte, and Miami or further afield. Severance from place often indicates a focus on the issues that Pérez Firmat sees as central for exiles: cultural continuity, family loyalty, and personal identity (*Next Year*, 12), issues that have always been central in U.S. Southern cultures. As he states, his words, feelings, experiences are both his and the community's and are resonant with "shared experiences and expectations" (13).

Family dominates virtually all Cuban American novels, just as it does in U.S. Southern narrative. Particularly important in kin structure is the figure of the *abuela*, the grandmother. Both Pérez Firmat and Suarez recount loving, sometimes comic, stories about their *abuelas*, but the extended kin—*tias, tios,* and their children especially—also populate these crowded family epics. Cuban American writers seem to delight in the idiosyncrasies of their relatives just as much as do Eudora Welty, Rita Mae Brown, and Raymond Andrews.

As *Next Year in Cuba* proceeds, we see Miami becoming a simulacrum of Havana, especially along and around Callé Ocho. As Pérez Firmat states, "In some ways Miami was closer to the heart of Havana than Havana itself" (85). Today, however, as many Cubans have prospered, they, like other ethnic groups in large Northern cities before them, have moved out to the suburbs, to other parts of the state, or, like Pérez Firmat, to far away Northern and Western cities.[13] Pérez Firmat admits he misses the old ethnic enclave. "With its boarded-up storefronts and faded signs, Callé Ocho has become little more than a promotional gimmick for European tourists" (89), and he laments that Cubans are losing distinctiveness through the influx of many other Latinos/as from Central and South America. For him, this means losing Havana twice.

There are moments in Cuban American writing such as these when Southern mythology infects the Cuban. Speaking of his mother, Pérez Firmat remembers she did not miss Cuba as much as she did their old neighborhood in Havana and their house. "She once told me, 'Remember what Scarlett O'Hara says—she doesn't say she wants to go back to Atlanta. She always says, "I want to go back to Tara." Kohly [her old neighborhood] was my Tara'" (166). Much later in the book, we learn that Pérez Firmat has a Confederate flag on his desk (269), a signal of the ways in which the days "befoh' the wah" in the U.S. South have an affinity for the supposedly golden years in Cuba before Castro.

Pérez Firmat's ruminations on Miami need to be aligned with his presentation of Latino/a Southern identity in his fiction. There are indications that he originally planned his novel, *Anything but Love* (2000), as an extended take on the U.S. South and its comparison with Cuba, as the novel was originally going to be titled *My Life as a Redneck*. In his short story by that name, Pérez Firmat's adulterous narrator/double, who is married to a fellow Cuban American, describes a holiday he and his Anglo-American mistress Cat take during spring break to Cedar Key, Florida, the "Redneck Riviera." On the way down, they stop at Southern landmarks like Lanier's Oak and the historic city of St. Augustine. In Gainesville, they find copies of the Southern writer Harry Crews's books. Cedar Key turns out to be a "Key West without Hemingway or Jimmy Buffett" ("My Life," 1992, 233). After checking into the decrepit "Paradise Inn," the couple frequents the "L&M Bar," whose customers arrive in pickup trucks, eager to hear "Gordon and the Red Clay Rockers" play hits like "Betty Lou's Getting Out Tonight," which suddenly becomes "Betty Lou's Going Down Tonight." Later, the band plays "Happy Birthday" for the "Imperial Wizard of Chiefland" (a nearby town). The narrator keeps his mouth shut and enjoys "passing" as a redneck: "For several hours the L&M Bar was the center of our universe. We were two diminutive stars in a veritable galaxy of bare midriffs, bleached blonde hair, and jeans. I drank Myer's on the rocks, which I'm not sure is a redneck drink" (234). In 1992, the editors of *Iguana Dreams* indicated that this story would be part of Pérez Firmat's novel-in-progress by the same name. However, as noted, the published novel was called *Anything but Love* (2000) and most of the redneck material and references were jettisoned in favor of a dark tale involving the narrator's lover, and later wife, Cat, and her supposed sexual abuse while growing up, which forms the basis for the narrator's cruel behavior toward her. One wonders what the novel would have been like had Pérez Firmat followed his original plan, as the "Life as a Redneck" fragment offers further examples of his interest in making comparisons between the U.S. South, its subset of Miami, and his original Cuba. Elsewhere, Pérez Firmat has written, "I am myself a somewhat odd coupling of North and South, of Carolina and Caribbean, spic and hick in equal parts" ("Spic Chic," 1987, 20–22, 36–37).

The novel, *Anything but Love*, however, turned out quite differently, and one wonders if Pérez Firmat's reputation will be affected when and if critics get around to reading this short, little-discussed, perhaps little-read, work. In some ways, he is following a basic pattern noticeable in many Latino/a Americans novels written by the second generation—that is, the U.S.-born or mostly U.S.-raised children of the first immigrants. They usually share two things with their parents: a cultural memory of an Edenic, pre-Castro Cuba and a hatred of the Castro regime. They may or may not have a strong allegiance to the Spanish language, but virtually all of them write in English for an English-speaking audience. Most of these writers choose to set their fictions in the present rather than in the past, and the male writers almost always take on a strongly masculine tone, as they parade their macho heroes for the reader's inspection. Pérez Firmat provides readers with ethnic markers for his characters; they wear strong perfume and lots of gold, and the men all smoke cigarettes or cigars or both. Many, as is the case in other Cuban American narratives, eventually die of lung diseases. Here the appeal of the new country is seen in the Anglo mistress, while the ties of family and the old country are felt in the narrator's obligations to his Cuban wife and children.

The misogyny and priapic nature of this novel may be partly due to the extraordinary success of the Pulitzer Prize–winning novel *The Mambo Kings Play Songs of Love* (1990) of Cuban American Oscar Hijuelos. For a time, it seemed to become a kind of Rosetta Stone for male Latino/a writers, with its mix of fraternal struggle, generational conflict, Latin jazz and music, hot women, steamy sex, and fast living, scenes that alternate with quieter domestic tableaus populated by Latina mothers, sisters, and *abuelas,* often through kitchen portraits replete with ethnic food and steaming Cuban coffee. But there are also many highly sexual, orgiastic scenes worthy of Petronius, and it could be argued that this accounts for much of the *Mambo King*'s appeal to a general audience, which had reveled in the sexual hijinks of male characters of the preceding decades in the work of Philip Roth, Norman Mailer, and Saul Bellow.[14] Pérez Firmat has stated that he originally included this part of his life in the earlier memoir *Next Year in Cuba*, but his editors objected to it as "offensive," and he therefore expanded it into novel format. Nevertheless, he once claimed that "everything in it is true" (Dick 2003, 146). Pérez Firmat acknowledges that some readers have objected to the "machismo" of the book, but he does not comment on the fact that some readers see the narrative as exploitative of his wife. Ironically, Pérez Firmat claims in this same conversation that *Life on the Hyphen*, probably his most famous book, is a "250 page valentine to my wife Mary Anne" (his Anglo second wife and the model for Cat) (148). On the other hand, he talks frankly about his family's appalled reaction to *Next Year in Cuba*, particularly his mother's dislike of his accounts of his relations with his brother and their father. It is telling, however, that all the vexed relationships in these texts are related to the perils of acculturation and the divided identities of the characters/protagonists.

In both fiction and nonfiction, however, Pérez Firmat, concentrating on another vector of these struggles, voices his determination not to abandon his native language, despite the fact that he writes in English. Trained as a teacher of Spanish, his strongly linguistic bent made him determined to use his Anglophone fiction as a virtual blackboard for his native tongue. Over and over, in ingeniously appealing ways, he inserts Spanish into the text. His "translations" offer more than a mere paralleling of words; often accompanied by cultural mediation, these aspects of the narrative centrally locate meaning in language and thus offer a kind of heuristic metaphor for the extensive dialogue and discourse that his works feature. His interest in what has happened to Spanish during the history of the Hispanic and then Cuban diaspora is shared by many other Cuban American writers. In Cristina García's *The Agüero Sisters*, the character Reina, an immigrant to Miami from Cuba in the late twentieth century, compares her Spanish, "an explosive lexicon of hardship and bitter jokes at the government's expense," to that of her sister, who immigrated just after the Cuban Revolution: "a flash-frozen language, replete with outmoded words and fifties expressions. For Constancia, time has stood linguistically still. It's a wonder people can speak to each other!" (236). Southern literature, as many have noted, is a veritable gumbo of dialects, inflections, differing accents, and imported terms from other cultures, and the myriad tongues of Miami would seem to extend that tradition into the current century. Further, Southern writers, from the eighteenth century onward, have delighted in dialect, realizing that the special qualities of Southern life are abundantly present in the delightfully expressive vernacular, which is so often metaphor drenched, physical, and alternately comic or poignant.

A Portable Culture?

The 2008 collection *The Portable Island: Cubans at Home in the World*, edited by Ruth Behar and Lucía Suárez, features the voices and opinions of diasporic Cubans, including many writers and painters, thereby giving the diaspora an accurately diverse portrait. Since the Cuban Revolution, almost 15 percent of the island's citizens have left. As the editors demonstrate, however, the richness of Cuban culture has been evident in the repeated ways it has proved "portable" and has been re-created—albeit in differing forms— in sites around the world.

Many other scholars and writers have in the last two decades attempted to span the chasm between the original political split, between Castro's supporters and those that group termed *gusanos*, or worms. As Behar notes, the worms became *mariposas*—butterflies—after the family reunification program began in the 1970s, and then again after 1993 when the dollar was made a valid currency within Cuba. Bearing gifts, sending welcome checks, "*traidores* (traitors) became *traedólares* (dollar carriers)" (4). Unlike the more unforgiving exiles, Behar and Suárez have made repeated visits back to Cuba and were determined that their collection would include the perspectives not just of exiles but also of leading artistic figures who have stayed on the island, many of whom had not been previously published in the United States.

There is disagreement, however, among the more conservative writers about the exile community. The poet Ricardo Pau-Llosa, who has lived and taught in Miami for decades, becomes infuriated when fellow exiles bemoan the family business that was lost. He raises a hypothetical example: Venice is totally destroyed and someone laments the loss of the family bistro on the Grand Canal. "You've lost Venice! Who the fuck cares about your grand-mother's bistro! You've lost something far greater than some property." To Pau-Llosa, the revolution meant the loss of Cuba as a civilization and culture (Dick 2003, 135). Here we note an affinity, once again, with the myth of the lost civilization of the Old South. Southern apologists, of course, usually did not reflect on the fact that this glittering edifice was built on the backs of millions of slaves, and Pau-Llosa's vision of pre-Castro Cuba similarly emphasizes the positives—"a modern, capitalist, entrepreneurially alive Hispanic Latin José country . . . [without] Protestant hangups over sex and pleasure; it made money and had a very modern worldview" (134), while ignoring the rampant corruption and huge disparity between the people and the ruling class and the racial divisions. But these kinds of lapses are iden-tical to those who try to re-create the "Old South," which is the analogue to what exiled Cubans refer to as *Cuba de ayer* (Cuba of yesterday). The apologists of the Old South were fond of putting these kinds of expressions in the mouths of freed Africans, who even more than their deposed masters yearned for the days "befo' de wah," as Thomas Nelson Page's Marse Chan states in the story by that name (1881): "Dem wuz good ole times, marster— de bes' Sam ever see! Dey wuz, in fac'!" (1881, 10).

Another way of looking at this "lost cause" mentality is to reflect on the notion of the "chosen people" that Cubans seemingly share with Jews and old-line Southerners. As Ruth Behar has put it, "Our island is small, but ever since José Martí envisioned our independence in the nineteenth century, we have thought of ourselves as a chosen people with a unique purpose in the world. The Cuban Revolution, for better or for worse, took that megaloma-niac fantasy, what scholars politely call exceptionalism, a step further, and since 1959, we have become accustomed to being players on the world stage. We Cubans dared to imagine a great role for ourselves in history, and the rest of the world has not let us forget it" (*Portable*, 7). There is a parallel for this. During Reconstruction, many Southerners thought and/or wrote of them-selves as modern-day avatars of the children of Israel during the Babylonian captivity, as we saw in our examination of Woolson's fiction from that period. The parallel was never exact since no major relocation had taken place, but Southern society had indeed been razed, and the reign of the "godless" carpetbaggers, scalawags, and U.S. military and government agents was indeed seen as a captivity.[15] Similarly, Cuban exiles, endlessly awaiting "next year in Cuba," figuratively (and literally, in the case of musicians and writers) played on their lyres, lamenting their lost land, their separation from relatives on the island, and a way of life that was "gone with the wind." It was therefore more than ironic that the Elián González affair of 1999 coincided with the fortieth anniversary of the Cuban Revolution, a marker of forty years in the wilderness. Miguel de la Torre has provided a detailed account of how such constructs have been welded into a new religion, one that joins traditional spiritual discourse with politics, and how all this came into sharp new focus during the vigil outside Elián González's Miami home as the debate over his custody stretched into months. It was said that Elián, whose mother died trying to take him to asylum in the United States, was a sacred child, a new Moses drawn from the water, escaping from Pharaoh (Castro), and that he would lead his people back to the promised land (Cuba) (2003, 9).[16] When his Castroite father in Cuba successfully sued for his custody, the home within which his relatives sheltered him in Florida became a shrine.

The Elián affair exacerbated the rifts in the contemporary Cuban American community, confirming the continuing ways in which attitudes toward the revolution can literally split families apart. Pérez Firmat tells us of his reaction when his brother Pepe said that he did not begrudge the taking of the family's house and business by the revolution—that it was not theft but appropriation: "I want[ed] to strangle him . . . to eat his flesh and drink his blood" (*Next Year*, 1995, 173). This thematic of brother against brother—which of course makes the Cuban Revolution similar to the American Civil War—brings in parallels with the surrounding South.

The political aspect of Pérez Firmat's hatred of Castro and the revolution rears its head in his professional attitudes: "My personal history and conservative politics set me apart from many of my professors and most of my peers, who looked up to Fidel Castro and who spoke of the Cuban Revolution as a model for the rest of Latin America. . . . I was just another right-wing *gusano* from Miami towing the party line" (*Next Year*, 195). This grad school attitude lives on after tenure: "I know a *comemierda*, a shithead, when I see one, and American universities are chock full of them. . . . Every time I'm at a departmental meeting with my Ivy-poisoned colleagues, mostly worthless people with whom I'm pleased to have little in common, I real-

ize that I have gotten away with murder. . . . I sometimes think to myself—
you jargon-spouting, distinction-mongering, literature-hating, life-denying
comemierdas. . . . What the hell am I doing here with you?" (206).

At one point in his memoir, Pérez Firmat refers to his constant trips to
Miami as a kind of inoculation against Americanization, here treated as infection. But in the ultimate chapter, he admits, "Even though I love Miami
more than any other place I know, even though Miami remains home and
haven, I can't conceive of not having left. If I still lived in Little Havana, I'm
afraid I would be trapped by memory, the way my father is. Every time I'm
in Miami and run into someone I knew . . . I'm struck by how 'Cuban' they
look, dress, and sound. Take them out of Miami and they will wither as fast
as hibiscus in a desert. . . . As an exile from Little Havana, I say to myself
that it's better to live up to change than to try to live it down" (*Next Year*,
270). This passage proves revealing in several ways. First, Miami's Little Havana replicates its namesake city but not its current version. By seeking to
replace a past polity, a kind of stasis resulted and thus helped contribute to
the boarded-up shops of today. In this sense, Pérez Firmat's life story does
indeed prove to be communal and choral, as thousands more like him have
decided to follow the lead of their American children and opt for living up
to change.

The critical presidential election of 2000, however, underlined the increasing significance of both Miami and Florida in national affairs. The entire election ultimately hung on the disposition of the state's electoral votes,
and on thousands of disputed ballots, many of them cast in the greater
Miami area. Cuban American voters were crucial components of the Republican victory in the state. Conversely, Obama's narrow victories in Florida
in 2008 and 2012 were in part due to a dilution of the old Cuban American
vote.

Florida's rise to this demographic and political position is one of the most
amazing stories in Southern and circumCaribbean history. In 1950, the population of the state was 2.7 million; in 2000, it was 15.9 million (Mormino
2005, 2). At midcentury, the city was like most others in the South in ethnic
makeup: 13.1 percent of Dade County was black, and 4 percent was Latino.
The rest was white, and most were native Southerners (Croucher 1997, 28).
Miami was just as racially segregated as other Southern cities of the period,
and one could argue that racial divisions have festered longer there than in
any other Southern town, especially in light of the resentment of Southern
African Americans over their sense that Cuban immigrants have displaced
them in the marketplace and in political arenas, and, more recently, the per-

secution Haitian refugees have felt at the hands of Miami whites, Cubans, and Southern African Americans.[17] There have, however, also been fruitful exchanges between Southern blacks and Cuban émigrés, especially when they have gotten to know each other in the public schools. In 2010, the U.S. Census reported that the city was 15 percent white, 17 percent black, and 65 percent "Hispanic or Latino" (www.sfpc.com/census).

At the same time, however, the city prospered financially with the success of the now-dominant Cuban population and the installation in the city of hundreds of multinational corporations, both regional branches and international headquarters. Further, the U.S. government, in the Cuban Adjustment Act of 1965, guaranteed immediate residency and expedited citizenship to immigrant Cubans, an extraordinary advantage enjoyed by no other immigrant ethnic or national group. Concurrently, the port of Miami and Miami International Airport became central hubs for Latin America and indeed, the hemisphere. While most Americans rightly think of Miami as a major tourist destination for U.S. citizens, increasingly it has drawn millions of Central and South American tourists as well.

The Cuban diaspora has branched out considerably, with important communities of exiles in New York and Los Angeles and in cities in Australia, Argentina, and Russia. Concurrently, as we have seen, Miami has attracted many other groups of Latino/a immigrants, particularly from the Dominican Republic and Costa Rica and, most important, thousands from Honduras, thereby diluting the monocultural aspect of what was once a mostly Cuban Latino/a community.[18] Partly as a response to this, a popular bumper sticker reads, "Don't Call Me Hispanic, I'm Cuban" (Croucher 1997, 56). The writer Roberto Fernández has stated, "If you say I'm Hispanic, it denies me my whole Cuban culture. . . . And then they harp always on the race. The black, white, and Hispanic races. Hispanic is not a race. It's a cultural group or a make-believe entity" (Binder and Breinig 1995, 17).

To date, however, Miami is the only U.S. metropolis in which Cuban Americans have contributed forcefully to a city's literary heritage. Many Cuban American writers tend to locate part or all of their fictions there, even when, as sometimes is the case, the writer in question never, or only briefly, lived there. Cristina García, for instance, sets parts of her novels—particularly *The Agüero Sisters*—in Miami, but she was raised in New York and for some years has lived in Texas or California, her current home.

Cuban Americans have not all reacted positively to Miami, and the Cuban diaspora, which has spread to other countries, particularly to Spain, has been fed by this distaste. Perhaps the most famous of the island's expatriate writers, Reinaldo Arenas, who wound up in New York, always felt that Miami represented a strange intensification of some of Havana's worst qualities, particularly its machismo and its biases against *maricons* (homosexuals): "I did not want to stay too long in that place, which was like a caricature of Cuba, the worst of Cuba" (1993, 293). He paints a portrait of a city of bourgeois morality, conservative and reactionary, which was made evident when he was told that as a gay man, he had to act more masculine, because "the typical Cuban machismo has attained alarming proportions in Miami. . . ." For Arenas, Miami is a haunting nightmare: "the eternal gossip, the chicanery, the envy. I also hated the flatness of the scenery, which could not compare with the beauty of an island; it was like the ghost of our Island, a barren and pestiferous peninsula, trying to become, for a million exiles, the dream of a tropical island. . . . In Miami the obsession with making things work and being practical, with making lots of money . . . has replaced a sense of life" (292). For him, the city is "a plastic world, lacking all mystery. . . . I knew I could not live in Miami" (293). Arenas is not alone in his uneasiness with the new Havana; the historian Maria Cristina García has stated that "Miami . . . serves . . . as both a mirror and a lightning-rod: reflecting the best and the worst of Cuban culture, it both attracts and repels" (1996, 170).

Although she has written about Miami at length and has lived there, writer Cristina García characterizes her relation with the city that she terms "a political hothouse" as "uncomfortable." "I still have a love-hate relationship with Miami. . . . I always look forward to going, [but] thirty-six hours after . . . I get depressed . . . I don't belong. . . . To write about the Cuban experience I probably have to be, in some ways, as far away from it as possible" (Kevane and Heredia 2000, 71), an attitude shared by Pérez Firmat, even though he obviously loves Miami. Again, these sentiments could hardly be more Southern, with their strong echo of Quentin Compson's outcry, "I don't hate it! I don't."[19]

Virgil Suarez was born in Cuba in 1962 and came to the United States in 1974. Like his fellow academic Pérez Firmat, he has written in many forms, including poetry, novels, memoirs, and literary criticism, and he has also published several groundbreaking anthologies of Latino/a writing, particularly the often-used *Iguana Dreams* (1992, co-edited with his wife, Delia Poey). The son of garment workers, Suarez eked a way out of poverty by becoming a star student and by dazzling critics with his first novel, in 1989, *Latin Jazz*.[20] His 1996 novel *Going Under* is an excellent example of the ethnic yuppie novel, but it is also a Southern bildungsroman. It opens as upwardly mobile Xavier Cuevas fumes in his Volvo 240GL in a Miami traffic jam. Suarez lets us know, however, that this is an ethnically determined yuppie who is actually a YUCA—a young urban Cuban American. "In this magic city of Miami, the Sun Capital, countless deals waited to be made, and whoever struck first, struck big" (13).

Xavier does a good business—much of it via his ever-busy cell phone—translating between the two cultures, speaking Spanish to his Latino/a customers and English to the industry bigwigs. Throughout the novel, the omniscient narrator reads actual signs and then translates them, much like Xavier does with his customers. As he drives into his old neighborhood, the sign reads "Hialeah, The City of the Future," but the narrator/Xavier transforms it to "Cube City, U.S.A. Bienvenidos a Hialeah, la ciudad que progresa y tropieza, the city that progressed and stumbled" (18). This kind of comic and ethnic signification punctuates the novel. The extended skein of these jokes eventually becomes rather moving, as the reader sees that the yucas want their Americano affluence but also yearn for their comforting ethnic ambience.[21]

Suarez gives the flavor of the city in broad sketches. Wilfredo, high on Cubano coffee, speeds on the McArthur Causeway, "past the charter fishing boat docks, helicopter rides, Chalks Airline platforms, and trash-cluttered foliage. Flocks of sea birds swarmed over the docked cruise ships . . . a brown pelican glided as fast as the car moved. *Incredible, those bastards can really fly!*" (70).

Minor characters fill in the multicultural ambiance: Xavier's father Carlos Antonio's male companion Adolfo is a combat veteran of the Cuban excursions to Angola. Benito the yard man was one of the Mariel boatlift refugees. When business reverses and the hectic pace he keeps causes Xavier to have a breakdown, Carlos takes him to a *santera* (a priestess of Santería) named Caledonia, whose *botanica* on Callé Ocho is in the heart of Little Havana; it is filled with African and Catholic figures, charms, and powders. Her question, "Are you Cuban or American," forces his recognition that little of the Cuban remains in him. Her rituals involve Afro-Cuban chanting and the sacrifice of a live dove, summoning African orishas. Eventually, the spirit of Sonny Manteca, a celebrated and deceased Cuban conga player, appears to counsel Xavier to simplify his life. We learn that Manteca, a mulatto, died in exile from Cuba, bitter and depressed.

Within the family, bicultural tensions abound. A flashback reveals Xavier's cold Midwestern in-laws. The father warns, "You come from a different world than she does and you're bound to have disagreements. Lots of them" (124). Xavier's blond son Eric hates for his Cuban grandfather to call him Rubio ("blondie") and refuses to call him "Abuelo" (grandfather). Xavier's Anglo wife, Sarah, often asks herself how she got involved with this culture. Carlos and Eric *can* bond, however, through exploring the fuel-injection system of Abuelo's Mercedes. Xavier, however, decides he cannot understand the old-timers: "They live and die here with hopes of one day going back. They're just waiting" (114). He doesn't feel Cuban; Wilfredo tells him he's neither Cuban nor American, thereby setting up the classic dilemma of what in the culture is called an "iguana" state, or to use Pérez Firmat's term, "life on the hyphen." Yet Xavier yearns for "the salsa, the sabor, the zest" (119). He tries to find it by buying and playing congas, like the ghost who visits him did in life.

The novel ends ambiguously when Xavier, confused, alone, thinking of Sonny Manteca, drives instinctively south to Key West; along the way he meets a mysterious old man named Lazaro in a Cuban restaurant who claims he is a parable: "I am Cuban. Nothing but Cuban" (152). At road's end, facing Cuba, Xavier jumps into the sea and swims: "In the pursuit of the unattainable, Xavier Cuevas was swimming home" (155). Unlike the similar conclusion of Kate Chopin's *The Awakening*, this ending is ambiguous, in that rather than being an act of suicide, the immersion may in fact function more as a baptism, a rebirth into a new consciousness, one that accepts the liminality that the speaker's position afloat in the intervening sea signifies— life on the hyphen, indeed.

Some might object that this novel has nothing to do with Southern literature and that it would be best left to Latino/a studies. However, despite the lack of grits, the Klan, white-columned mansions, or old-time or even new-time Southern belles, the book is set in the South. The key role African-derived culture plays here echoes thematics of both black and white writers in other parts of the U.S. South, and the (post-) plantation cross-culturalism connects Cubans powerfully to that element of the region as well. Suarez, who has lived in Florida and Louisiana for much of his life, is currently a professor in Tallahassee, and as his various writings reveal, he has been powerfully affected by both the South and Cuba.

Roberto Fernández came to Miami from Cuba at the age of ten, and for some years he has lived in Tallahassee where he teaches alongside Virgil Suarez at Florida State, although he still considers Miami his home. His work constitutes an anomaly in Cuban American writing, in that it is highly satirical and sometimes surreal. His two novels in English are remarkable in that they attend to the strange conjunctions of the South and the Caribbean that bob up in the salsalike culture of South Florida. While these works could be termed comedies, their complexity and underlying sadness suggest a different aim. These are, in fact, quite difficult texts to comprehend, perhaps because they are attempting a radical postmodern approach to what we might call oppositional fiction. Doris Sommer has spoken of how narrative that "seems easy," that allows "possession without a struggle and cancels the promise of self-flattery for an expert reading," may make our hands "go limp at the covers. . . . We take up an unyielding book to conquer it and to feel enriched by the appropriation and confident that our cunning is equal to the textual tease that had, after all, planned its own capitulation" (1985, 11).

Fernández's *Holy Radishes!* (1995), despite its comic appeal, is in many ways "unyielding," especially for readers who do not know Spanish. The novel bases its satire in carnivalization, the turning upside down of social hierarchies, which was very characteristic for many members of the Cuban diaspora. While there were, as noted, many wealthy Cubans who managed to transfer much of their wealth to Miami banks, others lost everything and had to accept much-diminished living conditions and menial employment. One of the central figures of *Holy Radishes*, Nellie Pardo, in Cuba was the daughter of the affluent Don Andrés, who loves antiques, gourmet food, and dalliances with his female servants equally. The novel opens in Belle Glade, Florida, where Nellie has been exiled along with her two children and her husband, Nelson, who similarly was born into Cuban affluence.[22] Relieved that he did not have to run his wealthy father's business in Cuba, now he is a stocker for a truck agency, and Nellie works at a radish-processing plant. When she is at home, she watches *The Donna Reed Show* or goes through photographs of Cuba, which trigger memories. We learn of the many links between Cuba and the South before the revolution. One of Nellie's friends had attended a finishing school in Mobile; and a sugar mogul in pre-Castro Havana went to Tulane and met his New Orleans belle wife (jokingly named Fanny Fern) at a Mardi Gras debutante ball.

The Florida scenes, however, have their counterparts in flashbacks to Nellie's affluent days in Sagua la Grande, but they also have elements of the U.S. South. Before the revolution, Nellie's parties featured renditions of "When the Saints Go Marching In." After the revolution, the faithful servant Delfina forages for food for the family, bathes and coddles Don Andrés, and, after he is arrested, makes a new dress out of a linen tablecloth for Nellie to wear when she visits him. Delfina and Nellie strongly suggest Mammy and Scarlett in *Gone with the Wind*, especially in terms of the servant's inexplicable devotion and the echo of Mammy's making a fine dress for Scarlett out of

Mrs. O'Hara's green draperies. Later, as Nellie's Southern co-worker Mrs. B. shows pictures of her family's plantation, Fairview, she tells a tale of how her great-grandmother had to make a dress out of a curtain after General Sherman stole her dresses for his "ugly wife" (151), causing Nellie to declare, "Just like what happened to me," underscoring the "lost cause" echoes in the Cuban diaspora. As we saw in Lafcadio Hearn's *Youma*, servant/master relations in the circumCaribbean often have racial and familial aspects. Román de la Campa describes visiting his dead aunt's home in Havana, where her former black servant Ramona and her sister Hortensia now live amid pictures of de la Campa's family, which they regard as their own. As he tells us, many well-off white Cuban families before the revolution had "dear old [black] servants . . . [like Nellie's maid Delfina, who literally keeps the family alive]. The same pattern could be found in family histories in the South of the United States" (2000, 169). But, as he notes, these women, who were educated by the new government, are no longer servants, and indeed, they own his family's house.

The tragic and ironic aspects of Nellie's family's fall includes a shocking scene in which the old patriarch, knowing his luxurious house and its furnishings are going to fall into the hands of the mistress of one of Castro's henchmen, takes an axe and destroys precious antiques. Such scenes were not uncommon. Pérez Firmat discloses that his uncle ripped out toilets, wiring, and so on in order to spite the new owners who would take over his properties (*Next Year*, 1995, 32). This raging indulgence in the Fernández novel, however, ensures the old man's incarceration and slow death by starvation. As this episode indicates, despite the novel's sometimes cruel and raucous humor, Fernández provides a serious consideration of the suffering and disruption caused by the Cuban Revolution. Rolfo, the crude and vengeful epitome of the revolutionary leaders, while ridiculous in many respects, is all too believable in the outrages he performs on Nellie's affluent and haughty father, who pays dearly for smashing his fine house rather than let Rolfo and his superiors enjoy it. His plight also leads to Nellie's rape by Rolfo.

Of chief interest here, however, is the depiction of Florida, where Nellie and the other exiles settle, in the factory town of Belle Glade, which has a real equivalent in the state, not far from Miami. The decrepit and dangerous radish plant, the shabby dwellings the Cuban workers inhabit, and Nellie's backbreaking work dramatize what was a reality for many exiled Latina women, who often had to, and have to, take jobs that are dangerous, exhausting, low paying and, sometimes, humiliating. Women were preferred for such positions since they were paid at a lower level than immigrant men. By 1970, Cuban women represented the largest proportionate group of female workers in the United States (de la Torre 2003, 86).

This novel parallels Fernández's own life. His family, like Nellie's, was well-to-do in Cuba. They too settled in Belle Glade—his father worked in a sugar mill stockroom and his mother worked in a radish packroom. Fernández says it was fine because other members of the Cuban bourgeoisie worked beside his mother, wearing their jewelry, while working "next to the rednecks and other people but always with a sense of class" (Binder and Breinig 1995, 4). After ten years, his parents moved to New York, but Fernández stayed in Florida to attend Palm Beach Junior College, Florida Atlantic University, and then Florida State.

Fernández does not hesitate to needle contemporary Cubans. Resurrecting his sixty-year-old vamp Mirta from his first novel (*Raining Backwards*, 1988), he has her training for the invasion in the Everglades. There is much more—a scandalous fake Holocaust scam, Nellie's wedding in Cuba, where her pet pig, Rigoletto, serving as the ringbearer, chows down on the church's relics of a saint—but all the raucous and often surreal comedy proceeds out of dislocation and bizarre juxtapositions, be they caused by exile, poverty, lust, or simple madness. The underlying despair most of the characters feel, however, is given indelible expression in flashback scenes set in Cuba, where the shady British businessman Conway is graphically tortured, a dramatic shift that seriously dislocates the comic gravity the book at first has.

Belle Glade—also popularly called "Muck City"—is an interesting location for the story, in that it is part of a network of small rural towns in the South Florida counties of Palm Beach, Miami-Dade, and Hillsborough, where Latinization has paralleled more dramatic versions in the large cities of Miami, Tampa, and West Palm Beach. Famous for the rich "muck" of its soil, the region has also produced a legendary number of star Southern football players. It was immortalized by Zora Neale Hurston's classic *Their Eyes Were Watching God* (1937), in which the heroine, Janie, and her third husband, Tea Cake, come to the "Muck" as agricultural workers; while there, they suffer the onslaught of the notorious 1928 Okeechobee hurricane, in which thousands were killed. The radish-packing plant of Fernández's novel is a modern, mechanized version of the agricultural work sketched by Hurston, but the black and Caribbean workers in Hurston's text have largely been replaced by Cuban exiles. Interestingly, radishes were being shipped from the area as early as 1936, just before Hurston's novel was published in 1937. Before Nellie and her friends began work at the plant, however, the method of sorting and packing radishes had changed dramatically. Beginning in 1953, the vegetables were packed in plastic bags, completely changing the handling methods employed by the industry and dictating topped radishes. Modern washing methods using bleach (which ruined workers' hands) and conveyor belts and demanding, fast-moving machinery used for sorting made these plants more stressful for workers (Talbott 1954, 151–54).[23]

Nellie's strenuous work and child care and cooking duties, along with her fantasies of escaping to the mythical land of Mondovi (Italy perhaps?), keeps her ignorant of her husband's obsession with a prostitute named "The Squirrel." Mrs. James B. Olson from Tallahassee, Nellie's co-worker at the radish plant in Belle Glade, is a parody of the Southern belle, especially those who lost everything during the Civil War (later this story seems suspicious when we learn that Mrs. Olson frequents pig races and that her Daddy died of bad moonshine). In this (perhaps mythical) aspect, she echoes Tennessee Williams's Blanche DuBois, whose tragic loss of the family plantation, Belle Rive, rehearses Reconstruction narratives but also contradicts them in her unladylike fall into dissolution. Mrs. B., unlike Blanche, is married to her childhood sweetheart James B., a Southern good ole boy who was the star quarterback when Mrs. B. was a beautiful cheerleader and homecoming queen (which fits in with Belle Glade's actually glorious football history), memories that she encodes in poetry, as Nellie does with her recollections of Cuba, which Fernández, aiming for a mythical satire, renames Xawua. Now, however, James B. is a drunk who often beats his wife. Although Nellie came from the Cuban upper class, Mrs. B. sees her as her racial inferior but ultimately bonds with her in a Thelma and Louise–like conclusion, when they flee their husbands and the town for a better life. Throughout their friendship, Mrs. B.'s tale of her family's losses during the Civil War parallel Nellie's at the hands of the revolution. As Nellie puts it, "Mrs. James B.'s family lost it all during the Civil War. She has endured immense hardship like we are now, but there's still some class in her. Class is like matter; it can never be destroyed" (225), thereby providing a Cuban version of the myth of the Lost Cause.

Both accounts, however, are handled satirically and often fantastically, in ornate language. Fernández provides a Southern racial mix too, with the character of Naomi, a dialect-talking black woman who hails from Cordell, Georgia. While much of the comedy resembles wilder forms of sitcoms, elsewhere Fernández provides quite surreal humor, as when Mrs. B. and Nellie dress domestic animals to resemble those in zoos and charge admission, a counterpart to earlier scenes in Cuba when Nelson frequents a whorehouse where the women dress as animals. Fernández ought to be better known in postmodernist literary criticism, as he employs scrambled chronology, pastiche, mixed genres, multivocality, unreliable narrators, parody, satire, and a richly realized sense of the absurd. His first novel, *Raining Backwards* (1988), folds in clips from TV news shows, local newsletters, satiric poems, advice columns, menus, legal documents, recipes, chain letters, and a beauty contest application form. One of Fernández's most parodic touches is his creation of the local newsletter, "The Southern Pearl," which ostensibly unites exiles from the Cuban town of Cienfuegas (translated here as "One Hundred Fires"). Ricardo L. Ortiz has traced the publication's basis to a Los Angeles Cuban periodical, *La Villa*, which similarly addresses L.A. exiles from the Cuban town of Güines, but in actuality is read by many Cubans in Miami (Ortiz 2007, 8–9), as the many ads for businesses in that city attest. Fernández creates an "English supplement" for the "Pearl" featuring fractured "Spanglish," which is both creative and hilarious.[24] Throughout his novels—in both Spanish and English—Fernández delights in creating a linguistic bridge between English and Spanish, but it has been said by several critics that only bilingual readers can really appreciate this aspect of his work (see, for instance, Rivero Marín 2004).

The Olsens also appear in *Raining Backwards*, which is set in Miami's Little Havana. Mr. Olsen hates Cubans and calls them "tropical scum," perhaps a figuration on the epithet the first wave Cubans used for the *Marielitos* when they arrived during the 1980s.[25] In this novel, the extended Cuban family gets together for Christmas Eve pork dinners, but members of the "tribe" keep disappearing, many of them drifting off after marrying white Southerners. Mima, the hostess, swears that this is the last party and wistfully tells her husband, Jacinto, "I am tired of looking after you and everyone else. I should do like Emelina and move along to a place where no one will find me, like Kendall" (44), a Miami suburb, an oblique comment on the dilution of the Cuban American community. Most of the characters, in fact, are busy assimilating. Pepe's son Pepito is getting his real estate license; and Quinn Rodriguez, a priest, is nominated for bishop by his congregation, at the same time that his brother Keith is being arrested for possession of forty kilos of cocaine.

One of the most pathetic characters is the forty-something Mirta Vergara, whose memories of Cuba telescope into a fantasy memory of her liaison with an ideal lover on Veradero Beach. At one point in the novel, she transforms her bathroom with kitty litter (sand); blue-green dye (for "sea" in the bathtub); Alka-Selzer (to make foamy "waves"); and wallpaper featuring tropical sunsets and coconut palms. The claustrophobic and false aspect of this miniature "Havana" represents one of Fernández's sharpest criticisms of his beloved community's attempt to transform Miami into a simulacrum of Havana.

Raining Backwards does not make as many connections as *Holy Radishes* does to the circumambient quasi-Southern culture that surrounds its characters, but the thematics of Southern literature are everywhere.[26] The Cuban Americans suffer from bias against them, but they too are prejudiced against blacks, Jews, and other ethnic groups. The stories of Connie and Mirta both involve, despite the difference in the two characters' ages, the traditional virgin/whore roles for women in both the South and Cuba. Connie's love affair with the blond football player Billy Cloonen (née an Alabamian), who betrays her in favor of a silicone-implanted white cheerleader, brings up the Deep South mythology of high school football and all its accompanying scripts.

Fernández has commented on the combination of carnivalization and melancholy we noted earlier: "I always see it [his narratives] as a New Orleans carnival, or as a sort of happy funeral, but it is a funeral. There is a lot of pageantry, but you are getting ready to bury someone" (Binder and Breinig 1995, 16). His work offers a fine example of how parallels can be drawn between the defeated postbellum Southerners and the exiled Cubans. The U.S. South, which provided the first inhabitants of Miami, lived under the shadow of the Confederacy for many decades after the Civil War concluded. The popular motto "The South will rise again!" deflected defeat and reflected an effort among whites to regroup in order to resist the federal dictates (physically manifest during actual Reconstruction rule) and force African Americans back into a submissive position. The myth of the Lost Cause found expression in the Plantation School of Southern literature, particularly in the works of Thomas Nelson Page, Joel Chandler Harris, Thomas Dixon, and, later, Grace King. The Plantation South before the war was revisited and romanticized, often through the testimony of ex-slaves, who claimed a longing for the old days. The myth was used to construct a moral position akin to a religion, which led to the formation of a "chosen people" identity. Something of the same thing occurred with the exiled Cuban community in Miami, where any deviation from the group's absolute hatred for Castro and his regime and its dedication to working for his removal and an eventual return to the "promised land," where enduring and authentic Cuban values would be reinstalled, brooked no opposition. Several of the writers examined in this chapter have voiced objections to this stance, not so much to the virulent hatred of the Cuban Revolution but to its monolithic and absolutist consequences for any meaningful discussion of Cuban American identity or of dialogue with island Cubans that might contribute to eventual reunification between the groups. The posture of the older Miami exile community establishes it as a kind of "saving remnant." It is *they* who have preserved true *Cubanidad* within the ark of the covenant of Little Havana. Castro's early animosity to the Catholic Church provided an opening for Miami Cubans to don the mantle of religious restoration as well.

The resultant exceptionalism of Cuban Miami melded seamlessly with the preoccupations of the even-more-exceptionalist Cold War United States, which viewed the Communist enclave just off the nation's shore as both a danger (which it proved to be during the Cuban missile crisis) and a barrier to the nation's image as invincible in its own hemisphere. The Republican Party's return to millennial rhetoric—Reagan's reinstitution of the nation as a "city set upon a hill"—fit with the vision of "next year in Cuba," especially since successive Republican administrations, ever conscious of the crucial role Cuban Miamians continued to play in electoral college scenarios, refused to deal with Castro or to even consider lifting the embargo.

The issue of race, crucial to white Southerners before, during, and after the war, was revealed to be a factor in the Miami Cuban community, as well, during the Mariel boatlift, when a clear line of demarcation was drawn between the mostly darker, and sometimes criminal and/or homosexual, refugees and the supposedly "white" earlier exiles, who often characterized the *Marielitos* as "scum."[27]

Also, like the Reconstruction South, Miami's original Cuban population embraced a virtual public religion, which gave it a sense of identity and unity.[28] This stance, however, was constructed by a ruthless condemnation of "Others" within the Cuban diaspora who did not share these views, so much so that during the 1970s and 1980s, dissenters were persecuted, driven out, and sometimes assassinated. In 1989 alone, eighteen homes and businesses belonging to exiled Cubans calling for mediation with the island were bombed (de la Torre 2003, 14). We have seen how Arenas and García felt victimized by the Cuban majority, and even a more sympathetic Pérez Firmat, who views Miami as the Mecca he has to return to regularly, states he had to get away to get a real perspective on Cuban American identity and issues. Miguel A. de la Torre has traced the specifics of this civil religion within the Cuban American community in Miami and has provided a detailed examination of the sacral aspects of the Elián González episode, which continues to reverberate in South Florida. De la Torre sees a strong connection between the Babylonian captivity of the Hebrews in the Old Testament and this secular religion of Miami's exiled Cubans. "Rather than proclaiming 'next year in Jerusalem,' Exilic Cubans tell each other 'this year Castro will fall'" (2003, 70).

Fernández's difficult, semi-surreal, but often hilarious novels offer one of the best examples of the simulated aspect of Little Havana, as he simultaneously draws lines of comic connection between the twin lost causes of the Old South and Old Havana. Satire, however, rarely reaches the level of epic. Perhaps the most impressive Cuban American novel to date is Cristina García's *The Agüero Sisters* (1997), which approaches this level of mythic achievement.[29] The novel is set in both Havana and Miami, cities associated with the sisters Reina and Constancia Agüero, respectively, whose father, Ignacio, in a flashback to 1948, kills their mother, Blanca, during a bird hunt in a Cuban swamp in the first pages of the novel. This murder, never really explained satisfactorily, only gradually becomes known by the two sisters, whose modern-day story radiates back to this event, which occurred when they were children. In this respect, the novel resembles William Faulkner's masterful—and Caribbean-inspired—*Absalom*, which similarly yo-yos back repeatedly to Henry Sutpen's murder of his Haitian half brother, Charles Bon. A second parallel with Faulkner's work: Blanca has no real voice here, despite the burning relevance she has for the major figures, thereby replicating the silence of Caddie Compson in *The Sound and the Fury*.

Significantly, García's characters are not all from Havana. Blanca hails from a rural ranch in Camagüey; her six brothers—Aristides, Ernesto, Virgilio, Fausto, Cirilio, and Dámaso—all have literary names and in many ways echo the McCallum brothers in Faulkner's Yoknapatawpha sagas, whose backwoods virtues and classical names make them a strong contrast to the tormented town dwellers, the Sartorises and the Compsons. The revolutionary city of Havana and the commercial citadel of Miami find personification in the vocations of the two sisters. Reina, an Amazonian but definitely feminine wonder woman, is an electrician who lives in Cuba. Her dainty sister, Constancia, builds a cosmetics empire when her two husbands—a pair of brothers—prove, in turn, to be ineffective. The reunion of the sisters in Miami constitutes a kind of prefiguration of the eventual reunion of Havana and Miami, as do their respective daughters (one of whom is pregnant), who represent the future.

García has made it clear that Blanca's murder speaks for much of the book: "You can finally know the 'facts' of what happened, but you still don't know what happened. I'm not sure that Constancia or Reina finally knowing exactly what happened in the swamp brought them any closer to understanding *why* it happened. Although it was important for them to know the facts, it was only a springboard for speculation. At the center is Blanca, whiteness, the unknowable, and all you can hope to do is surround it and get close to the heat of it" ("Translation," 2002, 48).

The varied ways in which Ignacio's "lies" have led the world to forget Blanca sheds light on one of the book's two inscriptions, lines from Hart Crane: "Forgetfulness is white—white as a blasted tree, / And it may stun the sybil into prophecy, / Or bury the gods. / I can remember much forgetfulness." García appears to ponder the role of forgetting in the condition of exile. One of the conundrums of the Cuban American experience, which many have commented on, is the fact that it has gone on so long that the Cuba of 1959, which only the older exiles remember, no longer exists. Indeed, some have claimed that its only remaining essence lies in the simulacrum of Old Havana that Miami has become, but recently even that view has been challenged as the Cuban diaspora has thinned through its dispersal into the suburbs and also to other cities and states. Further, as Ana Menéndez has poignantly expressed in her superb short story "Her Mother's House" (2001), memories are inevitably mutable, and although they seem to represent the truth, they are all too often like Hart Crane's blasted tree, shorn of their living attributes.[30] García herself seems to think that her anti-Castro family's bitterness has distorted their memory: "When I first went back to Cuba, in 1984, I developed a strong relationship with my grandmother and realized how distorted those accounts from my mother were, how nostalgia and anger had clouded her version of events" (Kevane and Heredia 2000, 70).

Ignacio Agüero's beyond-the-grave meditations, all in italics, punctuate the late twentieth-century story of his two daughters. The family is distinguished by its doubly exiled history. Ignacio's father, Reinaldo, immigrated from Galicia to Cuba, where his refined education and relative poverty dictated a career as a lector at the El Cid factory. A figure who usually sat in a small balcony above a tobacco factory floor, the lector would go through a series of readings that would relieve the tedium of the manual labor of the strippers and rollers. The lector was usually, but not always, Hispanic. In yet another link between Southern and Cuban American writing, we recall that James Weldon Johnson, one of the elder statesmen of the Harlem Renaissance and the author of the pathbreaking novella *Autobiography of an Ex-Colored Man*, was reared in Jacksonville, which, like Tampa and other Florida cities, had its own cigar industry.[31] The unnamed narrator of his novel makes his living for a time as a lector. Although the lector read a variety of texts, he almost always favored novels.

García's Reinaldo chooses *Don Quixote, La Bête Humaine,* and *A Tale of Two Cities* for his texts. This trio represents, first, the romantic, mythic, and courtly Spanish heritage; second, the Zola naturalist classic as reflective of the sufferings of the Cuban people under colonialism, slavery, and U.S. imperialism; and, third, the Dickens as a code for the twin capitals of Havana and Miami, with Cubans in both metropolises living with the consequences of revolution.[32]

Reinaldo wanted to be a musician, and his musical training leads to his marriage to the sisters' grandmother Soledad, a flutist ten years his senior. The taste for musical sound transforms itself into their son's passion for birds, which leads to his career as an ornithologist. This aspect of the novel lends great beauty and gravity to the text, in that Ignacio's field trips with his strange wife, Blanca, acquaint us with the now-lost tropical jungles of the island and species that have since passed into extinction. This motif of loss and death (like Audubon, the romantic and mystical figure immortalized by Eudora Welty and Robert Penn Warren, Ignacio must kill the birds he loves in order to study them) extends to the mystery of Blanca's murder.

The power of these passages comes from García's meticulous research and particularly from her use of Thomas Barbour's 1945 study, *A Naturalist in Cuba.* The book's copious illustrations offer a glimpse of a lost Cuba that obviously fascinates García. She tips her hat to Barbour by naming her character Soledad after the plantation Barbour immortalized in his work. Like Barbour, she seems to lament the fact that it is only Havana that registers for outsiders, so the bird-gathering trips she creates offer an opportunity to take readers into the interior.[33] Her descriptions of the Zapata swamp closely follow those of Barbour, and her treatment of Ignacio's relation to wood ducks profits from Barbour's section "Resident Ducks" (1945, 121–26). However, García came to Barbour's books only after she became interested in bird-watching when living in Hawaii. This led her to the library, and ultimately, to the discovery that Cuba's natural history could be a way to get beyond the impasse the revolution has caused in terms of understanding the island's history: "I wanted to get away from the gravitational pull of the revolution and look at loss and memory and nostalgia and extinction and myth making through another prism. . . . I think the natural history there was useful that way" (Kevane and Heredia 2000, 79).

As we have seen, the swamp has functioned as a shifting metaphor in Southern literature, and García uses it similarly in this novel. However, there is an important analogue in Cuban literature as well, Luis Felipe Ro-dríguez's *Ciénaga* (1923), a searching portrayal of Cuban peasant life, which has many affinities with Claude McKay's *Banana Bottom* (1933), Jacques Roumain's *Masters of the Dew* (1944), and the "Muck" sections of Zora Neale Hurston's *Their Eyes Were Watching God* (1937). The swamp with its quag-mires is a major character in *Ciénaga*, and it offers a metaphor for Cuba's ills. It is also, as it is in Woolson's *East Angels* and Hurston's *Seraph on the Suwanee*, a metaphor for the human unconscious and the mysteries of sexu-ality. García employs all these strategies, and more. The succubus of the swamp—which is, conversely, a nursery of vital and often beautiful life forms—is a gigantic aviary whose myriad species of birds are both a pre-cious legacy to be preserved and symbols of freedom and movement.

Again and again, birds prove to be omens and also agents.[34] Ignacio's ducks save Reinaldo when thugs arrive to punish him for his role in a strike at the cigar factory. Conversely, as he lies gravely ill, the migrant birds from the United States create such a racket that his recovery is impaired.[35] Con-stancia's daughter Isabel, the *artiste*, in an eerie echo of her ornithologist grandparents, sends her parents a gift for their thirty-second anniversary (the last one they share). "Anniversary Birds" consists of birds preserved in formaldehyde, dressed in knitted outfits she made. More ominously, an electric blue dove descends on Blanca's coffin. Worse yet, when Constancia's son Silvestre flies to Miami from New York to meet his dying father, Gonzalo, a pigeon brushes by him in the hospital hallway: "He wonders whether the omen is good or bad. He can't afford neutrality" (245). Since he murders Gonzalo with a pillow, we must assume the omen was negative. Indeed, the entire narrative seems to proceed from auguries. In the flashbacks Ignacio provides, we learn his mother spotted a stygian owl, a bird of ill omen, who seemingly brings on her birthing pains and then flies away over a political crowd with the placenta, raining blood on the president below. This fantas-tic scene seemingly echoes the famous image of the eagle flying over ancient Mexico City with a serpent in its mouth, but it also prefigures the fated and mysterious element of the Agüero family history. As Ignacio tells it, "*Word of this incident quickly spread throughout Cuba. Mama told me that for once the priests' and the* santeros' *interpretations were in accord; the island was headed for doom*" (30).[36]

García's plot is infused with this Afro-Cuban heritage. As noted earlier, soon after the novel begins, Reina is struck by lightning while doing electri-cal work in Cuba, after black owls had ominously followed her. Surviving her burns by means of skin grafts from relatives, she attributes the lightning as coming from the African deity Changó, or from Oya, his wife, who stole fire from him. By associating the family members with disasters that have resonance for Cubans of all backgrounds, García thus seems to make the family she depicts emblematic of the island's destiny as a whole. Reina's burns also echo those of her mother, who suffered injuries as a chemist. But Blanca also receives a "curse" from nature, in that she is bitten on the heel by a reptile as she makes love to Ignacio in a tropical river. Later, the newborn Isabel too loses part of her heel when Constancia, unable to wake her baby, bites her there. Finally, Raku, Isabel's son, is born with a red birthmark on his heel. Thus omens of doom from nature collide with the mythical (Achilles, after all was dipped in the river Styx by his mother to make him invulnerable, but, held by his heel, he was unprotected there and died when Paris's arrow pierced him on the plains of Troy). The Agüeros, it seems, have a mystic connection in this sense, one that is appropriate, since their name means omen; the question seems to be whether the omen will prove adverse or propitious—is it fixed, one way or the other?

The sections devoted to Ignacio's forays into the wilderness are one part of García's dual presentation of her version of the tropical sublime. She writes the Zapata swamp passages knowing that much of this kind of terrain has been lost, and as such, she offers a physical equivalent to the rich history that has been eclipsed by the power of the revolution and the subsequent saga of Castro's Cuba. But these passages also align her with many of the other writers we have considered, especially Woolson, Hearn, and Bell, all of whom are both attracted to and to some degree repelled by the lush—and dangerous—growths of the jungles and the hidden menaces of the sea. But our knowledge of the swamps, and in particular what happened the day that Blanca died, does not come only from Ignacio's italicized monologues; we also get bits and pieces from the two sisters as they reflect back during their other activities. Constancia, for instance, at Hialeah Racetrack, remembers her parents' two horses, Gordita and Epictetus, who, her father told her, were driven mad by the mosquitoes of Zapata. We know better, having read an account of the murder in the first pages; the gunshot terrifies the horses, who run away and sink into quicksand. The two horses, male and female, respectively, clearly represent their owners, as Ignacio will die at his own hands soon after the murder. "Gordita," or the fat one, refers to the body and its appetites, while "Epictetus" summons up the stoic philosopher who felt life was fated and that freedom from passion was the only way to happiness. As he intoned, "Control thy passions lest they take vengeance on thee." Both horses, however, like their riders, end up the same way—in tragic, premature death.[37]

The inset story of Blanca's infidelity (which resulted in Reina's birth), coupled with her refusal to make love with Ignacio, would seem to be the motivation for her murder, when he lets his stoic sense of acceptance and rationality (expressed by taking the pregnant Blanca back) drop for a moment in the "swamp" of his passion, which had drawn him to Blanca to begin with: "How could I be logical when the very sight of this woman uprooted my heart?" (183).

Constancia's two husbands, the brothers Gonzalo and Heberto, both come to tragic ends. Gonzalo, near death already in a hospital room, is smothered by his estranged son, Silvestre. Heberto, who has been seduced by Gonzalo into joining the paramilitary group La Brigada Caimán, dies in yet another abortive attempt to invade Cuba and foment an antirevolution. Silvestre seems to be in the book to point out the folly of the "Pedro Pan" program, a group of youngsters who were sent by their parents in Cuba to live in the United States, in response to the rumor that Castro was going to send Cuban children to boarding schools in the Ukraine. Many of them never returned to the island and were often bitterly estranged from the parents who exiled them. Silvestre's deafness, which resulted from a fever he contracted in frigid Colorado, appears to relate to his inability to "hear" his parents.[38]

Part 1 of *The Agüero Sisters*, "Tropical Disturbances," is followed by Part 2, "A Common Affliction." The two verbs found at the root of these titles, "disturb" and "afflict," are emblematic of the originating rupture of the Cuban Revolution, which causes not only the exile of many of the book's key figures, but the utter transformation of the lives of Cubans who stay on the island, including the central figure, Reina Agüero.

The sisters' father recalls that his own sire, the exiled lector, found consolation in the writings of Marcus Aurelius, particularly the Roman's suggestion that man think hard about his relatively minor role in the world and the brevity of his time in it. The family seems to have a fondness for capsule philosophies, which stud the writings of Marcus Aurelius like raisins in a fruitcake. Indeed, the key figures of the narrative all have mottos. One of Reina's is *Vive de la vida lo sublime* (12). Another is "What we pass on is often as much a burden as a gift" (206). Her father's is "The quest for truth is far more glorious than the quest for power" (13). He also advises, "Tell me what you want, and I will tell you who you are" (67). The shrewd entrepreneur Constancia concocts a motto to go along with her cleverly labeled cosmetics: "Time may be indifferent, but you needn't be" (132). Perhaps the most telling expression of Ignacio's, however, could be "Only lost causes merit any effort" (179), a line that fits his frantic gathering of specimens of vanishing species, but also the cause of both the Cuban exiles and the Old South figures they resemble.

The flashbacks to Ignacio's training in ornithology and natural history occasion an elegy to a lost Cuba of tropical forests and innumerable unique species of animals, which is most noticeable during his apprenticeship in the swamp with a Harvard biologist, significantly named Dr. Forrest, "who bemoaned the loss of Cuba's lowland forests." Ignacio reluctantly shares a meal of roasted iguana with the good doctor, perhaps reflecting García's interest in Barbour's statement that the Cuban iguana is just as good to eat as the ones he consumed in Central America (1945, 55).

In the lyrical descriptions of Ignacio's journeys through Cuban forests, swamps, and caves, we find an analogue to Madison Smartt Bell's equally mournful re-creation of Haiti's lost flora and fauna as he traces Toussaint's journeys across the verdant mountains of the seventeenth-century island, even then a lost paradise, since the shell roads under the towering trees were created by the then already vanished Native Americans of the island. Both writers in turn echo the lament for the lost wilderness one finds in many American writers, such as James Fenimore Cooper, in the Florida tales we have examined by his niece Constance Fenimore Woolson, and most notably in William Faulkner's tragic *Go Down, Moses*, especially in "The Bear." In many respects, this "vanishing" aspect contributes forcefully to what I have been calling the "tropical sublime," particularly when the flora and fauna that are vanishing are depicted in rapturous, lush language. Importantly, this tone surfaces repeatedly in Barbour's work, not only in his Cuban volume, but even more so in his aptly named study of Florida, *That Vanishing Eden* (1944), which clearly influenced the way he would look at Cuba's topology in his later book on that island. He wrote this as an indictment: "Thirty years ago [1914] Florida was one of the most extraordinary states. . . . But being flat and quite park like . . . it was an easy state for man to ruin, and he has ruined it with ruthless efficiency. In the pages that follow, I have tried to recapture some of the original charm . . . [of] the Paradise which I know once existed. If you are interested in land-promotion schemes, horse racing, dog racing, night clubs, or other activities pandering to the purely carnal interests of man, do not read on" (3).

Cristina García partially follows this script in her portrait of Miami. Its natural beauty, lavishly landscaped gardens, and Mediterranean villas attract; on the other hand, when we are following Constancia or her son Silvestre on their freeway journeys, we see a semi-industrial wasteland: There are "faded clapboard and cement houses," "acres of flatness and whitewashed filth," and a hospital that is "a monstrosity" (1997, 244–45). After her restorative skin surgeries, Reina immigrates to Miami, providing García an opportunity to look at the city through new eyes: "Reina is bewildered each time she goes shopping in Miami. The displays of products she'd forgotten or didn't even know existed. . . . Everything, it seems, can be frozen or freeze-dried here. Instant, instant everything!" (163). This doubled descriptive refers to both the simulacrum of Old Havana and the new forms that mimicry has taken in the affluent immigrant community, which is also part of the larger tourist-driven pleasure dome, in turn founded on the imaginary of a tropical paradise—but one without the jungle's terrors.

Out for a ride with Constancia in Heberto's boat, Reina is initially indifferent to the mansions and yachts. "To have money and share this swamp with mosquitoes and water rats? *Por favor!* . . . she wouldn't choose to live like this, cheek by jowl with the pathological rich" (165). Although this scene takes place in Miami, it could stand in for New Orleans's Northshore or Houston's River Oaks. Above all, however, Reina sees, despite the bold talk she hears from the expatriate Cubans, "how ludicrous the idea of an invasion had been. It's the last thing on anyone's mind here. People are too busy making money, too busy sorting through the hysteria of what to purchase next" (199). Making money in the postmodern South involves media, and Constancia appears on several television shows to hawk her products. As a guest of *Mi Fortuna*, devoted to Latino/a success stories, she shares the stage with a formerly incarcerated credit card thief who has started a dating service and a liposuction entrepreneur. Miami's financial magazines run stories on her cosmetics empire (232).

Consumer/industrial society may be glamorous, but it has an ugly backside. Near the end of the book, Constancia plans a dangerous and solitary trip back to Cuba to retrieve her father's journal. When she and Reina follow the *santero*'s instruction to offer libations at Miami's river, they are constrained by ugly concrete banks and garbage: "Factories grind the night downriver. . . . The river itself has no margins or tides, no submarine life" (269). This plague, we learn, infected Cuba even earlier. Ignacio, revisiting his father's old cigar factory, is deafened by the whir of machines and the blare of radios, which have replaced the mellow cadences of the lector's edifying readings. García follows Barbour in tracing this pattern even further back. Describing Ignacio and Blanca's gathering expeditions in Cuba's remaining jungles and swamp, she relates: "The Agüeros often imagined what Cuba must have been like before the arrival of the Spaniards, whose dogs, cats, and rats multiplied prodigiously and ultimately wreaked havoc on the islands' indigenous creatures. Long ago Cuba had been a naturalist's dream. Why, then, had so much been sacrificed to successive waves of settlers and spreading monotony of sugarcane fields?" (4). This same lament—including the advent of Spaniards—could refer to Florida as well, as García, who had read Barbour, realized.

The Agüero sisters at first seem to represent a rather "pure" version of *Cubanos*, in that their grandfather migrated to the island from Spain, making them true "criollos." Because García has been faulted for not featuring racial distinctions more prominently in her narratives, her explosion of this initial perception of racial purity (which she creates seemingly in order to complicate) deserves inspection. García must have been struck by Barbour's reflections on race in the concluding chapters of his Cuban book. "The Cubans pride themselves that, among them, race prejudice does not exist. This is not by any means universally true. Many families are just as proud to maintain a pure white family tree in Cuba as in the United States. But there is a better understanding of and appreciation of what the Negro has contributed to civilization in Cuba than there is anywhere in North America" (1945, 274).

This thematic may not be developed in depth by García, but it is certainly there. Eventually we are told that Reina's father was a mulatto, which may have had something to do with Ignacio's reaction to Blanca's betrayal; further, before he has married Blanca, Ignacio learns from her brother that their mother was a mulatta descended from French colonists who fled revolutionary Haiti for Cuba. One wonders if this revelation—tinged with Haitian ancestry—reflects a partial debt on García's part to Faulkner's *Absalom*, in which Sutpen, like Ignacio, finds out that his chosen has African ancestry. This also means that all the Agüeros born after Ignacio have this heritage. But even if the Agüeros did not have this racial history, as Cubans they would still be, as all U.S. Southerners are, profoundly affected by African culture. Reina makes an offering to a dark-skinned Virgin in the novel's opening passages, whose alternate name, Oshún, refers to her African identity in the Santerían religion, which is practiced by all shades of Cubans. We also learn that Constancia believes in both astrology (which situates her, born on March 21, on the cusp of Aries and Pisces as a hybrid personality) and the wisdom of the soothsayers back in Cuba. Her favorite TV show is *La Hora de los Milagros* (The Hour of the Miracles).

Santeros, we learn, are also in Florida. Like Virgil Suarez and other Cuban American writers, García has been fascinated by this Afro-Cuban tradition that has infiltrated the lives of all Cubans, black, white, mestizo, rich, and poor. As she has stated in an interview, she herself created a shrine to the trickster god of the crossroads, Eshu/Elleguá, who, she notes, is the "messenger to the other *orishas*, the essence of potentiality, the only one who knows the past, present and future. . . . [His] vision surpasses that of the other gods yet he is often mischievous, a prankster, an eternal child. . . . He is opportunity chance, the unexpected. I want everything Elleguá represents to be reflected in my work" (Abani 2007, 37).

At a key point in the novel, when her husband, Heberto, has left on his ill-fated secret expedition with a military group to invade Cuba, Constancia consults a *santero*, who significantly lives off Martin Luther King Boulevard. She has been devastated, not just by Heberto's flight, but also by seeing her face transformed into her mother's. The ritual of divination is detailed and profoundly African; La Virgen is really, we learn, Oshún, the African orisha. Casting the cowrie shells, after praying in Yoruban, the *santero* proclaims that Constancia is cursed, and that no intervention is currently available.

As this indicates, although thoroughly modern and nonreligious in most ways, Constancia is superstitious; she keeps apples in bowls in her house, never eating them, just as the *santero* Oscar Piñango specified (176). She has him recite an oration to La Virgen de la Caridad del Cobre, light candles, and burn sacred fires in her cosmetics factory in order to drive out whatever is causing bloody chicken feathers, dead bats, and other omens to appear there.

Reina, on the other hand, eats the apples—but nevertheless, when Isabel's son is born, she gives him a charm to ward off the evil eye. The most spectacular use of Santería comes after Constancia receives a letter from her dead uncle revealing that her father's diary is buried in rural Cuba.[39] Before setting out to retrieve it, she has a very elaborate series of ceremonies with the *santero*, twelve days before Oshún's Yoruban celebration. Hard on the heels of this scene, a flashback takes up Ignacio's consultation with a *santera* when he is searching for Blanca after she leaves him following Constancia's birth. Here the elderly priestess prophesies correctly that Blanca will return with a second child who will be destined for the god Changó, an accurate prediction in that this is the Yoruban god of thunder, lightning, and force (Joseph M. Murphy 1988, 182), in keeping with Reina's vocation as electrician and with being struck by lightning.

Amparo Marmolejo-McWatt (2005) has argued persuasively that Blanca

Mestre represents the orisha Ochún and points out that García introduces us to the full panoply of African gods and goddesses in *The Agüero Sisters*, including Changó and Yemayá. Since Ochún is also identified with Our Lady of Charity of El Cobre, the Cuban patron saint, her doubled role involves both the Virgin and the African goddess of love, seeming opposites. We learn that Blanca "cast a spell" on many men, not just Ignacio. Indeed, one of them, Amado Savedra, hangs himself (183).

Her connection with the orishas explains much about her daughters too. Late in the novel, we find a clue that explains Constancia's vulnerability/ belief in the orishas. Ignacio's diary reveals that when Blanca deserted them, he hired a nurse, Beatriz, who was the niece of his own *santera*, Estér Salvet Llagunto (262). As he states, and Constancia would perhaps agree, "When logic fails, when reason betrays, there is only the tenuous solace of magic, of ritual and lamentation" (262). As for Reina, she has clearly inherited her mother's sexual appeal, as she too draws men to her, like Ochún, without any effort; her sexual encounters with them leave them helpless, exhausted, and gasping.

These displays of African-derived religious rituals have many counterparts in Southern literature, particularly in African American writing. As we have seen, Delany's *Blake* (1859) features a conclave of conjurors; Frederick Douglass relies on a hoodoo root for courage; and Charles Chesnutt's magically transformed characters often consult the title figure of *The Conjure Woman*. Zora Neale Hurston presented many aspects of hoodoo and voodoo in her circumCaribbean anthropological works, and versions of it appear in the costumed circumCaribbean novels of Frank Yerby as well. Ernest Gaines's great short story, "A Long Day in November" (1971), involves a consultation with a conjure woman, while Brenda Marie Osbey's long narrative poem, *Desperate Circumstance, Dangerous Woman* (1991), revolves around a hoodoo woman's role in two lovers' passionate but troubled relations. More recently, Jewel Parker Rhodes's *Voodoo Dreams* (1993) has capitalized on the appeal and terror associated with New Orleans religious traditions taken from Africa.

We have seen how García reinvigorates the narrative by viewing Miami anew through the eyes of recently arrived Reina. Initially, however, García makes us see Miami through Constancia's eyes. Constancia has just moved there after years in New York, and she knows she will never fit into the conservative exile community, which is aghast that she voted for the Democrat Jimmy Carter: "She shuns their habit of fierce nostalgia, their trafficking in the past like exaggerating peddlers" (45–46). This positioning might have

been seen as necessary by García, who needed to navigate her narrative between Miami and Havana rather than identify with the conservative enclave
in Florida. Dalia Kandiyoti has argued compellingly that nostalgia is "the key
to selling Cuban America," which she notes is ubiquitous in Cuban American
literature (2006, 81). García, however, shows us the myriad aspects of the
phenomenon, including its commodification—which is most evident here
in Constancia's cosmetics empire, "Cuerpo de Cuba." She shrewdly manipu-
lates Cuban American women's peculiar brand of nostalgia, which ironically
is opposed to her own abhorrence of the romanticization of the past (174).
The overall selling point is to summon up memories of the past through figuration of the Cuban woman's body as a synecdoche for the lost and verdant
Eden of Cuba. Certainly the feminization of the island by its various colonizers and the way in which Constancia is cleverly milking that tradition here
is also reflective of the ways in which other Cuban American entrepreneurs
employ nostalgia and gender stereotypes, quite similar to the many products
available in the U.S. South that cater to the image of the Southern belle.

This constellation of feminine forms of identity has a counterpart among
the men of the novel, including Constancia's two husbands. The Zapata
swamp that we encounter on the first pages of the novel finds its Southern
equivalent when Constancia's husband Heberto joins his brother Gonzalo's
band of guerrillas in the Everglades, as they train for an invasion of Cuba.[40]
Although he is punished by the "crushing sun . . . the drip and suck of the
swamp . . . the stinging heat . . . clots of incessant mosquitoes," he rejoices
that he is with "hundreds of militant, *ordained* men" (123). This passage
initiates a section of the novel entitled "Original Geographies," a seeming
reference to restorative, primeval earth, and it is telling that the Florida
Everglades offers passage to Cuba, and perhaps to the Zapata swamp as well.
We learn here, as war-crazed Heberto literally gets a hard-on and feels his
cojones contracting, that their older brother Leopoldo died in the Bay of Pigs
invasion, in which Gonzalo was crippled. These scenes remind us of the opportunity for heroism that Mrs. Pickens's American filibusters sought when
they joined Narciso Lopez in *his* attempted invasion.

The alternating narratives of the sisters are punctuated by first-person
narrations from their children, including Dulce Fuerte, Reina's daughter,
a sometime prostitute (like many other needy citizens) in the tourist sex
market of the Havana waterfront. Eventually, Dulce flees to Spain with an
elderly man she impulsively marries. Dulce's hip-and-knowing monologues
and jet-setting adventures offer a kind of relief from the past-ridden consciousness of the sisters. Then, too, her legendary father—a dead revolu-

tionary hero named José Luís Fuerte (who bears more than a passing resemblance to the real Che)—has put her on the spot, as people expect more from her (something she shares with Che's son, a classmate).[41] Since Dulce has an African heritage, her work as a *jinatera* relates her to the long Cuban fascination with the mulatta, the epitome of female beauty and seduction. A beautiful, near-white woman is the title figure of the Cuban national novel, Cerilo Villaverde's *Cecilia Valdés*. Moreover, Dulce's resort to marriage with a Spaniard and her subsequent (if temporary) relocation to Spain align her with one of the chief consequences (and goals) of *jinerismo*, since over 10,000 mixed-race Cuban women immigrated to Spain in the 1990s, many as wives of Spanish men they picked up in Havana (de la Campa, 2000, 163–64). Through Dulce's comic lament, we learn about the corruption of just about everyone in Havana; even the Santéria *babalawos (priests)* have become hustlers. Originally, the *babalawo* Cuenca had to keep his operations secret: "The occasional bleating of an illegal goat or the appearance of a horde of paralytics on his doorstep was the only clue to the secret power within." Now, however, his house sports a huge statue of St. Lazaro on the lawn, flags fly, and people openly carry pigeons, corn, and offerings up the street to him. "His best clients are referred to him by the government" (56). An authentic initiation goes for $4,000, with the government getting its cut—"anything for foreign exchange" (56).

Dulce, as the daughter of a revolutionary hero, perhaps is a gesture on García's part to honor the braver, better aspect of the revolution that her relatives who stayed in Cuba revered. Reina to a certain extent epitomizes this effort as well, although both she and Dulce leave Cuba during the course of the novel. García's evenhandedness here is somewhat unusual; as we have seen, most Cuban expatriate writers either reject Castro entirely or find his impoverished Cuba a betrayal of his goals.

When Isabel, pregnant and jilted, comes home to Constancia, Miami's mania for money infects her too. She tours her mother's factory and fantasizes about taking it over, "making a million dollars in no time flat. I'd buy one of those oceanfront fortresses, build a tennis court and a helipad, have a foot massage every night. What is it about this city that fosters such empty illusions?" (288). And the Cubans are not the only immigrants to Miami; Reina's love, Russ Hicks, arrives from Omaha intending to continue on to assist the Cuban Revolution, but he stays to become rich through stocks, real estate, and antique cars. His Chippewa, French, and German roots offer a reminder to us of Florida's, the South's, and the nation's immigrant past and provide a corrective to the idea that immigrant Miami is all Cuban.

Similarly, at Gonzalo's funeral, we meet his other wives, who are from San Domingo, Venezuela, and El Salvador.

Still, Reina's amazement over the differences between Cuba and Florida are counterpoised against her recognition of the similarities. The tropical foliage and weather of Miami and its strand of palm-lined beaches provide almost everything left behind in Cuba except the island's mountains and its mysterious caves. Foods central to Cuban cuisine grow easily in South Florida, and for those willing to look for it, a substantial Spanish history and heritage is everywhere, from the Tortugas to St. Augustine. But the past has morphed into the present, and into new Southern/Cuban configurations. Miami's transnational glamour is suggested repeatedly. Secretly following her husband in a car one day, Constancia passes sailboats and cruise ships on the flawlessly blue bay, and she notes the skyscrapers. She also sees tourist attractions along the way, including Bird Island and Hialeah racetrack.[42] Affluent since their New York days, she and Heberto live in a shiny new condominium by the beach and often celebrate at lavish yacht club parties. Her products are snapped up at tony new malls by elegantly clad Cuban matrons, and Constancia is always tastefully and expensively dressed and coifed.

Yet we also see the poignant tropical beauty of the city through Constancia's eyes. Driving down Rickenbacker Causeway with the top down, "the tide is low, and an army of iridescent crabs scrambles along the shore. Shirtless men in cut-off shorts gather the crabs in tin buckets as spirals of smoke rise up from barbecues on the beach. The fading light lingers on the water before dying altogether" (139). Yet the palms on Crandon Boulevard remind her of when she and her father drank water from the stems of Cuban palms and ate their seedpods.

Contrasts such as this between the past and the present remind us that the thematic of death and memory is everywhere in this novel. Going back before the Cuban Revolution to retrieve the island's past—particularly through the story of Ignacio and Blanca—is a mission of restoration and memorialization, particularly as the story of the characters intersects with the vanishing species of the island's flora and fauna, which we see in the subplot of the Agüero scientific expeditions. Further, the regional aspect of the tropical life we discover along with Ignacio and Blanca has strong affinities with that we see in Florida through Constancia and, later, Reina. There, too, a natural world is vanishing, and its "time"—its memory—deserves consideration and, if possible, retrieval, as with the Everglades.

Musing on the conundrum of memory as she wanders around Madrid, Dulce thinks of her dead ancestors and wishes she knew more of them, both the side that produced scientists and entrepreneurs and the other that led to her revolutionary and heroic father. She reflects, "I wonder if anyone still remembers them. . . . There should be rituals like in primitive societies, where the elders confer their knowledge on the descendants bit by bit. Then we could discuss all the false histories pressed upon us, accumulate our true history like a river in rainy season" (144). Soon after this reverie, in a flashback to Ignacio's father's death, we hear the latter's wife tell him, "Go, if you must, mi amor . . . your memory is safe with us" (151).[43]

The "us," ultimately, is the living, and Reina too, like her daughter, wonders, "Who will remember Mami in thirty years? Who will remember her father? Who, Reina wonders, will remember *her*? We hold only partial knowledge of each other, she thinks. We're lucky to get even a shred of the dark, exploding whole" (201). Similarly, Constancia, at the airport to pick up her pregnant daughter, thinks: "When you give birth . . . you cede your place to another. You say in effect, when I'm gone, you will live, you will remember. But what is it exactly they're supposed to remember?" (211).

Reina and Constancia have a discussion about memory, with Reina remarking, "I guess it's less painful to forget than to remember," but we know Constancia has forgotten nothing, really. She has, in fact, remembered her mother in her products, and she is forced to confront her daily now that her face has transformed into Blanca's. As Reina, perhaps cruelly, tells her sister, "Sometimes we become what we try to forget most" (173). Ultimately, Reina and Constancia retrieve their memories of their parents and interrogate them. The horror of their mother's murder is the price they must pay for the full burden of memory revealed.

· · · · ·

As my readings indicate, the word "return" occurs over and over in Cuban American fiction and prose. Although it more often than not implies "return" to Cuba—either now or in a post-Castro future—it surfaces quite often as a return to Miami, the simulacrum of Havana, as we have seen, or simply as a return to home, wherever that may be for diasporic Cubans as they navigate between various exile cities such as Houston, Madrid, or Mexico City.

Return, it seems, can be dangerous. We remember the ending of Suarez's *Going Under* and its ominous relation to the title, but also the penultimate chapter of *The Agüero Sisters*, where Reina and Constancia are in a boat a mile off Key West, performing rites the *santero* specified necessary for Constancia's subsequent solitary return to Cuba to retrieve her father's papers. Here, in and on the liminal space of the hyphenating waters between

Cuba and Florida, Reina finally tells her sister the truth about their mother's death, namely that their father shot her. Enraged, Constancia almost kills Reina with an oar and then prepares to watch her drown. She relents, however, saves her, and shares food the *santero* ordered her to bring with her to propitiate Oshún. This rite of sisterly communion overshadows the *santero*'s prescribed ones and seems to indicate a lifting of the curse the family suffers, as the sisters, who have until now been surrogates for their parents— Reina for Blanca, Constancia for Ignacio—face up to the tragedy their parents enacted directly and thus find a cleared space for a new relationship.

It is worth noting here that the notion of "return" is inextricably linked in Cuban American literature with nostalgia. That word, however, has two parts: *nostos* (return home) and *algia* (pain). By considering these two components separately, García is able to emphasize the dangers I have mentioned, but also to avoid the merely sentimental, which has marred too many narratives of exile in the past, especially when, as in Ana Menéndez's tartly but poignantly expressed short story, "Her Mother's House," sentiment can lead to fantasy.

It is tempting to suggest that Blanca and Ignacio's doomed union represents that of pre-Castro Cuba and the United States, with Ignacio constituting the colonizing, abusing dominant power. His refined, educated background as the son of an elegant, artistic émigré from Galicia situates him as an agent of the earlier colonizer, Spain; and his refusal to pay his wife adequate compensation for her work or to assist her in finding employment (and thus independence) elsewhere aligns gender with imperialism. Further, her African heritage and her ultimate betrayals of him with not only one but two men of color—once right before Ignacio's eyes—invokes the specter of race, which always tinged the centuries-old debate about annexing Cuba that occurred within the United States, as we have seen, particularly in the U.S. South in the days of Narciso Lopez and Mrs. Pickens.

The various lines of the narrative converge in Constancia's James Bond–like private invasion of the island (she has to swim ashore in a wetsuit). She has just learned of her husband Heberto's death in the commando raid on Cuba, and she will come ashore on Varadero Beach, where he died.[44] The trip to Camagüey to retrieve the diary, guided by Reina's ex-lover, pulls together the extracts from it we have already read. Nearing the island, Constancia crosses the imaginary line of the Tropic of Cancer, where there is good bone fishing, and we remember that Blanca carried a white bone around her neck. On the day that Constancia arrives at her ancestral village, she realizes it is her son's thirty-fourth birthday, and she is driven there in a Packard that echoes her father's. Apparently it is also the feast day of the Virgen de la Caridad del Cobre, as a procession passes with children bearing the sacred pumpkins. The convergence of these temporal lines creates a narrative crossroads, one consonant with the magic of the god of the crossroads, Esu Elegba, who is also the god of new beginnings.[45]

Constancia's successful retrieval of the family's heritage in the form of Ignacio's diary and Blanca's sacred bone thus constitutes a new beginning for the growing family, as now she and Reina can finally lay aside the differences they have had functioning as virtual avatars of Ignacio and Blanca, respectively. Her heroic efforts in doing this situate her as having metaphorical *cojones* and demonstrate, as Reina's career as an Amazonian electrician did earlier, that women can embody the virtues of what is called "machismo" better than men at times. Certainly Constancia's two husbands fail miserably in that department, as does her son Silvestre (Dulce and Isabel seem to have fared little better with their men, for that matter).[46]

Cuban American writing, for the most part, is ruptured from traditional Cuban narrative in several ways other than by the revolution. Historically, as Benítez-Rojo (1992) and Glissant (1989) have both observed, not just Cuban but Caribbean literature, like that of the U.S. South, has been marked by legacies from slavery and the plantation. For the most part, Floridian Cuban writers do not deal with this, although it needs to be said that Virgil Suarez's novel *The Cutter* (1998) returns to the agricultural peonage of his father.[47]

As we have seen, many of the narratives spun by Cuban American writers (particularly men) center on the betrayal (as they see it) of the revolution, the appropriation of private property, followed by flight to the United States, very often to Miami. Ensuing narratives center on the Cuban enclave of Little Havana, family life, and the myriad complications of exile, which nevertheless ultimately lead to acculturation of the U.S.-born generation. This is not the case with several women Cuban American writers, such as Cristina García and Ana Menéndez. The latter's wonderful book of short stories, *In Cuba I Was a German Shepherd* (2001), was followed by her fascinating novel *Loving Che* (2003), which is less hostile to the revolution and more focused on the realities of life on the island. Menéndez possibly got the idea for this novel from Roberto Fernández's wild satire, *Raining Backwards* (1988), in which the character Mima's son Keith is said to be the product of her affair with Che.

Loving Che's narrator breathlessly tries to communicate what the original insurrection was like: "Cataclysmic events, whatever their outcome, are as rare and transporting as a great love. Bombings, revolutions, earthquakes, hurricanes—anyone who has passed through one and lived, if they are honest, will tell you that even in the depths of their fear there was an exhilaration missing from their lives until then" (51–52).[48] This formula is expressive of the mixture of beauty, awe, and terror of the sublime. It is worth noting how often natural and manmade catastrophes such as hurricanes and revolutions rupture the fabric of society in Southern and Caribbean narratives, as we have seen in works by Delany, Woolson, Hearn, Hurston, Wright, McKay, and many others. In light of the havoc caused by the Cuban Revolution, the Bay of Pigs, the Cuban Missile Crisis, the Mariel boatlift, the Elián González case, and the many hurricanes and catastrophes at sea for boat people, it is strange that we have had few extended narratives about the revolution itself—a fact no doubt owing to the influence of the exiled Cubans, who have preferred to ignore or at least not valorize the uprising that transformed Cuban society, a silence similar to that of white Southerners during the Haitian insurrection.

In the preface to *Loving Che*, the first narrator (the daughter of the central figure, Teresa, who will tell the main story) reveals her fondness for collecting old photographs from prerevolutionary Cuba, for which she invents stories. "I know," she tells us, "that I'm playing a game with history" (1). The same might be said for every one of the writers addressed here, as the Cuban diaspora cannot be considered apart from its history. Menéndez, however, like García, wants to ensure that prerevolutionary Cuba not be eclipsed by the Castro era. In a related move, she emphasizes the verb "play," and there is in *Loving Che* an inventive playfulness that enables her skillful juggling of real events and figures with more fanciful forms and happenings. The major portion of the book consists of Teresa's rhapsodic memories of her lost lover and their assignations. Lyrical, sensual, yet in many ways rather abstract, these scenes depict a woman and man lost in a physical passion; their affair, however, does not abrogate either partner's continuing love for an absent spouse.

We know little of Teresa's early life; she seems to feel that she was launched into the world only with her marriage, in 1953, to Calixto de la Landre, a professor of Spanish who also writes for scholarly journals in Spain. Each has had, she says, "a cushioned upbringing," and both are lonely, in that he is estranged from his parents, her father is distant, and her mother is dead. Still, her father buys the young couple a house in El Vedado. While his young bride paints, Calixto increasingly becomes involved with young revolutionaries, which leads to important connections after the revolution. After Ernesto Guevara attends a party she hosts in a striking blue satin gown, her husband encourages her to develop a friendship with him: "The way things are, it's not a bad idea to have important friends" (57).

Menéndez creates a fascinating and amusing twist to her story. Just before the revolution, Teresa gets a commission to paint a seven-panel mural of scenes in Miami for a new hotel on the Isle of Pines. The developer, capitalizing on all the people moving to Miami, plans his development as a New Miami. Never having been to the Florida city, Teresa has to work from photographs and postcards. "There I stood in my studio in Havana, day after day trying to paint Miami as if it were a city of dreams; more truly, it was a city of lies" (63), a fascinating "Florida imaginary" that we can set beside the "Cuban imaginary" of earlier times.

Teresa's affair with Guevara is offset by the suspicion that Calixto too is having affairs. The concluding third of the book, however, returns us to the original narrator, Teresa's daughter, musing in Florida over Teresa's letters. "Miami was not a city for romantic heroes; here, an association with the Revolution was something to be hidden, denied, and ultimately forgotten" (158). But the narrator refuses to box away her dead mother's letter testimony, and she takes the trove to Dr. Caraballo at the University of Miami, a professor of Cuban history, who confirms that the language and images in Che's letters are similar to those found in his writings.

The narrator, as part of her research into her parents' affairs and Che's history, talks with Jacinto Alcazar, a photographer who fought in the mountains alongside Fidel and Che. He is full of memories but also says, "You know, nothing really died in the revolution. . . . Havana's pathologies and beauties came to splendor in Miami. Sometimes I think this exile has been little more than a brief passage through a mirror. . . . The owner of *El Tiempo* [a Havana newspaper] ended up publishing another little sheet in Miami . . . called *Libertad*. . . . In late October of 1975, he wrote an editorial in favor of political bombings. A few days later he was killed when his car blew up" (167). The narrator also consults an expert on Cuban art who assists the curator at Vizcaya, the legendary Miami mansion situated on the bay amid the mangroves. She knows nothing of the narrator's mother's paintings but provides a brief summary of Cuban modernism, indicating that the brain drain to the United States might be of benefit to Cuba's international aesthetic reputation.

On a more mundane level, when the narrator is being driven to the airport for a flight to Havana, her cabdriver at first berates her for providing money to Castro. He relents, however, when he hears she is seeking her mother, and he confides that his son is in Cuba with his mother and that he has not seen him in fourteen years. The narrator's trip to Cuba is her first in ten years, and the new tourism has transformed the city. Her hotel (for tourists only, to be sure) offers first-class food and service; new shops are everywhere; and dollars are the dominant currency. "I wondered how many of these tourists claimed sympathy to the revolution even as they savored the fruits that Batista had once tended so well. Everywhere, the socialist experiment seemed dead and buried, awaiting only the death and burial of its maximum leader" (184). She also finds a dollar store, one "as defined by Miami" (184). If Miami is a simulacrum of Old Havana, the new Havana seems busy morphing into a simulacrum of Miami. And, indeed, a pretty single mother, whose little boy cons the narrator into buying groceries, cooks for her and laments, "Without dollars in this country you're as good as dead . . . if you don't have relatives in Miami, if you don't know anybody in the counterrevolutionary Miami Mafia" (187). Menéndez has this young mother invert a popular joke in Miami: "Will the last American to leave Miami please bring the flag." She reveals that "these Cubans" had carefully hung a large suitcase on the outstretched arm of the statue of José Martí (189).

There is a pendant to this scene. The narrator also has dinner with an elegant older invalid and her attractive, intellectual son in their faded but once-grand apartment, and the repast is tended by a black servant. The narrator hopes that Caridad (an obvious reference to Cuba's patron saint, La Virgen de la Caridad del Cobre) is her mother, but she is not. From these characters, however, we learn that the poor but charming single mother was right—all good things do come from Miami, where Caridad's wealthy brother lives in Coral Gables (when he is not at his home in France). We see a picture of Caridad's niece standing in front of the Fontainebleau Hotel in South Beach.

Caridad's memories of the *really* affluent days before the revolution, however, cause the narrator to reflect that "nostalgia is not the exclusive province of exiles; or perhaps that one can be an exile without ever having left, can be an exile, so to speak, from time" (200). The narrator ultimately learns the truth; her mother was actually named Cueva, not de la Landre, and she spent her last years before her suicide still painting, mainly portraits of Che. She lived in a tiny apartment with an old friend and her son, and now they survive selling the paintings of Che to tourists. The lesson seems to be that genuine love—rather than nostalgia—can live on and be nourishing in a new way. The paintings and drawings are presented as having an integrity that the myriad photographs of Che in circulation—on T-shirts and coffee mugs and in countless advertisements—lack in an age of crass mechanical reproduction. Further, the artistic renderings seem to differ from even the original photographs of the legend. The narrator finds an old photograph of Che in a Paris antiquary shop; significantly, he wears a camera around his neck. The shop's owner refers to Roland Barthes's writing on photography: "He was correct . . . in our time, death more and more appears to reside most comfortably in the photograph" (224).

As this brief analysis suggests, *Loving Che* smartly equates the passions of the revolution with a great love, blending them in the narrator's affair with the Byronic Che, rebel, intellectual, military hero, leader, and lover. All these things were true of Castro too, as Barbara Walters's rapturous memories of her interviews with him reveal. Cristina García has remarked, "Castro for many years was a powerful sex symbol in Cuba. He did sleep with many women in Cuba and has many children scattered around the island. I think he represented a kind of sexual fantasy for many women" (Vorda 1993, 70).

Among the many non-Cuban Latino/a writers who have lived in Miami is the Puerto Rican Judith Ortiz Cofer, who for many years taught in Athens, Georgia. She told an interviewer in 2000 that although she often was asked by Southerners where she was from, such inquiries were a matter of interest because she was "exotic." However, during her ten years in Miami, this changed after the influx of "problematic" Latinos/as via the Mariel boatlift into the city. Formerly hospitable merchants became hostile: "The prejudice level rose for anyone looking Latino. I predict that's going to happen again in the deep South. When you're an exotic and no threat, you're an interesting thing to have around; when there's a lot of you and you pose a problem, like 'we don't want you in our neighborhood' or that sort of thing, the prejudice level rises" (Dick 2003, 113). And, in fact, since that interview, the migration of thousands of Latinos/as to Athens, Atlanta, Charlotte, and many other Southern cities (mainly from Mexico, but also from Columbia, Honduras, the Dominican Republic. and elsewhere) has indeed raised hackles.

Despite nativist fears, the various waves of immigrants from Cuba, which continue to this day, have constantly enriched and sustained the Latino/a enclaves in the United States (particularly in Miami) and also the multicultural makeup of the U.S. South. We might see the continual Latinizing of South Florida as similar in effect to the way in which refugees from Haiti, both black and white, contributed to an enrichment of Francophone and African elements in New Orleans, which has made that city one of the chief nodes of both African survivalisms and New World creativity, and the sole remaining rich repository of French heritage in the United States. New immigrants to Little Haiti in Miami are currently helping to establish a similar node in South Florida, and their communal organizations have learned some key lessons about the development of political and cultural power from their Cuban American neighbors.

All of these factors and events have found expression in the pages of new Southern writing, as more recent immigrants and exiles have added their voices to those who preceded them. Increasingly, Anglo Southern writers are turning to the intersection of the South and the Caribbean too, as in Peter Matthiessen's *Killing Mister Watson* (1990) and its two sequels and Madison Smartt Bell's magnificent trilogy on the Haitian Revolution. In the years to come, we will certainly hear more from the Cuban American writers of Miami and from the growing numbers of their neighbors in Little Haiti, especially the phenomenally talented Edwidge Danticat, who has started to write about her adopted city in her tragic memoir, *Brother, I'm Dying* (2007).

Glissant has asserted that national literature "must signal the self-assertion of new peoples, which one calls their rootedness, and which is today their struggle. That is its hallowing function, epic or tragic. It must express—and if this is not done (only if it is not done) it remains regionalist, that is moribund and folkloric—the relationship of one culture to another in the spirit of Diversity, and its contribution to the totalizing process. Such is its analytical and political function which does not operate without calling into question its own existence" (1989, 101).

Southern literature urgently needs to reconfigure "new people," like Florida's Cuban Americans, whose "rootedness" was until recently on the island they left. Now, however, new generations are rooted in both Cuba and Florida. Yet without the concept of a transnational South, this process cannot hope to succeed. Recently, critics have complained about the dominance of the concept of place in Southern literary studies, forgetting that place is far from static, and that it can, in fact, be portable. In the writings of Cuban Americans, we see rapid changes in the composition and character of Miami, an Afro/Anglo/Latino/a crossroads of the U.S. South that is also a Caribbean and hemispheric hub, where the mischievous orisha Eleggua, master of the crossroads, is surely inspiring new and seductive narratives for our entertainment and, one hopes, our cultural and national health.

Notes

Preface

1. Region and place are fluid and dynamic, not fixed, and both subjects in the Americas are inextricably bound up with issues of race, a topic Benedict Anderson addresses at length, asserting that nationalism "thinks in terms of historical destinies, while racism dreams of eternal contaminations, transmitted from the origins of time through an endless sequence of loathsome copulations: outside history . . . the dreams of racism actually have their origin in ideologies of *class*, rather than in those of nation: above all in claims to divinity among rulers and to 'blue' or 'white' blood and 'breeding' among aristocracies" (1991, 149). The thematic of race and contagion will be an issue of great interest to my argument.

2. The Southern-born and -raised African American writer Percival Everett moved to Miami from South Carolina when he was sixteen: "I remained a Southerner there, considering Florida is as far South as you can go in the United States. But it was there I got a foreign accent, in college where everyone around me was actually speaking Spanish. The character of Miami was not at all like South Carolina" (Julien and Tissut 2007, 230). Yet, as Everett states, Florida *is* the South, and Miami did not change his identity as a Southerner.

3. Before the big Cuban immigration to the city, the most numerous set of circum-Caribbean residents came from the Bahamas. Between 1900 and 1920, the period when my grandfather was beginning his Miami career, over 12,000 Bahamians migrated to the city, representing one-fifth of the entire population of the Bahamas (Gannon 1996, 399). It is no wonder that the anthropologist Zora Neale Hurston was so intrigued by the culture she found in the islands and the many parallels she saw between the African elements of that culture and her own.

Introduction

1. I also follow Ileana Rodríguez, who gathered with other Caribbean scholars in 1978 at the University of Minnesota to consider Caribbean unity. As she writes: "The Caribbean must be conceived as a differentiated structural totality which includes not only the island nations, but the east coast of mainland countries extending from the southern United States to Mexico, Central America and finally Columbia, Venezuela and the Guyanas" (1983, 19–20).

2. To understand the interplay of writers and artists from the South with those *farther* south, we need to become more proficient in French and Spanish and to more

vigorously pursue translations, which Werner Sollors and Marc Shell's Longfellow Institute at Harvard is in fact doing with classic texts written in what is now the United States in languages other than English.

3. Jeff Karem has authored a multilingual consideration (2011) of the effect of the Caribbean on U.S. culture since the Spanish American War. He sometimes considers writers who figure in this volume, particularly Zora Neale Hurston and Richard Wright. His work, which was published after I completed most of my original readings, is complementary rather than competing, because he usually does not draw the contrast between Caribbean writers and those of the U.S. South.

4. Promising new historians have also shown us the way to the kind of work I am doing here. During the course of my research for this book, I was happy to discover Matthew Pratt Guterl's *American Mediterranean: Southern Slaveholders in the Age of Emancipation* (2008), which provides a paradigm of transnational history, while echoing the point I made in my 2005 essay, "Calypso Magnolia," that the Caribbean in so many ways constitutes our hemisphere's version of the Mediterranean, and that the enforced African diaspora, which spilled over every kind of boundary, created a masterclass of capitalists, whose complex interactions in global trade brought new definitions to the concepts of New World freedom while simultaneously expanding and complicating chattel slavery.

5. *The Tempest* has repeatedly been employed by critics of circumCaribbean colonial and postcolonial cultures as a metaphor for Western domination. I refer to several of these studies in the course of my discussion, but two are of special note: the Cuban critic Robert Fernández Retamar's *Caliban and Other Essays* (1999) and Sandra Pouchet Paquet's classic *Caribbean Autobiography: Cultural Identity and Self-Representation* (2002). A secondary but also important Western text that has received "re-accentuation," and often parody, is Defoe's *Robinson Crusoe* (1719), which is masterfully dissected and inverted in Derek Walcott's play *Pantomime* (1978).

6. This concept of a culture of folklore and performance that circles around the Caribbean rim—and importantly includes the crucial city of New Orleans—has been adumbrated by Joseph Roach in his pathbreaking *Cities of the Dead: Circum-Atlantic Performance* (1991). In sociolinguistics, Roger Abrahams demonstrated the correspondences between the Caribbean and Southern "man of words," who variously talks "broad" or "sweet" to various audiences (1983).

7. Jewell Parker Rhodes, Internet interview with Maxine E. Thompson, Black Butterfly Press, *www.maxinethompson.com/Jewell.html* (n.d.), 1.

Chapter 1

1. This concept of a northern lover/protector operating in the interests of a southern, feminine captive had a broader application in the continental configurations of Arnold Guyot, whose 1849 study *The Earth and Man* asserted, "Each northern continent has its southern continent near by which seems more especially commended to its guardianship and laced under its influence. Africa is already European at both ex-

tremities; North America leans on South America, which is indebted to the example of the North for its emancipation and its own institutions" (307–8).

2. Other combatants from the U.S. South who wrote about the conflict include South Carolina's H. Judge Moore and Marcus Claudius Marcellus Hammond and Tennessee's George C. Furber. The most prolific reporter of the war, however, was Louisiana's Thomas Bangs Thorpe, the author of the celebrated story "The Big Bear of Arkansas" (1841). He ultimately published several volumes of war reportage. For an early discussion of the literature generated by the conflict, see Johannsen (1985, 241–69).

3. The literature of the Mexican American War has been productively analyzed over the past two decades. Shelley Streeby (2002) considers the many sensational novels set during the war as a reflection of crises in Northern U.S. cities; David Kazanjian (2003) provides a new interpretation of the war as an example of the complex manifestations of U.S. imperialism; Jesse Alemán (2006) focuses on the war's uncanny aspects; and Jaime Rodríguez (2010) concentrates on the various literary tropes or stereotypes generated in the war literature of both the United States and Mexico. None of these critics, however, configures the war with the peculiar brand of regionalism that was taking on dynamic new configurations in the U.S. South.

4. It is significant that the Mexican War novels and novelettes generated outside the South were not sectional. Although the term "yankee" was occasionally used and characters were identified as, for example, Kentuckians or Ohioans, very rarely were they presented as "Northern" or "Southern."

5. As I will employ the concept of the tropical sublime extensively in this study, we should pause to define it more closely. A new register of perception emerged in the eighteenth century, when Edmund Burke and Immanuel Kant revolutionized modes of writing about nature, in all its forms. Burke felt that the sublime was generated by "whatever is in any sort terrible, or is conversant about terrible objects, or operates in a man analogous to terror" (1757, 36). Terror could be caused by the awe one feels viewing a surging ocean, a misty mountain peak, or by terrible actions such as volcanoes or hurricanes. Sublime delight, however, is possible only when viewing the source of the terror from a safe distance. For Burke, the sublime may be found in beauty, but mere beauty, without an aspect of terror, is inferior to the sublime. Ultimately, the sublime is psychological. Further, "To make any thing very terrible, obscurity in general seems to be necessary" (1790, 54). The sublime, then, is inexpressible and can be embodied in words that seem tangible but are actually incomprehensible, such as heaven and hell.

6. Prescott's charge of Indian "degeneracy" would be echoed again and again. Bayard Taylor's account of his visit to Mexico City reports, "Faces of the pure Aztec blood are still to be found. . . . They have degenerated in everything but their hostility to the Spanish race" (1850, 301).

7. Ironically, Prescott, an ardent abolitionist, was adamantly opposed to the war, fearing it would lead to the spread of slavery; still, he reveled in the increased sales of his book.

8. For a classic presentation of this kind of language, see Annette Kolodny, *The Lay of the Land* (1975) and *The Land Before Her* (1984).

9. Prescott's influence on U.S. combatants is described in Johannsen (1985, 241ff.).

10. It is worth noting that the phrase "Manifest Destiny" was coined by John O'Sullivan as he discussed the annexation of Texas in 1844: "Other nations have undertaken to intrude themselves . . . limiting our greatness and checking the fulfillment of our manifest destiny to overspread the continent allotted by Providence." O'Sullivan situates Texas as an "untrodden space." Its sparse inhabitants were, he claims, eager for annexation, as most of them had migrated there from the United States. Their union with the nation was therefore "not only inevitable, but most natural" (1845, 5).

11. Kirsten Silva Gruesz has noted these gendered tropes of beauty as well; she discovers a tendency among U.S. commentators on the Mexican War to depict Mexicans as emasculated or overtly feminine. By contrast, Mexico itself was often feminized, sometimes to the point of idealization (as with Ellen, Falkner's *senorita* heroine). Clearly what is needed is a manly, equally beautiful mate to rescue this figuration of the land itself from, first, brute "Spanish" masters, yes, but also from ineffectual and weak Mexican men (2002, 73–74).

12. At times, bias against the Church of Rome took on more virulent forms. The doctrine of Manifest Destiny had always had a strongly anti-Catholic element in it, and the Catholic church became a chief target for marauding American soldiers, who beat and even killed priests, ripped up altar cloths and tomb covers, and stole crucifixes and implements of the mass. These outrages echoed similar ones that occurred during the struggle for Texas independence, a conflict that drew sustained outside support within the United States by Papist-hating Protestant sects. For a perceptive reading of the forms of anti-Catholicism prevalent in the United States during the Mexican War, see Haddox (2005, 7ff.).

13. On a related note, Kirsten Silva Gruesz has complained that recent transnational studies have tended to neglect the importance of Mexican, Yucatan, and Central American ports in favor of the island ports that were linked to Europe (2006, 474).

14. This restriction is similar to the shuttering of both China and Japan from outside trade in preceding centuries.

15. In her first novel, *Inez: A Tale of the Alamo* (1855), the teen-age Augusta Jane Evans, who would go on to become one of the South's most read romance writers, made use of her childhood in Texas to create a gothic potboiler about young girls menaced by an evil Catholic priest in San Antonio, just before the fall of the Alamo. The novel devotes most of its energies to a debate over Protestant and Catholic doctrine, to the neglect of its mostly maudlin romantic plots. But both of these narrative strands are far more important than the American engagement with the Mexicans, although real-life figures such as Santa Ana and Fanning appear eventually. The title figure, Inez, a "Spaniard," loves in vain a white Protestant doctor and abandons her

Catholicism as she fights the evil Italian priest, whose "swarthy" face links him with "Indians" as an ethnic other.

16. We need to recall here that many Latin American countries have had very convoluted, even chaotic, records of governance. Mexico and Nicaragua, two Caribbean countries of key interest for this study, were especially notorious for instability. From 1833 to 1855, Mexico had thirty-six presidents; Nicaragua has seemed to change presidents every year (Robert E. May 2002, 86).

17. The concept of colonization through amalgamation, however, was prevalent in the U.S. popular literature of the war and beyond. See especially the transnational marriages that conclude *Caballero*, a Mexican American novel by Jovita González and Eve Raleigh (written in the 1930s but not published until 1995). For a full discussion of that text, see Jaime Javier Rodríguez (2010, 213–37).

18. Accordingly, the naval commander Semmes offers a perspective that proceeds from a sense of the interconnectedness of the circumCaribbean through the seas, a concept in keeping with Glissant's two epigraphs for his *Poetics of Relation*: Barbadian poet Edward Kamau Brathwaite's axiom that the connections that bind the peoples of the Caribbean together are submarine and St. Lucia's Derek Walcott's declaration that "the sea is history" (Glissant 1990, vii).

19. Many writers seeking to convey the richness and potential of these "untrammeled" tropical landscapes regularly featured views from summits and were possibly influenced not only by Romantic writers addicted to the sublime but also by a Romantic historian, Prescott, who constantly describes sweeping views of valleys and farms, employing an "eye" that occupies the high realm of a superior culture.

20. Compare Semmes's account with that of the popular travel writer Bayard Taylor, who journeyed from Matanzas to Vera Cruz shortly after the conclusion of the war. Although he found Mexico City enchanting, Taylor repeated the usual stereotypes of rural Mexicans, reporting, "Notwithstanding the unsurpassed fertility of soil and genial character of climate, this region is very scantily settled, except in the broad river bottoms opening towards the sea. There, under the influence of a perpetual summer, the native race becomes indolent and careless of the future. Nature does everything for them" (1850, 256). Colonel Falkner may well have consulted the Mexico City portion of Taylor's *Eldorado; or, Adventures in the Path of Empire* (1850).

21. As Alemán reminds us, ruins can invoke a sublime past that inspires notions of a glorious future, as in José María Heredia's 1820s poem "Las sombras," wherein a pilgrim finds sublime inspiration from the ruins of Chapultepec. U.S. combatants—especially those familiar with Prescott, like Semmes—had similar reveries, piggybacking, so to speak, on the heroic/barbaric past of their enemy to imagine a new Mexican golden age (Alemán 2006, 407).

22. The tropical sublime must be differentiated from what has been called "tropicalism," a variant on Edward Said's formulation of "orientalism." The former term, according to Frances Aparicio and Susan Chávez-Silverman, refers to "a system of ideological fictions with which the dominant (Anglo and European) cultures trope

Latin American and U.S. Latino/a identities and cultures" (1997, 1). However, I would argue that this is far too restrictive, in that "tropicalization" has been used in this way to address cultures worldwide that fit into a "tropical" pattern, including South America, Polynesia, Africa, Southern and Southeast Asia, and the circumCaribbean (which includes the tropical U.S. South).

23. The Treaty of Guadalupe Hidalgo (1848) did nothing to change the oppression of Indians. Southerners at this time were completing the removal of Native Americans from Florida and Georgia; the Cherokees in Georgia were barriers to the exploitation of gold in the mountainous northern part of the state.

24. For a convincing reading of Cole's *The Course of Empire* as a conservative political allegory, see Angela Miller (1998).

25. Rob Wilson (1991) offers a valuable way of understanding how this concept of the sublime was generated by the Puritans. He traces the development of the genre up to Whitman but then leaps forward to consider Wallace Stevens and does not attempt to link the syndrome in any detail to the concept of Manifest Destiny. Further, although he claims to be addressing the "American" sublime, he considers no Southern writers except Poe. Conversely, Amy S. Greenberg, in her excellent study of manhood and Manifest Destiny (2005), reads travel narratives for ideology and gendered attitudes but ignores how aesthetic perceptions and formulations of the landscape relate to these issues.

26. Semmes's clear sense that the Mexican hacienda and the Southern plantation are analogues has found expansive and carefully qualified treatment recently in the work of José E. Limón (2000), Vincent Pérez (2006), and, especially, George Handley (2000).

27. This kind of racial mathematics appears frequently in the literature of sensation generated by the war. A character in George Lippard's *Bel of Prairie Eden* exclaims: "Fifty white men of Texas are equivalent to one thousand Mexicans any day" (1848, 113).

28. As we shall see, while Colonel Falkner's novel would provide gruesome details of combat, he chose not to emphasize the equally horrific but less romantic elements of disease, parasites, and privation.

29. This account of the hospitality and charm of Mexico after hostilities ceased was echoed by Ulysses S. Grant: "The people who remained at their homes fraternized with the 'Yankees' in the pleasantest manner. In fact, under the humane policy of our commander, I question whether the great majority of the Mexican people did not regret our departure as much as they had regretted our coming. Property and person were thoroughly protected, and a market was afforded for all the products of the country such as the people had never enjoyed before" (1990, 82).

30. For a full listing of the many literary works based on the war, see Streeby's exhaustive study (2002), chapter 7 of Johannsen (1985), and, especially, Rodríguez and Kazanjian (2003, 173–212).

31. For a compelling reading of Bird's novel, see Alemán (2006, passim).

32. Whether by coincidence or design, Falkner's novel, *The Spanish Heroine*,

echoes what Ralph Bauer has identified as three central tropes of early prose narratives about the Atlantic: shipwreck, captivity, and travel (2003, 9). As I will demonstrate, these tropes remained dominant in the literature of the Americas and are still major motifs and fascinations today.

33. Falkner had, however, been posted near Monterey, so he knew the city and the territory. Absent without leave, he was severely wounded by Mexican guerrillas and sent back to Mississippi to recuperate. He rejoined his company briefly in 1850 (it was stationed near Buena Vista), but when it became apparent that his prior injuries made him unfit for duty, he was discharged, on October 31, and he returned to Mississippi.

34. The poem seems to offer veiled confirmation of the Hindman charges of Falkner's "indecent" sexual behavior in Mexico: Falkner wrote: "Full well I know the feeling of lead / I have never fought, but freely bled, / Mexican soil hath drank my gore, / But I disgrace, instead of glory bore" ("Siege," canto I, stanza xi).

35. We now know that there were at least 400 cross-dressed female Civil War soldiers. For an extended account of these women and the narratives they created or inspired, see Elizabeth Young's chapter "Confederate Counterfeit: The Case of the Cross-Dressed Civil War Soldier," in her study, *Disarming the Nation* (1999, 149–94). See also Jesse Alemán's introduction to the reprint of Velasquez's story and the introduction he composed with Streeby for their anthology, *Empire and the Literature of Sensation* (2007); several of the texts there include cross-dressing heroines.

36. Here we remember that Mark Twain famously claimed that the South lost the Civil War because of its addiction to the romantic and chivalric novels of Sir Walter Scott (the "Sir Walter Scott disease" is pinpointed in chapters 40, 45, and 46 of *Life on the Mississippi* [1883]). Further, the wrecked steamboat *Walter Scott* functions importantly in *Adventures of Huckleberry Finn* (1885) as a symbol of the ruinous effects of romantic chivalry in contemporary life.

37. This thematic, as David Kazanjian has demonstrated (2003, 196–97), was present in several fictional treatments of the war, as in Harry Halyard's *The Heroine of Tampico* (1847), which, like *The Spanish Heroine* (and for that matter, Delany's *Blake*), concludes with several cross-cultural marriages. Often, as in Harry Hazel's (pen name of Justin Jones) novel *Inez, the Beautiful; or, Love on the Rio Grande* (1846), the fair U.S. soldier saves the heroine of "pure Castillian blood" from rape by a swarthy "serpent-like" Mexican. Inez, like Ellen, cross-dresses as a Mexican soldier. As Kazanjian states, "U.S. expansionism thus consolidates white nationalist masculinity by saving white women . . . from Mexican men" (196).

38. We note that Colonel Falkner's most popular and impressive work, *The White Rose of Memphis* (1881), takes place on a Mississippi riverboat, where a masked ball (a kind of Caribbean carnival afloat) animates all that follows in the narrative. In costume, the passengers, somewhat in the manner of Boccaccio's courtiers in *The Decameron*, begin telling tales that reflect gruesome realities of Southern life. The book went through seventeen editions and was more popular in its time than most of the Colonel's great-grandson's books. With its highly romantic frame and grue-

somely naturalistic inset tales, the novel replicates the same strange admixture of *The Spanish Heroine* but also similar configurations in Latin American fiction of the time.

39. Sudden revelations of noble birth were conventions of the early U.S. novel. Joseph Holt Ingraham's *The Quadroone* (1841), for instance, saves presumed black characters from disaster. Azèlie finds she is the daughter of a princess and a Castilian heiress, while Renault learns he is the heir of a marquis. Both are then free to marry the aristocratic Henrique and Estelle, respectively.

40. We can detect in Falkner's differentiation here confirmation of Ulysses S. Grant's assertions in a letter from Mexico to his friend John W. Lowe (to whom I am not related): "The people of Mexico are a very different race of people from ours. The better class are very proud and tyrannize over the lower and much more numerous class as much as a hard master does over his negroes, and they submit to it quite as humbly. The great majority of inhabitants are either pure or more than half blooded Indians, and show but little more signs of neatness or comfort in their miserable dwellings than the uncivilized Indian" (1990, 916).

41. This is not the only scene where Ellen proves rather bloodthirsty; earlier in the narrative, acting almost like the "Bride" in Quentin Tarantino's film *Kill Bill*, when she and her party are assaulted by Mexican bandits, Ellen kills two of them—one by decapitation. Shades of Judith and Holofernes!

42. At the battle of Buena Vista, the corpse of Arkansas colonel Yell was plundered just after he fell (Foos 2002, 100).

43. In 1912, working-class Mexicans calling themselves "Zapatistas" after one of their leaders, Emiliano Zapata, rose up and attacked haciendas, plantations, large farms, and industrial operations—especially mines—a series of actions strongly resembling those that occurred in Haiti in the 1790s. Eventually, the U.S. Navy intervened on behalf of President Huerta, who resigned in favor of Carranza, and against Villa and Zapata, taking the port of Vera Cruz in 1914. Subsequently, reforms on the part of the government and the military leadership of their general, Obregon, plus interventions by U.S. president Woodrow Wilson (including an invasion after Villa raided New Mexico), led to the defeat of the Villa and Zapatista forces and Obregon's own revolution against President Carranza, resulting in the former's elevation to the presidency in 1920, in which he espoused many of the goals that had motivated the now-assassinated Zapata and the defeated Villa and implemented the reform Constitution of 1917, which was the chief achievement of the revolution (Hart 2000, 465). Although he did not inspire violence, Louisiana governor Huey Long would rise up as the champion of the poor in Depression America, offering a challenge to Franklin Delano Roosevelt's hegemony. Like Zapata, Long was assassinated.

44. The Colonel's Mexican tale had parallels in Northern literary circles. Mrs. E.D.E.N. Southworth makes the war the nexus for several strands of her complicated plot in *The Hidden Hand* (1859), the story of the "madcap" Capitola. Mrs. Southworth made little use of the real Mexico, and Christopher Looby has suggested that she shifted her story there, rather late in the novel, to appeal to readers who had become interested in nostalgic fictions set during the war, which had become a stimulus to

further dreams of expansion and American glory. *The Hidden Hand* appeared serially in the *New York Ledger*, which ran a number of shorter works set during the war during the run of the novel, including "The Guerilla's Daughter, or the Fandango Fight," "The Bandit Queen," and "The Escape: An Episode of the Mexican War," all titles redolent of the thematics of Falkner's work (Looby 2004, 205–6). Mrs. Southworth, however, sidestepped the political aspects of the war, which she well knew had sharply divided readers, who were debating the specter of slavery spreading to new territories — and newer territories perhaps to come.

45. Curiously, religion was not so strong a factor in cross-national marriages. While we tend today to see attitudes of racial superiority as dominant among expansion-minded Americans of this time, in fact many obtained power and property in the new territories through intermarriage with wealthy Mexicans. This becomes a dominant motif in the aforementioned novel *Caballero*. Indeed, many of the early U.S. pioneers who settled Texas cooperated with the Mexican government and were sometimes opposed to the annexation of Texas by the United States. Obviously, the ultimate marriage of the poor — and Protestant — Appalachian Henry to the wealthy — and Catholic — Mexican Ellen in Falkner's novel is emblematic of this syndrome, and, indeed, of the "pioneering" myth that often underlay discourses of Manifest Destiny. Colonel Falkner is silent regarding who officiates at the multiple marriage ceremonies that conclude the novel, and he also does not give any indication of what the religious practices of any of the characters who ultimately reside in Kentucky might be.

46. As José E. Limón has noted, the U.S. South and northern Mexico had much in common, both culturally and structurally. Enslaved Africans had a counterpart in Indian peons; the bustling ranches and haciendas paralleled in many ways plantations; and cotton was grown productively in both regions. The Southern-driven war with Mexico resulted in a new ethnic population in the greater South — Mexican Americans — and destabilized Mexico, making it dependent in many ways on its connections to the United States, particularly the South. A paradoxical situation resulted, of the U.S. South participating in the U.S. imposition of federal authority on Mexico, when both the South and its southern neighbor saw themselves as culturally distinct and beleaguered by the North (2000, 13).

47. Clement Eaton some decades ago underlined the fact that the Texas Rangers and many of the American troops who came to their aid were, yes, Americans, but also *Southerners.* "The Mexican War was an adventure in imperialism of the South in partnership with the restless inhabitants of the West. It was provoked by a southern President and fought largely by Southern generals and Southern volunteers" (1949, 365).

Chapter 2

1. "Plácido" was the pseudonym of Gabriel de la Concepción Valdés (1809–44). For a detailed analysis of his importance to both Cuban arts and politics, see Sibylle Fischer (2004, 77–106). Ifeoma Nwankwo's *Black Cosmopolitanism* provides a telling explication of Plácido's most important verse (2005, 87–114).

2. Significantly, however, William Hickling Prescott, who similarly had never visited the Mexico he immortalized in *The Conquest of Mexico*, provided copious descriptions of the landscape, largely through utilizing the accounts of travelers, such as his friend Fanny Calderón de Barca. His depictions not only added an attractive element of sublime spatiality and romance to his accounts but also catered to the taste for landscape tradition that had been inculcated by a long procession of painters, writers, and poets. Further, as Donald Ringe has explained, the sublime landscape provided a striking and dramatic contrast to the barbarity of Aztec religious sacrifices, and also to the massacres and cruelties of the Spanish (1983, 572).

3. Later patriots like José Martí saw Lopez as little different from soldiers of fortune like William Walker, a filibuster who briefly seized the presidency of Nicaragua; and, indeed, as Rodrigo Lazo has noted in his excellent study of filibustering narratives, many have seen Lopez's expedition as a forerunner of the Bay of Pigs (2005, 194). Both Pickens and Delany were aware of other narratives that had been written about and by the filibusters, who were inevitably drawn into the discourse on slavery as they planned and executed their military expeditions.

4. Pickens practices what Srinivas Aravamudan calls the "self-valorization of the metropolitan subject." As he notes, Jean-Paul Marat's *Les chaines de l'esclavage* (1774) concerns the metaphorical bondage of the French people at the "pinnacle of plantation slavery," with no reference to the actual slavery France was employing abroad (Aravamudan 1999, 4).

5. As Edward Said has noted, it all depends on how you look at such figures: "If you conceive of one type of political movement . . . as being 'terrorist' you deny it narrative consequence, whereas if you grant it normative status . . . you impose on it the legitimacy of a complete narrative" (1993, 312).

6. The flag that Lopez used in his expedition, which forms the title of this novel, actually became the country's flag, which is still used today, so Lopez's expedition had at least one permanent and very visible legacy. Eric Hobsbawm has demonstrated that national traditions in the modern age require such symbols, and that sometimes old traditions—including old flags—can be grafted onto new ones (1983, 6). Clearly, Fidel Castro had no problem appropriating the same flag flown by his predecessor Batista, perhaps because the lone star echoed that on traditional communist flags.

7. Rodrigo Lazo thinks Pickens—who does use the term "dark"—emphasizes Lopez's racial otherness (which fits into Lazo's overall reading of the general run of depictions of Lopez in the press), but his evidence is based on the way the description contrasts with that of the filibuster/soldier/politician John Quitman. A careful reading of the various portraits of race rendered in the novel reveals that Pickens in fact "whitens" Lopez in this particular passage, and does so without making any reference to his actual color (Lazo 2005, 114).

8. "The Black Legend," as David J. Weber explains, had its origins in Renaissance Europe, where Hispanophobia generated propaganda directed against Spain's militant Catholicism and competing and successful colonialism. According to *la leyenda negra*, Spaniards came to be seen as "cruel, avaricious, treacherous, fanatical, super-

stitious, cowardly, corrupt, decadent, indolent, and authoritarian" (2005, 336). For a full account of this syndrome, see Deguzmán's impressive study, *Spain's Long Shadow: The Black Legend, Off-Whiteness, and Anglo-American Empire* (2005, passim), which ranges from the American Renaissance up through modernism and postmodernism. We might note here that Colonel Falkner employs virtually all of these pejorative stereotypes in his portraits of his "white" Mexicans who have "pure Castillian blood."

9. Ironically, also in 1854, the Georgia-born John Rollin Ridge/Yellow Bird (Cherokee) would publish *The Life and Adventures of Joaquin Murieta, the Celebrated California Bandit*, the first Native American novel and also the first published by a Southern Indian. Therein, he would detail the predatory appropriation of his Mexican hero's California property, the rape of his lover, and his subsequent career as a bandit. This text provides a cautionary contradiction to Pickens's tale, as it illustrates the predatory and often racist appropriation of native people's lands—colonization, in short—that Ridge had already felt personally when the Cherokees were ejected from Georgia, where gold had been discovered on their lands. The ironic repetitions of history are everywhere in his California narrative.

10. For a description of the myth of the biracial plantation as it was employed by U.S. Southern writers during and after Reconstruction, see my essay in *Bridging Southern Cultures* (2006).

11. He would ultimately reverse this position after his trip to Africa—which began in Liberia—in 1859 and 1860. Traveling on to Lagos and the Niger Valley, he and his associate Robert Campbell negotiated treaties with local chieftains enabling settlement of immigrant Americans of color. The onslaught of the Civil War, combined with increasing British colonization of West Africa, brought an end to these plans, however, and after Delany's service in the Union Army—from which he emerged as the first black major—he spent most of the rest of his life in South Carolina, initially working with the Freedmen's Bureau.

12. The fact that Delany relied heavily on Stowe's novel for structure, symbolic scenes, and characters does not mean he admired her overall perspective and achievement; he denounced her as a racist colonizer and bitterly resented the ascendency she enjoyed as a spokesperson for the race.

13. Double-generation predation without incest could occur too. In Delany's own time, the planter James Henry Hammond purchased a female slave, Sally, and her one-year-old daughter, Louisa, making the mother his concubine. His wife, Catherine, tolerated this, until he raped Louisa when she was twelve (Clinton 1991, 62).

14. We remember that Delany once edited a newspaper entitled *The Mystery*, and he may well have intended the ending of the novel (presumed lost) to be inconclusive, a "mystery." Indeed, John Ernest suggests that "what is finally most striking about the work is its air of mystery, of secrets suggested but untold, and of an organization powerful because it is, in fact, and will remain, a secret" (1995, 112).

15. This prefigures the thematic of Toni Morrison's *Beloved* (1987), but also Frank Yerby's *The Foxes of Harrow* (1946), in which a black slave woman from Africa tries to kill herself and her son, Inch, in the river rather than have him raised a slave.

16. The fact that there are four of them suggests a reference to the four evangelists of the New Testament, Matthew, Mark, Luke, and John. Henry's plan is for them to evangelize on every plantation: "Find one good man or woman . . . make them the organizers . . . they in like manner impart it to some other . . . it will spread like small-pox among them" (41). This "contagion of freedom" echoes the method that was used in the Haitian Revolution (1791–1804), which Delany clearly had studied. As we shall see, Delany interbraids references to the Old and New Testaments throughout *Blake*, creating a kind of doubled typology of deliverance and revelation. At this point, we should recall the language of the Ostend Manifesto, which feared the spread of Haitian-style revolution; there the metaphor was of a rampant fire, a stronger strain of Delany's smallpox/contagion metaphor, which is similarly based, in concept, on Haiti, whose revolution will be the focus of the following chapter.

17. Priscilla Wald, concentrating on mythologies and narratives that have been generated by actual epidemics such as typhoid and AIDS, has identified what she calls an "outbreak narrative." Her study, aptly titled *Contagious*, makes the point that "disease emergence dramatizes the dilemma that inspires the most basic of human narratives: the necessity and danger of human contact. . . . The outbreak narrative . . . follows a formulaic plot that begins with the identification of an emerging infection, includes discussion of the global networks through which it travels, and chronicles the epidemiological work that ends with its containment" (2008, 2). In Delany's narrative, these tropes are used by slaves as a metaphor for liberation and revolution and by slave owners as a negative signifier of racial pollution and insurrection. I will return to this doubled signification in the following chapter, as many narratives of the Haitian Revolution employ these images.

18. In a variation on this, Glissant asserts that "Whites in the South detest the Black race but love Negroes, and Whites in the North love the idea of the Black race but neither like nor associate with Negroes" (1999, 85).

19. This action, however, must be inferred—it is not presented—and Bruce A. Harvey has noted that this is, in fact, the only place in the novel where Henry is physically violent. In another passage he even watches passively as his wife is beaten, and he never foments revolt during the slave ship *Vulture*'s cruise. Harvey finds the hero's passivity in these and other episodes curious, in light of *Blake*'s revolutionary rhetoric and project (2001, 233).

20. We also note that Delany once asserted in a lecture that the Masons owed their founding to "a fugitive slave," Moses, who learned all his liberatory lore in African Egypt. Robert Levine has claimed, in fact, that Delany himself, throughout his career, conceived of himself in the tradition of Moses, an idea based on his understanding of Moses as African (1997, 9).

21. Ishmael Reed would use this metaphor in a joyful, mischievous way in his novel *Mumbo Jumbo*, wherein the "Jes Grew epidemic" is a comic vehicle for spreading the popularity of ragtime and jazz during the age of the New Negro. As Reed defines it, "The Jes Grew epidemic was unlike physical plagues. Actually Jes Grew was an anti-plague. Some plagues caused the body to waste away; Jes Grew enlivened

the host" (1972, 6). Reed's narrative links "Jes Grew" with the Caribbean and the black diaspora by considering the protracted U.S. occupation of Haiti. Further, "Jes Grew" begins in New Orleans, just as Henry's major conspiracy does. Like his plot, "Jes Grew" is viewed as a pollution and a threat by white culture.

22. For a recent and compelling analysis of the "swamp sublime" and its connection to maroon communities, see Allewaert (2008). We will return to her theories in a later chapter.

23. As Rodrigo Lazo notes, this event led to the exile/flight of many educated Cubans, many of them settling in New Orleans and New York. Well-to-do Cubans had been vacationing in the United States for some time, and many sent their children to the United States for an education. Conversely, Cuba was a popular vacation spot for Americans, particularly invalids, and many American writers wrote about their experiences there, in memoirs and novels, including William Henry Hurlbert, Mary Peabody Mann, and Julia Ward Howe (2005, 9).

24. For a complementary and helpful reading of both Plácido's works and his sometimes covert revolutionary stance, see Kutzinski (1993, 81–100).

25. José Limón has recently theorized that recoveries of folklore like this "may be seen as going beyond simple group affirmation to embody an imminent critique of capitalist modernity, racism and gender relations," even though they may further eroticize notions of primitivism, although from a positive stance (2000, 32).

26. This scene offers a horrifying expansion of similar incidents that were well known and echoes a famous painting by J. M. W. Turner, *Slavers Throwing Overboard the Dead and Dying: Typhoon Coming On (The Slave Ship)*, which John Ruskin owned. It was exhibited at the Royal Academy in 1840; Ruskin eventually sold it after finding it too painful to view. Now at the Museum of Fine Arts in Boston, it was based upon the 1781 tragedy of the slave ship *Zong*, whose captain had thrown 132 sick and dying slaves into the sea in order to collect insurance money. This atrocity led to a famous trial. For details of the incident and its consequences, legal and otherwise, see Baucom (2005, passim). The *Zong* massacre figures in several other novels, including Michelle Cliff's *Abeng* (1984) and Barry Unsworth's *Sacred Hunger* (1992), and in NourbeSe Philip's epic poem *Zong!* (2008).

27. Nevertheless, Carla L. Peterson has criticized Delany's hyper-masculine stance—and the relative weakness of his female characters—as a sign of his fixation on models of white capitalist production. She also asserts that African American women of the time had little interest in leaving the United States for an uncertain future in Africa (1995, 113–18).

28. This, in fact, is a variant on the scripture (Psalms 68:31), which reads, "Princes shall come out of Egypt; Ethiopia shall soon stretch out her hands unto God." Changing the words underlines the fact that, until now, the prophecy has not been fulfilled, but that it is inevitable. Ethiopian culture was a central subject in Pauline Hopkins's *Of One Blood; or, The Hidden Self* (1903), which concerns an archaeologist's expedition, during which he learns that he is a descendant of an Ethiopian culture, which then proclaims him king and marries him to the virgin Candace. This story, as Martin

Japtok argues, becomes problematic through Hopkins's fall into what he calls "the Darwinist trap," that is, judging the Africans as less "developed" because of their lack of technological and cultural accomplishments (2002, passim). I would add, however, that the novel's placement of its hero as king of the people, like *Blake* and William Walker's narrative, also argues for Western "correction" through Western "control," and at the very top, be it by white or black scientists/military figures.

29. This became obvious historically in mid-century. In light of the links between the stories of Narciso Lopez and Henry Blake, it is fascinating to note Delany's acknowledgment—through the quoted white "expert"—of the effect of Lopez on Spanish authorities. "In 1849, Roncall, the Captain General then in power, took advantage of the Dia de los Reyes to give the Creoles of Cuba a significant hint of what they might expect from the government if they gave any alarming degree of aid to the revolutionary operations of General Lopez. He prolonged for three days the privilege of the day to the Mucumis, the most warlike of the tribes of the African slaves in Cuba. . . . Many a Creole family shuddered . . . at the fearful illustration thus exhibited under their eyes of the standing threat that Cuba must be Spanish or African" (1859, 302).

Chapter 3

1. Glissant also approves the 1976 Caribbean Festival's organization around circumCaribbean heroes Toussaint-Louverture, José Martí, Benito Juárez, Simón Bolivar, and Marcus Garvey (1989, 67). Clearly, the ways in which Caribbean history has been shattered by Western institutions through the device of separation—that is, the forced creation of national rather than regional histories—has forestalled the potential power of a circumCaribbean historical foundation based on struggles with regional implications, such as those in Haiti, rather than forcing Barbadians to valorize British national heroes or Guadeloupeans to fixate on French epic narratives. But the list of heroes of the region also includes the great leaders of the U.S. civil rights movement, who inspired the rebels and people of the circumCaribbean as well, figures such as Andrew Young, Stokely Carmichael, Malcolm X, Angela Davis, Ralph Abernathy, Rosa Parks, Fannie Lou Hamer, Coretta Scott King, and Martin Luther King. As this grouping suggests, circumCaribbean unity often actually means black diasporic unity as well.

2. Throughout this chapter, I will rely on the many excellent histories of the Haitian Revolution that have been published in the past few decades. Laurent Dubois's several books on this subject, especially his magisterial studies, *A Colony of Citizens: Revolution and Slave Emancipation in the French Caribbean, 1787–1804* (2004), and *Avengers of the New World: The Story of the Haitian Revolution* (2004) forcefully present the importance of this monumental event in Caribbean, hemispheric, and world history, particularly in terms of the ways it reshaped discussion of basic human rights and the nature of social constructs and the ways in which it affected political and social events in the decades and centuries to come.

3. The original Western (French) description of vodoun was provided in Moreau de Saint-Méry's *Description topographique, physique, civil, politique et historique de la partie française de l'isle de Saint-Domingue* (1797). For influential modern readings, see Alfred Métraux (1959), Maya Deren (1953), Joan Dayan (1995, but also 1997), and especially Margarite Fernández Olmos and Lizabeth Paravisini-Gebert's edited volume, *Sacred Possessions* (1997). For a presentation of the African origins of New World African religions, see Thornton (1992, 235–71). Keith Cartwright's study of African elements in New World literature has much to say on this subject as well (2002).

4. This often-reported horror has been questioned by recent historians but was repeatedly presented as factual by earlier scholars. Madison Smartt Bell employs it as a key symbol in his trilogy, although he has acknowledged, in a recent interview, that he now understands that it may be mythical.

5. We now know that this narrative, previously attributed to Hannah, was the work of Leonora Sansay, Aaron Burr's mistress, who also wrote a novel based on the Haitian Revolution, *Zelica, the Creole: A Novel in Three Volumes* (London, 1820). For an extended reading of *Secret History*, see Michael Drexler (2003, 184–93). Smith-Rosenberg similarly explicates *Zelica* in *This Violent Empire* (2010, 441–64).

6. South Carolina's senator Robert Y. Hayne stated in 1824, "We never can acknowledge her [Haiti's] independence . . . which the peace and safety of a large portion of our union forbids us even to discuss" (Schmidt 1971, 28).

7. For an account of Saint Domingue's contribution to the American Revolution, see Steward (1899).

8. Indeed, for decades, historians have stated that Charles Deslondes was originally enslaved in Haiti. However, Gwendolyn Midlo Hall has recently proven that he was a Louisiana Creole (2007, 14).

9. Between 1840 and 1860, many of these figures established connections with Haiti and with leading figures in Africa, an early example of the Pan-Africanism Du Bois would later espouse, but in a more revolutionary mode (Genovese 1972, 97). Equally important, however, is Genovese's extensive documentation of the wide effect the revolt in Saint Domingue had for decades across the entire circumCaribbean.

10. We will remember Gayarré's "call" for a contemporary Scott later in this chapter when we turn to Madison Smartt Bell, whose historical fiction has powerfully commemorated the Haitian Revolution for readers everywhere.

11. This poignant description of the breaking of family ties echoes scenes of separation among the enslaved that abolitionists used in their campaigns.

12. King's origins in French Creole society and fluency in French made her aware of the Francophone diaspora in the New World, and her often sympathetic portrait of black Southerners linked her to fellow realists and influences William Dean Howells, Charles Dudley Warner, and Mark Twain.

13. Only a few years after *The Grandissimes* appeared, Maturin M. Ballou, who had already published *Due West; or, Round the World in Ten Months*, turned out *Due South; or, Cuba Past and Present* (1885). The book is based on an extensive trip the writer

made to the circumCaribbean, including the Bahamas, Veracruz, Trinidad, and other locations. Ballou is advised, however, to avoid "Hayti" by a "compagnon du voyage" who had lived in Port-au-Prince for two years: "'I advise you to avoid Hayti.' . . . He fully confirmed the reports of its barbarous condition, and declared it to be in a rapid decadence. . . . Voudou worship and cannibalism are quite common" (1885, 27).

14. As we shall see in a subsequent chapter, Cable's deep involvement in investigative reporting (which for a while brought him into regular contact with another Louisiana writer we will consider, Lafcadio Hearn) gave his writing a singular degree of realistic detail but also furnished him with an invigorating sense of social injustice. Both are present in his superb short story collection, *Old Creole Days* (1879), too often dismissed as mere "local color." Most of these stories, which I cannot examine here, are studded with references to the many Caribbean elements that were present in Cable's New Orleans.

15. The application of postcolonial theory to Southern/Caribbean literature is being explored by numerous scholars, many of whom met at a pathbreaking conference in Puerto Vallarta in 2002. Their papers appear in *Mississippi Quarterly* 56, no. 4, and 57, no. 1 (2003–4). My own essay, "Reconstruction Revisited: Plantation School Writers, Postcolonial Theory, and Confederates in Brazil," in *Mississippi Quarterly* 57, no. 1 (2003–4):5–26, suggests the possibilities of such an approach.

16. John Stuart Mill noted that Britain's colonies "are hardly to be looked upon as countries, carrying on an exchange of commodities with other countries, but more properly as outlying agricultural or manufacturing estates belonging to a larger community. Our West Indian colonies, for example, cannot be regarded as countries with a productive capital of their own. . . . [They are] the place where England finds it convenient to carry on the production of sugar, coffee and a few other tropical commodities. . . . The trade with the West Indies is hardly to be considered an external trade, but more resembles the traffic between town and country" (1965, 693).

17. My extended reading of both O'Neill's play and the screenplay that was created by the Charlestonian DuBose Heyward has appeared in *Philological Quarterly* (Lowe 2011). The film *The Emperor Jones* fascinates in that Heyward created a new first half that demonstrates the profoundly Southern heritage of the title character. The constant drumbeat of the play would also be used by Arna Bontemps in his novel about the Haitian Revolution, *Drums at Dusk* (1939). Like *The Free Flag of Cuba* and *Blake*, the film's first part is largely set in the U.S. South; the second part takes place in the Caribbean, the sole site of the original play.

18. Hurston was extremely well prepared for this research by her graduate work at Columbia University, where she was famously trained in anthropology during the 1920s by the founding father and mother of American anthropology, Franz Boas of Columbia and Ruth Benedict of Barnard. Hurston also had a course at Columbia under Melville Herskovits, who had done extensive research on the Caribbean's link to Africa; he would later author the seminal text *Life in a Haitian Valley*, which was published in 1937, the same year of Hurston's *Their Eyes Were Watching God*. Field work in the U.S. South (mostly in Louisiana and Florida) collecting African American

folklore and learning the intricacies of hoodoo was also invaluable preparation for Hurston's subsequent Caribbean research.

19. William Safran, writing in the first issue of *Diaspora* on "Diasporas in Modern Societies: Myths of Homeland and Return" (1991), begins with a basic unit, which he defines as "expatriate minority communities." Of course he is thinking of actual physical separation—often a far distance—between the subject people and the homeland. Safran then posits that diasporas are 1) dispersed from an original center to at least two "peripheral" places; 2) they maintain a "memory vision, or myth about their original homeland"; 3) they "believe they are not—and perhaps cannot be—fully accepted by their host country"; 4) they "see the ancestral home as a place of eventual return, when the time is right"; 5) they are "committed to the maintenance or restoration of this homeland"; and 6) their consciousness and solidarity as a group are "importantly defined" by this continuing relationship with the homeland (1991, 83–84).

20. For a helpful description of the U.S. occupation of Haiti, see chapter 5 of David Nicholls's study *From Dessalines to Duvalier* (1979). The definitive study, however, is Mary Renda's *Taking Haiti* (2001).

21. For a devastating critique of Hurston's attitude in *Tell My Horse*, see J. Michael Dash (1997, 58–60).

22. For an extensive reading of the novel, see my *Jump at the Sun: Zora Neale Hurston's Cosmic Comedy* (1994).

23. For an excellent complementary discussion of Johnson's connections to the Caribbean, see Keith Cartwright's *Sacral Grooves, Limbo Gateways* (2013, 66–83), which appeared too recently for full consideration here.

24. Georges Biassou has recently received attention from the historian Jane Landers, who corrects several misunderstandings about him, partly through a reading of a French captive in Biassou's camp, one M. Gros, who remarked on the African's apparent devotion to Catholicism and his orderly camp, which segued into the military precision of Toussaint, who began his military career as Biassou's camp physician. Ultimately, Biassou and Toussaint parted company when the latter deserted the Spanish forces they had both served to return to the French troops. When the Spanish forced black Haitians out, Biassou and his band migrated to St. Augustine, Florida. Here the exiled leader strutted through the streets in his fancy uniforms and medals. He was maintained until his death by the Spanish crown, established a plantation, and married his son to a leading black family of the town. When Biassou died suddenly, he was given an elaborate Catholic funeral, which was attended by the Florida governor (Landers 2010, 65–93).

25. For an informative and persuasive defense of *Drums at Dusk*, see Michael P. Bibler and Jessica Adams's introduction to their new edition of the novel (2009).

26. James had been influenced by the important demographic and cultural influences Haitian immigrants had on his island after the Haitian Revolution and beyond.

27. For a devastating critique of the effacement of Martinique's history through the imposition of that of France, see Glissant (1989, especially 88–95).

28. Roland Barthes has commented on the interplay between history and narrative, stating, "The narration of past events, commonly subject in our culture, since the Greeks, to the sanction of historical 'science,' placed under the imperious warrant of the 'real,' justified by principles of 'rational' exposition—does this narration differ, in fact, by some specific feature, by an indubitable pertinence, from imaginary narration as we find it in epic, the novel, the drama?" (1986, 127).

29. It is worth noting, however, that the most admired fictional treatment of the Haitian Revolution before Bell's was Carpentier's *The Kingdom of This World* (1949), and he too was a white writer. Bell has stated that he read this text only after completing *All Souls' Rising,* but there are indeed definite influences from Carpentier in *Master of the Crossroads* (2000).

30. It should be noted, however, that Walcott's *Henri Christophe* concerns the fate of Haiti after Toussaint's capture and death, detailing the intrigues that led to the monarchies of first Dessalines and then Christophe. Bell's trilogy ends with the establishment of the republic in 1804.

31. Riau also has many affinities with Carpentier's Ti Noel, the central figure in *The Kingdom of This World,* even though Bell, as noted, said he did not read that novel until after he completed *All Souls Rising.*

32. A cluster of essays discussing Bell's trilogy—positively—appeared in the key Caribbean journal *Small Axe* in 2007; contributors were Laurent Dubois, Charles Forsdick, Martin Munro, and Marie-José Nzengou-Tayo, all experts on Haitian literature and culture.

33. Riau, who consistently offers an African perspective, in passing tells us of Macandal, the Guinea-born poisoner who attempted the first insurrection in 1757. Clearly repeating a mythic narrative that has come down to him through his culture, Riau rehearses the scene on the LeNormand plantation when Macandal had his arm destroyed by the sugarcane press. Here his view "from below" usefully complements the account "from above" of the black rebel Oge's end, by Maltrot. As early as 1870, the Macandal legend was codified (in French) by Marie Joséphine Augustin, in her *Le Macandal.*

34. The roles of the *gros-bon-ange* and *ti-bon-ange* in Haitian culture are explained by Maya Deren in her *Divine Horsemen* (1953, 26). Bell would later expand on this in volumes 2 and 3, where *The Kingdom of This World*'s, Ti Noël's story parallels Riau's in many ways.

35. As Maya Deren tells us, many accounts of the vodoun rite that generated the Haitian Revolution state that an old black woman appeared, who sacrificed the black pig. She may have been the original Marinette, or the horse of that figure, who is the major goddess of terror in the Petro nation. The ritual is clearly Petro, both because it is conducted to foster death and because pig sacrifices are Petro (1953, 63n).

36. Bell intends to dramatize what C. L. R. James asserted in 1938: "The slaves destroyed tirelessly . . . the destruction of what they knew was the cause of their sufferings; and if they destroyed much it was because they had suffered much. They knew that as long as these plantations stood their lot would be to labour on them

until they dropped. The only thing to do was destroy them. From their masters they had known rape, torture, degradation, and, at the slightest provocation, death. They returned in kind" (1938, 88).

37. This aspect of the trilogy ought to give pause to the minority of critics who chastised Bell for not going to Haiti before starting his epic. As I have noted earlier, the physical world of the late eighteenth century re-created here has very little to do with today's island, which has been almost completely denuded of its once lush jungle foliage and rich fields.

38. For a chilling account of Jeannot's reign of terror, see Dubois (2004, 102–9). Joan Dayan explains this manifestation of Erzulie (1995, 63, 64).

39. This moving utterance, however, is based in a misunderstanding Bell had when writing the first book. Toussaint, born in Saint Domingue, was in fact free and owned slaves of his own, which Bell has incorporated into his subsequently published biography of Louverture. Of course we can still read this, however, as a misunderstanding on Riau's part.

40. Riau's literacy and obvious gift for narrative should be configured with Ishmael Reed's remark at the beginning of this chapter: "Guede got people to write."

Chapter 4

1. For an excellent and detailed discussion of the creation and publishing history of *Picturesque America* and of Woolson's various contributions to that volume, see Sue Rainey's *Creating Picturesque America* (1994).

2. For my extended analysis of the various accounts of travel on the Oklawaha that were written during the late nineteenth century, see my essay in Hobson and Ladd (forthcoming).

3. For the story of Confederates in Brazil, see my "Reconstruction Revisited" (2003–4).

4. Harilaos Stecopoulos has shown that the Southern states after the Civil War became the first colony of the North, and that methods employed in this venture led to subsequent colonization, particularly during and after the Spanish American War (2008, 3–4, 37–39).

5. Because of space limitations, I will not consider Woolson's other circum-Caribbean texts, the novels *Jupiter Lights* (1889), which takes place on an island off the Georgia coast, and *Horace Chase* (1894), which sets many scenes in St. Augustine.

6. Minorcans had been imported as indentured servants to work on indigo plantations as early as 1768. By the middle of the nineteenth century, they were a sizable minority of the St. Augustine area's population (Gannon 1996, 214, 392).

7. The thematic of consumptive Northerners coming to Florida in a desperate effort to shake their disease has a parallel in Louisiana literature around New Orleans, as there was a leper colony there in Carville, and leprosy has a similar role to play in one of George Washington Cable's classic stories, "Jean An-Poqueline" (1883), also a tale centered on one strong brother and one afflicted brother, who are devoted to

each other. They too live on the edge of a swamp, which eventually is drained as New Orleans advances. Since Woolson's story was published first, one wonders if there was an influence on Cable.

8. Here Woolson rehearses the thematic from Melville's great chapter in *Moby-Dick*, "The Mast-Head," where Ishmael warns "pantheists" at watch atop a ship against dreamily gazing at a moonlit sea and then falling to their deaths. Similarly, in a brilliant reading of the naturalist William Bartram's travels across the tropical South in the late eighteenth century, M. Allewaert notes how Bartram often "experienced his entanglement in the lowlands as a pleasurable loss of self" (2008, 342). This seems true for Carl as well, and, to a certain extent, for characters in Woolson's *East Angels*, as we shall see.

9. DeLoughrey, Gosson, and Handley's edited volume, *Caribbean Literature and the Environment* (2005), could profit from a consideration of writers such as Woolson and Hearn, who, though not Caribbean themselves, are detailing, with both admiration and repulsion, a topography that clearly must be considered, especially as Florida has become more, rather than less, Caribbean in both population and culture.

10. This figure is strongly predictive of Faulkner's Sam Fathers in *Go Down, Moses*, also a triracial hunter, guide, and spiritual reader of the wilderness.

11. These languages by no means remain pure; the hybrid/Caribbean aspect of Gracias-a-Dios culture is suggested in Woolson's description of the fishermen's language: "Their English was by no means clear, it was mixed with Spanish and West Indian, with words borrowed from the not remote African of the Florida negro, and even with some from the native Indian tongues; it was a very patchwork of languages" (180). The metaphor is an interesting one, in that this patchwork—a quilt—forms a unity, in fact a useful one. The reference is not to Babel or impurities, but rather to creative creolizations of language.

12. The Winthrops seemingly have a passion for travel. Evert, a veteran of the Civil War, has wandered widely in Europe; Mrs. Rutherford, Evert's aunt, has spent years traversing that continent and the Middle East; her husband, Evert, had gone to Central America and studied Aztec culture. However, the current Evert has a rather jaundiced view of travelers. Thinking of his aunt, he speculates that her visit to Florida "wore much of the air of an exploring expedition, the kind of tour through remote regions that people made sometimes, and then wrote books about—books with a great many illustrations" (65), Woolson's perhaps wry and self-mocking commentary on her own travel writing.

13. At another point, when Lucian Spenser brings his new wife, Rosalie, to East Angels, she refuses to see Garda as a Southerner: "Miss Thorne is Spanish . . . she doesn't come under the term southerner, as I use it, at all" (301). But Woolson clearly sees all her East Angels figures as Southern, including her criollos.

14. We should note, however, that the price may be due to the times. Garda hardly makes Florida attractive to Winthrop, for she states that cultivation of cotton and cane is impossible now without slaves, and that the new industry of orange growing would require advisers, who are not yet present. Moreover, there is the heat,

the swamps, the snakes. The first set of conditions, however, is due to the war and Reconstruction.

15. The recurring motif of contagion and infection that we have noted throughout this study in terms of African influences has special relevance to the damning charge of "indolence." J. M. Coetzee comments on the habit European travelers had of condemning the Boer settlers of South Africa, whose sloth "stand[s] for a rejection of the curse of discipline and labour in favour of an African way of life in which the fruits of the earth are enjoyed as they drop into the hand, work is avoided, as an evil, and leisure and idleness become the same thing" (1988, 44). Further, the reference to the untapped mineral resources that the natives have proven incapable of developing is an uncanny forerunner of the recent conversation about Afghanistan's vast mineral resources, also "neglected" and presumably ripe for development by Western industrial powers.

16. Here we recall the relevance of Pratt's extended observations on this topic, which I cited in the chapter on the Mexican American War.

17. Glissant puts this kind of contrast another way: "The forest of the maroon was thus the first obstacle the slave opposed to the *transparency* of the planter. There is no clear path, no *way forward*, in this density. You turn in obscure circles until you find the primordial tree. The formulation of history's yearned-for ideal, so tied up with its difficulty, introduces us to the dilemma of peoples today still oppressed by dominant cultures" (1989, 83).

18. In this respect, the narrative at this point recalls the roles played by Humphrey Bogart and Katherine Hepburn in the 1951 film *The African Queen*, another fated love story played out during a dangerous swamp voyage.

19. Katherine Swett reads this scene productively and suggests that it echoes the repressed sexuality present in Isabel Archer's erotic confrontations with Caspar Goodwood in Henry James's *The Portrait of a Lady* (1881). I believe the parallel is even stronger with the similarly configured relation of Christopher Newman and Claire de Cintré in James's earlier novel, *The American* (1877).

20. *Gombo Zhèbes* (1885) was one of three books Hearn brought out on New Orleans lore, hoping to capitalize on the crowds thronging to the city's Cotton Exposition of 1884. The others were *La Cuisine Creole* and *The Historical Sketch Book and Guide to New Orleans* (both 1885). Unfortunately, delays in printing led to publication after fairgoers had departed (Tinker 1925, 183). Professor William Henry headed a boy's school and was an expert on Creole patois. Alfred Mercier was an important Creole/Francophone writer; his most notable novel was *Habitation Saint-Ybars* (1881). Louis Claudel was a member of an old Creole family who had many anecdotes. Charles Gayarré was in his lifetime the most important historian of New Orleans culture.

21. Indeed, when Hearn finally got to St. Pierre, he wrote to his friend Elizabeth Bisland: "Imagine Old New Orleans, the dear quaint part of it, young and idealized . . . made all tropical . . . climbing the side of a volcanic peak . . . or descending in terraces . . . to the sea. . . . Fancy our Creole courts filled with giant mangoes and

columnar palms . . . everybody in a costume of more than Oriental picturesque-ness; — and astonishments of half-breed beauty" (Bisland 1906, 1:412).

22. Krehbiel prospered in New York and eventually published over twenty-five volumes of music criticism, including an admired three-volume biography of Beethoven. Like Hearn, he traveled to the Far East and wrote about its musical traditions. Throughout his long career (he died in 1923), he was fascinated by Creole and black diasporic cultural productions; one of his books was *Afro-American Folksongs* (1914). For more details, see Frost (1958, 164–69).

23. Hearn expressed his admiration for Gottschalk in a letter to Krehbiel in 1885: "I would touch upon the transplantation of negro melody to the Antilles and the two Americas, where its strangest black flowers are gathered by the alchemists of musical science, and the perfume thereof extracted by magicians like Gottschalk" (Bisland 1906, 1:356). For an excellent biography of Gottschalk, which explicates his circum-Caribbean aspects, see Starr (1995).

24. Hearn always yearned to visit Cuba and saw its African aspects as a key component of what we now call the African diaspora. His friend Dr. Mata had told him about the rich tradition of Cuban music and its strongly African heritage, which Mata claimed was also the case in Mexico (Bisland 1906, 1:380).

25. Hearn often equates the sense of the divine with landscape painting, particularly that of Claude Lorrain and Salvator Rosa, whose majestic canvases were also decidedly classically romantic. It should be noted that Claude Lorrain was also a favorite of Melville, who shared a similar sense of the sublime with Hearn.

26. As Hearn was well aware, however, Francophone researchers had already paved the way for him. He told Krehbiel of reading La Selve's study of "negro-creole dances and songs of the Antilles." He had also been enjoying French works on the Senegal griots and African music, including Jeannest's "Au Congo," Marche's "Afrique Occidentale," and Turiault's "Etude sur la Language Créole de la Martinique" (Bisland 1906, 1:353–54, 357).

27. This fascination with the myriad shades of Caribbean blue has a contemporary counterpart. In Cristina García's first novel, *Dreaming in Cuban* (1992), Pilar, an artist, sees light as the embodiment of the color blue and states: "Until I returned to Cuba, I never realized how many blues exist. The aquamarines near the shoreline, the azures of deeper waters, the eggshell blues beneath my grandmother's eyes, the fragile indigos tracking her hands. There's blue, too, in the curves of the palms, and the edges of the words we speak, a blue tinge to the sand and the seashells and the plumb gulls on the beach. The mole by Abuela's mouth is also blue, a vanishing blue" (233).

28. The trope of the sensual, lithe, and accommodating native woman of the tropics was an early signifier of the tourist industry. Adam Rothman perceptively observes that while Hearn shares the masculinist-imperialist mode of perceiving native women, his accompanying presentation of the feminized tropical landscape varies, in that other male writers see the islands as ripe for conquest and possession, while Hearn describes his passive "surrender to tropical nature's seductive, stupefying feminine power" (2008, 274).

29. During the swamp journey Margaret and Winthrop undertake in *East Angels*, they look inside a dilapidated hut. In the moonlight, Winthrop sees hundreds of writhing snakes and, ultimately, the bones of a dead man, a telling example of Woolson's expert use of gothic imagery, combining the haunted, isolated, ruined "castle," threatening, smothering nature, and darkness, death, and the threat of death. Woolson was far more adventurous in the wild than was Hearn. She tirelessly explored the swamps and was quite fascinated by snakes.

30. Hearn's transformation of a disability into an asset finds a parallel in Woolson's deafness, which, as we have seen, led her to see the benefits of silence.

31. Before Burke, Addison, speaking of monumentality, had claimed that "everything that is majestic, imprints an awfulness and reverence on the mind of the beholder, and strikes in with the natural greatness of the soul" (1970, 188).

32. Aravamudan asserts that by "demonstrating the pathological within the normative, theories of sublimity unite experience and ontology." Speaking of a boy whose sight was restored, he refines what the subject's sense of "delight" actually constituted, in that "delight is Burke's technical term for the relief from pain that is not the same as positive pleasure." Thus, when Hearn "delights" in tropical splendors that are simultaneously threatening, he is experiencing the Burkean dichotomy of the "perceptible sublime" and "the barely perceptible abject" (1999, 197).

33. The fiery eruption of volcanoes had a far more common parallel in the flooding and winds of hurricanes. As Hearn states in a footnote, the great storm of 1780 killed over 22,000 inhabitants of Martinique, St. Vincent, St. Lucia, and Barbados (140n1). A third menace of the islands is subsequently introduced: small pox, or *la vérette,* which can similarly wipe out thousands in only a few days. Readers in the U.S. South might not have experienced volcanoes, but they certainly knew about floods, hurricanes, and epidemics, particularly in the New Orleans Hearn had just left behind. All of these catastrophic disturbances are sites of the tropical sublime.

34. Hearn died only three years after the eruption and in 1903 wrote from Tokyo to his friend Ellwood Hendrick, who had sent him numerous newspaper clippings about the disaster. Hearn refers to the eruption as that "black day" (Bisland 1906, 2:484). Bisland noted, from her perspective in 1906, that Hearn's account of the city as he knew it comprised a "minute and astonishing record of the town and the population, now as deeply buried and utterly obliterated as was Pompeii." She projects forward to speculate on how valuable an archaeologist of the future might find this guide to a lost civilization (1:98).

35. In the sketch "Los Criollos" (1877), Hearn had remarked on the "colored Creole" community of New Orleans, "who still teach their children the songs—heirlooms of melody resonant with fetich words—threads of tune strung with *grisgris* from the Ivory Coast"; their "love philters hinted at in Creole ballads, and the deadly *ouanga* art as bequested to modern Voudooism by the black Locustas of the eighteenth century" (in *Inventing New Orleans*, 2001, 38).

36. This hymn to the original primitive beauty of the earth, a remnant of which is found in Martinique, has an echo in Woolson. In "The South Devil," she writes,

"The atmosphere was hot, and heavy with perfumes. It was the heart of the swamp, a riot of intoxicating, steaming, swarming, fragrant, beautiful, tropical life, without man to make or mar it. All the world was once so, before man was made" ([1880] 1886, 191–92).

37. This language—sensual and related to appetite—speaks to Hearn's lifelong preference for mixed-race women. Ironically, one of his early biographers used this aspect of Hearn to orientalize *him*: "The fancy for mulattos, Creoles and orientals, which he displayed all his life, is most likely to be accounted for as an inheritance from his Arabian and oriental ancestors on his mother's side. He but took up the dropped threads of his barbaric ancestry" (Kinnard 1912, 84).

38. Such passages align Hearn with the many Western writers who, as Edward Said has so memorably demonstrated in *Orientalism*, created a discourse of the Other, one that was useful for "dominating, restructuring, and having authority over the Orient" (1979, 3).

39. Hearn's friendship with the puritanical Gould, like that with Krehbiel, ended badly, and Gould later wrote a very long and quite venomous biography of the writer, stating baldly: "Hearn, mentally and spiritually, was most perfectly an echo. . . . He invented nothing. . . . [His] only originality was colour—a particular derivation of a maimed sense. . . . [He had] a lot of heathenish and unrestrained appetites" (1908, xiii).

40. This prophecy has relevance to Bell's mulatto character Choufleur, whose story, as we have seen, follows this script.

41. Here again we see Hearn's typical mix of attraction and repulsion, a dynamic that gave him a desired frisson. As he wrote in a letter during his New Orleans days, "I have pledged me to the worship of the Odd, the Queer, the Strange, the Exotic, the Monstrous. It quite suits my temperament. . . . Enormous and lurid facts are certainly worthy of more artistic study than they generally receive" (Bisland 1906, 1:328–29).

42. Hearn's early biographer, Nina H. Kinnard (1912), who was more familiar than we are with the popular literature of his time, compares the style of *Two Years in the French West Indies* to that in James Froude's *West Indies* and Sir Frederick Kreves's *Cradle of the Deep*.

43. A fascinated Hearn began a correspondence with Loti, who sent his note-books for Hearn to translate and publish in the *New Orleans Times-Democrat*, pieces that helped solidify Hearn's reputation (Temple 1974, 71), as they simultaneously acquainted him with an exotic style that he would employ in the tropics further south. Even after his move to Japan, Hearn followed Loti's strange career, extolling him as "the best writer of prose of any country in this world . . . a marvelous genius" (Bisland 1906, 2:385). For an excellent examination of Loti's bizarre life and florid writings, see Blanch (2004). A consideration of the links between Hearn and Loti would clearly confirm many of the points Elizabeth DeLoughrey has recently made about connections between the literatures and histories of the Caribbean and the Pacific in her study *Routes and Roots* (2007).

44. Writing to Krehbiel after his initial trip to the Caribbean, Hearn claims that his

trip was largely motivated by "the new style of Pierre Loti—that young marine officer who is certainly the most original of living French novelists" (Bisland 1906, 1:334).

45. While in New Orleans, Hearn translated six of Gautier's short stories, which were published under the title *One of Cleopatra's Nights* in 1882.

46. Hearn, like many travel writers before him—including Melville, whose *Typee* and *Omoo* were similarly constructed—obviously wrote with prior accounts of the island before him. Later in the narrative, he comments appreciatively on the earlier narratives of Père Du Tertre, Thibault de Chanvalon, the historian Dr. Etienne Rufz De Lavison, and others.

47. In such passages, Hearn refuses to accept the notion that Martinique's culture is that of the "motherland," France. His reconstruction of island history involves French figures like Père Labat, but he situates them as participants in the island's troubled history, rather than that of France. Woolson, similarly, took pains—especially in her travel narratives like "The Oklawaha"—to contradict the idea that the tropics are "blank" and have no meaningful human history. In that sketch, "the General" reconstructs the details of the Seminole War, paying tribute to the courage and cultures of both the Native Americans and the Union soldiers.

48. Hearn heard these reports from his servants in *Two Years in the French West Indies* (1890) but does not offer his own interpretation of the zombie. Years later, however, in Japan, Hearn wrote of touring Martinique with Louis, a "half breed" guide; one night they are awakened by the apparent visit in their room of an immensely tall woman, a zombie. Hearn presents this visitation ambiguously, as a dream that perhaps was not a dream. The passage resembles Hurston's encounter with a zombie in *Tell My Horse* (1938). Hearn's tale appears in *Exotics and Retrospectives in Ghostly Japan* (1923), 193–204 (under the title "Vespertina Cognitio").

49. This syndrome is most pronounced in melodrama, as in William Hill Brown's 1789 American novel *The Power of Sympathy*, Cirillo Villaverde's Cuban classic *Cecilia Valdés* (1882), and William Faulkner's *Absalom, Absalom!* (1936), where men and women who have the same father but different mothers are raised apart, meet, and fall in love through what Brown called the "power of sympathy," which in some ways bears a kinship to narcissism.

50. Hearn's eclectic library in New Orleans included books on Senegambian culture, which he declared threw "a torrent of light on the whole history of the songs and superstitions of American slaves" (cited in McWilliams 1946, 163).

51. Engravings were an essential element in travel writing of the time. King's *Great South* included over 430 (Greeson 2006, 498). Woolson's travel articles similarly featured detailed engravings.

52. Cyrillia's instruction and tales, along with her sexual bond with Hearn, situate her as satisfying Hearn's enactment of "reciprocity," that is, an exchange between cultures, which was often enfolded, in earlier tropical zone romances and travel accounts, with an amorous relationship between a white man and a native woman. As Peter Hulme has noted, such plots substitute sex for slavery, expressing "the ideal of cultural harmony through romance" (1987, 141). Mary Louise Pratt (who discusses

reciprocity from several angles (1992, 69–85) comments that these "romances" always break down, and Hearn deserts Cyrillia when he leaves the island, just as Colonel Pinkerton leaves Butterfly in Puccini's opera, the "type" of this genre. Hearn was also familiar with Pierre Loti's many variations on this, especially in his previously cited autobiographical novel, *Tahiti: The Marriage of Loti*. Cyrillia's relation with Hearn is the subject of Ina Césaire's *Moi, Cyrilia* (2009).

53. Indeed, much later in Japan (in 1898), Hearn asserted, "I find that, with the exception of West-Indian and a few New Orleans experiences, I remember nothing agreeable" (Bisland 1906, 2:398).

54. Such passages were not entirely consonant with Hearn's actual experiences. A local doctor, J. J. Cornilliac, a profound student of the Antilles, its culture and history, had a superb library, which he made available. Further, Hearn's bitterness about the lack of interest in literature could stem from the prolonged periods when he had no money coming in from his writing. At one point, his landlady was getting ready to throw him out into the street and take his property. He was saved, however, by a timely loan from the notary Léopold Arnoux (to whom *Two Years* is dedicated). Similarly, when Hearn fell ill of the fever, local Creoles nursed him back to health.

55. As Natalie Ring explains in her excellent essay on the tropical south, Huntington linked the U.S. South with the Caribbean and Latin America, thereby creating a miasmic and energy-sapping new region (2003, 619–20). For an expanded version of her argument, see her equally impressive volume *The Problem South* (2012).

56. This story of "Lys" was in fact a fragment from an entire novel that Hearn had written but was never able to place. It concluded with "Lys" dying of tuberculosis, longing for her tropical home (Tinker 1925, 291–22).

57. As he wrote to Krehbiel in 1885, Grand Isle had "a hybrid population from all the ends of heaven, white, yellow, red, brown, cinnamon-colour, and tints of bronze and gold. Basques, Andalusians, Portuguese, Malays, Chinamen, etc." (Bisland 1906, 1:350).

58. Hearn clearly saw a link between the tropical countries where yellow fever predominated. Writing to Krehbiel after "Yellow Jack" hit New Orleans in 1878, he thought he might have acquired immunity and therefore "could now live in Havana or Vera Cruz without fear of the terrible fevers which prevail there" (Bisland 1906, 1:195). This returns us to the triangular circumCaribbean nexus of the Mexican War, but also to Hearn's long-felt desire to leave New Orleans in pursuit of the even more tropical South of the South, which he saw not as necessarily different, but as a more intense and therefore more fascinating version of Louisiana.

59. At least one of Hearn's critics, Nina H. Kinnard, has claimed that Hearn heard the story that is the basic narrative of *Chita* from Dr. Matas, and, indeed, the book is dedicated to him. Later critics, however, such as Cott, argued that Cable was the source (Kinnard 1912, 102; Cott 1990, 193). Jean Temple states, in fact, that Cable was so angry when *Chita* came out using a story line he had shared with Hearn at a dinner party, that their relationship was ended (Temple 1974, 73). In any case, Hearn stated that "Chita was founded on the fact of a child saved from the Lost Island disaster

by some Louisiana fisher-folk, and brought up by them. Years after a Creole hunter recognized her, and reported her whereabouts to relatives. These, who were rich, determined to bring her up as young ladies are brought up in the South, and had her sent to a convent. But she had lived the free healthy life of the coast, and could not bear the convent;—she ran away from it, married a fisherman, and lives somewhere down there now,—the mother of multitudinous children" (Bisland 1906, 1:426–27).

60. Hearn wrote an essay on Poe, "Crimson Madness," for the *New Orleans Item* (November 20, 1878), in which he noted, "Crimson fires illuminate the vast mediaeval hall, where appears the apparition of the Red Death. . . . The moon . . . is also crimson in the last scene of the 'house of Usher.'" Hearn views Poe's strange passion for crimson as indicative of "a peculiar and abnormal condition of the imagination" (*Editorials*, 1926, 40). Another editorial, on a French translation of Poe by Baudelaire, demonstrates Hearn's admiration of that similar spirit too: "He found a certain reflection of himself—the same wild dreams, the same strange despair, the same madness of melancholy, the same idiosyncrasies of style" (*Editorials*, 1926, 64).

61. Hearn wrote to his friend Krehbiel in 1878: "George Cable, a charming writer, some of whose dainty New Orleans stories you may have read in *Scribner's Monthly*, is writing a work containing a study of Creole music. . . . I have helped Cable a little in collecting the songs" (Bisland 1906, 1:175). In 1883, again to Krehbiel, Hearn praised "Belles Demoiselles Plantation" and "Jean Ah-Poquelin" as two of Cable's greatest achievements (Bisland 1906, 1:289).

62. For a fascinating parallel, see Thomas Nelson Page's remarks on the "Mammy," in *Social Life in Old Virginia* (1897): "The Mammy was the zealous, faithful, and efficient assistant of the mistress in all that pertained to the care and training of the children. Her authority was recognized in all that related to them . . . second only to that of the Mistress and Master. . . . Her affection was undoubted. Her *régime* extended frequently through two generations, occasionally through three . . . the affection between her and the children she nursed being often *more marked* than that between her and her own offspring" (57, my emphasis).

63. The "da," like the U.S. "Mammy," was also a signifier of social position. James Weldon Johnson, the celebrated Harlem Renaissance writer, tells in his autobiography of his *white* mammy. It seems when his mixed-race mother took ill she could not nurse, and a white neighbor woman who had given birth about the same time suckled him. As he wryly reports, "I do not intend to boast about a white mammy, for I have perceived bad taste in those southern white people who are continually boasting about their black mammies. I know the temptation for them to do so is very strong, because the honor point on the escutcheon of Southern aristocracy, the *sine qua non* of a background of family, of good breeding and social prestige, in the South is the Black Mammy" (1933, 9, 10).

64. Hearn avidly researched the African heritage of both New Orleans and the Caribbean. In an 1884 letter to Krehbiel, he cites Bryan Edwards's *History of the West Indies* as confirmation of the African origins of New World musical instruments, claims that the Congo dances of New Orleans "are certainly importations from . . . the

Ivory Coast," and also comments on the African heritage of black West Indian dance traditions (Bisland 1906, 1:297). In 1884, he wrote Krehbiel excitedly about a new work on Senegambia—"home of the Griots"—and in a subsequent letter enthused about his Senegalese books, which had accounted for many slave songs, "superstitions and folklore. . . . Of course, you know the slaves were chiefly drawn from the *West Coast*; and the study of ethnography and ethnology of the West Coast races is absolutely essential to a knowledge of Africanism in America" (Bisland 1906, 1:332).

65. This "de-sexualization" of the "mammy" had a counterpart in the creation of figures such as Joel Chandler Harris's Uncle Remus and Page's elderly black males, who frequently function as the narrators of his stories, such as "Marse Chan" and "Meh Lady." Ole Uncle Billy in the latter story certainly could not have taken on the paternal role he does with his "little Missy" if he had been a young, virile figure. Emasculation was a given for "good black" figures in paternalistic white plantation narratives.

66. Since his two extended sojourns in former slave territories—in New Orleans and St. Pierre—were in former French colonies, his remarks on a story he read in *Scribner's* (and we should not forget that his impressions of the South and the Caribbean were shaped not only by his insights but also by his readings and research) are pertinent. Writing to Krehbiel in 1879, he remarked: "There is a New Orleans story in the last issue of *Scribner's Monthly*,—'Ninon,' which I must tell you is a fair exemplification of how mean French Creoles can be. The great cruelties of the old slave régime were perpetuated by the French planters" (Bisland 1906, 1:203).

67. See, for instance, Yu (1964, 74).

Chapter 5

1. For an account of McKay's connection of rural Morocco with his native Jamaica, see Wayne Cooper's biography, *Claude McKay* (1987, 273–90). Cooper does not, however, provide a detailed reading of *Banana Bottom*.

2. The valorization of the folk as the font of culture has recently returned to the fore in the work of Bakhtin; however, this kind of impetus has many venerable antecedents. Montaigne, for instance, declared, "The least contemptible class of people seems to me to be those who, through their simplicity, occupy the lowest rank, and they seem to show greater regularity in their relations. The morals and the talk of peasants I find commonly more obedient to the prescriptions of true philosophy than are those of our philosophers. *The common people are wiser, because they are as wise as they need be*" ("Of Presumption," 1957, 501). In all these respects, it is fascinating to compare *Banana Bottom* and *Their Eyes Were Watching God* with two other "peasant" novels that appeared shortly after *Their Eyes*, DuBose Heyward's *Star Spangled Virgin* (1939) and Jacques Roumain's *Masters of the Dew* (1944).

3. For similar readings, see Barbara Griffin, who condemns the novel for its "patriarchal layers" and McKay's "misty-eyed evocations of the old days of paternalistic

coziness." She complains that Bita's actions "do little to change the economic inequities heavily based on the rigid class structure of the island," and that she winds up in a "circumscribed existence" that "reduces her intellect into a commodity of personal enhancement and merges her identity with that of her husband's"—here Jubban is said to be (without any evidence at all) a man "whose entrenched routine rustic life and sociopolitical apathy in no way threaten the colonial subtext of the narrative. . . . With him Bita will be subdued and isolated" (1999, 504–6). While there are many problems with this reading, the principal one is that the potential patriarchs here— Jordan, Squire Gensir, and Jubban—all work actively to foster Bita's agency and are hardly part of white colonial paternalism.

4. Similarly, in her autobiography, Hurston makes it clear that the tropical bounty of the land also contributed to her family's well-being. Surrounded by flowering plants, they also had "plenty of orange, grapefruit, tangerine, guavas and other fruits in our yard. We had a five-acre garden with things to eat growing in it, and so we were never hungry. We had chicken on the table often; home-cured meat, and all the eggs we wanted. . . . There was plenty of fish in the lakes" (*Dust Tracks*, 1942, 26–27).

5. Bita's seven-year "exile" echoes that of McKay, whose parents sent him at the age of six to live with his brother near Montego Bay, where he was subjected to a strict English education. He eventually became absorbed with his brother's philosophical books, as Bita does in the library of her white patron, Squire Gensir. Earlier, his sister had also been sent away for study and had returned home a very fashionable young lady, making people say that "she was too 'highly-educated' for a village man," which is also said of Bita (*My Green Hills*, passim).

6. The British missionaries, the Craigs, constitute a perfect example of Frantz Fanon's description of white religion's role in colonization: "The Church in the colonies is the white people's Church, the foreigner's Church. She does not call the native to God's ways but to the ways of the white man, of the master, of the oppressor" (1963, 42).

7. He corresponds to Earl, Arvay Henson's challenged son in Hurston's last novel, *Seraph on the Suwanee* (1948), and may well have been that character's inspiration.

8. Josh Gosciak (2006) has given the fullest account of McKay's relationship with Jekyll, who was the brother of the famous horticulturist Gertrude Jekyll (1843–1932). She encouraged her brother's interest in Caribbean flora and fauna. Walter's veiled homosexuality may have been McKay's gateway to his own bisexuality. Unaccountably, Gosciak makes almost no mention of *Banana Bottom*, or Jekyll's alter ego there, Squire Gensir. For another view of this relationship, see Cobham (1992, passim).

9. Despite the initial resistance of the Jamaican government to the recruitment of their citizens for work on the canal, only Barbadians exceeded the number of Jamaicans in the canal workforce. Many Jamaicans were skilled workers, serving as teachers, policemen, and artisans. The canal builders naturally preferred English-speaking workers. For a full discussion of Jamaicans in the isthmus workforce, see Greene (2009, especially 65, 128–29, 148–49, 341–42).

10. For detailed descriptions of Esu's role in cultures of Africa and its diaspora, see Gates (1988) and Euba (1989).

11. Bita's and Janie's scenes before the mirror echo Delany's pride in being a black man. Frederick Douglass famously said of him, "I thank God for making me a man simply; but Delany always thanks him for making him a *black man*" (Levine 1997, 6).

12. Garvey's "court" and the elaborate costumes worn by him and his followers inspired Eugene O'Neill's depiction of Emperor Brutus Jones's court.

13. Although Garvey had not gone to Africa when he founded his "empire," he had done extensive research on African culture in London before World War I. Langston Hughes had actually been to Africa, if briefly, as a merchant seaman. For a detailed examination of Garvey's legacy and his role in Pan-Africanism, see Stein (1986).

14. Walter Jekyll was an important anthologist of the Anancy stories, which have many parallels with trickster tales of the Old U.S. Southwest. For a comparison of the traditions, see my essay "Anancy's Web" (2013).

15. This episode, like many others in the novel, came from an incident in McKay's hometown of Sunny Ville, where Edwin Thatcher is discovered hiding under the bed of Edith and is pulled out by his leg—thus, Yoni's last name, Legge, in the book is a signification on an actual event (*My Green Hills*, 51).

16. Although McKay was most probably thinking of the 1760 revolt, there was another one in 1736 on Antigua, led by the slave Court, aka Tacky. Like many of the insurrection leaders of the period, including Jamaica's figure of the same name, Antigua's Tacky was a Coromantee. The carefully planned and extensive revolt he led in Antigua almost came to fruition and, as in the later insurrection in Jamaica, was laid out in conjunction with Obeahmen, including two named Caesar and Quawcoo. The latter was also a Coromantee, and court records specify the elaborate rituals that were employed (Gaspar 1978, 322), which in several ways are similar to the ones that McKay ascribes to Wumbe.

17. Banana production in Jamaica in the late nineteenth century was led by the Boston Fruit Company, which merged with Minor Keith's Latin American and Caribbean operations in 1899 to become the United Fruit Company. The extensive range of the operation meant that hurricane damage, as reflected in McKay's novel, could be offset by production in a neighboring island/country. The banana industry has always been dominated by Northern capital, as the complex system of production, speedy overseas shipment, and ripening procedures demanded a unified and well-financed operation. A labor-intensive crop, bananas quickly became a natural replacement for sugar production, which declined in value with the rise of the beet-sugar industry in Europe. For a full analysis of the complex interplay between this banana production and colonial and postcolonial operations, see Wiley (2008).

18. Winston James (1998) draws attention to this passage in the novel and relates it to general anger in the population against legislators who, in effect, operated against their own people in order to benefit their own light-skinned children. McKay and his brother, U. Theo McKay, knew many such "traitors." James also cites Garvey's 1913 heated opposition to the policy and that of the venerable, passionate, and dark-

skinned Rev. E. Ethelred Brown, who denounced this very policy in Harlem before the Jamaican Progressive League in 1936.

19. For a detailed examination of the economic structures and arguments in the novel, see David Nicholl's excellent essay (1999).

20. Derek Walcott, musing on many of these issues, includes a character based on Philoctetes in his epic poem, *Omeros*.

21. The hurricane section drew heavily on McKay's own experiences. He relates how "a fierce hurricane would sweep everything before it . . . destroying the best crops of bananas. . . . The aftermath was sheer misery . . . the villages were faced with starvation. Somehow I recall that we always used to pull through" (*My Green Hills*, 3). Further, the death of the two friends, as Jordan struggles to save Malcolm, recalls the swimming death of the young married couple in D. H. Lawrence's *Women in Love* (1920), a book McKay admired. Similarly, Hurston had experienced the terrible 1928 hurricane that lifted Lake Okeechobee over its banks, killing thousands, and she had also been through another terrible hurricane in the Bahamas in 1929, which she described in her autobiography.

22. In opera, this pattern finds a notable example in the pairing of Tamino/Pamina (the "nobles") and the bird-catcher Papagano/Papagena in Mozart's *The Magic Flute*.

23. As Dash demonstrates, the key text of this type was Jacques Roumain's *Gouverneurs de la rosée* (1944), known in English translation as *Masters of the Dew*. The novel's hero, Manuel, returns to Haiti after participating in collective revolt in Cuba. Roumain, like Hurston and McKay before him, was strongly influenced by anthropologists and folklorists such as Jean Price-Mars, Melville Herskovits, and Alfred Métraux, whose investigations of African survivalisms—especially in the religious practices of vodoun—brought about a new respect for the complexities of diasporic culture among the intelligentsia. Roumain limns a folk culture in times of stress—a terrible drought—but also describes patterns of migration, the onslaughts of finance capitalism from abroad, and "the emergence of new diasporic revolutionary identities" (Dash 2008, 38).

24. This issue has continued to surface in Caribbean literary studies, particularly in responses to the patrician—and very Western—attitudes of the esteemed Jamaican writer John Hearne. The argument for and against any one strand of culture in the region, however, was eloquently countered by the writer Sylvia Wynter: "To insist as we have hitherto done on any one part—i.e. the European—to the total exclusion of *any* or *all* of the others, is to humiliate and exile a part of ourselves. . . . To understand West Indian history, we must turn to the history of Africa, Asia, of the indigenous peoples of the American continent, [and of] Europe" (cited in Nettleford 1979, 67).

25. For a compelling recent reading of *Moses* as a circumCaribbean work, see Sam Vásquez's *Humor in the Caribbean Literary Canon* (2012).

26. In "Folklore and Music," Hurston would further state, "Also in Florida are the Cuban-African and the Bahamian-African folk tales. It is interesting to note that the same Brer Rabbit tales of the American Negro are told by these islanders. One also

finds the identical tales in Haiti and the British West Indies. . . . The wide distribution denotes a common origin in West Africa" (1995, 891–92), and, one notes, the net of connections the African diaspora draped over the circumCaribbean.

27. It seems likely that Hurston's original knowledge of the Anancy stories came from a reading of Walter Jekyll, who indeed may have been brought to her attention by McKay. Certainly Franz Boas knew this important resource. Her collection work in Jamaica, however, brought the stories into a more dynamic and immediate dimension.

28. When Hollywood offered to make his play into a film, O'Neill turned to the white Charleston writer DuBose Heyward, who had had success writing about black Southern characters. His novel *Porgy* (1928) became a Broadway play, which O'Neill admired; it later became the basis for George Gershwin's celebrated opera, *Porgy and Bess*. Heyward's screenplay for *The Emperor Jones* (1930) melds in a new first half, mainly set in the U.S. South, which situates Jones as a gospel-singing, womanizing, but profoundly Southern black, who knows both folklore and subversive modes of signifying. The two halves of the film thus constitute an early example of a modernist text that compares the South and the Caribbean, drawing lines of both connection and contrast. See my article on the screenplay in *Philological Quarterly* (2011).

29. Hurston's time in Harlem was also the era of the aforementioned back-to-Africa black nationalist Marcus Garvey and his Universal Negro Improvement Association. His retinue included talented writers such as Wilfred Domingo, who edited Garvey's *Negro World*. Although there were few writers of the time who took Garvey seriously (McKay had nothing but scorn for his fellow Jamaican), his movement increased awareness of Caribbean people and culture and helped expand the sense of the diaspora that was so prominent in Alain Locke's monumental edited volume, *The New Negro* (1925).

30. Hurston had made it a point to study the historic maroon community of Apopong in Jamaica in *Tell My Horse* (1938).

31. Nanny, the maroon heroine, plays a key role in Michelle Cliff's Jamaica novel, *Abeng* (1984).

32. The acquisition of land, rather than empty consumerism, is repeatedly put forward by McKay as a wise strategy for peasant investment. Jordan carefully adds to his acreage, and after his death, Bita and Jubban buy adjoining plots with the money she is willed by Squire Gensir.

33. This episode should be kept in mind in regard to the economic argument of the book, in which McKay makes it plain that "peasant" wisdom can also lead to financial benefits.

34. In addition to Smith, see Southerland (1979), Pavlić (2004), Lowe (1998), and especially Cartwright (2013), who offers the most extended reading of African religious references in the novel. His discussion appears in a different form in Jennings's edited volume on *Their Eyes Were Watching God* and Haiti (2013).

35. For two views of Tea Cake's presentation through Eastern mythology, see Lowe (1994, 195–96) and Pondrom (1986, passim).

36. On the other hand, Nanny's poignant and wrenching memories of her travails

during slavery and afterward with Janie's wayward mother, Leafy, never seem to move Janie, whose lack of education and thus sense of history limits her to a certain extent. It is time for us to wonder if Hurston agreed with Janie's assessment of Nanny and her story; after all, Hurston created it. On a related note, to my mind, one of the several egregious mistakes in the recent film of *Their Eyes Were Watching God* was the omission of Nanny's speech, which reduced her to a cipher, a double shame since she was portrayed by the magnificent actress Ruby Dee.

37. Hurston's account of Janie's teenage years similarly has her briefly enamored, after romantic reveries, with a Hopping Dick–type figure: "Through pollinated air she saw a glorious being coming up the road. In her former blindness she had known him as shiftless Johnny Taylor, tall and lean. That was before the golden dust of pollen had be-glamored his rags and her eyes" (25).

38. Apparently, Tea Cake was based on what Hurston called "the real love affair of my life," with a son of West Indian parents, a graduate of City College who was working on his master's degree at Columbia, who had very little money. He had "nothing to offer but what it takes—a bright soul, a fine mind in a fine body, and courage" (*Dust Tracks*, [1942], 1984, 255). But after he receives his degree, she gets a Guggenheim and sails off for Jamaica, the first leg of two years in the Caribbean, where she writes *Their Eyes Were Watching God* (1937), in an effort "to embalm all the tenderness of my passion for him" (260). In light of this model, it is interesting that Tea Cake, like Jubban, has no apparent formal education.

39. As she recorded in her autobiography, "I lived through that terrible five-day hurricane of 1929. It was horrible in its intensity and duration. I saw dead people washing around on the streets when it was over. You could smell the stench from dead animals as well. More than three hundred houses were blown down in the city of Nassau alone" (*Dust Tracks*, [1942], 1984, 203).

Chapter 6

1. We should also pay attention to the complicated relationship between Lamming and Wright. As we have seen, Wright had a keen interest in the Caribbean arena of the black diaspora, and his enthusiastic introduction to *In the Castle of My Skin* in 1953 was appreciated by Lamming, who of course admired Wright as one of the preeminent modern writers. According to Wright's most recent biographer, however, Wright was disturbed when he came home one day and found the handsome Lamming in deep conversation with Ellen Wright. Always jealous of his wife, despite his own well-known philandering, Wright again got upset when he returned home a week later and Ellen was not there, which led him to have Vivian Mercer call Lamming's hotel to find out where he was (Rowley 2008, 478–79). It seems likely, however, that Lamming never knew of this aspect of their relationship, for he dedicated his 1972 novel, *Natives of My Person*, to Margaret Gardiner and in memory of Richard Wright.

2. The line comes from Walcott's *Epitaph for the Young* (1949).

3. We should not be surprised that Wright was eager to read Lamming's book. Always interested in the lives of other people of color in foreign lands, during the early days of World War II, Wright wrote Claude Barnett, who headed the Associated Negro Press, that he wanted to cover the war in Russia, China, or India: "I would like to get stories of how the brown, red and yellow people are faring, what they are hoping for, and how their attitudes are likely to influence the outcome of the war in Europe" (Rowley 2008, 235).

4. For a reading of Wright's unpublished 1950 "Haitian Biographies," see Karem (2011, 234–36).

5. In making this argument, I am inspired by Edward Said's examination of Beethoven's late works (2006), which he situates as operating against the concept of "art as document." In this study, his own last work, Said reminds us that aesthetic elements can—and often do—operate in tandem with other objectives, including propaganda.

6. For a superb example of this tradition, see John Pearson's "train sermon" in Hurston's first novel, *Jonah's Gourd Vine* (1934).

7. This aspect of his work has been given close examination by Claudia Tate (1998).

8. Certainly one of the more remarkable aspects of Wright's final years was his creation of thousands of haiku poems, which were collected in *Haiku: The Other World* (1998). In a moving foreword to that book, Wright's daughter Julia suggests that the Japanese-inspired poems gave Wright a forum in which to link his mourning for recently deceased friends and his mother with his yearning for the Southern landscapes of his youth. As she puts it, "A form of poetry which links seasons of the soul with nature's cycle of moods enabled him to reach out to the black boy part of himself still stranded in a South that continued to live in his dreams" ("Introduction," 1998, xi). These intricately wrought and deceptively short poems take us back to the artistry of *Black Boy*, whose pages subject us to painfully detailed scenes of suffering and oppression, but also to wonderfully poignant renditions of the Southern landscape in short, one-sentence reflections.

9. Here Wright points to the way scarce resources lead to divisions and violence within the community. Further, a related scene in *Black Boy* in which white men cause black boys to fight each other (which later formed the nexus of Ralph Ellison's famous "Battle Royal" scene in *Invisible Man*) has a counterpart in *Castle*, where the white "gentlemen" toss coins into the harbor for black boys to dive and fight for.

10. While my discussion here juxtaposes *Black Boy* and *Castle*, Lamming was also inspired by Wright's achievement in *Twelve Million Black Voices*, which I am situating in this presentation as a kind of corollary to the earlier biography.

11. Similarly, Yoshinobu Hakutani has suggested that in *Black Boy* Wright is intent on displaying his experiences "with naturalistic objectivity, rather than from a personal point of view" (1996, 115). I concur.

12. The Italian composer Giuseppe Verdi once remarked, "To imitate truth may be a good thing but to invent truth is better" (cited in Kimbell 1994, 501), a sentiment both Wright and Lamming would approve.

13. Lamming's point might be reversed as well. The riots did indeed lead to mod-

ernization and correction of the more egregious problems of the time (Nair 1996, 101). Lamming's subsequent presentation of this history, coupled with his much fiercer nonfictional speeches and essays that followed, affected the political and literary climates of the Caribbean. There is no question that *Black Boy* and many of Wright's other works had a similar effect in the United States and, later, abroad. Still, we should remember that both *Black Boy* and *Castle* conclude with figures leaving the land. "Richard" flees to Chicago, while Pa, Trumper, and "G." all vacate Creighton village for disparate new locations. The peasant spokesman, the shoemaker, also disappears. In the long light of history, however, readers today see these earlier struggles and flights as prelude to the independence of Caribbean nations, the monumental achievements of the civil rights movement in the United States, and the advent of a New New South that has fomented a reverse migration of African Americans back to the Southern locales of their ancestors. For an engrossing account of this movement, see Stack (1996, passim).

14. In terms of a mother's pain, one becomes fascinated by the similar scene in Hurston's autobiography, *Dust Tracks on a Road* (1942), when the dying Lucy Hurston's final wish to avoid folk-centered traditions for deaths (the position of the bed, veiling mirrors, and so on) are violated, even though the child tries valiantly to carry them out. Hurston, too, waxes poetic and also uses the scene as a predictor of the future: "The Master-Maker in His making had made Old Death. Made him with big, soft feet and square toes. Made him with a face that reflects the face of all things, but neither changes itself, nor is mirrored anywhere. Made the body of Death out of infinite hunger. Made a weapon for his hand to satisfy his needs. This was the morning of the day of the beginning of things" (87).

15. In an interview with George Kent, Lamming referred to Wright's *Black Boy* as a model for what he was seeking, a "backward glance" that would serve as a narrative of both immigration and return. "Speaking of Wright, the other day I came across an exercise book I used as a young boy . . . which would probably have a date like 1948, and I found pages and pages of *Black Boy* written out in ink. I remember very well this very long section where Wright is reflecting about leaving for the North" (Kent 1992, 97).

16. In this effort, she is following the vanguard of postnationalist studies by Sandra Pouchet Paquet (2002), Belinda Edmondson (1999), and A. J. Simoes Da Silva (2000).

17. Jeff Karem, who has also examined the links between Lamming and Wright, has suggested that *Castle* in fact influenced *The Long Dream* in some respects (Karem 2011, 242–46).

18. This echoes the prejudiced statements of the near-white Mrs. Turner in Hurston's *Their Eyes Were Watching God*, whose damnation of "My People" is in fact more color based: "Who wants to be mixed up wid uh rusty black man, and uh black woman goin' down de street in all dem loud colors, and whoopin' and hollerin' and laughin' over nothin'? . . . Always singin' ol' nigger songs! . . . If it wuzn't for so many black folks it wouldn't be no race problem. De white folks would take us in wid dem. De black ones is holdin' us back" ([1937], 1974, 210).

19. Although there is no evidence that Lamming knew Wagner's opera *Die Meister-singer*, which centrally concerns "heilige deutsche Kunst" (holy German art), which proceeds from the folk, he puts much of the narrative's central philosophies into the mouth of the village shoemaker. Wagner's Hans Sachs, a Meistersinger/poet himself, as shoemaker knows all the people in the town and like Lamming's artisan, thus has a more communal view than others.

20. One wonders at the strong parallel between this inserted story and the book-length treatment of the same topic in the U.S. Virgin Islands in DuBose Heyward's *Star Spangled Virgin* (1939), which similarly depicts uneducated peasants struggling with new social pressures to marry (see the discussion of this thematic in the preceding chapter).

21. Despite the debts I have traced on Lamming's part to Wright's *Black Boy*, two important Lamming critics have not drawn this connection, although both Supriya Nair and Sandra Pouchet Paquet speak briefly of Lamming's reliance on the "collective characters" Lamming employs, who in this regard resemble Wright's Bigger Thomas of *Native Son* (Wright said this character was based on "many Biggers" [Paquet 1982, 5; Nair 1996, 6]). It is important, however, that Nair points to the ways in which Lamming's angry narrative attempts to create a history for the "historyless," that is, the colonized peoples whose place in Western chronicles has been erased by the colonizer. Nair reminds us of Frantz Fanon's pronouncement that it is the settler who "makes history" in the colonized land, but a history the settler always identi-fies as part of the mother country's. Thus, Fanon charges, the "settler" "skims off . . . violates and starves" (1963, 51). Nair adds that this skimming of history parallels the skimming of material resources (1996, 79–80), and both Wright and Lamming illus-trate this point again and again in their "alternate" histories.

22. Edward Baugh has provided an extensive examination of *Castle* as an alter-native history, one that disrupts the received history of the colonizer, which has muted or erased the voices and experiences of the various colonized people (1977, 6). See also Supriya Nair's rehearsal of this issue (1996, 8ff.).

23. For a detailed explanation of the operations of the "speakerly text" in *Their Eyes Were Watching God* (1937), see Gates (1988).

24. This important vision has a very real counterpart early in *Castle*, when Lam-ming critiques the assembly-line colonial educational system: "There were nine squads . . . a thousand boys . . . packed close. . . . Seen from the school porch the spec-tacle was that of an enormous ship whose cargo had been packed in boxes" (1953, 28).

25. The passage is also proleptic of Aunt Esther's similar re-creation of the Middle Passage in August Wilson's play *Gem of the Ocean* (2003).

26. On the other hand, two late letters from Wright to his editor outlined the third novel in his Fishbelly series, in which Fish chooses Yvette over Marie-Rose and settles for a time in Africa, where their son is born shortly after Fish's mother arrives. The entire family then returns to the United States, hoping for a final and true integra-tion into American life. The novel was to conclude with the choices faced by Fish's son—life in Europe, in New York, or in Mississippi with his grandmother (summary

from Fabre 1973, 486). The projected trilogy would have pulled in the three points of the Black Atlantic, and by circling back to a presumably transformed United States, it would have ended the trilogy, which began, typically for Wright, in fear, but ended in some kind of hope, a trajectory perhaps prompted by a kind of wistfulness on Wright's part at the end of his life. We might see a sort of a parallel in Lamming's eventual return to the Americas.

Chapter 7

1. Most of the events I am summarizing here are discussed in much greater detail in Louis A. Pérez Jr.'s essential history of the island and its culture; see especially his comparison and contrast of Havana and Miami (2008, 432–44).

2. Gustavo Pérez Firmat's *The Havana Habit* (2010) is a lively and informative study of the fascination with all things Cuban in American popular culture of the twentieth century. His focus, however, is the relationship of Cuba—usually Havana— to the United States, rather than that of the island to the U.S. South.

3. For detailed presentation of these events, see Helg (1995).

4. For a contrasting reading of the Mariel boatlift exodus, see de la Campa (2000, 94 ff.).

5. New Orleans, another circumCaribbean city we have visited, of course has a counterpart in its gumbo, which uses local chicken, sausage and/or seafood, Caribbean spices, French roux, and African okra ("gumbo"). Louisianans often refer proudly to their "cultural gumbo."

6. For an exhaustive survey of Cuba's place in the U.S. imperialist imaginary, see Louis A. Pérez Jr.'s book on the subject (2008).

7. Scott Romine (2008) has suggested that the *entire* postmodern South of today is in many ways a "fake" copy of what it thinks it formerly was. He argues that our "South" is variously simulated, virtual, and/or commodified, which leads him ultimately to wonder if the notion of an "authentic" South ever really existed. This question would seem to be moot, however, if we recognize that culture—of whatever type and locale—is never static but always dynamic. His argument, however, fits well with many conceptions of both "Little Havana" and Miami as a whole.

8. García's presentation—some say misrepresentation—of Santería has been one of the chief criticisms of her work; a minority of critics have generally faulted her for not being raised in a Cuban neighborhood, and for missing nuances of the culture. Interestingly, Virgil Suarez, who also makes use of Santería in his fiction but has closer ties with the Miami community, has thus far not been criticized on this basis. For an example of these criticisms, see Pascha A. Stevenson (2007), whose argument verges on "biological insiderism." Detailed presentation of the many versions of Santería may be found in Pérez Sarduy and Stubbs's *Afrocuba* (1993) and in Joseph M. Murphy's *Santería* (1988).

9. For a detailed account of this subset of the Cuban diaspora, which figures importantly in many works of Cuban American literature, see Conde (1999).

10. As earlier chapters of this book indicate, Miami is not alone in this regard. Houston, New Orleans, Atlanta, and even Charlotte now offer examples of the effects of the new immigration, which has greatly complicated the Old South binary of plain black and white. Latinos/as of every nationality—especially Mexicans—have migrated to virtually every area of the South in the past decade. Even tiny Dillard in northern Georgia has a booming bodega nestled amid its mountain craft shops. There are more Mexican and Caribbean restaurants around these days than there are the traditional meat-and-threes of the past.

11. *Next Year in Cuba* (1995) now has a sequel, *Scar Tissue* (2005), a volume chiefly devoted to the writer's affliction with prostate cancer and the death of his father, a key figure in the earlier memoir.

12. Another novel by a woman writer that provides a strong counterpoint to *Next Year in Cuba* in this respect is Ivonne Lamazares's *The Sugar Island* (2000). The first half of the tale unfolds in Cuba. The narrator's mother was a youthful and fiery supporter of Fidel who joined the revolutionaries in the mountains. Returning home pregnant, she subsequently descends into a life of poverty and despair. The second part of the novel details her desperate flight across the choppy waters with her daughter to Florida.

13. The identification of a certain ethnic community within a larger Southern city with a particular street is also found in Atlanta, where Auburn Avenue, "Sweet Auburn," was for many years the main artery of bustling black Atlanta. In both cities, these ethnic cores became diminished—after the civil rights movement in Atlanta and after rising prosperity for Cubans in Miami inevitably led to dispersal to wealthier surrounding suburbs (in Atlanta, more affluent blacks have migrated to outlying communities like Stone Mountain). Still, as with Little Italy and the Lower East Side in New York, where Italian and Jewish Americans, respectively, return for a dose of ethnic sustenance, these fabled enclaves continue to enjoy mythic status within the community's ethnic imaginary.

14. It should be mentioned that Virgil Suarez's first novel, *Latin Jazz* (2002), displays some of this priapic energy, and the book many would highlight as the most radical in the Cuban American canon, Reinaldo Arenas's *Before Night Falls* (1993), is filled with sex (most of it male/male).

15. Although, as we have noted, there were significant colonies of exiled Confederates established in several countries, most prominently in Brazil and Mexico.

16. Interestingly, de la Torre throughout his study emphasizes Cuba's *mestizaje* (mixed) culture, particularly as seen in exilic Cuban religion, which he represents by the term *ajiaco*, a Cuban stew, which, as previously noted, bears an affinity to the South's fabled gumbo.

17. It should be noted that most of Miami's African Americans migrated there from northern Florida, Georgia, and Alabama, maintain strong contacts with those areas, and continue to be part of a dynamic black Southern folklore and culture (see Stepick et al. 2003, 24). It has also been observed that the immigrant Haitian community

has tended to eventually acculturate with this component of the Miami population, although frictions that developed between African American and Haitians during the first wave of immigration have continued, despite intermarriage and intermingling of cultural traditions. Figures on the current racial makeup of Miami are cited in the text of this chapter.

18. Virgil Suarez's novel *Havana Thursdays* (1995), which I will not discuss here, displays the spread of the diaspora. The matriarch of the Torres family still lives in Florida, but in the suburb of Kendall not in Little Havana, and two of her children reside in Buenos Aires and in Maryland.

19. On the other hand, García's character Reina Agüero, a recent immigrant to Miami, writes to her daughter Dulce in Madrid that Miami's seas and skies are just like Cuba's, only fresher, bluer (1997, 209). Further, Reina immediately finds a host of eager lovers, and then work, first at her sister Constantia's cosmetics factory and then fixing up old cars.

20. I will not consider *Latin Jazz* here, since its major stateside setting is Los Angeles.

21. In *Life on the Hyphen*, Gustavo Pérez Firmat defines the YUCA as "a self-consuming vegetable. An English-speaking YUCA who parks his beamer, hooks a beeper onto his belt (or slings a cellular phone into her purse) and goes into a pricey Coral Gables restaurant also called Yuca to eat *nouvelle cuisine ajiaco* is not less Cuban but more American" (1994, 16).

22. Junot Diaz pays a tribute to Fernández in his 2007 Pulitzer Prize–winning *The Brief Wondrous Life of Oscar Wao*, where he names a minor character Nelson Pardo. Like Fernández, Diaz includes much untranslated Spanish in his fiction and has been praised for creating a kind of "Spanglish."

23. Belle Glade, a town of 15,000 in 2008, has never been an affluent town and has suffered from the miseries of poverty. During the 1980s, it became notorious for having the highest rate of AIDS infection in the nation. In 2003, it had the second-worst violent crime rate in the country (Gonzalez 2008, 5C).

24. For interesting and revealing analyses of Fernández's linguistic invention in the "Pearl" sections, consult Ortiz (2007, 14–16) and Alvarez-Borland (1998, 100).

25. In one of the many subplots of *Holy Radishes*, Coach Olsen joins a party of rednecks who dress as Indians and torch a local business where a Jew and a Cuban work, ostensibly to drive out the Cuban community, which is taking good jobs from whites at the radish factory. The raid is absurd in every way, but the comic elements are mounted on both a parody of the Boston Tea Party and the grim history of the Klan, whose exploits this group mimics, thereby equating the Cuban workers with Southern African Americans.

26. I totally agree with Rosanna Rivero Marín, however, that the overwhelming majority of the literary references (many of them pretty well hidden) are from Spanish and Latino/a literatures, some of them bordering on plagiarism, as in a wholesale lifting from Sor Juana Inés de la Cruz in some of Connie's passages (2004, 41–42, 60–61).

27. In the 1880s, influential white Southerners inveighed against the increasing numbers of foreign immigrants, who were perceived as pollutants and threats to the purity of Southern civilization. These intruders were viewed as "red-handed anarchists and God-defying atheists," terms not too dissimilar from those used against the "polluting" *Marielitos*. Dissenters within the community, however, were also branded, usually as communists, regardless of their particular political affinities.

28. Civil religions of this sort are by no means unique to Miami Cubans and Reconstruction whites of the U.S. South. Émile Durkheim stated that all societies have spiritual dimensions, that they see many aspects of their shared culture as sacred, and that many citizens may even see that culture as holy (1912, 52, 56, 59, 261). For exhaustive surveys of the "Lost Cause" of the U.S. South, see Charles Reagan Wilson's *Baptized in Blood: The Religion of the Lost Cause* (1980) and Gaines Foster's *Ghosts of the Confederacy* (1987).

29. García's widely praised and often-taught first novel, *Dreaming in Cuban* (1992), also impresses, but I will not treat it here since the characters in that book relocate not to Florida but to the Northeast.

30. False memory can wind up as lies. García has claimed that she wants "to explore all the lying that goes on in Cuban history" (Kevane and Heredia 2000, 70).

31. More recently, Nilo Cruz's Pulitzer Prize–winning play *Anna in the Tropics* (2002), set in Tampa in the 1920s, features a love triangle involving a lector, whose elegance attracts the factory owner's daughter, with disastrous results. The story includes an early reference to a Southern belle from Atlanta who eloped with a lector from Guanabacoa, a story that is compared, like the central one, with the love triangle of Tolstoy's *Anna Karenina*, which the lector reads to the workers. One of the themes of the play is the looming elimination of the lectors as workers are replaced by machines. In García's novel, in one of Ignacio's flashbacks to his father's career as a lector, he states that, while some workers have lost their jobs because of falling prices, "those who remained were fearful of losing them to the modern cigar-rolling machines from America" (113).

32. Reading the classics to a "class" of workers replicates the structure of the academy, and, indeed, as Michel de Certeau reminds us, a lector "was, in the Middle Ages, the title of a kind of University Professor" (1984, 225n11).

33. Interestingly, Barbour's passion was not birds but reptiles. His book, however, contains chapters on Cuban birds, much of it based on the earlier collecting career of the German naturalist Juan/Johannes Gundlach, whose collections from the east of the island became the property of the Museum of the Institute of Havana (installed there in 1895). García's shift permits her to relate Ignacio's naturalist activities to his parents' musical tradition but also sets up the Audubon parallel of killing the beautiful birds in order to immortalize them, just as he kills his wife. Both reptiles and birds, however, are found in the Zapata swamp, Gundlach's favorite site, which indeed is the setting Ignacio prefers for his collecting.

34. Israel Reyes has noted this motif, reminding us that "an *aguëro* [which translates as augury or omen] can signal good or bad luck, as in the commonly used *buen*

or *mal agüero*," and *un pájaro de mal agüero* [bird of ill omen] prefigures calamitous events" (2002, 224).

35. Barbour notes that the native bird populations of Cuba are often invaded by migrating flocks from the United States: "Many will find it hard to believe that there are so many redstarts or black-throated blue warblers" (1945, 112), precisely the migratory birds that bother Reinaldo.

36. Barbour (1945, 159) reports that Gundlach, his great predecessor, speaks of the diminished numbers of the Stygian owls as a result of deforestation "and of the fact that they are killed whenever possible, as being birds of ill omen." Further, Ignacio states that the bird is known to "fly about late at night, stealing people's souls, and striking them deaf" (29), and decades later, Ignacio's grandson Silvestre is struck deaf by a fever.

37. The terror of the horses and their subsequent death enhances the power of this apocalyptic scene, but it does not fit with the realistic source for the expedition, Dr. Barbour's journal. There he tells us that a steady, sure-footed horse, who won't shy after a gunshot, is crucial for bird-gathering expeditions (Barbour 1945, 141). On the other hand, he also quotes the Cuban naturalist Fermín Cervera, who stated that the Zapata swamp was rife with quicksand, "where one may sink up to one's neck" (Barbour, 1945, 180).

38. Román de la Campa's memoir (2000) details his experience as a "Pedro Pan" recruit. The program relocated over 14,000 children to various cities in the United States.

39. This motif is in keeping with revolutionary narrative. As Édouard Glissant has noted, "The French Revolution reaching the Antilles, the victorious Haitian Revolution, and the Civil War in the American South were occasions for secret burials of gold, jewels, and silver. Add to that the penchant for mystery, in a *buena suerte* manner, and for West Indian *quimbois*. The hysterical search for buried treasure is like the quest for Knowledge, a deep search, an effort that cannot be shared, and indubitable" (1999, 90).

40. Interestingly, Barbour calls the Zapata swamp "Cuba's counterpart of the Florida Everglades" (1944, 248). Elsewhere, he notes that Key West "has always been a half-Cuban town, [and] many of the savory creole dishes handed down from Old Spain add their spice to the table. The queer little unpainted houses, many of them said to have been brought from the Bahamas, with their typical West Indian jalousy blinds, and the tales of old wrecking days, make this town to me a center of real charm" (1944, 196).

41. Havana's burgeoning sex industry, featuring male and female prostitutes (*jinateras* and *jinteros*—jockeys), is described in some detail in Román de la Campa's memoir, *Cuba on My Mind* (2000, 162–66). Andrei Codrescu's travelogue *Ay, Cuba!* (2001) also considers this industry, especially as it is practiced on Cuba's beaches (1999, 113–18). See also Coco Fusco's "Jinateras en Cuba" (1997).

42. The avian thematic is heightened as we learn that Constantia has visited there to hear the stories of the *guajiro* (peasant), who tells her of the birds of Florida, Peru,

and, of course, Cuba. Hialeah racetrack is famous, too, for the huge flock of flamingos that inhabit the lake inside the track, and indeed, "flamingos are everywhere, awkwardly preening" (80).

43. The sociologist W. Lloyd Warner has noted that when the living think of the deaths of others, they necessarily express some concerns about their own deaths (1959, 280). By consciously shaping and then policing the boundaries of the "saving remnant" with the instruments of a new kind of civil religion, the Cuban exile community seeks a kind of immortality and helps ward off the fear that this last vestige of true *Cubanidad*, which no longer exists on the island, will wither away in exile.

44. Heberto's commandos have had numerous real-life equivalents, an echo of the filibusters we considered in an earlier chapter, but with a more intense, semireligious dedication to *la lucha* (the struggle). There were guerrilla camps near Miami in the 1980s where training was conducted for possible operations in Cuba, Nicaragua, and Panama (de la Torre 2003, 44).

45. Eleggua (one of many spellings) is the name of the orisha; when he appears as a *lwa* (notably in Haiti) the name is either Legba or Elegba.

46. For a fascinating examination of the ways in which virtually every aspect of Cuban society has been affected by the cult of *machismo*—and, especially, *la lucha* (the struggle against Castro)—see de la Torre (2003, particularly 83–117). The concept is also considered repeatedly by Arenas (1993); see also de la Campa (2000, especially 45–46). For an in-depth treatment of *machismo*'s roots in the nineteenth century, see Kutzinski (1993, 163–98).

47. This does not mean that Cuban American writers are not dealing with postplantation realities, such as gated communities, "stand your ground" laws, butterfly ballots, and divestment in social programs and infrastructure. Some of this, as I have noted, appears prominently in García's work.

48. How similar this is to Faulkner's Drusilla of *The Unvanquished*, who says of the Civil War that has devastated her South, "Who wants to sleep now, with so much happening, so much to see? Life used to be so dull, you see, stupid. . . . It's fine now; you don't have to worry now about the house and the silver, because they get burned up and carried away; and you don't have to worry about the Negroes, because they tramp the roads all night. . . . You don't have to worry about getting children to bathe and feed and change, because the young men can ride away and get killed in the fine battles" (1938, 114–15).

Sources Consulted

Abani, Chris. "Cristina García." *Bomb* 99 (2007): 34–37.

Abrahams, Roger. *The Man-of-Words in the West Indies: Performance and the Emergence of Creole Culture.* Baltimore: Johns Hopkins University Press, 1983.

Addison, Joseph. *Critical Essays from The Spectator.* Edited by Donald F. Bond. New York: Oxford University Press, 1970.

Alemán, Jesse. "The Other Country: Mexico, the United States, and the Gothic History of Conquest." *American Literary History* 18, no. 3 (2006): 406–26.

Alemán Jesse, and Shelley Streeby, eds. *Empire and the Literature of Sensation: An Anthology of Nineteenth-Century Popular Fiction.* New Brunswick: Rutgers University Press, 2007.

Alexis, Jacques Stéphen. "Où va le roman?" *Présence africaine* 13 (1957): 87–101.

Allewaert, Monique. *Ariel's Ecology: Plantations, Personhood, and Colonialism in the American Tropics.* Minneapolis: University of Minnesota Press, 2013.

——. "Swamp Sublime: Ecologies of Resistance in the American Plantation Zone." *PMLA* 123, no. 2 (2008): 340–57.

Allred, Jeff. "From Eye to We: Richard Wright's *Twelve Million Black Voices,* Documentary, and Pedagogy." *American Literature* 78, no. 3 (2006): 549–83.

Alvarez Borland, Elizabeth. *Cuban-American Literature of Exile: From Person to Persona.* Charlottesville: University of Virginia Press, 1998.

Alvarez Borland, Elizabeth, and Lynette M. F. Bosch. *Cuban-American Literature and Art.* Albany: State University of New York Press, 2009.

Anderson, Benedict. *Imagined Communities: Reflections on the Origin and Spread of Nationalism.* Rev. ed. London: Verso, 1991.

Aparicio, Frances R., and Susana Chávez-Silverman, eds. *Tropicalizations: Transcultural Representations of Latinidad.* Hanover, N.H.: University Press of New England, 1997.

Aptheker, Herbert. "Maroons within the Present Limits of the United States." In *Maroon Societies: Rebel Slave Communities in the Americas,* edited by Richard Price, 151–68. 3rd ed. Baltimore: Johns Hopkins University Press, 1996.

Aravamudan, Srinivas. *Tropicopolitans: Colonialism and Agency, 1688–1804.* Durham: Duke University Press, 1999.

Arenas, Reinaldo. *Before Night Falls.* Translated by Delores Koch. New York: Viking, 1993.

Arjomand, Said Amir, and Edward A. Tiryakian, eds. *Rethinking Civilizational Analysis.* London: Sage, 2004.

Auerbach, Erich. *Mimesis: The Representation of Reality in Western Literature.* Translated by Willard Trask. New York: Anchor-Doubleday, 1957.

Augustin, Marie Joséphine. *Le Macandal.* 1870; reprint, Shreveport, La.: Editions Tintamare/Centenar, 2010.

Bakhtin, Mikhail. *The Dialogic Imagination: Four Essays.* Edited and translated by Caryl Emerson and Michael Holquist. Austin: University of Texas Press, 1981.

———. *Problems of Dostoevsky's Poetics.* Edited and translated by Caryl Emerson. Minneapolis: University of Minnesota Press, 1984.

Barbour, Thomas. *A Naturalist in Cuba.* Boston: Little, Brown, 1945.

———. *That Vanishing Eden: A Naturalist's Florida.* Boston: Little, Brown, 1944.

Barth, Fredrik. Introduction to *Ethnic Groups and Boundaries: The Social Organization of Culture Difference*, edited by Fredrik Barth, 9–38. Boston: Little, Brown, 1969.

Barthes, Roland. "The Discourse of History." In *The Rustle of Language*, translated by Richard Howard, 127–40. Oxford: Blackwell, 1986.

Baucom, Ian. *Specters of the Atlantic: Finance Capital, Slavery, and the Philosophy of History.* Durham: Duke University Press, 2005.

Baudrillard, Jean. *Selected Writings of Jean Baudrillard.* Edited by Mark Poster. Palo Alto: Stanford University Press, 1988.

Bauer, K. Jack. *The Mexican War, 1846–1848.* Lincoln: University of Nebraska Press, 1974.

Bauer, Ralph. *The Cultural Geography of Colonial American Literatures: Empire, Travel, Modernity.* Cambridge: Cambridge University Press, 2003.

Baugh, Edward. "The West Indian Writer and His Quarrel with History." *Tapia* 8, no. 9 (1977): 6.

Behar, Ruth, and Lucía M. Suárez. *The Portable Island: Cubans at Home in the World.* New York: Palgrave, 2008.

Bell, Archie. *The Spell of the Caribbean Islands.* New York: L. C. Page, 1926.

Bell, Madison Smartt. *All Souls' Rising.* New York: Pantheon, 1995.

———. "Engaging the Past." In *Novel History*, edited by Mark C. Carnes, 197–208. New York: Simon and Schuster, 2001.

———. *Master of the Crossroads.* New York: Pantheon, 2000.

———. *The Stone That the Builder Refused.* New York: Pantheon, 2004.

———. "True Morality." In *Outside the Law: Narratives on Justice in America*, 32–42. Boston: Beacon, 1997.

Benedict, Clare, ed. *Constance Fenimore Woolson.* London: Ellis, 1930.

Benítez-Rojo, Antonio. *The Repeating Island: The Caribbean and Postmodern Performance.* Translated by James E. Maraniss. Durham: Duke University Press, 1992.

Benjamin, Walter. "The Work of Art in the Age of Mechanical Reproduction." In *Illuminations: Essays and Reflections*, 214–18. Edited by Hannah Arendt. translated by Harry Zohn. London: Fontana, 1968.

Bennett, Tony. "Texts in History: The Determinations of Readings and Their Texts."

In *Reception Study: From Literary Theory to Cultural Studies*, edited by James L. Machor and Philip Goldstein, 61–79. New York: Routledge, 2001.

Bhabha, Homi. *The Location of Culture.* New York: Routledge, 1994.

Bibler, Michael P., and Jessica Adams. Introduction to Arna Bontemps, *Drums at Dusk*, vii–lii. Baton Rouge: Louisiana State University Press, 2009.

Binder, Wolfgang, and Helmbrecht Breinig, eds. *American Contradictions: Interviews with Nine American Writers.* Hanover, N.H.: Wesleyan University Press, 1995.

Bisland, Elizabeth. *The Life and Letters of Lafcadio Hearn.* 2 vols. Boston: Houghton Mifflin, 1906.

Blanch, Lesley. *Pierre Loti: Travels with the Legendary Romantic.* London: Tauris Parke, 2004.

Boas, Franz. *The Mind of Primitive Man.* 1916; rev. ed., New York: Macmillan, 1938.

Bongie, Chris. *Exotic Memories: Literature, Colonialism, and the Fin de Siècle.* Stanford: Stanford University Press, 1991.

———. *Islands and Exiles: The Creole Identities of Post/Colonial Literature.* Stanford: Stanford University Press, 1998.

Bonner, Sherwood. "The Hoodoo Dance." In *Library of Southern Literature*, edited by Edwin Anderson Alderman, Joel Chandler Harris, and Charles William Kent, 1:458. Atlanta: Martin and Hoyt, 1907.

Bontemps, Arna. *Drums at Dusk: A Novel.* New York: Macmillan, 1939.

Bordelon, Pamela, ed. *Go Gator, and Muddy the Water: Writings by Zora Neale Hurston from the Federal Writers' Project.* New York: Norton, 1999.

Brathwaite, Edward Kamau. "The African Presence in Caribbean Literature." *Daedelus* 103, no. 2 (1974): 73–109.

———. *The Development of Creole Society in Jamaica.* Oxford: Oxford University Press, 1971.

———. "History, the Caribbean Writer, and X/Self." In *Crisis and Creativity in the New Literature in English*, edited by Geoffrey V. Davis and Hena Maes-Jelinek, 23–46. Amsterdam: Rodopi, 1990.

Braudel, Fernand. *The Mediterranean and the Mediterranean World in the Age of Philip II.* 1949; rev. ed. 2 vols., translated by Sian Reynolds. New York: Harper, 1972.

Braziel, Jana Evans, and Anita Mannur, eds. *Theorizing Diaspora: A Reader.* London: Blackwell, 2003.

Brickhouse, Anna. *Transamerican Literary Relations and the Nineteenth-Century Public Sphere.* Cambridge: Cambridge University Press, 2004.

Brodber, Erna. "Making a Living in Jamaica, 1923–1980." Ph.D. diss., University of the West Indies, Jamaica, 1987.

Brodhead, Richard H. *Cultures of Letters: Scenes of Reading and Writing in Nineteenth-Century America.* Chicago: University of Chicago Press, 1993.

Brown, Sterling. *The Negro in American Fiction: Negro Poetry and Drama.* New York: Arno Press, 1969.

Brown, William Wells. *St. Domingo: Revolutions and Its Patriots.* 1855; reprint, Afro-American History Series Collection 4: *Pioneer Drama and Poetry*, Wilmington, Del.: Scholars Resources, n.d.

Browning, Barbara. *Infectious Rhythm: Metaphors of Contagion and the Spread of African Culture.* New York: Routledge, 1998.

Burke, Edmund. *A Philosophical Inquiry into the Origin of Our ideas of the Sublime and the Beautiful.* 1757; reprint, New York: Oxford University Press, 1998.

Burton, Orville Vernon, and Georgeanne B. Burton. Introduction to *The Free Flag of Cuba*, edited by Orville Vernon Burton and Georgeanne B. Burton, 1–48. Baton Rouge: Louisiana State University Press, 2002.

Cable, George Washington. "Belles Demoiselles Plantation." In *Old Creole Days*, 121–45. 1879; reprint, New York: Scribner's, 1927.

———. *The Creoles of Louisiana.* New York: Scribner's, 1910.

———. *The Grandissimes.* 1880; reprint, New York: Penguin, 1988.

Caminero-Santangelo, Marta. *On Latinidad: U.S. Latino Literature and the Construction of Ethnicity.* Gainesville: University Press of Florida, 2007.

Carby, Hazel. "The Politics of Fiction, Anthropology, and the Folk: Zora Neale Hurston." In *New Essays on* Their Eyes Were Watching God, edited by Michael Awkward, 71–93. Cambridge: Cambridge University Press.

Carnes, Mark. *Novel History: Historians and Novelists Confront America's Past (and Each Other).* New York: Simon and Schuster, 2001.

Carpentier, Alejo. *The Kingdom of This World.* 1949; translated by Harriet De Onís, New York: Farrar, Straus and Giroux, 1957.

Cartwright, Keith. *Reading Africa into American Literature: Epics, Fables, and Gothic Tales.* Lexington: University of Kentucky Press, 2002.

———. "Re-Creolizing Swing: St. Domingue Refugees in the *GOVI* of New Orleans." In *Reinterpreting the Haitian Revolution and Its Cultural Aftershocks*, edited by Martin Munro and Elizabeth Walcott-Hackshaw, 102–22. Kingston, Jamaica: University of the West Indies Press, 2006.

———. *Sacral Grooves, Limbo Gateways: Travels in Deep Southern Time,* Circum-Caribbean *Space, Afro-Creole Authority.* Athens: University of Georgia Press, 2013.

Casid, Jill H. *Sowing Empire: Landscape and Colonization.* Minneapolis: University of Minnesota Press, 2005.

Castro, Max. "The Trouble with Collusion: Paradoxes of the Cuban-American Way." In *Cuba, the Elusive Nation: Interpretations of National Identity*, edited by Damián J. Fernández and Madeline Cámara Betancourt, 292–309. Gainesville: University Press of Florida, 2000.

Cave, Damien. "U.S. Overtures Find Support among Cuban-Americans." *New York Times*, April 22, 2009.

Certeau, Michel de. *The Practice of Everyday Life.* Translated by Steven Rendell. Berkeley: University of California Press, 1984.

———. *The Writing of History*. Translated by Tom Conley. New York: Columbia University Press, 1988.

Césaire, Aimé. *Discourse on Colonialism*. 1955; translated by Joan Pinkham, New York: Monthly Review Press, 2000.

———. *La Tragédie du roi Christophe*. Paris: Présence Africaine, 1970.

Césaire, Ina. *Moi Cyrilia, gouvernante de Lafcadio Hearn; 1888: Un échange de paroles à Saint-Pierre de la Martinique*. Bordeaux, France: Elytis, 2009.

Chaffin, Tom. *Fatal Glory: Narciso Lopez and the First Clandestine U.S. War against Cuba*. Baton Rouge: Louisiana State University Press, 1996.

Charnov, Elaine S. "The Performative Visual Anthropology Films of Zora Neale Hurston." *Film Criticism* 23, no. 1 (1998): 38–47.

Chellappan, K. "Cultural Dualism in *Banana Bottom*: An Indian Perspective." In *Claude McKay: Centennial Studies*, 32–40. New Delhi: Sterling Publishers, 1992.

Clifford, James. *The Predicament of Culture: Twentieth-Century Ethnography, Literature, and Art*. Cambridge: Harvard University Press, 1988.

———. *Routes: Travel and Translation in the Late Twentieth Century*. Cambridge: Harvard University Press, 1997.

Clifford, James, and George E. Marcus. *Writing Culture: The Poetics and Politics of Ethnography*. Berkeley: University of California Press, 1996.

Clinton, Catherine. "'Southern Dishonor': Flesh, Blood, Race, and Bondage." In *In Joy and in Sorrow: Women, Family, and Marriage in the Victorian South, 1830–1900*, edited by Carol Bleser, 52–68. New York: Oxford University Press, 1991.

Clymer, Jeffery A. "Martin Delany's *Blake* and the Transnational Politics of Property." *American Literary History* 15, no. 4 (2003): 709–31.

Cobham, Rhonda. "The Background." In *West Indian Literature*, edited by Bruce King. London: Macmillan, 1979. 9–29.

———. "Jekyll and Claude: The Erotics of Patronage in Claude McKay's *Banana Bottom*. *Caribbean Quarterly* 38, no. 1 (1992): 55–78.

Codrescu, Andrei. *Ay, Cuba! A Socio-Erotic Journey*. New York: Picador, 2001.

Coetzee, J. M. *White Writing: On the Culture of Letters in South Africa*. New Haven: Yale University Press, 1988.

Cohn, Deborah. *History and Memory in the Two Souths*. Nashville: Vanderbilt University Press, 1999.

———. "'Of the Same Blood as This America and Its History': William Faulkner and Spanish American Literature." In *South to a New Place: Region, Literature, Culture*, edited by Suzanne W. Jones and Sharon Monteith, 44–57. Baton Rouge: Louisiana State University Press, 2002.

Conde, Yvonne. *Operation Pedro Pan*. New York: Routledge, 1999.

Cook, David, and Michael Okenimkpe. *Ngugi wa Thiong'o: An Exploration of His Writings*. London: Heinemann, 1983.

Cooper, Wayne. *Claude McKay: Rebel Sojourner in the Harlem Renaissance*. Baton Rouge: Louisiana State University Press, 1987.

———, ed. *The Passion of Claude McKay: Selected Poetry and Prose, 1912–1948*. New York: Schocken, 1973.

Cooper, Wyn. "About Madison Smartt Bell." *Ploughshares* 25, no. 4 (1999): 205–9.

Cott, Jonathan. *Wandering Ghost: The Odyssey of Lafcadio Hearn*. New York: Knopf, 1990.

Cox, John D. *Traveling South: Travel Narratives and the Construction of American Identity*. Athens: University of Georgia Press, 2005.

Craige, John Houston. *Cannibal Cousins*. New York: Minton, Balch, 1934.

Crapanzano, Vincent. "Hermes' Dilemma: The Masking of Subversion in Ethnographic Description." In *Writing Culture: The Poetics and Politics of Ethnography*, edited by James Clifford and George E. Marcus, 51–76. Berkeley: University of California Press, 1996.

Cronin, Justin. "A Conversation with Madison Smartt Bell." *Four Quarters* 9, nos. 1, 2 (1995): 13–24.

Croucher, Sheila. *Imagining Miami: Ethnic Politics in a Postmodern World*. Charlottesville: University of Virginia Press, 1997.

Cruz, Nilo. *Anna in the Tropics*. New York: Theatre Communications Group, 2003.

Dalleo, Raphael, and Elena Machado Sáez. *The Latino/a Canon and the Emergence of Post-Sixties Literature*. New York: Palgrave, 2007.

Darwin, Charles. *Voyage of the Beagle*. London: Penguin Classics, 1989.

Dash, J. Michael. "Fictions of Displacement: Locating Modern Haitian Narratives." *Small Axe* 12, no. 3 (2008): 32–41.

———. *Haiti and the United States: National Stereotypes and the Literary Imagination*. 2nd ed. New York: St. Martin's Press, 1997.

———. Introduction to Édouard Glissant, *Caribbean Discourse: Selected Essays*. Translated by J. Michael Dash. Charlottesville: University of Virginia Press, 1989.

———. *The Other America: Caribbean Literature in a New World Context*. Charlottesville: University of Virginia Press, 1998.

———. "The Peasant Novel in Haiti." *African Literature Today* 9 (1978): 77–90.

Davidson, Basil. *The Black Man's Burden and the Curse of the Nation-State*. New York: Times Books, 1992.

Davis, David Brion. "Impact of the French and Haitian Revolutions." In *The Impact of the Haitian Revolution in the Atlantic World*, edited by David P. Geggus, 3–9. Columbia: University of South Carolina Press, 2001.

Davis, Thadious M. *Southscapes: Geographies of Race, Region, and Literature*. Chapel Hill: University of North Carolina Press, 2011.

Dayan, Joan. *Haiti, History, and the Gods*. Berkeley: University of California Press, 1995.

———. "Vodoun, of the Voice of the Gods." In *Sacred Possessions: Vodou, Santería, Obeah, and the Caribbean*, edited by Margarite Fernández Olmos and Lizabeth Paravisini-Gebert, 13–36. New Brunswick: Rutgers University Press, 1997.

Dean, Sharon L. *Constance Fenimore Woolson: Homeward Bound*. Knoxville: University of Tennessee Press, 1995.

Deguzmán, Maria. *Spain's Long Shadow: The Black Legend, Off-Whiteness, and Anglo-American Empire*. Minneapolis: University of Minnesota Press, 2005.

de la Campa, Román. *Cuba on My Mind: Journeys to a Severed Nation*. New York: Verso, 2000.

Delany, Martin R. *Blake; or, The Huts of America*. 1859; reprint, Boston: Beacon, 1970.

——. *The Condition, Elevation, Emigration and Destiny of the Colored People of the United States*. Philadelphia: published by the author, 1852.

——. *Martin R. Delany: A Documentary Reader*. Edited by Robert S. Levine. Chapel Hill: University of North Carolina Press, 2003.

de la Torre, Miguel. *La Lucha for Cuba: Religion and Politics on the Streets of Miami*. Berkeley: University of California Press, 2003.

DeLoughrey, Elizabeth M. *Routes and Roots: Navigating Caribbean and Pacific Island Literatures*. Honolulu: University of Hawai'i Press, 2007.

DePietro, Thomas. *Conversations with Don DeLillo*. Jackson: University Press of Mississippi, 2005.

Deren, Maya. *Divine Horsemen: The Living Gods of Haiti*. Kingston, N.Y.: McPherson, 1953.

Dick, Bruce Allen. *A Poet's Truth: Conversations with Latino/Latina Poets*. Tucson: University of Arizona Press, 2003.

Didion, Joan. *Miami*. New York: Simon and Schuster, 1987.

Donaldson, Susan V. "Southern Narrative and Haitian Shadows." Unpublished essay.

Douglas, Anne. *The Feminization of American Culture*. New York: Knopf, 1977.

Douglass, Frederick. "The Revolution of 1848." In *Frederick Douglass: Selected Speeches and Writings*, edited by Philip S. Foner and Yuval Taylor, 103–11. New York: Lawrence Hill Books, 1999.

Drexler, Michael. "Brigands and Nuns: The Vernacular Sociology of Collectivity after the Haitian Revolution." In *Messy Beginnings: Postcoloniality and Early American Studies*, edited by Malini Johar Schueller and Edward Watts, 175–99. New Brunswick: Rutgers University Press, 2003.

Duberman, Martin Bauml. *Paul Robeson*. New York: Knopf, 1988.

Dubois, Laurent. *Avengers of the New World: The Story of the Haitian Revolution*. Cambridge: Harvard University Press, 2004.

——. *A Colony of Citizens: Revolution and Slave Emancipation in the French Caribbean, 1787–1804*. Chapel Hill: University of North Carolina Press, 2004.

——. "Capturing Louverture." *Small Axe* 12, no. 1 (2007): 177–83.

Duck, Leigh Anne. *The Nation's Region: Southern Modernism, Segregation, and U.S. Nationalism*. Athens: University of Georgia Press, 2006.

——. "'Rebirth of a Nation': Hurston in Haiti." *Journal of American Folklore* 117, no. 464 (2004): 127–46.

Duclos, Donald Philip. "Son of Sorrow: The Life, Works and Influence of William C. Falkner, 1825–1889." Ph.D. diss., University of Michigan, 1962.

Durkheim, Émile. *The Elementary Forms of the Religious Life.* 1912; reprint, New York: Free Press, 1965.

Eaton, Clement. *A History of the Old South.* New York: Macmillan, 1949.

Edelman, Marion Wright. *The Measure of Our Success: A Letter to My Children and Yours.* Boston: Beacon, 1992.

Edmondson, Belinda. *Making Men: Gender, Literary Authority, and Women's Writing in Caribbean Narrative.* Durham: Duke University Press, 1999.

Ernest, John. *Resistance and Reformation in Nineteenth-Century African-American Literature: Brown, Wilson, Jacobs, Delany, Douglass, and Harper.* Jackson: University Press of Mississippi, 1995.

Euba, Femi. *Archetypes, Imprecators, and Victims of Fate: Origins and Developments of Satire in Black Drama.* New York: Greenwood, 1989.

Evans, Augusta Jane. *Inez: A Tale of the Alamo.* New York: Mershon, 1858.

Fabre, Michel. *The Unfinished Quest of Richard Wright.* 1973; 2nd ed., translated by Isabel Barzun, Urbana:: University of Illinois Press, 1993.

———. *The World of Richard Wright.* Jackson: University Press of Mississippi, 1985.

Falkner, William Clark. *The Siege of Monterrey.* Cincinnati: J. Hart, 1851.

———. *The Spanish Heroine: A Tale of War and Love.* Cincinnati: J. Hart, 1851.

Fanon, Frantz. *Black Skin, White Masks.* Translated by Charles Lam Markmann. New York: Grove Weidenfeld, 1967.

———. *The Wretched of the Earth.* Translated by Constance Farrington. New York: Grove Weidenfeld, 1963.

Faulkner, William. *Absalom, Absalom!* 1936; reprint, New York: Vintage, 1972.

———. *The Unvanquished.* 1938; reprint, New York: Vintage, 1966.

Fernández, Roberto G. *Holy Radishes!* Houston: Arte Publico Press, 1995.

———. *Raining Backwards.* Houston: Arte Publico Press, 1988.

Fick, Carolyn E. "The French Revolution in Saint Domingue: A Triumph or a Failure?" In *A Turbulent Time: The French Revolution and the Greater Caribbean,* edited by David Barry Gaspar and David Patrick Geggus, 51–75. Bloomington: Indiana University Press, 1997.

———. *The Making of Haiti: The Saint Domingue Revolution from Below.* Knoxville: University of Tennessee Press, 1991.

Fischer, Sibylle. *Modernity Disavowed: Haiti and the Cultures of Slavery in the Age of Revolution.* Durham: Duke University Press, 2004.

Foner, Philip S., and Yuval Taylor, eds. *Frederick Douglass: Selected Speeches and Writings.* New York: Lawrence Hill Books, 1999.

Foos, Paul. *A Short, Offhand, Killing Affair: Soldiers and Social Conflict during the Mexican-American War.* Chapel Hill: University of North Carolina Press, 2002.

Forbes, Curdella. *From Nation to Diaspora: Samuel Selvon, George Lamming, and the Cultural Performance of Gender.* Kingston, Jamaica: University of the West Indies Press, 2005.

Forsdick, Charles. "Madison Smartt Bell's Toussaint at the Crossroads: The Haitian Revolutionary between History and Fiction." *Small Axe* 12, no. 1 (2007): 194–208.

Foster, Gaines M. *Ghosts of the Confederacy: Defeat, the Lost Cause, and the Rise of the New South*. New York: Oxford, 1987.

Freehling, William W. *The Road to Disunion, Volume II: Secessionists Triumphant, 1854–1861*. New York: Oxford University Press, 2007.

Freud, Sigmund. *Civilization and Its Discontents*. Translated and edited by James Strachey. New York: Norton, 1961.

Frost, O. W. *Young Hearn*. Tokyo: Hokuseido Press, 1958.

Furé, Rogelio Martínez. "Imaginary Dialogue on Folklore." In *Afrocuba: An Anthology of Cuban Writing on Race, Politics, and Culture*, edited by Pedro Pérez Sarduy and Jean Stubbs, 109–16. Melbourne: Ocean Press, 1993.

Fusco, Coco. "Jinateras en Cuba." *Encuentro* 4, no. 5 (1997): 53–64.

Gaga [Mark S. Johnson]. "Interview with Ishmael Reed." In *Conversations with Ishmael Reed*, edited by Bruce Dick and Amritjit Singh, 51–58. Jackson: University Press of Mississippi, 1995.

Gaines, Steven. *Fool's Paradise: Players, Poseurs, and the Culture of Excess in South Beach*. New York: Crown, 2009.

Gannon, Michael, ed. *The New History of Florida*. Gainesville: University Press of Florida, 1996.

García, Cristina. *The Agüero Sisters*. New York: Ballantine, 1997.

——. *Dreaming in Cuban*. New York: Ballantine, 1992.

——. "Translation as Restoration." In *Voice-Overs: Translation and Latin American Literature*, edited by Daniel Balderston and Marcy Schwartz, 45–48. Albany: State University of New York Press, 2002.

García, Maria Cristina. *Havana USA: Cuban Exiles and Cuban Americans in South Florida, 1959–1994*. Berkeley: University of California Press, 1996.

Garcia Márquez, Gabriel. "William Faulkner 1897/1997." In *A Faulkner 100: The Centennial Exhibition, with a Contribution by Gabriel Garcia Márquez*, edited by Thomas M. Verich. University: University of Mississippi Library Special Collections, 1997.

Gaspar, David Barry. "The Antigua Slave Conspiracy of 1736: A Case Study of the Origins of Collective Resistance." *William and Mary Quarterly*, 3rd ser., 35, no. 2 (1978): 308–23.

Gates, Henry Louis, Jr. *The Signifying Monkey: A Theory of Afro-American Literary Criticism*. New York: Oxford University Press, 1988.

Geertz, Clifford. *The Interpretation of Cultures*. New York: Basic Books, 1973.

Geggus, David P., ed. *The Impact of the Haitian Revolution in the Atlantic World*. Columbia: University of South Carolina Press, 2001.

Genovese, Eugene. *From Rebellion to Revolution: Afro-American Slave Revolts in the Making of the Modern World*. Baton Rouge: Louisiana State University Press, 1972.

Gikandi, Simon. *Writing in Limbo: Modernism and Caribbean Literature*. Ithaca: Cornell University Press, 1992.

Gilroy, Paul. *The Black Atlantic: Modernity and Double Consciousness*. Cambridge: Harvard University Press, 1993.

Girard, René. *Violence and the Sacred*. Translated by Patrick Gregory. Baltimore: Johns Hopkins University Press, 1977.

Glissant, Édouard. *Caribbean Discourse: Selected Essays*. Translated by J. Michael Dash. Charlottesville: University of Virginia Press, 1989.

——. *Faulkner, Mississippi*. Translated by Barbara Lewis and Thomas C. Spear. New York: Farrar, Straus and Giroux, 1999.

——. *Monsieur Toussaint: A Play*. Translated by J. Michael Dash and Édouard Glissant. Boulder, Colo.: Lynne Rienner, 2005.

——. *Poetics of Relation*. Translated by Betsy Wing. Ann Arbor: University of Michigan Press, 1997.

Godden, Richard. *Fictions of Labor: William Faulkner and the South and the South's Long Revolution*. New York: Cambridge University Press, 1997.

Gonzalez, Antonio. "Florida Football Town's Future Looks Grim." *Baton Rouge Advocate*, August 12, 2008, 5C.

Gordon, Lyndall. *A Private Life of Henry James: Two Women and His Art*. New York: W. W. Norton, 1999.

Gosciak, Josh. *The Shadowed Country: Claude McKay and the Romance of the Victorians*. New Brunswick: Rutgers University Press, 2006.

Goudie, Sean X. *Creole America: The West Indies and the Formation of Literature and Culture in the New Republic*. Philadelphia: University of Pennsylvania Press, 2006.

Gould, George M. *Concerning Lafcadio Hearn*. London: T. Fisher Unwin, 1908.

Grady, Henry. "The New South." 1886; reprinted in *Georgia Voices*, edited by Hugh Ruppersburg, 2: 205–13. Athens: University of Georgia Press, 1994.

Grant, Ulysses S. *Ulysses S. Grant: Memoirs and Selected Letters, 1839–1865*. New York: Library of America, 1990.

Greenberg, Amy S. *Manifest Manhood and the Antebellum American Empire*. Cambridge: Cambridge University Press, 2005.

Greene, Julie. *The Canal Builders: Making American Empire at the Panama Canal*. New York: Penguin, 2009.

Greeson, Jennifer. "Expropriating *The Great South* and Exporting 'Local Color': Global and Hemispheric Imaginaries of the First Reconstruction." *American Literary History* 18, no. 3 (2006): 496–520.

——. *Our South: Geographic Fantasy and the Rise of National Literature*. Cambridge: Harvard University Press, 2010.

Griffin, Barbara. "The Road to Psychic Unity: The Politics of Gender in Claude McKay's *Banana Bottom*." *Callaloo* 22, no. 2 (1999): 499–508.

Gruesz, Kirsten Silva. *Ambassadors of Culture: The Transamerican Origins of Latino Writing*. Princeton: Princeton University Press, 2002.

——. "The Gulf of Mexico System and the 'Latinness' of New Orleans." *American Literary History* 18, no. 3 (2006): 468–95.

Guterl, Matthew Pratt. *American Mediterranean: Southern Slaveholders in the Age of Emancipation*. Cambridge: Harvard University Press, 2008.

Guyot, Arnold. *The Earth and Man: Lectures on Comparative Physical Geography, in Its Relation to the History of Mankind.* Boston: Gould, Kendall, and Lincoln, 1849.

Haddox, Thomas F. *Fear and Fascinations: Representing Catholicism in the American South.* New York: Fordham University Press, 2005.

Hakutani, Yoshinobu. *Richard Wright and Racial Discourse.* Columbia: University of Missouri Press, 1996.

Hale, Sarah Josepha. *Liberia; or, Mr. Peyton's Experiment.* 1853; reprint, Upper Saddle River, N.J.: Gregg Press, 1968.

Hall, Gwendolyn Midlo. "Franco-African Peoples of Haiti and Louisiana." *Southern Quarterly* 44, no. 3 (2007): 10–17.

Hall, Stuart. "Cultural Identity and Diaspora." In *Theorizing Diaspora: A Reader*, edited by Jana Evans Braziel and Anita Mannur, 233–46. London: Blackwell, 2003.

Hamner, Robert. "Dramatizing the New World's African King: O'Neill, Walcott, and Césaire on Christophe." *Journal of West Indian Literature* 5, nos. 1, 2 (1992): 30–47.

Handley, George B. *Postslavery Literature in the Americas: Family Portraits in Black and White.* Charlottesville: University of Virginia Press, 2000.

Hanger, Kimberly S. "Origins of New Orleans's Free Creoles of Color." In *Creoles of Color of the Gulf South*, edited by James H. Dormon, 3–27. Knoxville: University of Tennessee Press, 1996.

Harris, Trudier. "Celebrating Bigamy and Other Outlaw Behaviors: Hurston, Reputation, and the Myth of Feminism." In *Approaches to Teaching Hurston's* Their Eyes Were Watching God *and Other Works*, edited by John Lowe, 67–80. New York: Modern Language Association, 2009.

Harris, Wilson. *Tradition, the Writer, and Society.* London: New Beacon, 1973.

———. *The Womb of Space: The Cross-Cultural Imagination.* Westport, Conn.: Greenwood Press, 1983.

Hart, John Mason. "The Mexican Revolution, 1910–1920." In *The Oxford History of Mexico*, edited by Michael C. Meyer and William H. Beezley, 435–65. New York: Oxford University Press, 2000.

Harvey, Bruce A. *American Geographics: U.S. National Narratives and the Representation of the Non-European World, 1830–1865.* Palo Alto: Stanford University Press, 2001.

Hassel, Mary. *Secret History; or, The Horrors of St. Domingo.* 1808.

Hathaway, Heather. *Caribbean Waves: Relocating Claude McKay and Paule Marshall.* Bloomington: Indiana University Press, 1999.

Hearn, Lafcadio. *An American Miscellany.* Edited by Albert Mordell. New York: Dodd, Mead, 1925.

———. *Chita: A Memory of Lost Island.* 1888; reprint, edited by Delia Barr. Jackson: University Press of Mississippi, 2003.

———. *Editorials.* Edited by Charles Woodward Hutson. New York: Houghton Mifflin, 1926.

——. *Exotics and Retrospectives in Ghostly Japan*. Boston: Little, Brown, 1905.

——. *Inventing New Orleans: Writings of Lafcadio Hearn*. Edited by S. Frederick Starr. Jackson: University Press of Mississippi, 2001.

——. "A Study of the Half-Breed Races in the West Indies." In *An American Miscellany*, edited by Albert Mordell, 2:221–31. New York: Dodd, Mead, 1925.

——. *Two Years in the French West Indies*. 1890; reprint, Northampton, Mass.: Interlink Publishing, 2001.

——. *Youma: The Story of a West-Indian Slave*. 1890; reprint, Alhambra, Calif.: C. F. Braun, 1951.

Hegeman, Susan. "Franz Boas and Professional Anthropology: On Mapping the Borders of the 'Modern.'" *Victorian Studies* 41, no. 3 (1998): 455–83.

Helg, Aline. *Our Rightful Share: The Afro-Cuban Struggle for Equality, 1886–1912*. Chapel Hill: University of North Carolina Press, 1995.

Herskovits, Melville J. *Franz Boas: The Science of Man in the Making*. New York: Scribner's, 1953.

——. *Life in a Haitian Valley*. New York: Knopf, 1937.

Herzog, Kirstin. *Women, Ethnics, and Exotics: Images of Power in Mid-nineteenth Century American Fiction*. Knoxville: University of Tennessee Press, 1983.

Heyward, Dubose. "Charleston: Where Mellow Past and Present Meet." *National Geographic Magazine* (March 1939): 273–312.

——. *Porgy*. New York: George H. Doran, 1928.

——. *Star Spangled Virgin*. New York: Farrar and Rinehart, 1939.

Hiassen, Carl. "On the Beach." Review of *Fool's Paradise: Players, Poseurs, and the Culture of Excess in South Beach* by Stephen Gaines. *New York Times Book Review*, February 22, 2009, 1.

Hijuelos, Oscar. *The Mambo Kings Play Songs of Love*. New York: Harper, 1990.

Hobsbawm, Eric. "Introduction: Inventing Traditions." In *The Invention of Tradition*, edited by Eric Hobsbawm and Terence Ranger, 1–15. Cambridge: Cambridge University Press, 1983.

Hogan, Ron. Interview with Madison Smartt Bell, 1997. www.beatrice.com/interviews/bell.

Holly, James. "Thoughts on Hayti." *Anglo-African Magazine* 1 (1859): 365.

Homer. *The Odyssey*. Translated by Robert Fagles. New York: Penguin, 1996.

Hospital, Carolina, and Jorge Cantera, eds. *A Century of Cuban Writers in Florida: Selected Prose and Poetry*. Sarasota: Pineapple Press, 1996.

Hulme, Peter. *Colonial Encounters*. Cambridge: Cambridge University Press, 1987.

Hunt, Alfred N. *Haiti's Influence on Antebellum America: Slumbering Volcano in the Caribbean*. Baton Rouge: Louisiana State University Press, 1988.

Hurston, Zora Neale. *Dust Tracks on a Road*. 1942; 2nd ed., Urbana: University of Illinois Press, 1984.

——. "Folklore and Music." In *Folklore, Memoirs, and Other Writings*, 875–94. New York: Library of America, 1995.

——. "How It Feels to Be Colored Me." 1928; reprinted in *I Love Myself When I*

Am Laughing: A Zora Neale Hurston Reader, edited by Alice Walker, 152–55. Old Westbury, N.Y.: Feminist Press, 1979.

———. *Jonah's Gourd Vine*. 1934; reprint, New York: HarperCollins, 1990.

———. *Mules and Men*. 1935; reprint, Bloomington: Indiana University Press, 1978.

———. "Proposed Recording Expedition into the Floridas." In *Go Gator, and Muddy the Water: Writings by Zora Neale Hurston from the Federal Writers' Project*, edited by Pamela Bordelon. New York: Norton, 1999.

———. "Review of *Harlem: Negro Metropolis*." *Common Ground* 1 (1941): 95–96.

———. *Seraph on the Suwanee*. 1948; reprint, New York: HarperCollins, 1990.

———. *Tell My Horse: Voodoo and Life in Haiti and Jamaica*. 1938; reprint, New York: HarperCollins, 1990.

———. *Their Eyes Were Watching God*. 1937; reprint, Urbana: University of Illinois Press, 1974.

Hurston, Zora Neale, collector and annotator. *Caribbean Melodies*. Philadelphia: Oliver Ditson, 1947.

Hutchisson, James M. *Dubose Heyward: A Charleston Gentleman and the World of Porgy and Bess*. Jackson: University Press of Mississippi, 2000.

Ingraham, Joseph Holt. *The Quadroone; or, St. Michael's Day*. 2 vols. New York: Harper and Brothers, 1841.

Jacknis, Ira. "Franz Boas and Photography." *Studies in Visual Communication* 10, no. 1 (1984): 2–60.

Jackson, Maurice, and Jacqueline Bacon, eds. *African Americans and the Haitian Revolution: Selected Essays and Historical Documents*. New York: Routledge, 2010.

Jacobs, Karen. "From 'Spy-glass' to 'Horizon': Tracking the Anthropological Gaze in Zora Neale Hurston." *Novel* 30, no. 3 (1997): 329–60.

Jahn, Janheinz. *Muntu: African Culture and the Western World*. 1958; translated by Marjorie Grene, New York: Grove Weidenfeld, 1961.

James, C. L. R. *The Black Jacobins: Toussaint L'Ouverture and the San Domingo Revolution*. 1938; rev. ed., New York: Random House, 1989.

James, Henry. "Miss Woolson." In *Constance Fenimore Woolson*, edited by Clare Benedict, 1–14. London: Ellis, 1930.

James, Winston. *Holding Aloft the Banner of Ethiopia: Caribbean Radicalism in Early Twentieth-Century America*. New York: Verso, 1998.

Jan Mohamed, Abdul R. *The Death-Bound Subject: Richard Wright's Archaeology of Death*. Durham: Duke University Press, 2005.

Japtok, Martin. "Pauline Hopkins's *Of One Blood*, Africa, and the "Darwinist Trap." *African American Review* 36, no. 3 (2002): 403–15.

Jefferson, Thomas. Letter to Lydia Huntley Sigourney, Monticello, July 18, 1824. *Magazine of American History* 21 (1891): 481.

———. *The Writings of Thomas Jefferson*. Vol. 5. Washington, D.C.: Jefferson Memorial Society, 1905.

Jekyll, Walter. *Jamaican Song and Story: Annancy Stories, Digging Songs, Ring Tunes, and Dancing Tunes*. London: David Nutt, 1907.

Jennings, La Vinia Delois, ed. *Zora Neale Hurston, Haiti, and* Their Eyes Were Watching God. Evanston: Northwestern University Press, 2013.

Johannsen, Robert W. *To the Halls of the Montezumas: The Mexican War in the American Imagination.* New York: Oxford University Press, 1985.

Johnson, James Weldon. *Along This Way: The Autobiography of James Weldon Johnson.* New York: Viking, 1933.

———. *Social, Political, and Literary Essays.* Vol. 2 of *The Selected Writings of James Weldon Johnson.* Edited by Sondra Kathryn Wilson. New York: Oxford University Press, 1995.

———. "The Truth about Haiti: An N.A.A.C.P. Investigation." *Crisis* 5 (September 1920): 217–24.

Julien, Claude, and Anne-Laure Tissut. *Reading Percival Everett: European Perspectives.* Tours, France: Presses Universitaires François Rabelais, 2007

Kandiyoti, Dalia. "Consuming Nostalgia: Nostalgia and the Marketplace in Cristina García and Ana Menéndez." *MELUS* 31, no. 1 (2006): 81–97.

Kant, Immanuel. *Critique of Judgment.* 1790; translated by Werner S. Pluhar, Cambridge: Hackett, 1983.

Kaplan, Amy. "Manifest Domesticity." *American Literature* 70, no. 3 (1998): 581–606.

Karem, Jeff. *The Purloined Islands: Caribbean-U.S. Crosscurrents in Literature and Culture, 1880–1959.* Charlottesville: University of Virginia Press, 2011.

Kazanjian, David. *The Colonizing Trick: Imperial Citizenship in Early America.* Minneapolis: University of Minnesota Press, 2003.

Kelley, Robin D. G. "A Poetics of Anticolonialism." Introduction to *Discourse on Colonialism,* by Aimé Césaire (1933). Reprint, translated by Joan Pinkham. New York: Monthly Review Press, 2000.

Kennedy, John Pendleton. *Swallow Barn: A Sojourn in the Old Dominion.* 1853; reprint, New York: Hafner, 1962.

Kent, George. "A Future They Must Learn." In *Conversations: George Lamming: Essays, Addresses, and Interviews, 1953–1990,* edited by Richard Drayton and Andaiye, 4–14, 88–97. London: Karia Press, 1992.

Kevane, Bridget, and Juanita Heredia. *Latina Self-Portraits: Interviews with Contemporary Women Writers.* Albuquerque: University of New Mexico Press, 2000.

Kimbell, David R. B. *Italian Opera.* Cambridge: Cambridge University Press, 1994.

King, Grace. *New Orleans: The Place and the People.* New York: Macmillan, 1915.

Kinnamon, Keneth, and Michel Fabre. *Conversations with Richard Wright.* Jackson: University Press of Mississippi, 1993.

Kinnard, Nina H. *Lafcadio Hearn.* New York: Appleton, 1912.

Kolodny, Annette. *The Land Before Her: Fantasy and the Experience of the American Frontiers, 1630–1860.* Chapel Hill: University of North Carolina Press, 1984.

———. *The Lay of the Land: Metaphor as Experience and History in American Life and Letters.* Chapel Hill: University of North Carolina Press, 1975.

Konzett, Delia Caparoso. *Ethnic Modernisms: Anzia Yezierska, Zora Neale Hurston, Jean Rhys, and the Aesthetics of Dislocation.* New York: Palgrave, 2002.

Kraidy, Marwan M. *Hybridity, or the Cultural Logic of Globalization.* Philadelphia: Temple University Press, 2005.

Kreyling, Michael. *The South That Wasn't There: Postsouthern Memory and History.* Baton Rouge: Louisiana State University Press, 2010.

Kroeber, Alfred. Review of *Patterns of Culture* by Ruth Benedict. *American Anthropologist* 37 (1935): 689–90.

Kutzinski, Vera. "Borders and Bodies: The United States, America, and the Caribbean." *New Centennial Review* 1, no. 2 (2001): 55–88.

——. *Sugar's Secrets: Race and the Erotics of Cuban Nationalism.* Charlottesville: University of Virginia Press, 1993.

Ladd, Barbara. "Dismantling the Monolith: Southern Places—Past, Present, and Future." In *South to a New Place: Region, Literature, Culture*, edited by Suzanne W. Jones and Sharon Monteith, 44–57. Baton Rouge: Louisiana State University Press, 2002.

——. *Nationalism and the Color Line in George W. Cable, Mark Twain, and William Faulkner.* Baton Rouge: Louisiana State University Press, 1996.

——. *Resisting History: Gender, Modernity, and Authorship in William Faulkner, Zora Neale Hurston, and Eudora Welty.* Baton Rouge: Louisiana State University Press, 2007.

Lamazares, Ivonne. *The Sugar Island.* Boston: Houghton Mifflin, 2000.

Lamming, George. *In the Castle of My Skin.* 1953; reprint, Ann Arbor: University of Michigan Press, 1991.

——. *Natives of My Person.* 1972; reprint, Ann Arbor: University of Michigan Press, 1995.

——. *The Pleasures of Exile.* 1960; reprint, London: Allison and Busby, 1984.

Landers, Jane G. *Atlantic Creoles in the Age of Revolutions.* Cambridge: Harvard University Press, 2010.

Langley, Lewis D. *The Americas in the Age of Revolution, 1760–1850.* New Haven: Yale University Press, 1996.

Lanier, Sidney. *Florida: Its Scenery, Climate, and History, with an Account of Charleston, Savannah, Augusta, and Aiken, and a Chapter for Consumptives; Being a Complete Hand-Book and Guide.* Philadelphia: Lippincott, 1875.

Larsen, Nella. *Quicksand* and *Passing.* New Brunswick: Rutgers University Press, 1986.

Lazo, Rodrigo. "Filibustering Cuba: *Cecilia Valdés* and a Memory of Nation in the Americas." *American Literature* 74, no. 1 (2002): 1–30.

——. *Writing to Cuba: Filibustering and Cuban Exiles in the United States.* Chapel Hill: University of North Carolina Press, 2005.

Levine, Robert S. *Martin Delany, Frederick Douglass, and the Politics of Representative Identity.* Chapel Hill: University of North Carolina Press, 1997.

Limón, José E. *American Encounters: Greater Mexico, the United States, and the Erotics of Culture*. Boston: Beacon, 2000.

Lippard, George. *Bel of Prairie Eden: A Romance of Mexico*. 1848; reprinted in *Empire and the Literature of Sensation: An Anthology of Nineteenth-Century Popular Fiction*, edited by Jesse Alemán and Shelley Streeby, 107–200. New Brunswick: Rutgers University Press, 2007.

Loichot, Valérie. *Orphan Narratives: The Postplantation Literature of Faulkner, Glissant, Morrison, and Saint-John Perse*. Charlottesville: University of Virginia Press, 2007.

———. *The Tropics Bite Back: Culinary Coups in Caribbean Literature*. Minneapolis: University of Minnesota Press, 2013.

Lomeli, A. Francisco. "Po(l)etics of Reconstructing and/or Appropriating a Literary Past: The Regional Case Model." In *Recovering the U.S. Hispanic Literary Heritage*, edited by Ramón A. Gutiérrez and Genaro M. Padilla, 1:221–40. Houston: Arte Publico Press, 1993.

Long, A. L. *Memoirs of Robert E. Lee: His Military and Personal History*. New York: J. M. Stoddart, 1886.

Long, Edward. *The History of Jamaica*. Vol. 2. London, 1774.

Looby, Christopher. "Southworth and Seriality: *The Hidden Hand* in the *New York Ledger*." *Nineteenth-Century Literature* 59, no. 2 (2004): 179–211.

Lowe, John. "Anancy's Web/Sut's Stratagems: Humor, Race, and Trickery in Jamaica and the Old Southwest." In *Beyond Southern Frontier Humor: New Approaches*, edited by Ed Piacentino, 171–92. Jackson: University Press of Mississippi, 2013.

———. "Calypso Magnolia: The Caribbean Side of the South." *South Central Review* 22, no. 1 (2005): 54–80.

———. "Creating the Circum-Caribbean Imaginary: Du Bose Heyward's and Paul Robeson's Revision of *The Emperor Jones*." *Philological Quarterly* 90, nos. 2, 3 (2011): 317–39.

———. *Jump at the Sun: Zora Neale Hurston's Cosmic Comedy*. Urbana: University of Illinois Press, 1994.

———. "Not So Still Waters: Early Travelers to Florida and the Tropical Sublime." In *The Oxford Handbook of the American South*, edited by Fred Hobson and Barbara Ladd. New York: Oxford (forthcoming).

———. "Reconstruction Revisited: Plantation School Writers, Postcolonial Theory, and Confederates in Brazil." *Mississippi Quarterly* 57, no. 1 (2003–4): 5–26.

———. "Re-creating a Public for the Plantation: Reconstruction Myths of the Biracial Southern 'Family.'" In *Bridging Southern Cultures: An Interdisciplinary Approach*, edited by John Lowe, 221–53. Baton Rouge: Louisiana State University Press, 2006.

———. "'Seeing Beyond Seeing': Zora Neale Hurston's Religion(s)." *Southern Quarterly* 36, no. 3 (1998): 77–87.

Luis, William. "Hurricanes, Magic, Science, and Politics in Cristina García's *The*

Agüero Sisters." In *Contemporary U.S. Latino/a Literary Criticism,* edited by Lyn Di Orio Sandín and Richard Pérez. New York: Palgrave, 2007. 144–64.

Luis-Brown, David. *Waves of Decolonization: Discourses of Race and Hemispheric Citizenship in Cuba, Mexico, and the United States.* Durham: Duke University Press, 2008.

Lukács, Georg. *The Historical Novel.* 1936. Translated by Hannah Mitchell and Stanley Mitchell. Lincoln: University of Nebraska Press, 1962.

Lyotard, Jean-François. *The Postmodern Condition: A Report on Knowledge.* Translated by Geoff Bennington and Brian Massumi. Manchester: Manchester University Press, 1984.

Manigault, Arthur Middleton. *Mexican War Narrative,* edited by Warren Ripley and Arthur M. Wilcox. In *A Carolinian Goes to War: The Civil War Narrative of Arthur Middleton Manigault, Brigadier General, C.S.A.,* edited by Lockwood Tower. Columbia: University of South Carolina Press, 1983.

Manring, M. M. *Slave in a Box: The Strange Career of Aunt Jemima.* Charlottesville: University of Virginia Press, 1998.

Marmolego-McWatt, Amparo. "Blanca Mestre as Ochún in *The Agüero Sisters. Afro-Hispanic Review* 21, no. 12 (2005): 89–101.

Marsh-Lockett, Carol P. "Martin Robinson Delany." In *Afro-American Writers before the Harlem Renaissance,* vol. 50 of *Dictionary of Literary Biography,* edited by Thadious Davis, 74. Farmington Hills, Mich.: Gale, 1986.

Martí, José. "Our America." In *The Heath Anthology of American Literature,* vol. 2, 4th ed., edited by Paul Lauter et al., 879–86. New York: Houghton Mifflin, 2002.

Matthews, John. "Recalling the West Indies: From Yoknapatawpha to Haiti and Back." *American Literary History* 16, no. 2 (2004): 238–62.

May, Robert E. *Manifest Destiny's Underworld: Filibustering in Antebellum America.* Chapel Hill: University of North Carolina Press, 2002.

———. *The Southern Dream of a Caribbean Empire, 1854–1861.* Athens: University of Georgia Press, 1989.

McCaffrey, James M. *Army of Manifest Destiny: The American Soldier in the Mexican War, 1846–1848.* New York: New York University Press, 1992.

McCall, Dan. *The Example of Richard Wright.* New York: Harcourt, Brace and World, 1969.

McCarthy, Lloyd D. *"In-Dependence" from Bondage: Claude McKay and Michael Manley: Defying the Ideological Clash and Policy Gaps in African Diaspora Relations.* Trenton, N.J.: Africa World Press, 2007.

McClennen, Sophia. "Inter-American Studies or Imperial American Studies?" *Comparative American Studies* 3, no. 4 (2005): 393–413.

McElya, Micki. *Clinging to Mammy: The Faithful Slave in Twentieth-Century America.* Cambridge: Harvard University Press, 2007.

McKay, Claude. *Banana Bottom.* New York: Harper, 1933.

———. *Banjo: A Story without a Plot.* 1929; reprint, New York: Harcourt, 1957.

——. *Constab Ballads*. Kingston, Jamaica: Aston W. Gardner, 1912.

——. *Gingertown*. New York: Harper, 1932.

___. *Home to Harlem*. New York: Harper, 1928.

——. *Harlem: Black Metropolis*. New York: E. P. Dutton, 1940.

——. *A Long Way from Home*. New York: Lee Furman, 1937.

——. *My Green Hills of Jamaica and Five Jamaican Short Stories*. Edited by Mervyn Morris. Kingston, Jamaica: Heinemann, 1979.

——. *The Negroes in America*. Translated from the Russian by Robert J. Winter. Edited by Alan L. McLeod. Port Washington, N.Y.: Kennikat Press, 1979.

——. *Songs of Jamaica*. Kingston, Jamaica: Aston W. Gardner, 1912.

McWilliams, Vera. *Lafcadio Hearn*. New York: Houghton Mifflin, 1946.

Mead, Margaret. Preface to *Patterns of Culture* by Ruth Benedict, v–x. New York: Mentor, 1959.

Melville, Herman. "The Encantadas." In *The Complete Stories of Herman Melville*, edited by Jay Leyda, 49–117. New York: Random House, 1949.

——. *Moby-Dick*. 1851; New York: Hendricks House, 1962.

Menéndez, Ana. *In Cuba I Was a German Shepherd*. New York: Grove Press, 2001.

——. *Loving Che*. New York: Grove Press, 2003.

Métraux, Alfred. *Voodoo in Haiti*. Translated by Hugo Charteris. New York: Schocken, 1959.

Mignolo, Walter. *Local Histories/Global Designs: Coloniality, Subaltern Knowledges, and Border Thinking*. Princeton: Princeton University Press, 2000.

Mill, John Stuart. *Principles of Political Economy*. Vol. 3. Edited by J. J. Robson. Toronto: University of Toronto Press, 1965.

Miller, Angela. "Thomas Cole and Jacksonian America: *The Course of Empire* as Political Allegory." In *Critical Issues in American Art: A Book of Readings*, edited by Mary Ann Calo, 59–76. Boulder: Westview, 1998.

Miller, David C. *Dark Eden: The Swamp in Nineteenth-Century American Culture*. New York: Cambridge University Press, 1989.

Minh-ha, Trinh T. "Strategies of Displacement for Women, Natives and Their Others: Intra-views with Trinh T. Minh-ha." *Women's Studies Journal* 10, no. 1 (1994): 5–25.

——. *Woman, Native, Other: Writing Postcoloniality and Feminism*. Bloomington: Indiana University Press, 1989.

Montaigne, Michel de. "Of Presumption." In *The Complete Essays of Montaigne*, translated by Donald M. Frame, 478–502. Palo Alto: Stanford University Press, 1957.

Moore, John Preston. "Pierre Soulé: Southern Expansionist and Promoter." *Journal of Southern History* 21 (1955): 203–23.

Moore, Rayburn. *Constance Fenimore Woolson*. New Haven: Twayne, 1963.

Moreau de Saint-Méry, M. L. E. *Description topographique, physique, civil, politique et historique de la partie française de l'isle de Saint-Domingue*. 3 vols. 1797; reprint, Paris: Société de l'historie des colonies françaises, 1959.

Mormino, Gary R. *Land of Sunshine, State of Dreams: A Social History of Modern Florida*. Gainesville: University Press of Florida, 2005.

Morrison, Toni. *Playing in the Dark: Whiteness and the Literary Imagination*. Cambridge: Harvard University Press, 1992.

Morson, Gary Saul, and Caryl Emerson. *Mikhail Bakhtin: Creation of a Prosaics*. Stanford: Stanford University Press, 1990.

Moses, Wilson Jeremiah. *The Golden Age of Black Nationalism, 1850–1925*. Hamden, Conn.: Archon Books, 1978.

Murphy, Gretchen. *Hemispheric Imaginings: The Monroe Doctrine and Narratives of U.S. Empire*. Durham: Duke University Press, 2005.

Murphy, Joseph M. *Santería: African Spirits in America*. Boston: Beacon, 1988.

Murray, Paul. *A Fantastic Journey: The Life and Literature of Lafcadio Hearn*. Ann Arbor: University of Michigan Press, 1993.

Nair, Supriya. *Caliban's Curse: George Lamming and the Revisioning of History*. Ann Arbor: University of Michigan Press, 1996.

Nettleford, Rex. *Caribbean Cultural Identity: The Case of Jamaica: An Essay in Cultural Dynamics*. Los Angeles: Center for Afro-American Studies, 1979.

Nicholls, David G. "The Folk as Alternative Modernity: Claude McKay's *Banana Bottom* and the Romance of Nature." *Journal of Modern Literature* 23, no. 1 (1999): 79–94.

Nicholls, David. *From Dessalines to Duvalier: Race, Colour, and National Independence in Haiti*. Cambridge: Cambridge University Press, 1979.

Nishizaki, Ichiro, ed. "Newly Discovered Letters from Lafcadio Hearn to Dr. Rudolph Matas." *Studies in Arts and Cultures* 8 (March 1956): 85–118.

Nixon, H. C. *Forty Acres and Steel Mules*. Chapel Hill: University of North Carolina Press, 1938.

North, Michael. *The Dialect of Modernism: Race, Language, and Twentieth-Century Literature*. New York: Oxford University Press, 1994.

Northup, Solomon. *Twelve Years a Slave*. Edited by Sue Eakin and Joseph Logsdon. 1853; Baton Rouge: Louisiana State University Press, 1968.

Nwankwo, Ifeoma Kiddoe. *Black Cosmopolitanism: Racial Consciousness and Transnational Identity in the Nineteenth-Century Americas*. Philadelphia: University of Pennsylvania Press, 2005.

Nzengou-Tayo, Marie-José. "Haitian Gothic and History: Madison Smartt Bell's Trilogy on Toussaint Louverture and the Haitian Revolution." *Small Axe* 12, no. 1 (2007): 184–93.

Olmos, Margarite Fernández, and Lizabeth Paravisini-Gebert, eds. *Sacred Possessions: Vodou, Santería, Obeah, and the Caribbean*. New Brunswick: Rutgers University Press, 1997.

Olney, James. "The Ontology of Autobiography." In *Autobiography: Essays Theoretical and Critical*, edited by James Olney, 235–67. Princeton: Princeton University Press, 1990.

Ortiz, Ricardo L. *Cultural Erotics in Cuban America*. Minneapolis: University of Minnesota Press, 2007.

Ostendorf, Berndt. "Creoles and Creolization." In *Louisiana Culture, from the Colonial Era to Katrina*, edited by John Lowe, 103–35. Baton Rouge: Louisiana University Press, 2008.

O'Sullivan, John. "Annexation." *Democratic Review* 42 (July 1845): 5–10.

Ott, Thomas O. *The Haitian Revolution, 1789–1804*. Knoxville: University of Tennessee Press, 1973.

Page, Thomas Nelson. "No Haid Pawn." In *In Ole Virginia*, 169–93. New York: Scribner's, 1887.

——. *In Ole Virginia*. New York: Scribner's, 1881.

Paquet, Sandra Pouchet. *Caribbean Autobiography: Cultural Identity and Self-Representation*. Madison: University of Wisconsin Press, 2002.

——. *The Novels of George Lamming*. London: Heinemann, 1982.

Paravisini-Gebert, Lizabeth. "'He of the Trees': Nature, Environment, and Creole Religiosities in Caribbean Literature." In *Caribbean Literature and the Environment: Between Nature and Culture*, edited by Elizabeth M. DeLoughrey, Renee K. Gosson, and George B. Handley, 183–96. Charlottesville: University of Virginia Press, 2005.

Pavlić, Edward M. "'Papa Legba, Ouvrier Barriére Por Moi Passer': Esu in *Their Eyes Were Watching God* and Zora Neale Hurston's Diasporic Modernism." *African American Review* 38, no. 1 (2004): 61–85.

Paz, Octavio. *The Labyrinth of Solitude*. Translated by Lysander Kemp, Yara Milos, and Rachel Phillips Belash. New York: Grove Press, 1985.

Pérez, Louis A., Jr. *Cuba in the American Imagination: Metaphor and the Imperial Ethos*. Chapel Hill: University of North Carolina Press, 2008.

——. *On Becoming Cuban: Identity, Nationality, and Culture*. Chapel Hill: University of North Carolina Press, 1999.

Pérez Firmat, Gustavo. *Anything but Love*. Houston: Arte Publico Press, 2000.

——. *The Cuban Condition: Translation and Identity in Modern Cuban Literature*. Cambridge: Cambridge University Press, 1990.

——. *The Havana Habit*. New Haven: Yale University Press, 2010.

——. *Life on the Hyphen: The Cuban-American Way*. Austin: University of Texas Press, 1994.

——. "My Life as a Redneck." In *Iguana Dreams: New Latino Fiction*, edited by DeliaPoey and Virgil Suarez, 221–34. New York: Harper, 1992.

——. *Next Year in Cuba: A Cubano's Coming-of-Age in America*. New York: Anchor Books, 1995.

——. "The Rights of the Aesthetic." *South Atlantic Review* 73, no. 4 (2008): 67–71.

——. "Spic Chic: Spanglish as Equipment for Living." *Caribbean Review* 15, no. 3 (1987): 20–22, 36–37.

——. *Tongue Ties: Logo-Eroticism in Anglo-Hispanic Literature*. New York: Palgrave, 2003.

———, ed. *Do the Americas Have a Common Literature?* Durham: Duke University Press, 2000.

Pérez Sarduy, Pedro, and Jean Stubbs, eds. *Afrocuba: An Anthology of Cuban Writing on Race, Politics, and Culture*. Melbourne: Ocean Press, 1993.

Pérez, Vincent. *Remembering the Hacienda: History and Memory in the Mexican American Southwest*. College Station: Texas A&M University Press, 2006.

Peterson, Carla L. *"Doers of the Word": African American Women Speakers and Writers in the North (1830–1880)*. New York: Oxford University Press, 1995.

Pickens, Lucy Holcombe. *The Free Flag of Cuba*. 1854; edited by Orville Vernon Burton and Georgeanne B. Burton, Baton Rouge: Louisiana State University Press, 2002.

Pondrom, Cyrena N. "The Role of Myth in Hurston's *Their Eyes Were Watching God*." *American Literature* 58, no. 2 (1986): 181–82.

Poniatowska, Elena. *Las Soldaderas: Women of the Mexican Revolution*. El Paso: Cinco Puntos Press, 2006.

Powell, Timothy. "Postcolonial Theory in an American Context: A Reading of Martin Delany's *Blake*." In *The Preoccupation of Postcolonial Studies*, edited by Kalpana Seshadri-Crooks and Fawzia Azfal-Kahan, 347–65. Durham: Duke University Press, 2000.

Praeger, Michèle. *The Imaginary Caribbean and Caribbean Imaginary*. Lincoln: University of Nebraska Press, 2003.

Pratt, Mary Louise. "Fieldwork in Common Places." In *Writing Cultures: The Poetics and Politics of Ethnography*, edited by James Clifford and George E. Marcus, 27–50. Berkeley: University of California Press, 1986.

———. *Imperial Eyes: Travel Writing and Transculturation*. New York: Routledge, 1992.

Prescott, Henry H. *History of the Conquest of Mexico*. Edited by John Foster Kirk. 3 vols. Philadelphia: Lippincott, 1873.

Price, Richard, ed. *Maroon Societies: Rebel Slave Communities in the Americas*. 1979; rev. ed., Baltimore: Johns Hopkins University Press, 1996.

Quinn, Arthur Hobson. *American Fiction: An Historical and Critical Survey*. New York: D. Appleton-Century, 1936.

Rainey, Sue. *Creating Picturesque America: Monument to the Natural and Cultural Landscape*. Nashville: Vanderbilt University Press, 1994.

Ramchand, Kenneth. *The West Indian Novel and its Background*. 2nd ed. London: Heinemann, 1983.

Ramesh, Kotti Sree, and Kandula Nirup Rani. *Claude McKay: The Literary Identity from Jamaica to Harlem and Beyond*. Jefferson, N.C.: McFarland, 2006.

Reed, Ishmael. *Flight to Canada*. New York: Macmillan, 1976.

———. *Mumbo Jumbo*. New York: Doubleday, 1972.

Reid-Pharr, Robert. "Violent Ambiguity: Martin Delany, Bourgeois Sadomasochism, and the Production of a Black National Masculinity." In *Representing Black Men*, edited by Marcellus Blount and George P. Cunningham, 73–94. New York: Routledge, 1996.

Reilly, John M. "Richard Wright Preaches the Nation: *12 Million Black Voices*." *Black American Literature Forum* 16, no. 3 (1982): 116–19.

Renda, Mary A. *Taking Haiti: Military Occupation and the Culture of U.S. Imperialism, 1915–1940*. Chapel Hill: University of North Carolina Press, 2001.

Retamar, Robert Fernández. *Caliban and Other Essays*. Translated by Edward Baker. Minneapolis: University of Minnesota Press, 1999.

Reyes, Israel. "De-facing Cuba: Translating and Transfiguring Cristina García's *The Agüero Sisters*." In *Voice-Overs: Translation and Latin American Literature*, edited by Daniel Balderston and Marcy Schwartz, 224–34. Albany: State University of New York Press, 2002.

Rieff, David. *The Exile: Cuba in the Heart of Miami*. New York: Simon and Schuster, 1993.

———. *Going to Miami: Exiles, Tourists, and Refugees in the New America*. New York: Penguin, 1987.

Ring, Natalie J. "Inventing the Tropical South: Race, Region, and the Colonial Model." *Mississippi Quarterly* 56, no. 4 (2003): 619–31.

———. *The Problem South: Region, Empire, and the New Liberal State, 1880–1930*. Athens: University of Georgia Press, 2012.

Ringe, Donald A. "The Function of Landscape in Prescott's *The Conquest of Mexico*." *New England Quarterly* 56, no. 4 (1983): 569–77.

Rivero Marín, Rosanna. *Janus Identities and Forked Tongues: Two Caribbean Writers in the United States*. New York: Peter Lang, 2004.

Roach, Joseph. *Cities of the Dead: Circum-Atlantic Performance*. New York: Columbia University Press, 1991.

Roberts, Diane. *The Myth of Aunt Jemima: Representations of Race and Region*. New York: Routledge, 1994.

Rodríguez, Ileana. "The Literature of the Caribbean: Initial Perspectives." In *Process of Unity in Caribbean Society: Ideologies and Literature*, edited by Ileana Rodriguez and Marc Zimmerman, 13–24. Minneapolis: Institute for the Study of Ideologies and Literatures, 1983.

Rodríguez, Jaime. *Literatures of the U.S.-Mexican War: Narrative, Time, and Identity*. Austin: University of Texas Press, 2010.

Rodríguez, Luis Felipe. *Ciénaga*. 1923; rev., 1937; reprint, Miami: Mnemosyne, 1969.

Rohlehr, Gordon. "The Calypsonian as Artist: Freedom and Responsibility." *Small Axe* 9 (2001): 1–26.

Rollin, Frank A. *Life and Public Services of Martin R. Delany, Sub-assistant Commissioner Bureau Relief of Refugees, Freedmen, and of Abandoned Lands, and Late Major 104th U.S. Colored Troops*. Boston: Lee and Shepard, 1868.

Romine, Scott. *The Real South: Southern Narrative in the Age of Cultural Reproduction*. Baton Rouge: Louisiana State University Press, 2008.

Rothman, Adam. "Lafcadio Hearn in New Orleans and the Caribbean." *Atlantic Studies* 5, no. 2 (2008): 265–83.

Roumain, Jacques. *Masters of the Dew*. 1944; translated by Langston Hughes and Mercer Cook, London: Heinemann, 1947.

Rowley, Hazel. *Richard Wright: The Life and Times*. Chicago: University of Chicago Press, 2008.

Rushdie, Salman. *Imaginary Homelands: Essays and Criticism, 1981-1991*. London: Granta, 1991.

———. *The Satanic Verses*. New York: Viking, 1989.

Russ, Elizabeth Christine. *The Plantation in the Postslavery Imagination*. New York: Oxford University Press, 2009.

Safran, William. "Diasporas in Modern Societies: Myths of Homeland and Return." *Diaspora* 1, no. 1 (Spring 1991): 83-99.

Said, Edward W. *Culture and Imperialism*. New York: Random House, 1993.

———. *On Late Style: Music and Literature against the Grain*. New York: Vintage, 2006.

———. *Orientalism*. New York: Vintage, 1979.

———. *Reflections on Exile and Other Essays*. Cambridge: Harvard University Press, 2000.

Saldivar, Ramon. "Looking for a Master Plan: Faulkner, Paredes, and the Colonial and Postcolonial Subject." In *The Cambridge Companion to Faulkner*, edited by Philip M. Weinstein, 96-120. Cambridge: Cambridge University Press, 1995.

Sansay, Leonora. *Secret History; or, The Horrors of St. Domingo, in a Series of Letters, Written by a Lady at Cape Francois*. Philadelphia: 1808.

———. *Zelica, the Creole: A Novel in Three Volumes*. London: 1820.

Savin, Ada. "Between Island and Mainland: Shifting Perspectives in Cristina García's *The Agüero Sisters*." *Revue française d'etudes américaines* 96 (2003): 60-73.

Schama, Simon. *Landscape and Memory*. New York: Knopf, 1995.

Scherr, Arthur. *Thomas Jefferson's Haitian Policy: Myths and Realities*. Lanham, Md.: Lexington Books, 2011.

Schmidt, Hans. *The United States Occupation of Haiti, 1915-1934*. New Brunswick: Rutgers University Press, 1971.

Schoelcher, Victor. *Vie de Toussaint Louverture*. Paris: Karthala, 1982.

Schomburg, Arthur A. "General Evaristo Estenoz." *Crisis* (July 1912): 143-44.

Seabrook, William B. *The Magic Island*. New York: Literary Guild of America, 1929.

Séjour, Victor. "The Mulatto." In *The Norton Anthology of African American Literature*, edited by Henry Louis Gates Jr. and Nellie McKay, 287-99. New York: Norton, 1997.

Semmes, Raphael. *Service Afloat and Ashore during the Mexican War*. Cincinnati: William H. Moore, 1851.

Severens, Martha R. *The Charleston Renaissance*. Spartanburg, S.C.: Saraland Press, 1998.

Shaw, Philip. *The Sublime*. New York: Routledge, 2006.

Shell-Weiss, Melanie. *Coming to Miami: A Social History*. Gainesville: University Press of Florida, 2009.

Simoes Da Silva, A. J. *The Luxury of Nationalist Despair: George Lamming's Fiction as Decolonizing Project*. Amsterdam: Rodolfi, 2000.

Smith, Maria T. *African Religious Influences on Three Black Woman Novelists: The Aesthetics of "Vodun."* Lewiston, Maine: Edwin Mellen Press, 2007.

Smith-Rosenberg, Carroll. *This Violent Empire: The Birth of an American National Identity*. Chapel Hill: University of North Carolina Press, 2010.

Sommer, Doris. *Proceed with Caution, When Engaged by Minority Writing in the Americas*. Cambridge: Harvard University Press, 1985.

Southerland, Elease. "The Influence of Voodoo on the Fiction of Zora Neale Hurston." In *Sturdy Black Bridges: Visions of Black Women in Literature*, edited by Roseann Bell et al., 172–83. Garden City, N.Y.: Anchorage-Doubleday, 1979.

Spencer, Warren F. *Raphael Semmes: The Philosophical Mariner*. Tuscaloosa: University of Alabama Press, 1997.

Spurr, David. *The Rhetoric of Empire: Colonial Discourse in Journalism, Travel Writing, and Imperial Administration*. Durham: Duke University Press, 1993.

Stack, Carol. *Call to Home: African Americans Reclaim the Rural South*. New York: Basic Books, 1996.

Stallybrass, Peter, and Allon White. *The Politics and Poetics of Transgression*. Ithaca: Cornell University Press, 1986.

Starr, S. Frederick. *Bamboula! The Life and Times of Louis Moreau Gottschalk*. New York: Oxford University Press, 1995.

Stecopoulos, Harilaos. *Reconstructing the World: Southern Fictions and U.S. Imperialisms, 1898–1976*. Ithaca: Cornell University Press, 2008.

Stein, Judith. *The World of Marcus Garvey: Race and Class in Modern Society*. Baton Rouge: Louisiana State University Press, 1986.

Stepan, Nancy Leys. *Picturing Tropical Nature*. Ithaca: Cornell University Press, 2001.

Stephens, Jack. "Madison Smartt Bell." *Bomb* 73 (2000): 1–8.

Stephens, Michelle Ann. *Black Empire: The Masculine Global Imaginary of Caribbean Intellectuals in the United States, 1914–1962*. Durham: Duke University Press, 2005.

Stepick, Alex, Guillermo Grenier, Max Castro, and Marvin Dunn, eds. *This Land Is Our Land: Immigrants and Power in Miami*. Berkeley: University of California Press, 2003.

Stepto, Robert. *From Behind the Veil: A Study of African-American Literature*. Urbana: University of Illinois Press, 1979.

———. "I Thought I Knew These People: Richard Wright and the Afro-American Literary Tradition." *Massachusetts Review* 18 (1977): 525–41.

Stevenson, Elizabeth. *Lafcadio Hearn*. New York: Macmillan, 1961.

Stevenson, Pascha A. "Dreaming in Color: Race and the Spectacular in *The Agüero Sisters* and *Praisesong for the Widow. Frontiers* 28, no. 3 (2007): 141–59.

Steward, T. G. "How the Black St. Domingo Legion Saved the Patriot Army in the Siege of Savannah, 1779." *American Negro Academy, Occasional Papers* 5 (1899): 1–15.

Stimson, Frederick S. *Cuba's Romantic Poet: The Story of Plácido.* Chapel Hill: University of North Carolina Press, 1964.

Stott, William. *Documentary Expression and Thirties America.* New York: Oxford University Press, 1973.

Stowe, Harriet Beecher. *Dred: A Tale of the Great Dismal Swamp.* 2 vols. Boston: Phillips, Sampson, 1856.

Stowe, Harriet Beecher. *Uncle Tom's Cabin: or, Life Among the Lowly.* 2 vols. Boston: John P. Jewett, 1852.

Streeby, Shelley. *American Sensations: Class, Empire, and the Production of Popular Culture.* Berkeley: University of California Press, 2002.

Suarez, Virgil. *Going Under.* Houston: Arte Publico Press, 1996.

———. *Havana Thursdays.* Houston: Arte Publico Press, 1995.

———. *Spared Angola: Memories from a Cuban-American Childhood.* Houston: Arte Publico Press, 1997.

Sundquist, Eric. *To Wake the Nations: Race in the Making of American Literature.* Cambridge: Harvard University Press, 1993.

Sweatt, Katherine. "Corinne Silenced: Improper Places in Constance Fenimore Woolson's *East Angels.*" In *Constance Fenimore Woolson's Nineteenth Century: Essays,* edited by Victoria Brehm, 161–71. Detroit: Wayne State University Press, 2001.

Talbott, George M. "Radish Production in Florida." *Journal of the Florida State Horticultural Society* (1954): 151–53.

Tate, Claudia. *Psychoanalysis and Black Novels: Desire and the Protocols of Race.* New York: Oxford University Press, 1998.

Taylor, Bayard. *Eldorado; or, Adventures in the Path of Empire.* 1850; reprint, Lincoln: University of Nebraska Press, 1988.

Taylor, Patrick. *The Narrative of Liberation: Perspectives on Afro-Caribbean Literature, Popular Culture, and Politics.* Ithaca: Cornell University Press, 1989.

Temple, Jean. *Blue Ghost: A Study of Lafcadio Hearn.* New York: Haskell House, 1974.

Thompson, Krista A. *An Eye for the Tropics: Tourism, Photography, and Framing the Caribbean Picturesque.* Durham: Duke University Press, 2006.

Thompson, Mark Christian. "Voodoo Fascism: Fascist Ideology in Arna Bontemps's *Drums at Dusk. MELUS* 30, no. 3 (2005): 154–77.

Thoreau, Henry David. "Walking." 1862; reprinted in *Walden and Other Writings,* edited by William Howarth. New York: Modern Library, 2000.

Thornton, John. *Africa and Africans in the Making of the Atlantic World, 1400–1680.* New York: Cambridge University Press, 1992.

Thorpe, Thomas Bangs. "The St. John's and Ocklawaha Rivers, Florida." *Appleton's Journal* (November 12, 1870): 577–84.

Tinker, Edward Larocque. *Lafcadio Hearn's American Days*. London: John Lane/ The Bodley Head, 1925.

Toole, John Kennedy. *A Confederacy of Dunces*. Baton Rouge: Louisiana State University Press, 1980.

Torgovnick, Marianna. *Gone Primitive: Savage Intellects, Modern Lives*. Chicago: University of Chicago Press, 1990.

Trefzer, Annette. "Possessing the Self: Caribbean Identities in Zora Neale Hurston's *Tell My Horse*." *African American Review* 34, no. 2 (2000): 299–312.

Trouillot, Michel-Rolph. *Silencing the Past: Power and the Production of History*. Boston: Beacon, 1995.

Tuan, Yi-Fu. *Space and Place: The Perspective of Experience*. Minneapolis: University of Minnesota Press, 1977.

Vanderwood, Paul. "Betterment for Whom? The Reform Period: 1855–1875." In *The Oxford History of Mexico*, edited by Michael C. Meyer and William H. Beezley, 371–96. New York: Oxford University Press, 2000.

Vasquez, Josefina Zoraida. "War and Peace with the United States." In *The Oxford History of Mexico*, edited by Michael C. Meyer and William H. Beezley, 339–69. New York: Oxford University Press, 2000.

Vásquez, Sam. *Humor in the Caribbean Literary Canon*. New York: Palgrave, 2012.

Vauthier, Simone. "'Textualité et stéréotypes': Of African Queens and Afro-American Princes and Princesses: Miscegenation in *Old Hepsy*." In *Regards sur la littérature noire américaine*, edited by Michel Fabre, 65–107. Paris: Publications du Conseil Scientifique de la Sorbonne Nouvelle–Paris, 1980.

Velazquez, Loreta Janeta. *The Woman in Battle: The Civil War Narrative of Loreta Velazquez, Cuban Woman and Confederate Soldier*. 1876; reprint, Madison: University of Wisconsin Press, 2003.

Vorda, Allan, ed. *Face to Face: Interviews with Contemporary Novelists*. Houston: Rice University Press, 1993.

Walcott, Derek. *Epitaph for the Young*. Bridgetown, Barbados: Advocate, 1949.

———. *Omeros*. New York: Farrar, Strauss and Giroux, 1990.

———. "What the Twilight Says: An Overture." In *Dream on Monkey Mountain and Other Plays*, 3–40. New York: Farrar, Straus and Giroux, 1970.

Wald, Priscilla. *Contagious: Culture, Carriers, and the Outbreak Narrative*. Durham: Duke University Press, 2008.

Walker, Daniel E. *No More, No More: Slavery and Cultural Resistance in Havana and New Orleans*. Minneapolis: University of Minnesota Press, 2004.

Walker, William. *The War in Nicaragua*. 1860; reprint, Detroit: Blaine Etheridge, 1971.

Wallerstein, Immanuel. *The Modern World System*. Vol. 2, *Mercantilism and the Consolidation of the European World-Economy, 1600–1750*. Berkeley: University of California Press, 2011.

Warner, W. Lloyd. *The Living and the Dead: A Study of the Symbolic Life of Americans*. New Haven: Yale University Press, 1959.

Webb, Constance. "Interview with Ralph Ellison." February 3, 1963. In Richard Wright Collection, Schomburg Center for Research in Black Culture, New York Public Library, New York, N.Y.

Weber, David J. *The Spanish Frontier in North America.* New Haven: Yale University Press, 1992.

Welch, Kimberly. "Our Hunger Is Our Song: The Politics of Race in Cuba, 1900–1920." In *The African Diaspora: African Origins and New World Identities,* edited by Isidore Okpewho, Carole Boyce Davies, and Ali A. Mazrui, 178–96. Bloomington: Indiana University Press, 2001.

Wertheimer, Eric. *Imagined Empires: Incas, Aztecs, and the New World of American Literature, 1771–1876.* Cambridge: Cambridge University Press, 1999.

West, Alan. *Tropics of History: Cuba Imagined.* Westport, Conn.: Bergin and Garvey, 1997.

White, Hayden. *Tropics of Discourse: Essays in Cultural Criticism.* Baltimore: Johns Hopkins University Press, 1978.

Wiley, James. *The Banana: Empires, Trade Wars, and Globalization.* Lincoln: University of Nebraska Press, 2008.

Wilmott, Glenn. *Modernist Goods: Primitivism, the Market, and the Gift.* Toronto: University of Toronto Press, 2008.

Wilson, Anthony. *Shadow and Shelter: The Swamp in Southern Culture.* Jackson: University Press of Mississippi, 2006.

Wilson, Charles Reagan. *Baptized in Blood: The Religion of the Lost Cause, 1865–1920.* Athens: University of Georgia Press, 1980.

Wilson, Rob. *American Sublime: The Genealogy of a Poetic Genre.* Madison: University of Wisconsin Press, 1991.

Winders, Richard Bruce. *Mr. Polk's Army: The American Military Experience in the Mexican War.* College Station: Texas A&M University Press, 1997.

Wood, Gordon. *Empire of Liberty: A History of the Early Republic, 1789–1815.* New York: Oxford University Press, 2009.

Woodward, C. Vann. *Thinking Back: The Perils of Writing History.* Baton Rouge: Louisiana State University Press, 1986.

Woolson, Constance Fenimore. *East Angels.* New York: Harper and Brothers, 1886.

———. *Jupiter Lights.* 1889; reprint, New York: AMS Press, 1971.

———. "The Oklawaha." *Harper's New Monthly Magazine* 52 (January 1876): 161–79.

———. *Rodman the Keeper: Southern Sketches.* 1880; reprint, New York: Harper and Brothers, 1886.

Wright, Julia. Introduction to Richard Wright, *Haiku: The Other World,* edited by Yoshinobu Hakutani and Robert L. Tener, vii–xii. New York: Arcade, 1998.

Wright, Richard. *Black Boy.* New York: Harper and Brothers, 1945.

———. *Black Power: A Record of Reactions in a Land of Pathos.* 1954; reprint, New York: HarperCollins, 1995.

———. "Blueprint for Negro Writing." 1937; reprinted in *Richard Wright Reader,* edited by Ellen Wright and Michel Fabre. New York: Harper and Row, 1978.

——. "The Handiest Truth to Me to Plow Up Was in My Own Hand." *P.M. Magazine* (April 4, 1945): 3.

——. Introduction to George Lamming, *In the Castle of My Skin,* ix–xii. New York: McGraw-Hill, 1953.

——. *Letters to Joe C. Brown.* Edited by Thomas Knipp. Kent, Ohio: Kent State University Libraries, 1968.

——. *The Long Dream.* Garden City, N.Y.: Doubleday, 1958.

——. *Pagan Spain.* New York: Harper, 1957.

——. *Twelve Million Black Voices.* 1941; reprint, New York: Thunder's Mouth Press, 1988.

——. *White Man, Listen! Lectures in Europe, 1950–1956.* 1957; reprint, New York: HarperCollins, 1995.

Wurdemann, John George F. *Notes on Cuba.* 1844; reprint, New York: Arno Press, 1971.

Young, Elizabeth. *Disarming the Nation: Women's Writing and the American Civil War.* Chicago: University of Chicago Press, 1999.

Yu, Beongcheon. *An Ape of Gods: The Life and Thought of Lafcadio Hearn.* Detroit: Wayne State University Press, 1964.

Yúdice, George. *The Expediency of Culture: Uses of Culture in the Global Era.* Durham: Duke University Press, 2003.

Žižek, Slavoj. *The Sublime Object of Ideology.* London: Verso, 1989.

Index

Abernathy, Ralph, 352 (n. 1)

Abolitionists, 84, 101–4, 195, 353 (n. 11)

Abrahams, Roger, 340 (n. 6)

Aesop, 221

Africa: black return to, 13, 67, 71–74, 89, 219, 236, 278, 282, 349 (n. 11), 370 (n. 29); Cuba influenced by, 14, 63, 64, 114, 233, 286, 290, 291–92, 325, 360 (n. 24); as origin of imported slaves, 16, 62, 71–72, 74, 82, 85–86, 90, 94–95, 97–99, 101, 117, 121, 134, 146; Creoles and, 79, 171; New Orleans influenced by, 89–90, 102, 104, 179–80, 182, 185, 186, 327, 337; Haiti influenced by, 108, 110–11, 114, 123, 128, 134, 137, 181, 233; circum-Caribbean influenced by, 114, 141, 204, 360 (n. 24), 360 (n. 26), 369 (n. 24); Martinique influenced by, 114, 183, 184, 186, 233; contagion/infection rhetoric and, 142–43; travel writing and, 146, 147; Florida influenced by, 201–4; Jamaica influenced by, 206, 212; agriculture and, 231

African American writers: rhizomelike circumCaribbean cultural connections and, 10; Haitian Revolution and, 16–17, 93, 104, 105, 123, 142; U.S. South / circumCaribbean connections and, 59; African-inspired religions and, 98, 327; African diaspora and, 112–13, 114; slavery and, 120–21; Reconstruction and, 150–51; swamp imagery and, 158, 328; dance as gestural language and, 217; Southern Studies and, 284. *See also specific writers*

African diaspora: creation of new circumCaribbean culture and, 8, 14–15, 62, 113; return to Africa and, 13, 67, 71–74, 89, 219, 236, 278, 282, 349 (n. 11), 370 (n. 29); parallels among diasporic peoples, 18, 248, 250, 255, 256, 267; black colonization and, 60, 71–74, 89, 91–92; Delany's *Blake; or, The Huts of America* and, 85; Sherwood Bonner and, 106; Zora Neale Hurston and, 112–15; Florida and, 114, 233; Bell's *All Souls' Rising* and, 123; Haitian Revolution and, 123–24; valorization of peasant culture and, 198; circumCaribbean folklore and, 235, 369–70 (n. 26); exile and, 249; slave narrative and, 249; George Lamming and, 250, 267, 282; Richard Wright and, 250, 254–57, 266–67, 267, 282; loss of black identity and, 252; Wright's *Black Boy* and, 252

African-inspired religions: circum-Caribbean and, 13, 81, 117, 141; Catholic Church and, 89, 98, 116, 124, 133, 138, 184, 308; African American writers and, 98, 327; Haiti and, 98–99, 102, 114, 117, 124, 130, 132–34, 141; Zora Neale Hurston and, 114–17, 124, 233, 242–43, 327, 363 (n. 48); U.S. South and, 117, 141, 182; Jamaica and, 117, 199, 212, 232; Cuba and, 117, 293; Madison Smartt Bell and, 139;

Benjamin, Walter, 292

Bhabha, Homi, 5, 178, 274–75

Biassou, Georges, 120, 355 (n. 24)

Bierstadt, Albert, *The Landing of Columbus*, 36

Bird, Robert Montgomery, *Calavar; or, The Knight of the Conquest*, 42–43

Birth of a Nation (film), 267

Bisette, Cyrille, 104

Bisland, Elizabeth, 359–60 (n. 21)

Black Atlantic: Davis's *The Black Atlantic*, 8, 203; Martin Delany and, 59–60; Delany's *Blake; or, The Huts of America* and, 72, 78; Zora Neale Hurston and, 114; Constance Fenimore Woolson and, 154, 156; Richard Wright and, 248–49, 374 (n. 26)

Black Boy (Wright): Lamming's *In the Castle of My Skin* and, 18, 248–53, 269, 270–78, 280, 283, 373 (n. 10), 373 (n. 13), 373 (n. 15), 374 (n. 21); as tour guide for whites, 251–52; "restoration" and, 255; as aesthetic presentation vs. autobiography, 256, 264, 265, 268, 270; biblical references, 256–57; hunger themes and, 257, 258, 264, 266, 268, 274; racism and, 258–62; cruel mother themes and, 259, 262, 276; masculinity and, 259–60, 276; silence/uproar dichotomy and, 260, 264; Freudian sexuality and, 260–61, 372 (n. 7); visual imagery and, 261, 263, 372 (n. 8); education and, 263, 264, 280–81; community violence caused by scarce resources and, 263, 372 (n. 9); negative portrayals of blacks, 264–66, 277; as "speakerly text," 266; U.S. South and, 268, 272, 373 (n. 15); South to North migration and, 272, 282–83; exile themes and, 274, 282–83; prosperity themes and,

275; shame and public surveillance themes, 275, 277; "historyless" aspect of colonized cultures and, 276; humor and, 278, 279

Black identity, 252, 257

Black nationalism, 96, 134, 249, 370 (n. 29)

Blackness: "unchangeable uselessness" trope and, 9; contagion/infection themes and, 96; Madison Smartt Bell and, 126, 144; Haitian Revolution and, 141; Hearn's *Two Years in the French West Indies* and, 177, 178; McKay's *Banana Bottom* and, 208; poverty and, 250

Black Studies, 4–7, 10, 19, 152, 250

Blake; or, The Huts of America (Delany): Cuba and, 16; Falkner's *The Spanish Heroine* and, 44; black domesticity and, 51, 67, 88–89; wedding scenes, 51, 88, 226, 345 (n. 37); U.S. South / Caribbean links and, 59, 72, 77, 78, 79, 82, 85, 91; Plácido and, 59, 83–84, 86–88, 90, 351 (n. 24); slavery and, 71–92; Black Atlantic and, 72, 78; Maroons and, 72, 80, 82, 236; biblical references, 79, 243, 350 (n. 16), 351–52 (n. 28); comic elements of, 85; carnival themes and, 89–90; "pure" African traditions and, 213; African-derived religions and, 221, 327; sugar production and, 288; hurricanes and, 334

Bloch, Marc, 19

Boas, Franz, 115, 200, 220–21, 354 (n. 18), 370 (n. 27); *The Mind of Primitive Man*, 221

Bobadillo, Rosa, 53

Bogart, Humphrey, 359 (n. 18)

Bolivar, Simón, 352 (n. 1)

Bongie, Chris, 183

Bonner, Sherwood, "The Hoodoo Dance," 106

Bontemps, Arna, 6, 17; *Black Thunder*, 120; *Drums at Dusk*, 120, 354 (n. 17)

Booth, Edwin, 26

Boukman (vodoun priest), 99

Bourke-White, Margaret, *You Have Seen Their Faces*, 266

Boyer, Jean-Pierre, 104

Brancusi, Constantin, 220

Brathwaite, Edward Kamau, 95, 164, 343 (n. 18)

Braudel, Fernand, 10, 12; *The Mediterranean and the Mediterranean World in the Age of Philip II*, 19–20, 152

Breckenridge, John C., 288

Brer Rabbit stories, 235, 369–70 (n. 26)

Brickhouse, Anna, 62, 104

Brodber, Erna, 231

Brooks, Cleanth, 19

Brown, E. Ethelred, 368–69 (n. 18)

Brown, Joe, 253

Brown, John, 63

Brown, Rita Mae, 299

Brown, Sterling, 199

Brown, William Hill, *The Power of Sympathy*, 363 (n. 49)

Brown, William Wells, *St. Domingo*, 100

Browning, Barbara, 142, 143

Buchanan, James, 64

Buntline, Ned, 45; *The Volunteer; or, The Maid of Monterey*, 42

Burke, Edmund, 137, 177, 341 (n. 5), 361 (n. 31)

Burr, Aaron, 353 (n. 5)

Bustamente, Anastasio, 24

Byron, Lord, 45; *Don Juan*, 44

Cable, George Washington, 6, 106, 107–9, 172; *The Grandissimes*, 107–8, 353–54 (n. 13); *The Creoles of Louisiana*, 108; "The Freedman's Case in Equity," 109; *Old Creole Days*, 171, 354 (n. 14); "Belles Demoiselles

Plantation," 191, 365 (n. 61); "Jean Ah-Poqueline," 357 (n. 7)

Cabrera, Lydia, 293

Calderón de Barca, Fanny, 348 (n. 2)

Caldwell, Erskine: *Tobacco Road*, 203; *You Have Seen Their Faces*, 266

Calhoun, John C., 30

California, 69–70

Calypso mythology, 13

Campbell, Robert, 59

Camus, Albert, 264, 272

Candomble, 13. *See also* African-inspired religions

Cantera, Jorge, 288; *A Century of Cuban Writers in Florida*, 287

Capitalism, 32, 56, 92

Carby, Hazel, 200–201, 224, 229

Carera Infante, Guillermo, 293

Caribbean identity, as hybrid, 228–29

Caribbean Literature and the Environment, 358 (n. 9)

Caringa/calinda dance, 14

Carmichael, Stokely, 352 (n. 1)

Carnival: Delany's *Blake; or, The Huts of America* and, 89–90; demonic carnivalization and, 135, 138–39; Lafcadio Hearn and, 185; Roberto Fernández and, 315

Carondelet, Francisco Luis Hector de, 101

Carpentier, Alejo, 17, 127, 141; *The Kingdom of This World*, 93, 121, 131, 356 (n. 29), 356 (n. 31), 356 (n. 34); *Toussaint L'Ouverture*, 93

Carranza, Venustiano, 346 (n. 43)

Casid, Jill H., 80

Castro, Fidel: Cuban diaspora and, 18, 58, 288, 294, 296, 300, 302, 315–17, 329; Cuban Revolution and, 91, 285–86, 289, 304; communism and, 100; Mariel boatlift and, 290–91; Catholic church and, 316; Cristina García and, 318, 329, 337, 378 (n. 30); "Pedro

Caribbean connection and, 2, 3, 4, 57, 146, 179; travel writing and, 17; and Southern writing's Northern animus, 38, 150; Mexican American War and, 40, 55, 56–57; female warriors and, 44, 345 (n. 35); Haitian Revolution and, 100, 103, 105, 118; Florida and, 145; tourism and, 146; slavery and, 156; Woolson's *East Angels* and, 162; Confederate relocation to Cuba, 288; Cuban Revolution and, 304, 313, 315; hidden family treasures and, 379 (n. 39)

Class: plantation economy and, 2–3; dramatization of history through conflicts of, 54; racial aspects of, 55

Claudel, Louis, 170, 359 (n. 20)

Cliff, Michelle, *Abeng*, 351 (n. 26), 370 (n. 31)

Clifford, James, 8, 112, 151, 296

Cobham, Rhonda, 94, 231

Cockfighting, 32

Code Noir, 108, 128

Codrescu, Andrei, *Ay, Cuba!*, 379 (n. 41)

Coetzee, J. M., 359 (n. 15)

Cofer, Judith Ortiz, 14, 337

Coffee production, 101

Cole Thomas, *The Course of Empire*, 35

Colonialism: England and, 2, 3, 4, 6, 8, 152, 161, 177, 208, 230, 232, 273, 278; Spain and, 2, 3, 4, 8, 16, 27–28, 35, 38, 43, 46, 91, 152, 157, 161, 288, 348–49 (n. 8); France and, 2, 3, 4, 8, 16, 104, 123, 152, 161, 199; United States and, 8, 16, 72, 167, 224; "tropicopolitans" and, 9; Cuba and, 16, 74, 108, 290; circum-Caribbean identity and, 20, 151–52; feminization/eroticization and, 21, 23, 39, 41–42, 46, 161, 340–41 (n. 1), 342 (n. 11); degeneracy and, 23, 33, 36–37, 46, 167, 178, 341 (n. 6,7), 342 (n. 11); Mexican American War and,

28, 31; improvement of mismanaged resources and, 28, 167, 178, 359 (n. 15); racial amalgamation and, 30, 343 (n. 17); ruin imagery and, 35, 36; slavery and, 35, 37, 121, 152; industrialization and, 38; domesticity and, 52, 67; black colonization and, 60, 71–74, 89, 91–92; colonizing gaze, 60, 116, 160, 178, 271; "self-cloaking" aspects of, 72; Haitian Revolution and, 95, 103, 116, 352 (n. 1); Faulkner's *Absalom, Absalom!* and, 109–11; Haiti's African heritage and, 123; "historyless" aspect of colonized cultures and, 123, 250, 276, 356 (n. 28), 374 (n. 21); postcolonialism and, 150, 154, 354 (n. 15); anti-imperialist writing and, 151; silencing of colonized people, 153–54; Woolson's *Rodman the Keeper* and, 156–57; tourism and, 157, 161, 165–66; Woolson's "Felipa" and, 160; Hearn's *Two Years in the French West Indies* and, 186; valorization of peasant culture and, 198; McKay's *Banjo* and, 199; Jamaica and, 204, 210, 212, 224, 229, 232, 234, 265; white religions' role, 206; McKay's *Banana Bottom* and, 209–11, 215, 228–29, 230–32, 244, 247; fruit industry and, 223–24, 368 (n. 17); disruption of natural economies and, 226; focus on agricultural production and, 231; Hurston's *Their Eyes Were Watching God* and, 231–32, 244, 247; philistinism and, 232; racial stereotyping and, 232; suppression of local narratives and, 247; Caribbean writers' arguments against, 248; racial division and, 248; Lamming's *In the Castle of My Skin* and, 250, 252, 271, 276, 278, 374 (n. 21, 22); Jim Crow America and, 255; "third space" between colonizer and colonized, 275

58, 288, 294, 296, 300, 302, 315–17, 329; Southern literature and, 18–19; Narciso Lopez and, 91; Miami and, 285–87, 289, 297, 306, 316, 335; anti-Cuban prejudice and, 286, 291, 293, 305–6, 315, 337; "Pedro Pan" children and, 293, 322, 379 (n. 38); return to Cuba and, 294, 295–97, 309; lost cause themes and, 297, 303, 311, 313, 317, 323; Spanish language and, 302; Cuban Revolution and, 302–4, 316, 333–34; "chosen people" narrative and, 303–4, 315; international character of, 306, 329–30, 377 (n. 18); upending of social hierarchies and, 310, 312, 313; undesirable jobs and pay for women and, 311–12; Fernández's *Raining Backwards* and, 314; ethnic prejudices of, 315, 316, 378 (n. 27); civil religions and, 315–16, 378 (n. 28), 380 (n. 43); philistinism and, 316; Republican Party and, 316

Cuban Revolution: Fidel Castro and, 91, 285–86, 289, 304; Cuba/Florida connections and, 285–86, 288, 293; Miami and, 285–86, 289, 289–90, 319, 336; Havana and, 292, 319; Gustavo Pérez Firmat and, 296, 298, 304–5, 311; García's *The Agüero Sisters* and, 302, 318, 319, 322, 329–30; Cuban diaspora and, 302–4, 316, 333–34; Civil War and, 304, 313, 315; Fernández's *Holy Radishes* and, 311, 313; Menéndez's *Loving Che* and, 333–37; Ana Menéndez and, 334–35

Cullen, Countee, 219

Cyrillia (Hearn's mistress), 184, 187, 363–64 (n. 52)

Damballah (voodoo deity), 81, 98, 116, 132, 235

Dance, 14, 217

Danger: cultural and racial mixing and,

25, 27, 48, 52, 63, 220, 350 (n. 17); tropical sublime and, 34, 36, 40, 145, 148, 152, 158–59, 168–69, 175, 197, 321; philistinism and, 232

Danticat, Edwidge, 14; *Brother, I'm Dying*, 338

D. Appleton and Company, 147

Darwin, Charles, 23, 29

Dash, J. Michael, 13–14, 90, 129, 142, 210, 228, 237, 369 (n. 23)

Daumier, Honoré, 174

Davis, Angela, 351 (n. 1)

Davis, David Brion, 105

Davis, Jefferson, 70

Davis, Thadious, *Southscapes*, 203

Dayan, Joan, 353 (n. 3)

De Beauvoir, Simone, 272

Decolonization, 103, 135, 198

Dee, Ruby, 371 (n. 36)

Defoe, Daniel, *Robinson Crusoe*, 340 (n. 5)

Degeneracy, as justification for colonialism, 23, 33, 36–37, 46, 167, 178, 341 (nn. 6–7), 342 (n. 11)

De la Campa, Román, 286, 293–94, 311; *Cuba on My Mind*, 293, 379 (n. 38), 379 (n. 41)

Delany, Alexandre Dumas, 88

Delany, Charles Lenox Redmond, 88

Delany, Ethiopia Halle, 88

Delany, Fastin Soluque, 88

Delany, Martin: Southern Studies and, 6; Black Atlantic and, 59–60; Cuba and, 59–62, 76, 292; Lucy Holcombe Pickens and, 59–63, 66, 72; tropical sublime and, 60; U.S. South / circum-Caribbean linkages, 60, 74–75, 77, 91; Caribbean settings and, 60–62; slavery and colonialism themes and, 60–62, 67, 71–92, 348 (n. 3), 349 (n. 11), 349 (n. 13), 349 (n. 15), 350 (nn. 16–17); John Brown and, 63; Harriet Beecher Stowe and, 67, 75,

Durkheim, Émile, 378 (n. 28)

Duvalier, François "Papa Doc," 120

Duvalier, Jean-Claude "Baby Doc," 120, 123

Early, Jubal A., 288

Eastman, Mary Henderson, *Aunt Phillis's Cabin*, 195

Eaton, Clement, 56, 347 (n. 47)

Edelman, Marian Wright, 257, 258

Edmondson, Belinda, 230, 373 (n. 16)

Education themes: McKay's *Banana Bottom* and, 205, 206, 207, 222, 223, 227–30, 237, 240; Hurston's *Their Eyes Were Watching God* and, 213, 237–38, 240, 242; Wright's *Black Boy* and, 263, 264, 280–81; Lamming's *In the Castle of My Skin* and, 280–81, 374 (n. 24)

Edwards, Bryan, *History of the West Indies*, 365–66 (n. 64)

Edwards, Harry Stillwell, 150

El Hablitor (newspaper), 27

Ellison, Ralph, 134, 265; *Invisible Man*, 372 (n. 9)

Emancipation: labor exploitation and, 4; Cuba and, 67, 92, 290; literacy and, 83; Haitian Revolution and, 101, 102, 103, 105, 128, 140; African American writers and, 105; McKay's *Banana Bottom* and, 105; racism and, 155; sugar production and, 178; Martinique and, 196, 197; Hearn's *Youma* and, 196, 311; effects of slavery after, 282; slavery's lasting effects after, 282

Emerson, Ralph Waldo, 201

"Empty" landscapes, 32, 36, 151, 158

England: colonialism and, 2, 3, 4, 6, 8, 152, 161, 177, 208, 230, 232, 273, 278, 354 (n. 16); Haitian Revolution and, 16, 99; Barbados and, 250, 251, 260, 265, 278; racial codes in, 283

Equiano, Olaudah, 83

Ernest, John, 349 (n. 14)

Erzulie Freida (Rada god), 98–99, 117, 130, 137, 242

Escalera insurrection, 84, 87

Eshu/Elleguá (trickster god of the crossroads), 326, 380 (n. 45)

Esu-Elegba (trickster), 242, 243, 333, 380 (n. 45)

Esu-Eleggua (orisha), 212, 338, 380 (n. 45)

Etienne, Mambo, 117

Evans, Augusta Jane, 60; *Inez: A Tale of the Alamo*, 342–43 (n. 15)

Evans, Walker, *Let Us Now Praise Famous Men*, 266

Everett, Percival, 293

Exile: African diaspora and, 249; George Lamming and, 249–51, 252, 271–75, 282–83, 296, 374 (n. 26); Richard Wright and, 249–51, 253, 271–75, 282–83, 374 (n. 26); Lamming's *In the Castle of My Skin* and, 270, 274, 282–83; McKay's *Banana Bottom* and, 274; Wright's *Black Boy* and, 274, 282–83; U.S. South and, 298; García's *The Agüero Sisters* and, 318, 322–23, 327

Fabre, Michel, 254

Falkner, William Clark: Southern Studies and, 6; Mexican American War and, 16, 21–22, 24–26, 38–39, 42–45, 56, 344 (n. 28), 344–45 (n. 32), 345 (nn. 33–34); tropical sublime and, 24, 33, 50–51, 54; William Faulkner and, 24, 43, 44, 109; amalgamation of races and, 37; tropics viewed through Southern lens, 43, 44, 53, 189; U.S. imperialism and, 45; portrayal of native women, 45–47, 49, 51, 68, 342 (nn. 10–11); male beauty and, 45–47, 68, 342 (nn. 10–11); Mexican/Spanish differentiation, 49, 52, 346 (n. 40);

cross-national marriages and, 51–52, 54, 347 (n. 45); European travels, 53; history dramatized through class conflict and, 54
—works of: *The Spanish Heroine*, 24, 42, 44–53, 68, 83, 109–10, 344–45 (n. 32), 345–46 (n. 38); *The Siege of Monterey*, 44, 45; *Rapid Ramblings in Europe*, 53; *The White Rose of Memphis*, 345–46 (n. 38)
False histories, 121
Fanon, Frantz, 103, 135, 216, 230, 250, 367 (n. 6), 374 (n. 21)
Faulkner, William: Southern identity and, 5; transnational aspects of works, 5, 6; Southern Studies and, 6; U.S. South / Caribbean linkages, 11, 58, 112, 121; notoriety of, 19; William Clark Falkner and, 24, 43, 44, 109; tropical sublime and, 33; Mexican Revolution (1910–20) and, 53; incest themes and, 76; interracial sexuality and, 105, 111, 363 (n. 49); Haitian Revolution and, 109–11, 141; Michael Kreyling and, 129; racial conflict and, 134; Lafcadio Hearn and, 195; "backwoods" themes and, 211; García's *The Agüero Sisters* and, 317
—works of: *Absalom, Absalom!*, 6, 46, 58, 109–11, 196, 317, 325, 363 (n. 49); *The Unvanquished*, 44, 52, 380 (n. 48); *Go Down, Moses*, 76, 323, 358 (n. 10); *Light in August*, 111; *The Sound and the Fury*, 317
Febvre, Lucien, 19
Federal Writers' Project, 233
Ferguson, Sally Ann, 245
Fernández, Roberto, 6, 18, 285, 298, 306, 309, 377 (n. 22), 377 (n. 24); *Holy Radishes*, 310–14, 315, 377 (n. 25), 377 (n. 26); *Raining Backwards*, 312, 314–15, 317, 333, 377 (n. 26)

Fernández Olmos, Margarite, 353 (n. 3)
Fick, Carolyn, 131; *The Making of Haiti*, 128
Filibusters: Cuba and, 3, 16, 58, 332, 380 (n. 44); New Orleans and, 16, 58, 172; slavery and, 28, 57; liberation narratives and, 59, 70, 91; black colonization and, 60, 72, 91; Delany's *Blake; or, The Huts of America* and, 75; contagion/infection rhetoric and, 79. *See also* Lopez, Narciso; Walker, William
Fillmore, Willard, 66
Finn, Harry, 147
Fischer, Sybille, 100
Florida: Spain and, 2, 58, 147, 158, 161, 163, 189–90, 289, 330; circum-Caribbean writers and, 14, 16, 145, 146; circumCaribbean immigration to, 113–14, 229; polyglot hybrid population of, 114, 164, 229, 233, 284; Constance Fenimore Woolson and, 145, 149, 151–53, 157–59, 161, 164, 166–67, 170, 186, 204, 323, 358 (n. 8), 358 (n. 12); *Picturesque America* and, 147; Sidney Lanier and, 147–48; Zora Neale Hurston and, 198, 200, 229, 232–33, 237, 369–70 (n. 26); African influences and, 201, 204; Latino/a writers and, 284; Cuban American writers and, 285; Cuban Revolution and, 285–86, 288, 293; Mariel boatlift and, 286, 290–91, 316, 337, 378 (n. 27); Cuban migration to, 287–88, 338; Southern identity and, 298; presidential elections and, 305, 316; U.S. South / Caribbean conjunctions in, 309–10; Fernández's *Holy Radishes* and, 310–13. *See also* Miami, Florida
Florida State University, 298
Florit, Eugenio, 293
Foley, Alethea "Mattie," 175
Folklore: performative style and, 14,

Church and, 87, 94, 122, 124; literary legacy of, 93–96, 100, 103, 144, 168–69; slavery and, 93–98, 100–105, 108, 110, 118–19, 120–21, 124, 127–29, 130, 134–35, 139, 196; colonialism and, 95, 103, 116, 352 (n. 1); suppression of narrative, 95–96, 100, 105, 108, 123, 353 (n. 6); voodoo/vodoun and, 96, 98–99, 102, 109–10, 122–23, 124, 353 (n. 3), 356 (n. 35); liberating narrative and, 96–97; massacres of whites and, 98–101, 134–35, 139; African-inspired religions and, 99, 141; Civil War and, 100, 102–3, 105, 118; United States and, 102, 103, 104, 111, 127, 254; George Washington Cable and, 107–9; William Faulkner and, 109–11, 141; Madison Smartt Bell and, 117, 120, 123–26, 127–29, 133, 139–43, 323, 353 (n. 4); Creoles and, 119, 130, 134, 141; Bontemps's *Drums at Dusk* and, 120; Césaire's *The Tragedy of King Christophe* and, 122–23; French Revolution and, 133, 137; Lafcadio Hearn and, 181, 196; buried family treasures and, 379 (n. 39)

Hakutani, Yoshinobu, 372 (n. 11)

Hale, Sarah Josepha, 89; *Liberia*, 67; *Northwood*, 67

Hall, Gwendolyn Midlo, 353 (n. 8)

Hall, Stuart, 144

Halyard, Harry: *The Buccaneer of the Brazos*, 42; *The Warrior Queen*, 42; *The Heroine of Tampico*, 42, 345 (n. 37)

Hamer, Fanny Lou, 352 (n. 1)

Hammond, James Henry, 349 (n. 13)

Hammond, Marcus Claudius Marcellus, 341 (n. 2)

Handley, George, 9, 344 (n. 26), 358 (n. 9)

Hardimann, H. M. *See* Pickens, Lucy Holcombe

Harding, Warren, 117

Hardy, Thomas: *Tess of the D'Urbervilles*, 211; *Far from the Madding Crowd*, 212

Harlem Renaissance: Haitian Revolution and, 17; McKay's *Home to Harlem* and, 18; circumCaribbean writers and, 113; James Weldon Johnson and, 117, 318; Arna Bontemps and, 119; Zora Neale Hurston and, 198; Claude McKay and, 198, 220, 237, 250; dance and, 217; primitivism and, 218, 219; folk wisdom and, 247; West Indian immigration to Harlem and, 250

Harper, Frances Ellen, 89

Harris, Joel Chandler, 66, 105, 315, 366 (n. 65); *Nights with Uncle Remus*, 232

Harris, Trudier, 241

Harris, Wilson, 10, 232

Hartman, Geoffrey, 204

Harvey, Bruce A., 350 (n. 19)

Havana, Cuba: New Orleans and, 11, 65, 89–90; Mexican American War and, 21, 26, 29, 31–32, 58; St. Augustine and, 58; slavery and, 74, 90; Miami as simulacrum of, 285–87, 289–90, 292, 295, 298, 299, 307, 315–18, 324, 331, 335–36, 375 (n. 7); as metaphor for entire country, 286; tourism and, 289, 294; Cuban Revolution and, 292, 319; García's *The Agüero Sisters* and, 302, 306, 317–18, 327–30; Menéndez's *Loving Che* and, 335–36

Hawthorne, Nathaniel, *The Scarlet Letter*, 44

Hayne, Robert Y., 353 (n. 6)

Hazel, Harry, *Inez, the Beautiful; or, Love on the Rio Grande*, 345 (n. 37)

Hearn, Lafcadio: Southern Studies and, 6; travel writing and, 17, 145–46, 147, 153, 173–74, 363 (n. 46); "local color" articles, 145–46, 153; Constance Fenimore Woolson and, 146, 148–49, 151, 190; tropical sublime and, 148,

171, 173–77, 179, 180, 183, 189, 195,
321, 360 (n. 25), 360 (n. 27), 361 (nn.
32–33); Martinique and, 149, 174,
177–82, 188; hurricanes and, 149,
188, 190, 190–91, 361 (n. 33); U.S.
South / circumCaribbean connections and, 151, 183, 189; music and,
170, 171–72, 190, 360 (nn. 22–24),
360 (n. 26), 365 (n. 61), 365–66
(n. 64); Creole culture and, 170–73,
179, 193, 359 (n. 20), 359–60 (n. 21),
360 (nn. 22–24), 360 (n. 26), 361
(n. 35), 365 (n. 61), 366 (n. 66); New
Orleans and, 170–74, 179–82, 186,
187–89, 192, 197; folklore and, 171,
184–85, 195, 363 (n. 50); vision problems of, 173–74, 176–77, 361 (n. 30),
362 (n. 39); lure of the Caribbean for,
174–75, 360 (n. 27); representations
of women and, 175, 177, 182–83,
185–87, 360 (n. 28), 362 (n. 37);
womanizing of, 175, 187, 360 (n. 28),
362 (n. 37); racial biases of, 177–78,
181, 184, 186–87, 195–96, 211; colonizing gaze of, 178; debilitating effect of
tropical climate and, 178, 187–88, 364
(nn. 53–55); Mt. Pelée eruption and,
179, 361 (nn. 33–34); orientalization
and, 180, 362 (n. 38); racial mixing
and, 180–82, 185, 186–87; Haitian
Revolution and, 181, 196; attraction/
repulsion dynamic and, 181–82, 362
(n. 41); Pierre Loti and, 182, 193, 197,
362 (n. 43), 362–63 (n. 44), 363–64
(n. 52); bilingualism and, 183, 192;
Catholic church and, 183–84; Jean-
Baptiste Labat and, 183–84, 363
(n. 47); zombies and, 184, 363 (n. 48);
Antilles carnival and, 185; Florida
and, 189–90; yellow fever and, 190,
193, 364 (n. 58); *da*/Mammy parallels
and, 193–95, 197, 365 (n. 63), 366
(n. 65); racial philistinism and, 194;

African influences on the Caribbean
and, 195, 365–66 (n. 64); slavery and,
195–97, 366 (n. 66); African aspects
of Cuba and, 360 (n. 24)
—works of: "Saint Malo," 148–49;
Collected Works, 149; *Chita*, 149–50,
174, 189–93, 364–65 (n. 59); *Gombo
Zhèbes*, 170, 359 (n. 20); "Los Crio-
llos," 172, 361 (n. 35); *Two Years in the
French West Indies*, 174, 177–82, 186,
188, 362 (n. 42), 363 (n. 48); *Youma*,
189, 193–97, 311; *La Cuisine Creole*,
359 (n. 20); *The Historical Sketch
Book and Guide to New Orleans*, 359
(n. 20); *Exotics and Retrospectives in
Ghostly Japan*, 363 (n. 48)
Hearne, John, 369 (n. 24)
Hendrick, Ellwood, 361 (n. 34)
Henry, William, 170, 359 (n. 20)
Hepburn, Katherine, 359 (n. 18)
Heredia, José María, 343 (n. 21)
Herrera, Petra "Pedro," 53
Herskovits, Melville, 114, 369 (n. 23);
Life in a Haitian Valley, 354 (n. 18)
Heteroglossia, 11–12, 340 (n. 3)
Heyward, DuBose, 200, 247, 354 (n. 17);
Star Spangled Virgin, 366 (n. 2), 374
(n. 20); *Porgy*, 370 (n. 28)
Hiaasen, Carl, 294
Hijuelos, Oscar, *The Mambo Kings Play
Songs of Love*, 301
Hindman, Robert Holt, 43, 345 (n. 34)
Hindman, Thomas C., 43, 345 (n. 34)
HIV virus, 141
Hobsbawm, Eric, 348 (n. 6)
Holland, Edwin C., 101
Holland, Josiah Gilbert, 147
Holland, 2, 8, 152
Holly, James, 134
Homeland. *See* Return/restoration
themes
Homer, *Odyssey*, 11
Homoeroticism, 37, 49

Immersion narratives, 203–5, 213, 230

Imperialism: concept of "eye" and, 32; "empty" landscapes and, 32, 36; ruin imagery and, 33; Mexican American War and, 45, 56; United States / Cuban relationship and, 59, 67, 78–79, 292; filibusters and, 60; "self-cloaking" stratagems for, 72; slavery and, 111; Reconstruction and, 151; tourism and, 157; loss of locality and, 224; cultural authenticity / physical terrain narrative and, 228; gender and, 332

Incest themes, 76, 105

Industrialization: sugar production and, 3, 288; García's *The Agüero Sisters* and, 4, 231, 324, 378 (n. 31); Caribbean as a blank slate and, 13–14; colonization and, 38; development of middle class and, 145; cigar industry and, 378 (n. 31)

Ingraham, Joseph Holt, *The Quadroone*, 346 (n. 39)

Interracial sexuality: slavery and, 47, 111, 195–96; Martin Delany and, 76, 349 (n. 13); William Faulkner and, 105, 111, 363 (n. 49); Madison Smartt Bell and, 131, 138–39, 140–41. *See also* Rape

In the Castle of My Skin (Lamming): Richard Wright and, 18, 248, 252–53, 277, 282, 371 (n. 1); Wright's *Black Boy* and, 18, 248–53, 269, 270–78, 280, 283, 372 (n. 10), 372–73 (n. 13), 373 (n. 15), 374 (n. 21); United States / Caribbean links and, 250; "historyless" aspect of colonized cultures and, 250, 276, 374 (n. 21); as alternative history, 250, 279–80, 374 (nn. 21–22); as tour guide for whites, 251–52; masculinity and, 260, 273–76, 279; silence/uproar dichotomy and, 260; as aesthetic presentation

vs. autobiography, 270; exile themes in, 270, 274, 282–83; castle symbology and, 271, 276; South to North migration and, 272, 282–83; gender metaphors and, 273, 275–76, 279; valorization of peasant culture in, 274, 280; shame and public surveillance themes in, 275, 276–77, 373 (n. 18); cruel mother themes in, 276, 278; comic aspects of, 278–79; education and, 280–81, 374–75 (n. 24); mythology of oversexed blacks and, 281; slavery and, 281–82; community violence caused by scarce resources and, 372 (n. 9); Wright's *The Long Dream* and, 373 (n. 17)

Irving, Washington, 29

Jackson, Andrew, 35, 80

Jahn, Janheinz, 130

Jaloff people, 108

Jamaica: U.S. ties to, 2, 14, 232; Zora Neale Hurston and, 18, 113, 200, 203–4, 219, 232, 234–36; Claude McKay and, 18, 198–206, 208, 210, 217, 219, 221, 224, 228–32, 366 (n. 1); African-inspired religions and, 117, 199, 212, 232; colonialism and, 204, 210, 212, 224, 229, 232, 234, 265; African influences, 206, 212; Panama Canal and, 211; slavery and, 222, 234; Tacky's Rebellion and, 222, 368 (n. 16); fruit industry and, 223–24, 368 (n. 17); modernist economics and, 224; agriculture and, 224, 226, 229, 231

James, C. L. R., 17, 99, 121, 127, 141, 250, 355 (n. 26), 356–57 (n. 36); *The Black Jacobins*, 93, 121, 125, 254

James, Henry, 145, 149–50, 154, 160–61, 169; *The American*, 157, 359 (n. 19); *The Portrait of a Lady* and, 359 (n. 19)

James, Winston, 369 (n. 18)

Lukács, Georg, 54
Lyell, Charles, 29
Lyotard, Jean-François, 137, 177
Lytle, Andrew, 5

Macandal, François, 130, 132, 356
  (n. 33)
Maceo, Antonio, 290
Machado, Gerardo, 289
Machismo, 301, 307, 333, 380 (n. 46)
Magruder, John B., 288
Mailer, Norman, 301
Malcolm X, 87, 352 (n. 1)
Male beauty, 45–47, 68, 342
  (nn. 10–11), 351 (n. 27). *See also*
  Masculine identity
Mammy: stereotype of, 193, 195, 365
  (n. 63), 366 (n. 65); *da*/Mammy
  parallels and, 193–95, 197, 365
  (n. 63), 366 (n. 65)
Manet, Eduardo, 293
Manifest Destiny doctrine: Mexico
  and, 23, 28, 39, 70; Texas and, 27,
  342 (n. 10), 342 (n. 12), 347 (n. 45);
  aestheticization of, 36; homoeroti-
  cism and, 37; Cuban annexation and,
  64, 65, 69, 70, 79; slavery and, 67;
  "incapability" of natives to govern
  themselves and, 79; the sublime and,
  344 (n. 25)
Manigault, Arthur, 6, 16, 21, 24, 33, 38,
  40–41, 45; *Mexican War Narrative*,
  40, 54
Mann, Mary Peabody, 351 (n. 23)
Marat, Jean-Paul, 348 (n. 4)
Marcus Aurelius, 322
Mariel boatlift, 286, 290–91, 316, 334,
  337, 378 (n. 27)
Marinette/Erzulie Mapionne (Petro
  god), 98, 356 (n. 35)
Marmolejo-McWatt, Amparo, 326–27
Maroon culture: Delany's *Blake; or, The
  Huts of America* and, 72, 80, 82, 236;

U.S. South / Caribbean affinities and,
  82, 105, 108, 238; Zora Neale Hurston
  and, 113, 117, 201, 235, 236–37, 370
  (n. 30); Madison Smartt Bell and, 117,
  126, 130, 133, 134, 137; Arna Bontemps
  and, 120; Haitian Revolution and,
  120, 130, 133, 134, 137, 141; Constance
  Fenimore Woolson and, 168
Marshall, Paule, 14
Martí, José, 288–90, 303, 336, 348
  (n. 3), 352 (n. 1)
Martin, Lawrence, 253
Martin, Sylvia, 253
Martínez Furé, Rogelio, 14
Martinique: Louisiana ties, 2; French
  identity of, 12–13, 97, 181, 363 (n. 47);
  African influences on, 114, 183, 184,
  186, 233; Lafcadio Hearn and, 149,
  174, 177–82, 188; Haitian Revolution
  and, 181, 196; emancipation and,
  196, 197
Masculine identity: Southern Studies
  and, 5; colonizing narrative and,
  46; manhood myths, 58, 61; Claude
  McKay and, 199, 215–16, 222, 240,
  367 (n. 8); slave narrative and, 205;
  Richard Wright and, 259–60, 276;
  George Lamming and, 260, 273–76,
  279; Cuban American writers and,
  300, 307; Gustavo Pérez Firmat and,
  301; Fidel Castro and, 337; Manifest
  Destiny doctrine and, 344 (n. 25).
  See also Male beauty
Mason, John, 64
Matamoros, Mexico, 25
Matas, Rudolph, 173, 190, 364–65
  (n. 59)
Matoso, Diego Ferrer, 83
Matthews, John T., 110
Matthiessen, Peter, *Killing Mister
  Watson*, 338
Maximilian (emperor of Mexico), 55
McCall, Dan, 269

341 (n. 3), 347 (n. 46); literary legacy of, 16, 21–22, 24, 38, 341 (n. 3), 341 (n. 4); William Clark Falkner and, 16, 21–22, 24–26, 38–39, 42–45, 56, 344 (n. 28), 344–45 (n. 32), 345 (nn. 33–34); gender metaphors and, 21, 23, 39, 41–42, 46, 58, 340–41 (n. 1), 342 (n. 11); Havana and, 21, 26, 29, 31–32, 58; "degeneracy" of Mexicans as justification for, 23, 33, 36–37, 46, 167, 178, 341 (nn. 6–7), 342 (n. 11); United States and, 24, 27, 29–31, 35, 38–39, 42, 45, 52, 54–55, 72; Texas and, 24, 27, 342 (n. 10); international romances and, 25, 37, 39–40, 45–47; soldiers' reactions to local religious practices, 26; Mexico City and, 26, 28, 40, 44, 50, 331, 341 (n. 6), 343 (n. 20); Catholic Church and, 26, 28, 48, 342 (n. 12), 342–43 (n. 15); racism and, 28, 30–31, 35, 45, 53–54; colonizing "improvement" of mismanaged resources as justification for, 28, 31; casualties from, 40; Civil War and, 40, 55, 56–57; depictions of native women and, 41–42, 49, 50, 51, 68, 342 (nn. 10–11); female warriors and, 42, 44, 49, 51, 52–53

Mexican Revolution (1910–20), 53

Mexico: migration to United States and, 8, 142; Indian heritage in, 12, 23, 29, 33–35, 38–40, 43, 46, 49, 54, 55; multilingualism and, 12, 339–40 (n. 2); colonization and, 16; Spain and, 16, 22, 24, 35, 43, 46, 49, 52, 346 (n. 40); feminization/eroticization of, 21, 23, 39, 41–42, 46, 58, 340–41 (n. 1), 342 (n. 11); racial variety of population, 25; mongrelization of population, 28; slavery and, 28, 30, 37, 45, 54–57, 346–47 (n. 44); ruin imagery and, 32–33, 36; dependent capitalism and, 56; as wasteful custo-

dian of rich lands, 70; Richard Wright and, 253–54

Mexico City, Mexico, 26, 28, 40, 44, 50, 331, 341 (n. 6), 343 (n. 20)

Miami, Florida: Spanish culture and, 2; circumCaribbean immigration to, 158, 294, 306, 337–38, 376 (n. 10); Southern identity and, 284–85, 293, 305, 315; Cuban American writers and, 285, 338; Atlanta and, 285, 376 (n. 13); Cuban Revolution and, 285–86, 289, 289–90, 319, 336; Cuban diaspora and, 285–87, 289, 297, 306, 316, 335; as simulacrum of Havana and, 285–87, 289–90, 292, 295, 298, 299, 307, 315–18, 324, 331, 335–36, 375 (n. 7); Cuban migration to, 289, 333, 335, 337; Afro-Cuban oppression and, 291; polyglot population of, 291, 302; García's *The Agüero Sisters* and, 302, 306, 317–18, 324, 327–30; presidential election of 2000 and, 305, 316; racial segregation and, 305–6; Haitian immigration to, 306, 376–77 (n. 17); Cristina García and, 306–7, 315–18, 323–24, 327–28, 377 (n. 19); Reinaldo Arenas and, 307; Virgil Suarez and, 308; Roberto Fernández and, 314, 317; Menéndez's *Loving Che* and, 335

Michaels, Walter Benn, 150

Middle Passage, 11, 139, 250, 266, 281–82, 374 (n. 25)

Mignolo, Walter, 92

Millet, Jean-François, 186

Minh-ha, Trinh T., 8, 231

Missouri Compromise, 73

Mitchell, Margaret, *Gone With the Wind*, 8, 107, 191, 292, 310–11

Monroe, James, 58

Montaigne, Michel de, 366 (n. 2)

Monterey, Mexico, 44, 45, 345 (n. 33)

Montes Huidobro, Marías, 293

Montezuma (emperor), 22

Moore, H. Judge, 341 (n. 2)

Moore, Thomas Overton, 288

Moreau de Saint-Méry, M. L. E., 108

Morris, Willie, *North Towards Home*, 297

Morrison, Toni, 20; *Sula*, 127, 213; *Song of Solomon*, 236; *Tar Baby*, 237; *Beloved*, 282, 349 (n. 15)

Mourning, 150, 151, 154, 155, 173, 264, 323

Mozart, Wolfgang Amadeus, *The Magic Flute*, 369 (n. 22)

Multilingual abilities: U.S. South / Caribbean linkages and, 11–12, 183, 284, 339–40 (n. 2); "Felipa" and, 160, 358 (n. 11); Woolson's *East Angels* and, 163–64; Lafcadio Hearn and, 183, 192; Fernández's *Holy Radishes* and, 310; *The Brief Wondrous Life of Oscar Wao* and, 377 (n. 22)

Munro, Martin, 356 (n. 32)

Music: Mexico and, 25; Reed's *Mumbo Jumbo* and, 96; African influence on circumCaribbean and, 114, 360 (n. 24), 360 (n. 26); Woolson's "The South Devil" and, 158–59; Lafcadio Hearn and, 170, 171–72, 190, 360 (nn. 22–24), 360 (n. 26), 365 (n. 61), 366 (n. 64); McKay's *Banana Bottom* and, 206, 210, 220, 223, 225, 226, 227; "primitive" cultures and, 221; Hurston's *Their Eyes Were Watching God* and, 245; Cuba and, 285, 286, 287, 289, 304; García's *The Agüero Sisters* and, 319

The Mystery (newspaper), 349 (n. 14)

Naipaul, V. S., 250

Nair, Supriya, 374 (n. 21)

Napoleon III (emperor of France), 55, 94, 100, 106

Native Americans: contact and conquest, 2; Mexico and, 12, 23, 29, 33–35, 38–40, 43, 46, 49, 54, 55; U.S. wars against, 49, 349 (n. 9); Hispaniola and, 97, 99; slavery and, 97, 101, 121, 137, 152; as "indolent," 167; Constance Fenimore Woolson and, 167, 359 (n. 15), 363 (n. 47); Southern Studies and, 284

Nature/culture dialectic, 12–13

The New Negro (Locke), 370 (n. 29)

New Orleans, Louisiana: plantation economy and, 2; French culture and, 2, 94, 97–98, 101–2, 337; as Mediterranean, 11; Havana and, 11, 65, 89–90; Cuba and, 14, 64, 83, 172, 288, 289, 298; filibusters and, 16, 58, 172; Mexican American War and, 21–22, 26–27, 31–32, 42, 48, 54, 55, 58; Spanish control of, 58; slavery and, 74, 76, 90, 102, 172, 366 (n. 66); African influences, 89–90, 102, 104, 179–80, 182, 185, 186, 327, 337; Haitian Revolution and, 94, 100, 101–2, 104, 106–9; Creoles and, 101–2, 109, 170–71, 359 (n. 20), 359–60 (n. 21); Lafcadio Hearn and, 170–74, 179–82, 186, 187–89, 192, 197; carnival and, 185, 315; hurricane Katrina and, 246; voodoo/vodoun and, 327, 361 (n. 35); folklore and, 340 (n. 6)

Nicaragua, 21, 65

Nixon, Herman Clarence, *Forty Acres and Steel Mules*, 266, 267

Noble savage, 160

North, Michael, 230

Northop, Solomon, *Twelve Years a Slave*, 77

North Star (newspaper), 73

Novás Calvo, Lino, 293

Nwankwo, Ifeoma, 83, 84

Nzengou-Tayo, Marie-José, 356 (n. 32)

Obama, Barack, 305

Obeah, 117, 202, 219, 220–22, 238, 242, 368 (n. 16)

Civil War and, 2, 3, 4, 57, 146, 179; annexation of circumCaribbean lands,
3–4, 67, 76; circumCaribbean trade
networks and, 4, 26, 298; disregard
for circumCaribbean texts, 4–7, 10,
19, 152, 250; and Southern identity,
5, 20, 169, 284–85, 293, 298, 303–5,
315; Mexican American War and,
7, 21–22, 31, 42, 45, 54–56, 58, 341
(n. 3), 347 (n. 46); African diaspora
and, 8, 14, 255; plantation system
and, 8, 99, 112, 253, 333; Mexican
migration to, 8, 157–58; Cuban
influence, 8, 285, 289, 299; circum-
Caribbean's lure of fortunes to be
made and, 11, 58; exclusion of other
cultures from the biracial concept
of, 12; tropical sublime and, 15, 189;
Reconstruction and, 17; Mexican
similarities to, 26; chivalric tradition
and, 45, 345 (n. 36); dependent capitalism and, 56; miscegenation and,
69, 96, 142–43; Haitian Revolution
and, 94, 96–97, 100, 101, 103, 104,
110–11, 117–21, 123–24, 139, 144; Jim
Crow laws and, 107, 203, 254, 255,
260, 271, 273, 277; African-inspired
religions and, 117, 141, 182; civil rights
movement and, 140, 248; African
influences on, 141, 147, 236, 309, 325;
stereotyping and scapegoating people
of color, 142, 193, 195, 232, 265, 365
(n. 63), 366 (n. 65); circumCaribbean
literature and, 142–44, 146; as
colony of North, 147, 150, 151, 167,
357 (n. 4); black/white racial binary
and, 152, 228, 376 (n. 10); silencing
of colonized people and, 154; circum-
Caribbean immigration to, 158; West
Indies islands and, 179–80; climate's
debilitating effects on, 188; and
valorization of peasant culture, 199,
203; "basket of crabs" syndrome and,
207, 239; and blacks' immigration
to the North, 219, 266, 274, 275, 277;
philistinism and, 232; hoodoo and,
233; Richard Wright and, 258, 265,
272, 274; George Lamming and, 272,
274; class distinctions among blacks
and, 278; mythology of oversexed
blacks and, 281; anti-Cuban prejudice
and, 286, 291, 293, 305–6, 315, 337;
Southern imaginary and, 292, 324,
335, 376 (n. 13); as scapegoat for
U.S. problems, 293; Cuban trade
and, 298; exile narratives and, 298;
literary variety of dialects and, 302;
re-creation of the "Old South," 303;
"chosen people" narrative and,
303–4, 315; Fernández's *Holy Radishes*
and, 310; Emancipation and, 311;
Roberto Fernández and, 315; South-
ern/Cuban parallels, 315; nostalgia
and, 328; reverse migration of blacks
to, 372–73 (n. 13); as simulacrum,
375 (n. 7); anti–foreign immigrant
bias and, 378 (n. 27). *See also* Florida;
Louisiana; Texas
Unsworth, Barry, *Sacred Hunger*, 351
(n. 26)

Vandercook, John W., *Black Majesty*,
119, 120
Varela, Félix, 288
Vauthier, Simone, 139
Vázquez, Concepción, 83
Velasquez, Loreta Janeta, *The Woman
in Battle*, 44
Vera Cruz, Mexico, 21–22, 26–28,
30–32, 38, 40, 44, 48, 54–55, 58, 343
(n. 20)
Verdi, Giuseppe, 372 (n. 12)
Vesey, Denmark, 101
Viaud, Louis Marie Julien. *See* Loti,
Pierre
Villa, Pancho, 346 (n. 43)